SIUA
SIWA

SAUṠPİDNA KATATSĠOVABMIS
A DESCRIPTIVE GRAMMAR

Étienne L. Poisson

Second print

§1 Foreword 2
§2 The Alopian People 4
　§2.1 Origin of the Alopian People 6
　§2.2 The Alopian People in North-America 8
　§2.3 The Alopian Family Tree 10
　§2.4 The Siwa People 13
　　§2.4.1 Siwa Territory 13
　　　§2.4.1.1 Geography 14
　　§2.4.2 Sociolinguistic Situation 14
§3 Phonology 16
　§3.1 Vowels 16
　　§3.1.1 Short Vowels 18
　　　§3.1.1.1 Short Open Vowels 18
　　　§3.1.1.2 Short Closed Vowels 19
　　　§3.1.1.3 The Archiphoneme <ɨ> 19
　　§3.1.2 Long Vowels 20
　　§3.1.3 Diphthongs 20
　　　§3.1.3.1 Diphthong Contraction 22
　　§3.1.4 Semi-vowels 23
　　§3.1.5 Triphthongs 23
　　　§3.1.5.1 Diphthong and Long Vowel Coalescence 23
　　§3.1.6 Vowel Apocope 26
　　§3.1.7 Vowel Prothesis 26
　　§3.1.8 Vowel Polarity Inversion 27
　§3.2 Stress 29
　§3.3 Orthographic Conventions Regarding Vowels 30
　§3.4 Consonants 31
　　§3.4.1 Consonants & Allophones 31
　　　§3.4.1.1 Allophony and Sound Changes 33
　　§3.4.2 Long Consonants 56
　　§3.4.3 Palatalized Consonants 56
　　§3.4.4 Glottalized Consonants 56
　　§3.4.5 Preaspirated Consonants 56
　　§3.4.6 Initial Consonant Clusters 57
　　§3.4.7 Internal Consonant Clusters 58
　　　§3.4.7.1 Anaptyctic Pronunciation 64
　　　§3.4.7.2 Ejective Pronunciation 67
　　§3.4.8 Lenition 67
　§3.5 Diachronic Phonology 75
　　§3.5.1 Consonants 75
　§3.6 Prosody 78
　§3.7 Tśebġeka 79
§4 Nouns 81
　§4.1 Animacy 82
　　§4.1.1 Inanimate 83
　　§4.1.2 Animate 84
　　§4.1.3 Ambiguous Nouns 89
　　§4.1.4 Honorific Nouns 89
　§4.2 Marked Form 89

§4.2.1 Inanimate Marked Form......89
  §4.2.1.1 Vowel-Final 90
    §4.2.1.1.1 A-declension 91
    §4.2.1.1.2 E-declension 95
    §4.2.1.1.3 I-declension 101
    §4.2.1.1.4 O-declension 106
    §4.2.1.1.5 U-declension 112
    §4.2.1.1.6 Y-declension 115
  §4.2.1.2 Marked Consonant-Final Form 119
    §4.2.1.2.1 S-declension 120
    §4.2.1.2.2 N-declension 120
    §4.2.1.2.3 T-declension 121
    §4.2.1.2.4 L-declension 122
    §4.2.1.2.5 Honorifics in -ts 124
  §4.2.1.3 Diphthong Coalescence Declension 124
§4.2.2 Inanimate Plural 125
  §4.2.2.1 Collective Plural 127
  §4.2.2.2 Plural Nouns 128
§4.2.3 Animate Marked Form 128
  §4.2.3.1 Overview 143
  §4.2.3.2 Dual Nouns 144
  §4.2.3.3 Action Nominals 146
§4.3 Irregular Nouns 148
§4.4 Approbation 149
  §4.4.1 Marking 149
  §4.4.2 Approbative 151
  §4.4.3 Pejorative 153
§4.5 Cases 154
  §4.5.1 Agentive Case 155
  §4.5.2 Patientive Case 157
  §4.5.3 Genitive Case 158
  §4.5.4 Dative Case 160
    §4.5.4.1 Dative vs. Genitive 163
  §4.5.5 Locative Cases 163
    §4.5.5.1 Inessive, Illative and Elative 164
    §4.5.5.2 Adessive, Allative and Ablative 165
    §4.5.5.3 Locative Cases for Indirect Objects 166
    §4.5.5.4 Abessive, Instrumental and Essive 169
§4.6 Double Case Marking 170
§4.7 Indeclinable and foreign words 176
§5 Adjectives 177
§5.1 Function of Verbal and Participial Forms 179
  §5.1.1 Translative Verbal and Adjectival Forms 181
§5.2 Function of Adjectival and Copular Forms 184
  §5.2.1 Copular coalescence 184
§5.3 Predicative Adjectives 185
  §5.3.1 Object Predicative 187
  §5.3.2 Subject Predicative 188
§5.4 Attributive Adjectives 189

§5.5 Adjective Formation 192
§5.6 Declension 197
§5.7 Formation of Verbal Forms from Non-Derived Adjectival Forms 197
§5.8 Degrees of Comparison 199
   §5.8.1 Comparative 199
       §5.8.1.1 Mitigative Comparative..201
       §5.8.1.2 Ultimate and Terminative Comparatives 201
   §5.8.2 Superlative...203
       §5.8.2.1 Ultimate Superlative 204
       §5.8.2.2 Mitigative Superlative 204
   §5.8.3 Equative 205
   §5.8.4 Comparative and Superlative of Non-Adjectives 205
§5.9 Compound Adjectives..207
§5.10 Nominalization of Adjectives 209
§5.11 Non-Numeral Quantifiers 211
   §5.11.1 Comparative and Superlative 216
§6 Adverbs..218
§6.1 Adverbial Form of Adjectives 218
§6.2 Adverbial Form of Verbs...221
   §6.2.1 Participial Adverbs 221
   §6.2.2 Verbal Adverbs..222
§6.3 Adverbial Form of Non-Numeral Quantifiers 223
§6.4 Comparative and Superlative 224
§6.5 Locative Adverbs/Postpositions 226
   §6.5.1 Cardinal Directions..228
   §6.5.2 Up and Down 231
   §6.5.3 Over and Under...235
   §6.5.4 In, On and Out...237
   §6.5.5 Before, Behind, In The Middle and Through 239
   §6.5.6 At, Near, Away...242
   §6.5.7 Amongst, Next To and At The Edge Of..............................244
   §6.5.8 Across and On The Other Side 246
§6.6 Temporal adverbs 248
§6.7 Indeclinable Adverbs 254
   §6.7.1 Indeclinable Adverbs of Degree 254
   §6.7.2 Indeclinable Adverbs of Time 255
   §6.7.3 Other Indeclinable Adverbs 256
§6.8 Negation Adverbs...257
§7 Conjunctions 258
§7.1 Proper Conjunctions 258
   §7.1.1 Coordinators 258
   §7.1.2 Subordinating Conjunctions 260
   §7.1.2 Correlative Conjunctions 263
§7.2 Coordinating Particles 264
§8 Postpositions...270
§9 Verbs..283
§9.1 Verb morphology 283
§9.2 Verb Structure 286
   §9.2.1 Independent Verbs..286

§9.2.1.1 Prefix slots 286
    §9.2.1.1.1 Slot -3 286
    §9.2.1.1.2 Slot -2 287
    §9.2.1.1.3 Slot -1 287
§9.2.1.2 Verb Stem 288
    §9.2.1.2.1 Slot 1 288
    §9.2.1.2.2 Slot 2 289
    §9.2.1.2.3 Slot 3 and 4 289
    §9.2.1.2.4 Impersonal Verbs and Verbal Adjectives 294
    §9.2.1.2.5 Slot 5 296
    §9.2.1.2.6 Slot 6 297
    §9.2.1.2.7 Slot 7 298
    §9.2.1.2.8 Slot 8 298
    §9.2.1.2.9 Slot 9 298
§9.2.2 Split Stems 299
  §9.2.2.1 Split Stem Concord 301
§9.3 Verbal Personal Pronouns 302
  §9.3.1.1 Inclusive vs. Exclusive 302
  §9.3.1.2 Obviative vs. Proximate 303
  §9.3.1.3 Fourth Person 305
 §9.3.2 Agentive Pronouns 309
 §9.3.3 Recipient Pronouns 309
 §9.3.4 Patientive Pronouns 310
 §9.3.5 Unagentive Pronouns 311
 §9.3.6 Overview 314
§9.4 Agentivity 315
 §9.4.1 Unagentive Verbs 315
  §9.4.1.1 Patientive Verbs 317
 §9.4.2 Agentive Verbs 317
 §9.4.3 Ambiguous Agentivity 318
 §9.4.4 Double Agentivity 319
  §9.4.4.1 Causative Double Agentivity 321
§9.5 Valency 321
 §9.5.1 Transitive 322
  §9.5.1.1 Non-Valent Triggers of Transitivity 324
 §9.5.2 Intransitive 324
  §9.5.2.1 Intransitive Syncope 326
 §9.5.3 Translative 327
 §9.5.4 Subjective 329
 §9.5.5 Ditransitive 331
  §9.5.5.1 Subjective Directional 334
 §9.5.6 Passive 335
 §9.5.7 Impersonal Verbs 336
 §9.5.8 Prefix Coalescence 338
§9.6 Evidentiality 338
 §9.6.1 Assertive 339
 §9.6.2 Inferential 339
§9.7 Mood 341
 §9.7.1 Indicative 342

- §9.7.2 Conditional Realis 342
- §9.7.3 Conditional Irrealis 345
- §9.7.4 Optative 347
- §9.7.5 Obligative 349
- §9.7.6 Imperative 350
  - §9.7.6.1 Imperative Obviative 352
- §9.8 Postverbal Vowel Coalescence 352
- §9.9 Aspect 360
  - §9.9.1 Conclusivity 360
    - §9.9.1.1 Verbal Inconclusive 361
    - §9.9.1.2 Copular Inconclusive 362
    - §9.9.1.3 Telicity 363
  - §9.9.2 Habitual 365
  - §9.9.3 Perfective 366
  - §9.9.4 Secondary Aspectual Markers 367
    - §9.9.4.1 Reversive 368
    - §9.9.4.2 Semelfactive 369
    - §9.9.4.3 Persistive 372
    - §9.9.4.4 Frequentative 373
    - §9.9.4.5 Inchoative 374
    - §9.9.4.6 Subitive 374
    - §9.9.4.7 Habilitive 376
    - §9.9.4.8 Diminutive 377
- §9.10 Tense 378
  - §9.10.1 Past Form 380
    - §9.10.1.1 Past Marking on Vowel-Final Verbs 380
      - §9.10.1.1.1 Vowel-final Stem Coalescence 382
      - §9.10.1.1.2 Vowel-Final Verbs 383
      - §9.10.1.1.3 Diphthong-Final Verbs 391
    - §9.10.1.2 Past Marking on Consonant-Final Verbs 391
      - §9.10.1.2.1 Strong Consonant-Final Verbs 391
      - §9.10.1.2.2 Weak Consonant-Final Verbs 397
    - §9.10.1.3 Irregular verbs 399
      - §9.10.1.3.1 Augmented Verbs 400
      - §9.10.1.3.2 Syncoped Verbs 401
      - §9.10.1.3.3 Proper Irregular Verbs 401
- §9.11 Tense-Aspect Coalescence 404
- §9.12 Location and Movement 405
  - §9.12.1 Primary Locative Markers 406
  - §9.12.2 Definite Secondary Locative Markers 407
  - §9.12.3 Relative Secondary Locative Markers 407
- §9.13 Preverbal Adverbs 409
  - §9.13.1 Locative Preverbal Adverbs 409
    - §9.13.1.1 With Transitive Verbs 410
    - §9.13.1.2 With Semantically Passive Verbs 411
    - §9.13.1.3 With Paritciples 411
    - §9.13.1.4 Modifying the Verb 412
  - §9.13.2 Simlpe Preverbal Adverbs 416
- §9.14 Absolutive Descriptives 429

§9.14.1 -AHP- 432
§9.14.2 -AHT- 435
§9.14.3 -ATST- or -ADDJ- 439
§9.14.4 -IB- or -IDB- 442
§9.14.5 -IKS- 444
§9.14.6 -IPR-/-IBĜ- or -IUL- 446
§9.14.7 -JUP/-YP-/-EB- 448
§9.14.8 -OHN/-ÕHN- 451
§9.14.9 -OHK- 453
§9.15 Complementization 456
§9.15.1 Short Forms 458
§9.15.1.1 Short Forms in Direct Speech 459
§9.16 Copula 459
§9.16.1 Independent Copula 460
§9.16.1.1 There-Existential Phrases 461
§9.16.1.2 To Be 464
§9.16.1.3 Relative Clauses 467
§9.16.1.3.1 Subjective Relative Clauses 470
§9.16.1.3.2 Objective Relative Clauses 472
§9.16.1.3.3 Possessive Relative Clauses 475
§9.16.1.3.4 Locative Relative Clauses 476
§9.16.1.3.5 Link Constructions 479
§9.16.1.3.5.1 Temporal Link Constructions 480
§9.16.1.3.5.2 Goal Link Constructions 486
§9.16.1.3.5.3 Adverbial Link Constructions 488
§9.16.1.3.5.4 Copular Link Constructions 491
§9.16.2 Dependent Copula 492
§9.16.2.1 Copular Endings 497
§9.16.2.2 Defective Copular Verbs 498
§9.16.2.3 Coalescence 500
§9.16.2.4 Use 502
§9.16.2.5 Miscellaneous 503
§9.17 Participles 504
§9.17.1 Active Participles 506
§9.17.2 Patientive Participles 510
§9.17.3 Temporal Participles 512
§9.18 Infinitives 514
§9.18.1 Nominal Infinitive 519
§9.18.1.2 Verb Stem and Nominal Infinitive Coalescence 520
§9.18.2 Copular Infinitive 526
§9.18.2.1 Time And Evidentiality 527
§9.18.2.2 Bare Infinitives 528
§9.18.2.3 Locative Infinitives 529
§9.19 Conjugation Paradigm 533
§10 Pronouns and Determiners 535
§10.1 Personal Pronouns 536
§10.1.1 First Person 538
§10.1.2 Second Person 538
§10.1.3 Third Person 539

x

- §10.1.3.1 Disambiguative Third Person 540
- §10.1.4 Fourth Person 541
- §10.1.5 Self 541
- §10.2 Demonstrative Pronouns 542
  - §10.2.1 Independent Pronouns 544
  - §10.2.2 Attributive Pronouns 547
- §10.3 Adverbial Pronouns or 'Pro-Adverbs' 550
- §10.4 Question Words 553
- §10.5 Interrogative Adverbs 555
- §10.6 Indefinite Pronouns 557
  - §10.6.1.1 Known To Speaker 559
  - §10.6.1.2 Unknown To Speaker 559
  - §10.6.1.3 Non-Specific 559
  - §10.6.1.4 Polar Question 560
  - §10.6.1.5 Conditional 560
  - §10.6.1.6 Indirection Negation 560
  - §10.6.1.7 Direct Negation 560
  - §10.6.1.8 Comparison 561
  - §10.6.1.9 Free Choice 561
  - §10.6.1 Known Existential Pronouns 561
  - §10.6.2 Unknown Existential Pronouns 563
  - §10.6.3 Elective Pronouns 565
  - §10.6.5 Known Negative Pronouns 566
  - §10.6.6 Unknown Negative Pronouns 567
- §10.7 Universal and Distributive Pronouns 569
  - §10.7.1 Distributive Pronouns 569
  - §10.7.2 Universal Pronouns 571
- §10.8 -ni Determiners 572
  - §10.8.1 -ni Determiners on Pronouns 573

§11 Numerals 575
- §11.1 Cardinal Numerals 575
- §11.2 Ordinal Numerals 578
  - §11.2.1 Halves and Fractions 579
- §11.3 Nominal Numerals 580
- §11.4 Collective Numerals 580

§12 Interjections 582
§13 Interrogation 583
§14 Derivation 584
- §14.1 Derivational Phonological Changes 584
  - §14.1.1 Fronted Vowels 585
  - §14.1.2 Lengthened Vowels 586
  - §14.1.3 Shortened Vowels 588
  - §14.1.4 Overview of Vowel Changes 589
- §14.2 Derivational Endings 590
  - §14.2.1 Nominal Derivational Endings 590
    - §14.2.1.1 Non-Productive Endings 599
  - §14.2.2 Deverbalizers 600
    - §14.2.2.1 Verbal Derivational Endings 601

§15 Syntax 612

§15.1 General Word Order	612
§15.2 The Noun Phrase	614
§15.3 The Adjectival Phrase	615
§15.4 The Adverbial Phrase	615
§15.5 Interrogative Phrase	616
§15.6 Topicalization	617
§16 Dialects	618
§17 Texts	624
Nitśaka Siųiko	624
17.1 English Version	631
§18 Lexicon	638
§19 Glossing	709
§20 Siwa Swadesh List	710
§21 Map	713
Appendix A: Modernization	714

§1 Foreword

Siwa is a constructed language or *conlang* that came to be as the result of many years of exploration, imagination and hard work. The original project started sometime before 2005 when I decided to catalog my ideas for a new language in the form of a journal. The project bore the name *Glossopoiesis* and although the result you will find in this book has little to do with the original project, there is an unbroken chain of work, ideas and documents that extend over 10 years and have culminated in the form of this book.

The hobby of creating languages is called conlanging. It is a difficult idea to explain to the uninitiated or those who have never considered language creation as a tool for creativity. As I came to find out, language creation is very much a form of art, disguised in linguistic terms and abstract grammatical ideas. There is beauty in using the infinitely complex and diverse phenomenon of language, which is available to us all, and turn in into something distinctly private and personal. There is also a fundamental problem with conlanging – this hobby is often only ever fully appreciated by its creator. It would be foolish for anyone setting out creating a language to think that there will be an audience for the creation. Indeed it is quite far from the point of this book. Instead, the satisfaction I get from having created my own language lies in my ability to express my thoughts and ideas in a way uniquely tailored to my taste, my aesthetics, my view of the world. Conlanging is a lonely and selfish hobby, which is perhaps why so few dare to share their work with the world.

I started conlanging at a young age, first by designing and modifying all types of alphabets. I was still young when I discovered an old family heirloom, a book on Ancient Greek grammar, passed down from father to son for 200 years. The alphabet fascinated me and it stimulated my imagination. I was able to express myself through the creation of alphabets. All my school books were covered in various indecipherable scribblings. My curiosity quickly turned to languages, which took up most of my interest throughout my teens. I read through every language book I could find and I was assiduously studying Icelandic and Finnish with perfect fluency as my goal. The more I learned about foreign languages and their grammar, the more inspired I became to make my own language, using what I liked about the many languages I was studying to create something uniquely mine. The result was the first systematic attempt to describe the creation of a conlang, which many years later would lead to the birth of Siwa.

Siwa, and my goal of finishing this book, widened my horizons and introduced me to exciting subjects; anthropology, botany, biology, genetics, human prehistory and most importantly linguistics. Of the languages I have studied, a few have left a very important mark on Siwa, namely Finnish, Northern Sámi and Georgian.

Now, more than 700 pages later, Siwa is a functional, rich, realistic apriori conlang with a large vocabulary and one speaker. A fully operational machine capable of expressing any thought beautifully, set in a detailed culture and landscape of pre-Columbian Native America.

Although the medium I chose to express myself artistically is unusual, I hope I have succeeded in capturing my vision of Siwa so that those who wish to peer into it may learn about it, appreciate it and even find out something new about the world.

Étienne L. Poisson
Reykjavík, 2014

§2 The Alopian People

The Siwa people are a pre-columbian North-American semi-nomadic people who inhabit a 525 km long belt of land in central Quebec, mostly centred around lake Mistassini (**Sipsi**) and westward along the Rupert River (**Sengi**) to the shores of the James Bay. Siwa and their relatives form the Alopian language family (from the Ancient Greek ἀλωπός 'male fox', a common symbol amongst these people).

The Alopian family contains seven languages grouped in three branches on the basis of their development, mutual intelligibility, cultural contact and shared features:

> **Forest Alopian** [Inland Alopian]
>   Siwa
>   Sigori
> **Tundra Alopian**
>   Eastern Onori
>   Western Onori
> **Coastal Alopian** — Central Olma @ pg. 5
>   Coastal Olma
>   Southern Olma

The Forest and Tundra Alopian branches are grouped together as the Inland Alopian branch. The Alopian language family is of no genetic or linguistic relation to any other language or language family in North America and the surrounding Algonquian and Iroquoian languages.

Compared to their neighbours, the Alopian languages have a remarkably different morphology and phonology – the languages are not typical of the northeastern native american linguistic profile; Alopian languages show distinction between voiced and unvoiced consonants; certain languages have rounded vowels; all Alopian languages have fixed initial stress, etc. On the other hand, there is much homogeneity between all Alopian languages, and even the most divergent languages, for example the linguistically and geographically distant Eastern Onori and Southern Olma languages, are not as distant from each other as English and Russian – their similarities and dissimilarities are more comparable to those of English to Swedish. Physically, the Alopians are not similar to their Algonquian neighbours. Alopians are short, have large elevated flat cheekbones, somewhat small noses,

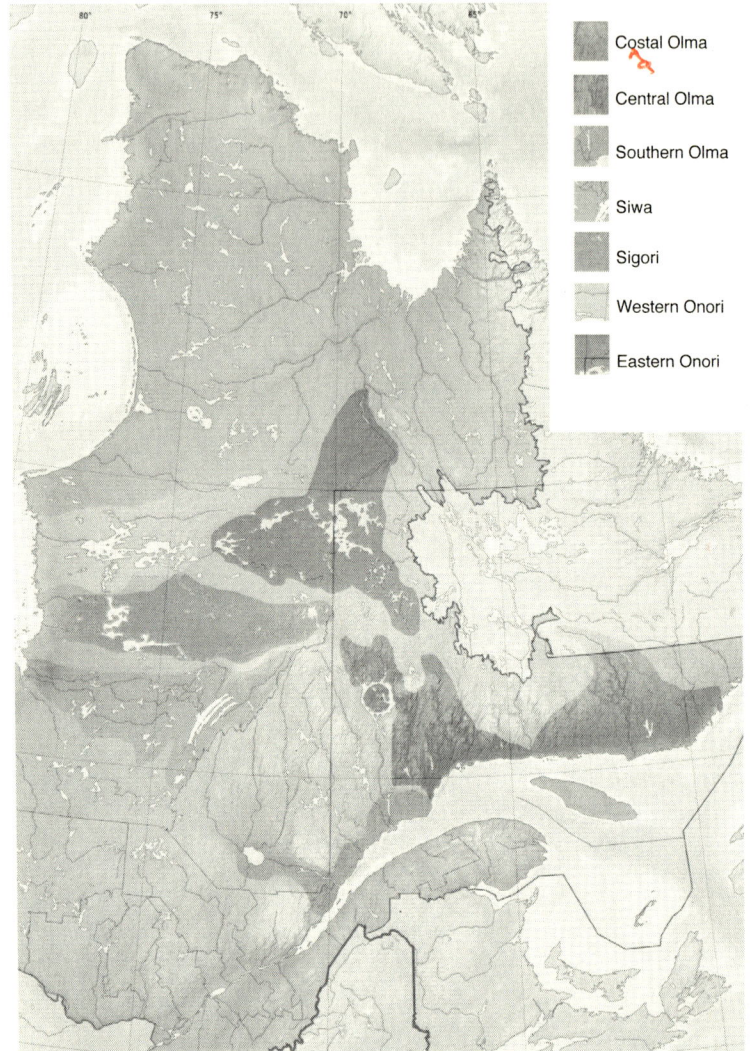

heavy but bare brow and brown hair. However, unlike other native populations, Alopian people sometimes display curly hair in much lighter shades, freckles, pale brown to green eyes and a paler complexion.

Genetically, Alopians are atypical in that they exhibit the highest rate of the X mtDNA haplogroup in the Americas, with as much as 45% of the population carrying the X haplogroup. They are followed by the Algonquian people (their neighbours to the west) with a frequency of as much as 25%. The X haplogroup is the only founding haplogroup of Native Americans (the others are A, B, C and D) which is found in Europe, specifically in Near East, Caucasus and Mediterranean Europe. This, along with other clues discussed elsewhere in this book, points to an ultimately European origin for the Alopian people and languages.

§2.1 Origin of the Alopian People

It has been proposed that the Alopian people arrived in Quebec from Europe sometime after the beginning of the Holocene epoch roughly 10,000 years ago when most of Quebec was still covered by a thick layer of ice. These people who settled the northeastern part of America would have likely spoken a single language, which quickly took to diverging into the present Alopian languages over a period of 2500-3500 years. Viewed in concert with the range of with their domain, the arrival of the Alopian people in North-America can be placed 5,000-4,000 years ago, during the late Boreal or early Atlantic periods of the Holocene epoch. This places the present Siwa people and their relatives in time at around 2,500 years ago.

The reconstructed proto-language, ancestor of the Alopian languages, is likely to have been spoken somewhere in Eurasia to the west of the Ural mountains. This generally supported scenario indicates that Proto-Alopians moved westward and likely encountered the early Uralic or Finno-Ugric people in or east of Scandinavia. This interaction would have lasted for some time to allow for the incorporation of several loanwords into the early proto-Alopian language. Eventually proto-Alopians are thought to have traveled across the Atlantic Ocean and settled what is known today as Quebec. The means of this migration over the Atlantic ocean are unknown, but travel by boat is possible, especially in view of the advanced boat making skills displayed by the Olma people, who build boats strong enough to go fishing great distances out into the Atlantic.

The evidence for this migration from Europe to America is composed of a few borrowings from a very early Uralic language as well as traits generally dissimilar to the native american cultures that surround Alopian people and similar traits to many Siberian reindeer herders. This theory, if correct, would make the Alopian people the only genetic and linguistic group to have settled America from the Atlantic Ocean.

Due of the great time depth involved in reconstructions of proto-Uralic languages (proto-Finnic, proto-Saamic and/or proto-Finno-Permic. depending on the classification) which appear to go back to the earliest stages of proto-Uralic, it is not possible to confirm a time or area of contact between the proto-Alopian and early Uralic peoples – if it occurred at all.

However, it seems very likely that these two groups were at one point in Sprachbund with geographical proximity and sociolinguistic contact. Genetic or otherwise, evidence of community or contact includes cultural terms common to the Uralic language. The proto-Uralic *wäśkä (sometimes termed a Wanderwort) resembles the proto-Alopian form *(v/m?)ōski (cf. SIWA *moski* 'wild copper' and OLMA *vaišk* 'golden, reddish, yellow'). Similarly, the proto-Uralic *yïŋsi 'bow' is similar (but not identical or regularly derivable) to the proto-Alopian *ɨksɨ (cf. SIWA *ÿksy* 'bow').

Further evidence places the movement of the proto-Alopian people in a migration course near the Baltic sea, such as the extensive use of amber in graves, large ceramic containers decorated with fine lines, using of large tipis and wooden houses common to the Comb-Ceramic or Pit-Comb culture of neolithic Scandinavia, which places a proto-Alopian presence there at 7000 years ago.

This is coherent with apparent loanwords from a Uralic language:

proto-Uralic	*suksi	'ski'
proto-Alopian	*süs:i-ba	
Siwa	sohpa	'ski'

proto-Uralic	*suksi	'ski'
proto-Alopian	*süs:i	
Siwa	syhhi	'bent tree'

proto-Uralic	*mekši	'bee'
proto-Alopian	*mēši	
Siwa	meihho 'beehive'	

proto-Uralic	*wäŋe	'brother-in-law'
proto-Alopian	*veŋe	
Siwa	vi	'male visitor who is allowed to sleep with host's daughter'

proto-Uralic	*puwe	'wood'
proto-Alopian	*pümi	
Siwa	pymi	'unedible cambium'

proto-Uralic	*jikä	'age'
proto-Alopian	*j:ecæ	
Siwa	gjekes	'year'

proto-Uralic	*repä	'fox'
proto-Alopian	*re<te>pa	
Siwa	retema 'fox'	

proto-Uralic	*päjwä	'sun'
proto-Alopian	*pej-pe	
Siwa	peibi	'full-moon'

proto-Uralic	*hi-	'polish'
proto-Alopian	*hex-	
Siwa	heġl-	'to polish, to make smooth/even'

proto-Uralic	*tuŋke	'push'
proto-Alopian	*toŋ-ka	
Siwa	tōkka	'it will give birth to it (of animals)'

These correspondences are however at a time depth too deep for more than speculation on whether these words are true borrowings or convergent coincidence.

§2.2 The Alopian People in North-America

Proponents are currently divided over proposals on the mechanism of proto-Alopian migration, currently into two separate camps; the most likely route of settlement is along the southern margins of the Atlantic sea ice (early settlement theory) or by crossing the ocean on boat (late settlement theory).

An agricultural force such as the Corded-Ware culture might have forced the hunter-gathering proto-Alopian people to migrate westward. Most of the present Alopian territory would have been unaccessible or covered in a large lake (the Tyrrell sea) 9000 years ago. Proto-Alopian people would have first settled in the eastern Woodlands and subsequently moved up into the Shield Archaic cultural region as the Laurentide Ice Sheet recessed. Unlike the Algonquian people, who are believed to have come from the west and have more or less always been part of the Shield Archaic culture, Proto-Alopians would have gone through a cultural switch, going from semi-nomadic forest hunting and light agriculture to a much more nomadic lifestyle of forest and sea hunting and a heavy dependence on caribou herding.

Many terms related more or less to the lifestyle of the Shield Archaic culture found in Alopian languages are borrowed from an early Algonquian language:

proto-Algonquian	*ahp-	'dark blue, bruise'
proto-Alopian	*o-ōp-i	
Siwa	òbi	'X gets a bruise'
proto-Algonquian	*ameθkwa	'beaver'
proto-Alopian	*meskwa	
Siwa	misko	'beaver meat'
proto-Algonquian	*pešiwa	'lynx'
proto-Alopian	*pišwe	
Siwa	pisvi	'lynx'
proto-Algonquian	*nepi-	'water'
proto-Alopian	*niiw-	
Siwa	nivvon	'wet'
proto-Algonquian	*ašk-	'unripe'
proto-Alopian	*ŏsk-ama	
Siwa	ohkama	'raw'
proto-Algonquian	*-axkw-	'wood'
proto-Alopian	*-ōga-	(in certain tree names)
Siwa	serula	'larch'

	iruoga	'larch wood'[1]
proto-Algonquian	*eθkwe-	'woman'
proto-Alopian	*iskwe	
Siwa	*iski*	'woman'
proto-Algonquian	*ka:wa:ntakwa	'white spruce'
proto-Alopian	*kauwa:ta	
Siwa	*kumora*	'white spruce'
proto-Algonquian	*mahkate:w	'black'
proto-Alopian	*mōka-si	
Siwa	*moasi*	'black bear (taboo word)'
proto-Algonquian	*namewa	'sturgeon'
proto-Alopian	*nomwa	
Siwa	*nommo*	'sturgeon'
proto-Algonquian	*na:pe:ya:kwa	'male porcupine'
proto-Alopian	*nobeja	
Siwa	*nobia*	'porcupine'
proto-Algonquian	*oxpwa·kana	'pipe'
proto-Alopian	*ōbwa·kon	
Siwa	*uboko*	'pipe'
proto-Algonquian	*se:hse:ka:ntakwa	'black spruce'
proto-Alopian	*seseka:ta	
Siwa	*seskora*	'tree used to find one's way'
proto-Algonquian	*weθkwani	'his forehead'
proto-alopian	*oskwan	
Siwa	*oskon*	'male moose'
proto-Algonquian	*wesa:w	'yellow'
proto-alopian	*osū	
siwa	*usu*	'smoked'[2]

---

[1] (cf. *sijula* 'fir' > *ijuoga* 'fir wood' and *nipi* 'dwarf birch' *neuoga/neyoga* 'drift wood' (proto-Siwa *nīw-ōga, contaminated by *neyo* 'sand')

[2] (reanalyzed as *os-u, cf. *toski* 'it keeps for a long time' from *os-k and *oskima* 'durable')

§2.3 The Alopian Family Tree

The diagram below shows how Alopian languages are thought to have evolved from the proto-Alopian language and how they are related to each other.

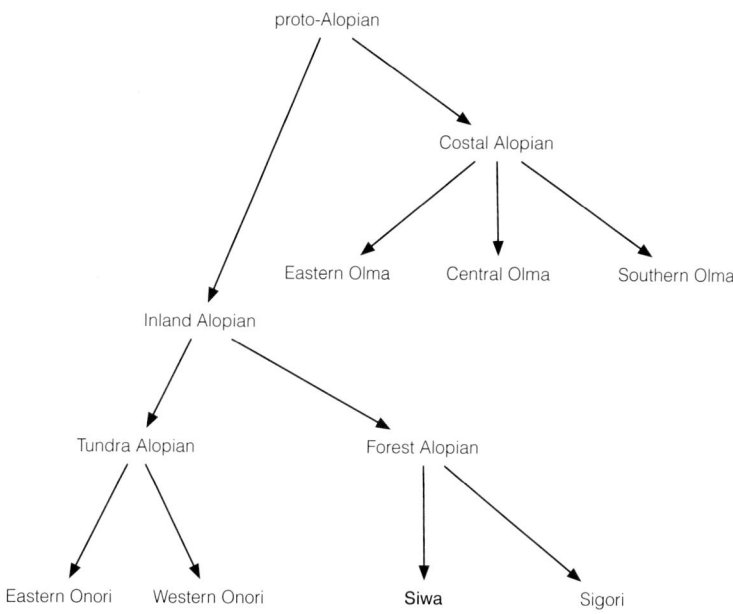

The Alopians are organized in 3 main groups according to both a cultural and geographical separation; the nomadic caribou herders of the north (the Tundra Alopians); the semi-nomadic hunter gatherers of the Boreal Forest (the Forest Alopian speakers), and the semi-settled fishermen, farmers, traders and hunters of the southern territory (the Costal Alopian speakers). The settled Costal Alopians have been influenced by the extended North-Eastern cultural area of North-America and are thus similar to Iroquoian people. The nomadic and semi-nomadic Forest and Taiga Alopians of the North belong to the Subarctic hunter-gatherer cultural area. Despite large cultural differences, the Alopian peoples recognize their distinct culture, ethnicity and linguistic relationship. This is supported by an intricate system of cooperation, intertribal visitations, intermarriage and trade.

	Proto-Alopian	Forest Alopian			Tundra Alopian			Costal Alopian		
		Siwa	Sigori		Eastern Onori	Western Onori	Southern Olma	Central Olma	Costal Olma
fish	*sira	sira	sina		si:/si:s	sina	siesa	si:s	sicci
berry	*sudo	suvo	suo/suju		su:j	su:	suol	su:ru	suli
firewood	*tine	tinin	čie/čieni		čeni	čini	cien	čen	čiem
honey	*siwe	sivi	sibi		še:j	šie	sieb	si:b	šep
cedar	*tsxi:	tsgin	tsuhi/tso:		tsømø	tši	čiše	čiši	či:š
guts	*tio:di-un	tsoadjun	čo:čan/čo:nu		čo:čunu	čo:čo	čua?nu	čuo?nu	ča?nu
snowshoes	*jɨku-m	gjykin	čikom/čika		čyka/kyka	čykyn	cöca	žöča	žačča
aspen	*säl-ka	solka	sanaka		sauk/sauka	salka	sauka	so:ka	solk
maple	*ma:hi	maihhi	mauhi/ma:fi		ma:š/ma:ši	ma:š	ma:j	ma:bi	maub

	Proto-Alopian	Forest Alopian		Tundra Alopian			Costal Alopian		
		Siwa	Sigori	Eastern Onori	Western Onori	Southern Olma	Central Olma	Costal Olma
smoke	*obena	**obena/ obeno**	obna/ wabna	wo:na/ wo:ni	oʔna	vuapi	wapi	wapin
fat	*bi:li	**bieli**	bieli/biali	be:w/be:j	bieli	pieja	paja	paja
fly (n.)	*mɨrɨ	**myry**	mini	myry/myny	myry	mana	mana	mana
forest fire	*sãθ-bi	**saḍbi**	soppi	saspi/ sappi	saspi	saumpi	sampi	sauppi
hunter	*ta-mãθ-si	**tamosi**	tamoši/ tamoš	tamši	tamši	tama:š	tamo:š	tamo:š
one	*migi	**mî**	mje	meč	mič	mag	max	meg
two	*eši	**eṡi**	iš	iiš	iiš	aš	aš	eš

12

§2.4 The Siwa People

The Siwa people call themselves *Siuragi* in their language, Siwa (*Siu̯a*). There are various endonyms used for different parts of the Siwa territory. These two names are clearly etymologically related (siu- and siu̯-), though the ultimate origin is unclear. Siwa themselves consider that the words originate from *sivva* 'foxes', as they strongly associate with the arctic fox (*vulpes lagopus*). However, another possibility is that the two cognates could be related to the word sivi 'honey'. In Siwa mythology, the world came from a drop of honey that was shattered by lightning. This is also supported by various words with a positive conotation derived from honey (*sivusomi* 'honeyman' means a righteous, good man) and the central role that honey plays in Siwa culture – honey is considered a holy substance, a cure and even a form of payment.

As a people, the Siwa are united by their way of life, their mythology, stories, songs, skills and dialects. All Siwa are semi-nomadic, constantly moving during the winter and regrouping in permanent villages during the summer months. Siwa society is organized around multiple units formed of one or many families living together in communities around lakes and rivers. These communities are home to children and woman all year round, with the men and boys being away from the communities for up to 9 months of the year.

Siwa people survive thus through hunting and the keeping of caribou (or at the very least the hunting of caribou) and some light forms of agriculture (certain communities grow beans, berries and squashes). Great hunting and fishing skills and an extensive knowledge of the flora in which they live has allowed Siwa to grow and expand over a large territory and diversify into specific regional communities. For example, the western communities are known for their seal hunting while eastern communities exceed at weaving baskets and shoes from birch bark.

§2.4.1 Siwa Territory

Siwa territory contains four main regions, each of which have their own dialects, culture and own ethnonyms. They are the western, mid-western, mid-eastern and eastern territories. Eastern Siwa people call themselves *Tatimragi* (shore-people, cf. temmu 'shore'), mid-easterners are called *Aslaragi* (antler-people, cf. *salama* 'antlers'), mid-westerners are called *Densigi* (arrow-people, cf. *deno* 'arrow'), and easterners are called *Hesṡigi* (salt-people, cf. *hego* 'salt'). Mid-eastern and mid-western territories are sometimes refered to as *Masmoski* (game-people). These ethnonyms reflect characteristic features of those who live in each territory.

There are 22 main Siwa communities spread over the whole territory, with many more smaller settlements and temporary camps. The most populous community is the city of *Aingo*, whose dialect is the basis for the language described in this book. The communities and territories are organized as such:

    Western communities (Hesṡigi):
        Ėdnu
        Riekka
        Nenniu̯auki
        Regna

Mid-western communities (**Denṡigi**)
    Tsōki
    Hadlġoi
    Kola
    Sủkụisġa

Mid-eastern communities (**Aslaragi**)
    Sarsirit
    Onnjụ
    Saihken

Eastern communities (**Tatimragi**)
    Aingo
    Jekla and **H**okla
    Rihri
    Kelṡin
    Neụihesko
    Kjevvi
    Kjuomṡin
    Sorhi
    Nupiddima
    Suṡtaṡen

§2.4.1.1 Geography

The geography of Quebec was quite different 3000 years ago than it is today. The water levels of lakes and rivers was higher, the climate was wetter and slightly cooler than today. Flora and fauna found more to the north were common in the south of Quebec. The Boreal Forest also began further south than it is today. Wetlands, quagmires, bogs and marshes were much more common than today. The Tundra, Open Boreal Woodland, Mid Taiga and South Taiga vegetation/climate belts would have been respectively shifted to the south, such that the Tundra belt of today would have been found where today's Open Boreal Woodland belt is, and the Open Boreal Woodland belt would have been where the Mid Taiga belt is today, and so on. The tundra area would have been treeless, perhaps similar to northern Finland and its *tunturi*.

§2.4.2 Sociolinguistic Situation

It is estimated that are about 30,000–60,000 Siwa people. About half of the males speak at least another language, most commonly Sigori. Some may be able to communicate with neighboring Algonquian peoples. Siwa people recognize their close ties with the Sigori, and the continuum between the two languages can become unclear in the dialect of Siwa which closest resemble Sigori, namely the *Sorhi* dialect.

Siwa is best thought of as a continuum composed of 8 dialect groups spoken in 22 areas, which are generally separated into East and West. The grammar contained in this book is based mainly on the eastern dialects, especially that of Aingo, which belongs to the Sapsi dialect. To illustrate how the dialects differ from each other, the phrase *the man burned himself in the fire* is shown in each dialect:

Western Dialects
   Far Western, spoken in **Ėdnu**, **Riekka**, **Nenniyauki** and **Regna**

   asayi nobetta ot sonka

   Mid Western, spoken in **Tsōki**, **Hadlġoi**, **Kola** and **Sùkyisġa**

   asavi nobenda at sonka

Eastern Dialects
   Mid Eastern, spoken in **Sarsirit**, **Onnju** and **Saihken**

   yasayi noyenda ot sōkko

   Sapsi dialects, spoken in **Jekla**, **Rihri** and **Kelsin**

   osayi noemta oġta somġo

   South-Sapsi, spoken in **Aingo**, **Nupiddima** and **Suśtaśen**

   osavvi noimmita otta sōkko

   North-Sapsi, spoken in **Neyihesko**

   osayi noyemta otta sonko

   Far Eastern, spoken in **Kjevvi** and **Kjuomśin**

   usavvi noyenda okta songu

   North Eastern, spoken in **Sorhi** (called **Saroġ**)

   yasaddi noyemba yaġta sōmko

The western dialects have most heavily been influenced by surrounding Algonquian languages; they contain more loanwords, are less conservative than eastern dialects and are generally regarded as less proper by eastern dialect speakers.

§3 Phonology
§3.1 Vowels

The table below shows all vowels of Siwa, both phonemes (in //) and allophones (in []).

	front	near-front	mid	near-back	back
close	/i · y/		/ɨ/		/u/
near close	/e · ø/	[ɪ]		[ʊ]	
close mid					/ɔ/
open mid	[ɛ · œ]				/ɔ̃/
near open	/æ/				
open	[a]				/ɑ/

Siwa has a phonemic distinction between short and long vowels:

SHORT
/ɑ æ e i ɔ u ø y ɔ̃/
<a ę e i o u ů y õ>

LONG
/æː eː iː ʊː uː øː yː ɔ̃ː/
<å ė i̇ ȯ u̇ ėu ẏ õu>

The former are either 'open' or 'closed', and the latter are always 'long' vowels. The two semi-vowels are /j w/ <i̯ u̯>. The semi-vowels can also be long, then spelled gj [jː] and vv [wː]. The short vowels are pronounced as follow in closed syllables (before two consonants or before a word-final consonant, though not before long consonants):

/a ɛ ɪ ɔ ʊ œ œ ɔ̃/
<a e i o u ů y õ>

The vowel /æ/ <ę> does not exist in closed syllables, being instead replaced by [ɛ] <e>, and <y ů> being being pronounced [œ] when in closed syllables.

Siwa also has a vowel which lacks its own surface form – it is a phoneme which has no fixed pronunciation; an archiphoneme. This archiphoneme is <ɨ> (not to be confused with the anaptyctic [ɨ]). Its pronunciation is dependent on the preceding vowels. It is not found in stressed syllables (see *§3.1.3*). It is sometimes found written as <ȯ>, especially when transcribing certain eastern dialects which have kept it as the phoneme [ɯ] or [ɤ], e.g. *kigjini* [ˈcʰijːini] 'youngest child' vs. *kigjôni* [ˈcʰiːjːɯni]. However, since this is restricted to only a few dialects, it will not be used here.

Below is a chart summing the vowels and their orthography:

	short		long	
	open	closed	open	closed
/a/	[ɑ] a	[a] a	[æː] à	
/æ/	[æ] ę	Ø	[æː] à	
/e/	[e] e	[ɛ] e	[eː] è	
/i/	[i] i	[ɪ] i	[iː] i	
/o/	[o] o	[ɔ] o	[ʊː] or [ɯː] ò	
/u/	[u] u	[ʊ] u	[uː] ù	
/y/	[y] y	[œ] y	[yː] ẏ	
/ø/	[ø] û	[œ] û	[øː] èu	
/ɔ̃/	[ɔ̃] õ		[ɔ̃ː] õu	

The terms 'open' and 'closed' refer to the type of syllable the vowels appear in. Open syllables are of the type V.(C)(V), where the coda of the first syllable is followed by another syllable without onset. Closed syllables are of the type VC# (word-final coda other than -s) and V.CC. For example, **at.a** [ˈɑta] is open, **at** [ˈat] is closed and so is **an.ta** [ˈanta]. Note however, that -CC- must be composed of two different phonemes – long consonants and the sounds [tɬ tɕ dʑ] and [ts] do not cause a syllable to be closed.

gedli	[ˈɟetɬi]	'X will work' (rarely [ˈɟɛtɬi])
hiddjuja	[ˈhidʑːuja]	'X will stack Y up' (never *[ˈhɪdʑːuja])
katsa	[ˈkʰatsa]	'outside'

The quality of a vowel (short open, short closed, but **not** long) changes only allophonically when in a stressed syllable, i.e. the vowel's realization changes but it maintains the same phonemic value, if short:

	dàdna	[ˈdæːʔtna]	'pillow'
→	*dànaka*	[ˈdæːnɑga]	'pillow GEN.'
	ehhama	[ˈehːɑma]	'seam'
→	*ehhakka*	[ˈehːaʔka]	'seam GEN.'

§3.1.1 Short Vowels
Short vowels are:

    in open syllables   in closed syllables
    [ɑ æ e i ɔ u y ø ɔ̃]   [a ɛ ɛ ɪ ɔ ʊ œ œ ɔ̃]
    <a ę e i o u ů y õ>   <a e e i o u y ů õ>

Short /ø y/ respectively are not phonetically distinguished in closed environments, but they remain distinguished through orthography. In the Regna dialect, /ø/ in closed syllables can be realized as [ɤ] or [ɵ]. The nasal /ɔ̃/ has no allophonic variation in closed or open syllables.

    gagi [ˈgɑɟi] 'with'   *kulu* [ˈkʰulu] 'cloudy'
    galmot [ˈgalmɔʔ] 'soft'   *nuppua* [ˈnʊʔpua] 'X will snatch Y'

    kęmes [ˈcʰæmɛs] 'happy'
    megi [ˈmeɟi] 'I'   *půdů* [ˈpʰødø] 'log'
    netra [ˈnɛtxa] 'really'   *sůtrů* [ˈsœtxø] 'frustrated'

    nitśa [ˈnitɕa] 'X will teach Y'   *tygi* [ˈtʰyɟi] 'poison'
    pilra [ˈpʰɪlra] 'copper'   *ymni* [ˈœmnːi] 'early fall'

    pohi [ˈpʰɔʔi] 'chubby'   *kõhi* [ˈkʰɔ̃ʔi] 'memory'
    sġodna [ˈsxɔʔtna] 'shade'   *kõdga* [ˈkʰɔ̃ðga] 'bear cub'

§3.1.1.1 Short Open Vowels
Short open vowels are those which appear in front of a single consonant, a long geminated unvoiced stop ([pː] <bb> [tː] <dd> [kː] <gg>), any geminated sonorant or [tɕ] <tś ti> [dʑ] <dj di> [tɬ] <dl> and [ts] <ts>, followed by another vowel – in an open syllable.

        ata   [ˈɑta]   'open mouth'
→   *atra*   [ˈatxa]   'open mouth GEN.'
        (short open vowel in open syllable into closed syllable)

        sukno   [ˈsʊʔnɔ]   'large isolated conifer'
→   *sungoma*   [ˈsuŋːɔma] 'large isolated conifer GEN.'
        (short closed vowel in close syllable into open syllable)

        hallu   [ˈhɑlːu]   'electricity'
→   *haluka*   [ˈhɑluga]   'electricity GEN.'
        (unaffected by geminated /l/)

The vowels /a/ is realized as [a] <a> word finally for most speakers. More elevated speech may have [ɑ].

§3.1.1.2 Short Closed Vowels
Short closed vowels are those which appear in front of a single consonant word finally, or next to two consonants word internally, i.e. a closed syllable. Short closed vowels never appear in originally open syllables, with the exception of /æ/ (though not as an allophone of /ɑ a/). They can only be in open syllables as the result of a shift in the syllable structure, in which case they become open.

	gedna	[ˈɹɛʔtna]	'nut'
→	genari	[ˈɹenɑri]	'nut GEN.'
	kuspo	[ˈkʰʊspɔ]	'skunk'
→	kusoui	[ˈkʰusɔwi]	'skunk GEN.'
	edġe	[ˈɛðxe]	'air'
→	eteri	[ˈeteri]	'air GEN.'

§3.1.1.3 The Archiphoneme <i̇>
The archiphoneme <i̇> has no pronunciation of its own. It is not written, but it is its own phoneme. It is never found in stressed position, and is found in a number of derivative suffixes. Its pronunciation is dependent on the preceding vowels:

o a	e i ę å	u y i̇	ů
u/o	i/e	y/u/ů	ů

For example, the derivational suffix -in marks large objects (and causes lengthening of the stressed vowel):

	tahha	[ˈtʰɑhːa]	'tree'
→	toahhun	[ˈtʰɔɑhːʊn]	'large tree' (underlying *toah·i̇n)
	gasi	[ˈgɑsi]	'moon'
→	gausun	[ˈgɑusʊn]	'full moon' (underlying *gaus·i̇n)
	gei	[ˈɹei]	'snout'
→	geġiin	[ˈɹejːɪn]	'big snout' (underlying *geġi·i̇n)
	kyṡi	[ˈcʰyɕi]	'squirrel'
→	kůiṡůn	[ˈcʰœɪɕœn]	'big squirrel' (underlying *kůiṡ·i̇n)

§3.1.2 Long Vowels
Long vowels are always:

[æː eː iː ʊː uː øː yː ɔ̃ː]
<à è ì ò ù èu ỳ õu>

Long vowels are found in both open and closed syllables.

màra	[ˈmæːra]	'we'
màhra	[ˈmæhra]	'bear'
pèsi	[ˈpʰeːsi]	'maternal uncle'
pèbmui	[ˈpʰeːʔpmui]	'X will bounce'
pìni	[ˈpʰiːni]	'corn'
pìdna	[ˈpʰiːʔtna]	'direction'
pòbi	[ˈpʰʊːbi]	'seal'
tòhni	[ˈtʰʊːhni]	'late spring'
ùma	[ˈuːma]	'a lot of'
ùdno	[ˈuːʔtnɔ]	'angelica'
èu	[ˈøː]	'sand'
èulbi	[ˈøːlbi]	'hoof'
ỳ	[ˈjyː]	'end, ending'
mỳhni	[ˈmyːhni]	'wolverine'
kõuba	[ˈkʰɔ̃ːba]	'the most'
õut	[ˈɔ̃ʔ]	'newly fallen snow'

§3.1.3 Diphthongs
Siwa has a rich system of diphthongs. Diphthongs in Siwa can only consist of two short vowels. A long vowel can be combined with any other vowel, in which case the result are two separate syllables, e.g. *sì.ubmi* [ˈsiːʊʔpmi] 'hungry'. Below is a table of all possible vowel combinations and/or the result of two vowels coming in direct contact with each other.

When vowels come in contact through consonant syncope, they form diphthongs or monophthongs according to the table below. Diphthongs may change when they find themselves in a closed syllable. This open syllable diphthong is shown above, with the closed (or contracted) version below. Contracted diphthongs are irregularly used and vary greatly across speakers and dialects. They may be ignored completely, but they form the basis of many dialects.

Note that in many cases, when vowels come together, a consonant may be inserted between them or the result may not be that which is presented in the table below. This happens with prefixes as well as suffixes. The changes are tied to grammatical or morphological markings - they happen when two vowels or more come together as the result of a morphological coalescence, for example adding preverbal vowels. Because these are function specific in nature (i.e. each change is particular to a grammatical function), they will be explained in the relevant chapters (see §4.3.1.7, §4.4, §5.3 and §5.4.4)

	a-	ę-	e-	i-	o-	u-	y- / ů-
-a							ůa [œa]
	à [æ:]			ia [ia]	oa [ɔa]	ua [ua]	ẏ [y:]
-ę							ůa [œa]
							ẏ [y:]
-e	ai [ai]	ei [ei]	è [e:]	ie [ie]	oi [ɔi] or ue [ue]	ui/ue or y [ui/ue] [y]	ůi [œɪ]
							ẏ [y:]
-i	ai [ai]	ei [ei]		i̇ [i:]	oi [ɔi]	ui or y [ui] [y]	ůi [œɪ]
							ẏ [y:]
-o	au [au]	eu [eu]	io [iɔ]			uo [ʊɔ]	
-u	au [au]	ay [æœ]	eu [eu]	iu [iu]	ou [ɔu]	u̇ [u:]	
-y/-ů	ay [æœ]		ey [ɛœ]	iů [iø]		u̇ [u:]	ẏ [y:]

21

Notice that [ø:] is always spelled <ėu>. The diphthong <ue> is mostly found with inanimate nouns ending in -o with a stressed -e-.
　　　　Dialectal variation in diphthong is great and often constitutes the basis on which one can identify them. It is worth noting that the following diphthongs are pronounced differently in closed syllables:

<au oa eu ia ie io iu iů ou ua ui ay ey>
[aʊ ɔa ɛʊ ɪa ɪɛ ɪɔ ɪʊ ɪœ ɔʊ ʊa ʊɪ æœ ɛœ]

aubmi	'knot'	[ˈaʊʔpmi]
koakvi	'call'	[ˈkʰɔakwːi]
neulkio	'ant'	[ˈnɛʊlcɪɔ]
nianso	'creek'	[ˈnɪansɔ]
riehpi	'wife'	[ˈrɪɛhpi]
diuksi	'icicle'	[ˈdɪʊksːi]
miout	'warmth'	[ˈmɪɔʊʔ]
yanuahmo	'lichen covered spot GEN.'	[ˈwɑnʊahmɔ]
vuihli	'X will whistle'	[ˈvʊɪhɬi]
gaykka	'X will satisfy Y'	[ˈɟæœʔka]

§3.1.3.1 Diphthong Contraction

The segment -oy̨- and -uy̨- are affected by lenition, in which case they change to ů (or ėu is stressed) and similarly, -iy̨- changes to y (or ẏ if stressed) after lenition. The semi-vowel y̨ is not pronounced after t- d- n- k- and g- because it shows palatalization:

　　　　　　　　　　　　LENITION
-ov-V　　-oy̨-V　　　→　　　　-ėu- or -ů-
-uv-V　　-uy̨-V　　　→　　　　-ėu- or -ů-
-iv-V　　-iy̨-V　　　→　　　　-y- or -ẏ-

　　　suvi　　　　['suvi]　　　'flow'
→　sůimo　　　['sœimɔ]　　'flow GEN.'
　　(suvi → *sui-mo → *syi-mo → sůimo)

　　　huy̨o　　　['huwɔ]　　　'fog'
→　huoma　　['huɔma]　　'fog GEN.'
　　(huy̨o → *huo-ma → *hyo-ma → huoma)

With other diphthongs, the process is irregular, unpredictable and is disappearing as a productive change. It is still found in derivational processes, but as a productive and regular change, it is mostly only found in elevated speech or in the speech of older speakers of the eastern dialects, especially in the north-east (**Sorhi** and **Kjuomṡin**, and rarely in **Kjevvi**).

§3.1.4 Semi-vowels
Siwa has two semi-vowels or glides, ɥ and ʝ. They behave like consonants in most respects - they are not affected by other vowels (no contraction). They can also be found as long, then [w:] <vv> and [j:] <gj>. The long semi-vowel <vv> is more common in stressed positions than its short counterpart <ɥ>.

	igjut	[ˈijːʊʔ]	'mood'
	luvvù	[ˈluwːuː]	'intense heat'
EAST	oɥala	[ˈɔwala]	'wide'
WEST	ovvala/oula	[ˈɔwːala/ˈɔʊla]	'wide'

The semi-vowel ʝ is written without its diacritic if it is the onset of a syllable not directly after a stressed syllable, i.e. third syllable from the beginning of the word. This is to reflect the pronunciation of most speakers, though it might not occur if a speaker is speaking in a more elevated register.

§3.1.5 Triphthongs
Siwa allows the following triphthongs:

/iau iai iei ieu iue ioi oai eui uoi uei/
<iau iai iei ieu iue ioi oai eui uoi uei>

The diphthongs <iei ieu iue> may be pronounced with a glide or [ɪ] in both open or closed syllables. Other diphthongs are also subject to change in closed syllables. Not all dialects have <eui>, some have <eɥi>, <ey> or <evvi> instead.

tsgiauga	[ˈtsxiauɣa]	'cedar wood'
tõkkiauki	[ˈtʰɔ̃ʔciauʝi]	'litter'
tieibid	[ˈtʲjeibɪdʑ] or [ˈtʲɪeibɪdʑ]	'twig GEN.'
mieumi	[ˈmjeumi] or [ˈmɪeumi]	'leg GEN.'
niue	[ˈnjue] or [ˈnɪue]	'sand GEN.'
toaika	[ˈtʰɔaiga]	'urine GEN.'
peuiskvi	[ˈpʰɛʊɪskwːi]	'slippery jack
		(*Suillus luteus*)'
(also peɥiskvi~peyskvi~pevviskvi)		
ruoiknei	[ˈrʊɔɪʔŋei]	'X wakes up a little'

§3.1.5.1 Diphthong and Long Vowel Coalescence
Siwa has a complex system of rules that govern how certain diphthongs and long vowels behave when they coalesce with other vowels. They are especially important in the creation of new words, and for inanimate nouns whose stressed syllable

contains a long vowel or a diphthong, and whose consonant coda disappears completely through lenition.

The rules are fairly simple, but many exceptions exist. Generally, diphthongs ending in -u will lose this sound and have -m-, or -b- (before -o/-i/-ů/-y), whereas diphthongs in -i change to -i̯, or -gi̯ before -i/-ů/-y. The diphthong ay is reduced to ęm- or -ęb-, and both eu and ey change to ům- or ůb-. Diphthongs with a front rounded vowel cause -u to change to -ů.

Suffixes beginning with a -i̯ are grouped under suffixes in -i. However, the glide -i̯ disappears and only leaves -gi̯-, -b- or -i-. For example, the word hi̯ůbaka 'tidal pool' was formed by adding the ending -i̯aka (causing vowel fronting) to hi̯ů 'sea water' – thus, one could infer the original form *hi̯ůb·i̯aka.

	back			front		rounded
	-a	-o	-u	-e	-i	-y/-ů
ai-	-ai̯a	-ai̯o	-ai̯u	-ai̯e	-agi̯i	-ey
oi-	-oi̯a	-oi̯o	-oi̯u	-oi̯e	-ogi̯i	-oi̯ů
ui-/ue-	-ui̯a	-ui̯o	-ui̯u	-ui̯e	-ugi̯i	-ůgi̯ů
ei-	-ei̯a	-ei̯o	-ei̯u	-ei̯e	-egi̯i	-ei̯ů
ie-	-igi̯a	-igi̯o	-igi̯u	-iė	-iei	-igi̯y
ůi-	-ůi̯a	-ůi̯o	-ůgi̯ů	-ůi̯e	-ůgi̯i	-ůgi̯ů
ay-	-ęma	-ębo	-ębů	-ęme	-ębi	-ębů
uo-	-uma	-ubo	-umu	-ume	-ubi	-ůbů
au-	-ama	-abo	-amu	-ame	-abi	-amů
ou- **oa-**	-oma	-obo	-omu	-ome	-obi	-omů
eu-/ey-	-ůma	-ůbo	-ůbů	-ůme	-ůbi	-ůbů
iu-	-ivva	-ibo	-ibu	-ivve	-ibi	-ivvů
ȧ-	-ęi̯a	-ęi̯o	-ęi̯u	-ęi̯e	-ęgi̯i	-ey
ȯ-	-oma	-obo	-omu	-ome	-obi	-omů
ů̇-	-uma	-ubo	-ubu	-ume	-ubi	-ůbů
ė-	-evva	-evvo	-evvu	-egi̯e	-egi̯i	-ey

	back			front		rounded
	-a	-o	-u	-e	-i	-y/-ů
i-	-ivva	-ivvo	-ivvu	-igje	-igji / -iddji	-igjy
ẏ-	-yma	-ybo	-yby	-yme	-ybi	-yby
ėu-	-ůma	-ůbo	-ůbů	-ůme	-ůbi	-ůbů

Here are examples of this process:

	gàgi	[ˈɹæːji]	'summer solstice'
→	gẹjagi	[ˈɹæjɑji]	'summer solstice GEN.'

(·gi is a plural marker, < *gà+a)

	gei	[ˈɹei]	'snout'
→	geje	[ˈɹeje]	'snout GEN.' (< *gei+e)

	goi	[ˈgoi]	'sharp edge'
→	gojo	[ˈɹɔjɔ]	'sharp edge GEN.' (< *goi+o)

	hego	[ˈhegɔ]	'salt'
→	hivve	[ˈhiwːe]	'salt GEN.' (< *hiu+e, < *heo+e) (also hiobi)

	keugo	[ˈcʰeuɣɔ]	'burden, load'
→	kůbue	[ˈcʰøbue]	'burden, load GEN.' (< *keu+o+e)

	niuba	[ˈniuba]	'despair'
→	nivvadi	[ˈniwːɑdʑi]	'despair GEN.' (< *niu+a+di)

	maidi	[ˈmɑidʑi]	'measure unit (±30cm)'
→	magjika	[ˈmɑjːiga]	'measuring unit GEN.' (< *mai+i+ka)

	saiyu	[ˈsɑiwu]	'pot'
→	sajuka	[ˈsɑjuga]	'pot GEN.' (< *sai+u+ka)

	tiegibi	[ˈtʰejibi]	'twig'
→	tieibid	[ˈtʰieibɪdʑ]	'twig GEN.' (< *tie+ibi+d)

	tuobi	[ˈtʰuɔbi]	'juniper'
→	tubimo	[ˈtʰubimɔ]	'juniper GEN.' (< *tuo+i+mo) (also tuovvumi)

	vebo	[ˈvebɔ]	'knot'
→	vivve	[ˈviwːe]	'knot GEN.' (< *viu+e) (also *viobi*)

§3.1.6 Vowel Apocope
Final vowel sometimes go through apocope, i.e. they are deleted before the addition of another vowel or consonant. This is especially productive in inanimate nouns, less so in animate nouns and fairly rare in adjectives. Vowel apocope occurs when the emerging consonant cluster is allowed. The complexity of the apocope may influence whether a animate noun or adjective will go through the change. More complex changes are less likely to occur. Apocope is especially common with the vowel -i-.

	tsammi	[ˈtsɑmːi]	'forest'
→	tsamġa	[ˈtsɑmxa]	'forest GEN.'
→	tsamṡita	[ˈtsɑmɕida]	'forest ILLAT.' (not *tsam·ġa·ita)

	sira	[ˈsira]	'fish'
→	sihdi	[ˈsiːhdʑi]	'fish GEN.' (not *sir·a·di)

	kori	[ˈkʰɔri]	'boy'
→	kohko	[ˈkʰɔhkɔ]	'boy GEN.' (not *koriko)

	pyry	[ˈpʰyry]	'gust of wind, wind'
→	pyhma	[ˈpʰœhma]	'gust of wind, wind GEN.'

Verbs with the postverbal vowel -i- may or may not go through apocope if the resulting cluster is allowed - both forms are usually in free variation.

sġaumkka	[ˈsxaʊmkːa]	'we will breathe' (also **sġaumigga**)
iltṡemkka	[iːlˈtɕɛmkːa]	'we will come crawling' (also **iltṡemigga**)

For a more detailed description of vowel apocope in nouns, see section §4.3.1.

§3.1.7 Vowel Prothesis
Vowel prothesis consists of the addition of a vowel to the beginning of a word. This happens regularly in certain dialects, especially those of the east. This is done to avoid initial consonant clusters which have become illegal in the eastern dialect. Vowel prothesis is usually analyzed as part of the root, as the examples below show, where the past tense preverbal vowel **a-** is added onto the already augmented form -omġ-, whereas commonly Siwa shows simply the (irregularly) syncoped root -mġ-.

Standard Siwa

moġa
['mɔxa]
Ø-moġ-a-Ø
TR-drink-ASS.CONCL.TR-3P.PAT
'X will drink Y'

amġa
[aˈmxa]
a-m<Ø>ġ-a-Ø
TR-drink.PAST-ASS.CONCL.TR-3P.PAT
'X drank Y'

Eastern Dialect

anomġa
[ɑnɔˈmxa]
an-o=m<Ø>ġ-a-Ø
TR-drink.PAST-ASS.CONCL.TR-3P.PAT
'X drank Y'

See section *§4.3* on irregular verbs.

§3.1.8 Vowel Polarity Inversion

Vowels may see their polarity inverted. In Siwa grammar, a vowel has two polarities - its default polarity and its inverted polarity. In other words, the inverted polarity of a vowel is its opposite within the context of Siwa phonology. Most vowels have more than one inverted polarity. In the case where one is rounded and one is not, the rounded vowel will be found after another rounded or a high front vowel. In other cases, it is not quite possible to predict the outcome.

	polarized
a	i/e (o before -i/-e in western dialects)
à	ie/ei
ę	u
e	u/o
ė	uo/ù(vv)
i	u/y

	polarized
i̇	uo/ẏ
o	i/y
ȯ	i̇/ẏ
u	e/ai
u̇	ę/ey
y	oi/ů
ẏ	uo/ui
ů	i/ei
ėu	i̇

Polarity inversion is an important derivational strategy. Many words are derived or even combined with inverted polarity. For example, many nouns have a poetic or higher-register counterparts derived from the noun by using polarity inversion and the ending -ts, whose genitive also requires polarity inversion. Adjectives can freely be derived from nouns by polarizing the last vowel and adding a suffix. Most nouns, when attached to another to form a compound, have a polarized final vowel.

	tsammi 'forest'		
→	tsammuts	'forest' (high-register)	(i→u)
→	tsamebme	'forest GEN' (high-register)	(u→e)
→	tsammuha	'of the forest, sylvan' (-ha adjectival marker)	(i→u)
	ni̇pi	'dwarf birch (betula nana)'	
→	ni̇pyts	'dwarf birch' (high-register)	(i→y)
→	ni̇poibme	'dwarf birch GEN.' (high-register)	(y→oi)
	mavvu	'meat'	
→	mavvedna	'meaty' (-dna adjectival marker)	(u→e)

	gauta	'colour'	+ mehiu	'painted'
→	gautumehiu	'colourfully painted'		

	bansi	'today'	+ belmo	'chore, work'
→	bansubelmo	'today's chore'		

	ono	'lichen'	+ kelta	'ground'

→	onikeltuha	'having a lichen covered ground' (-ha adjectival marker)
	njuhhi	'old woman' + ri 'tooth'
→	njuhhuryhha	'having teeth like an old woman' (-ha adjectival marker)

Polarity inversion is also commonly used as a genitive marker for personal names and place names, e.g. *Surri-śini* 'Surro's daughter', rather than *śini Suddji* (true genitive).

§3.2 Stress

Stress is fixed on the initial syllable of a root word. Prefixes do nto affect stress. Only when affixes create new words may stress change.

entiebbie [ɛnˈtiepːie] 'I should'
Root is -tiebb- 'to ought' with prefix **en-**.

mohjeimeni [mɔˈhjeimeni] 'I am hot'
Root is -hjeimen- 'to feel hot' with personal
prefix **m-** and subjective preverbal vowel -o-.

osikkami [ɔˈsɪʔkɑmi] 'I will sneak'
Root is -sikk- 'to sneak' with subjective preverbal vowel -o-.

ogauldigge [ɔˈgaʊldʑicːe] 'we will talk together'
but *ogalen* [ˈɔgalɛn] 'conversation'
The verb has the affix o- while the noun has incorporated the affix into the root and allows it to carry stress.

Certain words saw their prefixes assimilated and stress was shifted to the first syllable.

asġa [ˈasxa] 'ashes'
cf. *sahha* [ˈsɑhːɑ] 'X will burn Y'
Here with syncope of **a** in the root **sahh-** 'to burn'.

Note that in certain dialects, especially in the east, the word-initial consonants [pʰ tʰ kʰ/ cʰ] <p t k> may be found as ejectives if they are preceded by suffixes.

entiebbie [ɛnˈtiepːie] 'I should'
or [ɛnˈt'iepːie]

§3.3 Orthographic Conventions Regarding Vowels

Siwa orthography is fairly regular and logical, but it presents certain difficulties to those who are not familiar with it. Two vowels have special rules regarding their orthography: – the vowel [ø] <ů> cannot take diacritics - instead, it is written [ø:] <èu> when long. Siwa orthography can sometimes express the same sound in more than a single way. For example, [œ] can be written both <y> and <ů>. This means that there are homophones which are only distinguishable through their written forms, e.g. *nǔdna* and *nydna* are both pronounced [nœʔtna], but the former means 'wave' while the latter means 'adult (of women)'. Siwa contains the following orthographic exceptions:

The suffix -ha of the possessive case is pronounced [ɑ] not [ha]. Hyphenated clitics do not change the word boundaries but the word and the clitic read as one unit.

   màhra-nen [ˈmæːhranɛn] 'one's bear'
not   *[ˈmæːhrɑnɛn]

§3.4 Consonants
The table below shows all consonants of Siwa.

	bilabial	dental	alveolar	post alveolar	palatal	velar	glottal
nasal	m (m̥)		n (n̥)		ɲ	ŋː	
plosive	p · b (p')		t · d (t')		c · ɟ	k · g (k')	ʔ
fricative	v	ð	s (z)	ɕ		x · ɣ	h
affricative			tɕ · dʑ (tɕ')				
trill			r · ɾ				
lateral			l~ɬ · tɬ (tɬ')				

§3.4.1 Consonants & Allophones
Siwa consonants are:

[m p b v n t d ð ː s ɕ tɕ dʑ r tɬ c ɟ ŋː ɲ k g x h ʔ]
<m p b v n t d ḍḍ s ś tś dj r dl ki gi ng ni k g ġ hh h>

The table below shows all the phonemes with their allophonic variation. Explanations for special cases are below.

	stressed front vowel	stressed back vowel	unstressed -i	unstressed	long	palatalized	glottalized stressed
/m/		[m] m			[mː] mm		[ʔpm] bm
/p/	[pʰ] p- [p] -p-			[b] p	[ðb] ḍb		[ʔp] pp
/b/		[b] b			[pː] bb		

	stressed front vowel	stressed back vowel	unstressed -i-	unstressed	long	palatalized	glottalized stressed
/v/			[v] v		[w:] vv		
/n/			[n] n		[n:] nn	[ɲ] nj	[ʔtn] dn
/t/	[t] -t- [tʰ] t-	[d] t [tɕ] -ti-	[d] t		[ð:] ḋḋ	tś [tɕ]	[ʔt] tt
/d/	[d] d	[d~ɾ~l] d [dʑ] -di-	[ð] [ɾ] d		[t:] dd	dj [dʑ]	
/ð/	∅	∅	[ð:] ḋḋ		[ð:] ḋḋ		
/s/			[s] s		[s:] ss	[ɕ] ś	
/ɕ/			[ɕ] ś		[ɕ:] śś		
/tɕ/	[tɕ] tś	[tɕ] tś -ti-	[tɕ] tś		[dʑ:] ddj		
/dʑ/	[dʑ] dj o	[dʑ] dj- di-	[dʑ] dj				
/r/			[r] r		[r:] rr		
/l/			[l] l		[l:] ll		
/tɬ/			[tɬ] dl				[ʔtɬ] kl
/ŋ:/	∅		[ŋ:] ng				[ʔŋ] kn
/ɲ/			[ɲ] nj		[ɲ:] nnj	[ɲ] nj	
/k/	[cʰ] k- [c] -k-	[kʰ] k- [k] -k-	[ɟ] k	[g] k	[ðg] ḋg	[c]/[cʰ] kj	[ʔk] kk
/g/	[ɟ] g	[g] g	[ɟ] g [j] -gi-	[ɣ] g	[k:] gg	[j:] gj	
/c/	[cʰ] k- [c] -k-	[cʰ] kj- [c] -kj-	[ɟ] k	[ɟ] kj			

	stressed front vowel	stressed back vowel	unstressed -i	unstressed	long	palatalized	glottalized stressed
/ɟ/	[dz] gi- [j:] -gi-	[ɟ] gi- [j:] -gi-	[j:] gi		[ɟ:] ggi	[ɕ] ṡ	
/x/	[x] ġ	[x] ġ	[ɕ] ṡ or [x] ġ	[x] ġ	[x:] ġġ		
/ʔ/	∅		[ʔ] ḥ		[ʔ:] ḥḥ		
/h/	[h] h- [h:] -hh-		[h:] hh			[h:j] hhi̯	[ʔ] h

§3.4.1.1 Allophony and Sound Changes

Siwa sounds interact with each other in a dynamic and complex system of allophonic variation and sound changes. Due to changes that occur inside and between Siwa words, consonant that were once apart often come together. Special rules govern how sounds fuse together or coalesce, if they can do so at all. Below is a description of how consonants change and interact with other sounds. Only relevant phonemes' allophonic changes are given below (those not included do not show any significant allophonic variation).

/m/

The sound /m/ can be found short as [m] <m>, long as [m:] <mm> or glottalized as [ʔpm] <bm> (sometimes simply [ʔm]). It can also be preaspirated as [hm] <hm>.

moni	['mɔni]	'path'
ḷohma	['lɔhma]	'infectious'
mamma	['mɑm:a]	'leg'

When /m/ comes in contact with /n/, they form the cluster [mn:] or [m:n] <mn>.

umna	['ʊmn:a]	'the place below'
ymni	['œmn:i]	'early fall'
hjòmno	['hjʊ:mn:ɔ]	'the place below'
imni	['ɪmn:i]	'to produce smoke'

Note that although /p/ is voiced in unstressed position, when /m/ precedes it, the cluster it forms is pronounced [mp].

| kůimpa | ['cʰœɪmpa] | 'pair of boots' |

Similarly, when /m/ precedes /ʔk kː/ <kk gg>, they combined to form the cluster [mkː] or [m̥kː] <mkk>. This often occur with the first person plural pronouns in -gga/-gge.

tŭmkki	[ˈtʰœmcːi]	'boulder'
ljemkka	[ˈljɛmkːa]	'to infect'
sġaumkka	[ˈsxaʊmkːa]	'we will breathe' (< sġaum·i·gga)
iltśemkka	[iːlˈtɕɛmkːa]	'we will come crawling' (< il·tśem·i·gga)

If /m/ finds itself next to /k g/, there are three possible outcomes - [mx] <mġ> or [mk] <mk> after /m: ʔpm/ or a long vowel, or [ʔk] <kk> especially in inanimate nouns and adjectives. This is not always predictable. However, /m/ and /x g/ always combine to [mx] <mġ>. The cluster <mġ> regularly changes to [mɕ] <mś> before an unstressed <i> (note the exception *semgia* 'cod').

	damu	[ˈdɑmu]	'skin with fur'
→	*damġa*	[ˈdɑmxa]	'skin with fur GEN.' (< *dam·ka)
	kaibmu	[ˈkʰaɪʔpmu]	'walking stick'
→	*kaimka*	[ˈkʰaɪmka]	'walking stick GEN.' (< *kaim·ka)
but	*tsammi*	[ˈtsɑmːi]	'forest'
→	*tsamġa*	[ˈtsɑmxa]	'forest GEN.' (< *tsamm·ka)
→	*tsamśia*	[ˈtsɑmɕia]	'forest INESS.' (<*tsamm·ġ·ia)
	ehhama	[ˈehːama]	'seam'
→	*ehhakka*	[ˈehːaʔka]	'seam GEN'. (< *ehham·ka)
	gjaukama	[ˈjɑugama]	'down'
→	*gjaukakka*	[ˈjɑugaʔka]	'down GEN.' (< *gjaukam·ka)

If /m/ is combined with /t ts tsx/ <t ts tsġ>, then it changes to /n/ <n> forming the clusters <nt nts ntsġ>. Note that -om- and -um- turn to -õ- before <t ts tsġ>. This is sometimes not the case with inanimate nouns and adjectives whose genitive form ends in -mV - apocope of the vowel does not necessarily cause the /m/ to change in the illative. /m/ and /ɕ/ combine to form [mɕ] <mś>.

	tama	[ˈtʰama]	'many'
→	*taintsġi*	[ˈtʰaɪntsxi]	'numerous' (< *taim·tsġi)

Similarly, when /m/ combines with /d/, it may become [md] <md> or [nd] <nd>in unstressed position.

	dimma	[ˈdiːmːa]	'treeless mountain'
→	*dindi*	[ˈdiːndʑi]	'treeless mountain GEN.' (< *dim·di)

	kinaubmi	[ˈcʰinaʊʔpmi]	'foreign'
→	kinaundi	[ˈcʰinaʊndʑi]	'foreign GEN.' (< *kinaum·di)

/p/ and /b/

The sound /p/ can be found short as [p] or [b] (in unstressed position) <p>, long as [ðb] <d̨b>, glottalized as [ʔp] <pp> or as an ejective [p'] when in non-initial syllables, whereas /b/ can only be found as short [b] <b> or long [p:] <bb>. Both /p/ and /b/ can be preaspirated as [hp] <hp> and [hb] <hb>. Word initially, /p/ is aspirated as [pʰ] <p>.

pila	[ˈpʰila]	'red'
laipin	[ˈlaibɪn]	'bitter'
mėppi	[ˈmeːʔpi]	'knee'
oadbi	[ˈɔaðbi]	'gums'
loba	[ˈlɔba]	'dregs'
ijeppi	[ˈijɛpˈi]	'sticky'
haihpo	[ˈhaɪhpɔ]	'strong, spicy'
tiehba	[ˈtɪɛhba]	'hands GEN.'

When /p/ is combined with /v w w:/ <v ų vv>, the cluster becomes [p:] <bb>.

onębbi	[ɔˈnæpːi]	'X wants to get caught' (< *o·nęp·ųi)

When /p/ and /b/ combines with /m/, they form the cluster [ʔpm] or [ʔm] <bm>. However, if instead of /p/ one has /ʔp p:/ <pp bb>, the resulting cluster will be [pm:] or [p:m] <pm>.

nubmi	[ˈnʊʔpmi]	'X is angry' (< nupi 'X will be angry')
tsåpmi	[ˈtsæːpːmi]	'X is bleeding'

Both /p/ and /b/ cannot stand before /n/, in which case the cluster they form becomes [mnː] <mn>. When /p/ is next to /s/, they combine as [bs] or [ps] <bs>, but next to /ɕ/, the outcome is [pɕ] <pṡ> or [bɕ] <bṡ>. However, if /ʔp p:/ <pp bb> combine with /s/, the cluster is [ps:] or [p:s] <ps>.

nypsiri	[ˈnœpsːiri]	'they usually stick out' (< *nypp·s·i·ri)
tsåpsiri	[ˈtsæːpsːiri]	'they usually bleed' (< *tsåbb·s·i·ri)

If /p/ precedes /t/, the resulting cluster is [mt] <mt>, while /b/ and /t d/ combine to form [ð:] <d̨d̨>. Both /p/ and /b/ combine with /k/ to form [ðg] <d̨g>.

If /p/ or /b/ and /h r/ combine, they become [px] <pr>. In certain dialects, /p/ and/or /b/ and /g x/ combine to [bɣ] <bġ>, but other dialects (mainly western dialects) only have [px] <pr>.

tśipra　　　　['tɕɪpxa]　　　'X will write Y'

If /p/ or /b/ and /s/ <s> combine, they become [bs] or [ps] <bs>. Similarly, /p b ʔp p:/ and /ɕ/ <ś> form [bɕ] or [pɕ] <bś> and [pɕ:] or [p:ɕ] <pś>. However, /ʔp p:/ <pp bb> and /s/ become [ps:] or [p:s] <ps>. Western dialects do not differentiate between <ps> and <bs>.

elepśia　　　['elɛpɕ:ia]　　　　'in bloom'
gabśi　　　　['gabɕi] or ['gapɕi]　'fool'

The combination of /p/ and /k/ is [ðg] <ḑg>.

　oapi　　　　['ɔabi]　　　　'help'
→　*oaḑgo*　　　['ɔaðgɔ]　　　'help GEN.' (< *oap·ko)

　rapa　　　　['rɑpa]　　　　'hill'
→　*raḑga*　　　['rɑðga]　　　 'hill GEN.' (< *rap·ka) (also *rapra* ['rapxa])

/v/

The sound /v/ can be found short as [v] or [ʊ] <v> or long as [w:] <vv>.

vimi　　　　['vi:mi]　　　 'X will scream'
savi　　　　['sɑvi]　　　　'than'
seuvvi　　　['seuw:i]　　　'sweat'

When /v/ or [w:] <vv> precedes the consonants /p m n ɲ t l s k/ <p m n nj t l s k>, the resulting sounds are geminated as [ɖb m: n: ɲ: ð: l: s: ðg] <ḑb mm nn nnj ḑḑ ll ss ḑg>, with the stops /p t k/ becoming affricates.

　sůivvi　　　['sœɪw:i]　　　'proof, sign'
→　*sůimmo*　　['sœɪm:ɔ]　　 'proof, sign GEN.' (< *sůiv·mo)

　tussa　　　　['tʰus:a]　　　 'to turn' (< tuv·sa)
　tymmi　　　['tʰym:i]　　　'is heavy' (< *tyv·mi)

When /v/, whether it is short or long, precedes /ʔp ʔt ʔk/ <pp tt kk>, they combine to form /p: t: k:/ <bb dd gg>. This is not a common sound change, but may appear as the result of vowel apocope.

	śidda	['ɕitːa]	'stay!' (< śiv·i·tta)
	tudda	['tʰutːa]	'turn!' (< tuv·i·tta)

In addition, /v/ and [wː] <vv> may combine with /h hː/ to form the cluster [hːw] <hhy̨>.

	kehno	['cʰɛhnɔ]	'pine'
→	kehhya	['cʰehːwa]	'pine GEN.'

/n/

The sound /n/ can be found short as [n] <n>, long as [nː] <nn>, palatalized short as [ɲ] <nj>, palatalized long as [ɲː] <nnj> or glottalized as [ʔtn] or [ʔn] <dn>. It can also be preaspirated as [hn] <hn>. It is found word finally, sometimes causing nasalization of <o u>.

	netuba	['netuba]	'lily'
	tona	['tʰɔna]	'West'
	kinji	['cʰiɲi]	'fringes'
	nja	['ɲa]	'now'
	hanna	['hɑnːa]	'fair, pale'
	kůnnjůli	['cʰɵɲːøli]	'X will settle down'
	lidna	['liːʔtna]	'great'
	ihna	['ɪhna]	'certainly'
	hiamın	['hiɑmɪn]	'milk and honey drink'
	hihlon	['hiɬːɔn]	'shelter'

If /n/ precedes /m/, they can either combine through metathesis as [mnː] <mn>, or more commonly, they become [mː] <mm>, especially in unstressed positions and in inanimate nouns and adjectives.

	mamna	['mamnːa]	'center' (< *man·ma)
	obeno	['ɔbɛnɔ]	'smoke'
→	oimma	['ɔimːa]	'smoke GEN.' (< *oben·ma)
	ono	['ɔnɔ]	'lichen'
→	omma	['ɔmːa]	'lichen GEN.' (< *on·ma) (also omna)
	sumana	['sumɑna]	'irritated, sore'
→	sumamma	['sumɑmːa]	'irritated, sore GEN.' (< *suman·ma)

When /n/ finds itself next to /s/, three things may happen: least commonly, they simply form [ns] <ns> (though this is not common in Siwa), metathesis resulting in the cluster [hn] <hn>, or most commonly they will combine to form [nt] <nt> (however, the forms -ont- and sometimes -unt- change to -ōt-). Similarly, /n/ and /ɕ/ combine to /ntɕ/ <ntṡ>, /nɕ/ <nṡ> or [ɔ̃tɕ] <ōtṡ> and /n/ and /ts/ or /tsx/ combine to [ntsx] <ntsġ> or [ɔ̃tsx] <ōtsġ>.

	noni	[ˈnɔni]	'X will swim'
→	*nōtsen*	[ˈnɔ̃tɕɛn]	'X can't swim' (< non·i·ṡen)
	koni	[ˈkʰɔni]	'X will walk'
→	*kōtsiṡi*	[ˈkʰɔ̃tsiɕi]	'X can't walk' (< kon·i·siṡi)
→	*kōtṡi*	[ˈkʰɔ̃tɕi]	'X can walk' (< kon·i·ṡi)
	bansi	[ˈbansi]	'today'
	mani	[ˈmɑni]	'X will come'
→	*mansi*	[ˈmɑnsi]	'X came'
	untsi	[ˈʊntsi]	'along the bottom' (< *un·tsi)

If /n/ precedes /k/, the resulting cluster is [ŋk] <nk>, while if it precedes /g/, the resulting cluster is [ŋː] <ng>. However, if /n/ is followed by /k/ in an unstressed syllable in inanimate nouns or adjectives, the resulting cluster is like to be [ʔk] <kk>. This is always true after /ʔk kː/ <kk gg>.

	bana	[ˈbɑnɑ]	'place'
→	*banka*	[ˈbɑŋkɑ]	'place GEN.' (< *ban·ka)
	janna	[ˈjɑnːɑ]	'accumulated snow'
→	*janka*	[ˈjɑŋkɑ]	'accumulated snow GEN.' (< *jan·ka)
	rakana	[ˈrɑkɑnɑ]	'fragile'
→	*rakakka*	[ˈrɑkɑʔkɑ]	'fragile GEN.' (< *rakan·ka)
	atana	[ˈɑtɑnɑ]	'big'
→	*atakka*	[ˈɑtɑʔkɑ]	'big GEN.' (< *atan·ka)

If /n/ precedes /h/, the resulting cluster is either [nh] <nh> (especially after apocope in inanimate nouns and adjectives), or may irregularly go through metathesis and become [hn] <hn>.

	lonis	[ˈlɔnɪs]	'short walk'
→	*lonhi*	[ˈlɔnhi]	'short walk GEN.' (< *lon·hi)
			(also *lōhhi* [ˈlɔ̄hːi] or *lohni* [ˈlɔhni])
	bunus	[ˈbunʊs]	'small squash'

→ bunhi [ˈbʊnhi] 'small squash GEN.' (< *bun·hi)
(also bōhhi [ˈbōhːi] or buhni [ˈbʊhni])

/t/

The sound /t/ can be found short as [tʰ] <t> word initially, [t] <t> in stressed position, [d] <t> in unstressed position before all vowels except /i/, and [tɕ] <t> before /i/ in unstressed syllables. It can also be long as [ð:] <ḍḍ>, glottalized as [ʔt] <tt> or as an ejective [t'] in non-initial stressed syllables. /t/ can be preaspirated as [ht] <ht>. /t/ is found word-finally, and is usually pronounced as [ʔ] or [ʔV] where the preceding vowel is repeated, or also commonly as [x], unless preceded by /i/, in which case it is often found as [tɕ].

tatami	[ˈtʰatami]	'wolf'
eita	[ˈeida]	'X will build Y'
itita	[ˈiːtɕida]	'later'
kŭitton	[ˈcʰœɪʔtɔn]	'boot'
sàhta	[ˈsæːhta]	'lung'
soḍḍos	[ˈsɔðːɔs]	'evening'
hjokot	[ˈhjɔkɔʔ(ɔ)]	'care'
ŭat	[ˈœaʔa]	'this'
hait	[ˈhaɪʔɪ]	'that'
sirit	[ˈsɪrɪʔ]~[ˈsɪrɪtɕ]	'fish stock, amount of fish in a lake'

When /t/ comes in contact with /m/, the resulting cluster is [ʔbm] or [ʔm] <bm>. However, /ʔt/ combines with /m/ to form [pm:] or [p:m] <pm>.

tata	[ˈtʰata]	'X will think'
→ tabmi	[ˈtʰaʔpmi]	'X is thinking'

Similarly, when /t/ comes in contact with /n/, the resulting cluster is [ʔtn] or [ʔn] <dn>, and /ʔt/ combines with /n/ to form [tn:] or [t:n] <tn>.

ùdno	[ˈuːʔtnɔ]	'angelica'
→ ùtva	[ˈuːtwːa]	'angelica GEN.'
nẏdednjukli	[ˈnyːðɛˈʔtnʊklːi]	'fern head, furled frond' (< nẏdet+njukli)
hetna	[ˈhɛtnːa]	'to scatter'

When /t/ comes in contact with /s/, the resulting cluster is [ts] <ts>, which is a phoneme. It can combine to form the clusters [tsw: tsm: tsn: tst: tsk: tsx] or [ts:v ts:m ts:n ts:t ts:k tsx] <tsv tsm tsn tst tsk tsġ>.

atsio	[ˈatsiɔ]	'glade'
kotsmi	[ˈkʰɔtsmːi]	'walking path'

tetsni	[ˈtʰɛtsn:i]	'dried fish'

When /t ʔt/ come in contact with /l/, the resulting cluster is [tɬ] or [t:ɬ] <dl>. A number of words have <dl> initially. The combination is actually a phoneme and does not cause closed syllable. It is also found in the clusters [tɬw: tɬm: tɬn: tɬk: tɬx] <dlv dlm dln dlk dlġ>.

	idla	[ˈi:tɬa]	'late'
	dlei	[ˈtɬei]	'X will itch'
	ġyadlmi	[ˈxwatɬmi]	'rainbow'
	seidlġa	[ˈsɛɪtɬxa]	'pregnant fish'
	půadlva	[ˈpʰœatɬw:a]	'otter'
	setula	[ˈsetula]	'X will push Y'
→	*sedla*	[ˈsetɬa]	'X pushed Y'

If /t/ or /ʔt/ precedes /v w/ or [w:] <vv>, they combine to form [t:v] or [tw:] <tv>, which is found word-initially as [tʰv]. Similarly, with /ts/ the resulting cluster is [tsw:] or [ts:w] <tsv>. Note that <tv> can be preaspirated to [htw:] or [h:tw] <htv>.

kotvi	[ˈkʰɔtw:i]	'X wanted to walk' (< *kott·ɥi)
notvi	[ˈnɔtw:i]	'X wanted to swim' (< *nott·ɥi)
beitsvi	[ˈbɛɪtsw:i]	'X wants to spend the day' (< *beits·ɥi)
tvimyn	[ˈtʰvi:mœn]	'vagina'

If /t/ precedes /h r g/, they combine to form [tx] <tr>, while /ts/ and /hts/ form [tsx] and [htsx] <tsġ htsġ>. However, with /ʔt/, the resulting cluster is [t:x] (or less commonly [tx:]) <tġ>, and similarly /t/ and /ɣ/ <ġ> also form the same cluster, but this is a rare occurrence and is not found in all dialects. Inanimate nouns and adjectives having an unstressed /t/ which should normally get the marked ending -ka/-ko get instead -ra/-ro (originally *-ġa/-ġo). This is the most common cause of this allophonic change.

	gauta	[ˈgɑuda]	'color'
→	*gautra*	[ˈgɑʊtxa]	'color GEN.' (< *gaut·ġa, < *gaut·ka)
	nauto	[ˈnɑudɔ]	'vertigo'
→	*nautra*	[ˈnɑʊtxa]	'vertigo GEN.' (< *naut·ġa, < *naut·ka)
	seta	[ˈseta]	'X will place Y'
→	*setġa*	[ˈsɛt:xa]	'X will place Y' (< *set·ġa, semelfactive)

When /t/ precedes /k ʔk k:/ <k kk gg>, the resulting cluster is [tk] <tk>. Similarly, /ts/ and /hts/ combine with /k ʔk k:/ <k kk gg> to form [tsk:] <tsk> or [htsk:] <htsk>.

otka	[ɔˈtka]	'we will unite' (< o·t·i·gga)
tsotka	[ˈtɕotka]	'we will cooperate' (< tsot·i·gga)
biohtska	[ˈbɪɔhtskːa]	'we will play' (< biohts·i·gga)

/d/

The sound /d/ can be found short as [d] <d> in stressed position, [d] or [r] or [ð] or [l] or not pronounced at all, but written <d> in unstressed position before all vowels except /i/ (including consonant clusters ending in -d), and [dʑ] <d> before /i/ in unstressed syllables. It can also be long as [tː] <dd> (never palatalizes) or palatalized as [dʑ] <dj>. /d/ can be preaspirated as [hd] <hd>. A handful of words begin with [tɬ] <dl>. Word finally, /d/ is pronounced [dʑ] after /e i/. The sound /d/ can be found word-finally, only if preceded by /i/, in which case it is pronounced [dʑ] <d>. /d/ as a stressed coda is commonly pronounced as a flat and written <r>.

dedna	[ˈdɛʔtna]	'village'
djė	[ˈdʑeː]	'grey'
ida	[ˈida]	'X will fall'
iedot	[ˈiedɔʔ / ˈieðɔʔ / ˈierɔʔ / ˈielɔʔ / ˈieɔʔ]	
		'deciduous'
kendita	[ˈcʰɛndʑida]	'early'
lingid	[ˈliːŋːɪdʑ]	'splinter GEN.'
dlei	[ˈtɬei]	'X will itch'
tieibid	[ˈtʰieibɪdʑ]	'twig GEN.'
kodi~kori	[ˈkʰɔdi~ˈkʰɔri]	'X walked'
edi~eri	[ˈedi~ˈeri]	'X sat'

Like its unvoiced counterpart, /d/ and /m/ form the cluster [ʔpm] or [ʔm] <bm>. However, [tː] and /m/ form the cluster [pmː] or [pːm] <pm>.

tiobmi	[ˈtʰɪɔʔpmi]	'to hold' (< *tiod·a·mi)
kahùbmi	[ˈkʰɑʔuːʔpmi]	'to decorate with shells' (< *kahùd·a·mi)
kebmi	[ˈcʰɛʔpmi]	'to carry' (< *ked·a·mi)

When /d/ and /v w wː/ combine, they form [ðwː] or [ðːw] <ḍv>.

meḍvi	[ˈmɛðwːi]	'eyelid'
loḍvot	[ˈlɔðwːɔʔ]	'delayed, long, slow'

Similarly, /d/ combines with /n/ to form [ʔtn] or [ʔn] <dn>, and [tː] and /n/ form [tnː] or [tːn] <tn>.

idnu	[ˈɪʔtnu]	'to fall badly' (< *id·i·nu)
keidna	[ˈcʰɛɪʔtna]	'to light oneself a fire' (< *keid·i·na)
so sitna-a?	[sɔˈsɪtnːaː]	'did you understand?' (< so sidd·i·na-a)
s-otoatna-a	[sɔˈtɔatnːaː]	'did you come along?' (< so otoadd·i·na-a)

When /d/ comes in contact with /p b/ and /k g/, the respective resulting clusters are [ðb] <ḍb> and [ðg] <ḍg>. However, /d/ combines with /kː/ to form the cluster is [ðkː] <ḍk>, while /d/ and [x] combine to form [ðx] <ḍġ>. Note that /tː/ combine with /k kː ʔk g/ to form [tkː] or [tːk] <tk>.

	bàdi	[ˈbæːdʑi]	'pain'
→	*bàḍga*	[ˈbæːðga]	'pain GEN.' (< *bàd·ka)
	gidu	[ˈɟidu]	'X will dry in the open air'
→	*gieḍbi*	[ˈɟɪɛðbi]	'drying frame'
	tsotka	[ˈtɕɔtka]	'we cooperated' (< tsodd·i·gga)
	noḍka	[ˈnɔðka]	'we will sing' (< nod·i·gga)
	sidġami	[ˈsiðxami]	'I suddenly understand' (< sid·i·ga·mi)
	otoatka	[ɔˈtɔatka]	'we came along' (< o·toadd·i·gga)

When /d/ is followed by /h r/, the resulting cluster is [tx] <tr>. However, in certain cases where apocope is involved, /d/ combines with /h/ to form [lh] <lh>.

	sitri	[ˈsɪtxi]	'they will understand' (< sid·i·ri)
	guokveitri	[ˈgʊɔkwːɛɪtxi]	'they will play hard to catch' (< guokveid·i·ri)
	niedas	[ˈnieðas]	'fir'
→	*nielhi*	[ˈnɪɛlhi]	'fir GEN.' (< *nied·hi)
	puodus	[ˈpʰuɔðʊs]	'navel'
→	*puolhi*	[ˈpʰʊɔlhi]	'navel GEN.' (< *puod·hi)

Finally, /d/ and [tː] combine with /l/ to form [tɬ] or [tːɬ] <dl>.

	geudlu	[ˈɟeutɬu]	'to be worth doing, to be possible' (<geud·lu)
	maudli	[ˈmautɬi]	'maple sap' (< *maud·li)

/ð/

The sound /ð/ is always found as long [ðː] <ḍḍ> or may be short in consonant clusters.

oḍḍo	['ɔð:ɔ]	'night sky'
saḍḍa	['sað:a]	'fire'
sieḍḍo	['sieð:ɔ]	'foot'
iḍmi	[ɪðm:i]	'raven'

When /ð/ comes in contact with /m/, they become [ðm:] or [ð:m] <ḍm>.

daḍmi	['daðm:i]	'to answer' (< *daḍḍ·a·mi)
heiḍmi	['hɛɪðm:i]	'X was appetizing' (< *heiḍḍ·i·mi)
koḍmi	['kʰɔðm:i]	'guest'
→ *koḍḍa*	['kʰɔð:a]	'guest GEN.' (< *koḍḍ·ta)

When /ð/ precedes /p b/, /t d/ and /k g/, the respective resulting clusters are [ðb] <ḍb>, [ð:] <ḍḍ> and [ðg] <ḍg>. However, before glottalized or long consonants, /ð/ becomes /h/ and devoices the following consonant, except in the case of /ð/ and /k:/, which form the cluster [ðk:] <ḍk>. Similarly, /ð/ and /v/ or /v:/ combine to form the cluster [ðw:] or [ð:w] <ḍv>.

jeḍka	['jɛðk:a]	'we will run' (< jeḍḍ·i·gga)
siḍbi	['sɪðbi]	'shoe' (cf. *sieḍḍo* 'foot')
veḍgo	['vɛðgɔ]	'crow' (cf. *uḍḍ·emi* 'black bird')
veḍvo	['vɛðw:ɔ]	'X would have wanted to be'

If /ð/ and /l/ come in contact, they form the cluster [tɬ] <dl>. Before /s/, /ð/ changes to /h/, forming [hs] <hs>.

udlu	['utɬu]	'for the night sky to clear up' (< *uḍḍ·lu)
jehsa	['jɛhsa]	'to run' (< *jeḍḍ·i·sa)

In some dialects, syllables in -VḍḍV- are found as -VḍV-.

/s/

The sound /s/ can be found short as [s] <s> or long as [s:] <ss>. It can also become palatalized as [ɕ] <ṡ>. /s/ can be found word-finally.

sara	['sara]	'good'
ussù	[us:u:]	'smoked fish'
misas	[misas]	'rock'
mimŭkis	['mimøµs]	'butterfly'

When /s/ is followed by /v w w:/ <v ų vv>, the resulting cluster can either be [sv] <sv> or [sw] <sų>.

	svaḍma	[ˈsvaðmːa]	'foam'
	okjasvi	[ˈɔcasvi]	'X wants to hurry up' (< *o·kjas·ui)

In a few cases, /s/ and /m/ will combine to form [hm] <hm> instead of the expected [sm] <sm>. This is especially true of the second person pronoun -sa- before the first person pronoun -mi-.

		nujahmi	[ˈnujahmi]	'I will see you' (< nuj·a·sa·mi)
		lugjuahmi	[ˈlujːʊahmi]	'I love you' (< lugju·a·sa·mi)
but				
		kjasmi	[ˈcʰasmi]	'to speed up' (< *kjas·a·mi)
		njosma	[ˈɲɔsma]	'deaf GEN.'

Similarly, if /s/ is followed by /n/, the resulting cluster is often [nt] <nt> (or nasalized <õt>) instead of the expected [sn].

	kjanta	[ˈcʰanta]	'to hurry up' (< *kjas·na)

The cluster /sl/ is also allowed as [sl] or more commonly [sɫ] or [stɫ] <sl>.

	josli	[ˈjɔs(t)ɫi]	'complication, knot, lump'

When /s/ is followed by /ʔk kː/ <kk gg>, they form [skː] or [sːk] <skk>, while /s/ and /r g x h/ <r g ġ h> form [sx] <sġ>, which is the most common word initial cluster.

	okjaskka	[ˈɔcaskːa]	'we will hurry up' (< *beits·ui)
	moski	[ˈmɔsci]	'wild copper'
→	*moskko*	[ˈmɔskːɔ]	'wild copper GEN.' (< *mosk·ko)
	sappiska	[ˈsaʔpɪska]	'paw'
→	*sappiskka*	[ˈsaʔpɪskːa]	'paw GEN.' (< *sappisk·ka)
	keltaus	[ˈcʰɛltɑuse]	'terrestrial'
→	*keltausġi*	[ˈcʰɛltɑʊsxi]	'terrestrial GEN.' (< *keltaus·ri)

In addition, /s/ is found in the cluster [skwː] or [skv] <skv>.

miaskvi [ˈmɪaskwːi] or [ˈmɪaskvi] 'X wants to celebrate'

/ɕ/

The sound /ɕ/ can be found short as [ɕ] or [ʃ] <ś> or long as [ɕː] or [ʃː] <śś>. Certain eastern dialects allow word-final <ś>.

śeira	[ˈɕeira]	'bearberry'
tośmi	[ˈtʰɔɕmːi]	'X is young'
seyiś	[ˈsewɪɕ]	'little river (eastern dialect)'

The sound /ɕ/ can combine with /p v t k/ to form [ɕp] <śp>, [ɕv] <śv>, [ɕt] <śt> and [ɕk] <śk>, in addition to being found in the cluster [ɕkwː] or [ɕːkv] <śkv>.

iśpa	[ˈiːɕpa]	'grandparents'
piśkeli	[ˈpɪɕceli]	'X will be in a coma'
kośtet	[ˈkʰɔɕtɛʔ]	'wood-work, art'
nuśkva	[ˈnʊɕkwːa]	'hail'

When /ɕ/ comes in contact with /r h x/ <r h ġ>, the resulting cluster is [ɕː] <śś>. This is common in verbs ending in -ś in the habitual.

	kyśa	[ˈcʰyɕa]	'X will try Y'
→	kyśśa	[ˈcʰyɕːa]	'X usually tries' (< *kyś·h·a)

/tɕ/ and dʑ/

The sounds /tɕ /dʑ/ can be found short as [tɕ] <tś> and [dʑ] <dź> or long as [tɕː dʑː] <tts ddj>. They are not found in any clusters and do not come in contact with other consonants. The long <ddj> may be pronounced as the ejective [tɕ'] in non-initial syllables.

	tśieka	[ˈtɕiega]	'snake'
	tśoairu	[ˈtɕoɑiru]	'will rot'
	vetśo	[ˈvetɕo]	'rash'
and			
	djoki	[ˈdʑɔci]	'trap in snow'
	djata	[ˈdʑɑta]	'X will mourn Y'
	hjŭdja	[ˈhjødʑa]	'pregnant'
	oaiddji	[ˈɔɑidʑːi]	'along the south-west'
	hiddjuja	[ˈhidʑːuja]	'X will stack Y up'

/r/

The sound /r/ can be found short as [r] <r> or long as [rː] <rr>. It may also be found preaspirated as [hr] <hr>.

rabma	[ˈraʔpma]	'canoe'
riehpi	[ˈrɪɛhpi]	'wife'

	sira	[ˈsira]	'fish'
	u̇arro	[ˈœɑrːɔ]	'wild turkey'
	ohra	[ˈɔhra]	'god, deity'

When /r/ is next to /v wː/, the resulting cluster is [rwː] or rarely [rːw] <rv>.

| | *tervima* | [ˈtʰɛrwːima] | 'it is twilight' |

When /r/ precedes /m/, the resulting cluster usually goes through metathesis to become [m(b)r] <mr>. However, [rm] <rm> is also possible, whereas in unstressed position and sometimes stressed position, they combine to form [hm] <hm>.

	tomri	[ˈtɔmri]	'velvet'
	kimra	[ˈcʰɪmra]	'in the morning'
also	*kirma*	[ˈcɪrma]	'in the morning'

| | *kobbomora* | [ˈkʰɔpːɔmɔra] | 'salamander' |
| → | *kobomohmo* | [ˈkʰɔbɔmɔhmɔ] | 'salamander GEN.' (< *kobomor·mo) |

| | *myry* | [ˈmyry] | 'fly' |
| → | *myhma* | [ˈmœhma] | 'fly GEN.' (< *myr·ma) |

| | *su̇ro* | [ˈsuːrɔ] | 'berry bush' |
| → | *su̇hma* | [ˈsuːhma] | 'berry bush GEN.' (< *su̇r·ma) |

When /r/ precedes /p b/, the resulting clusters may either be [hp hb] <hp hb> especially in unstressed position, or in stressed position [rb] or [rp] <rp>. However, before /ʔp bː/ <pp bb>, the resulting cluster is always [rpː] <rpp>.

| | *sihpi* | [ˈsiːhpi] | 'whale' |
| → | *sirumi* | [ˈsiːrumi] | 'whale GEN.' (< *sir·pi) |

| | *orpi* | [ˈɔrpi] or [ˈɔrbi] | 'X will misbehave' |
| | *ḳurppo* | [ˈcʰʊrpːɔ] | 'hollow' |

Similarly, when /r/ precedes /t d/, the resulting clusters may either be [ht hd] <ht hd> (this is also true of /tɕ dʑ/ and /ts tsw: tsx/), especially in unstressed position, or in stressed position [rt] or [rd] <rt>. However, before /ʔt tː/ <tt dd>, the resulting cluster is always [rtː] <rtt>.

| | *lu̇ri* | [ˈløri] | 'scum, dirt' |
| → | *lu̇hdi* | [ˈlœhdʑi] | 'scum, dirt GEN.' (< *lu̇r·di) |

| | *tèrhi* | [ˈtʰeːrhi] | 'sun' |

→	tėhtśa	[ˈtʰeːhtɕa]	'SUN GEN.' (< *tėr·tśa)
	artaita	[ˈartɑida]	'compared to'
	ġertto	[ˈxɛrtːɔ]	'threshold'
	njėrtteni	[ˈɲeːrtːeni]	'X will hurt'

When /r/ precedes /n/, the resulting cluster may be [hn] <hn>, [rn] <rn> more commonly [nr] or [ndr] <nr~ndr>. When /r/ precedes /l/, the resulting cluster may be [l(d)r] <lr> (with metathesis) or less commonly [rl] or [rtɬ] <rl>.

	tsulra	[ˈtsʊlra]	'pressed/vapour-moulded wood' (also tsurla)

As with the other stops, when /r/ precedes /k/, the resulting clusters may either be [hk] <hk>, especially in unstressed position, or in stressed position [rk] or [rg] <rk> (this mainly occurs as the result of [rː] <rr> coming in contact with /k/). However, before /ʔk kː/ <kk gg>, the resulting cluster is always [rkː] <rkk>. This often occur with the first person plural pronouns in -gga/-gge.

	gjori	[ˈʝɔri]	'doubt'
→	gjohko	[ˈʝɔhkɔ]	'doubt GEN.' (< *gjor·ko)
	toarra	[ˈtʰɔɑrːa]	'root vegetable'
→	toarka	[ˈtʰɔarkːa]	'root vegetable GEN.' (< *toarr·ka)
	tsoairkka	[ˈtsɔairkːa]	'we will go by ski' (< tsoair·i·gga)
	erkka	[ˈɛrkːa]	'we will be careful' (< er·i·gga)

If /r/ precedes /g x h/ <g ġ h> however, the resulting cluster is usually [rh] <rh>, though some dialects have [hr] <hr>.

	jairha	[ˈjaɪrha]	'X will suddenly row' (< jair·i·ga)
	joairha	[ˈjɔaɪrha]	'calm, easy to row (of water)' (< *joair·ġa)
	kiras	[ˈcʰiras]	'early morning'
→	kirhi	[ˈcʰɪrhi]	'early morning GEN.' (< *kira·hi)

Eastern dialects have the cluster [rx] <rġ>, whereas western dialects usually simply have [rh] or [hr] <rh hr>.

	njorġa	[ˈɲɔrxa]	'duck' (also njorha)
	birġo	[ˈbɪrxɔ]	'beam' (also birho)

/N/

The sound /l/ can be found short as [l] <l> or long as [l:] <ll>. It may also be found preaspirated as [hl] or [ɬ:] <hl>[1]. /l/ may be found word-finally, especially in adverbs – some dialects do not allow final /l/. Many speakers tend to devoice /l/ to [ɬ] before unvoiced stops. /l/ can be palatalized as [lj] <lj>.

lahton	[ˈlahton]	'mitten'
ljasa	[ˈljɑsa]	'X will lacerate Y'
svilla	[ˈsvilːa]	'braid'
sohla	[ˈsohla~ˈsɔɬːa]	'best'
vihla	[ˈvɪhla~ˈvɪɬːa]	'flesh'
pigjil	[ˈpʰijɪl]	'health' (more commonly *pigji*)
ljȯ	[ˈljʊː]	'resin'

When /l/ precedes /p b/, the resulting clusters may be [lp lb] <lp lb>, but not all dialects have both versions (<lb> is more common in dialects with only either [lp] or [lb]). However, before /ʔp bː/ <pp bb>, the resulting cluster is always [lpː] <lpp>. Certain speakers pronounce <lp> as [ɬp] and <lb> as [lp].

tsalbi	[ˈtsalbi] or [ˈtsalpi]	'rarely'
tyry	[ˈtʰyry]	'son'
→ *tolba*	[ˈtʰɔlba] or [ˈtʰɔlpa]	'son GEN.'
delpia	[ˈdɛlpia] or [ˈdɛlbia] or [ˈdɛɬpia]	'X will turn Y over'
jȧlppi	[ˈjæːlpːi]	'hare'
nalppa	[ˈnalpːa]	'snout'

Similarly, when /l/ precedes /t d/, the resulting clusters are [ɬt~lt ld~lt] <lt ld> (this is also true of /tɕ dʑ/ and /ts tsx/). However, before /ʔt tː/ <tt dd>, the resulting cluster is always [ltː] <ltt>.

ylta	[ˈœlta] or [ˈœɬta]	'for/to/before the night'
kilda	[ˈcʰiːlda] or [ˈcʰiːlta]	'again'
killa	[ˈcʰilːa]	'all'
→ *kildi*	[ˈcʰɪldʑi]	'all GEN.'
suikildi	[ˈsuiɲldʑi]	'X will live together'
noaltta	[ˈnɔaltːa]	'tooth, pike'
keltta	[ˈcʰɛltːa]	'ground'

---

[1] A great deal of speakers pronounce <hl> as an unvoiced l [ɬ] often spelled <ł>, which in many cases causes lengthening of the preceding vowel. This explains variations of *sohla* 'best' such as *soała*, *svała*, *sóła* and *souła*, for example. Western dialects tend to simply geminate the vowel phoneme (then with <˳>): *vı̥ła* [vɪːɬa] 'flesh' (far western dialects).

	njelli	[ˈɲelːi]	'chief'
→	njeltśa	[ˈɲɛltɕa]	'chief GEN.'
	koalgi	[ˈkʰɔalʝi]	'paternal aunt'
→	koaltsa	[ˈkʰɔaltsa]	'paternal aunt GEN.'
	vilo	[ˈvilɔ]	'maternal aunt'
→	viltsa	[ˈvɪltsa]	'maternal aunt GEN.'

As with the other stops, when /l/ precedes /k g/, the resulting clusters may either be [ɬk lg~lk lg] <lk lg>. However, before /ʔk kː/ <kk gg>, the resulting cluster is always [lkː] <lkk>. This often occur with the first person plural pronouns in -gga/-gge.

	kjala	[ˈcʰɑla]	'land'
→	kjalka	[ˈcʰalka] or [ˈcʰaɬka]	'land GEN.' (< *kjal·ka)
	kolkon	[ˈkʰɔlkɔn] or [ˈkʰɔɬkɔn]	'bread'
	noalgi	[ˈnɔalʝi] or [ˈnɔalci]	'tar kiln'
	olkko	[ˈɔlkːɔ]	'temple'
	otśilkka	[ɔˈtɕɪlkːa]	'we will dry ourselves' (<o·tśil·i·gga)
	kůnnjůlkka	[ˈcʰøɲːœlkːa]	'we will settle down' (< kůnnjůl·i·gga)

When /l/ precedes /s h/ <s h>, the resulting cluster is [lh] <lh> or [xɬ] <ġl> with <ġ>.

	peles	[ˈpʰælɛs]	'stuffed stomach'
→	pelhi	[ˈpɛlhi]	'stuffed stomach GEN.' (< *pel·hi)
	gosù	[ˈgɔsuː]	'calm'
→	gosulha	[ˈgɔsʊlha]	'calm ADJ' (< *gosul·ha)
	nelġi	[ˈnɛlxi]	'X will suddenly bud' (< nel·i·ġa)

Many dialects allow for /l/ to be in final position, especially eastern dialects. It is often found unvoiced then.

/ŋ/

The sound /ŋ/ is always found long intervocally as [ŋː] <ng>. It is also found glottalized as [ʔŋ] <kn>, which some speakers pronounced long as [ʔŋː].

	angi	[ˈɑŋːiː]	'seed'
	bengomu	[ˈbeŋːɔmu]	'roof'

ekni	[ˈɛʔŋi] or [ˈɛʔŋːi]	'way'

If /ŋ/ precedes /m/, the resulting cluster is [ŋmː] or [ŋːm] <gm>.

tsegma	[ˈtɕɛŋmːa]	'child'
omigmi	[ɔˈmɪŋmːi]	'I will get ready' (< o·ming·i·mi)
muogmi	[ˈmʊɔŋmːi]	'I will stay the night' (< muong·i·mi)

If /ŋ/ precedes /n/, the resulting cluster is [ŋnː] or [ŋːn] <gn>.

gegna	[ˈɟɛŋːa]	'den'
migna	[ˈmɪŋnːa]	'to get ready' (< *ming·i·na)
muogna	[ˈmʊɔŋnːa]	'to stay the night' (< *muong·i·na)

If /ŋ/ precedes /ʔk kː/, the resulting cluster is [ŋkː] <nkk>, while /ŋ/ and /k g/ form [ŋ̊k] <nk>.

	ominkka	[ɔˈmɪŋkːa]	'we will get ready' (< o·ming·i·gga)
	muonkka	[ˈmʊɔŋkːa]	'we will stay the night' (< muong·i·gga)
	lainga	[ˈlɑiŋːa]	'bait'
→	*lainka*	[ˈlɑɪŋka]	'bait GEN.'

/k/

The sound /k/ is always palatalized to [c] before before /i e æ y ø/ <i e ę/à y ů>. It can be found short as [kʰ] <k> word initially or palatalized as [cʰ] <k>, [k] <k> or palatalized as [c] <k> in stressed position, [g] <k> or palatalized as [ɟ] <k> in unstressed position. It can also be long as [ðg] or palatalized as [ðɟ] <ḍg>, glottalized as [ʔk] or as an ejective [k'] in non-initial syllables, or palatalized as [ʔc] <kk>. /k/ can be preaspirated as [hk] or palatalized as [hc] <hk>. In addition, /k/ can be palatalized to [cʰ] word initially, [c] in stressed position and [ɟ] in unstressed position as <kj>. This is not indicated before /i e æ y ø/ <i e ę/à y ů> as they already cause palatalization.

kaibmu	[ˈkʰaɪʔpmu]	'walking stick'
kokve	[ˈkʰɔkːve]	'light'
kàhlo	[ˈcʰæːhɬɔ]	'high'
hokoma	[ˈhɔkɔma]	'back and forth'
euka	[ˈeuga]	'X will produce Y'
maiki	[ˈmɑiɟi]	'white'
koḍga	[ˈkʰɔðga]	'twin brothers'
kaḍgju	[ˈkʰaðɟu]	'fresh wood'
mokkuo	[ˈmɔʔkuɔ]	'beak'
kykky	[ˈcʰœʔcy]	'voice'

	nahkara	[ˈnahkɑra]	'louse'
	ohki	[ˈɔhci]	'deep'
	kehkjo	[ˈcʰɛhcɔ]	'birch bark canoe'
	atakka	[ˈatakʼa]	'big GEN.'

If /k/ comes in contact with /m/, the resulting cluster is usually [hm] <hm>, especially in unstressed syllables. However, /ʔk/ and in some cases /k/ usually combine with /m/ to form [km:] or [gm:] or [k:m] <km>.

	odjikmi	[ɔˈdʐɪkmːi] or [ɔˈdʐɪgmːi]	'I will show off' (< o·djikk·i·mi)
→	õka õkmo	[ˈõka] [ˈõkmːɔ] or [ˈõgmːɔ]	'tundra' 'tundra GEN.' (also commonly õhmo)
	djikma sokmi	[dʐɪkmːa] or [ˈdʐɪgmːa] [ˈsɔkmːi] or [ˈsɔgmːi]	'on display, obvious' 'seagull'

When /k/ precedes /w/, the resulting cluster is [kw] <kʉ>, but [kw:] before /w: v/ <vv v>. In unstressed position, however, /k/ and /v w/ usually combine to [kv] or [gv] <gv>, or may also simply be [kw] <kʉ>. If /ʔk/ combines with /v w w:/ <v ʉ vv>, the result is always [kw:] or [k:v] <kv>.

	ijuakvimi	[ˈijuˈakwːimi]	'I want to cut boughs' (< *iju·ak·ʉi·mi)
	odjikvi	[ɔˈdʐɪkwːi]	'X wants to show off' (< *o·djikk·ʉi)
	guokvo obinugvi	[ˈgʊokwːɔ] [ɔˈbinʊgvi]	'frog' 'X wants to become wealthy' (< *o·inuk·ʉi, also found as obinukʉi)

When /k ʔk/ precede any bilabial stop (/p b ʔp p:/ <p b pp bb>), the resulting cluster is always [hp] <hp>. Similarly, /k ʔk/ combine with all dental stops (/t d ʔt t:/ <t d tt dd>) to form [ht] <ht>.

	riehpi riekumi	[ˈrɪɛhpi] [ˈrɪɛgumi]	'wife' 'wife ADJ' (<*riek·pi)
→	jikia jihta	[ˈjiːʝia] [ˈjiːhta]	'in the west' 'to the west' (< *jik·ta)

When /k ʔk/ precede /n ŋ/ <n ng>, the resulting cluster is [ʔn] <kn>.

	osoaki	[ɔˈsɔɑɟi]	'X will build itself a house'

→	soakna	[ˈsɔaʔŋa]	'to build oneself a house' (<*soak·i·na)
	ilotśieki	[iːlɔˈtɕieɹi]	'X will crawl on ice'
→	iltśiekna	[iːlˈtɕɪɛʔŋi]	'to crawl on ice' (< *il·tśiek·i·na)

Both /l/ and /r/ combine with /k ʔk/ to form [klː] or [kːl] <kl>. Many speakers pronounce <kl> as [kɬː], and outside of the Aingo dialect, it is very commonly preglottalized as [ʔtɬ] or even [tɬʼ][1]. However, in unstressed position, /k/ combines with /r/ to form [x] <ġ> or [xː] <ġġ>.

	njukli	[ˈɲʊklːi] or [ˈɲʊkːli] or [ˈɲʊkɬːi]	'hook, finger'
	goka	[ˈgɔka]	'sheath'
→	goakla	[ˈgɔakːla] or [ˈgɔaklːa]	'*mollusca*' (< *gok·ra)

If /k ʔk/ and /s/ come together, the resulting cluster is [ksː] <ks> or also [kːs]. The same is true of /ɕ/, forming [kɕː] <kś> or [kːɕ].

tŭnŭkśi	[ˈtʰønœkɕːi] or [ˈtʰønœkːɕi]	'attack leader'
y̌ksy	[ˈyːksːy] or [ˈyːkːsy]	'bow'

/g/

The sound /g/ always palatalizes before before /i e æ y ø/ <i e ẹ/à y ů> in stressed position. It can be found short as [g] <g> word initially and in stressed position or palatalized as [ɟ] <g>. In unstressed position, /g/ is always pronounced [j] <g> before /i/, but [ɣ] or [x] before other vowels. It can also be long as [kː] or palatalized as [cː] <gg>. /g/ can also be palatalized before /i e æ y ø/ <i e ẹ/à y ů> word-initially to [ɟ]. Word-internally, <gj> always represents the sound [jː].

goi	[ˈgɔi]	'point, edge'
giga	[ˈɟiga]	'goose'
kigge	[ˈcʰiːcːe]	'spark'
poagga	[ˈpʰɔakːa]	'seal meet GEN.'
oaiga	[ˈɔaiɣa]	'X will hook Y'
kinagi	[ˈcʰinaji]	'foreigner'
gjosmi	[ɟɔsmi]	'is tired'
gjekes	[dzecɛs] or [ˈzecɛs]	'year'
gjykin	[dzycɪn] or [ˈzycɪn]	'snowshoes'

---

[1] Many dialects used λ where this orthography uses kl for the preglottalized or ejective pronunciation of this phoneme, e.g. *kekli* can be pronounced [ˈcʰɛklːi], [ˈcʰɛkːli], [ˈcʰɛ(ː)gɨlːii], [ˈcʰɛkɬːi] or [ˈcʰɛʔtɬi] while the orthography *keλi* can be pronounced [ˈcʰɛʔtɬi] or [ˈcʰɛtɬʼi]

gogja	[ˈgɔj:a]	'X will adze Y'
hogjů	[ˈhɔj:ø]	'nonsense'

When /g/ precedes /m/, the resulting cluster is [hm] <hm> or occasionally [ŋm:] <gm>. However if /k:/ <gg> precedes /m/, the resulting cluster is [km:] or [gm:] or [k:m] <km>.

	kega	[ˈcʰega]	'X will hide Y'
→	*kehmi*	[ˈcʰɛhmi]	'to hide' (< *keg·a·mi)
	suga	[ˈsuga]	'X will visit Y'
→	*suhmi*	[ˈsʊhmi]	'to visit' (< *sug·a·mi)
	tsuogga	[ˈtsuɔk:a]	'X will hope for Y'
→	*tsuokmi*	[ˈtsʊɔkm:i]	'to hope'
	or	[ˈtsʊɔgm:i]	

Similarly, when /g/ precedes /n/, the resulting cluster is [hn] <hn>, and if /k:/ <gg> precedes /n/, they combine to [ʔŋ] <kn>.

	okegi	[ɔˈceɟi]	'X will hide itself'
→	*kehna*	[ˈcʰɛhna]	'to hide oneself' (< *keg·i·na)
	imůiggi	[iˈmœɪc:i]	'X will hold on to'
→	*můiknin*	[ˈmœɪʔŋɪn]	'to hold on to' (< *můigg·i·nin)

When /g/ precedes /v w w:/ <v ᶣ vv>, they combine to form [kv] or [gv] <gv>, but /k:/ forms [kw:] or [k:v] <kv>.

piagvi	[ˈpʰɪakvi] or [ˈpʰɪagvi]	'X wants to fall asleep' (< *piag·ɥi)
imůikvi	[iˈmœɪk:vi] or [iˈmœɪkw:i]	'X wants to hold on to' (< *i·můigg·ɥi)

When /g/ precedes stops, it preaspirates them, except in the case of /k ʔk k:/ <k kk gg>, which combine to form [k:] <gg>. This is not especially common, however.

okegga	[ɔˈcek:a]	'we will hide ourselves'
		(more commonly *okegigga*)

When /g/ precedes /s/, they form [ks] or [gs] <gs>. This is common in the genitive form of inanimate nouns, as <ks> is lenited to <gs>. However, /k:/ <gg> combines with /s/ to form [ks:] or [k:s] <ks>.

diugsid	[ˈdrʊksɪdʑ] or [ˈdrʊgsɪdʑ]	'icicle GEN.'
rugsoma	[ˈrʊksɔma] or [ˈrʊgsɔma]	'circle GEN.'

Similarly, /g/ and /l/ combine to form [gl] or [kl] <gl>. This is common in the genitive form of inanimate nouns, as <kl> is lenited to <gl>. However, /k:/ <gg> combines with /l/ to form [kl:] or [k:l] or [kɬ:] <kl>.

suglimo	[ˈsʊglimɔ] or [ˈsʊklimɔ]	'protection GEN.'
syglyma	[ˈsœglyma] or [ˈsœklyma]	'team GEN.'

If /g/ and /h r x/ <h r ġ/g> combine, the result is [x] <ġ>, though /g/ and /r/ may combine to [rh] <rh> through metathesis.

	giga	[ˈɟiga]	'goose'
→	*girha*	[ˈɟiːrha]	'flock of geese' (< *gig·ra)
	iruoga	[ˈiruɔɣa]	'coniferous wood'
→	*iruorha*	[ˈirɔːrha]	'made of coniferous wood' (< *iruog·i·ha)

/x/

The sound /x/ is pronounced [x] <ġ> word initially. Intervocally, it is pronounced [x] <ġ>, but all western dialects have <ġ> change to [ɕ] <ś> before front vowels in unstressed position. It can also be palatalized, in which case it turns to [hj] <hj> or more commonly [hːj] <hhj> in stressed position, though this is mostly a historical change. In eastern dialects, some inanimate nouns ending in non-front vowel may have a word final -ġ in the plural, usually pronounced [x]. The phoneme /x/ is most commonly found in clusters such as <sġ> and <tsġ>. It can be found long as [x:] or [ɣ:] or even [q:ˈ] <ġġ>.

ġemi	[ˈxemi]	'X will shake'
ġoli	[ˈxɔli]	'hilltop'
iġa	[ˈixa]	'X will accept Y'
moġa	[ˈmɔxa]	'X will drink Y'
neuġi	[ˈneuxi]	'birch wood GEN.' (standard/eastern dialects)
neuśi	[ˈneuɕi]	'birch wood GEN.' (western dialects)
sevaġi	[ˈsevɑxi]	'burnt embers GEN.' (standard/eastern dialects)
sevaśi	[ˈsevɑɕi]	'burnt embers GEN.' (western dialects)
boaihhji	[ˈbɔɑihːji]	'floating weeds in lake, algae' (cf. **boġi** 'branch with leaves')

tapaġ	['tʰapax]	'bulbs' (eastern dialects)
kyġga	['cʰyx:a]	'mouse'

When /x/ precedes /m/, they form [xm] or [xm:] <ġm> or in unstressed position [hm] <hm>. Similarly, /x/ and /n/ form [xn] or [xn:] <ġn> or [hn] <hn> in unstressed position, and with /l/, the resulting cluster is [xl] or [xɬ:] <ġl> or [hl] or [ɬ:] <hl> in unstressed position. These clusters are fairly uncommon and speakers may replace them with their preaspirated counterparts.

iġmi	['ɪxmi] or ['ɪxm:i]	'to accept' (< *iġ·a·mi)
moġmi	['mɔxmi] or ['mɔxm:i]	'to drink' (< *moġ·a·mi)
soġli	['sɔxli] or ['sɔxl:i]	'X will thaw'
kuoġni	['kʰʊɔxni] or ['kʰʊɔxn:i]	'X will argue'

Before /s/ and /r/, /x/ becomes [h] <h> to form [hs] <hs> and [hr] <hr>.

mohsa	['mɔhsa]	'to drink' (< *moġ·i·sa)
moahrit	['mɔahrɪ?]	'drinkable water supplies' (cf. *moaġa* 'drinkable water')

If /x/ precedes /h/, the /h/ is dropped and only /ɣ/ remains.

seġu	['sexu]	'barren land'
→ *seġa*	['sexa]	'barren' (< *seġe·ha)

/ʔ/

The sound /ʔ/ is mainly found before other consonants, namely [ʔt ʔp ʔk ʔŋ ʔm ʔn] <tt pp kk kn bm dn>, but intervocally it is found as [ʔ] <h> in stressed syllables or <ḥ> in unstressed syllables. The glottal stop can also be found long, then [ʔ:] and written <ḥḥ>[1].

kihaha	['cʰiʔaʔa]	'there is something very large'
kahi	['kʰaʔi]	'shell'
koahi	['kʰɔaʔi]	'enough'
minihi	['miniʔi]	'common snipe GEN.'
miha	['miʔa]	'X smoked Y'
pjaha	['pjaʔa]	'healer, shaman'

---

[1] One of the more famous tongue twisters of Siwa is:

Aḥḥitaḥḥina iḥḥen tkiḥḥen puoḥḥua det, koaḥḥorena ju
[aʔ:iˈtʰaʔ:ina ˈiʔɛn ˈtciʔ:ɛn ˈpʰʊɔʔ:ua dɛʔ ˈkʰɔaʔ:ɔrenaju]
'if you can keep squeezing it that way, you will split it in half'

saiha	[ˈsaiʔa]	'X warned Y'
tahama	[ˈtaʔama]	'world'
neḥḥe	[ˈneʔːe]	'well, you see, hm...'
puḥḥu	[ˈpʰuʔːu]	'woosh, go away!'

/h/

The sound /h/ is always found long as [hː] <hh> in stressed position (though not word initially). In unstressed syllables, it is found short as [h] <h>. It can be palatalized as [hːj] <hhi̯> in stressed position and [hj] <hi̯> in unstressed position.

hai	[ˈhai]	'glue'
hi̯ỏmno	[ˈhjʊːmnɔ]	'midwife'
ihha	[ˈihːa]	'just, only'
kegahi	[ˈcʰegahi]	'fœtus GEN.'
kohhi̯a	[ˈkʰohːja]	'X will rip Y'
gi̯ekehi̯i	[ˈdzecehji]	'birthday GEN.'

The sound /h/ is found as the first sound in preaspirated consonants (see *§3.4.5*)

§3.4.2 Long Consonants

The long consonants are [mː pː vː nː tː ðː sː ɕː dʑː jː rː lː kː xː ŋː hː ʔː] <mm bb vv nn dd ḍḍ ss śś ddi̯ gi̯ rr ll gg ġġ ng hh ḥḥ>. Long consonants do not count as CC but Cː (thus not closing syllables). All long consonants occur intervocally. The voiceless stops /p t k/ have unusual long allophones, [ðb ðː ðg] <ḍb ḍḍ ḍg>.

§3.4.3 Palatalized Consonants

The palatalized consonants are [tɕ dʑ ɕ ɲ c ɟ] <tś dj ś ni̯ ki̯ g-i/e> in stressed syllables but [tɕ dʑ ɕ ɟ j] <tś/t-i/e dj/d-i/e ś ki̯/k-i/e g-i/e> in unstressed syllables. Stressed palatalized consonants are the result of historical palatalization. True productive palatalization only occurs in certain case in weak syllables before /j/ or diphthongs whose first sound is /i/.

§3.4.4 Glottalized Consonants

Only the voiceless stops /p t k/ and the nasals /m n ŋː/ are glottalized. They are written <pp tt kk bm dn kn> and pronounced [ʔp ʔt ʔk ʔpm ʔtn ʔkŋː]. They are found intervocally only.

§3.4.5 Preaspirated Consonants

Siwa has the following preaspirated consonants:
[hp hb ht hd hk hm hn hl hs hr hts htsk: htsx htv htx hːw hːj]
<hp hb ht hd hk hm hn hl hs hr hts htsk htsġ htv htr hhu̯ hhi̯>

ihpi	[ˈiːhpi]	'arrowhead'
ůihba	[ˈœɪhba]	'the least'

hehta	['hɛhta]	'completely'
nigjehdi	['nijːɛhdʑi]	'X will do summer work'
ohkama	['ɔhkɑma]	'raw'
sohma	['sɔhma]	'in the evenings'
kehno	['cʰɛhnɔ]	'pine tree'
kihli	['cʰiɬːi]	'thread'
vahsu	['vahsu]	'X will grow stronger'
lehra	['lɛhra]	'straw'
sihtsa	['sɪhtsa]	'X will look for Y'
oahtska	['ɔahtskːa]	'from the edge of'
rahtsġi	['rahtsxi]	'X will run (on four legs)'
mihtvi	['mɪhtwːi]	'X will whisper'
sehhy̨e	['sehːwe]	'eager'

Note that the consonant cluster <hl> can be pronounced as two morphemes [hl] or [hɬ] or alternatively as a geminate [ɬː]. The latter is quite common in all dialects, especially in younger speakers.

§3.4.6 Initial Consonant Clusters

A number of initial consonant clusters are allowed in Siwa. They are [sv sx sxw ts tsv tsx tsxw tɬ tv kv km kn xv] <sv sġ sġv ts tsv tsġ tsġv dl tv kv km kn>. Many dialects lack <km kn> entirely, e.g. *kmŭti~mŭti* 'bustle, turmoil'. Certain more conservative dialects of the far east have also kept two other clusters which have vanished from all other dialects, [tm tk sm mx] <tm tk sm mġ>: SORHI DIALECT *tmisas* ['tmisas] but standard is *misas* ['misas] 'rock', or *sma* 'X ate Y' instead of standard *ma* and *mġegi* [mxeɟi] 'I', *mġàri* [mxæːri] 'we'. Higher registers commonly include <mġ>, perhaps due to it being found in fairly common words[1].

.[1] Some of the more common words with *mġ-* found in high register are:
    mġegi 'I' (*mġeidġi* GEN., *mġŭta* PREC.)
    mġa- 'me'
    mġàri/mġàra 'we' (*mġendra/mġendri* GEN., *mġŭtra/mġŭtri* PREC.)
    mġari-/mġeri- 'us'
    mġoġ- 'drink'
    mġiegj- 'to herd' (*mġiedju* 'herd' and *mġŭjŭmi* 'herder')
    mġotona 'claw'
Words in **km- kn- tm- tk- sm-** include:
    kmaitsa 'toe'
    kmanda 'type of priest'
    knes 'sour drink'
    knabi 'small mushroom'
    tmisas 'stone'
    tmetvi 'cow vetch'
    tmŭgla 'type of mushroom'
    tkihḥen 'without stopping, steadily, ongoing'
    tky̨aggi 'wood duck'
    smairu·i 'X smiles' (usually mairo-)
    smoro 'landsnail'

Certain western dialects include the clusters <mh nh> initially, then rendered as voiceless [m̥ n̥], sometimes spelled <m̊ n̊>. This is non-standard, e.g. *mahatru* 'I ought to' can be found as *m̊atru* in the west.

§3.4.7 Internal Consonant Clusters
Internal consonant clusters can either be anaptyctic, glottalized, preaspirated or non-anaptyxis (normal clusters). Normal clusters are (excluded are preaspirated clusters and the long voiceless stops <ḍb ḍd ḍg>):

mp [mp]
jampo [ˈjampɔ] 'on the other side'
kůimpa [ˈcʰœɪmpa] 'pair of boots'
sompo [ˈsɔmpɔ] 'swift'

mn [mnː] or [mːn]
umna [ˈʊmnːa] 'space below'
homna [ˈhɔmnːa] 'quiet waters in stream'
imni [ˈɪmnːi] 'X will produce smoke'

mt [mt]
uḍḍemta [ˈuðːɛmta] 'black bird GEN.'
ůpimta [ˈøpɪmta] 'ungulate ILLAT.' (also *ůpimita*)
dotsġamta [ˈdɔtsxamta] 'idea ILLAT.' (also *dotsġamita*)

ms [ms]
oamsu [ˈɔamsu] 'X will get snowed in'
jamsi [ˈjamsi] 'along the other side'

mst [mst]
omste [ˈɔmste] 'type of knot'
Tatimstagi [ˈtʰatɪmstaji] 'Eastern-Siwa (.GEN)'

mś [mɕː]
simśi [ˈsɪmɕi] 'human'
śimśi [ˈɕɪmɕi] 'bear ritual'
tomśiko [ˈtʰɔmɕigɔ] 'velvet GEN.'

mr [mr]
otomrōti [ɔˈtɔmrɔ̄tɕi] 'X will rub its antlers off'
aimra [ˈaɪmra] 'wrongly'

giamra [ˈɟamra] 'one hundred thousand'

mk [mk]
haumka [ˈhaʊmka] 'bright GEN.'
kaimka [ˈkʰaɪmka] 'walking stick GEN.'
nȯmka [ˈnʊːmka] 'sturgeon GEN.'

mkk [mkː]
nẏmkka [ˈnyːmkːa] 'X will pile Y up'
tůmkki [ˈtʰœmcːi] 'boulder'
tśemkka [ˈtɕɛmkːa] 'X will diminish Y'

mġ [mx]
damġa [ˈdamxa] 'skin with fur GEN.'
gamġa [ˈgamxa] 'character GEN.'
jamġa [ˈjamxa] 'the other side GEN.'

mh [mh]
liamhi [ˈlɪamhi] 'hat GEN.'
tśimhi [ˈtɕɪmhi] 'chain GEN.'

pm [pmː] or [pːm]
tśuopmo [ˈtɕʊɔpmːɔ] 'shallow GEN.'
sůpma [ˈsuːpma] 'black GEN.'

ps [psː] or [pːs]
dapsa [ˈdapsːa] 'younger sister'
hopsai [ˈhɔpsːai] 'X will vomit'
kepsi [ˈcʰɛpsːi] 'mushroom'

pś [pɕː] or [pːɕ]
elepśia [ˈelɛpɕia] 'in bloom'
hůpśi [ˈhœpɕːi] 'purple finch'

pr [px] or [px']
ipro ['ɪpxɔ] 'carcass'
kiprirui ['cʰiːpxirui] 'X will chirp'
moaksapri ['mɔaksːapxi] 'it is time for ptarmigan hunting'

bm [ʔpm] or [ʔm]
nebmia ['nɛʔpmia] 'perhaps'
nibma ['niːʔpma] 'birch bark'
rabma ['raʔpma] 'one-man canoe'

bs [ps] or [bs]
tsebsue ['tsɛpsue] 'a little GEN.'
kebsie ['cʰɛpsie] 'mushroom GEN.'

bṡ [pɕ] or [bɕ]
miebśi ['mɪɛpɕi] 'fat person/animal'
gabśi ['gapɕi] 'fool'

nt [nt] or [ntɕ]
hantui ['hantui] 'X will lie'
inta ['ɪnta] 'yes'
muontia ['mʊɔntɕia] 'X decided Y'

nts [nts]
tontsori ['tʰɔntsɔri] 'puffin'
gogantsi ['gɔgantsi] 'X will limp'

ntsġ [ntsx]
taintsġi ['taɪntsxi] 'numerous'

nd [nd] or [ndʑ]
hindu ['hɪndu] 'X died in combat.'
india ['ɪndʑia] 'X was scattered around'

ndl [ntɬ]
ġundli ['xœntɬi] 'X will sigh'

ns [ns]
kansi ['kʰansi] 'female moose'
keukonsimo ['cʰeukɔnsimɔ] 'band, marching band'
mansi ['mansi] 'X came'

nṡ [nɕ]
enśi ['ɛnɕi] 'early winter.'
onśi ['ɔnɕi] 'channel catfish'

nr~ndra [nr] or [ndr]
benra ['bɛn(d)ra] 'dog GEN.'

nk [ŋk]
rjanka ['rjaŋka] 'hip GEN.'
sinka ['sɪŋka] 'a long time ago'
tonkua ['tʰɔŋkua] 'sinew'

nh [nh]
benho ['bɛnhɔ] 'dog'
minhi ['mɪnhi] 'black spruce'

tv [twː] or [tːv]
hŭtva ['hœtwːa] 'X will hit Y'
mitvo ['mɪtwːɔ] 'night frost'

tn [tnː]
bùtni ['buːtnːi] 'cast of bad weather'
hetna ['hɛtnːa] 'to scatter'

ts [ts] (has the value of a single phoneme)
ėtsi ['eːtsi] 'wall'
etsa ['eːtsa] 'X will start Y'
gaitsa ['gaitsa] 'star'

tsv [tswː] or [tsːv]
beitsvi ['bɛɪtswːi] 'X wants to spend the day'

tst [tstː]
itsta ['iːtstːa] 'lifetime GEN.'
kijutsta ['cʰijʊtstːa] 'room GEN.'
nesotsta ['nesɔtstːa] 'green GEN.'

tsl [tslː] or [tsɬ]
matsli ['matslːi] 'bastard'
tetsli ['tʰɛtslːi] 'american coot'

tsm [tsmː] or [tsːm]
kotsmi ['kʰɔtsmːi] 'walking path'

latsma [ˈlatsmːa] 'log-bridge'

tsn [tsnː] or [tsːn]
tetsni [ˈtʰɛtsnːi] 'dried fish'
mitsni [ˈmɪtsnːi] 'cabin'

tsk [tskː] or [tsːk]
nitski [ˈnɪtscːi] 'unit'
otski [ˈɔtscːi] 'laced'
patskon [ˈpʰatskːɔn] 'inconsiderate'

tskv [tskwː] or [tsːkv]
meitskva [ˈmɛɪtskwːa] 'spruce sprout'
kotskven [ˈkʰɔtskwːɛn] 'wooden ring to tie skins around'

tsġ [tsx]
pitsġa [ˈpʰɪtsxa] 'X will scold Y'
tsġiame [ˈtsxiɑme] 'cedar strips'
katsġi [ˈkʰatsxi] 'jam'

tsġv [tsxw]
batsġvi [ˈbatsxwi] 'X will look for Y'
tsġatsġva [ˈtsxatsxwa] 'bug'

tr [tx]
netro [ˈnɛtxɔ] 'pistil'
retro [ˈrɛtxɔ] 'northern pike'

tk [tk]
rietki [ˈrɪɛtci] 'where the forest ends'
saitki [ˈsaɪtci] 'X will disappear'
tatkatka [ˈtʰatkːatka] 'inside out'

tkv [tkwː] or [tːkv]
piatkvi [ˈpʰɪatkwːi] 'X wanted to go to sleep'
okitkvi [ɔˈcɪtkwːi] 'X wanted to take a break'

tġ [tːx]
tsutġasi [ˈtsʊtːxɑsi] 'lunar eclipse'
setġa [ˈsɛtːxa] 'X will place Y'
rytġy [ˈrœtːxy] 'hammer'

ḍm [ðmː]
svaḍma [ˈsvaðmːa] 'foam'
taḍma [ˈtʰaðmːa] 'furthest back'

dn [ʔtn] (or [ʔn])
hudna [ˈhuːʔtna] 'steam hut'
lidna [ˈliːʔtna] 'great'
nidna [ˈniːʔtna] 'hut'

dl [tɬ] (single phoneme)
sudlu [ˈsutɬu] 'X will bear berries'
tsodli [ˈtɕɔtɬi] 'late summer'
ġidli [ˈxiːtɬi] 'X will crackle'

ḍk [ðkː] or [ðːk]
iḍka [ˈɪðkːa] 'we will fall' (also *idigga*)
keiḍka [ˈcʰɛɪðkːa] 'we will start a fire' (also *keidigga*)

ḍv [ðw] or [ðːw]
meḍvi [ˈmɛðwːi] 'eyelid'
loḍvot [ˈlɔðwːɔʔ] 'delayed, long, slow'

dġ [ðx]
nedġi [ˈnɛðxe] 'X will sit down'
edġe [ˈɛðxe] 'air'
jodġi [ˈjɔðxi] 'X will yelp'

sm [sm]
miasma [ˈmɪasma] 'peace'
njosma [ˈɲɔsma] 'deaf GEN.'

sp [sp]
ispa [ˈiːspa] 'X will pinch Y'
kuspo [ˈkʰʊspɔ] 'skunk'

sv [sv]
osve [ˈɔsve] 'sour'
svotta [ˈsvɔʔta] 'mother GEN.'
svohka [ˈsvɔhka] 'X will slam Y'

st [st]

tusta [ˈtʰʊsta] 'barricade, steep hill'
ẏstůa [ˈyːstøa] 'X will kiss Y'
estot [ˈɛstɔʔ] 'first'

sl [sl] or [stɬ]
kislo [ˈcʰiːslɔ] 'noose'
aisla [ˈaɪsla] 'X will drag Y'

sk [sk]
hesko [ˈhɛskɔ] 'small bay'
iski [ˈiːsci] 'woman'
kieska [ˈcʰɪɛska] 'X will watch Y'

skl [sklː] or [sːkl]
eiskla [ˈɛɪsklːa] 'X interviews Y'
Tasklabi [ˈtʰasklːabi] 'toponym'

skv [skwː] or [sːkv]
miaskvi [ˈmɪaskwːi] 'X wants to celebrate'
peuiskvi [ˈpʰɛʊɪskwːi] 'slippery jack'
toskvi [ˈtʰɔskwːi] 'caribou without antlers'

skk [skː]
tsaskka [ˈtsaskːa] 'X forgot Y'
pjeskko [ˈpʰjɛskːɔ] 'snowflake'
siskki [ˈsɪscːi] 'it thundered'

sġ [sx]
tausġon [ˈtʰaʊsxɔn] 'rigid'
hausġa [ˈhaʊsxa] 'edible'
kesġamo [ˈcʰɛsxamɔ] 'teacher'

sġv [sxw]
sġvelmi [ˈsxwɛlmi] 'gland'
kesġven [ˈcʰɛsxwɛn] 'chickadee'

śm [ɕm]
kośma [ˈkʰɔɕma] 'strong wind'
nośmo [ˈnɔɕmɔ] 'pouch'
siśmu [ˈsɪɕmu] 'bottom'

śp [ɕp]
iśpa [ˈiːɕpa] 'grandparents'

tśyśpi [ˈtɕœɕpi] 'X speaks with an accent'

śv [ɕv]
iśva [ˈiːɕva] 'grandparents GEN.'
gośvari [ˈgɔɕvari] 'oakwood'

śk [ɕk]
kiśka [ˈcʰɪɕka] 'away ELAT.'
loiśko [ˈlɔɪɕkɔ] 'leech GEN.'
śůśků [ˈɕœɕcø] 'nipple'

śkv [ɕkwː] or [ɕːkv]
nuśkva [ˈnʊɕkwːa] 'hail'
śeśkvo [ˈɕɛɕkwːɔ] 'slush'

rm [rm]
jorma [ˈjɔrma] 'young bull GEN.'
kirma [ˈcʰɪrma] 'in the morning' (also *kimra*)

rp [rp] (or [rb])
orpi [ˈɔrpi] 'X will misbehave'
rarpo [ˈrarpɔ] 'angry'

rpp [rpː]
suorppi [ˈsʊɔrpːi] 'X will drink (animal)'
varppi [ˈvarpːi] 'rude'

rv [rwː] or [rv]
tervima [ˈtʰɛrwːima] 'it is twilight'
ůrvi [ˈœrwːi] 'surroundings'

rt [rt] (or [rd])
artaita [ˈartaida] 'compared to'
ġertobi [ˈxɛrtɔbi] 'threshold GEN.'

rtt [rtː]
torttiu [ˈtʰɔrtːiu] 'paralyzed'
ġertto [ˈxɛrtːɔ] 'threshold'

rk [rk] (or [rg])
ůrkyno [ˈœrcynɔ] 'close to'

virke [ˈviːrce] 'short, stumpy'

rkk [rkː]
liarkko [ˈlɪarkːɔ] 'guest bench'
sarkka [ˈsarkːa] 'X will break Y'

rġ [rx], also **rh** [rh]
njorġa [ˈɲɔrxa] 'duck' (also *njorha*)
birġo [ˈbɪrxɔ] 'beam' (also *birho*)

rh [rh]
ẏrhů [ˈyːrhø] 'X will grow (of scars)'
birho [ˈbiːrhɔ] 'canidæ'
erho [ˈɛrhɔ] 'careful'

lm [lm]
galmot [ˈgalmɔʔ] 'soft'
kolmo [ˈkʰɔlmɔ] 'esker GEN.'

lp [lp] or [lb] or [ɬp]
holpo [ˈhɔlpɔ] 'dull'
jálpika [ˈjæːlpiga] 'hare GEN.'
nalpaka [ˈnalpaga] 'snout GEN.'

lpp [lpː]
gjylppa [ˈdzœlpːa] 'wet snow'
jálppi [ˈjæːlpːi] 'hare'
nalppa [ˈnalpːa] 'snout'

lb [lb]
kelba [ˈcʰɛlba] 'shoulders'
kilbi [ˈcʰɪlbi] 'usually'
nalbi [ˈnalbi] 'husband' (also *nalvi*)

lv [lv]
telvu [ˈtʰeːlvu] 'X will clear up'
tulvi [ˈtʰʊlvi] 'nutrient'
bialvuni [ˈbɪalvuni] 'cray fish, crustacean'

ln [ln]
okůlni [ɔˈcœlni] 'X will make its nest'
ulnuma [ˈuːlnuma] 'milky way'
kelne [ˈcʰɛlne] 'more'

lt [lt] or [ɬt] (or [ld])
loalta [ˈlɔalta] 'to the back'
noaltaka [ˈnɔaltaga] 'tooth GEN.'

ltt [ltː]
keltta [ˈcʰɛltːa] 'ground' (also *kelta*)
njolttima [ˈɲɔltːima] 'X is sick'
noaltta [ˈnɔaltːa] 'tooth'

lts [lts] or [ɬts]
viltsa [ˈvɪltsa] 'maternal aunt GEN.'
koaltsa [ˈkʰɔaltsa] 'paternal aunt GEN.'

ltsv[1] [ltsw] or [ɬtsw]
Meltsva [ˈmɛɬtswa] 'toponym'

ltsġ [ltsx] or [ɬtsx]
ġiltsġa [ˈxɪɬtsxa] 'disgust'

ltsġv [ltsxw] or [ɬtsxw]
Teltsġvi [ˈtʰɛɬtsxwi] 'toponym'

ld [ld] or [ldʑ]
ajelda [ˈajelda] 'marrow GEN.'
bieldi [ˈbɪɛldʑi] 'fat GEN.'
kilda [ˈcʰiːlda] 'again'

lś [lɕ]
salśinhi [ˈsalɕɪnhi] 'caribou head sacrifice'

ltś [ltɕ] or [ɬtɕ]
eultśai [ˈɛʊltɕai] 'high grasses GEN.'
njeltśa [ˈɲɛltɕa] 'chief GEN.'

ldj [ldʑ]

---

[1]The clusters <ltsv ltsġ ltsġv> are also found as -uts-/-yts- in other dialects. The river *Teltsġvi* is also commonly called *Teytsġvi*.

tśildjui [ˈtɕɪldʑui] 'X screamed'

lr [lr] or [ldr]
gilra [ˈɟɪlra] 'wet weather'
olra [ˈɔlra] 'fewest'

lk [lk] or [ɬk] (or [lg])
kolkon [ˈkʰɔlkɔn] 'bread'
gagulka [ˈɡɑɡʊlka] 'community'

lkk [lk:]
olkko [ˈɔlk:ɔ] 'temple'
hialkko [ˈhɪalk:ɔ] 'wound'

lg [lɡ]
noalgi [ˈnɔalʝi] 'tar kiln'
jàlgi [ˈjæːlʝi] 'male rite of passage'

lġ [lx]
půlġůn [ˈpʰœlxœn] 'bud'
ġalġa [ˈxalxa] 'callus'

lh [lh]
kelho [ˈcʰɛlhɔ] 'dried meat'
nielhi [ˈnɪɛlhi] 'fir GEN.'

dlv [tɬwː]
ġedlvi [ˈxɛtɬwːi] 'thick fog'
radlva [ˈratɬwːa] 'X will disturb Y'
půadlva [ˈpʰœatɬwːa] 'otter'

dlm [tɬmː]
ġyadlmi [ˈxwatɬmːi] 'rainbow'
sodlmot [ˈsɔtɬmːɔʔ] 'snowdrift'

dln [tɬnː]
hadlna [ˈhatɬnːa] 'sea ice'
nõdlni [ˈnõtɬnːi] 'it will be flooding/overflowing'

dlk [tɬkː]
kodlken [ˈkʰɔtɬcːɛn] 'firefly'
midlkis [ˈmɪtɬcːɪs] 'crab'

dlġ [tɬx]
seidlġa [ˈsɛɪtɬxa] 'pregnant fish'
ůdlġůt [ˈœtɬxœʔ] 'throat'
sġidlġa [ˈsxɪtɬxa] 'reins' (pl.)

km [kmː] or [gmː] or [kːm]
djikma [ˈdʑɪkmːa] 'on display, obvious'
sokmi [ˈsɔkmːi] 'seagull'

kv [kwː] or [kːv]
guokvo [ˈɡʊɔkwːɔ] 'frog'
kokve [ˈkʰɔkwːe] 'light'
leikva [ˈlɛɪkwːa] 'slippery'
kvia [ˈkʰviːa] 'X will feel Y'

kn [ʔŋ] or [ʔŋː]
ljekna [ˈljɛʔŋa] 'snowless'
nakna [ˈnaʔŋa] 'X will break Y'
sykni [ˈsœʔŋi] 'generation'

ks [ksː] or [kːs]
tůnůksi [ˈtʰønœksːi] 'attack leader'
ẏksy [ˈyːksːy] 'bow'

ksk [kskː]
nùkskon [ˈnuːkskːɔn] 'eternal'

ksl [kstɬ]
saksla [ˈsakstɬa] 'loose ice in river'
teyksla [ˈtʰɶœkstɬi] 'X will punish Y'

kś [kɕː] or [kːɕ]
akśi [ˈakɕːi] 'death'
pikśima [ˈpɪkɕːima] 'X is hurt'

kl [klː] or [kɬː] or [kːl]
rokloma [ˈrɔklːɔma] 'round'
saykla [ˈsæœklːa] 'X will protect Y'

gm [ŋmː] or [ŋːm]
tśegma [ˈtɕɛŋmːa] 'child'
igmo [ˈɪŋmːɔ] 'rapidly changing weather'

gv [kv] or [gv]

kyegvia [ˈkʰwɛkvia] 'X will call Y (animal)'
sigvima [ˈsɪkvima] 'it is dusk'

gn [ŋnː] or [ŋːn]
gegna [ˈɟɛŋnːa] 'den'
migna [ˈmɪŋnːa] 'to get ready'

gs [ks] or [gs]
diugsid [ˈdɾʊksɪd͡ʑ] 'icicle GEN.'
rugsoma [ˈrʊksɔma] 'circle GEN.'

gl [kl] or [gl]
tsġoglimo [ˈtsxɔklimɔ] 'rakovalkea'
njuglimo [ˈɲʊklimɔ] 'finger GEN.'

ġm [xm] or [xmː]
iġmi [ˈɪxmi] 'to accept'
moġmi [ˈmɔxmi] 'to drink'

ġv [xv] or [xwː] (usually <hv> [hv])
aġvi [ˈaxvi] 'X stayed' (also ahvi)

ġn [xn] or [xnː]
kuoġni [ˈkʰʊɔxni] 'X will argue'

ġl [xl] or [xlː]
soġli [ˈsɔxli] 'X will thaw'

§3.4.7.1 Anaptyctic Pronunciation

Certain internal consonant clusters may be pronounced with anaptyxis (insertion of a vowel to break up a cluster), and are called anaptyctic consonant clusters or the anaptyctic pronunciation. This is commonly the case where the latter part of the cluster is geminated (Siwa tends to geminate the second consonant). This trait is common in both dialects and can be in free variation in speakers, but is somewhat more common in older speakers. There is much variation in the pronunciation of anaptyctic clusters. One finds an anaptyctic /ɨ/ (or also commonly /ə/) inserted between the consonants and usually lengthening or glottalization of the of the second consonant and voicing of the first consonant. In the east, the vowel /ɨ/ is not present or very short, and only lengthening occurs, whereas in the wear, /ɨ/ is present (or may be pronounced as a schwa) and voiceless stops are glottalized (most common) or lengthened.

Anaptyctic clusters are the following:

<mn mkk pm ps pś tv tn tsv tsm tsn tst tsk tskv tsġ tk tkv tġ dk dv dġ skv skk śkv rpp rv rtt rkk lpp ltt lkk dlv dlm dln dlġ km ks ksk kś kv kl gm gn ġm ġv ġn ġl>

They are all clusters normally pronounced with the second consonant being geminated. Anaptyctic pronunciation breaks down the clusters to the following:

[mɨnː mɨʔk bɨm: bɨsː bɨɕː dɨwː dɨnː dzɨw: dzɨm: dzɨn: dzɨʔt dzɨʔk dzɨkw:/tsɨgw: dzɨx: dɨʔk dɨkw:/dɨgw: dɨx: ðɨʔk ðɨw: ðɨɣ: skɨw: sɨʔk ɕkɨw: rɨʔp rɨw: rɨʔt rɨʔk lɨʔp lɨʔt tɬɨw: tɬɨm: tɬɨn: tɬɨx: gɨm: gɨs: gɨsk:/ksɨʔk: gɨɕː gɨwː gɨlː/gɨɫ: ŋɨm: ŋɨn: ɣɨm: ɣɨw: ɣɨn: ɣɨlː]

Note that anaptyctic clusters have a strong tendency to phonologically lengthen the preceding vowel (though not <skv śkv>) without affecting its pronunciation, i.e. the vowel remains unchanged but is lengthened. The following examples show normal pronunciation and its anaptyctic counterpart. Anaptyctic pronunciation is sometimes transcribed into Siwa's orthography (though not gemination), especially when writing western dialects.

	homna	[ˈhɔmnːa]	'quiet waters in stream'
→		[ˈhɔːmɔnːa]	
	tůmkki	[ˈtʰœmcːi]	'boulder'
→		[ˈtʰœːmɨ?cːi]	
	sůpma	[ˈsuːpmːa]	'black GEN.'
→		[ˈsuːbɨmːa]	
	dapsa	[ˈdapsːa]	'younger sister'
→		[ˈdaːbɨsːa]	
	hůpśi	[ˈhœpɕːi]	'purple finch'
→		[ˈhœːbɨɕːi]	
	hůtva	[ˈhœtwːa]	'X will hit Y'
→		[ˈhœːdɨwːa]	
	hetna	[ˈhɛtnːa]	'to scatter'
→		[ˈhɛːdɨnːa]	
	beitsvi	[ˈbɛɪtswːi]	'X wants to spend the day'
→		[ˈbɛːɪdzɨwːi]	
	nesotsta	[ˈnesɔtstːa]	'green GEN.'
→		[ˈnesɔːdzɨ?tːa]	
	nitski	[ˈnɪtscːi]	'unit'
→		[ˈnɪːdzɨ?cːi]	
	saitki	[ˈsaɪtcːi]	'X will disappear'
→		[ˈsaːɪdɨ?cːi]	
	toskvi	[ˈtʰɔskwːi]	'caribou without antlers'
→		[ˈtʰɔskɨwːi]	
	pjeskko	[ˈpʰjɛskːɔ]	'snowflake'
→		[ˈpʰjɛːsɨ?kːɔ]	
	nuśkva	[ˈnʊɕkwːa]	'hail'

→		[ˈnʊɕkɨwːa]	
	varppi	[ˈvarpːi]	'rude'
→		[ˈvaːrɨʔpːi]	
	ūrvi	[ˈœrwːi]	'surroundings'
→		[ˈœːrɨwːi]	
	ġertto	[ˈxɛrtːɔ]	'threshold'
→		[ˈxɛːrɨʔtːɔ]	
	sarkka	[ˈsarkːa]	'X will break Y'
→		[ˈsaːrɨʔkːa]	
	jàlppi	[ˈjælpːi]	'hare'
→		[ˈjæːlɨʔpːi]	
	noaltta	[ˈnɔaltːa]	'tooth'
→		[ˈnɔːalɨʔtːa]	
	olkko	[ˈɔlkːɔ]	'temple'
→		[ˈɔːlɨʔkːɔ]	
	sokmi	[ˈsɔkmːi]	'seagull'
→		[ˈsɔːgɨmːi]	
	guokvo	[ˈgʊɔkwːɔ]	'frog'
→		[ˈgʊːɔgɨwːɔ]	
	tūnūksi	[ˈtʰʊnœksːi]	'attack leader'
→		[ˈtʰʊnœːgɨsːi]	
	akṡi	[ˈakɕːi]	'death'
→		[ˈaːgɨɕːi]	
	saykla	[ˈsæœklːa]	'X will protect Y'
→		[ˈsæːœgɨɫːa]	
	tṡegma	[ˈtɕɛŋmːa]	'child'
→		[ˈtɕɛːŋɨmːa]	
	gegna	[ˈɟɛŋːa]	'den'
→		[ˈɟɛːŋɨnːa]	

Younger generations also tend to pronounce preglottalized consonants as -ʔVC- where the -V- is either anaptyctic or a copy of the preceding vowel.

kekken
[ˈcʰɛʔɛcɛn] or [ˈcʰɛʔɨcɛn]

Not everyone geminates or preglottalizes the second sound of a cluster. Clusters containing <v> are especially likely to geminate the first consonant: <skv> can be [skɨw:], [skw:] or [s:kv]~[skv]~[skw].

§3.4.7.2 Ejective Pronunciation
The Siwa consonant clusters [tx px tsx] <tr pr tsġ> may be pronounced as [tʼqʼ pʼqʼ tsʼqʼ], that is to say as ejectives. This pronunciation sometimes extends to <tġ> and <bġ> being pronounced as [tːʼ pːʼ] and even <ġġ> as [qːʼ]. This is especially common in eastern dialects and higher language registers. It is associated with more archaic language, and may be used as a form of hypercorrection.

The consonants <pp tt kk ddj dl> are commonly found as (geminated) ejectives [pʼ tʼ kʼ tɕʼ tɬʼ] in non-initial syllables or when directly before a stressed syllable.

§3.4.8 Lenition
Lenition is a phonological process by which the intervocalic coda (most commonly) of the stressed syllable in inanimate nouns is changed or 'weakened' as part of case marking. The sound changes range from loss of gemination, consonant cluster simplification to consonants disappearing all together. Lenition **only** affects inanimate nouns.

As a general rule, if lenition occurs, vowel apocope before case endings is less likely. However, geminate sonorants do not always obey this.

		agentive	genitive
		Geminated Voiced Stops	
[pː] **bb**	[b] **b**	*sabbas* [ˈsapːas] 'sole'	*sabahi* [ˈsabahi]
[tː] **dd**	/d/ **d**	*saddama* [ˈsatːama] 'callus'	*sadakka* [ˈsadaʔka]

/k:/ **gg**	/g/ **g**	keggas ['cʰek:as] 'foetus'	kegahi ['cʰegahi]
/x:/ **ġġ**	/x/ **ġ**	naiġġa ['naix:a] 'thicket'	naiġaka ['naixaga]

			Long Sonorant
/j̇/ **gj̇**	[j] **j̇**	nygjis ['nyj:ɪs] 'spirit'	nyjihi ['nyjihi] (also nẏhhi̇)
[m:] **mm**	[m] **m**	nẏmmi ['ny:m:i] 'heap, hill'	nẏmdi ['ny:mdʑi]
[l:] **ll**	[l] **l**	tśellu ['tɕel:u] 'catkin'	tśelue ['tɕelue]
/n:/ **nn**	[n] **n**	kinna ['cʰin:a] 'fist, hand'	kindi ['cʰɪndʑi]
[r:] **rr**	[r] **r**	kẹrru ['cʰær:u] 'suspicion'	kẹrume ['cʰærume]

			Uvular Stops

[bx] **bġ** *or* [px] **pr**	[p] **p**	*ipro* [ˈɪpxo] 'carcass'	*ipodi* [ˈipɔdʑi]
[ðx] **dġ** *or* [tx] **tr**	/t/ **t**	*edġe* [ˈɛðxe] 'air'	*eteri* [ˈeteri]
			glottalized Stops
[ʔpm] **bm**	[m] **m**	*sibma* [ˈsɪʔpma] 'claw'	*simadi* [ˈsimɑdʑi]
[ʔtn] **dn**	[n] **n**	*nŭdna* [nœʔtna] 'wave'	*nŭnamo* [nønɑmɔ]
[ʔŋː] **kn**	[ŋ] **ng**	*akna* [ˈaʔŋa] 'trace'	*angaka* [ˈɑŋːɑga]
			Consonant Clusters
[tɬ] **dl**	[l] **l**	*idlu* [iːtɬu] 'sprout'	*iludi* [ˈiːludʑi]
[lpː] **lpp**	/lp/ **lp**	*gjylppa* [ˈdzœlpːa] 'wet snow'	*gjylpamo* [ˈdzœlpɑmɔ]

[lt:] **ltt**	/lt/ **lt**	*noaltta* ['nɔalt:a] 'tooth'	*noaltaka* ['nɔaltɑga]
/lk:/ **lkk**	/lk/ **lk**	*hialkko* ['hɪalk:ɔ] 'wound'	*hialkodi* ['hɪalkɔdʑi]
[rp:] **rpp**	[rp] **rp**	*kjurppo* [cʰʊrp:ɔ] 'hollow'	*kjurpoma* [cʰʊrpɔma]
[rt:] **rtt**	/rt/ **rt**	*njėrtta* ['ɲe:rt:a] 'sharp pain'	*njėrtari* ['ɲe:rtɑri]
/rk:/ **rkk**	/rk/ **rk**	*liarkko* ['lɪark:ɔ] 'guest bench'	*liarkodi* ['lɪarkɔdʑi]
[ps:] **ps**	[ps] **bs** *or* [p:s] **ps**	*tsepsu* ['tsɛps:u] 'tiny bit'	*tsebsue* [tsɛpsue]
/mk:/ **mkk**	/mk/ **mk**	*tůmkki* ['tʰømc:i] 'boulder'	*tůmkimo* ['tʰœmcimɔ]
[kl:] **kl**	[kl] **gl**	*tsġokli* [tsxɔkl:i] 'rakovalkea'	*tsġoglimo* [tsxɔklimɔ]

[kw:] **kv**	[kv] **gv**	koakvi [ˈkʰɔakwːi] 'call'	koagvika [ˈkɔakviga]
[ks:] **ks**	[ks] **gs**	diuksi [ˈdɪʊksːi] 'icicle'	diugsid [ˈdɪuksɪdʑ]
/sk:/ **skk**	/sk/ **sk**	pjeskko [ˈpʰjɛskːɔ] 'snowflake'	pjeskue [ˈpʰjɛskue]

Voiced Consonants

[v] /w/ **v ŭ**	Ø	sivi [ˈsivi] 'honey'	sid [ˈsiːdʑ]
[w:] **vv**	Ø or [w] **ŭ**	nivvi [ˈniwːiː] 'humidity'	niŭila~nila [ˈniwila/ niːla]
[b] **b**	Ø	tśibes [ˈtɕibɛs] 'sign'	tśiehhi [ˈtɕiehːi]
/d/ **d** + back vowel	[l] **l**	puodus [ˈpʰuɔðʊs] 'navel'	puolhi [ˈpʰʊɔlhi]

/d/ **d** + front vowel	Ø	*hide* [ˈhide] 'hair'	*hiedi* [ˈhiedʑi]
/g x/ **g ġ** + back vowel	[v] **v** or [w:] **vv**	*ougu* [ˈouɣu] 'hook'	*oumma* [ˈɔum:a]
/g x/ **g ġ** + front vowel	Ø	*tiogi* [ˈtiɔji] 'dam'	*tśoid* [ˈtɕɔɪdʑ]
/ʔ/ **h/ḥ**	Ø	*vihi* [ˈviʔi] 'dirt'	*vid* [ˈviːdʑ]
			Consonant -i
[ri] **ri**	[ɕi] **śi**	*iri* [ˈiri] 'bark'	*iśid* [ˈiɕːɪdʑ] (also *ihdi*)
[xi] **ġi**	[ɕi] **śi**	*boġi* [ˈbɔxi] '(deciduous) branch and leaves'	*bośko* [ˈbɔɕkɔ]
[ɲi] **nji**	[jːi] **gji**	*kinji* [ˈcʰiɲi] 'fringes on clothes'	*kigjid* [ˈcʰijːɪdʑ]

[h:ji] **hḥji**	[ɕi] **śi**	boaihḥji ['bɔɑih:ji] 'floating weeds in lake'	boaiśka ['bɔɑɩɕka]

Long Voiceless Consonants			
[ðb] **ḍb**	[p] **p**	moḍbi ['mɔðbi] 'hunting territory'	mopiko ['mɔpɩgɔ]
[ð:] **ḍḍ**	[h:] **hh**	saḍḍa ['sɑð:a] 'fire (in a forest or house)'	sahhaka ['sɑh:aga]
/ðg/ **ḍg**	/k/ **k**	kõḍga ['kʰɔ̃ðga] 'bear cub'	kōkamo ['kʰɔ̄kamɔ]

Semi-Vowel			
[ɔw uw] **oų uų**	/ø/ **ů**	oųis ['ɔwɪs] 'turtle'	ẙhhi ['y:h:i]

Note that in conservative language, the cluster <ng> disappears between two identical vowels under lenition: *tingi* 'mating period' can be found as *tingid* or *tid* in the genitive.

Below is a table that summarizes lenition and offers more examples.

Table of consonant lenition

			Examples
bb	→	b	nebbi : nebie 'trap'
dd	→	d	saiddon : saidonta 'big catch'
gg	→	g	tsoggis : tsogihi 'hope'
gg	→	g	keyggün : keygüs 'big birch'
gj	→	j	tigjo : tijodi 'irritation'
mm	→	m	svaimmet : svaimetta 'responsibility'
ll	→	l	lillot : lilotsta 'p. uncle's house'
nn	→	n	senni : senie 'time period'
rr	→	r	rerreki : reregge 'change of mind'
bg/pr	→	p	soapri : soapika 'split'
dg/tr	→	t	edge : eteri 'air'
db	→	p	eidbi : eipie 'carver'
p	→	hh	soddos : sohhohi–sohhi 'evening'
dd	→	k	ködga : kökamo 'bear cub'
dg	→	m	rybmy : rymyma 'dress'
bm	→	n	ridni : rinid 'choru'
dn	→	n	akna : angaka 'traces'
kn	→	ng	seidlo : seilue 'push'
dl	→	l	jalppi : jalpika 'hare'
lpp	→	lp	noaltta : noaltaka 'tooth'
ltt	→	lt	olkko : olkoma 'temple'
lkk	→	lk	sorppo : sorpoma 'drink, slurp'
rpp	→	rp	gertto : gertue 'threshold, limit'
rtt	→	rt	erkka : erkari 'fork'
rkk	→	rk	tümkki : tümkimo 'boulder'
mkk	→	mk	pjeskko : pjeskue 'snowflake'
skk	→	sk	tsgokki : tsgoglimo 'rakovalkea'
kl	→	gl	sakva : sagvaka 'soap'
kv	→	gv	diuksi : diugsid 'icicle'
ks	→	gs	kepsi : kebsie 'mushroom'
ps	→	bs	sivi : sid 'honey'
v/u	→	Ø	tsibes : tsiehhi 'sign'
b	→	Ø	dahama : damga 'jawbone'
h/h	→	Ø	nagit : naitta 'dry branch'
g	→	Ø	puodus : puolhi 'navel'
d-a/o/u	→	Ø	hide : hiedi 'hair'
d-e/i/ü/y	→	Ø	sogabi : sovabiko 'insult'
g-a/o/u	→	v/vv	mige : mied 'crystall'
g-e/i/ü/y	→	Ø	giri : gisid 'leather pants'
ri/gi	→	si	kinji : kigjid 'fringes'
nji	→	gii	hyhhjys : hysyhi 'mumble'
hhj	→	s	moji : myko 'grandpa'
ou/uu	→	ü	

sabbas : sabahi 'sole'	kobbomora : kobomohmo 'salamander'	nüabbü : nüabüma 'bump'
saddama : sadakka 'callus'	süddü : südüma 'infection'	medde : mederi 'corner'
daiggi : daigika 'humid weather'	süiggi : süigid 'dry weather'	geggus : geguhi 'quack'
soggot : sogota 'bad burning wood'	hyeggü : huegie 'sunny weather'	jeyggü : jeygüma 'nap'
ygii : yjima 'spike'	igiut : ijutsta 'mood'	oagjon : oajonta 'memory'
voamme : voameka 'ghost'	tsoammus : tsoamuhi 'unit'	kvemmet : kvemetsta 'heather'
kvlli : kvliid 'sperm'	mjoallus : mjoaluhi 'particle'	hoalleri : hoalehka 'court'
unnaska : unaskamo 'vocabulary'	monnu : monuma 'damage'	kjennut : kjenutsta 'mallard duck'
eirro : eirue 'work'	irri : irid 'arrow'	arroma : arokka 'side of table'
loabgis : loapiha 'shirt'	gabgas : gapahi 'larva'	gibgi : gipid 'wire'
neidgeme : neitemme 'chair'	südgü : sütüma 'fizz, froth'	modgori : motohdi 'police'
ridbi : ripid 'socket'	lodbo : lopoma 'jelly'	gadbi : gapiko 'vase'
hudge : huhhemo 'light'	jeiddo : jeihhue 'run'	sadda : sahhaka 'fire (in house)'
diedge : diekedi 'little girl'	neudge : neukie 'light snow'	todgo : tokoma 'tree trunk, torso'
pübma : pümamo 'level, degree'	pelbmus : peimuhi 'ass'	haibmoki : haimokka 'depression'
ydni : ynid 'character'	oadni : oanika 'look'	peidni : peinie 'return'
ekni : engie 'way'	gakna : gangaka 'net'	keknuli : kengulie 'organizer'
idlu : iludi 'sprout'	saidli : sailika 'burnt food'	rudlu : ruluma 'wrinkle'
giylppa : giylpyma 'wet snow'	nalppa : nalpaka 'snout'	alppot : alpotta 'entry beam'
eltta : eltari 'steam house, sauna'	keltta : keltari 'ground'	mittet : miitetsta 'little) mush'
hialkko : hialkodi 'wound'	sailkko : sailkoka 'swelling'	lülkki : lülkimo 'hot (pool of) water'
varppi : varpika 'rude (person)'	kjurppo : kjurpoma 'hollow (in tree)'	tsarppa : tsarpaka 'button'
njertta : njertari 'sharp pain'	hartta : hartaka 'crown'	airtti : airtika 'vase'
garkken : garkenta 'substance, liquid'	kirkkyt : kirkytsta 'pine warbler'	nerkke : nerkie 'chorus'
imkki : imkid 'swallow'	somkkoro : somkohmo 'larva'	kümkkü : kümkümo 'snot'
giskku : giskyma 'spark, shock'	üskky : üskyma 'fold, roll'	risskotan : riskotas 'joke'
njukli : njuglid 'finger'	koklu : koglumo 'boat landing'	taikla : taiglaka 'snail'
kvikvon : kvigvos 'riddle'	rikvu : rigvud 'parcel'	gokvali : gogvalmo 'stubborn (man)'
yksy : ygsyma 'bow'	vieksо : viegsodi 'high-pitch noise'	müksü : mügsüma 'winter down'
hepsa : hebsari 'jewel'	gapsan : gabsanta 'placenta'	mipsi : mibsid 'thief'
kvavi : kvaika 'sleet'	avohi : auhika 'membrane'	myv : mymo 'girl, little girl'
giba : giadi 'small problem'	gjuebis : gjueihhi 'poke'	hebi : hegjie 'chick'
vihi : vid 'dust, dirt'	laihu : lajuka 'straw'	mohe : moimo 'loaf'
gaguika : gaulkka 'community'	dege : deri 'little boat'	haga : haka 'quill'
niedas : nielhi 'fir'	tsida : tsilala 'rabbit'	kadas : kalhi 'helmet'
kode : koimo 'shoulder blade'	gade : gaika 'rake'	gidi : gid 'newborn bird'
vogon : vovvonta 'sample'	huguna : huvvummo 'uhnus'	pago : pavvoka 'pest'
tsygy : tsyima 'reach (of a throw)'	tsgage : tsgaiko 'hammer'	gigi : gid 'kid'
piri : pisid 'nugget'	ügi : üsimo 'unedible berry'	reri : resie 'bladder on heel'
jenji : jegjie 'snake, viper'	manji : magjiko 'broken weapon/tool'	hynji : hygjid 'sponge'
sihhjiksus : sisiksuhi 'whizz'	mahhji : masiko 'fallen bear'	rehhji : resie 'secret'
oujis : yhhi 'turtle'	eџot : üboddja 'unimportant person'	guujis : gyhhi 'grape'

§3.5 Diachronic Phonology
Going through all of the changes from Proto-Alopian to modern Siwa would be of little use to the learner. However, certain consonants are worth examining as they may help recognize cognates and may shed light on the development of Siwa.

§3.5.1 Consonants
Below are given some of the relevant sound changes in consonants that have occurred in earlier stages of Siwa.

*/b/
Proto-Siwa */b/ sometimes disappeared intervocally or changed to */m/, especially before */ī ē/. This can be seen in the Siwa pair *bieli* ['bieli] 'fat, blubber' (PROTO-SIWA *bili) vs. *mielo* ['mielɔ] 'rot, mildew' (PROTO-SIWA *bīl·u). Before */o u/ it generally remained */b/, but sometimes became */w/ and sometimes it became */m/ (usually because of a neighbouring dialect's influence which kept the */m/ variant only), e.g. *voli* ['vɔli] 'arthritis' (PROTO-SIWA *bol-) cf. *malva* ['malva] 'sprain' (PROTO-SIWA *bŏl·wa).

*/w/
Proto-Siwa */w/ went through complicated sound changes. It most often changed to /v/ (before a stressed front vowel). Sometimes it fell together with */b/ and changed to /m/ before /ī ē/, cf. *vebo* ['vebɔ] 'knot' (PROTO-SIWA *wep-/wap-) but *mėpsemi* ['me:psemi] 'to make knots' (PROTO-SIWA *wīp-). */w/ usually disappeared all together between identical vowels.

*/d/
Proto-Siwa */d/ changed to */v/ before /a o/ intervocally, which can be seen in words such as *suvo* ['suvɔ] 'berry' (PROTO-SIWA *sud-) and *sudlu* ['sutɬu] 'to blossom' (PROTO-SIWA *sud·l-). Similarly, */d/ changed to */w/ before */u/, but it also sometimes disappeared, e.g. *saiyu* [sɑiwu] 'pot' (PROTO-SIWA *sād-) and *sayna* [sæœna] (PROTO-SIWA *sād·ina) 'hiding place'.

*/n/
Proto-Siwa */n/ changed to */j/ after a long front vowel, e.g. *tinin* ['tʰinɪn] 'firewood' (PROTO-SIWA *tini-) cf. *tiegibi* ['tʰiejibi] 'twig' (PROTO-SIWA *tīn·ibi).

*/θ/
Proto-Siwa /θ/ has the most number of reflexes in modern Siwa. It is perhaps worth describing all of them:

	-θa	-θo / -θu	-θe	-θi	-θj-
	-hha-	-vv-/-b-	-ḍḍe-	-Ø i-	-g-
a-/o-/u-	sahha (<*saθ·a) 'X will burn Y'	savvu (<*saθ·u) 'a burn' saubus (<*saθ·isa) '(small) flame, candle'	uḍḍemi (<*oθ·emi) 'black bird'	oi (<*oθ·i) 'moon light'	saugeni (<*saθ·jen) 'X smells burnt'
	-hha-	-vv-/-b-	-ḍḍe-	-b-	-g-
y-/ů-	nyhha (<*nyθ·a) 'X will make Y curl/bend'	nůbů (<*nøθ·ø) 'ring finger'	njůḍḍe (<*njøθ·e) 'coil'	ybi (<*oθ·i) 'cloudless'	njůgůkka (<*njøθ·økka) 'X will coil Y'
	-hha-	-hh-/-Ø-	-ḍḍe-	-hhi-/-Ø i	-g-/-ṡ-
e-/i-	rehha (<*reθ·a) 'X pull Y'	sieḍbi 'eagle' → siehhumi 'eagle gen' (< *sīθ·) tigjo (<*tīθ·o) 'skin irritation'	saiḍḍe (<*sāθ·e) 'burning sensation'	tiddji (<*tīθ·i) 'stimulus, frustration'	segaka (<*seθ·jaka) 'embers'

Before /h/ it became /ʔ/ (deleting the /h/):
    omoḥi   [ˈɔmɔʔi]   'game' (< *o-măθ·ʔi)

Before /s/ it disappeared:
    tamosi   [ˈtʰamɔsi]   'hunter' (< *ta-măθ·si)

Before /k g/ it became [s] <s>:
    maski   [ˈmasci]   'people' (< *maθ·ki)

It lengthened /p b/ to [ðb] <ḍb> and /t d/ to [ðː] <ḍḍ>:
    kaḍgju   [ˈkʰaðɟu]   'fresh wood' (< *kaθ·kil)

The cluster /θr/ became [tx] <tr>:
    utra   [ʊtxa]   'crowberry' (< *oθ·ra)

The cluster */θl/ became [tɬ] <dl>:
    sadlu   [satɬu]   'to burn in a pot' (<*saθ·lu)

*/s/

The cluster */sr/ changed to /sx/ <sġ> in Siwa. In some cases, */s/ changed to [h:] <hh> between /i y/ and /i/, e.g. *kyhhisi* [ˈcʰyhːisi] 'mink' and *kuspo* [ˈkʰʊspɔ] 'skunk' both from PROTO-SIWA *kus- (possibly 'stinky animal').

*/l/

Proto-Siwa */l/ sometimes palatalized to /ʎ/, but this became /ʃ/ in neighbouring languages as well as some eastern dialects, as can be seen from pairs such as Siwa ljemi [ˈljemi] 'infection' and *śi* [ˈɕiː] 'pus' from ŠUMO *šin* 'wound' from PROTO-SIWA *ljem- (most likely a borrowing from an unknown language).

*/ʃ/

Proto-Siwa */ʃ/ often became Siwa /ɕ/ but after diphthongs is usually changed to /h/ or /ʔ/, e.g. *aihha* [ˈɑihːa] 'thorn, sewing needle' cf. *aiskami* [ˈɑɪskɑmi] 'to sew' (PROTO-SIWA *āʃ-, earlier SIWA *aiśka*)

*/c/

As a general rule, Proto-Siwa */c/ palatalized to [tɕ] <tś> especially before long front vowels or /j/. Sometimes, it remained /c/, cf. *Kjuomśin* [ˈcʰʊɔmɕɪn] 'Kjuomśin' and *tśiempa* [ˈtɕɪɛmpa] 'sinuous', both from *cōm- 'sinuous, twisting'.

*/ŋ/

Proto-Alopian */ŋ/ remained as is in Siwa except between two identical vowels, in which case it disappeared, e.g. *tuo* [ˈtʰuɔ] 'carrot' (PROTO-SIWA *toŋo) cf. laddonga [ˈlaðːɔŋːa] 'root soup' (PROTO-SIWA *luθ·tong-).

§3.6 Prosody

Spoken Siwa has a variety of language registers, ranging from every day language, hunter-speech or *amisaśmi*, story telling to jocular or emphasized speech. Parallel to this are the differences between men's and women's speech.

The most elevated form of Siwa is ceremonial story-telling or emphatic speech called *ujoaimi* (lit. 'correctly told'). *Ujoaimi* is characterized by monotonous and long stretches of speech with a fixed rhythm. Phonetically, *Ujoaimi* is unusual in having most prefixes and certain suffixes clearly separated from the word they attach to by a glottal stop, [ʔ]. Also, unvoiced plosives are often aspirated even in non-stressed position. For example:

katitsġovahmi
[kʰatiˈtsxɔvahmi]
or [ˈkʰatʰʔiˈʔtsxɔvaʔhiʔmi]
'I will tell you about it'

Perhaps the most deviating register is *amisaśmi* or hunter-speech. It is the characteristic speech of hunters, typically used when talking amongst themselves. The main feature of *amisaśmi*, illustrated in the name, is the syncope of unstressed vowel (see §3.6). For example, the phrase *katsa satakana* 'you will whistle at me outside' is normally pronounced [ˈkʰatsa ˈsatakana], but in **amisaśmi**, it becomes *katsa stakna* [ˈkatsa ˈstagna]. Men also more often than women drop the copula in infinitive clauses.

Men tend to turn [wa] into [ɔ] after <p t k s l n>. This also applies to /oa/. Thus, men would tend to pronounced *nitkyat* 'gender-based role singing' as [ˈniːtkɔʔ]. Women usually lengthen the first sound of diphthongs and also have the lax versions of diphthongs with /i/, then pronounced /e/, e.g. *hiamin* 'milk and honey drink' [ˈheːamɪn] or [ˈheːamn].

§3.7 Tśebġeka

Siwa is occasionally written using a syllabic script called Tśebġeka. Its use is limited, and as this grammar aims to introduce a standardized orthography, it will not be used here.

Tśebġeka has 29 consonants and 8 vowels. Each of the 29 consonants has a specific character for each of the 9 vowels, for 261 different characters. The table below is adapted for Siwa and English as well as other Alopian languages, which also occasionally use Tśebġeka.

Punctuation

Diacritics
- geminated consonant
- long vowel
- -w ~ -u
- w- ~ u-
- -j ~ -i
- j- ~ i-

Here is a sample of Siwa written in the Tśebġeka script.

[Tśebġeka script text]

Romanization:

Isohhieita, batsġvia kialka saumi, saigi te olluli, golki tamosuldōria gejori ki taneġġuhka kehhia. Sia katta kokve kialka oḍḍa tśadnami. Îndvi ijultsamśia to saigi, hejerime meruen te eletka te miukime oaila, rendli kobai dajo. Îndvi ōgmoja to saumi, tå hejerime magja te omudna dajo, koka heruen te taja ono, mieri te elepuma elepśia kobai rendluki oaila, tå tsůiruma rekkot dajo utasuśuke kimi kemamomittaki gagi deja. Îndvi katta tsamśia ġvivid t-ôlhamo to olluli, tama kunna te suvuma muki oaila.

English:

Once a long time ago, a caribou, a moose and a deer were looking for land where all three could live together as friends. But such a place is not easy to find.
        The moose wanted to live in a spruce forfest with mild winters and pastures and bogs where he could graze in the summer.
The caribou wanted to live in the tundra, where winters are white and snowy, with cold summers and lots of lichen, moss and blooming flowers to eat and large open spaces to travel with his brothers and sisters.
        But the deer wanted to live in a big leafy forest, with lots of oaks and berries to eat.

§4 Nouns

Siwa nouns form an open category with a complex agentive derivation system. The following description is valid for all substantives and proper nouns as well as all attributive and post-positive adjectives.

Nouns are marked for case (agentive/dative, patientive/genitive, inessive, illative, elative, adessive, allative and ablative), number (singular, plural, collective) and can be marked for topic or approbation (approbative or pejorative). A small number of nouns also require a verbal personal marking or possession marker. They are called action nominals (see *§4..3.3.3*). Nouns also have animacy – they are either animate, inanimate or both.

Siwa nouns have two basic forms: an unmarked form, corresponding to the agentive and dative case, and a marked form, corresponding to the patientive and genitive case. The inessive, illative, elative, adessive, allative and ablative are grouped together as the locative cases, and they are added onto the genitive form of the noun, such that the locative case markings are considered to be secondary to the unmarked and marked forms.

unmarked cases
    agentive
    dative

marked cases
    patientive
    genitive
    locative cases
        inessive
        illative
        elative
        adessive
        allative
        ablative

This means that one only has two learn two basic forms of a noun to be able to decline it in all of its cases. Take for example the word *somi* 'man':

	singular	plural
unmarked form	*somi*	*somigi*
marked form	*sõkko*	
locative forms		
inessive	*sõkkia*	
illative	*sõkkita*	
elative	*sõkkika*	
adessive	*sõkkima*	
allative	*sõkkibma*	

ablative   *sõkkiska*

Plural marking is not required and is not usually found on the marked form of a noun. The collective is marked regularly through a clitic ending. Likewise, the approbative and pejorative markers are found as prefixed clitics:

approbative   *sussomi*   'good man/fellow'
pejorative   *ussomi*   'bad man'

Nominal declensions thus consist of two major forms, the unmarked and marked, with additional cases being formed from the marked form. Animacy only becomes visible through the marked form, i.e. a noun's animacy is not obvious from its default unmarked form. This explains why some nouns, whose marked forms are compatible with both animacies may freely go from animate to inanimate.

§4.1 Animacy

Animacy refers to whether a noun is considered to be living (animate) or non-living (inanimate), though animacy also covers cultural salience and personal importance. Animate nouns decline according to their ending, and the animate declensions only contain a fix set of 33 endings, while inanimate nouns decline according to both their stressed vowel and word-final vowel or only on their word-final consonant. However, inanimate nouns which happen to end in one of the 33 animate endings may have both an inanimate and animate marked form. Inanimate nouns are affected by lenition in their marked form (see *§3.4.8*)

For example, the word *eleba* 'flower' has both animacies – the ending -**ba** is one of the 33 animate endings. Its marked form can thus be either *eleu* (animate) or *elepri* (inanimate). The choice may be contextual or up to the speaker. The animate marked form implies a living, perhaps personified flower, while the inanimate form implies a flower, or perhaps a dried/picked flower. This is called perceived animacy.

The majority of nouns are inanimate. Animacy is not restricted to biological animacy. Animate nouns are generally perceived as being culturally more salient or important. In fact, importance is a major factor in choosing animacy for ambiguous nouns, and may greatly help in determining a noun's inherent animacy.

A small set of nouns have asymmetrical animacy, i.e. they are animate nouns whose singular marked form is inanimate, but whose plural unmarked form is animate. These include:

	singular	animate plural	inanimate plural
'man'	*somi*	*somigi*	*somie*
'woman'	*iski*	*iskigi*	*iskie*
'boy'	*kori*	*korigi*	*korie*
'girl'	*dida*	*didagi*	*didua*

Many speakers have more nouns in this category – biologically animate but morphologically inanimate nouns with an animate plural. The inanimate plural is usually translated into English without the definite article:

> *somigi*   'the men'
> *somie*   'men (in general)'

§4.1.1 Inanimate

Inanimate nouns include most lifeless things. They have two main groups of declensions – a change of ending to consonant-final words (consonant declensions), or an ending dependent on a combination of the stressed vowel and the word-final vowel (vowel declensions).

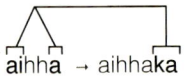

Inanimate nouns are optionally marked for plural and use a different plural marker than animate nouns. Inanimate nouns include:

aihha	'sewing needle, thorn'
àli	'wound'
bana	'place'
dedna	'village'
ekni	'way'
gjykin	'snowshoe'
hamit	'metal'
juoku '	enclosure'
kaibmu	'walking stick, support'
kykky	'call'
leuvva	'reindeer moss'
meků	'river banks'
nůjů	'knife'
omi	'snow'
opsi	'cup'
pjoki	'flint'
rapa	'small hill'
somora	'gold'
sugagi	'pea'
tśalta	'clay'
tsammi	'forest'
tȯ	'stone'
uja	'water'
ėu	'sand'

ygji	'spike'
và	'lake'

However, many inanimate nouns are biologically animate:

hapri	'flock of birds'
helon	'pregnant animal'
heutsġo	'burbot'
jȧlppi	'hare'
idlu	'sprout'
iski	'woman'
keggas	'fœtus'
kei	'lynx'

Such morphologically inanimate nouns may be referred to with animate pronouns, especially words referring to humans (*iski* 'woman', *somi* 'man', *dida* 'girl', *kori* 'boy', etc.).

Ambiguous nouns perceived as inanimate are usually non-specific, or may also imply that the noun is of lesser or 'lowered' importance. The former is especially true of many ambiguous nouns referring to animal or plant species. For example, *guokvo* 'frog', if perceived inanimate, may refer to frogs in general, e.g.;

so hana-a guogvoma	'do you eat frog?'	(inanimate)
so hana-a guokoui	'will you eat the frog?'	(animate)

§4.1.2 Animate

Animate nouns typically include living things, people or culturally important, holy or salient objects. They differ from inanimate nouns in their declensions and the fact that they are always marked for plural in the unmarked form (-gi/-hi-/ṡi or -i), with a separate marker from the inanimate plural. Animate nouns see their last syllable change, and no animate noun ends in a consonant. Animate nouns do not go through lenition. The animate endings are:

-ma	-mi	-mo
-ba	-bi	-bo
-pa	-pi	-po
-va	-vi	-vo
-na	-ni	-no
-la	-li	-lu
-ra	-ri	-ro
-ṡi		
-sa	-si	-so
-ta	-ti/-te	-to

-ka	-ki/-ke	-ko
-ha	-hi/-i	-ho
-ga	-gi	-go

Animate nouns include:

ajosi	'open ocean' or the impersonation of the sea
amoi	'blood'
bialvuni	'shrimp'
dapsa	'younger sister'
demo	'bone'
eulhi	'field'
eleba	'flower'
gasi	'moon'
helva	'female caribou'
hemi	'bird'
iḍmi	'raven'
iṡpa	'grandparents'
kansi	'female moose'
ko	'summer'
kyṡi	'squirrel'
manta	'world'
moasi	'black bear (taboo word)'
nůirhi	'adults, parents'
nommo	'sturgeon'
oadi	'palate'
ohra	'god'
peilki	'trout'
retema	'fox'
sira	'fish'
ṡimi	'bear head'
tàs	'nose'
ůdno	'angelica'
ůrjůni	'female wolf'
yṡi	'salmon'

Many specific species names are animate (though the majority are in fact ambiguous, but more commonly found as animate nouns). For example, *kjoḍma* 'auk bird' is any bird of the auk family and it is an inanimate noun. However, *tontsori* 'puffin' is animate. The same goes for plants: a coniferous tree is *piġo* and is an inanimate noun, but *minhi* 'black spruce', *kumora* 'white spruce' and *serula* 'larch' are all animates.

Most kinship words in Siwa are animate (marked form given in italics):

kembo
kàmoųi
'grandfather'
kàmaka **kàmasa**
kàmġaka *kàmġasa*
'my grandfather' 'your grandfather'

sambo
sàmoųi
'grandfather'
sàmaka **sàmasa**
sàmġaka *sàmġasa*
'my grandfather' 'your grandfather'

niebini
nieiġia
'grandmother'
nieųaka **nieųasa**
nieųaśka *nieųassa*
'my grandmother' 'your grandmother'

piddani
pittśa
'grandmother'
pittśaka **pittśasa**
pittśaśka *pittśassa*
'my grandmother' 'your grandmother'

lillu **koalgi**
lilda *koaltsa*
'paternal uncle' 'paternal aunt'

pėsi **vilo**
pėta *viltsa*
'maternal uncle' 'maternal aunt'

atri
attśa
'father'
ataka **atasa**
atkaka *atkasa*
'my father' 'your father'

suosa
suotta
'mother'
sòka **sòsa**
sòmaka *sòmasa*
'my mother' 'your father'

tyry
tolba
'son'

śini
śiśa
'daughter'

kośi
gasta
'older brother'
kosoka **kososa**
kottaka *kottasa*
'my older brother' 'your older brother'

toabi
daumi
'older sister'
tobika **tobisa**
toumika *toumisa*
'my older sister' 'your older sister'

karsa
karta
'younger brother'

dapsa
daḍḍa
'younger sister'

In addition, the Siwa seasons are also animate:

tęli	'spring'
ȧlni	'early spring'
tȯhni	'late spring'
ko	'summer' (also commonly inanimate)
ini	'early summer'
tsodli	'late summer'
ġi	'fall'
ymni	'early fall'
guni	'late fall'
hejeri	'winter'
enśi	'early winter'
jatkini	'late winter'

Below is how the Siwa year is organized into seasons.

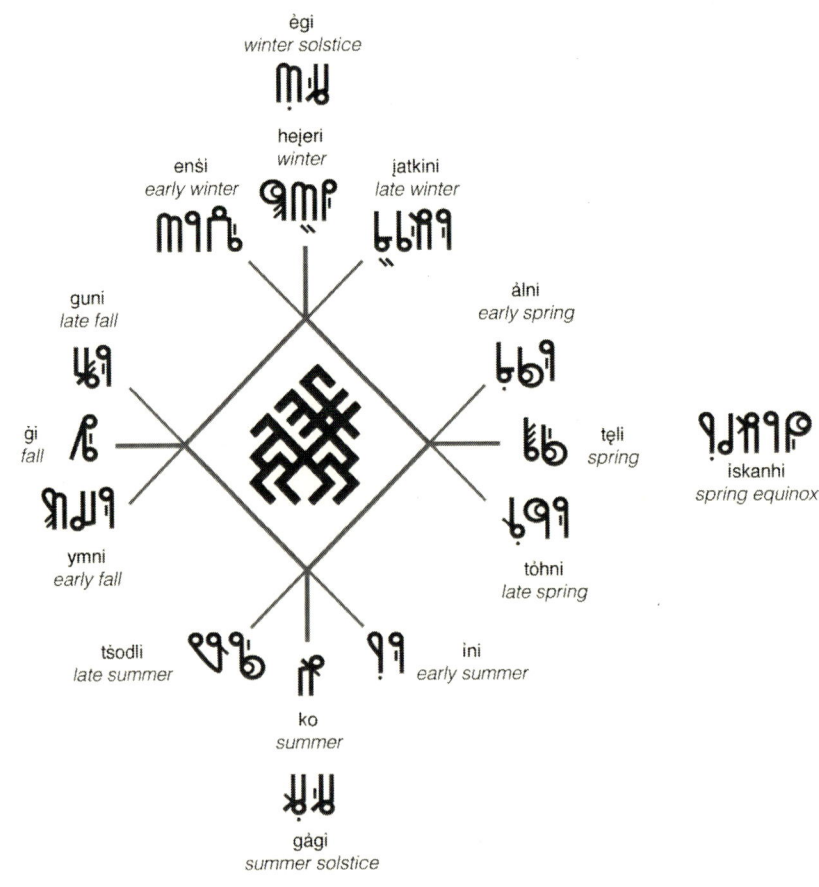

Words for important events in the Siwa year also have the animate form as well as the animate plural marker -gi/-ġi/-ṡi/-hi (thus all plural nouns):

tserogi	'sweat lodge ceremony'
aumulhi	'female menstruation ceremony'
jȧlhi	'male rite of passage'
salṡinhi	'caribou head sacrifice'
ìskanhi	'vernal equinox'
umuigi	'autumnal equinox'

Note that the following nouns are inanimate:

gȧgi	'summer solstice'
ėgi	'winter solstice'
gjekesġi	'birthday'
maisagi	'winter hunt start ceremony'
ṡimṡi	'bear ritual'.

The animate noun class also contains many body parts, most of which are irregular (marked form given in parentheses here):

totami	(*todatta*)	'head'
sata	(*savva*)	'ear'
saḍba	(*saubba*)	'ears'
kita	(*kivva*)	'eye'
kiḍba	(*keubba*)	'eyes'
njarri	(*njaret*)	'nose'
lisġi	(*lihḥji*)	'nostrils'
kuki[1]	(*kutṡa*)	'mouth'
kėppa	(*kėhu*)	'arm (from shoulder to wrist)'
tṡeḍḍa	(*tṡevva*)	'arm (from elbow to wrist)'
tiemo	(*tieka*)	'hand'
tiebba	(*tiehba*)	'hands'
miebi	(*mieumi*)	'leg (from hip to ankle)'
mamma	(*mamṡi*)	'leg (from knee to ankle)'
sieḍḍo	(*sievva*)	'foot'
mìppa	(*mihu*)	'feet'

---

[1] Note that *kuki* exists both as an animate and inanimate noun (then *kugmo* in the marked form). When used as an inanimate noun, it is slightly less polite.

§4.1.3 Ambiguous Nouns
Ambiguous nouns are those which have one animate and one inanimate marked form. Generally, ambiguous nouns perceived to be animate are given more importance, made to be more salient, more specific, personified, or in the case of many words referring to species of plants and animals, perceived animate nouns refer to an individual plant or animal rather than the species in general. Thus, ambiguous nouns are more commonly inanimate when plural (whether overt or not). Any noun ending in one of the animate noun endings may decline as an ambiguous animate noun. This is not consistently done but it can be done to underline the personification of an inanimate noun (such as when an inanimate noun is given life in narratives).

ėhtuma	'balsam poplar'	
kȧhloita elhi ėhtumari	'balsam poplars grow tall'	(inanimate)
kȧhloita edli ėhtuka	'the balsam poplar grew tall'	(animate)
miniso	'common snipe'	
viviksui minihi	'the common snipe winnows'	(inanimate)
viviksui ministi	'common snipes winnow'	(animate)

Ambiguous nouns include most tree species, many plants and many fish, bird and animal species.

§4.1.4 Honorific Nouns
Honorific speech in Siwa, used in certain ritualized circumstances (speaking before a council, addressing elders or sometimes young women or children) is characterized by absolute animacy – all nouns capable of being animate are declined as as such, even those which are normally never animate. For examples, the word *pjoki* 'flint' has the marked form *pjokko*, but if one were to present flint as a gift or in a ritualized circumstance, the marked form would be *pjotṡa*, which is otherwise not heard.

§4.2 Marked Form
Siwa nouns have two basic forms; unmarked and marked. The marked form corresponds to the genitive and/or the patientive case. Animate and inanimate nouns form the two groups of declensions. Note that adjectives follow inanimate declensions and will be included as examples here. Inanimate nouns undergo lenition in marked form.

§4.2.1 Inanimate Marked Form
Inanimate declensions are separated into two groups: consonant-final and vowel-based. Both groups go through consonant lenition, if possible. In vowel-based declensions, the stressed vowel of a word as well as its final vowel govern the shape of the case marker. The final vowel of a noun is very often deleted when the case

marker is added, though -o and -e generally remain unchanged before locative endings. However, nouns which undergo consonant lenition usually keep their final vowels, i.e. apocope is not generally allowed on lenited stems (though words in -i are more prone to apocope, as well as sonorants). Syllable count may also influence the shape of a marked noun – polysyllabic words obey different rules than bi- or monosyllabic words. The locative case markers delete the last vowel of the marked form in most cases. These changes are explained in more detail below.

§4.2.1.1 Vowel-Final

Vowel final declensions regroup bi- and polysyllabic words ending in vowels. The ending for the marked form is dependent on the stressed vowel and the final vowel of the verb.

    Endings may assimilate differently to the word depending on the syllable count of the word, or whether it contains a stressed diphthong. Words with a stressed diphthong or long vowel, or with three or more syllables (polysyllabic) are called *weak nouns* (W), while bisyllabic words with a simple stressed vowel are called *strong nouns* (S). In some cases, stressed diphthongs and long vowels and simple consonants may behave differently than their polysyllabic counterparts, and are then called *long nouns* (L).

weak nouns	nobe**mo**, ra**i**bma, rìdni
strong nouns	g**a**ma, b**a**na, ġ**u**pa
long nouns	h**au**ma, r**á**mi

final vowel → stressed vowel ↓	-a	-e	-i	-o	-u/-y/-ů
A-declension a á au ai oa ay		-ka or -ġa/-ra			
E-declension e ė ę ei ey	-ri/-ġi	-e		-e or -obi	-me
I-declension i í ie ia		-id or -di			
O-declension o ó ou oi	-mo	-ko or -ġo			

final vowel → stressed vowel ↓	-a	-e	-i	-o	-u/-y/-ů
U-declension u ů uo ui		-mo			-ma
Y-declension y ẏ ů ėu eu ůi ůa	-mo		-id or -di		

§4.2.1.1.1 A-declension

This declension includes all nouns whose stressed vowel is a à au ai and oa. This is one of the simpler declensions. Generally speaking, the ending is -ka or -ġa. Below are the rules for this declension. The marked form has its locative in -i- (-a is deleted).

Words ending in -mV or -mmV can either have the form -kka for weak nouns, -mġa for strong noun, which becomes -mṡ- before the -i- of locative cases, or or -mka after a stressed diphthong or a long vowel.

A-declension			unmarked	marked	locative
s	marked	locative	gama 'character'	gam·ġa	gam·ṡi-
	-mġa	-mṡi-	tsammi 'forest'	tsam·ġa	tsam·ṡi-
			hauma 'bright'	haum·ka	haum·ki-

A-declension			unmarked	marked	locative
-mV	L	-mka	-mki-	*saumi* 'caribou'	*saum·ka*	*saum·ki-*
				ràmi 'protruding rock'	*ràm·ka*	*ràm·ki-*
	W	-kka	-kki-	*sasame* 'tipi'	*sasa·kka*	*sasa·kki-*
				jasuma 'fear'	*jasu·kka*	*jasu·kki*
				salama 'antlers'	*sala·kka*	*sala·kki*

Words ending in -nV or -nnV can either have the form -nka or -kka. Weak nouns in -nV usually have the form -kka. Strong nouns in -nV or -nnV usually take -nka (and in some cases, this changes to -nṡ- before the -i- of locative cases, but not always).

A-declension				unmarked	marked	locative
		marked	locative			
-nV	S	-nka	-nṡi- / -nki-	*bana* 'place'	*ban·ka*	*ban·ṡi-*
				janna 'piled-up snow'	*jan·ka*	*jan·ṡi*
	W	-kka	-kki-	*atana* 'big'	*ata·kka*	*ata·kki-*
				saihkena 'point, cap'	*saihke·kka*	*saihke·kki-*

Words ending in -pV can have the form -pra or -ḍga. Weak nouns in -pV or -bV usually have the form -ḍga. Strong nouns in -pV take -pra (and in some cases, this changes to -pṡ- before the -i- of locative cases, but not always).

		A-declension		unmarked	marked	locative
-pV -bV	s	marked	locative	rapa 'small hill'	rap·ra	rap·ṡi-
		-pra	-pṡi-/-pri-	habi 'nipple'	hap·ra	hap·ṡi-
	w	-ḍba	-ḍbi-	natabi 'hemlock'	nata·ḍga	nata·ḍgi-
				saipi 'race'	sai·ḍga	sai·ḍgi-

Words ending in -tV can have the form -tka or -tra. Weak nouns in -tV or -dV have the form -tra. Strong nouns in -tV take -tka (and in some cases, this changes to -tṡ- before the -i- of locative cases, but not always). A small number of words with -tV have the ending -tra where one would expect -tka and vice-versa.

		A-declension		unmarked	marked	locative
-tV	s/w	marked	locative	ata 'mouth'	at·ra	at·ri-
		-tra	-tri-	gauta 'color'	gaut·ra	gaut·ri-
	w	-tka	-tṡi-	jata 'carved bowl'	jat·ka	ja·tṡi-

Weak nouns in -rV have the form -hka.

	A-declension		unmarked	marked	locative
	marked	locative	oari 'edge'	oa·hka	oa·hki-
-rV w			kalara 'hole'	kala·hka	kala·hki-
	-hka	-hki-	takeri 'person'	take·hka	take·hki-

Words ending in -vvV have -gga.

	A-declension		unmarked	marked	locative
	marked	locative	mavvu 'meat'	ma·gga	ma·ggi-
-vvV			poavvi 'seal'	poa·gga	poa·ggi-
	-gga	-ggi-	davva 'past'	da·gga	da·ggi-

Words in -lkV -rkV -skV get -lkka -rkka -skka.

	A-declension		unmarked	marked	locative
	marked	locative	aurko 'lake trout'	aur·kka	aur·kki-
-CkV			gagulka 'community'	gaul·kka	gaul·kki-
	-Ckka	-Ckki-	tasko 'woods'	tas·kka	tas·kki-

Other endings and most words that go through consonant lenition simply have the form -ka (with deletion of final vowel after sonorants).

A-declension			unmarked	marked	locative
-CCV	marked	locative			
	-CCVka	-ki-	kalsa 'oven, insides'	kalsa·ka	kalsa·ki-
			dàdna 'pillow'	dàna·ka	dàna·ki-
			màhra 'bear'	màhra·ka	màhra·ki-
			aihmi 'nesting hole in snow'	aihmi·ka	aihmi·ki-
			gaitsa 'meteor'	gaits·ka	gaits·ki-
	-Cka	-Cki-	aihha 'needle'	aih·ka	aih·ki-
			soalu 'fragrance, smell'	soal·ka	soal·ki-

§4.2.1.1.2 E-declension

This declension includes all nouns whose stressed vowel is e ė ę ei and ay/eu. The declension has three categories of ending; for words ending in -a or -e, for words ending in -i or -o, and for words ending in -u, -y or -ů. Marked endings in -e are always kept before locative endings (-eita, -eika, etc.).

-a/-e

Words in -a or -e which do not go through apocope of their last vowel get the ending -ri.

E-declension -a/-e			unmarked	marked	locative
	marked	locative	dida 'tear'	dia·ri	dia·ri- dia·h-

E-declension -a/-e			unmarked	marked	locative
-a -e	-ri	-ri -h-	helva 'female moose'	helva·ri	helva·ri- helva·h-
			dje 'gray'	dje·ri	dje·ri- dje·h-
			edġe 'air'	ete·ri	ete·ri- ete·h-

Words ending in -na or -ne have the marked form -di, which turns to -h- before the illative, elative and abessive (-hta, -hka and -hma) and in -i- before the allative and ablative (-ibma and -iska), but remain -d- before the inessive (-dia).

E-declension -a/-e				unmarked	marked	locative
-na -ne	s	marked	locative	hejona 'weak'	hejo·di	hejo·di- hejo·i- hejo·h-
		-di	-di- -h- -i-	merana 'difficult'	mera·di	mera·di- mera·i- mera·h-

Words in -ba/-be have the marked form -pri (sometimes -bġi), which becomes -pṡi- before locative endings.

E-declension -a/-e			unmarked	marked	locative
-ba -be	marked	locative	eleba 'flower'	elep·ri	elep·ṡi-
	-pri -bġi	-pṡi-	netuba 'lilly'	netup·ri	netup·ṡi-

Words in -ka/-ke have the marked form -ġi and -ṡi- before locative endings.

E-declension -a/-e			unmarked	marked	locative
-ka **-ke**	marked	locative	segaka 'burnt embers'	seva·ġi	seva·ṡi-
	-ġi	-ṡi-	teuke 'silhouette'	teu·ġi	teu·ṡi-
			neitrike 'proboscis, trunk'	neiti·ġi	neiti·ṡi-

Words in -ma/-me have the marked form -mmi, unchanged before the locative cases.

E-declension -a/-e			unmarked	marked	locative
-ma **-me**	marked	locative	teroma 'twilight'	tero·mmi	tero·mmi-
	-mmi	-mmi-	gegeme 'hem'	gè·mmi	gè·mmi-
			bename 'leather pouch'	bena·mmi	bena·mmi-

Words in -va/-ve have the marked form -rri, those in -tsa/-tse have -tsġi, in -sa/-se have -sġi, and -la/-le have -lli. All are unchanged before locative endings.

E-declension -a/-e			unmarked	marked	locative
-va **-ve**	marked	locative	neivi 'cone'	nei·rri	nei·rri-
	-rri	-rri-			
-tsa **-tse**	-tsġi	-tsġi-	letse 'pole'	lets·ġi	lets·ġi-

E-declension -a/-e			unmarked	marked	locative
-ta **-te**	-tri	-tri-	jeita 'structure'	jeit·ri	jeit·ri-
-sa **-se**	-sġi	-sġi-	hesse 'shovel'	hes·ġi	hes·ġi-
-la **-le**	-lli	-lli-	nevala 'diligent'	neva·lli	neva·lli-
			biele 'fat'	bie·lli	bie·lli-
-ha/-he **-ġa/-ġe**	-ġġi	-ġġi-	keiġe 'birch'	kei·ġġi	kei·ġġi

-i/-o
Words ending in -i or -o get the ending -e (changing -o to -ue). The ending -ue is also found as -obi in more conservative language or dialects.

E-declension -i/-o			unmarked	marked	locative
	marked	locative	ekni 'way, path'	engi·e	engi·ei-
-i	-ie	-iei-	elki 'high grasses'	elki·e	elki·ei-
			kepsi 'mushroom'	kebsi·e	kebsi·ei-

E-declension -i/-o			unmarked	marked	locative
-o	-ue -obi	-uei- -obi-	benho 'dog'	benh·ue benho·bi	benh·uei- benho·bi-
			rento 'grain'	rent·ue rento·bi	rent·uei- rento·bi-
			vebo 'knot'	v·ivve v·iobi	v·ivvei- v·iobi-

Words ending in -mi, -pi/-bi, -vi, -ni, -ri, -li, and -ki/-gi become -mme, -bbe -vve, -nne, -rre, -lle and -gge respectively.

E-declension -i/-o			unmarked	marked	locative
	marked	locative			
-mi	-mme	-mmei-	ljemi 'infection'	lje·mme	lje·mmei-
			seumi 'soil, land'	seu·mme	seu·mmei-
			tśemmi 'animal tracks'	tśe·mme	tśe·mmei-
-pi **-bi**	-bbe	-bbei-	reibo 'beam of light'	rei·bbe	rei·bbei-
-vi	-vve	-vvei-	teivi 'nit'	tei·vve	tei·vvei-
-ni	-nne	-nnei-	tetśõka (< *tetśuni-ka) 'guts'	tetśu·nne	tetśu·nnei-
			nekõka (< *nekuni-ka) 'crumbs'	neku·nne	neku·nnei-
			teuriri 'a couple'	teuśi·rre	teuśi·rrei-

E-declension -i/-o			unmarked	marked	locative
-ri	-rre	-rrei-	*eluri* 'great, fantastic'	*elu·rre*	*elu·rrei-*
-li	-lle	-llei-	*meuli* 'blue'	*meu·lle*	*meu·llei-*
-ki **-gi**	-gge	-ggei-	*keggeki* 'boasting'	*kege·gge*	*kege·ggei-*
			rerreki 'sudden change of mind'	*rere·gge*	*rere·ggei-*

-u/-y/-ů

Words in -u, -y or -ů which do not go through apocope of their last vowel get the ending -me.

E-declension -u/-y/-ů			unmarked	marked	locative
	marked	locative	*detku* 'quality'	*detku·me*	*detku·mei-*
-u **-y** **-ů**	-me	-mei-	*tsepu* 'unfrozen'	*tsepu·me*	*tsepu·mei-*
			enṇju 'pole for nagivation'	*enju·me*	*enju·mei-*

The most common endings that go through apocope are in -mV and -nV, which get the marked ending -**mme**, and -kV, which get the marked ending -**gme** (strong nouns) or -**hme** (weak nouns).

E-declension -u/-y/-ů				unmarked	marked	locative
-mu -my -mů -nu -ny -nů		marked	locative	temmy 'shore'	te·mme	te·mme-
				demy 'mucus'	de·mme	de·mme-
		-mme	-mme-			
				deumu 'bone'	deu·mme	deu·mme-
-ku -ky -ků	s	-gme	-gme-	seky 'cliff'	seg·me	seg·me-
				meků 'river banks'	meg·me	meg·me-
-ku -ky -ků	w	-hme	-hme-	njeiku 'frown'	njei·hme	njei·hme-

§4.2.1.1.3 I-declension

This declension includes all nouns whose stressed vowel is i į and the diphthongs ia ie io iu. The declension has two main endings, -di for all final vowels except -i, which have the form -id for words that do not go through apocope. Those in -di have change to -h- before the illative, elative and abessive (-hta, -hka and -hma) and in -i- before the allative and ablative (-ibma and -iska), but remain -d- before the inessive (-dia).

I-declension			unmarked	marked	locative
	marked	locative	dida 'girl'	dia·di	dia·di- dia·h- dia·i-

-V	-Vdi	-di- -h- -i-	idlu 'sprout'	ilu·di	ilu·di- ilu·h- ilu·i-
			hide 'hair'	hie·di	hie·di- hie·h- hie·i-
-i	-id	-idi-/-i- -ih- -i-	ridni 'thorn'	rini·d	rini·di-/ rin·i- rini·h- rin·i-
			mihki 'frost'	mihki·d	mihki·di-/ mihk·i- mihki·h- mihk·i-
			ki 'new'	ki·d	ki·d- ki·h- ki·-/kiddji-

Words in **-mV** and **-nV** have the marked form **-ndi**, unchanged before the locative cases. Note that certain adjectives in **-bmi** have **-ndi** in the marked form. Notice that words in **-umV/-omV** and **-unV/-onV** have the marked for **-ōdi**.

I-declension		unmarked	marked	locative
marked	locative	dimma 'treeless mountain'	di·ndi	di·ndi-

-mV **-nV**	-ndi	-ndi-	*ilama* 'facade, place in front'	ila·ndi	ila·ndi-
			kinaubmi 'foreign'	kinau·ndi	kinau·ndi-
			inina 'rich'	inin·di	inin·di-
			kinna 'fist, paw'	kin·di	kin·di-
-umV **-omV** **-unV** **-onV**	-õdi	-õdi-	*istoma* 'scalp, brain'	ist·õdi	ist·õdi-
			siehhumi 'dried meat'	siehh·õdi	siehh·õdi-
			gikuni 'cartilage'	gik·õdi	gik·õdi-

Note that *kinaubmi* goes through lenition *and* apocope despite being an adjective.

Words in -vV and -gV have the marked form -ḍḍi, but when combined with the elative, form -ḍga, and with the abessive, form -ḍma. Note that words in -gV may also have a marked form in -hdi.

I-declension			unmarked	marked	locative
-vV **-gV**	-ḍḍi	marked	locative	tsģiauga 'cedar wood'	tsģiau·ḍḍi	tsģiau·ḍḍi- tsģiau·ḍ- tsģiau·v-
		-ḍḍi- -ḍ- -v-	giga 'goose'	gi·ḍḍi	gi·ḍḍi- gi·ḍ-
			kinagi 'foreigner'	kina·ḍḍi	kina·ḍḍi- kina·ḍ-

Words in -sV have the marked form -sti.

I-declension			unmarked	marked	locative
-sV	-sti	marked	locative	sisi 'thunder'	sis·ti	sis·ti-
		-sti-	imisi 'animal'	imis·ti	imis·ti-
			kyhhisi 'mink'	kyhhis·ti	kyhhis·ti-

Words in -rV, -hV -kV and sometimes in **-gV** have the marked form **-hdi**.

I-declension			unmarked	marked	locative
-rV **-hV** **-kV** **-gV**	marked	locative	*mieri* 'moss'	*mie·hdi*	*mie·hdi-*
	-hdi	-hdi-	*sira* 'fish'	*si·hdi* (irr. -i-)	*si·hdi-*
			siseri 'south'	*sise·hdi*	*sise·hdi-*
			syhhi 'bent tree'	*syh·di*	*syh·di-*
			bieluha 'fat'	*bielu·hdi*	*bielu·hdi-*
			miuki 'bog'	*miu·hdi*	*miu·hdi-*
			niujaka 'sand dune'	*niuja·hdi*	*niuja·hdi-*
			iruoga 'coniferous wood'	*iruo·hdi*	*iruo·hdi-*

Words in -IV have the marked form -ldi.

I-declension			unmarked	marked	locative
-IV	marked	locative	*mielo* 'mildew'	*miel·di*	*miel·di-*
	-ldi	-ldi-	*milla* 'soggy spot'	*mil·di*	*mil·di-*
			pila 'red'	*pil·di* or *pil·di*	*pil·di-* or *pil·di-*
			sijula 'spruce'	*sijul·di*	*sijul·di-*

§4.2.1.1.4 O-declension

This declension includes all nouns whose stressed vowel is **o ò ō ou ōu** and **oi**. The declension has three endings, **-mo** after vowels **-a** and **-e**, or **-ko** after **-i** and **-ma** after **-u**, **-y** or **-ů**. Endings in **-o** tend to keep the vowel before the locative endings (-oita, -oika, etc.), but **-a** is deleted and **-o** can also be deleted, but less commonly in higher speech registers. Adjectives always keep the **-o**.

-a/-e

Words in **-a** or **-e** which do not go through apocope of their last vowel get the ending **-mo**.

O-declension -a/-e			unmarked	marked	locative
-a **-e**	marked	locative	*doba* 'handle'	*doa·mo*	*doa·moi-*
			dotsġa 'idea, thought'	*dotsġa·mo*	*dotsġa·moi-*
	-mo	-moi-	*kokve* 'light'	*kokve·mo*	*koḑge·moi-*
			osve 'sour'	*osve·mo*	*osve·moi-*

Words in **-ba/-be** and **-ta/-te** have the marked form **-bmo**.

O-declension -a/-e			unmarked	marked	locative
-ba **-be** **-ta** **-te**	marked	locative	*nịobba* 'beard'	*nịob·mo*	*nịob·moi-*
			hobbe 'earwax'	*hob·mo*	*hob·moi-*
	-bmo	-bmoi-	*koita* 'cocoon'	*koib·mo*	*koib·moi-*
			doịote 'dispute'	*doịob·mo*	*doịob·moi-*

Words in **-va/-ve**, **-ma/-me** and **-na/-ne** have the marked form **-mmo**.

O-declension -a/-e			unmarked	marked	locative
-va **-ve** **-ma** **-me** **-na** **-ne**	marked	locative	*hoivva* 'flooding river'	*hoi·mmo*	*hoi·mmoi-*
	-mmo	-mmoi-	*ḷoive* 'fin'	*ḷoi·mmo*	*ḷoi·mmoi-*
			ohkama 'raw'	*ohka·mmo*	*ohka·mmoi-*
			mome 'slope'	*mo· mmo*	*mo·mmoi-*
			onona 'little'	*ono·mmo*	*ono·mmoi-*
			boina 'belt'	*boi·mmo*	*boi·mmoi-*
			gonne 'rind'	*go·mmo*	*go·mmoi-*

Words in -ra/-re, -ha/-he and -ga/-ge have the marked form -hmo.

O-declension -a/-e			unmarked	marked	locative
-ra **-re** **-ha** **-he** **-ga** **-ge**	marked	locative	*somora* 'gold'	*somo·hmo*	*somo·hmoi-*
	-hmo	-hmoi-	*tokura* 'amphibian'	*toku·hmo*	*toku·hmoi-*
			ȯliha 'leafy'	*ȯli·hmo*	*ȯli·hmoi-*
			lohhe 'bob'	*lo·hmo*	*lo·hmoi-*
			toge 'eyelash'	*to·hmo*	*to·hmoi-*

Strong nouns in -ka/-ke, have the marked form -gmo, while weak nouns have -hmo.

O-declension -a/-e				unmarked	marked	locative
-ka **-ke**	s	marked	locative	goka 'sheath'	go·gmo	go·gmoi-
		-gmo	-gmoi-	oka 'forefather'	o·gmo	o·gmoi-
				õka 'tundra'	õ·gmo	õ·gmoi-
-ka **-ke**	w	-hmo	-hmoi-	somuka 'manly, courageous'	somu·hmo	somu·hmoi-

Words in -la/-le have the marked form -lmo.

O-declension -a/-e			unmarked	marked	locative
-la **-le**	marked	locative	kola 'ridge, esker'	kol·mo	kol·moi-
	-lmo	-lmoi-	oyala 'wide'	oyal·mo	oyal·moi-

-i
Words of the O-declension whose final vowel is -i- get the ending -ko if no apocope occurs. The ending -ko behaves exactly like the ending -ka of weak nouns of the A-declension.

O-declension -i			unmarked	marked	locative
-i	marked	locative	tosmi 'hay'	tosmi·ko	tosmi·koi-
	-ko	-koi-	moḍbi 'hunting territory'	mopi·ko	mopi·koi-
			sokmi 'seagull'	sokmi·ko	sokmi·koi-

Words in -mi, -ni, -ki and -gi get -kko, as well as those in -lki, -rki and -ski/-sġi, becoming -lkko, -rkko and -skko. Most nouns have -oi- before locatives, but forms in -Vkko- often have -Vkki- before locatives.

O-declension -i			unmarked	marked	locative
-mi -ni -ki -gi	marked	locative	somi 'man'	sõ·kko	sõ·kki-
	-kko	-kkoi- -kki-	moni 'path'	mõ·kko	mõ·kki-
			djoki 'trap in snow'	djo·kko	djo·kki-
			pjoki 'flint'	pjo·kko	pjo·kki-
			hogi 'pearl, ball'	ho·kko	ho·kki-
-lki	-lkko	-lkkoi- -lkki-	molki 'erosion'	mol·kko	mol·kkoi-
-rki	-rkko	-rkkoi- -rkki-	kjorki 'blue jet'	kjor·kko	kjor·kkoi-
-ski -sġi	-skko	-skkoi- -skki-	moski 'wild copper, ore'	mos·kko	mos·kkoi-
			mosġi 'mammal'	mos·kko	mos·kkoi-

The other most common endings that undergo apocope are -li, -ri, -ṡi/-hhji and -hi.

O-declension -i			unmarked	marked	locative
-li	marked	locative	holi 'stem, core'	hol·ko	hol·koi-
	-lko-	-lkoi-	voli 'arthritis'	vol·ko	vol·koi-
-ri **-hi**	-hko-	-hkoi-	gjori 'doubt'	gjo·hko	gjo·hkoi-
			mori 'a little'	mo·hko	mo·hkoi-
			tsoihhi 'sleigh'	tsoih·ko	tsoih·koi-
-ṡi **-hhji**	-ṡko-	-ṡkoi-	loiṡi 'leech'	loiṡ·ko	loiṡ·koi-
			ȯhhji 'evening'	ȯṡ·ko	ȯṡ·koi-

-o/-u/-y/-ů

Words in -o, -u, -y or -ů which do not go through apocope of their last vowel get the ending -ma, which is reduced to -mi- before locative endings, and sometimes -n- (especially before the illative and elative). The ending -ma behaves exactly as the -ma of words in -a/-e/-i, with the exception of endings in -kV generally always marked as -hma in both strong and weak nouns.

O-declension -o/-u/-y/-ů			unmarked	marked	locative
-o **-u** **-y** **-ů**	marked	locative	hogjů 'nonsense'	hojů·ma	hojů·mi- hojů·n-
	-ma	-mi- -n-	jobu 'sheaf'	jou·ma	jou·mi- jou·n-
			osmu 'smell of fire'	osmu·ma	osmu·mi- osmu·n-
			monnu 'damage'	monu·ma	monu·mi- monu·n-

Words in -bV/-pV and -tV/-dV have the marked form -bma.

O-declension -o/-u/-y/-ů			unmarked	marked	locative
-bV **-pV** **-tV** **-dV**	marked	locative	opo 'individual'	o·bma	o·bmi-
	-bma	-bmi-	hoto 'peel, layer'	ho·bma	ho·bmi-

Words in -vV, -mV and -nV have the marked form -mma.

O-declension -o/-u/-y/-ů			unmarked	marked	locative
-vV **-mV** **-nV**	marked	locative	obeno 'smoke'	oi·mma	oi·mmi-
			ono 'lichen'	o·mma	o·mmi-
	-mma	-mmi-	nobemo 'fire'	noi·mma	noi·mmi-
			tȯmo 'people'	tȯ·mma	tȯ·mmi-

Words in -rV, -hV, -gV and -kV have the marked form -hma.

O-declension -o/-u/-y/-ů			unmarked	marked	locative
-rV **-hV** **-gV** **-kV**	marked	locative	tokorů 'fox (white)'	toko·hma	toko·hmi-
			roihho 'droplet'	roih·ma	roih·mi-
	-hma	-hmi-	koro 'headwear'	ko·hma	ko·hmi-
			notśoko 'hollow, cavity'	notśo·hma	notśo·hmi-

Words in -lV have the marked form -lma.

O-declension -a/-e			unmarked	marked	locative
-lV	marked	locative	*kolo* 'cloud'	*kol·ma*	*kol·mi-*
	-lma	-lmi-			

§4.2.1.1.5 U-declension

This declension includes all nouns whose stressed vowel is **u ù uo** and **ui**. This declension is identical to the O-declension, with the exception of the O-declension ending **-ko** for words ending in **-i**, which is lacking in U-declensions. Instead, one finds **-ma**. The declension has two endings, **-mo** after vowels **-a** and **-e** and **-i**, or **-ma** after **-o**, **-u**, **-y** or **-ù**. Note that many dialects only have **-mo** for this group.

U-declension -a/-e/-i			unmarked	marked	locative
-a **-e** **-i**	marked	locative	*butta* 'bad weather'	*butta·mo*	*butta·moi-*
			kuilva 'drizzle'	*kuilva·mo*	*kuilva·moi-*
	-mo	-moi-	*lùlkki* 'hot water, hot pool'	*lùlki·mo*	*lùlki·moi-*
			njukli 'finger, hook'	*njugli·mo*	*njugli·moi-*
			uitse 'aquatic'	*uitse·mo*	*uitse·moi-*

Words in -bV/-pV and -tV/-dV have the marked form -bmo.

U-declension -a/-e/-i			unmarked	marked	locative
-bV -pV -tV -dV	marked	locative	*huopi* 'spy, scout'	*huo·bmo*	*huo·bmoi-*
	-bmo	-bmoi-	*nubba* 'eyelid'	*nu·bmo*	*nu·bmoi-*
			ututa 'still'	*utu·bmo*	*utu·bmoi-*

Words in -vV, -mV and -nV have the marked form -mmo.

U-declension -a/-e/-i			unmarked	marked	locative
-vV -mV -nV	marked	locative	*huvvi* 'comfortably cold'	*hu·mmo*	*hu·mmoi-*
	-mmo	-mmoi-	*jùtsuma* 'fear, paralysis'	*jùtsu·mmo*	*jùtsu·mmoi-*
			puna 'deer skin'	*pu·mmo*	*pu·mmoi-*

Words in -rV, -hV, -gV and -kV have the marked form -hmo.

U-declension -a/-e/-i			unmarked	marked	locative
-rV -hV -gV -kV	marked	locative	*kumora* 'white spruce'	*kumo·hmo*	*kumo·hmoi-*
	-hmo	-hmoi-	*njuhhi* 'old woman'	*njuh·mo*	*njuh·moi-*
			huoka 'drunk'	*huo·hmo*	*huo·hmoi-*

Words in -IV have the marked form -lmo.

U-declension -a/-e/-i			unmarked	marked	locative
-IV	marked	locative	tuvala 'heavy'	tuval·mo	tuval·moi-
	-lmo	-lmo-			

-o/-u/-y/-ů

Words in -o, -u, -y or -ů which do not go through apocope of their last vowel get the ending -ma, which is reduced to -mi- before locative endings, and sometimes -n- (especially before the illative and elative). The ending -ma behaves exactly as the -ma of words in -a/-e/-i.

U-declension -o/-u/-y/-ů			unmarked	marked	locative
-o **-u** **-y** **-ů**	marked	locative	u̇dno angelica	u̇no·ma	u̇no·mi- u̇no·n-
	-ma	-mi- -n-	ulju 'serious'	ulju·ma	ulju·mi- ulju·n-
			ůd̦vů 'whetstone'	ůd̦vů·ma	ůd̦vů·mi- ůd̦vů·n-

Words in -bV/-pV and -tV/-dV have the marked form -bma.

U-declension -o/-u/-y/-ů			unmarked	marked	locative
-bV **-pV** **-tV** **-dV**	marked	locative	ġupo 'vine'	ġub·ma	ġub·mi-
	-bma	-bmi-	hjutu 'necklace'	hju·bma	hju·bmi-

Words in -vV, -mV and -nV have the marked form -mma.

U-declension -o/-u/-y/-ů			unmarked	marked	locative
-vV -mV -nV	marked	locative	tuono 'the same'	tuo·mma	tuo·mmi-
	-mma -mmo	-mmi- -mmoi-	nunna 'angry'	nu·mmo	nu·mmoi-
			umu 'fog'	u·mmo	u·mmoi-

Words in -rV, -hV, -gV and -kV have the marked form -hma.

U-declension -o/-u/-y/-ů			unmarked	marked	locative
-rV -hV -gV -kV	marked	locative	juoku 'caribou enclosure'	juo·hma	juo·hmi-
	-hma	-hmi-	sùro 'berry bush'	sù·hma	sù·hmi-
			uboko 'pipe'	uo·hma	uo·hmi-

Words in -lV have the marked form -lma.

U-declension -o/-u/-y/-ů			unmarked	marked	locative
-lV	marked	locative	puilo 'nerve'	puil·ma	puil·mi-
	-lma	-lmi-			

§4.2.1.1.6 Y-declension

This declension includes all nouns whose stressed vowel is y ỳ ů èu ey ůa and ůi. The declension has three endings; -mo for words ending in -a, -di or -id for words ending in -i or -e, and -ma for words ending in -o, -u, -y or -ů, and is thus identical to the O-declensions, with the exception of -ko for words ending in -i. Generally, the final vowels -y and -ů are less often deleted. Many dialects do not have the endings -di or -id and use instead -ma.

-a
Words in -a which do not go through apocope of their last vowel get the ending -mo.

Y-declension -a			unmarked	marked	locative
-a	marked	locative	nůdna 'wave'	nůna·mo	nůna·moi-
	-mo	-moi-	nydna 'adult, mature (female)'	nydna·mo	nydna·moi-
			půbma 'point'	půma·mo	půma·moi-

Words in -va, -ma and -na have the marked form -mmo.

Y-declension -a			unmarked	marked	locative
-va -ma -na	marked	locative	ůrůma 'place near'	ůrů·mmo	ůrů·mmoi-
	-mmo	-mmoi-	sygjana 'summer camp'	syja·mmo	syja·mmoi-
			sůrůna 'rough'	sůrů·mmo	sůrů·mmoi-
			kymina 'nice'	kymi·mmo	kymi·mmoi-

Words in -ra, -ha, -ga and -ka have the marked form -hmo.

Y-declension -a			unmarked	marked	locative
-ra -ha -ga -ka	marked	locative	sẏgjaka 'branches of river'	sẏjah·mo	sẏjah·moi-
	-hmo	-hmo-	sůra 'part'	sů·hmo	sů·hmoi-
			dyra 'turn (river)'	dy·hmo	dy·hmoi-

Words in -la have the marked form -lmo.

Y-declension -a			unmarked	marked	locative
-la	marked	locative	tylla 'little brother'	tyl·mo	tyl·moi-
	-lmo	-lmoi-			

-i

Words of the Y-declension whose final vowel is -i- get the ending -id or -di, i.e. they behave exactly like nouns of the I-declension. This is not found in all dialects. Some have -i words following the same pattern as words in -a. Refer to the I-declension for a more extensive description.

Y-declension -i			unmarked	marked	locative
-V -C	-di	-di- -h- -i-	kyni 'nest'	kyn·di	kyn·di-
			lůri 'scum'	lů·hdi	lů·hdi-
			pymi 'hard bark'	pyn·di	pyn·di
			tsġůli 'skull'	tsġůl·di	tsġůl·di-
-i	-id	-idi-/-i- -ih- -i-	nieugi 'ground mist'	niůb·id	niůb·idi- niůb·ih- niůb·i-
			tygi 'poison'	tůi·d	tůi·di- tůi·h- tů·i-

-o/-u/-y/-ů

Words in -o, -u, -y or -ů which do not go through apocope of their last vowel get the ending **-ma**, which is reduced to **-mi-** before locative endings, and sometimes **-n-** (especially before the illative and elative). The ending **-ma** behaves exactly as that of the O-declension. Refer to it for a more extensive description.

Y-declension -o/-u/-y/-ů			unmarked	marked	locative
-o -u -y -ů	-ma	-mi- -n-	kydly 'bell'	kyly·ma	kyly·mi- kyly·n-
			mynty 'animal track'	mynty·ma	mynty·mi- mynty·n-
			nůjů 'knife'	nůjů·ma	nůjů·mi- nůjů·n-

Words in -vV, -mV and -nV have the marked form -mma.

Y-declension -o/-u/-y/-ů			unmarked	marked	locative
-vV -mV -nV	marked	locative	ůtůna 'rough'	ůtů·mma	ůtů·mmi-
	-mma-	-mmi-	ymina 'lost'	ymi·mma	ymi·mmi-
			ymy 'terrible'	y·mma	y·mmi-
			tȯmo 'people'	tȯ·mma	tȯ·mmi-

Words in -rV, -hV, -gV and -kV (weak nouns) have the marked form -hma. Unlike the O-declension, however, strong nouns in -kV do not go through apocope, cf. **gyky** 'still weather' → **gykyma**.

Y-declension -o/-u/-y/-ů			unmarked	marked	locative
-rV -hV -gV	marked	locative	myry 'fly'	my·hma	my·hmi-
	-hma	-hmi-	tygyha 'poisonous'	tygyh·ma	tygyh·mi-

Words in -lV have the marked form -lma.

Y-declension -a/-e			unmarked	marked	locative
-lV	marked	locative	jůlů 'sweat'	jůl·ma	jůl·mi-
	-lma	-lmi-			

§4.2.1.2 Marked Consonant-Final Form

For consonant-final nouns, the declension groups are much fewer and simpler. The marked form is shown by altering the final consonant. Nouns of the S-declension show considerable variation, often metathesis and apocope simultaneously.

§4.2.1.2.1 S-declension

This declension includes all nouns whose final consonant is -s. The marked for changes the -s to -hi or in stressed syllables, -hhi (which are shortened to -h- before the illative, elative and abessive, becoming -hta, -hka and -hma respectively). Many diminutives end in -s. Note that nouns in -ćVs have the marked form -lhi. Certain dialects have endings in -kVs become -hki in the marked form. Some dialects have a marked form in -i, which is common in poetic language.

	UNMARKED	-s
	MARKED	-hi -i -hØi

bidjis	'puppy, small dog'	→	*bijihi*
bunus	'small squash'	→	*bunuhi* or *bunhi* or *bõhhi*
gikis	'shard'	→	*gikihi* or *gihki*
hylys	'little or thin person'	→	*hylhi* or *hẏlhi*
ikos	'small axe'	→	*ikohi* or *ihki*
kiras	'morning'	→	*kirahi* or *kirhi*
kobas	'freckle'	→	*koahhi*
lagjas	'ingredient, flour'	→	*lajahi*
misas	'stone'	→	*misahi*
			(also irregular as *misġi*)
mȯs	'a little bit'	→	*mȯhhi*
nokos	'stick'	→	*nokohi* or *nohki*
rovus	'shore of lake'	→	*rẏhhi*
tohhus	'young'	→	*tohhuhi*
ůs	'young fish'	→	*ůhhu*
ųeśis	'any young animal'	→	*ųeśihi*
niedas	'fir'	→	*nielhi*
puodus	'navel'	→	*puolhi*

§4.2.1.2.2 N-declension

This declension includes all nouns whose final consonant is -n. The marked form changes the -n to either -s or -nta. Words whose stressed vowel is a o or u (most commonly o) have -nta, whereas words whose stressed vowel is e i y or ů have -s. Marked forms in -onta do changed to -õr- before the locative cases. Words ending in -n often depict a pejorative or larger version of another word.

UNMARKED		-n
MARKED	a o u	-nta (-onta → -õri-LOC)
	e i y ů	-s

a o u

hokon	'large boulder, ball'	→	hokonta
	(cf. hokõribma 'onto the large boulder')		
jokon	'large caribou herd'	→	jokonta
	(cf. jokõrika 'out of the large herd')		
kotson	'shock, scare, fright'	→	kotsonta
	(cf. kotsõria 'in shock')		
okon	'big old man'	→	okonta
	(cf. okõrima 'on the big old man')		
oskon	'male moose'	→	oskonta
	(cf. oskõriska 'off the male moose')		
toron	'big bear'	→	toronta
	(cf. torõrita 'into the big bear' i.e. 'into a trap/danger')		

e i y ů

bilin	'liver'	→	bilis
din	'barren field'	→	dis
ehhon	'nuance, difference'	→	ehhos
gegin	'mouth (vulgar)'	→	geis
helon	'pregnant mammal'	→	helos
ilun	'young'	→	ilus
leren	'pile'	→	leres
pirin	'nugget'	→	pisis
sinin	'big fish'	→	sinis
sinnen	'lake'	→	sines

§4.2.1.2.3 T-declension

This declension includes all nouns whose final consonant is -t. The marked for changes the -t to either -tsta (also found as -ddja or less commonly -tsitta) or -tta. Words whose stressed vowel is a o or u have -tta, whereas words whose stressed vowel is e i y or ů have -tsta.

UNMARKED		-t
MARKED	a o u	-tta
	e i y ů	-tsta -ddja

A subgroup of this declension, which is only found in the eastern dialects, have the form -Vut in the agentive, and take the form -Ida in the patientive. Not many words are part of this subgroup.

a o u   -t   -tta

    agjeut   'heart, center, marrow'   →   ajelda

                                                                                       (also ajeutta)

	aihhot	'thorny plant'	→	*aihhotta*
	baut	'butter'	→	*balda*
				(also *bautta*)
	hamit	'metal'	→	*hamitta*
	koat	'born during the summer'	→	*koatta*
	kolot	'womb, placenta'	→	*kolotta*
	lungit	'steam'	→	*lungitta*
	oṡot	'amount of fish'	→	*oṡotta*
	õut	'newly fallen snow'	→	*õutta*
	sasat	'protective spirit'	→	*sasatta*

e i y ů   **-tsta/-ddja**

djet	'a gray haired man'	→	*djetsta* or *djeddja*
elet	'open grassland'	→	*eletsta* or *eleddja*
ėt	'swampy ground'	→	*ėtsta* or *ėddja*
hingut	'ghost'	→	*hingutsta* or *hinguddja*
igjut	'humor, personality, mood'	→	*ijutsta* or *ijuddja*
kėut	'violence, war'	→	*kůlda* (also *kėutsta*)
miout	'warmth, energy'	→	*miolda* (also *mioutta*)
mykyt	'path following a river'	→	*mykytsta* or *mykyddja*
nitkyat	'team-story telling singing'	→	*nitkyatsta* or *nitkyaddja*
sirit	'the fishstock of a lake'	→	*siritsta* or *siriddja*
ůdůt	'power or energy left'	→	*ėutta*

§4.2.1.2.4 L-declension

This declension has up to four possible forms: one in a long vowel, one in -Vu/-Vů, one in -Vl and with -il, the form -ir is also found:

-ȧ	or	-au	or	-al
-ė	or	-eu	or	-el
-i̇	or	-iu/-iů	or	-il/-ir
-ȯ	or	-ou	or	-ol
-u̇	or	-ul		
-ẏ	or	-yl		
-ėu	or	-ėul/-ůl		

The marked form changes the long vowel to a short one followed by -la or -ri. Words whose stressed vowel is **a o** or **u** have -ri, whereas words whose stressed vowel is **e i y** or **ů** have -la. Many abstract nouns formed from adjectives are part of this declension.

UNMARKED		-VV -l -r -u
MARKED	a o u	-ri
	e i y ů	-la

a o u

angi̇~angir~angil	'pit, seed'	→	angiri
amȧ~amau~amal	'snot'	→	amari
gosu̇~gosul	'calm, cerenity'	→	gosuri
hjù~hjul	'sea water'	→	hjuri
luvvu̇~luvvul	'intense heat'	→	lùri
korù~korul	'pot'	→	koruri
njù~njul	'desire, lust'	→	njuri
okù~okul	'origin, source'	→	okuri
savvù~savvul	'goal, destination'	→	sauri
uvvù~uvvul	'abundance'	→	ùri

e i y ů

bė~beu~bel	'acid'	→	bela
dė~deu~del	'roll, tube'	→	dela
ė~el	'plant'	→	ela
jė~jeu~jel	'growth, success'	→	jela
hejù~hejul	'shiver'	→	hejula
i~iu~iddji~il~ir	'pitch dark'	→	ila or i̇la
kėu~kėul	'attack, fight'	→	kůla
migji̇~migjiu~migjiů middji̇~migjil~migjir	'dew'	→	mijila
pigji̇~pigjiu~pigjiů piddji̇~pigjil~pigjir	'health'	→	pijila
ymmẏ~ymmyl	'good fishing waters'	→	ymyla

§4.2.1.2.5 Honorifics in -ts

Certain nouns can be modified by adding an honorific or poetic ending in **-ts**. This ending polarizes the last vowel of the noun. The marked form of such nouns has a polarized version of the already polarized vowel and **-bme**.

	njelli	'chief'	
→	*njelluts*	'chief'	(honorific)
→	*njellebme*	'chief GEN'	(honorific)
	himha	'she'	
→	*himhets*	'she, mam'	(honorific)
→	*himhobme*	'she GEN'	(honorific)
	rogo	'he'	
→	*rogyts*	'he, sir'	(honorific)
→	*rogoibme*	'he GEN'	(honorific)
	tsammi	'forest'	
→	*tsammuts*	'forest'	(honorific)
→	*tsamebme*	'forest GEN'	(honorific)
	nipi	'dwarf birch (betula nana)'	
→	*nipyts*	'dwarf birch'	(honorific)
→	*nipoibme*	'dwarf birch GEN.'	(honorific)

§4.2.1.3 Diphthong Coalescence Declension

A few (usually monosyllabic) words ending in -ai -ei -ie -oi -ui -ůi -au -ay -eu -ey -iu -à -ȯ -ů and -ẏ go through vowel-specific changes in the marked form, which is realized by adding the copied stressed vowel to the word. Because most of the words are monosyllabic, the first vowel of the diphthong is usually the copied vowel. The chart of diphthong and long vowel coalescence in *§3.5.1* is how these nouns decline.

Words whose last syllable begins with a consonant which goes through gradation and disappears may leave a diphthong, in which case the noun may join this declension group. This is not always the case, and only a limited number of words do so.

eu	'scab, scar'	→	*eme*
gei	'snout'	→	*geje*
goi	'edge, point'	→	*gogjo*
hie	'pile, mount'	→	*hiddji*
hȯ	'ember'	→	*hobo* (also *honomi*)
ie	'crack'	→	*iddji*
iu	'older relative'	→	*ibi*
kei	'lynx'	→	*keje*

madu	'pregnancy'	→	*mama*
nige	'mud at the bottom of a lake'	→	*niddji*
rù	'limit of territory'	→	*rumu*
ȯ	'bruise'	→	*obo* or *ȯbo*
tey	'egg'	→	*tůme* or *tůe*

§4.2.2 Inanimate Plural

Inanimate nouns are generally only marked for plural in their unmarked forms. Marked forms may be pluralized, but more commonly with nouns whose marked form ends in -s -t -n -l.

Pluralization is done in two ways. Inanimate nouns ending in -s, -t, -n or a long vowel/-l (L-declension) gain -ka in the plural. Note that in nouns of the L-declension, the final vowel is shortened and the underlying -l appears before the addition of -ka. This plural is called the consonant-final plural. Note that monosyllabic words in diphthongs also belong to this group. Here are examples of pluralized consonant-final nouns:

gikis	'shard'	→	*gikiska*
misas	'stone'	→	*misaska*
nokos	'stick'	→	*nokoska*
sinin	'big fish'	→	*sininka*
hingut	'ghost'	→	*hingutka*
ėt	'swampy ground'	→	*ėtka*
angi/angil	'seed'	→	*angilka*
ė	'plant'	→	*elka*
kėu	'attack'	→	*kůlka*
eu	'scar'	→	*euka*
kei	'lynx'	→	*keika*

The second plural marker is used for all nouns ending in short vowels. Dialects differ greatly in how the plural is marked onto vowel-final words. The -n plural of western dialects is more common amongst younger generations and is spreading in the east as well. Below is a table illustrating this:

final vowel	plural form	
	Eastern dialects	Western dialects
-a	-ua	-uma / -ō
-e	-ie	-ime / -en
-i		
-o	-uo	-umo / -ō
-u		
-ů	-ůa	-ůmů / -ůn
-y		

Certain eastern dialects also have a plural in -ṡ (after -e and -i) and -ġ (pronounced [x]). This usually implies an uncertain, undefined or vague amount, and it may be considered to be impolite to use this plural in certain contexts:

    siraġ   ['sirax]   'a bunch of fish'
    kepsiṡ ['cʰɛpsːɪɕ] 'a couple of mushrooms'

It is not generally used when talking about things owned by people. Western dialects lack this distinction. Another feature of eastern plurals is that the stops **p t k** and endings in -ua and -uo join to form -ba -da -ga (from -ua) and -bo -do -go (from -uo), though not after diphthongs or long vowels.

Here are examples of vowel-final noun pluralization:

singular	eastern	western
eleba 'flower'	*elebua* / *elebaġ*	*elebuma* or *elebõ*
gauta 'color'	*gautua* / *gautaġ*	*gautuma* or *gautõ*
gjori 'doubt'	*gjorie* / *gjoriṡ*	*gjorime* or *gjoren*
hemi 'bird'	*hemie* / *hemiṡ*	*hemime* or *hemen*
jasuma 'tanned skin'	*jasumua* / *jasumaġ*	*jasumuma* or *jasumõ*
kahi 'shell'	*kahie* / *kahiṡ*	*kahime* or *kahen*
kepsi 'mushroom'	*kepsie* / *kepsiṡ*	*kepsime* or *kepsen*

	singular	eastern	western
	natabi 'hemlock'	*natabie / natabiś*	*natabime* or *nataben*
	oari 'edge, point'	*oarie / oariś*	*oarime* or *oaren*
	rukso 'circle'	*ruksuo / ruksoġ*	*ruksumo* or *ruksõ*
	sasame 'tipi'	*sasamie / sasameś*	*sasamime* or *sasamen*
	seky 'cliff'	*sekuo* or *sekůa* or *sego / sekyś*	*sekůmů* or *sekůn*
	sůddů 'infection'	*sůddůa / sůddůś*	*sůddůmů* or *sůddůn*
	tapa 'bulb'	*tapua* or *taba / tapaġ*	*tapuma* or *tapõ*

Pluralization of inanimate nouns in Siwa is optional and not especially common, as well as being quite emphatic. Nouns are not pluralized after numbers or quantifiers, but if they are, it is usually equivalent to an article in English.

neġvi mahhii	'three fallen bears'
tama eleba	'many flowers'
tama elebua	'the many flowers'
eura suvo	'few berries'

§4.2.2.1 Collective Plural

The collective plural is a historical plural marker that is still found in certain expressions. More commonly, the collective plural appears as an unproductive derivative ending creating words for packs or groups of things. Its form was originally -(V)rV, where -V- marks the same vowel as the preceding one. As a productive marker, it can be found on the marked form of nouns as well as after locative cases.

eu	'scab, scar'	→	*emre* or *ůre*	'rash, skin disease'
hemi	'bird'	→	*hamri/hapri*	'flock of birds'
giga	'goose'	→	*girha*	'flock of geese'
kepsi	'mushroom'	→	*kůsġi*	'place where many mushrooms grow together, agglomeration'
kuilla	'drizzle'	→	*gilra*	'wet weather'
neno	'pollen'	→	*netro*	'pistil or stamen'
seky	'cliff'	→	*seġu*	'barren land'
ůs	'young fish'	→	*ůrhu*	'bank of fish'

This has been especially productive in creating words describing species of plants, trees, insects and animals based on a common characteristic:

benho	'dog'	→	*bìrho*		'canidae'
eulbi	'hoof'	→	*ůbġi*		'ungulate'
kahi	'shell'	→	*tatskairi*		'scarab beetles'
ḳioḍma	'auk bird'	→	*ḳioro*		'sea bird'
mahhji	'bear'	→	*mosġi*		'mammals'
salama	'antler'	→	*solra*		'cervidae'
suvo	'berry'	→	*sůro*		'berry bush'

The collective plural marker -(V)rV is used in a few expressions to mean 'the many':

rìdni	'thorn'	→	*idi rìditara*	'be out of luck (lit. to fall in the (many) thorns)'
dyra	'turn (in river)'	→	*riebmala dyrara*	'be experienced (lit. to have navigated (the many) turns in rivers)'

§4.2.2.2 Plural Nouns

Certain nouns in Siwa are always pluralized. Because the plural of nouns is often marked by changing the final vowel, plural nouns may be misleading, as their final vowel is not representative of the group or subgroup to which they belong. Only a handful of words are always plural. They include:

henetka	'birch shoes'	(*henet)	→	*henetsta*
kutkuska	'flooring/bough'	(*kutkus)	→	*kutkuhi*
mokkuo~mokvo	'beak'	(*mokko)	→	*mokkoma*
pẏka	'canvas, material'	(*pẏ)	→	*pyby*
tetśõka	'gut'	(*tetśun)	→	
tetśunne				
tokkilka	'fish trap'	(*tokki)	→	*tokkiri*
tonkua	'sinew'	(*tonka)	→	*tonkamo*
tẏska	'joint'	(*tẏs)	→	*tẏhhi*
varrua/varva	'ladle'	(*varro)	→	*varoka*
dirva	'gills'	(*dirra)	→	*dirdi*
bytsva	'slime mold'	(*bytsa)	→	*bytsamo*

§4.2.3 Animate Marked Form

Nouns belonging to the animate group always have a final syllable in the shape -CV, which changes in the marked form as the table below illustrates. Most of animate nouns can also be declined as inanimate nouns (ambiguous). Certain endings may have a more or less specific function, e.g. -**ha**/-**ho** nouns generally depict feminine things, while -**mo**/-**ma**/-**ro** generally depict masculine things.

Note that the plural marker -gi changes the preceding -i- into -ę in western dialects:

  somi   'man'   →   *somigi~somęgi*   'men'.

-mo/-ma

This ending is particularly common with nouns depicting masculine agents, especially nouns of the form t-Ø-mo. It is also the form of nominalized present participles, i.e. present participles in -mo/-ma which are declined as animate nouns. Nouns with a stressed o or u get the marked form -śi.

unmarked		marked	
singular	plural	singular	plural
-mo	-mogi	-ka or -śi (if stressed o u)	-kagi or -śigi
-ma	-magi		
tȧhma 'heart'	tȧhmagi	tȧhka	tȧhkagi
takeulmo 'righteous man, real man'	takeulmogi	takeulka	takeulkagi
tiselmo 'experienced person'	tiselmogi	tiselka	tiselkagi
totomma 'family member'	totommagi	totośśi	totośśigi
tottamo 'trader'	tottamogi	tottaśi	tottaśigi

-mi

This ending is not strongly associated with any specific function. Nouns of the form -Vmi have the plural form -Vmhi or -Vmśi.

	unmarked		marked	
	singular	plural	singular	plural
	-mi	-migi -mśi / -mhi	-ta -tta	-tagi -ttagi
	totami 'head'	*totamśi*	*todatta* (irr. -d-)	*todattagi*
	ůhtakemi 'balsam fir'	*ůhtakemśi*	*ůhtaketa*	*ůhtaketai*
	kinapośmi 'guest, foreigner'	*kinapośmigi*	*kinaposta*	*kinapostagi*
	milmi 'lip'	*milmigi*	*miltta*	*milttagi*

-ba/-pa/-va

These endings are commonly found in words denoting pairs, though a number of these words, especially jointed body parts, are excluded from this due to their irregular declension. The ending -ba is quite common in flowers and flower bearing plants:

netuba	'lily'
monoba	'indian pipe'
kinuba/kinulba	'thistle'
tiba	'salsify'
velba	'dandelion'

	unmarked		marked	
	singular	plural	singular	plural
	-ba -pa -va	-bagi -pagi -vagi	-u	-ugi
	mippa 'two feet'	Ø	*mihu*	Ø

	unmarked		marked	
	singular	plural	singular	plural
	sohpa 'skis'	Ø	*sohhu*	Ø
	eleba 'flower'	*elebagi*	*eleu*	*eleugi*
	njulva 'muskox'	*njulvagi*	*njulu*	*njulugi*

-bi/-pi/-vi

These endings are not especially common, but are found in bird names:

tsimpi	'woodpecker'
miḍbi	'grey jay'
mankobi	'red-winged black bird'
polbi	'northern cardinal'

Nouns of the form **-Vbi/-Vpi** have the plural form **-Vbṡi**.

	unmarked		marked	
	singular	plural	singular	plural
	-bi -pi -vi	-bigi / -bṡi -pigi / -bṡi -vigi	-umi	-umṡi
	riehpi 'wife'	*riehpigi*	*riekumi*	*riekumṡi*
	sieḍbi 'eagle'	*sieḍbigi*	*siehhumi*	*siehhumṡi*
	nalvi / nalbi 'husband'	*nalvigi / nalbigi*	*nalumi*	*nalumṡi*
	moksabi 'ptarmigan'	*moksabigi / moksabṡi*	*moksaumi*	*moksaumṡi*

-bo/-po/-vo

These endings are not especially common or associated with any particular type of nouns.

unmarked		marked	
singular	plural	singular	plural
-bo -po -vo	-bogi -pogi -vogi	-oųi	-ośi
sambo 'maternal grandfather'	sȧmbogi (irr. -ȧ-)	sȧmoųi	sȧmośi
kembo 'paternal grandfather'	kȧmbogi (irr. -ȧ-)	kȧmoųi	kȧmośi
kuspo 'skunk'	kuspogi	kusoųi	kusośi
subo 'fruit'	subogi	suoųi suovvi	suośi
guokvo 'frog'	guokvogi	guokoųi	guokośi

-na/-no

These endings are not especially common. They often refer to elongated objects or sharp or pointy things at one end:

motona	'(sharpened) nail (on men)/claws'
ehrena	'sharpened stick used to hunt fish'
nomono	'fang'

unmarked		marked	
singular	plural	singular	plural
-na -no	-nagi -nogi	-va / -ųa -vva	-vagi / -ųa -vvagi
hjȯmno 'midwife'	hjȯmnogi	hjȯmųa	hjȯmųagi

unmarked		marked	
singular	plural	singular	plural
kehno 'pine'	kehnogi	kehhy̨a	kehhy̨agi
atkana 'tail'	atkanagi	atkavva	atkavvagi

-ni

This ending is somewhat common and often indicates a member/part of a group or periods of time, especially seasons and many ceremonies (usually in the plural). The plural unmarked form has either **-nhi** or **-nśi** after vowels, and **-nigi** otherwise.

unmarked		marked	
singular	plural	singular	plural
-ni	-nigi / -nśi / -nhi	-ja	-jagi
jatkini 'late winter'	jatkinśi	jatkija	jatkijagi
mẏhni 'wolverine'	mẏhnigi	mẏhhja	mẏhhjagi
peilni 'eldest male of group'	peilnigi	peilja	peiljagi
∅	salśinhi 'caribou head sacrifice'	∅	salśijagi
∅	iskanhi 'vernal equinox'	∅	iskajagi

-ta/-to

These endings are common in words denoting one of a pair, especially body parts. The ending **-y̨a** is used where illegal clusters would arise with **-va**, and **-vva** is used intervocally as the coda of a stressed syllable.

	unmarked		marked
singular	plural	singular	plural
-ta -to	-tagi -togi	-va / -ya -vva	-vagi / -ya -vvagi
kita 'eye'	kitagi	kivva	kivvagi
liota 'bear/large animal mother'	liotagi	liovva	liovvagi
sàhta 'lung, breath'	Ø	sàhhya	Ø
naihto 'infectious disease'	naihtogi	naihhya	naihhyagi

-te/-ti

These endings are uncommon.

	unmarked		marked
singular	plural	singular	plural
-te -ti	-tegi -tsi	-ika	-ikagi
mjuti 'finger tip'	mjutsi	mjuika	mjuikagi
ġotroti 'bullfrog'	ġotrotsi	ġotroika	ġotroikagi

-sa/-so

These endings are common in words for relative or female relatives. In words referring to humans, the marked form is -tta, while non-humans get -hi or -ḥi.

	unmarked		marked
singular	plural	singular	plural
-sa -so	-sagi -sogi	-hi (-ḥi) -tta	-higi (-ḥigi) -ttagi
miniso 'common snipe'	minisogi	minihi	minihigi
suosa 'mother'	suosagi	suotta svotta	suottagi svottagi
dapsa 'younger sister'	dapsagi	daḍḍa	daḍḍagi
karsa 'younger brother'	karsagi	kartta	karttagi

-si

This ending is not common and is nearly exclusively found in words denoting a masculine agent.

	unmarked		marked
singular	plural	singular	plural
-si	-sigi -sġi	-tta	-ttagi
okkomosi 'fellow, poor fellow'	okkomosġi	okkomotta	okkomottagi
pèsi 'maternal uncle'	pèsġi	pètta	pèttagi
tamosi 'friend, man'	tamosġi	tamotta	tamottagi

-ṡi

This ending is not common. It is found with certain agent words, birds, fish and smaller animals. The marked form is **-ohta** after consonants or **-hta** after vowels.

	unmarked		marked	
	singular	plural	singular	plural
	-śi	-śigi	-hta -ohta	-htagi -ohtagi
	tůnůkśi 'attack leader, general'	tůnůkśigi	tůnůkohta (form.) tůnůhta	tůnůkohtagi tůnůhtagi
	yśi 'salmon'	yśigi	yhta	yhtagi
	hůpśi 'purple finch'	hůpśigi	hůppohta	hůppohtagi
	simśi 'human, person, Siwa'	simśigi	simohta	simohtagi

-ro/-ra/-la

These endings are somewhat common and are not associated with any particular function. Most berries in -ra can be treated as animate nouns, but are more commonly inanimate.

	unmarked		marked	
	singular	plural	singular	plural
	-ro -ra -la	-rogi -ragi -lagi	-sta	-stagi
	sira 'fish'	siragi	sista (irr. -i-)	sistagi
	Siura 'Siwa'	Siuragi	Siusta	Siustagi
	tosġora 'reject, outlaw'	tosġoragi	tosġosta	tosġostagi
	Ø	tserogi 'sweat lodge ceremony'	Ø	tsestagi

-ri/-li

These endings are somewhat common in plural nouns denoting ceremonies and plural agents or groups. The unmarked plural form is -rhi or -lhi after vowels and -rigi or -ligi after consonants.

unmarked		marked	
singular	plural	singular	plural
-ri -li	-rigi / -rhi -ligi / -lhi	-tśa	-tśagi
Ø	aumulhi 'first menstruation ceremony'	Ø	aumutśagi
Ø	nůirhi 'adults, parents'	Ø	nůitśagi
Ø	taulhi 'army'	Ø	tautśagi
tauri 'soldier'	Ø	tautśa	Ø
tśodli 'last summer'	tśodligi 'past'	tśoddja tśyddja	tśoddjagi tśyddjagi

-lu

This ending is not especially common, but is found in a few words denoting male agents and a few words descriptive of bad or strong smelling things and remedies. The unmarked plural form is in -lhi after vowels and -lugi otherwise.

unmarked		marked	
singular	plural	singular	plural
-lu	-lugi -lhi	-da	-dagi

unmarked		marked	
singular	plural	singular	plural
koklu 'place where boat is lowered'	*koklugi*	*kohda*	*kohdagi*
holu 'spirit, ghost, soul'	*holhi*	*hoda*	*hodagi*
lillu 'paternal uncle'	*lillugi*	*lilda*	*lildagi*
ohlu 'death, decomposition, smell of death'	Ø	*ohda*	Ø
aumlu 'smell of blood'	Ø	*aumda*	*aumdagi*

-ka/-ko

These endings are commonly found in words denoting animals and in proper names. Many long or forked objects, or animals with tails, end in **-ka** or **-ko**.

unmarked		marked	
singular	plural	singular	plural
-ka -ko	-kagi -kogi	-uni	-unhi
aurko 'lake trout'	*aurkogi*	*auruni*	*aurunhi*
ḳuhko 'beaver'	*ḳuhkogi*	*ḳuhhuni*	*ḳuhhunhi*
ṇjaikka 'racoon'	*ṇjaikkagi*	*ṇjaikuni*	*ṇjaikunhi*
Siskko 'thunder deity'	Ø	*Siskuni*	Ø

unmarked		marked	
singular	plural	singular	plural
Nilkka 'personal name'	∅	Nilkuni	∅

unmarked		marked	
singular	plural	singular	plural
-ka -ko	-kagi -kogi	-uni	-unhi
aurko 'lake trout'	aurkogi	auruni	aurunhi
kjuhko 'beaver'	kjuhkogi	kjuhhuni	kjuhhunhi
njaikka 'racoon'	njaikkagi	njaikuni	njaikunhi
Siskko 'thunder deity'	∅	Siskuni	∅
Nilkka 'personal name'	∅	Nilkuni	∅

-ki

This ending is not especially common and is associated with animals or things containing a hardened or protective material:

keidgi   'helmet'   (cf. *keppi* 'head')
nykki   'nail'   (cf. *njukli* 'finger')
paikki   'turtle'   (cf. *pagi* 'backside')

The unmarked plural form is -kṡi after vowels and -kigi otherwise.

unmarked		marked	
singular	plural	singular	plural
-ki	-kigi / -kṡi	-tṡa	-tṡagi

	unmarked		marked	
	singular	plural	singular	plural
	kuki 'mouth'	*kukśi*	*kutśa*	*kutśagi*
	milki 'fish skin'	*milkigi*	*miltśa*	*miltśagi*
	õki 'tundra'	Ø	*õtśa*	Ø
	peilki 'trout, fish'	*peilkigi*	*peiltśa*	*peiltśagi*

-ga/-go/-gi

These endings are not common with nouns but common in names. Generally, humans have marked forms in -tsa (note that *kinagi* has *kinaubi*). A number of male names end in -go/-ġo or -ho and are part of this declension:

Samho (GEN *Samtsa*)
Talgo (GEN *Taltsa*)
Menho (GEN *Mentsa*)
Sotsġo (GEN *Sotsa*)
Vogo/Uohho (GEN *Votsa/Uohtsa*).

	unmarked		marked	
	singular	plural	singular	plural
	-ga -go -gi	-gagi -gogi -gigi	-ubi -tsa	-ubigi / -ubśi -tsagi
	giga 'goose'	*gigagi*	*giubi*	*giubigi* *giubśi*
	kinagi 'foreigner'	*kinagigi*	*kinaubi*	*kinaubigi* *kunaubśi*
	koalgi 'paternal aunt'	*koalgigi*	*koaltsa*	*koaltsagi*

unmarked		marked	
singular	plural	singular	plural
rogo 'man, character, he'	rogogi	rotsa	rotsagi

Notice that the honorific *rogyts* has the plural form *rogytsġi*.

-ha/-ho

These endings are common and generally refer to feminine ideas or agents. One can often assume the feminine form (usually pregnant or adult) of an animal to end in -ha:

yṡi	'salmon'
ohha	'female salmon'
salama	'caribou'
solha	'female caribou having had a calf before'
belha	'female/pregnant lobster/crab/spider'

unmarked		marked	
singular	plural	singular	plural
-ha -ho	-hagi -hogi	-ra	-ragi
himha 'woman, character, she'	himhagi	himra	himragi
kenho 'virgin'	kenhogi	kenra	kenragi
dailha 'pregnant woman'	dailhagi	dailra	dailragi
eirha 'female animal'	eirhagi	eirra	eirragi

-hi/-i

These endings are not common. A few words for trees and plants or otherwise other slow growing things end in -hi or -i. A number of female names ending in -i or -y/-ẏ join this declension:

Irhi (GEN *Ihtśa*)
Sẏ (GEN *Sytśa*)
Syly (GEN *Syltśa*)
Temhi (GEN *Temtśa*)
Vengy (GEN *Ventśa*)

unmarked		marked	
singular	plural	singular	plural
-hi -i/-y	-higi -igi	-tśa	-tśagi
maihhi 'maple tree'	*maihhigi*	*maitśa*	*maitśagi*
minhi 'black spruce'	*minhigi*	*mintśa*	*mintśagi*
oi 'moon light'	∅	*otśa*	∅
rì 'tooth'	*rìgi*	*ritśa*	*ritśagi*
tėrhi 'sun'	∅	*tėhtśa* (irr. -htś-)	∅
Muihti 'god'	∅	*Muihtśa*	∅

§4.2.3.1 Overview
Below is a reference table for the declension of animate nouns:

unmarked		marked	
singular	plural	singular	plural
-mo	-mogi	-ka or -śi (if stressed o u)	-kagi or -śigi
-ma	-magi		
-mi	-migi -mśi / -mhi	-ta -tta	-tagi -ttagi
-ba -pa -va	-bagi -pagi -vagi	-u	-ugi
-bi -pi -vi	-bigi / -bśi -pigi / -bśi -vigi	-umi	-umśi
-bo -po -vo	-bogi -pogi -vogi	-oųi	-ośi
-na -no	-nagi -nogi	-va / -ųa -vva	-vagi / -ųa -vvagi
-ni	-nigi / -nśi / -nhi	-ja	-jagi
-ta -to	-tagi -togi	-va / -ųa -vva	-vagi / -ųa -vvagi
-te -ti	-tegi -tsi	-ika	-ikagi
-sa -so	-sagi -sogi	-hi (-ḥi) -tta	-higi (-ḥigi) -ttagi
-si	-sigi -sġi	-tta	-ttagi
-śi	-śigi	-hta -ohta	-htagi -ohtagi
-ro -ra -la	-rogi -ragi -lagi	-sta	-stagi

unmarked		marked	
singular	plural	singular	plural
-ri -li	-rigi / -rhi -ligi / -lhi	-tśa	-tśagi
-lu	-lugi -lhi	-da	-dagi
-ka -ko	-kagi -kogi	-uni	-unhi
-ki	-kigi / -kśi	-tśa	-tśagi
-ga -go -gi	-gagi -gogi -gigi	-ubi -tsa	-ubigi / -ubśi -tsagi
-ha -ho	-hagi -hogi	-ra	-ragi
-hi -i/-y	-higi -igi/-ygi	-tśa	-tśagi

§4.2.3.2 Dual Nouns

A handful of nouns referring to pairs (body parts) have special declensions. They do not have a distinct plural form. Dual nouns are generally found with singular pronouns. The most common of these nouns are:

unmarked		marked	
dual	non-dual	dual	non-dual
ataḍga 'father and son'	∅	*atagga*	∅
ataḍba 'father and daughter'	∅	*atabba*	∅
bahpa 'testicles'	*bahhjo* 'testicle'	*baġa*	
iṡpa 'grandparents'	∅	*iṡva*	∅

unmarked		marked	
dual	non-dual	dual	non-dual
ilkima 'temples'	Ø	*ilkia*	Ø
kelba 'shoulders'	*ketku* 'shoulder'	*kedma*	*ketkume*
kiḏba '(both) eyes'	*kita* 'eye'	*keubba*	*kivva*
koḏga 'twin brothers'	Ø	*kȯgga*	Ø
koḏba 'brother and sister'	Ø	*kȯbba*	Ø
ků̇impa 'pair of boots/ shoes'	*ků̇itton* 'shoe/boot'	*kygju̇a/ky̆bba*	*ků̇ittos*
leḏba 'mittens'	*lahton* 'mitten'	*ledma*	*lahtos*
oaḏbi 'gums'	*oadi* 'palate, tongue'	*vaubbi/vaubba*	*vaika*
omna 'married couple'	Ø	*ȯbba*	Ø
rjaḏba 'hips'	*rjanna* 'hip'	*rjaubba*	*rjanka*
sȧhpa 'lungs'	*sȧhta* 'lung'	*sȧmġa*	*sȧhhu̧a*
saḏba '(both) ears'	*sata* 'ear'	*saubba*	*savva*
suoḏga 'mother and son'	Ø	*suogga/svogga*	Ø

	unmarked		marked	
	dual	non-dual	dual	non-dual
	suoḏba 'mother and daughter'	Ø	*suobba/svobba*	Ø
	tiebba 'hands'	*tiemo* 'hand'	*tiehba*	*tieka*
	toaḏba 'twin sisters'	Ø	*daubba*	Ø
	umpa '(both) knees'	*uba* 'knee'	*u̇ppa*	*oama*

§4.2.3.3 Action Nominals

Action nominals are a small set of nouns that are found with a patientive pronoun coalesced with an animate ending. These are mostly words for older relatives and a few nouns seen to be common to the whole of the Siwa people or a specific group of people or of personal importance. The patientive pronouns are:

1P. SG	·ka	1P. PL.INCL	·ba	1P. PL.EXCL	·be
2P. SG	·sa	2P. PL	·ha		
3P. SG	·ta	3P. PL	·ja	3P. OBV.	·no
4P.	·i/·ja				

The most common action nominals are:

unmarked		marked	
action nominal	animate	action nominal	animate
ata·ka 'my father'	*atri* 'father'	*atka·ka*	*addja*
sȯ·ka 'my mother'	*suosa* 'mother'	*sȯma·ka*	*suotta/svotta*

	unmarked		marked	
	action nominal	animate	action nominal	animate
	tobi·ka 'my older sister'	toabi 'older sister'	toumi·ka	daumi
	koso·ka 'my older brother'	kośi 'older brother'	kotta·ka	gasta
	kȧma·ka 'my paternal grandfather'	kembo 'paternal grandfather'	kȧmġa·ka	kȧmoui
	sȧma·ka 'my maternal grandfather'	sambo 'maternal grandfather'	sȧmġa·ka	sȧmoui
	nieya·ka 'my patnernal grandmother'	niebini 'paternal grandmother'	nieyaś·ka	niegja
	piddja·ka 'my maternal grandmother'	piddani 'maternal grandmother'	piddjaś·ka	piddja
	kjal·ba 'our land, Siwa land'	∅	kjalka·ba	∅
	pjap·pa 'our shaman'	∅	pjar·pa	∅
	saśi·ba 'Siwa language, our language'	∅	saśka·ba	∅
	tȯm·ba 'our people, Siwa people'	∅	tȯmma·ba	∅

Less common nouns include:

ik·ka	(GEN. *ikih·ka*)	'my axe'
nůi·ka	(GEN *nůjům·ka*)	'my knife',
sel·ka	(GEN *seus·ka*)	'my herd'
lu̯i·ka/lu̯h·ka	(GEN *lu̯juk·ka/lu̯juh·ka*)	'my love, my darling'.

§4.3 Irregular Nouns

A number of nouns fall outside of any pattern of declension. The most common irregular nouns are given here. Note that dual nouns and kinship terms are omitted.

unmarked	marked	animacy
bahhi 'day' (WEST)	*baski*	INA
kili 'wood, tree'	*kidli*	INA
ko 'summer'	*koba*	INA/ANI
lisġi 'nostril(s)'	*lihhi̯et*	ANI
misas 'stone'	*misġi / miski*	INA
oadi 'palate, tongue'	*vaika*	INA
nàrri (WEST) 'nose'	*ne̯re̯t*	ANI
nj̯arri (EAST) 'nose'	*nj̯aret*	ANI
tyry 'son, boy'	*tolba*	ANI
retema 'fox'	*revva*	ANI
y̯alo/valo 'tea'	*vàlka*	INA

§4.4 Approbation

Siwa nouns, adjectives and even verbs may be marked with one of two markers; the approbative (emphasizing the positive aspect of the word) and the pejorative (emphasizing the negative aspect of the word). Their use is quite common and may be difficult to illustrate fully, as both the markers cover a wide range of functions.

§4.4.1 Marking

The approbative and pejorative are marked through prefixes. The clitics are either hyphenated to the beginning of words or added directly. Approbation involves reduplication of either the whole of the first syllable of a word, or only its vowel. Reduplication takes the initial syllable of a word, copies it (the voiced consonants p- t- and k- are reduplicated as -bb- -dd- and -gg-). The reduplicated vowel is determined by the stressed vowel:

stressed	reduplicated
a	-a-
o u õ	-u- or -o-
e ẹ i	-e-
y ů	-y-

All initial consonants become geminate or change in the reduplicated form and no hyphen is used. The initial vowel clusters tsġ- and ts- are replaced by -tsk- and -tst-. Others are unaffected. Words beginning with a vowel have the reduplicated vowel separated from the initial vowel by -ḥ- (always hyphened).

The approbative is shown by the clitic aḣ- before vowels. For words starting with a consonant, both the approbative and the pejorative use reduplication – the approbative reduplicates the whole syllable (including the consonant), whereas the pejorative reduplicates only the vowel. Stress remains on the original initial syllable. The reduplicated vowel of the pejorative may not be pronounced in speech, leaving an initial geminate or otherwise changed consonant or consonant cluster. [1]

initial vowel	reduplicated form		examples
	approb.	pejo.	
a		aḥ-	ata 'open mouth'→ aḥ-ata 'jaw of an animal, dirty mouth' (PEJ)

---

[1] The ejective pronounciation is common with approbation markings, especially when used as a vocative with names, e.g. **Taddalgo!** [tʰɑt':algɔ] 'Talgo!'.

initial vowel	reduplicated form		examples
	approb.	pejo.	
o u õ	ȧḥ-	uḥ-	ȯ 'bruise'→ uḥ-ȯ 'a bad bruise' (PEJ)
e ę i		eḥ-	ėt 'swampy ground'→ eh-ėt 'dangerous/hunted swamp' (PEJ)
y ů		yḥ-	yhhy 'salmon'→ ȧḥ-yhhy 'good salmon, Oh Salmon' (APPR)

initial consonant	reduplicated form		examples
	approb.	pejo.	
p- / b-	pVbb-	Vbb-	benho 'dog'→ ebbenho 'bad dog' (PEJ)
			benho 'dog'→ pebbenho 'good dog' (APPR)
m-	mVmm-	Vmm-	mykyt 'path following a river'→ ymmykyt 'dangerous path following a river' (PEJ)
v- / ų- / oa-	vVvv-	Vvv-	oari 'edge'→ vavvari 'good/sharp edge' (APPR)
n- / nį-	nVnn-	Vnn-	neno 'pollen'→ enneno 'bad pollen, damned pollen' (PEJ)
ts- / tsġ-	tVtst- tVtsk-	Vtst- Vtsk-	tsamma 'forest'→ tatstamma '(our) forest, Oh Forest, the good old forest' (APPR)
t- / d-	tVdd-	Vdd-	tiemo 'hand'→ eddiemo 'bad hand, injured hand' (PEJ)
			tiemo 'hand'→ teddiemo 'good hand' (APPR)

initial vowel	reduplicated form		examples
	approb.	pejo.	
s- / sġ- / ṡ-	sVss-	Vss-	sȧhpa 'lungs'→ assȧhpa 'bad lungs, old lungs' (PEJ)
tṡ- / dj̣-	tṡVddj̣-	Vddj̣-	dj̣et 'a grayhaired man'→ tṡeddj̣et 'old man (respectful)' (APPR)
r-	rVrr-	Vrr-	roko 'hollow'→ urroko 'empty-head' (PEJ)
l-	lVll-	Vll-	luvvù 'intense heat'→ ulluvvù 'damned intense heat' (PEJ)
k- / g-	kVgg-	Vgg-	kjoro 'sea bird'→ koggjoro 'good (catch) sea bird, good old sea bird' (APPR)
j̣-	j̣Vgj̣-	Vgj̣-	jokon 'large caribou herd'→ jogjokon 'good herd, herd (polite)'
h- / ġ-	hVhh-	Vhh-	hingut 'ghost'→ ehhingut 'bad ghost' (PEJ)
			hingut 'ghost'→ hehhingut 'good ghost' (APPR)

§4.4.2 Approbative

The approbative emphasizes the positive aspect of a noun. It may be used to give praise, as a vocative, to underline the protagonistic role of the noun in a narrative or to give an impression of familiarity. It can also be polite to use the approbative when addressing other people's belonging or when the speaker wants to emphasize his inferior/humble position. It is also often used when words are described with a positive epitaph or are called a positive nickname. The Siwa word for bandleader is nj̣elli, but when addressing one's bandleader, one would use the form nennj̣elli. When talking about one's own herd, one may say jokon, but when addressing someone else's, it may be polite to refer to it as jogjokon. Ambiguous nouns are most commonly animate in the approbative.

pendodnani-dat kiggigagi
[ˈpʰɛndɔʔtnɑnidaʔ cʰiˈɟːigaji]
pen<nd>-o-dna-ni–dat ki–giga-Ø-gi
return.PAST-INFER.ITR.CONCL-REVERS-TRANSLO–SENS APPR–goose-AGT-PL
'the good old geese have returned, I see'

inta-ḥa gigjese àḥ-ikid
[ˈiːntaʔa ˈɟijːese æːʔˈicɪdʑ]
in=ta–ḥa giges-e àḥ–iki-d ha
still–ASS sharp-COP.INFER APPR-axe-PAT
'(your/the) good old axe is still sharp, I see'

saskuo nja toddoronta
[ˈsaskuɔ ˈnja tʰɔˈtːorɔnta]
sask-uo nja to-<dd>oron-ta
wake.up-INFER.OPT.ITR now APPR-big.bear-PAT
'wake up, now, Oh Big Bear'

jestui meġi rurrogo!
[ˈjɛstui ˈmexi ruˈrːɔgɔ]
jest-u-i meġi ru-<rr>ogo-Ø
succeed-PAST-ASS.CONCL.ITR fortunately APPR-he-AGT
'he fortunately succeeded!'

iġue ilkiumi rirrikimi
[ˈixue ˈiːlciumi riˈrːicimi]
iġ-ue ilk-i-u-Ø-mi ri-<rr>ikimi-Ø
accept-INFER.OPT.TR offer-PAST-PASS.PART-DAT-1P.AG.SG APPR-host-AGT
'may the kind host accept my offer'

Sassamho irrukita
[sɑˈsːamhɔ ˈiːruˈcita]
sa-<ss>amho-Ø irru=kita-Ø
APPR-Samho-AGT arrow=eye-AGT
'Arrow-Eye **Samho**'

taju nona yhmita memmiebṡiṡi inoni suvokurita nente
[ˈtʰɑju ˈnɔna ˈœhmida meˈmːɪɛbɕiɕi iˈnɔni ˈsuvˈɔkurida ˈnɛnte]
ta=ju n-on-a yhhy-m=ita mem–miebṡi=ṡi-Ø i-non-i suv=oku-ri=ta non-nin nent-e
then PAST.AUGM-tell-ASS.CONCL.TR salmon-ILLAT APPR-fat.neck=old-AGT DIT-swim-ITR stream=origin-ILLAT COP.IMP-INFER
'then the old fat bear told the salmon to swim to its home stream'

The last example illustrates one other use of the approbative – to show the theme or topic of a narration. In the example, the old fat bear (*miebṡiṡi*) is obviously the theme or topic of the story, meaning one can assume that it has been mentioned before. It is put in the approbative here because it is a nickname and because it shows that the bear is the protagonist of the phrase/story.

A few words were historically in the approbative but became reanalyzed as otherwise. For example, the word *kiddu* 'done' had the form *kiggiddu* as an answer to a superior when promising to do something. This was shortened to *iggidd* or *gidd* (pronounced [ˈcːʰitː], or as if it was written *gkidd), meaning 'yes' or 'affirmative', especially when answering to a demand or a request.

§4.4.3 Pejorative

The pejorative emphasizes the negative aspect of a noun. It may be used to show anger, as a negative vocative, to underline the antagonistic role of the noun in a narrative or to show that the noun is bad, worthless, hurt, dangerous or has another negative connotation. It can also be impolite to use the pejorative when addressing other people's belonging or when in an superior position. It may also be used to show modesty about one's own belonging or actions. It is also often used when words are described with a negative epitaph or are called a negative nickname. The Siwa word for a dog is **benho**, but when addressing a disobedient dog, one would use the form **ebbenho**. Below are more examples of the use of the pejorative:

oa-ḥa agigjomadna eḥ-ikid
[ˈɔaʔa aˈɟijːɔmaʔtna eʔˈicɪdʐ ha]
oa–ḥa a-gigj-o-ma-dna eḥ–iki-d ha
already-ASS TRANSL-be.sharp-INFER.TRANSL-INCONCL-REVERS PEJ-axe-PAT
'my damned axe is already becoming dull, I see'

ennikodemõ
[eˈnːikɔˈdemõ]
e-<nn>iko=dem-õ-Ø
PEJ-dead=bone-PL-AGT
'deadbones! (*insult*[1])'

---

[1] Siwa burn their dead, and by insinuating that someone's bones are left after death is a powerful insult to their honor.

kyha osikka maggita tśilutta gaita annjaikka
[ˈcʰyʔa ɔˈsɪʔka ˈmɑːːida ˈtɕilʊʔta ˈgɑida ɑˈɲːaɪʔka]
ky<h>-a o-sikk-a ma<gg>-ita tśil-u-tta g-a-ita an-njaikka-Ø
try.PAST-ASS.TR SUBJ-sneak-TR meat-ILLAT hang-PAT.PART-GEN
COP.PAST.CONCL-ASS-INESS PEJ-racoon-AGT
'the damned racoon tried to sneak into the drying meat'

gogantsujaka avvama
[ˈgɔgantsujɑga ɑwˈːɑma]
gogantsuj-a-ka a-<vv>a-ma
make.limp-ASS.CONCL.TR-1P.PAT.SG PEJ-knee-PAT
'my damned/bad/injured knee is making me limp'

avvakibma!
[ɑˈwːɑcɪʔbma]
av-oak=ibma
PEJ-home.ADESS
'go home! (impolite)'

The last example is also found as a shortened expression, *yaki* or *yagi*. It is used to signify to something to go away, for examples a mosquito or a dog. The word *yaki* was analyzed as translocative, and the cislocative analogy *yani* also came to be, and it means the same as *yaki*, but with movement towards the speaker. An angry mother might call her child by saying *yani*. It can also be used in a less impolite matter, for examples when asking someone to pass something over.

§4.5 Cases

Siwa nouns are found in the following cases: agentive, patientive, genitive, dative, inessive, illative, elative, adessive, allative and ablative. Of these, the inessive, illative, elative, adessive, allative and ablative are grouped together as locative cases. The patientive and genitive share their form, as do the agentive and dative cases. That is to say, the two pairs of cases differ syntactically but not morphologically – they have the same surface form, but different functions. While nouns and adjectives are identical in the agentive, patientive, genitive and dative, they are not marked for locative cases when attributive but are instead found in the genitive. Siwa thus has two cases for the subject (agentive and patientive) and two cases for the object (dative and genitive). The diagram below shows the relationship between case, word order and markedness.

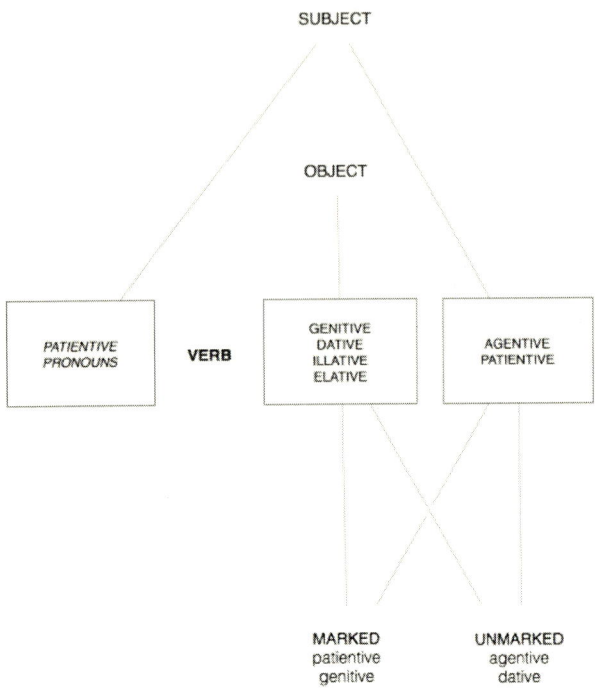

Subjects can be found as patientive pronouns affixed onto the verb, or in the marked form (patientive case) or the unmarked form (agentive case) at the end of the phrase. Objects can be found between the verb and the subject, in either the marked form (genitive case, or in the case of ditransitive verbs the illative or elative) or the marked form (dative case). There are four cases with two overt forms distinguished by word order.

In addition, Siwa makes use of double case marking. A noun may be marked primarily for one case, and secondarily for another one. Double marking endings are set and are usually added onto the genitive of a noun. Double case marking is explained in *§4.6*.

§4.5.1 Agentive Case

The agentive case is the default form of a noun. It is used to show that the noun is an agentive subject. This means that when ever a noun is performing an action willingly or with control, it is found in the agentive case (unless the verb requires a patientive subject). As it was mentioned above, the agentive case shares its form with the dative. However, it is quite easy to determine whether a noun is in the agentive or the dative case, given context – nouns in the agentive case are not found in the same slot as nouns in the dative in the Siwa phrase. In other words, word order can help identify the syntactical function of a noun int he unmarked form. Additionally, the agentive case is used with adjectival verbs and in certain other constructions where an unagentive subject would be expected, such as with existential copular verbs.

nùtta, jàlppi!
['nuː?ta 'jælpːi]
nù=tta jàlppi-Ø
see=SUBIT hare-AGT
'look, a hare!'

etsta nodi gaita dida
['ɛtsta 'nɔdi 'gɑida 'dida]
e<sk>-a nod-i g-a-ita dida-Ø
start.PAST-ASS.CONCL.TR sing-ITR COP.PAST-ASS-ILL.AT young.girl-AGT
'the girl started to sing'

ista tamoskita maggika kori
['iːsta 'tʰamɔscida 'macːiga 'kʰɔri]
i-i<st>-a tamos-k=ita ma<gg>-ika kori-Ø
dit-thank.past-ass.concl.tr hunter-illat meat-elat boy-AGT
'the boy thanked the hunter for the meat'

da seskora to syhhi-ůt
[da 'sɛskɔra tʰɔ 'syhːɪœ?]
d-a seskora me syhhi-Ø–ůt
COP-ASS tree.to.find.one's.way this.ANI.AG bent.tree-AGT–DET.PROXI
'this bent tree is used to find one's way' (lit. 'this bent tree is a **seskora**')

magjua kůnů
['mɑjːua 'cʰønø]
magja-a kůnů-Ø
white-COP.ASS milk-AGT
'milk is white'

da ataka ůat
[da 'ɑtɑga 'œa?]
d-a ata-Ø-ka ůat-Ø
COP-ASS father-AGT-1P.PAT.SG this.PROXI-AGT
'this is my father'

himi mitabe
['hiːmi 'miːdɑbe]
himi-i mitabe-Ø
warm-COP.PAST.ASS yesterday-AGT
'yesterday was warm'

Nouns in the agentive are often separated from the rest of the phrase by independent pronouns (§10.1), especially if the object is also a noun. This is preferred to pronouns marking the object, but it may happen especially with the dative if the subject is encoded onto the verb.[1]

	nega dida to kori	'the boy saw the girl'
	nega tsi dida	'X saw the girl' (dative **tsi**)
or	*nega dida to*	'X saw the girl' (agentive **to**)

§4.5.2 Patientive Case

The patientive case is found in the marked form. It is used to show that the noun is an unagentive subject – it is in direct opposition with the agentive case. This means that when ever a noun is performing an action unwillingly or without control, it is found in the patientive case. The same form as the patientive case is also used to mark the partitive object (i.e. only partially affected by the verb) – then, however, it is called the genitive case (see below).

etsta ojui gaita tsid
[ˈɛtstːa ˈɔjui ˈgɑida ˈtɕiːdʑ]
e<sk>-a oju-i g-a-ita tśi<Ø>i-d
start.PAST-ASS.CONCL.TR cry-ITR COP.PAST-ASS-ILLAT baby-PAT
'the baby started to cry'

tsaskka ihhja tamoskita maggika gaika kohko
[ˈtsaskːa ˈiːhːja ˈtʰamɔscida ˈmacːiga ˈgɑiga ˈkʰɔhkɔ]
tsa<sk>-a i-ihhj-a tamos-k=ita ma<gg>-ika g-a-ika kor-ko
forget.PAST-ASS.CONCL.TR DIT-thank-TR hunter-ILLAT meat-ELAT COP.PAST-ASS-ELAT boy-PAT
'the boy forgot to thank the hunter for the meat'

akjuobmu jànka unka seskosta
[ɑˈcʰʊɔʔpmu ˈjæːŋka ˈʊŋka ˈsɛskɔsta]
a-kjuo<bm>-u jàn-ka un=ka sesko-sta
TRANSL-bend.PAST-ASS.CONCL.TRANSL snow-GEN under-FROM tree.to.find.one's.way-PAT
'the **seskora** became bent under the snow'

maikjukkas desigi kůnůma
[ˈmaiɟʊʔkas ˈdeɕiji ˈcʰønøma]
maikjukk-a-s de-śi-gi kůnů-ma
whiten-ASS.CONCL.TR-HAB bone-GEN-PL milk-PAT
'milk whitens the bones' (cf. **demogi magja** 'strong bones', lit. 'white bones')

---

[1] Some western dialects have a reduced form of the pronouns *to/ta* as -t [ʔ/t] hyphened to the preceding word or the noun qualified: *nega dida t-kori*. Similarly, tsi may be -tsi hyphened to the preceding word: *nega-ts dida*.

nikli atkaka
['nɪklːi 'atkɑga]
nik-l-i at-ka-ka
die-PERF-ASS.CONCL.ITR father-PAT-1P.PAT.SG
'my father has died'

sindi mitaid
['sɪndʑi 'miːdaɪdʑ]
si<nd>-i mita<∅>e-d
last.long.PAST-ASS.CONCL.ITR yesterday-PAT
'yesterday was a long day' (lit. 'lasted for a long time')

§4.5.3 Genitive Case

The genitive case has the marked form of a noun. It serves two main functions - that of a proper genitive, and that of a partitive. Both share the same form and their distinction is purely a semantic one. In normal speech, the noun in the genitive follows what it qualifies. However, if the genitive is used with an adjective, it may precede it.

The proper genitive shows that the marked noun is the possessor of something:

rabma sõkko   'the man's (*sõkko*) canoe (*rabma*)'.

It may also show other kinds of relationships to other nouns, verbs or adjectives, such as:

composition	*irri pihra*	'an arrow made of yew'
origin	*maski obekka*	'a tribe from the north'
reference	*naipi sŭhhi*	'the banks of the river'

The genitive noun may come before an adjective if it qualifies it:

mahtsa sise	'tall as a bear'
kòma mu	'half eaten'
kehka hanna	'fair skinned' (lit. fair of skin)
mihu tàimo	'stable, strong on feet' (lit. standing of feet)
keubba mialha	'blue eyed'
tiehba ohhjo	'strong handed'

These words may also be written in one word; *mahtsasise*, *kòmomu*, *kehkahanna* and *mihutàimo*. Composition and origin usually considered to be part of the functions of the partitive genitive.

The partitive genitive, unlike the proper genitive, is one of the two cases that mark the object of a verb. A noun in the partitive genitive shows that only a part of it has been affected by the action and is generally associated with the inconclusive. However, conclusive verbs may also have their object in the partitive genitive, if for example, the object is uncountable (the phrase 'he drank milk' may be conclusive in that the agent is done drinking milk, but its object may be partitive because an unspecified amount of milk was drunk, as opposed to all of it). For a more detailed explanation on the role of the partitive genitive, see section *§5.4.1*.

proper genitive

rybmy iskid
[rœʔpmy 'iːscɪdʑ]
rybmy-Ø iski-d
dress-AGT woman-GEN
'the woman's dress'

kjutśi maskka
['cʰutɕi 'maskːa]
kjutśi-Ø maski-ka
territory-AGT tribe-GEN
'the tribe's territory'

miedju Samtsa
['miedʑu 'samtsa]
mie<dj>-u-Ø Sam-tsa
herd-PAST.PART-AGT Samho-GEN
'Samho's [m] herd'

nygjůa Natska iśid
['nyjːœa 'natskːa iɕɪdʑ]
nygjy-a-Ø Natsu-ka iśi-d
stanza-PL-AGT Natsu-GEN old-GEN
'Old Natsu's [f] stanza'

partitive genitive

ėmśi salulka
['eːmɕi 'salʊlka]
ėmśi-Ø sa<l>ul-ka
smell-AGT tar-GEN
'the smell of tar'

leren miehdi
['lerɛn 'mɪɛhdʑi]
leren-Ø mieri-di
pile-AGT moss-GEN
'a pile of moss'

kehhe unokkis iśid ojusta
['cʰehːe uˈnɔʔcɪs 'iɕɪdʑ 'ɔjʊsta]
kehhe-Ø u-nokk-i-s i<ś>i-d oju-sta
kehhe-DAT PASS-call-ASS.CONCL.ITR-HAB bark-PAT white.birch-GEN
'the bark of the white birch is called **kehhe**'

kůkiani magga poagga
['kʰøciani 'makːa 'pʰɔakːa]
kůk-i-a-ni mavv-ka poavv-ka
bring-PAST-ASS.CONCL.TR-3P.AG.PL meat-GEN seal-GEN
'they brought seal meat'

kokke diadi dahpika salla metġutta
['kʰɔʔce 'diadʑi 'dahpiga 'salːa 'mɛtːxʊʔta]
kokk-e-Ø di<Ø>a-di dahpi-ka salla me<tġ>-u-tta
like-INFER.CONCL.TR-3P.PAT young.girl-PAT clan-GEN well respect-PAST.PART-GEN
'X apparently likes a girl of a well respected clan'

A third function of the genitive is restricted to only certain words. It is called the temporal genitive, and incorporates the -i- of locative cases. It is used with words commonly found in time expressions, and indicates the time 'at which' or 'for which' an action was/is.

enet baski	'one day...' (cf. *huḍḍe baska* 'the light of day' WEST)
enehmõ kendai	'one day...' (cf. *huḍḍe kenda* 'the light of day' EAST)
ymjai	'early in the fall' (cf. *ymni* 'early fall', GEN. *ymja*)
gujai	'late in the fall' (cf. *guni* 'late fall', GEN. *guja*)
enohtai	'early in the winter'
	(cf. *enśi* 'early winter', GEN. *enohta*)
hejetśai	'in winter' (cf. *hejeri* 'winter', GEN. *hejetśa*)
jatkijai	'late in the winter' (cf. *jatkini* 'late winter', GEN. *jatkija*)
tȩtśai	'in spring' (cf. *tȩli* 'spring', GEN. *tȩtśa*)
àljai	'early in spring' (cf. *àlni* 'early spring', GEN. *àlja*)
tòhhjai	'late in spring' (cf. *tòhni* 'late spring', GEN. *tòhhja*)
kobai	'in the summer' (cf. *ko* 'summer', GEN. *koba*)

§4.5.4 Dative Case

The dative case shares its form with the agentive, the unmarked form. Typically, dative objects correspond to objects found with the determinants *the* in English.

Nouns in the dative case are often preceded by **otsi/ats** (ani/ina), **eksi** (pl.) or **ōtsi**, although most speakers simply use the reduced form **tsi**, though the marking is preferably found on the subject (**to/ta/ki/ōrō**) if both participants are nouns. The dative is found in objects which have some of the three following characteristics:

1. The noun is completely affected by the action

    sahrami (tsi) nokos
    [ˈsahrɑmi (tsi) ˈnɔkɔs]
    sa‹hr›-a-mi (tsi) nokos-Ø
    burn.PAST-ASS.CONCL.TR-1P.AG.SG (3PRON.INA.DAT) stick-DAT
    'I burnt the (whole) stick'

    ma meihhi to kōḍga
    [ma ˈmeihːi (tʰɔ) ˈkʰɔ̄ðga]
    m-a meihhi-Ø (to) kōḍga-Ø
    eat.PAST-ASS.CONCL.TR honeycomb-DAT (3PRON.ANI.AGT) bear.cub-AGT
    'the bear cub ate the (whole) honeycomb'

    kieḍgia lagjas oggori
    [ˈcʰɪɛðɟia ˈlɑjas ɔˈkːɔri]
    kieḍg-i-a lagjas-Ø o-‹gg›ori-Ø
    steal-PAST-ASS.CONCL.TR flour-DAT PEJ-boy-AGT
    'the damned boy stole (all) the flour'

    milkōtumana sira
    [ˈmɪlkɔ̄dumɑna ˈsira]
    milkōt-um-a-na sira-Ø
    scale-OBLI-ASS.CONCL.TR-2P.AG.SG fish-DAT
    'you must scale the (whole) fish'

2. The noun is the object of a conclusive verb, i.e. the action is completed or done to completion. It may be possible to translate some of the examples above differently – one could change *all* or *whole* for *completely*. Conclusive verbs with dative objects may also carry a notion of having completed the action correctly or successfully.

    milkōtumana sira
    [ˈmɪlkɔ̄dumɑna ˈsira]
    milkōt-um-a-na sira-Ø
    scale-OBLI-ASS.CONCL.TR-2P.AG.SG fish-DAT
    'you must scale the fish (completely)'

sahrami nokos
['sahrɑmi 'nɔkɔs]
sa<hr>-a-mi nokos-Ø
burn.PAST-ASS.CONCL.TR-1P.AG.SG stick-DAT
'I burnt the stick completely'

sauddia kuilis tsegma
['sɑutːia 'kʰuilts 'tɕɛŋmːa]
saudd-i-a kuilis-Ø tsegma-Ø
catch.with.hands-PAST-ASS.CONCL.TR tadpole-DAT child-AGT
'the child (successfully) caught the tadpole'

gikkia kilge tamosi
['ɲiːʔcia 'cʰɪlʝe 'tʰamɔsi]
gikk-i-a kilge-Ø tamosi-Ø
sharpen-PAST-ASS.CONCL.TR blade-DAT hunter-AGT

'the hunter sharpened the blade (completely)'

3. The noun goes through a change of state. This includes most causative and translative verbs.

sopria pŭdŭ esita
['sɔpxia 'pʰødø 'eɕida]
sopr-i-a-Ø pødø-Ø esi=ta
split-PAST-ASS.CONCL..TR-3P.AG.SG log-DAT two.INA-ILLAT
'X split the log in two'

aiga nokos mioldita
[ɑ'iga 'nɔkɔs 'mɪoldʑida]
a-i-g-a-Ø nokos-Ø miol-di=ta
PAST.AUGM-throw-PAST-ASS.CONCL.TR-3P.AG.SG stick-DAT flame-ILLAT
'X threw a stick into the flames'

sodda kori kiḑgami
['sɔtːa 'kʰɔri 'cʰɪðgami]
so<dd>-a-Ø kiḑg-a-mi
give.PAST-ASS.CONCL.TR-3P.AG.SG boy-DAT pick.up-TR-INFI.AG.TR
'the boy made X pick it up'[1]

---

[1] Although the sentence may also be understood to mean 'X made the boy pick it up', one will most commonly hear the object preceded by *(o)tsi* such an ambiguous phrase:

sodda kori kiḑgami   *sodda tsi kori kiḑgami*
'the boy made X pick it up'   'X made the boy pick it up'

§4.5.4.1 Dative vs. Genitive
When a noun can be both in the genitive or the dative, its most salient feature will be represented by its case. If a conclusive verb has a partitive object, it will generally correspond to 'X is/was/will be doing Y to (some) Z' while a dative object will generally correspond to 'X is/was/will be doing Y to (the/the whole/all the).

> *ma mavvu*
> [ma 'maw:u]
> m-a mavvu-Ø
> eat.PAST-ASS.CONCL.TR-3P.AG.SG meat-DAT
> 'X ate (the/the whole/all the) meat'
>
> *ma magga*
> [ma 'mak:a]
> m-a mavv-ka
> eat.PAST-ASS.CONCL.TR-3P.AG.SG meat-GEN
> 'X ate (some) meat'

The difference between a dative and genitive object affects the general meaning of the phrase greatly (see *§9.11* on tense-aspect coalescence)

§4.5.5 Locative Cases
The locative cases are formed by adding regular endings to the marked form. In certain cases, some changes occur, but generally the locative case endings are added directly to the marked form of a noun or with the vowel -i-.

The locative cases can be separated in two classes - the inessive, illative and elative show location in or at something, and the adessive, allative and ablative show location on or at something. The in-locative cases are commonly used with less concrete spaces or ideas:

> *tsamsia*   'in a forest'
> *nindia*   'in a hut'
> *sùhmia*   'in a berrybush'

As a general rule, more concrete surfaces are used with the on-locative cases, as well as wide open spaces:

> *eitsġima*   'on a wall'
> *misahima*   'on a rock'
> *ùkima*   'on the water'
> *sùpimima*   'at a winter camp'
> *atsiokima*   'in a glade'.

In addition, the illative is used with nouns to show the recipient of a ditransitive verb, i.e. to mark the indirect object;

> *ista diahta eleba kori*
> [ˈɪsta ˈdɪahta ˈeleba ˈkʰori]
> i-s<Ø>t-a di<Ø>a-ri=ta eleba-Ø kori-Ø
> DIT-give.PAST-ASS.CONCL.TR little.girl-ILLAT flower-DAT boy-AGT
> 'the little boy gave the little girl a flower'

Below is a table showing the form of the locative cases:

locative cases		
inessive	illative	elative
-ia	-ita, -ta	-ika, -ka
adessive	allative	ablative
-ima	-ibma	-iska, -ska

Certain dialects also include an instrumental (meaning 'with') with the ending -**igla** or -**gla** (sometimes also -**ila**/-**la** or -**ira**/-**ra**) and an abessive (meaning 'without') in -**usi**. One may find certain words with the ending -**imi**/-**emi**/-**ebi**/-**iu**/-**eu**/-**ů**. This is a fairly new case that has yet to spread to all dialects, but which represents the essive (showing a state in or as something).

§4.5.5.1 Inessive, Illative and Elative

The three interior cases, inessive, illative and elative, all function more or less in the same way – the inessive denotes a static position in or inside, illative shows movement to or into and elative shows movement from or out of.

> -ia   'in'
> -ita   'into'
> -ika   'out of'

The interior cases shows location in or at something. It generally refers to interiors and spaces which are not considered surfaces:

> *dindia*   'in/on the mountain(s)'
> *tsamṡita*   'into the forest'
> *ėnuja*   'in the bay, in the water'

koruria	'in a pot'
mantakia	'in the world'
õkkia	'in the snow'
sůhhika	'from the river'.

The interior cases also refer to states. Many words (nouns and adjectives) are found in the inessive as postpositions or adjectival/adverbial phrases:

angakia	(lit. in remains) 'to be dead, to have passed away (eastern dialects), to have a rash, to be sick, to have a disease (western dialects)'
bilisia	(lit. in liver) 'at the right place, in luck, at stake' (hence **bilitse** 'lucky')
djikma	(lit. in show) 'on display, obvious, visible'
elepsia	'in bloom, blooming'
gaskia	(lit. in moon) 'during the night time, secretly, in secret' (hence **goskka** 'X will betray Y')
hjůdja	'pregnant'
kolia	'strained, tensed, stretched, tight'
kůia	'afloat, floating, going, in a good state'
letkuika	(lit. from the paddle) 'confused, lost, astray'.
mihuja	(lit. in feet) 'winning, superior, ready, steadfast'
mihkidia	'frosty, covered in frost'
tamykkia	'happy, joyful'

The elative and the ablative are used to show possessors in possessive relative clauses (for a more detailed description of this, see *§5.10.1.2.3*).

§4.5.5.2 Adessive, Allative and Ablative

The three surface cases, adessive, allative and ablative, all function more or less in the same way – the adessive denotes a static position on a surface, allative shows movement onto a surface and ablative means movement off a surface.

-ima	'on'
-ibma	'onto'
-iska	'off, of'

The surface cases shows location on, over, in or at something. They have a more narrow meaning than the interior cases, and usually refer more precisely to surfaces or open spaces:

umima	'on the ground'
õkkiska	'from (off) the tundra'

atsiokima	'in the glade'
oakima	'at home'
bengommeima	'on the roof'
rỳhhima	'at the shore' (but *temmeja* 'id.')
sùpimibma	'to the winter camp'

Surface cases are also used to express possession, unalienable genitive relations – Siwa lacks a verb denoting ownership of most possessions, and those close to the owner or unalienable are usually in the surface cases, as well as with certain possessive relations where the possessee is perceived to come from or off the possessor:

sappiskua màhrakiska	'the bear's paws (lit. the paws off the bear)'
jùtsuma osiska	'your fear (lit. fear off you)'
èmsi kehkiska	'the smell of (your) skin (lit. the smell off the skin)'
hide todattaiska	'the head's hair (lit. the hair off the head).

§4.5.5.3 Locative Cases for Indirect Objects

The illative and allative paired with the elative and ablative are used with ditransitive verbs or verbs with an indirect object, recipient or benefactor. The nature of the exchange with the indirect object is coded in the case usage. These always come before the direct object:

VERB ... Ø-ita/-ika ... D.OBJ ... SUBJ

ona toatsita oadni	'X tells a story to someone'
isyvva toatsita toaḍḍi	'X shows something to someone'
isota toatsita isto	'X gives someone something'
initsa toatsita sauhhjahi	'X teaches a language to someone'
irahka toatsibma kesku	'X gives advice (on)to somsone'
iviḍḍa toatsi(s)ka riehpi	'X steals someone's wife'

Illative

ista diahta eleba kori
[ˈɪsta ˈdɪahta ˈeleba ˈkʰɔri]
i-s<Ø>t-a di<Ø>a-ri=ta eleba-Ø kori-Ø
DIT-give.PAST-ASS.CONCL.TR little.girl-ILLAT flower-DAT boy-AGT
'the little boy gave the little girl a flower'

ilkia nȧtṡaita gagama pjaha
['iːlcia 'næːtɕaida 'gagama 'pʰjaʔa]
i-ilk-i-a nȧ-tṡa=ita gagama-Ø pjaha-Ø
DIT-offer-PAST-ASS.CONCL.TR widow-ILLAT condolence-DAT healer-AGT
'the healer offered his condolences to the widow'

nitṡanin toatsita kůira
['nitɕanɪn 'tʰɔatsida 'cʰøira]
nitṡ-a-nin toa-ts=ita kůira-Ø
inform-TR-INFI.DIT someone.KNOWN.ANI-ILLAT issue-DAT
'to inform someone about the issue'

onnin toatsita
['ɔnːɪn 'tʰɔatsida]
on-nin toa-ts=ita
tell.story-INFI.DIT someone.KNOWN.ANI-ILLAT
'to tell someone a story'

Elative

neskanin toatsika oaḑgo
['nɛskanɪn 'tʰɔatsiga 'ɔaðgɔ]
nesk-a-nin toa-ts=ika oapi-ko
ask-TR-INFI.DIT someone.KNOWN.ANI-ELAT help-GEN
'to ask help *from* someone'

koaibmanon toatsika nitṡiyama
['kʰɔaɪʔpmanɔn 'tʰɔatsiga 'nitɕiwama]
koaibma-a-non toa-ts=ika nitṡiya-m-a-Ø
tire-TR-INFI.DIT.UNAG someone.KNOWN.ANI-ELAT interest-INCONCL-PRES.PART.UNAG-DAT
'to lose interest (lit. to tire *from* someone the interest)'

Usually, when the action is perceived to be benefactive to the object, or the object is a gift or intended as a service, the indirect object will be in the allative (**-ibma**/**-bma**) in the case of an exchange to/for the benefactive, or the ablative when the exchange is in the opposite direction. The ablative is especially common with possessions.

Allative

tonkanin toatsibma tulmu
['tʰɔŋkanɪn 'tʰɔatsɪʔpma 'tʰʊlmu]
tonk-a-nin toa-ts=ibma tulmu-Ø
sew-TR-INFI.DIT someone.KNOWN.ANI-ALLAT clothing-DAT
'to sew clothes *onto* someone'

onnin toatsibma
[ˈɔnːɪn ˈtʰɔatsɪʔpma]
on-nin toa-ts=ibma
tell.story-INFI.DIT someone.KNOWN.ANI-ALLAT
'to tell a story *onto* someone' (to an audience)

rahkanin toatsibma kesku
[ˈrahkɑnɪn ˈtʰɔatsɪʔpma ˈcʰɛsku]
rahk-a-nin toa-ts=ibma kesku-Ø
send-TR-INFI.DIT someone.KNOWN.ANI-ALLAT advice-DAT
'to give advice (lit. to send advice *onto* someone)'

soatskanin ohhistaibma
[ˈˈsɔatskːɑnɪn ˈɔhːɪstaɪʔpma]
soatsk-a-nin ohh-ista=ibma
pray-TR-INFI.DIT deity-ALLAT
'to pray *onto* a deity'

Ablative

kieḑganin toatsiska nůjů
[ˈcʰɪɛðgɑnɪn ˈtʰɔatsɪska ˈnøjø]
kieḑg-a-nin toa-ts=iska nůjů-Ø
steal-TR-INFI.DIT someone.KNOWN.ANI-ABLAT knife-DAT
'to steal the knife *from* someone'

geunnin toatsiska meiḑgi
[ˈɟeunːɪn ˈtʰɔatsɪska ˈmɛɪðɟi]
geun-nin toa-ts=iska meiḑgi-Ø
diminish-INFI.DIT someone.KNOWN.ANI-ABLAT respect-DAT
'to lose respect for someone (lit. to diminish the respect *from* someone)'

tśilnin toatsiska śavvi
[ˈtɕɪlnɪn ˈtʰɔatsɪska ˈɕawːi]
tśil-nin toa-ts=iska śavvi-Ø
hang-INFI.DIT someone.KNOWN.ANI-ABLAT courage-DAT
'to make someone lack the courage to (lit. to hang the courage *from* someone [to dry])'

§4.5.5.4 Abessive, Instrumental and Essive

The abessive, instrumental and essive cases are marginally used by certain dialects or in a few fixed expressions. The most commonly used of these is the instrumental, which is fairly common in most dialects but not in everyone's speech. The essive is an case with uneven distribution – it is most common in the west. In regular speech, the essive is replaced by the clitic -mi.

Abessive (-usi)

The abessive shows the lack of something. It generally forms adverbs, which may describe both verbs and nouns.

neinkobiusi errisa	'to work carelessly' (cf. *neinko* 'care')
ġylkymausi saśisa	'to speak monotonously' (cf. *ġylky* 'peak')
piśisusi	'not at all' (cf. *pirin* 'nugget')
nŭnamousi	'still, calm' (cf. *nŭdna* 'wave')
nongamousi	'endless(ly)' (cf. *nokna* 'end')
miteuhiusi	'unnecessarily' (cf. *miteus* 'reason')

Instrumental (-igla, -gla, -ġla, -ġil, -ġel, -ġġeli)

The instrumental shows with what something is done. It is a shortened form of the postposition *gala* with the same meaning (which is often reduced to [kla] or [xla] in pronunciation). The resulting word is generally considered an adverb. Eastern dialects often allow -ġeli to be added to endings in -ma (then -mġeli) and -d (then -tsġeli).

ikigla~ikitsġeli soprami	'to split X with an axe' (cf. *iki* 'axe')
nylymigla~nylymġeli ėhhami	'to sniff X with a snout' (cf. *nyly* 'snout')
kykkymigla~kykkymġeli habmaka saśśa	'to speak with a deep voice' (cf. *kykky habma* 'deep voice')
ioila/joira[1]	'with difficulty' (cf. *iɥo* 'difficult task')
goikoigla~goikoiġla jairsa	'to row with oars' (cf. *gobi* 'oar')

Essive (-imi/-emi and -iu/-eu/-ŭ)

The essive endings regroup two sub-cases. The forms in -imi/-emi have a comparative or semblative meaning (X is similar/like Y). The endings -iu/-eu/-ŭ rarer or not found in the western dialects. The -iu/-eu/-ŭ endings have an equative meaning (X is the same as Y):

-imi/-emi	'like, similar to, reminiscent of'
-iu/-eu/-ŭ	'the same as, in the same way as (eastern dialects only)'

---

[1] This word shows great variation: *joiġla~joġil~joġel~joġġeli*

The essive endings are added onto the marked form of the noun. Marked forms in -a/-e have the -emi or -eu forms (unless the preceding vowel is y or ů, then -ů). Marked forms in -i(d) have the -imi and -iu forms:

-a/-e	**-i/-id**
-emi	-imi
-eu	-iu
-ů	

Equative (eastern dialects only)
    mairui iskidiu   'X laughs like a woman'
    sahhi moaika mioldiu   'the drink burns like fire'
    osoakiskke tevutsiu-uri   'we build our houses the same way as our ancestors'
    nidlumina atkeusa   'you must do just like your father'

Semblative
    mairui iskidimi   'X laughs like a woman'
    saimnisa lůkkůmů   'to run like rapids'
    tåsa seskostemi   'to stand like a **seskora**'
        (i.e. to be very obvious)
    inįisa kejemi   'to sneak silently, to be unnoticed
        (lit. to sneak like a lynx)'
    rarpo ůrįůjemi/ůrįůjů   'madly furious' (lit. furious like a female wolf)

The essive case exists as a hyphened clitic (-mi) commonly used with verbs like *unoksi* 'is called (as a nickname)' and *tatska* 'considers':

    unokkika on Talgo, unoksika Toggon-mi
    'my name is **Talgo** but I called (as) **Toggon**'

§4.6 Double Case Marking

Siwa allows for double case marking on nouns, pronouns, adjectives and in certain cases adverbs. The secondary case markers are not unique to double case marking as they are found in many indefinite pronouns (see *§10.6*), and exist for primary cases, but the locative cases are added onto a single double case marker. Secondary case markers are added directly onto the genitive form of nouns and adjectives and to the locative form of pronouns. The table below illustrates the endings.

	locative cases
case	ending
	-ni
agentive	*da onta totonta to mů̱jů̱mi saumka-ůt, atsa katta haidni* [daõnta 'tʰɔtonta tʰɔ 'møjømi 'saʊmkæœʔ 'atsa 'kʰaʔta 'haɪʔtni] d-a onta toton-ta to mů̱jů̱mi-Ø saum-ka–ůt ad=sa ba hait-ni COP-ASS ONTA family-GEN this.ANI.AG herder-AGT caribou-GEN–DET.PROXI COP.ASS=NEG but this.MEDI-SECOND.AGT 'This caribou's owner is in my family, but this one's isn't'
	-y̨a/-va-/-vva
patientive	*kōtśi on tyry kottaka, set ka toumikay̨a* ['kʰōtɕiõ 'tʰyry 'kʰɔʔtaga sɛʔka 'tʰoumigawa] kon-ś-i on tyry-Ø ko=tta-ka set ka tou=mi=ka-y̨a walk-HABIL-ASS.CONCL.ITR ON son-AGT older.brother.GEN-1P.PAT.SG not KA older.sister-GEN-1P.PAT.SG-SECOND.PAT 'my older brother's son can walk but not my older sister's'
	-si, -ḍḍi
dative	*saskitśu sa, sǵoasmi ki̱ōhō bidjiska belra-ůt te poskitśu tevu sa, ki̱ōhō belrasi-t* ['sascitɕu sa 'sxɔasmi 'cʰɔ̃ʔɔ̃ 'bidʑɪska 'bɛlræœʔ de 'pʰɔscitɕu tevu sa 'cʰɔ̃ʔɔ̃ 'bɛlrɑsɪʔ] sask-i-tśu s-a, sǵo-a-s-mi ki̱ōhō bidjs-Ø-ka me ben-ra–ůt te posk-i-tśu tevu s-a ki̱ōhō ben-ra-si–t wake-ITR-LINK.TEMP COP.HAB-ASS feed-ASS.CONCL.TR-HAB-1P.AG.SG this.ANI.PL.DAT puppy-DAT-PL dog-GEN–det.PROXI and go.sleep-ITR-LINK.TEMP before COP.HAB-ASS this.ANI.PL.DAT dog-GEN-SECOND.DAT-DET.MEDI 'I feed these dogs' puppies when I wake up and those's before I go to sleep'
	-hō / -rō / -ġu (also -hon/-ron)
genitive	*da ie bengommeja soakka-go te nonia sõkkohō te* [da ie 'benːɔmːeja 'sɔaʔkagɔ de 'nɔnia 'sɔ̃ʔkɔhõde] d-a ie-Ø bengo<mm>e-ia soak-k=ia-go te non-ia somi-ko-hō te COP-ASS leaking.creack roof-INESS house-GEN-1P.POSS.SG and 3P.INA-INESS man-GEN-SECOND.GEN too 'there is a leak in the roof of my house and there is one in the man's [house's roof] as well'

	locative cases
	-tsi- *-tsia, -tsita, -tsika* *-tsima, -tsibma, -tsiska*
locative cases	*ga on tetsotsi rymymima djikami sopra, aksa ka nonitsima dela osġami* [gaõ ˈtʰetsɔtsi ˈrymymima ˈdʑikɑmi ˈsɔpxa, aksːaka ˈnɔnitsima ˈdela ˈɔsxɑmi] g-a on t=ets=o-tsi ry\<m>y-m=ima djika-m-i sopra-Ø ak-sa ka non-its=ima del-a o-sġa-mi COP.PAST-ASS ON some=of.many.INA-LOC dress-ADESS ornament-INCONCL-AGT.PART.AG.PL golden-AGT 3P.INA-SECOND.ADESS NEG-COP.PAST-ASS ka wear-TR REL-COP.PAST.HAB-tr-1P.AG.SG 'some dresses had golden ornaments, but the one I used to wear did not'
	istana tentsita? Daḍḍatsita istami [ɪˈstana ˈtʰɛntsida? ˈdaðːatsida ɪˈstami] i-s\<Ø>t-a-na ten-ts=ita? da-dda-tsi=ta i-s\<Ø>t-a-mi DIT-give.PAST-ASS.CONCL.TR-2P.AG.SG who.ILLAT little.sister-GEN-SECOND.ILLAT DIT-give.PAST-ASS.CONCL.TR-1P.AG.SG 'to whose did you give it? I gave it to (my) little sister's'

The ending -ya and -va are added to consonant clusters and after unstressed vowels, whereas -vva is added to stressed vowels. The genitive endings -hõ/-hon come following vowels, -ġu after **t b s m** and -rõ/-ron after **r** and **h**. Many dialects prefer -ġu to the other endings. Some pronouns replace -ġu by -t.

Double case marking has two functions – to form nouns that stand for a dropped noun phrase and to create words that carry a meaning of 'one who/of/like' or 'that which'.

For example, the phrase **This mushroom's flesh is poisonous, but this mushroom's [flesh] is edible** would make use of the double case marking onto the word **mushroom's**, which is both in the genitive and active (as the argument of the copula);

tygyhua on ůn mine kebsie-ůt, uhi ka ůn kebsiehõ-t sa
[ˈtʰyɟyhuãõ œn ˈmine ˈcʰɛpsiɛœ? uˈhi ka œn ˈcʰɛpsiehõ? sa]
tygyha-a on ůn mine-Ø kepsi-e–ůt ba u-h-i me ke\<bs>i-e-hon–t s-a
poisonous-COP.ASS ON this.ANI.GEN flesh-AGT mushroom-GEN–DET.PROXI PASS-eat-ITR KA this.ANI.GEN mushroom-GEN-SECOND.PAT–DET.MEDI COP.HAB-ASS
'This mushroom's flesh is poisonous, but that mushroom's [flesh] is edible'

The second function can be seen with first person plural locative stem **momṡi-** yielding **momṡini** 'one of us, one like us, ours' as in:

tsalbi unuji momṡiva
[tsalbi uˈnuji ˈmɔmɕiva]
tsalbi u-nuj-i momṡi-va
rarely PASS-see-ASS.CONCL.ITR 1P.PL-SECOND.PAT
'people like us are rarely seen'

Similarly, the fourth person locative stem *ni-* yields *nini* 'one's own';

serjeni nitsia
[serjeni ˈnitsia]
serjen-i ni-tsi=ia
feel.good-ASS.CONCL.ITR 4P-SECOND.INESS
'it feels good to be in one's own (privacy/comfort)'

Double case markers can be used with postpositions to create words like:

(*ůatta*)*maggjani*	'the one in this case, this particular'
	(cf. *ůatta maggja* 'in this case' or 'in the case of this')
roġoni	'the one in the way'
	(cf. *roġo* 'in the way')
tatsůini	'the additional one'
	(cf. *tatsůi* 'in addition')
kiḍḍjani	'the one within sight'
	(cf. *kiḍḍja* 'within sight')
tevuni	'the one before, the former'
	(cf. *tevu* 'before')
ahhani	'the one after, the latter'
	(cf. *ahha* 'after')

These words function either as nouns or as adjectives, in which case only the locative ending is used with a head noun in one of the locative cases.

sia hausġa ė maggjani
[ˈsia ˈhaʊsxa eː ˈmɑcːɑni]
si-a hausġa ė-Ø maggja-ni
COP.NEG-ASS.CONCL edible plant-AGT in.case-SECOND.AGT
'the plant in this case is not edible'

sikkui toboita roġotsi
[ˈsɪʔkui ˈtʰɔbɔida ˈrɔxɔtsi]
sikk-u-i-Ø t<obo>-ita roġo-tsi
kick-PAST-ASS.CONCL.ITR-3P.AG.SG rock-ILLAT in.the.way-SECOND.LOC
'X kicked the rock that was in the way'

mante tatsůisi koḍmi
[ˈmante ˈtʰatsøisi ˈkʰɔðmːi]
mant-e tatsůi-si koḍmi-Ø
take-INFER.CONCL.TR in.addition-DAT guest-AGT
'the guest shall take the additional one'

tsalbi angitubilua kiḍḍjani
[ˈtsalbi ˈaŋːidubilua ˈcʰið:jani]
tsalbi a<ngit>-u-ila-a kiḍḍja-ni
rarely desire.PAST-PAT.PART-SUPER-COP.ASS.CONCL within.sight-SECOND.AGT
'the most desired one is rarely the one in sight'

peljekkemi on tevusi, oskemi ka ahhasi
[ˈpʰeljɛʔcemiɔ̃ ˈtʰevusi ˈɔscemika ˈɑhːɑsi]
peljekk-e-mi on tevu-si osk-e-mi ka ahha-si
cook-INFER.CONCL.TR-1P.AG.SG on former-SECOND.DAT, smoke-INFER.CONCL.TR-1P.AG.SG ka latter-
SECOND.DAT
'I will cook the former but I will smoke the latter '

Double case endings are also found in certain words which otherwise have no primary case endings. These words those formed by adding the double case markers to pronouns and adverbs, for example *ůvvihni* 'the one (from) around here' (from *ůvvika* 'from around here') or *nini* 'one's own' (derived from the locative form of the fourth person). Similar to quantifiers of the type *ovva/havva/jovva* (such as this, such as that) can be formed with double case markers:

ůadni		'like this one, this one('s)'
	PAT.	*ůatva*
	DAT.	*ůatsi*
	GEN.	*ůadġu*
	LOC.	*ůatsi-*
eygni		'like these one', these ones(')'
	PAT.	*eyhtva*
	DAT.	*eyhtsi*
	GEN.	*eyhtõ*
	LOC.	*eyhtsi-*

sġůġju nuhlami it ůadġõ
[ˈsxøjːu ˈnuɬːami ˈiːʔi ˈœæðxɔ̃]
sġůġju nuhl-a-mi i=t ůat-rõ
never see.PERF-ASS.CONCL.TR-1P.AG.SG nothing.INA.GEN this.PROXI.2D.GEN

'I've never seen anything like this'

Compare to the quantifier *ovva*.

sġůgju nuhlami it ovva
['sxøj:u 'nuɬ:ami 'i:ʔi 'ɔw:a]
sġůgju nuhl-a-mi i=t ovva
never see.PERF-ASS.CONCL.TR-1P.AG.SG nothing.INA.GEN such.PROXI
'I've never seen such a thing'

haidna		'like that one, that one's'
	PAT.	*haitva*
	DAT.	*haitsi*
	GEN.	*haidġu*
	LOC.	*haitsi-*

kvagni		'like those one', those ones'
	PAT.	*kvahtva*
	DAT.	*kvahtsi*
	GEN.	*kvahtõ*
	LOC.	*kvahtsi-*

siduma kvahtsi
['siduma 'kʰvahtsi]
sid-um-a kvaht=si
understand-OBLI-ASS.CONCL.TR that.MED.PL-SECOND.GEN
'one must be understanding of these things'

iodna		'like that one there, that one's there'
	PAT.	*iotva*
	DAT.	*iotsi*
	GEN.	*iodġu*
	LOC.	*iotsi-*

gaugni		'like those one there', those ones(') there'
	PAT.	*gauhtva*
	DAT.	*gauhtsi*
	GEN.	*gauhtõ*
	LOC.	*gauhtsi-*

tsaupri iotva
['tsaʊpxi 'ɪotwːa]
tsaupr-i iot-va
happen.rarely-ASS.CONCL.ITR that.DIST-SECOND.PAT
'things like that happen rarely'

§4.7 Indeclinable and foreign words

A small number of words are not declined. This includes foreign words and a handful of words, of which most are adverbs that may be used as nouns. These words are not declined in so far as they lack any endings. However, many are found in the marked form with an inverted final vowel polarity. This is especially true of foreign words and names in modernized vocabulary. Such foreign words generally have an unmarked form in -(h)i (if the word ends in a consonant or diphthong) and a marked form in -(h)u. Some speakers may chose to decline foreign words as though they were normal inanimate nouns.

unmarked form
mẏtẏ
'yesterday night' (NO or ADV)

marked form
mẏtẏ~mẏtai
(*mẏtẏita* '[until] yesterday night')

atkenka
'day after tomorrow' (NO or ADV)

atkenki

aimra
'the wrong way' (NO or ADV)

aimri

Lontoni~Lonton
'London'

Lontonu~Lontonta

Leo~Leoḥi
'Leo'

Leo~Leoḥu~Leue/Leobi

§5 Adjectives

Adjectives in Siwa are similar to both verbs and nouns – some forms of adjectives can be declined similarly to a noun, or exactly like a noun, while other forms may have tense, clitical personal pronouns and other elements typically associated with verbs. Most adjectives either have predominantly a verbal form, an adjectival form (also called true attributive) or both. Adjectives differ greatly depending on whether they are attributive or predicative.

Essentially, verbal forms are predicative forms that are used for impersonal constructions or temporary and/or unagentive states for animate nouns[1] (found with the inconclusive marker -m-), while adjectival forms can be used with both animate and inanimate nouns and usually have a more general meaning and can be both attributive or predicative. In addition, the verbal form can also have a participial form to be used attributively (this is strictly speaking a complementized participle).

Compare the following forms of the adjective:

Verbal form

    root cannot stand alone

	her-	'cold'
	kęm-	'happy'

    -m- inconclusive marker

	hehmi	'it is cold'
	kęmmi	'X is happy'

    patientive topic, generally living or animate

	gjosmika	'I am tired'
	hehmi kohko	'the boy is cold'

    temporary/temporal meaning

	kęmmika	'I feel happy'
cf.	*kęmesami*	'I am (a) happy (person)'

    impersonal verbs or verbs of weather

	sihmi	'it rains'
	hùmmi	'it is windy'

    predicative only, no number agreement

	gjosmi kohko	'the boy(s) is/are tired'

    complementized if attributive (-ot·i·m-), number agreement

	kori gjosotima	'the tired boy'
	korigi gjosotimi	'the tired boys'

---

[1] Inanimate nouns are not ungrammatical when found with verbal adjectives, but semantically, verbal nouns most commonly apply to living experiencers.

Adjectival form
> non-verbal form, can stand alone
> > *heje*   'cold'
>
> can be predicative and attributive
> > *da uja heje*   'there is cold water'
> > *hejia uja*   'the water is cold'
>
> uses copula
> > *hejiata*   'it is cold'
>
> non-temporal meaning
> > *somi heje*   'a cold(-natured) man'

Verbal:	*hehmi*	'it is cold' (root *her-*, impersonal verb)
	hehmika	'I am cold' (temporary state)
Participial:	*tamosi herotima*	'a cold hunter' (i.e. a hunter who is cold)
Adjectival:	*heje*	'cold' (cf. *tamosi* **heje** 'a cold hunter', i.e. a hunter with a cold nature)

An essential notion to have in mind when looking at adjectives is whether it is predicative or attributive. A predicative adjective is usually linked to what it describes by the copula. For example, in the phrase **this foreign language is difficult**, the adjective **difficult** is predicative. The adjective **foreign**, on the other hand, is attributive, meaning that it is part of the noun phrase. This is important because of how predicative and attributive adjectives work in very different ways. The verbal form of adjectives is closely related to impersonal verbs, and in most regards, can be considered to be exactly that (with some restrictions), while adjectival forms are like nouns in that they are declinable (with some restrictions) and independent from any supplementary morphemes.

The way adjectival and verbal forms are derived from each other is not entirely regularly predictable – changes in the form of an adjective from verbal to adjectival are often irregular. All adjectives having a verbal form also have a participial form, which itself is regularly formed by complementization in attributive position only and is the only form that overtly shows number agreement.

The adjectival form is often considered the default form of adjectives. When predicative, the adjectival form is called copular, because it fuses with the copula. Thus, the various forms of adjectives are as follow:

predicative	
copular (adjectival + copula) (heje)	verbal (her-)
heįia edġe 'the air is cold'	hehmi 'it is cold'
	so hehmisa-a? 'are you feeling cold?'
attributive	
adjectival	participial (verbal + complementizer)
edġe heje 'cold air'	somi herotima~herven 'a man (who is) cold'

§5.1 Function of Verbal and Participial Forms

The verbal form has two main functions.

Firstly, it is mostly used with animate nouns whose predicative adjective denotes a temporary and/or involuntary state, and it is used in impersonal constructions, such as **it's cold** or **it's late**. Impersonal constructions use impersonal verbs (see section *§5.3.4* for a complete look at impersonal verbs), which are very similar to verbal adjectives.

Secondly, the verbal form is used to create the participial form, which is used attributively and always found with a complementizer and as present inconclusive participle. It has the form -(t)otima, -(t)otimi or corresponding short forms -(t)oima/-(t)ųima/-(t)vima or -ųen/-ųin~-ven/-vin. The participial form is the only form of an adjective which agrees in number with the head noun. However, because participial adjectives are in fact relative clauses, they do not agree in case with the head noun, e.g.:

	somi atetotima	a sick man
or	*somi atetoima*	
or	*somi ateųen*	
	somigi atetotimi	sick men
or	*somigi atetoimi*	
or	*somigi ateųin*	
	sõkkita atetotima	to a sick man

sõkkita atetotimi   to sick men

When used with a predicative adjective denoting the temporary and/or involuntary state of an animate noun (X is as/in the state of being Y), the verbal form differs from an impersonal verb in that it may in fact take person markings. The subject of these temporary adjectival verbs is usually in the patientive, both for pronouns and nouns, and it is always in the inconclusive. Thus, these adjectives are in fact very similar to actual verbs. Compare the table below showing predicative verbal adjectives and the attributive participial adjectives:

predicative		attributive
verbal with pronoun	verbal with noun	participial
gjosmika ['jɔsmiga] gjos-m-i-ka tired-INCONCL-ASS.ITR-1P.PAT.SG 'I am tired'	*gjosmi kohko* ['jɔsmi 'kʰɔhkɔ] gjos-m-i kori-ko tired-INCONCL-ASS.ITR boy-PAT 'the boy is tired'	*kori gjosotima* ['kʰɔri 'jɔsɔtɕima] kori-Ø gjos-ot-i-m-a boy-AGT tired-COMPLE-ASS.ITR-INCONCL-AGT.PART.UNAG.SG 'a tired boy'

Not all adjectives have verbal forms, although they might describe a temporary or involuntary state. And similarly, not all verbal adjectives actually have a corresponding adjectival form. In the latter case, these verbal adjectives differ from verbs in their use of the inconclusive (because regular verbs, except impersonal verbs, usually do not use the inconclusive marker -m-). Typically, adjectives that apply to humans or animate things *or* that refer to weather and topological features have both verbal and adjectival forms.

Often, verbal adjectives have both corresponding adjectival and participial forms. When both exist, the participial form usually bears an underlying affective or temporary meaning, while the adjectival form is more or less neutral with respect to duration, or may be taken to have a broader, more general meaning:

VERBAL
(temporal)

dapmi~dappima (dapp-)
'alone'

hokjami (hokja-)
'blinded'

ADJECTIVAL
(general)

dappo
'alone, lonely, lonesome'

hokju
'blind'

motommi (moton-) 'feeling sad'	*moton* 'sad, unhappy'
siubmi (siut-) 'hungry'	*siudna* 'hungry, gluttonous'
hoatsmi (hoats-) 'taken a back'	*hoadna* 'surprised'
kęmmi (kęm-) 'feeling happy'	*kęmes* 'happy'
nubmi (nup-) 'feeling angry'	*nunna* 'angry, hostile'
sůtromi (sůtro-) 'feeling frustrated'	*sůtrů* 'frustrated, annoyed, stuck'
tůhmi (tůhh-) 'feeling anxious'	*tůhna* 'anxious, stressed'
voammi (voavv-) 'afraid'	*voakna* 'fearful'

The formation of adjectives is described in *§5.5*.

§5.1.1 Translative Verbal and Adjectival Forms

Both verbal and adjectival forms can take on a translative meaning. Because not all adjectives exist in either forms, and not all who do can be used to derive a translative verb, this forms a fairly small group of adjective roots. However, adjectival forms can fairly freely become translatives if they do not have a corresponding verbal forms.

The distinction between a general state (adjectival forms like *kęmes* 'happy') and a more temporal form (verbal adjectives like *kęmmi* 'feeling happy') allows for two different derived translative forms.

The adjectival translative is formed from the the adjectival form by adding the preverbal **a-** and the translative postverbal **-u/-ů**. These forms may correspond to a slow change of state, not placed in a specific time or the adjectival form become more like what it describes. Such adjectival forms often loose final vowels, and in some cases final endings may also be deleted (-na, -la, -es, -us, -ot, e.g.: *gigies* 'sharp' becomes *a·gigj·u*):

dappo	'lonely'	*a·dapp·u*	'become isolated'
atana	'big'	*an·atan·u*	'become bigger'

Because of their translative nature however, their agent is always unagentive.

The structure of the translative verbal and adjectival forms can be illustrated as such:

		Form
General		
	adjectival form	Ø
	translative adjectival verb	a-Ø-u
Temporal		
	verbal adjective	Ø-mi
	translative verbal adjective	Ø-u

Few adjectives display all of these forms. Some common adjective roots are shown here to illustrate the differences in meaning that arise between four forms.

General		Temporal	
Adjectival form	Translative adjectival verb	Verbal adjective	Translative verbal adjective
kęmes·a·ta	*t·a·kęmes·u*	*kęm·m·i*	*ta·kęm·ů*
'X is happy'	'X becomes happy/happier' (slow change)	'X is feeling happy'	'X gets happy' (i.e. mood change)
moton·a·ta	*t·a·moton·u*	*motom·m·i*	*ta·moton·u*
'X is unhappy'	'X becomes unhappy/ unhappier' (slow change)	'X is feeling sad'	'X gets sad' (i.e. mood change)
voaknu·a·ta	*t·a·voakn·u*	*voam·m·i*	*t·voavv·u*
'X is fearful'	'X becomes fearful' (slow change)	'X is scared'	'X gets scared'
nunn·u·a·ta	*t·a·nunn·u*	*nub·m·i*	*ta·nup·u*
'X is angry'	'X becomes angry' (slow change)	'X is angry'	'X gets mad'
atan·u·a·ta	*t·a·n·atan·u*	*atah·m·i*	*t·atar·u*

'X is big'	'X becomes bigger' (slow change)	'X is pregnant'	'X gets pregnant'
piegjinu·a·ta	*t·a·piegjin·(adn·)u*	*pigj·i·ma*	*ta·pigj·u*
'X is in good health'	'X regains good health' (slow change)	'X is feeling healthy'	'X gets healthy' (sudden change)
dappu·a·ta	*t·a·dapp·u*	*dap·m·i*	*ta·dapp·u*
'X is alone'	'X becomes isolated' (slow change)	'X is lonely'	'X becomes lonely'
laipin·a·ta	*t·a·laipin·u*	*laib·m·i*	*d·laip·u*
'X is bitter'	'X becomes embittered'	'X is feeling jealous'	'X becomes jealous'
njòdn·u·a·ta	*t·a·njòdn·u*	*njoltt·i·ma*	*ta·njoltt·u*
'X is ill'	'X becomes ill' (slow change)	'X is feeling unwell'	'X becomes ill' (sudden change)
sůtr·éu·ta	*t·a·sůtr·ů*	*sůtro·m·i*	*t·sůtr·ů*
'X is frustrated'	'X grows frustrated'	'X is feeling annoyed'	'X becomes annoyed'
Defunct translatives			
		os·m·i	*t·os·u*
	∅	'X is feeling ashamed'	'X is embarrassed'
mybi·a·ta		*myb·m·i*	*ta·myb·ů*
'X is silent'	∅	'X is calm'	'X calms down'
		ay·m·i	*ęb·ů*
	∅	'X is feeling disgusted'	'X is disgusted'

§5.2 Function of Adjectival and Copular Forms

Adjectival forms are used attributively with all inanimate nouns and in some cases with animate nouns. In contrast to verbal forms, adjectival forms usually do not bear a meaning of temporary or involuntary state. They do not have a nuance of duration or state, but rather (often) simply state something more general about the thing they describe, e.g. *njòlttima* 'sick' (participial) has an underlying meaning of 'X is afflicted by disease', whereas *njòdna* (adjectival) simply means 'sick' or 'unhealthy'. However, because the primary meaning of the adjective is mostly stative, one can use *njòdna* without it having an inherent or permanent quality.

The adjectival form follows the head noun and agrees with its head noun in case but cannot take locative case markings. If the head noun is in a locative case, the adjective is found in the genitive. The adjectival form is only ever found in locative cases if the head noun is not present and the adjectival form functions as a nominal, e.g.:

	istami njòdnamoita	'I gave it to the sick one'
but	*istami kohkoita njòdnamo*	'I gave it to the sick boy'.

The adjectival form is used to create the copular form, simply by adding the copula to the adjective. The copular form is used with animate and inanimate nouns alike when the quality of the adjective is inherent, and with inanimate nouns for temporary qualities as well. Moreover, the copular form is used when the adjective is predicative, except for participial adjectives which are derived from verbal adjectives (verbal form used instead of a predicative phrase). Pronouns, complementizers and other parts of the verbal phrase are added directly to the adjective, though pronouns are commonly found standing independently. The copular form has a special negative form using the copular verb **si-** (or emphatically **hjed-**) (see defective copular verbs *§9.16.2.2*).

gjosina somi	'the man is tired'
sia gjosin somi	'the man isn't tired'
hjeda gjosin somi	'the man is in no way tired/not tired at all/**not** tired'

§5.2.1 Copular coalescence

The copula, when added to adjectives, coalesce with final vowels in specific ways. The table below illustrates these changes (adjective endings vertically, copula horizontally).

copula → adjective ↓		-a-	-o-	-u-	-e-	-i-
back	-a		-ua-		-ai-	
	-o	-ua-		-ù-		-ui-
	-u					
front	-e	-ia- / -ja-	-io- / -jo-	-iu- / -ju-	-ė-	
	-i					-i-
rounded		-y/-ů	(-ůa-)	-eu-		-ẏ-

    heje 'cold'   *hejia* 'X is cold'   *hegji* 'X was cold'
    piegjino 'healthy'   *piegjinua* 'X is healthy' *piegjinoi* 'X was healthy'
    seuvvi 'sweet'   *seuvvia* 'X is sweet'   *seuvvi* 'X was sweet'

See section §9.17.2 for a description of the dependent copula and §9.17.2.1 for a description of copula-adjective coalescence.

§5.3 Predicative Adjectives

Predicative adjectives are those which are typically found as the argument of the copula, such as 'X is big'.

    atanua tȯ   'the rock is big' (*atana* 'big')
    ononua kyśi   'the squirrel is small' (*onona* 'small')
    himia leḓba   'the mittens are warm' (*himi* 'warm')

When describing an animate noun, predicative adjectives can be found either in their adjectival or verbal form. Respectively, these correspond to inherent and temporary qualities. When describing an inanimate noun, however, predicative adjectives are found in their adjectival form. Certain inanimate nouns may be found in the patientive as the object of an impersonal verbal adjective. This is often the case with adjectives describing topological features:

    ohkia ůkia
    [ˈɔhcia ˈuːjia]
    ohki-a ů=k-ia
    deep-COP.ASS water-INESS
    'the water is deep' (lit. it is deep in the water)

kàhlua sehmeiska
[ˈcʰæːhɬua ˈsɛhmɛɪska]
kàhlo-a se<h>-me=iska
high-COP.ASS cliff-ABLAT
'the cliff is high' (lit. it is high from the cliffs - said from the top of the cliff)

The table below illustrates predicative adjectives, their form and function.

		predicative	
		inherent	temporary
		copular	verbal
animate		*atanua saigi* [ˈɑtɑnua ˈsaiji] atana-a saigi-Ø big-COP.ASS moose-AGT 'the moose is big'	*atahmi kansika* [ˈɑtahmi ˈkʰansiga] atar-m-i kansi-Ø big-INCONCL-ASS.ITR female.moose-PAT 'the moose is pregnant'
		njòdnua saigi [ˈɲʊːʔtnua ˈsaiji] njòdna-a saigi-Ø sick-COP.ASS I moose-AGT 'the moose is sick' (or 'it is not a healthy moose')	*njolttima saitsa* [ˈɲɔltːima ˈsaɪtsa] njolt-i-ma saigi-Ø sick-ASS.ITR-INCONCL moose-PAT 'the moose is sick' (right now)
		hokjù tśeddjet [ˈhɔcuː ˈtɕɛdʑːɛdʑ] hokju-a tśeddjet-Ø blind-COP.ASS I old.man-AGT 'the old man is blind'	*hokjami tśeddjeddja* [ˈhɔcami ˈtɕɛdʑːɛdʑːa] hokja-m-i tśeddje-ddja blind-INCONCL-ASS.ITR old.man-PAT 'the old man is blinded/cannot see'
	inherent	temporary	impersonal
		copular	verbal
		atanua misas [ˈɑtɑnua ˈmisas] atana-a misas-Ø big-COP.ASS rock-AGT 'the rock is big'	*atahmi ùhhja śines kika* [ˈɑtahmi ˈœhːja ˈɕinɛs ˈcʰika] atar-m-i ùhhja śi<n>e-s kika big-INCONCL-ASS.ITR here lake-GEN over.ADESS 'the lake is big here (lit. here is big over/across the lake)'

	predicative	
inanimate	*taite leymai moaġundi* ['tʰaide 'lɛœmai 'mɔaxʊndʑi] tai=te leyma-i moaġundi-Ø then=too warm-COP.PAST.ASS sip-AGT '(his/her) sip was still warm'	*taite katsa leymuima* ['tʰaide 'kʰatsa 'lɛœmuima] tai=te katsa leym-u-i-ma then=too outside-ADV warm-PAST-ASS.ITR-INCONCL 'outside was still warm'
	pilai mavvu ['pʰilai 'mɑw:u] pila-i mavvu-Ø red-COP.PAST.ASS meat-AGT 'the meat was red'	*katsa pidlmi* ['kʰatsa 'pʰɪtɫmːi] katsa pi<dl>-m-i outside=ADV red.PAST-INCONCL -ASS.ITR 'outside, it was red'

§5.3.1 Object Predicative

When the object of a verb has a predicative adjective, it is called an object predicative. An example of this in English could be 'I ate it raw'.

When a predicative adjective refers to the object of a verb, it comes before the noun it qualifies, in the appropriate case. This is also the case with predicative adjectives referring to nouns modified by a post- or preposition.

If the object to which the predicative adjective refers is a pronoun, the adjective will follow the verb (in the case of verbal pronouns) and may be found with the clitic -mi or found in the essive (see *§4.5.5.4*) if the object is in the genitive, otherwise unmarked if the object is in the dative.

ohkama mami
['ɔhkama mami]
ohkama-Ø m-a-Ø-mi
raw-DAT eat.PAST-ASS.CONCL.TR-3P.PAT-1P.AG.SG
'I ate it raw' (also **ohkama-mi mami, ohkamemi mami**)

iljilimatta uluvvi
['iljilimaʔta u'luw:i]
iljil-i-m-a-tta u-lu<vv>-i-Ø
live-ITR-INCONCL-AGT.PART.UNAG-PAT PASS-boil.PAST-ASS.CONCL.ITR-3P.PAT
'it was boiled alive' (also **iljilimatta-mi uluvvi, iljilimattemi uluvvi**)

gigari tvonna mavvu
['ɟigari 'tʰvɔnːa 'mɑw:u]
g<ig>-a-ri tvonna-Ø mavvu-Ø
share.PAST-ASS.CONCL.TR-3P.AG.PL equal-DAT meat-DAT
'they shared the meat equally' (lit. equal)

sapohhjis rekkotsta atra gala
[sɑˈpʰɔhːjɪs ˈrɛʔkɔtstːa ˈatxakla]
sa-pohhj-i-s rekkot-sta at-ra gala
2P.UNAG-sleep-ASS.CONCL.ITR-HAB-3P.ACT open-GEN mouth-GEN WITH
'you sleep with your mouth open'

omestari pila nidlie-nen
[ɔˈmɛstɑri ˈpʰila ˈniːtɬienɛn]
o-me<st>-a-ri pila-Ø nidli-Ø-e–nen
SUBJ-paint.PAST-ASS.CONCL.TR-3P.AG.PL red-DAT face-DAT-PL-4P.POSS
'they painted their faces red'

but

omestari nidlie-nen pila
[ɔˈmɛstɑri ˈniːtɬienɛn ˈpʰila]
o-me<st>-a-ri nidli-Ø-e–nen pila-Ø
SUBJ-paint.PAST-ASS.CONCL.TR-3P.AG.PL face-DAT-PL-4P.POSS red-DAT
'they painted their red faces'

§5.3.2 Subject Predicative
Like object predicatives, subject predicatives are a predicative adjective describing the subject of a verb.

When predicative adjectives refer to the subject of the verb, they generally precede the subject, or the verb in the case of pronominal subjects. The adjective agrees in case with the subject. In more formal speech however, it is preferable to use the adverbial form of the adjective.

sisedi tvahsaiu
[ˈsisedʑi ˈtʰvahsɑju]
sise-di t-vahs-ai-u
tall-PAT 3P.UNAG-grow-PAST-ASS.CONCL.TRANSL
'X grew tall'

or

sis(v)en tvahsaiu
[ˈsisɛn ˈtʰvahsɑju]
sis-ven t-vahs-ai-u
tall-ADV 3P.UNAG-grow-PAST-ASS.CONCL.TRANSL
'X grew tall'

nidotita mahri
[ˈnidɔtɕida ˈmahri]
nidot-ita ma<hr>-i-Ø
masterful-ILLAT hunt-PAST-ASS.CONCL.ITR-3P.AG.SG
'X hunted (until X became) masterful'

or
> *niden mahri*
> ['nidɛn 'mahri]
> nid-en ma‹hr›-i-Ø
> masterful-ADV hunt-PAST-ASS.CONCL.ITR-3P.AG.SG
> 'X hunted masterfully'

A third and more common way of forming such subject predicative adjectives is to add the inessive -ita (for subjects perceived to be in or go into a state) and the elative -ika (for subjects perceived to leave a state) directly onto the unmarked form of the adjective.

> *siseita tvahsaiu*
> ['siseida 't̠ʰvahsɑju]
> sise-ita t-vahs-ai-u
> tall-ILLAT 3P.UNAG-grow-PAST-ASS.CONCL.TRANSL
> 'X grew tall'

A number of fixed expressions use this construction;

> *tsikimaika saitkisa*
> 'to disappear from view' (lit. from being visible, *tsik·i-*)

> *obůrůkimaita lomsa*
> 'to run very fast' (lit. to run oneself drowned, *ob·ůrůk·i-*)

> *tsengita sisa*
> 'to realize, to finally understand' (lit. to understand clear)

> *uinoita onami*
> 'to admit, to recognize' (cf. to tell (in)to true)

§5.4 Attributive Adjectives

Attributives adjectives are those which are typically found as part of the noun phrase, such as 'a big X'. In Siwa, all attributive adjectives are found after the head noun. Postpositions are usually found after the adjective though they also appear between the noun and the adjective, whereas possessives are more often found on the noun.

tȯ atana	'a big rock'
kyṡi onona	'a small squirrel'
leḑba himi	'warm mittens'
ṡines tṡebi ůrja	'close to the small lake'
soakkia-go atakka	'in my big house'

Attributive adjectives are generally in the adjectival form, but participial forms are also used to place emphasis on the temporary/stative/essive meaning of the adjective (X is as/in the state of being Y) when a corresponding verbal form exists. Certain adjectives' meaning changes significantly whether participial or adjectival. Animacy does not affect attributive adjectives. Attributive adjectives do **not** agree in number with the head noun.

Attributive adjectives in the adjectival form do not agree in number but agree in case with their head noun, but do not use any of the locative case markings. Thus, if a noun is in the inessive, its attributive adjective will simply be in the genitive.

    tòka atana   'the big rocks'
    kyṡigi onona   'the small squirrels'
    lehton hìmi   'a warm mitten'

and

    toboima atakka   'on a big rock'
    kyṡtima onommo   'on a small squirrel'
    leḍmaia hìmid   'in warm mittens'

Adjectives do not have their own set of declensions – they behave like nouns, but are generally more regular and less prone to certain sound changes. Thus, adjectives follow the same declensions as nouns, although they are less subject to irregularities. Adjectives, however, do not go through lenition:

    gegin lammon   'a bold mouth'
    geisika lammonta   'from a bold mouth'

The form **geisika lamōrika*, where **lamōrika* has both lenition and a locative ending is ungrammatical.

Attributive adjectives in the participial form agree only in number (-**ma** for singular and -**mi** or sometimes -**me** for plural).

    iski atarotima   'a pregnant woman'
    iskigi atarotimi   'pregnant women'

When an adjective which would normally be attributive lacks a head noun, it becomes a nominal adjective. Nominal adjectives behave like nouns, and differ from regular attributive adjectives in that they take locative endings and can be found in the plural. However, they may or may not go through lenition. Lenition of nominal adjectives is considered poor language, but it is somewhat used. It should be considered vulgar.

    atakkia   'in the big one'
    onommoima   'on the big one'
    hìmihta   'into the warm one'
    lammōrika   'from the bold one'

Attributive adjectives are not affected by animacy. However, a few adjectives can only be used with one animacy. For example, 'old' is expressed by the Siwa word *jeila* for inanimate nouns, but *iśi* for animate nouns. Similarly, *siehhin* 'long' is only used with inanimate nouns, and *sise* with animate nouns, then meaning 'long' or also 'tall'.

The table below illustrates attributive adjectives, their form and function.

	attributive	
	inherent	**temporary**
	adjectival	adjectival / participial
animate/ inanimate	*saigi atana* ['saiji 'atana] saigi-Ø atana-Ø moose-AGT big-AGT 'a/the big moose'	*saigi atarotima* ['saiji 'atarɔtɕima] saigi-Ø atar-ot-i-m-a moose-AGT big-COMPLE-ITR-INCONCL-AGT.PART.UNAG.AGT 'a/the pregnant moose'
	oaḍbi piegjino ['ɔaðbi 'pʰiejːinɔ] oaḍbi-Ø piegjino-Ø gums-AGT healthy-AGT 'healthy gums'	*oaḍbi pigjotimi* ['ɔaðbi 'pʰijːɔtɕimi] oaḍbi-Ø pigj-ot-i-m-i gums-AGT healthy-COMPLE-ITR-INCONCL-AGT.PART.UNAG.AGT.PL 'healthy looking/feeling gums'
	tàhma ohhjo ['tʰæːhma 'ɔhːjɔ] tàhma-Ø ohhjo-Ø heart-AGT strong-AGT 'a/the strong/powerful heart'	*ġyeni ohhjotima* ['xweni 'ɔhːjɔtɕima] ġyeni-Ø ohhj-ot-i-m-a wind-AGT strong-ITR-INCONCL-AGT.PART.UNAG.AGT 'a/the strong/powerful wind'
	totomma njòdna ['tʰɔtɔmːa 'ɲʊːʔtna] totomma-Ø njòdna-Ø family.member-AGT sick-AGT 'a/the sick/unhealthy relative'	*totomma njolttotima* ['tʰɔtɔmːa 'ɲɔltːɔtɕima] totomma-Ø njolt-ot-i-m-a family.member-AGT sick-COMPLE-ITR-INCONCL-AGT.PART.UNAG.AGT 'a/the sick relative'

§5.5 Adjective Formation

There are about 20 derivatives from which most adjectival forms are created. Certain derivational endings may only or mostly be used with one class of words, e.g. the derivative -bmot is generally only added to verb stems, while -ra to noun stems.

A few types may be formed with either polarization or vowel lengthening. As a general rule, lengthening is used with less concrete and more abstract qualities, or to form adjectives from abstract nouns. Not all adjectival forms are listed here. Note that many other endings are characteristic of adjectives – those presented below are productive derivational endings. Note that most derivative adjectives lack verbal forms all together. The types of derivatives are as follows:

type/function	formation	example
material	polarization + -ra (-hta GEN)	kili 'wood' → kilura 'wooden'
		tsalta 'clay' → tsaltira 'made of clay'
essential relation to	polarization + -ka/-ko (-hta GEN)	somi 'man' → somuka 'masculine'
		notsġomo 'shaman' → notsġomiko 'shamanic'
	lengthening + -na/-no	śavvi 'courage' → śainno 'courageous'
possessive	polarization + -ha/-ho	jůlů 'sweat' → jůliha 'sweaty'
		ȯlma 'leaf' → ȯliha 'leafy'
evocative	polarization + -V	lokna 'intense cold' → longiu 'icy'
		sira 'fish' → siriu 'fishy'
loosely characterizing	polarization + -m- + -V	hejeri 'winter' → hejomi 'winter-like'
		kjodma 'auk bird' → kjodmimu 'auk bird-like'

type/function	formation	example
animate participle	-bmot	*pitta* 'X pays attention to Y' → *pittabmot* 'attentive'
		tohḥa 'X is dexterous enough to do Y' → *tohḥabmot* 'dexterous'
inanimate participle	-bmis (-mha GEN)	*koahi* 'X is enough' → *koahibmis* 'sufficient'
origin	-mma or -ppa	Kjuomśin → *kjuomśimma* 'someone from Kjuomśin'
location	inessive -tse	*uja* 'water' → *uitse* 'aquatic'
	adessive -us(e)	*kelta* 'ground' → *keltaus* 'terrestrial'
time / length	-nihta	*ko* 'summer' → *konihta* 'one summer long/old/…'
abessive	shortening + -skon	*śavvi* 'courage' → *śevviskon* 'coward'
		pitta 'X pays attention to Y' → *patskon* 'inconsiderate'
abundance	polarization + -dna	*mavvu* 'meat' → *mavvedna* 'meaty'
	lengthening + -na	*śiba* 'X has enough energy for Y' → *śiabuna* 'energetic'
lack	polarization + -ġlen	*tulvi* 'nutrient' → *tulvuġlen* 'lacking in nutrient'
		hego 'salt' → *hegiġlen* 'unsalted, sweat (of water)'
similarity or shape	lengthening + -ke(na)	*kori* 'boy' → *garike* 'boyish'
		õri 'stump' → *virke* 'stumpy'

type/function	formation	example
		rìdni 'thorn' → *rjeinkena* 'thorny, shaped like a thorn'
distributive	lengthening + -lu	*yly* 'night' → *vellu* 'nightly'
		kengi 'day' → *keundlu* 'daily'
		keppi 'head' → *keullu* 'per person'
abstract implication of abundance	lengthening + -(s)ġi/-śi	*tama* 'many' → *taintsġi* 'numerous'
		ȯlma 'leaf' → *vilśi* 'verdant'
		piusti 'X thrives' → *piutġi* 'thriving'
descriptive of verb's facility/rapidity	lengthening + -(s)ġa/-ha	*tuvi* 'X bends' → *deusġa* 'bendable/flexible'
		jairi 'X rows' → *joairha* 'easy to row in'
		ha 'X eats Y' → *hausġa* 'edible'
		sahhi 'X burns' → *soaġa* 'which burns well'
descriptive verb's lack of facility/rapidity	shortening + -(s)ġon	*tuvi* 'X bends' → *tausġon* 'unbendable/inflexible/rigid'
		ha 'X eats Y' → *hosġon* 'inedible'
		sahhi 'X burns' → *soġġon* 'which does not burns well'

type/function	formation	example
descriptive of typical quality	polarization + -bmi	*soaki* 'house' → *soakubmi* 'homely/cozy'
		tšegma 'child' → *tšengibmi* 'childish'
moderative	polarization + -hma or -htsa	*huvvi* 'comfortable cold' → *huvvuhma* 'cool'
		bieluha 'fat' → *bieluhma* 'quite fat/plump'
descriptive	polarization + -ppa/-ppi	*rapa* 'small hill' → *rapuppa* 'hilly'
		iJuri 'sap' → *iJeppi* 'sticky'
		tŭrŭ 'fur' → *tŭrippi/tŭrŭppŭ* 'fluffy'

In addition to these, many adjectives are non-derived, i.e. they do not have any corresponding forms from which they have been derived. Common endings for non-derived adjectival forms are:

-la   (-ldi, -lle, -lmo)
   irela   'beautiful'   GEN. *ireldi*
   nevala   'nifty, diligent'   GEN. *nevalle*
   ou̯ala   'wide'   GEN. *ou̯almo*
   tuvala   'heavy'   GEN. *tuvalmo*

-na   (-kka, -di, -mmo)
   atana   'big'   GEN. *atakka*
   hejona   'weak'   GEN. *hejodi*
   itina   'late'   GEN. *itindi*
   kisina   'quick'   GEN. *kisindi*
   kymina   'nice'   GEN. *kymimmo*
   męrana   'difficult'   GEN. *męradi*
   nunna   'angry'   GEN. *nunnamo*
   onona   'small'   GEN. *onommo*
   opona   'alive'   GEN. *opommo*
   sarana   'narrow'   GEN. *sarakka*
   sumana   'irritated, sore'   GEN. *sumammo*

	temyna	'joyful'	GEN. *temydi*
	tsusina	'fresh'	GEN. *tsusimmo*
	voanna	'strange, scary'	GEN. *voakka*

-ot (pronounced [ɔʔ(ɔ)] or [ɔh]. In the west, sometimes [ʊɔ] or [wɔ] , then written -uo/ɥo) (-otta, -otsta)

aipiot	'enormous'	GEN. *aipiotta*
horiot	'tender'	GEN. *horiotta*
galmot	'soft, pregnant (with eggs)'	GEN. *galmotta*
konkot	'horrible'	GEN. *konkotta*
miohhot	'slender'	GEN. *miohhotsta*
sonnjot	'lukewarm'	GEN. *sonnjotta*
tohhot	'young'	GEN. *tohhotta*

-on (sometimes -ō) (-os, -onta)

likion	'awful'	GEN. *likios*
lammon	'bold'	GEN. *lammonta*
sogjon	'dry'	GEN. *sogjonta*
sopon	'evil'	GEN. *soponta*

-in (-is, -inta)

aurin	'crisp'	GEN. *aurinta*
laipin	'bitter'	GEN. *laipinta*
ȯmin	'stiff'	GEN. *ȯminta*
siehhin	'long'	GEN. *siehhis*
sukin	'straight'	GEN. *sukinta*

-ɥe/-ve (-ɥeka, -ɥie, -ɥemo)

ayɥe	'shrill'	GEN. *ayɥeka*
daiɥe	'moist'	GEN. *daiɥeka*
kalve	'stringent, tight'	GEN. *kalveka*
kokve	'light'	GEN. *kokvemo*
osve	'sour'	GEN. *osvemo*
sehhɥe	'fervent'	GEN. *sehhɥie*
ůilve	'pungent'	GEN. *ůilvemo*

-(p)po/-ppů (-ppoka, -ppoma, -ppue)

daippo	'damp'	GEN. *daippoka*
hȧppo	'broad, ample'	GEN. *hȧppoka*
holpo	'dull'	GEN. *holpoma*
haimpo	'strong, spicy, stinging'	GEN. *haimpoka*
loippo	'flat'	GEN. *loippomo*
rarpo	'aggressive, mad'	GEN. *rarpoka*
sompo	'swift'	GEN. *sompoma*
keheppo	'sulky'	GEN. *kehheppue*

tůppů	'clumsy'	GEN. tůppůma

-ḥi/-hi   (-ḥiko, -ḥika, -ḥid, -ḥie)

nohi	'smart'	GEN. nohiko
pohi	'chubby'	GEN. pohiko
roahi	'simple, normal'	GEN. roahika
sipoḥi	'entangled, confused'	GEN. sipoḥid
sehi	'thin'	GEN. sehie
tśihi	'tiny'	GEN. tśihid
auḥḥi	'gullible'	GEN. auḥḥika
utoḥi	'mellow'	GEN. utoḥid
nuiḥḥi	'spiteful, mean, nasty'	GEN. nuiḥḥid

Of these, the endings -na and -ot are the most common. Many western dialects usually replace -ot by -us, and -on by -ō. Central dialects have merged both -ot and -on to -ō.

Adjectives can be made negative by simply adding the prefix si- or sem-, or more emphatically hi̧e- or hi̧et- (or hi̧eḥ-).

kvisġot	'regular'
sikvisġot	'irregular'
uino	'true'
hi̧eḥuino	'(completely) untrue'

§5.6 Declension
As it was mentioned before, adjectives do not have a separate set of declension endings from inanimate nouns. Of the four types of adjectives (adjectival and copular, verbal and participial), only the adjectival form has a declension. They behave identically to nouns, with the exception that adjectives never undergo lenition (only inanimate nouns do). In addition, adjectival forms are not found in locative cases, unless they stand alone as nominal adjectives. See section §4.2.1 for a complete description of declensions.

§5.7 Formation of Verbal Forms from Non-Derived Adjectival Forms
Verbal forms can be regularly derived from non-derived adjectival forms. Adjectival forms in -la and -on which have the stressed vowel -o- and -u- often see it become -y- in the verbal form (including -au- changing to -ay- or -ey-):

tuvala	'heavy'	→	tymmi
moron	'thick'	→	myhmi

Other types of adjectives are usually not found in their verbal form, and no special derivation strategies exist for them. It can be impossible to tell what corresponding adjectival form a verbal form may have. It is thus preferable to learn the adjectival form first.

adjectival	verbal	example
-na/-no	-r- (-h- before -m-)	*atana* 'big'→ *atah·mi* 'X is big/pregnant'
		opona 'alive'→ *opoh·mi* 'X is (still) alive'
		hejona 'weak'→ *hejoh·mi* 'X is (feeling) weak'
		sarana 'narrow'→ *sarah·mi* 'it is/becomes narrow'
-la	-Ø- (+ fronting of -o/u- to -y-)	*tuvala* 'heavy'→ *tym·mi* 'X is heavy'
		oyala 'wide'→ *ẏm·mi* 'X is/becomes wide'
-ot	-i-/-Ø-	*horiot* 'tender'→ *hori·mi* 'X is tender/sore'
		aipiot 'enormous'→ *aipi·mi* 'X is bloated, very full'
		galmot 'soft, pregnant (with eggs)'→ *galmi·mi* 'X carrying eggs'
		holot 'thin'→ *hol·mi* 'X is malnourished/sickly'
-on	-Ø- (+ fronting of -o/u- to -y-)	*sogjon* 'dry'→ *suǐ·mi* 'X is dry'
		tausġon 'rigid'→ *taysġ·ima* 'X has muscle aches/sore muscles'
		ġumeskon 'depressed'→ *ġymesk·ima* 'X is depressed'
-in	-Ø-	*ȯmin* 'stiff'→ *ȯm·mi* 'X is stiff, reluctant'
		laipin 'bitter'→ *laib·mi* 'X is/feels resentful'
		siehhin 'long'→ *sieh·mi* 'it is long/elongated'
		ayye 'shrill'→ *ay·mi* 'X shudders/is disgusted'

adjectival	verbal	example
-ųe/-ve	-Ø- (+ gemination of consonant if possible)	sehhųe 'fervent' → seh·mi 'X is sexually aroused/horny'
		kokve 'light' → kokmi 'X is relieved'
		osve 'sour' → os·mi 'X has heartburn/X feels guilty'
-(p)po	-(p)p-	keheppo 'sulky' → keheb·mi 'X is sulky'
		rarpo 'mad' → rarp·ima 'X is mad/furious'
		daippo 'damp' → daib·mi 'X is (very) sweaty (from work)'
		loippo 'flat' → loib·mi 'it is flat'
		holpo 'dull' → holp·ima 'X is bored'
-hi	-h- (or -b- before -m-)	sipohi 'confused' → sipob·mi 'X is confused'
		hjihi 'slanted' → hjib·mi 'it is slanted/there is a slope' or 'X is leaning towards/favorable to'
		mohi 'slippery, elusive, evasive' → mob·mi 'X cannot understand/wrap one's head around'

§5.8 Degrees of Comparison

Adjectives can be marked for comparison. The comparative and superlative use suffixes (-ta and -la) while the mitigative forms of the comparative and the superlative (less and least) use either a separate word (onna and volda) or suffixes derived from the positive comparative and superlative forms. In addition, other levels of comparison are found in Siwa such as the ultimate comparative (more than ever), the terminative comparative (as much as possible), the ultimate superlative (the very most) and the equative (as much as).˙

§5.8.1 Comparative

Adjectival forms can be found in the comparative. The comparative is regularly formed by applying vowel polarization to vowel-final adjectives and adding the ending -ta. Adjectives ending in -na, -la, -ųe/-ve and -ḥi/hi have respectively -nta, -lta, -ḍḍa and -tta, unless their adjectival endings form a consonant cluster, in which case polarization is used.

Adjectives ending in -**on**, -**in** and -**ot** have respectively -**onta** (or -**ōta**/-**ōdda**), -**inta** and -**oḍḍa**. All comparative adjectives have the genitive form -**tanna** in the east and -**tammo** in the west. Note that adjectives in -**Cve** may also have the form -**Cotta** in the comparative, not -**Cvuta**.

adjectival form	comparative	comparative genitive
garike 'boyish'	*garikota* 'more boyish'	*garikotanna* / *garikotammo*
somuka 'manly'	*somukita* 'more manly'	*somukitanna* / *somukitammo*
taintsġi 'numerous'	*taintsġuta* 'more numerous'	*taitsġutanna* / *taintsġutammo*
irela 'beautiful'	*irelta* 'more beautiful'	*ireltanna* / *ireltammo*
atana 'big'	*atanta* 'bigger'	*atantanna* / *atantammo*
daiye 'moist'	*daiḍḍa* 'moister'	*daiḍḍanna* / *daiḍḍamo*
kokve 'light'	*kokvuta* / *kokotta* 'lighter'	*kokvutanna* / *kokvutammo* *kokottanna* / *kokottammo*
sehi 'thin'	*setta* 'thinner'	*settanna* / *settammo*
sogjon 'dry'	*sogjonta* / *sogjōta* / *sogjōdda* 'drier'	*sogjontanna* / *sogjontammo* *sogjōtanna* / *sogjōtammo* *sogjōddanna* / *sogjōddammo*
siehhin 'long'	*siehhinta* 'longer'	*siehhintanna* / *siehhintammo*
galmot 'soft'	*galmoḍḍa* 'softer'	*galmoḍḍanna* / *galmoḍḍammo*

A few adjectives have an irregular comparative form. These include:

adjectival form	comparative	comparative genitive
sara 'good'	sohta / saista / sairta 'better'	sohtanna / sohtammo saistanna / saistammo sairtanna / sairtammo
seba 'bad'	seutta / sŭtta / baitta 'worse'	seuttanna / seuttammo sŭttanna / sŭttammo baittanna / baittammo

To compare something to another, Siwa uses two constructions; the most common one is 'X *savi* Y' or 'X-er than Y', and the more uncommon construction is 'Y.ELATIVE X', e.g.

> *atantua to sira-ŭt savi hait*
> ['ɑtantua tʰɔ 'siræœʔ 'sɑvi 'haɪʔ]
> atan-ta-a to-Ø sira-Ø–ŭt savi hait-Ø
> big-COMP-COP.ASS 3P.ANI.SG.AGT fish-AGT–DET.PROXI than that.MEDI-AGT
> 'this fish is bigger than that one'

> *haittaika atantua to sira-ŭt*
> ['haɪʔtɑiga 'ɑtantua tʰɔ 'siræœʔ]
> hait=ta-ika atan-ta-a to sira-Ø–ŭt
> that.MEDI-ELAT big-COMP-COP.ASS 3P.ANI.SG.AGT fish-AGT–DET.PROXI
> 'this fish is bigger than that one'

§5.8.1.1 Mitigative Comparative
Mitigative or negative comparison expresses that the compared adjective is less than instead of more. Siwa generally simply uses the word *onna* (short form of *ondanna* 'less GEN.') before the compared adjective. However, in more elevated registers, one might replace the comparative ending -ta by -tonda (GEN. -tondat~-tondatta), e.g. *onna taintsġi* 'less numerous' or *taintsġutonda* (GEN. *taintsġutondat*). In negative comparative constructions, **onna** does not decline:

> *tsẏhmoibma onna kuohhidnamo*
> *tsẏhmoibma kuohhidnitondat*
> 'to a less noisy spot' (cf. *kuohhidna* 'noisy')

§5.8.1.2 Ultimate and Terminative Comparatives
The comparative forms can be combined with two prefixes to form the ultimate and ferminative comparative forms of adjectives. These constructions can also be found with certain nouns and participial forms of verbs.

VERB	teu-Ø-uita-Ø	ultimate comparative
VERB	tsġav-Ø-uita-Ø	terminative comparative
teu-NOUN		
tsġav-NOUN		

The form **teu-Ø-uita-Ø** (where **-uita-** is in fact a form of the past patientive participle in -u, and **teu-** is from **tevu** 'before') is commonly used in phrases equivalent to English 'more than ever (before)' and is added onto verbs (**teu**-VERB-**uita**-PRONOUN). The prefix **teu-** usually changes to **tem-** before vowels (like **keu-** and **kem-** 'with').

ma·mi teu·m·uita·mi	'I ate more than I ever ate before'
nega·mi teu·neg·uita·mi	'I saw more than I ever saw before'
jekki·mi teu·jekk·uita·mi	'I ran more than I ever ran before'

This construction is quite common in Siwa and may also simply be understood to be very emphatic. A similar construction involves adding **teu-** to the comparative form of the adjective to mean 'more X than ever':

temirelta	'more beautiful than ever'
teusetta	'thinner than ever'
teukvolda	'bigger than ever'
tematanta	'bigger than ever'

Parallel to these two constructions is **tsġav-Ø-uita-Ø** (or **tsġaC-**, where -C is a geminated consonant), having the meaning of 'as VERB as possible'.

ma·mi tsġam·m·uita·mi	'I ate as much as I could eat'
nega·mi tsġan·neg·uita·mi	'I saw as much as I could saw'
jekki·mi tsġag·jekk·uita·mi	'I ran as much as I could run'

A similar construction involves adding **tsġav-** to the comparative form of the adjective to mean 'as X as ever/possible' or 'very/extremely/so/typically'. A few adverbs can be found ending in -(n)tsġavven as an intensifier.

tsġavirelta	'as beautiful as ever, ever so beautiful'
tsġassehi	'as thin as possible'
tsġakkolla	'as much as possible'
tsġavatanta[1]	'as big as possible, ever so big, enormous'
tsġassiyikita	'purely/typically Siwa'
hymmintsġavven	'completely quietly'
kisintsġavven	'very quickly'

---

[1] Some dialects even have *tsġavatantsġavven* 'unbelievably, incredibly, very'.

§5.8.2 Superlative

Adjectival forms can be found in the superlative. The superlative is regularly formed by applying vowel polarization to vowel-final adjectives and adding the ending -ila or -ela after -i. Adjectives ending in -a polarize to -e. Adjectives in -Cye or -Cve get -Cla, and those in -in, -on and -ot respectively change to -illa, -olla and -olla. The genitive form of the superlative is -Vlda.

adjectival form	superlative	superlative genitive
garike 'boyish'	*garikoila* 'most boyish'	*garikoilda*
somuka 'manly'	*somukeila* 'most manly'	*somukeilda*
taintsġi 'numerous'	*taintsġuila* 'most numerous'	*taintsġuilda*
irela 'beautiful'	*ireleila* 'most beautiful'	*ireleilda*
atana 'big'	*ataneila* 'biggest'	*ataneilda*
daiye 'moist'	*daiyoila* 'moistest'	*daiyoilda*
kokve 'light'	*kokla* 'lightest'	*kokkulda*
sehi 'thin'	*sehuila* 'thinnest'	*sehuilda*
sogjon 'dry'	*sogjolla* 'driest'	*sogjolda*
siehhin 'long'	*siehhilla* 'longest'	*siehhilda*
galmot 'soft'	*galmolla* 'softest'	*galmolda*

A few adjectives have an irregular comparative form. These include:

adjectival form	superlative	superlative genitive
sara 'good'	saisla~saihla~sohla 'best'	saisilda~saitsilda~sairilda ~sorulda
seba 'bad'	baidla 'worse'	bailda

To make a superlative comparison, one can use the construction ġůt 'of anything (inani.)', ġůmġu 'of anyone (ani.)', śebśu 'of all (out of many)' and śośśi or śosu~śuśu 'of everyone (out of all.)'.

    śośśi ataneilua to sira-ůt
    [ˈɕɔɕːi ˈɑtɑneilua tʰɔ ˈsiræœʔ]
    śośśi atan<e>-ila-a me sira-Ø–ůt
    all-GEN big-SUPER-COP.ASS 3P.ANI.SG.AGT fish-AGT–DET.PROXI
    'this fish is the biggest one of all'

    śebśõ ataneilua tsato sira-ůt
    [ˈɕɛpɕɔ̃ ˈɑtɑneilua ˈtsɑtɔ ˈsiræœʔ]
    śebś-õ atan<e>-ila-a tsa-to sira-Ø–ůt
    all.OUT.OF.MANY-GEN big-SUPER-COP.ASS OF.MANY.3P.ANI.SG.AGT fish-AGT–DET.PROXI
    'this fish is the biggest one of all' (of/in a known group of fish)

§5.8.2.1 Ultimate Superlative
The ultimate superlative is a very emphatic form of the superlative such as 'the very Ø-est', and it is formed by the prefix **ro-** (behaves exactly like the subjective preverbal vowel, with forms in **rob-** and **rom-**, see *§9.5.8* on prefix coalescence).

    romestot   'the very first'
    robireleila   'the very beautifulest'
    romataneila   'the very biggest'

Some rarely emphatic forms of the superlative can sometimes be found with the prefix **teu-** meaning 'Ø-est ever':

    teuġvivuila   'the biggest ever'
    temireleila   'the most beautiful ever'

§5.8.2.2 Mitigative Superlative
To make a mitigative or negative superlative, such as in English 'least X', Siwa generally simply uses the word *volda/ůlda* (cf. *olla* 'least') before the adjective.

However, in more elevated registers, one might replace the superlative ending -(i/e)la by -(i/e)lolla (GEN. -(i/e)luhla), e.g.:

	ùlda taintsġi	'least numerous'
or	taintsġuilolla (GEN. taintsġuiluhla)	'least numerous'

§5.8.3 Equative

Siwa does not have a specific marking for equative comparisons, i.e. 'X is as Y as Z'. Instead, it uses various constructions. The most common of them are '*tavvi* X *te* Y', or alternatively '*totta* X *te* Y'. Another way to show that two adjectives are equal is to place the compared item in the elative followed by either *tavvi* or *totta*, i.e. Y.ELATIVE *tavvi/totta* Y'.

tavvi/totta atanua to sira-ůt te hait
[ˈtʰawːi/ˈtʰɔʔta ˈɑtɑnua tʰɔ ˈsiræœʔ de ˈhaɪʔ]
tavvi/totta atana-a to sira-Ø–ůt te hait-Ø
as big-COP.ASS 3P.ANI.SG.AGT fish-AGT–DET.PROXI and that.MEDI.AGT
'this fish is as big as that one'

haittaika tavvi/totta atanua to sira-ůt
[ˈhaɪʔtaga ˈtʰawːi/ˈtʰɔʔta ˈɑtɑnua tʰɔ ˈsiræœʔ]
hait=ta-ka tavvi/totta atana-a to sira-Ø–ůt
that.MEDI-ELAT big-COMP-COP.ASS 3P.ANI.SG.AG fish-AGT–DET.PROXI
'this fish is as big as that one'

This same construction can see the word *te* combined with other words, most commonly *tavvi/totta* X *sůite* Y 'Y as much as X';

tavvi ohhjuata sůite holpua
[ˈtʰawːi ˈohːjuɑda ˈsœide ˈhɔlpua]
tavvi ohhjo-a-ta sůite holpo-a
as strong-COP.ASS-3P.AG.SG by.as stupid-COP.ASS
'X is as strong as X is dumb'

§5.8.4 Comparative and Superlative of Non-Adjectives

Like adjectives, participles and postpositions as well as adverbs can be found in the comparative and superlative. However, neither the comparative nor the superlative cause polarization to participles, postpositions/adverbs or subject predicative adjectives. Instead, they coalesce much like the u- of the passive. Because postpositions and adverbs show a wide range of endings, it is worth pointing out that the comparative and superlative endings -ita and -ila coalesce with the final vowel of the word *as if* they were their geminate forms (see *§3.1.5.1*), or:

	-i
-a	-ęgji
-o	-obi
-u	-ubi
-e	-egji
-i	-igji / -iddji
-y	-ybi
-ů	-ůbi

Patientive participles:
    -u + ita   →   -ubita
    -u + ila   →   -ubila

angitu	'desired'	→	*angitubila*	'most desired'
mu	'eaten'	→	*mubita*	'more eaten'
sośidlu	'famous'	→	*sośidlubila*	'most famous'
metġu	'respected'	→	*metġubila*	'most respected'

Active participles:
    -o + ita   →   -obita
    -o + ila   →   -obila

koahlimo	'noisy'	→	*koahlimobita*	'noisier'
maivvimo	'smiling'	→	*maivvimobila*	'most smiling'
injimo	'sneaky'	→	*injimobila*	'most sneaky'

    -i + ita   →   -iddjita
    -i + ila   →   -iddjila

rodlimi	'adorned'	→	*rodlimiddjila*	'most adorn'
belmimi	'working'	→	*belmimiddjita*	'more working'
koahlimi	'noisy'	→	*koahlimiddjila*	'most noisy'

    -e + ita   →   -egjita
    -e + ila   →   -egjila

tàime	'victorious'	→	*tàimegjila*	'most victorious'
gakvame	'friendly'	→	*gakvamegjita*	'friendlier'

Locative postpositions or subject predicative:
-a + ita → -ęgjita or -amda
-a + ila → -ęgjila or -amla

The **-amda** and **-amla** forms are more common with subject predicatives. Some dialects use -àta and -àla instead.

henda	'up'	→	*hendęgjita*	'higher up'
tvunda	'down'	→	*tvundęgjita*	'further down'
kihta	'over'	→	*kihtęgjita*	'higher over'
tatśa	'inside'	→	*tatśęgjila*	'innermost'
katśa	'outside'	→	*katśęgjila*	'outermost'
il	'in front'	→	*ilęgjila*	'foremost'
ůrja	'near'	→	*ůrjęgjila*	'nearest'
suṡta	'far'	→	*suṡtęgjita*	'farther'
loalta	'behind'	→	*loaltęgjila*	'from farthest back'
siseita	'(grow) tall'	→	*siseitęgjita*	'(grow) taller'
		→	*siseitamda*	'id.'

§5.9 Compound Adjectives

Adjectives can be compounded with a noun, verb or an other adjective. Generally, the compound will have the adjective first, then the noun/verb/other, followed by an adjectival formant (most commonly -ha/-ho or -bmot). Some compound adjectives will lose their derivative and non-derivative endings, especially -na, -la (-on, -ot and -in lose their final consonant), -ha/-ho, -hma and sometimes -ka/-ko. Most other endings and usually all derivative endings causing vowel lengthening remain. The vowel of the last constituent of the compound is polarized before adding the adjective marker. Nouns are generally polarized when they are the first part of the compound. When endings are added to verb, the typical vowel marker (-a for transitive, -i for intransitive and -u for translative) are generally reduced to their shortened form, respectively -o/-Ø, -a/-Ø and -a/-o/-y.

ADJECTIVE + NOUN		most commonly **-ha**	
siehhin 'long' + *hide* 'hair'	→	*siehhihidoha*	'long haired'
huvvuhma 'cool' + *kemśi* 'morning'	→	*huvvukemśua*	'cool-morninged'
ijeppi 'sticky' + *tiemo* 'hand'	→	*ijeppitiekiha*	'sticky-handed'

deusġa 'flexible' + gama 'character' →	deusġagamiha	'flexible-minded'
jůliha 'sweaty' + liello 'palm' →	jůlilielliha	'sweaty-palmed'
ohhjo 'strong' + tȧhma 'heart' →	ohhjotȧhmiha	'strong-hearted'
taja 'much' + myry 'fly' →	tajamyroiha	'with a lot of flies'
hȧppo 'broad' + kelba 'shoulders' →	hȧppokelbiha	'broad-shouldered'

ADJECTIVE + VERB   most commonly -**bmot**

kisina 'quick' + nupu 'X gets angry' →	kisinupubmot	'quick-tempered' (quick-angry)
atana 'big' + erri 'X works' →	ata-erribmot	'hard-working' (lit. big-working)
nin 'self' + tȧi 'X stands' →	nintȧbmot	'independent'
taja 'much' + ahma 'X wants Y' →	taja-ahmabmot	'greedy'
mybi 'silent' + di 'X steps' →	mybidibmot	'sneaky, stealthy'
kalve 'tight' + geiga 'X shares' →	kalvegeigabmot	'cheap'

NOUN + NOUN

ono 'lichen' + kelta 'ground' →	onikeltuha	'lichen-bottomed'
nipi 'dwarf birch' + tsamma 'forest' →	niputsammiha	'birch-forested'
sivi 'honey' + tabbi 'kidney' →	sivutabbubmi	'nice, goodhearted pure/innocent'

NOUN + VERB

salama 'antlers' + koahi 'is enough' →	salekoahibmis	'which has enough heads' (of a herd)
kehhe 'birch bark' + kjoka 'X weaves' →	kehhokjokabmot	'birch bark weaving'

§5.10 Nominalization of Adjectives

Adjectives can be nominalized (made into nouns). The derivation process depends on the ending of the adjectival form. The general rule, however, is that the last vowel of the word is polarized and lengthened (by adding ˀ) or followed by -l (in the east). The result is a noun with a genitive in either (a o u)-ri or (e i y ů)-la, depending on the vowel:

	somuka	'masculine'
→	somukė	'masculinity' (GEN. somukeri)
	atana	'big'
→	atė	'size' (GEN. ateri)
	ki	'new'
→	kiů	'newness, novelty' (GEN. kiula)

Note that the vowel -a- is always polarized to -e-, not -i-, in this case.

adjectival	adverbal	example
-na	polarization + lengthening of final vowel	atana 'big' → atė 'size'
-la	polarization + lengthening of final vowel	tuvala 'heavy' → tuvė 'weight'
-ot	-i	horiot 'tender' → horji 'tenderness'
-on	-i	sogjon 'dry' → sogji 'dryness'
-in	-ů	ȯmin 'stiff' → ȯmů 'stiffness'
-ųe/-ve	-(v/ų)ů	ůilve 'pungent' → ůilů 'pungency'
-(p)po	-(p)pi	keheppo 'sulky' → keheppi 'sulkiness'
-hi	-hů	sipohi 'confused' → sipohů 'confusion'

adjectival	adverbal	example
-ra	-rė	kilura 'wooden'→ kilurė 'woodenness'
-ka/-ko	-kė/-ki	somuka 'masculine'→ somukė 'masculinity'
-na/-no	-nė/-ni	śainno 'courageous'→ śainni 'courageousness'
-ha/-ho	-hė/-hi	jůliha 'sweaty'→ jůlihė 'sweatiness'
-V -m- + -V	polarization + lengthening of final vowel	longiu 'icy'→ longiė 'iciness'
-bmot	-mi	pittabmot 'attentive'→ pittami 'attentiveness'
-bmis	-mů	koahibmis 'sufficient'→ koahimů 'sufficiency'
-mma or -ppa	-mmė / -ppė	kjuomśimma 'someone from Kjuomśin'→ kjuomśimmė 'Kjuomśinness.'
-tse	-tsů	uitse 'aquatic'→ uitsů 'aquaticness'
-us(e)	-usů	keltaus 'terrestrial'→ keltausů 'terrestriality'
-nihta	-nihtė	konihta 'one summer long/old'→ konihtė 'one summer length/age'
-dna	-dnė	kiludna 'woody'→ kiludnė 'woodiness'
-ġlen	-ġlů	tulvuġlen 'lacking in nutrients'→ tulvuġlů 'lack of nutrients'

adjectival	adverbal	example
-ke	-kù	*garike* 'boyish'→ *garikù* 'boyishness'
-lu	-lė	*boahlu* 'daily'→ *boahlė* 'dailiness'
-(s)ġi	-(s)ġù	*taintsġi* 'numerous'→ *taintsġù* 'numerousness'
-(s)ġa	-(s)ġė	*deusġa* 'flexible'→ *deusġė* 'flexibility'
-bmi	-bmù	*soakubmi* 'cozy'→ *soakubmù* 'coziness'
-hma or -htsa	-hmė / -htsė	*huvvuhma* 'cool'→ *huvvuhmė* 'coolness'
-ppa/-ppi	-ppė / -ppù	*ijeppi* 'sticky'→ *ijeppù* 'stickiness'

Another set of endings found in abstract nouns derived from adjectives is -lden, and it is often used for more general, more abstract versions of the nominalized adjective:

nintorha   'free, independent'
nintorhė   'independence'
nintorhelden   'freedom'

atana   'big'
atė   'size'
atelden   'size, proportion(s)'

tuvala   'heavy'
tuvė   'heaviness'
tuvelden   'weight, gravity'

§5.11 Non-Numeral Quantifiers

Non-numeral quantifiers are words like *much, little, few*. They can be found before nouns, adjectives or verbs. Before adjectives, they are always found in the genitive, but if they are found before a noun they agree in markedness with the noun, while adverbial forms are derived from the marked form somewhat irregularly. Not all quantifiers may stand before a verb.

kolla omi	'a lot of snow'	before a noun
komma heje	'very cold'	before an adjective
kommen hehmi	'it is very cold'	before a verb

Unlike true attributive adjectives, which always follow their head noun, non-numeral quantifiers usually precede their head noun. In most respects however, they behave like adjectives, in that they cannot take locative case markings when attributive:

komma õkkia	'in a lot of snow'
tammi soakkika	'from many houses'

Non-numeral quantifiers may not be used adverbially with intransitive verbs (see **§6.3**). Non-numeral quantifiers have three forms – one marked and unmarked form as well as an adverbial form called verbal quantifiers. The marked form is also called the adjectval quantifier when it serves that function, while it is called the nominal quantifier (can be in either unmarked or marked form depending on the phrase) if it is found before nouns. In other words, quantifiers can be found before nouns, before adjectives and before verbs:

	nominal quantifier	*kolla bỳ*	'a lot of food'
GEN	adjectival quantifying adverb	*komma sara*	'very good'
-en/-il	verbal quantifying adverb:	*kommen sihmi*	'it is raining a lot'

Non-numeral quantifiers do not show pluralization, but the head noun may do so.

The most common non-numeral quantifiers are:

QUANTIFIER	ADJECTIVAL QUANTIFIER (MARKED FORM)	VERBAL QUANTIFIER
taja	**taba~tava~tova**	**tagjen, tagjil**
'much, a lot'		

> *ma iohhja taja omi*
> [ˈma ˈiɔhːja ˈtʰaja ˈɔmi]
> m-a iohh=ja ta-ja omi-Ø
> COP.PAST.INCONCL-ASS there.DIST much-AGT snow-AGT
> 'there was much/a lot of snow there'

> *negami taba õkko*
> [ˈnegami ˈtʰaba ˈɔ̃ʔkɔ]
> n<eg>-a-mi ta-ba om-ko
> see.PAST-ASS.CONCL.TR-1P.AG.SG much-GEN snow-GEN
> 'I saw much/a lot of snow'

QUANTIFIER	ADJECTIVAL QUANTIFIER (MARKED FORM)	VERBAL QUANTIFIER
tama 'many'	tammi	Ø

> *ma soakkia tama tśegma/tśegmua*
> [ˈma ˈsɔaʔcia ˈtʰama ˈtɕɛŋmːa/tɕɛŋmːua]
> m-a soak-k=ia ta-ma tśegma-Ø/tśegma-Ø-a
> COP.PAST.INCONCL.ASS house-INESS many-AGT child-AGT/child-AGT-PL
> 'there were many children in the house'

> *negami tammi tśegmari*
> [ˈnegami ˈtʰamːi ˈtɕɛŋmːari]
> n<eg>-a-mi ta-mmi tśegma-ri
> see.PAST-ASS.CONCL.TR-1P.AG.SG many-GEN child-GEN
> 'I saw many/a lot of children'

QUANTIFIER	ADJECTIVAL QUANTIFIER (MARKED FORM)	VERBAL QUANTIFIER
euma 'little, few'	eukka	eukken, eukkil ůkken, ůkli

> *da todattaima-ha euma hirigi*
> [ˈda ˈtʰɔdaʔtaimaw ˈeuma ˈhiriji]
> d-a to<datta>=ima–ho euma-Ø hi-ri-gi
> COP.ASS.CONCL head-ADESS–POSS.3P.SG.ANI little-AGT hair-AGT-PL
> 'there are few hairs on X's head'

> *śinka tavvi eukka sůite ilmolkeśi*
> [ˈɕiːŋka ˈtʰawːi ˈɛʊʔka ˈsœiha iːlˈmɔlceɕi]
> śink-a-Ø tavvi eu-kka sůite il-molk-e-śi-Ø
> know.how-ASS.CONCL.TR-3P.AGT.SG as little-GEN by.as accomplish-INFER.CONCL.TR-HABI-3P.AGT.SG
> 'one will accomplish as little as one knows'

QUANTIFIER	ADJECTIVAL QUANTIFIER (MARKED FORM)	VERBAL QUANTIFIER
eura 'few' (countable)	eumo, ůmmo, ůmmů	Ø

> *tavvi kisil jeḍḍi eura somi*
> [ˈtʰawːi ˈcʰisɪl ˈjeðːi ˈeura ˈsɔmi]
> tavvi kisi-il jeḍḍ-i eura-Ø somi-Ø
> as quick-ADV run-ASS.CONCL.ITR few-AGT man-AGT
> 'few a man runs as quickly'

nuhlami eumo sõkko tavvi kisil jeḍḍotiśimo
[ˈnuɬːami ˈeumo ˈsɔ̃ʔko ˈtʰawːi ˈcʰisɪl ˈjeðːɔtɕiɕimɔ]
n<uhl>-a-mi eu-mo som-ko tavvi kisi-il jeḍḍ-ot-i-śi-m-o
see.PERF-ASS.CONCL.TR-1P.AG.SG few-GEN man-GEN as quick-ADV run-COMPLE-ITR-HABIL-INCONCL-AGT.PART.AGT
'I've seen few a man able to run as quickly'

QUANTIFIER	ADJECTIVAL QUANTIFIER (MARKED FORM)	VERBAL QUANTIFIER
kolla 'much, a lot'	komma	kommen, kommil

kolla hama sara
[ˈkʰɔlːa ˈhama ˈsara]
kolla-Ø h-a-m-a sara-Ø
much-AGT eat-TR-INCONCL-AGT.PART.UNAG.AG good-AGT
'eating much is good' (saying)

komma irela
[ˈkʰɔmːa ˈirela]
ko=mma irela-Ø
much-GEN beautiful-AGT
'very beautiful'

QUANTIFIER	ADJECTIVAL QUANTIFIER (MARKED FORM)	VERBAL QUANTIFIER
mòs 'slightly, a little'	mòhhi, mòhko	miullil, miullen tśut, tśuḥḥu, tśoa

mòhhi sogjon
[ˈmʊːhːi ˈsɔjːɔn]
mò-hhi sogjon-Ø
slight-GEN dry-AGT
'slightly dry'

nami mòhhi oummia
[ˈnami ˈmʊːhːi ˈɔumːia]
n-a-mi mò-hhi=i ou<mm>a
COP.INCONCL.ASS-1P.AG.SG slight-GEN hook-INESS
'I have a slight problem' (lit. I'm in a slight hook)

QUANTIFIER	ADJECTIVAL QUANTIFIER (MARKED FORM)	VERBAL QUANTIFIER
tśůġġen tśuġġon '(a) little'	tśůġġes tśuġġonta	miullil, miullen tśut, tśuḥḥu, tśoa

tsŭġġes istaki
['tɕøxːɛs ɪˈstaɟi]
tsŭġġe-s i-s<Ø>t-a-ki-Ø
little-GEN ASS.PART DIT-give.PAST-ASS.TR-1P.RECI.SG-3P.AG.SG
'X gave me a little'

QUANTIFIER	ADJECTIVAL QUANTIFIER (MARKED FORM)	VERBAL QUANTIFIER
edlen	edles, elles	Ø[1]
'quite'		

edles atana
[ˈetɬɛs ˈɑtɑnɑ]
edle-s atana-Ø
quite-GEN big-AGT
'quite big'

QUANTIFIER	ADJECTIVAL QUANTIFIER (MARKED FORM)	VERBAL QUANTIFIER
seppi	seppen	Ø
'very, exceedingly, quite (the)'		

seppi sira
[ˈsɛʔpi ˈsira]
seppi-Ø sira-Ø
quite-AGT fish-AGT
'quite the fish'

sira seppen atana
[ˈsira ˈsɛʔpɛn ˈɑtɑnɑ]
sira-Ø sepp-en atana-Ø
fish-AGT quite-GEN big-AGT
'quite a big fish'

QUANTIFIER	ADJECTIVAL QUANTIFIER (MARKED FORM)	VERBAL QUANTIFIER
koahi	koakka	koakken, koakkil
'enough, well'		kvakken, kvakkil

negami koahi
[ˈnegɑmi ˈkʰɔɑʔi]
n<eg>-a-mi koahi-Ø
see.PAST-ASS.CONCL.TR-1P.AG.SG enough-DAT
'I saw enough'

---

[1] More conservative dialects also allow a verbal quantifier with varied forms such as *elhen*, *elhil* and *ędlę* which can usually be translated to 'quite a lot' or 'verily'.

koakka negami
['kʰɔaʔka 'negɑmi]
koa-kka n<eg>-a-mi
enough-GEN see.PAST-ASS.CONCL.TR-1P.AG.SG
'I saw enough'

koakka atana
['kʰɔaʔka 'atɑna]
koa-kka atana-Ø
enough-GEN big-AGT
'big enough'

QUANTIFIER	ADJECTIVAL QUANTIFIER (MARKED FORM)	VERBAL QUANTIFIER
kekki 'too'	kekken	kekken, kekkil ket, keḥḥe, kekli

kekken atana
['cʰɛʔcɛn 'atɑna]
kekk-en atana-Ø
too-GEN big-AGT
'too big'

§5.11.1 Comparative and Superlative

Non-numeral quantifiers have comparative and superlative forms that are irregularly derived. Note that *tsúġġen/tsúġġon* and *mós* have a common comparative and superlative form. This excludes verbal quantifiers, whose comparative and superlative forms are shown in section *§6.4*.

quantifier	comparative	superlative
taja 'much'	*tata* (GEN. *tadna/tabmo*) 'more'	*talla* (GEN. *tahla*) 'most'
tama 'many'	*tonda* (GEN. *tondanna/tondammo*) 'more'	*tabba* (GEN. *tahpa*) 'most'
euma 'little'	*onda* (GEN. *ondanna/ondammo*) 'less'	*olla* (GEN. *uhla*) 'less'

quantifier	comparative	superlative
eura 'few'	ohta (GEN. ohtanna/ ohtammo) 'fewer'	olra (GEN. ouhra) 'fewest'
kolla 'much, a lot'	kvolda (GEN. kvoldanna/ kvoldammo) 'more'	kvobba (GEN. kvohpa or kvolra) 'most'
mȯs 'slight'	miudna (GEN. miudnanna/ miudnammo) 'a little less'	miudla (GEN. miuhla) 'least'
tśu̇ġġen / tśu̇ġġon 'slight, little'		
koahi 'well, enough'	koatta (GEN. koattanna/ koattammo) 'better, more enough'	kodla (GEN. kuhla) 'best, most enough'

The form *koatta* is generally only found in comparisons and usually means 'even more', while *kodla* similarly is usually translated as 'the very most'.

negami on koahi, nega ka koatta ataka te nega taga kodla kȧmaka
[ˈnegamiɔ̃ ˈkʰɔaʔi ˈnegaka ˈkʰɔaʔta ˈataga de ˈnegadaga ˈkʰɔt╪a ˈcʰæːmaga]
n<eg>-a-mi on koahi-Ø, n<eg>-a ka koa-tta ata-Ø-ka te n<eg>-a taga kodla-Ø kȧma-Ø-ka
see.PAST-ASS.CONCL.TR-1P.AG.SG ON enough-DAT see.PAST-ASS.CONCL.TR KA enough-COMP father-AG-1P.PAT.SG and see.PAST-ASS.CONCL.TR TAGA enough-SUP paternal.grandfather-AG-1P.PAT.SG
'while I saw enough/a lot, my father saw even more and my grandfather saw the most'

§6 Adverbs

Adverbs in Siwa can be found with various endings. They can be formed from preexisting stems or words, most commonly adjectives, verbs and least commonly nouns. The main marker for adverbs of manner is -en or -il, with variation in surface form. Other types of adverb include spacial/directional adverbs, temporal adverbs, quantitative adverbs as well as other types.

Adverbs come before the adjective or verb they describe. Adverbial phrases have the same order as nominal phrases, but the adverbs always come last.

>njuhhi ⌜ koba nibma oakima tuvavven ⌝ aiteilotima
>[ˈɲuhːi ˈkʰɔbaˈniːʔpma ˈɔaɟima ˈtʰuvɑwːɛn ˈaideilɔtɕima]
>njuhhi-Ø ko-ba nibma oaki=ma tuva-vven aiteil-ot-i-m-a
>old.woman-AGT summer-GEN over home-ADESS heavy-ADV be.severely.sick-COMPLE-ITR-INCONCL-ACT.PART.UNAG
>'the old woman (who has been) ⌜at home heavily sick over the summer⌝'

§6.1 Adverbial Form of Adjectives

All adjectival forms can be turned into adverbs. The process is regular for adjectives of the types described above. The basic adverbial marker is -en or in certain cases and widely in eastern dialects, -il (variants: -el, -ilda, -elda, -ir, -is) which may polarize the preceding vowel. Certain adjective endings are deleted completely before -il. Below is a table illustrating the most common adjectival endings and their corresponding adverbial forms. Both -il and -en forms are equally common, though -il forms may be considered to belong to a higher language register. Adjectives in -e/-u/-i lack -il endings

Certain adjectives can be used as adverbs by using locative endings directly onto the stem without using the marked form:

>kàhloita   'high' (to grow high)
>kàhlokita   'to the high one' (see §5.3.2).

adjectival	adverbal	example
-na	-i or -il	*atana* 'big' → *atai* 'largely'
-la	-v(v)en	*tuvala* 'heavy' → *tuvavven* 'heavily'
-ot/-ut	-en / -(V)ɥen or -il	*horiot* 'tender' → *horiɥen/ horil* 'tenderly'
-on	-en or -il	*sogjon* 'dry' → *sogjen/ sogjil* 'dryly'

adjectival	adverbal	example
-in	-en or -il	*olmin* 'stiff'→ *olmen/olmil* 'stiffly'
-ųe/-ve	-ven/ųen or -ůl	*ůilve* 'pungent'→ *ůilen/ůilůl* 'pungently'
-(p)po	-(p)pen	*keheppo* 'sulky'→ *keheppen* 'sullenly'
-hi	-hen	*sipohi* 'confused'→ *sipohen* 'confusedly'
-ra	-ren or -il	*kilura* 'wooden'→ *kiluren/kiluril* 'woodenly'
-ka/-ko	-ken or -kil	*somuka* 'masculine'→ *somuken/somukil* 'masculinely'
-na/-no	-nen or -gjil / -il	*śainno* 'courageous'→ *śainnen/śaigjil* 'courageously'
-ha/-ho	-hen or -gjil	*jůliha* 'sweaty'→ *jůlihen/jůligjil* 'sweatily'
-V -m- + -V	(BV)-vven or -gjil	*longiu* 'icy'→ *longiuvven/longiugjil* 'icily'
-bmot	-mmen or -mmil	*pittabmot* 'attentive'→ *pittammen/pittammil* 'attentively'
-bmis	-mmen or -mmil	*koahibmis* 'sufficient'→ *koahimmen/koahimmil* 'sufficiently'
-mma or -ppa	-mmen / -ppen or -mmil / -ppil	*kjuomśimma* 'someone from Kjuomśin'→ *kjuomśimmen* 'in the way of someone from Kj.'
-tse	-tsven	*uitse* 'aquatic'→ *uitsven* 'aquatically'

adjectival	adverbal	example
-us(e)	-usven	*keltaus* 'terrestrial'→ *keltausven* 'terrestrially'
-nihta	-nihten	*konihta* 'one summer long/old'→ *konihten* 'in the way of someone which is one summer long/old'
-dna	-dnen or -dnil	*kiludna* 'woody'→ *kiludnen/kiludnil* 'woodily'
-ġlen	-ġlenen or -ġlil	*tulvuġlen* 'lacking in nutrients'→ *tulvuġlenen/tulvuġlil* 'in a way lacking nutrients'
-ke	-kven	*garike* 'boyish'→ *garikven* 'boyishly'
-lu	-len	*boahlu* 'daily'→ *boahlen* 'daily'
-(s)ġi	-(s)ġen	*taintsġi* 'numerous'→ *taintsġen* 'numerously'
-(s)ġa	-(s)ġen or -(s)ġil	*deusġa* 'flexible'→ *deusġen/deusġil* 'flexibly'
-bmi	-mmen	*soakubmi* 'cozy'→ *soakummen* 'cozily'
-hma or -htsa	-hmen / -htsen or -hmil / -htsil	*huvvuhma* 'cool'→ *huvvuhmen/huvvuhmil* 'coolly'
-ppa/-ppi	-ppen or -ppil	*ijeppi* 'sticky'→ *ijeppen/ijeppil* 'stickily'

Adjectives which do not fit the types above usually simply get -**en**, which deletes any final vowel. Consonant-Final adjectives simply get -i(l).

mybi	'silent'	→	*myben*	'silently'
ymy	'horrible'	→	*ymen*	'horribly'
aji	'clear'	→	*ajen*	'clearly'

| heje | 'cold' | → | hejen | 'coldly' |
| gigjes | 'sharp' | → | gigjesil | 'sharply' |

Adjectives ending in -t (other than -ot) or ending in -dno/-dna have the adverbial form -ddil/-dden.

nėut	'wet'	→	nėudden/nėuddil	'wetly'
neidno	'wise'	→	neidden/neiddil	'wisely'
ůrkůt	'related, similar'	→	ůrkůdden/ůrkůddil	'relatedly, similarly'

Note that adjectives of the subtype -nna have -gjil/-gjen.

voanna	'strange'	→	voagjen/voagjil	'strangely'
hanna	'pretty'	→	hagjen/hagjil	'nicely'
hjȯnna	'careful'	→	hjȯgjen/hjȯgjil	'carefully'

The adverbial form of adjectives is regularly used with certain verb of seeming, looking or otherwise feeling X. They are particularly prone to having -il instead of -en; e.g.

gjosil mageki	'I seem tired' (lit. I seem tiredly)
hagjil sageki	'you look/seem pretty' (lit. you seem nicely)
kiludnil ėhhjeni	'X smells like wood' (lit. X smells woodenly)

§6.2 Adverbial Form of Verbs

Verbs can form adverbs in three ways; by turning active participles into adverbs (-ō, cf. -oma), by changing infinitive endings into verbal adverbs (-ōren, -osġen, -edlen cf. -mi -sa -lu), or by turning patientive participles into adverbs (-uvven, cf. -u).

§6.2.1 Participial Adverbs

Participial adverbs can be regularly formed from verbs. Their ending is -ō (or -ḥō after vowels). Their negative counter part is -eddō. This type of adverb is usually derived from intransitive verbs and corresponds to the function of adverbial gerunds (such as those ending in -ingly in English). These participial adverbs are synonymous to constructions with mi/avvi.

geki	'X will seem'	→	gekō	'seemingly'
hejoli	'X will shiver'	→	hejolō	'shivering(ly)'
ivi	'X will increase'	→	iviḥō	'increasingly'
lialsei	'X will drift'	→	lialseḥō	'adrift'
rada	'X will cease Y'	→	radeddō	'inceasingly'

kẹmesil gekõ pendi
['cʰæmesɪl 'ɟekõ 'pʰɛndʑii]
kẹmes-il gek-õ pe<nd>-i-Ø
happy-ADV seem-ADV arrive.PAST-ASS.CONCL.ITR-3P.AG.SG
'X arrived seemingly happy'
(same as *kẹmesil avvi geki a, pendi*)

ivihõ tsepu̇
['ivi?õ 'tsepu:]
ivi-hõ tsepu-u
increase-ADV CLEAR.OF.SNOW-COP.ASS.TRANSL
'it is becoming increasingly snowless'

alahrakima lialsehõ suddju holokkes
['alahraɟima 'lɪalse?õ 'sudʑ:u 'hɔlɔʔcɛs]
alahra-k=ima lialse-hõ su<ddj>-u holokke-s
floating.log-ADESS drift-ADV move.away.PAST-ASS.CONCL.TRANSL dragonfly-PAT
'the dragonfly was moving away adrift a floating log'

§6.2.2 Verbal Adverbs

A second class of adverbs formed from verbs can be found in Siwa called verbal adverbs. They can be formed from both agentive and patientive participles. Such adverbs are descriptive of the way with or by which the action is realized ('by VERB-ing'). Endings are valency dependent, having three forms.

TRANSITIVE	-õren[1]	or -enra
INTRANSITIVE	-osġen	or -esġa
TRANSLATIVE	-edlen	or -elra

bůlka	'X will preserve Y'	→	*bůlkõren*	'by preserving'
heja	'X will feed Y'	→	*hejõren*	'by feeding'
jairi	'X will row'	→	*jairosġen*	'by rowing'
kisġili	'X will work fast'	→	*kisġilosġen*	'by working fast'
ta·tśoairu	'X will rot'	→	*tśoairedlen*	'by rotting'
t·sadlu	'X will burn'	→	*sadledlen*	'by burning'

---

[1] The form *-õrõ* is also found instead.

kieskŏren kesajo
['cʰɪɛskɔ̄rɛn 'cʰɛsɑjɔ]
kiesk-ŏren kes-a-Ø-jo
watch-ADV.TR learn-ASS.CONCL.TR-3P.PAT-4.AG
'one learns by watching'

sihhjuita tvůtsti tsġiauḍḍi soprŏren euka tsġiandi iskigi
['sihːjuidɑ 't<super>h</super>vœtstːi 'tsxiɑuðːi 'sɔpxɔ̄rɛn 'eugɑ 'tsxɪɑndʑi 'iːsciji]
sihhju-ita tvůd=tsi tsġiau-ḍḍi sopr-ŏren euk-a tsġiam-di iski-Ø-gi
length-ILLAT down=along cedar.wood-GEN split-ADV.TR produce-ASS.CONCL.TR cedar.strip-GEN woman-AGT-PL
'by splitting cedar wood down along its length, the women produce **tsġiame** (cedar strips for weaving)'

Patientive participles derive their adverbial form by changing -u to -ubil or -uvven.

ayḍgubil~ayḍguvven lolnoskui jålppi
'the hare escaped wounded (lit. woundedly)'

§6.3 Adverbial Form of Non-Numeral Quantifiers

Here is a list of the adverbial quantifiers (also called verbal quantifiers), which are forms used to qualify verbs.[1] Adverbial quantifiers often trigger transitivity without actually being counted in the verb's valency. Some verbs are not affected by this however, such as *kòi* 'speak'.

quantifier	adverbial form
taja 'much'	*tagjen* or *tagjil* 'much'
	tagjil koki ['tʰɑjːɪl 'kʰɔci] ta=gjil k<ok>-i-Ø much-ADV speak.PAST-ASS.CONCL.ITR-3P.AG.SG 'X spoke a lot'
	eukken~ůkken or *eukkil* or *ůkli* 'a little'

---

[1] *tsůġ~tsůġ* is found parallel to **miullen~miullil** in lower registers.

quantifier	adverbial form
euma 'little'	*eukken huhri gatta* ['ɛʊʔcɛn 'hʊhri 'gaʔta] eu=kken hu‹hr›-i ga-tta little-ADV shine.PAST-ASS.CONCL.ITR moon-PAT 'the moon shone a little'
kolla 'much, a lot'	*kommen* or *kommil* 'much, a lot'
	kommen sihhi ['kʰɔmːɛn 'sihːi] ko=men sihh-i much-ADV rain-ASS.CONCL.ITR 'it is about to rain a lot'
mȯs 'slight' *tsu̇ġġen / tsu̇ġġon* 'slight, little'	*miullen, miullil, tsut, tsoa* 'a little'
	miullil suimi ['miulːɪl 'suimi] miullil s‹u›-i-mi little-ADV understand.PAST-1P.AG.SG 'I understood a little'
koahi 'well, enough'	*koakken~kvakken* or *koakkil* 'well, enough'
	koakkil mihkehi ['kʰɔaʔcɪl 'miːhcehi] koa=kkil mihkeh-i well-ADV be.frosty-ASS.CONCL.ITR 'it is quite/well frosty (enough)'

§6.4 Comparative and Superlative

Like adjectives, adverbs may be found in the comparative or the superlative. These are very regularly formed from their regular adverbial forms by adding **-ne** for the comparative and **-oba** for the superlative:

adverb	comparative (-ne)	superlative (-oba)
śaigjil 'courageously'	śagjine 'more courageously'	śaigjioba 'most courageously'
tuvavven 'heavily'	tuvavvine 'more heavily'	tuvavvioba 'most heavily'
męrail 'with difficulty'	męraine 'with more difficulty'	męraioba / męrajoba 'with most difficulty'
neiddil 'wisely'	neiddine 'more wisely'	neiddioba 'most wisely'

Adverbs derived from verbs through -õ have the comparative -õdne and the superlative -õba.

adverb	comparative	superlative
besġõ 'peacefully'	besġõdne 'more peacefully'	besġõba 'most peacefully'
elõ 'growingly'	elõdna 'more growingly'	elõba 'most growingly'
gekõ 'seemingly'	gekõdne 'more seemingly'	gekõba 'most seemingly'

Irregular adverbial comparatives and superlatives include (excluding adverbs formed from the irregular genitive of comparative/superlative adverbs);

adverb	comparative	superlative
salla 'well'	sahne 'better'	sagjoba / saiba 'best'
sůppi 'badly'	sůdne 'worse'	sůiba 'worst'

Adverbial non-numeric quantifiers are also irregular:

quantifier	comparative	superlative
tagjen or *tagjil* 'much'	*tainne* 'more'	*taiba* 'most'
eukken~ůkken or *eukkil~ůkli* 'little'	*ůkne* 'less'	*ůihba* 'least'
kommen or *kommil* 'much, a lot'	*kelme / komne* 'more'	*keilba / kõuba* 'most'
miullen or *miullil* 'a little'	*mylne / můlne* 'a little less'	*mylba / můlba* 'least'
koakken~kvakken or *koakkil* 'well, enough'	*koakne* 'better, more enough'	*koaiba* 'best, most enough'

A comparative construction that relates to adverbs is of the type 'the more X, the more Y', which in Siwa is:

∅-te tavvi da, ∅-te tainne da

hate tavvi dami, pohhjite tainne daka
'the more I eat, the more I sleep'

§6.5 Locative Adverbs/Postpositions

Locative adverbs may stand on their own or follow a noun. In the latter case, the adverbs function as/are considered postpositions, and thus follow the noun they qualify, which is in either the locative for destinal adverbs (those which show a movement to a destination) and in the genitive for directional adverbs (those which show a movement to a general direction) and most other postpositions. Postpositions follow a noun, but if a noun is qualified by an adjective or the noun phrase extends after the noun, postpositions may intersect the noun phrase by coming directly after the noun, or they may simply be found at the very end of longer noun phrases:

kvylhi sikven ġilkadi **gala**   'with bright yellow little flowers'
kvylhi **gala** *sikven ġilkadi*   'id.'

Below is a summary of the most common locative adverbs. Note that adverbs have a nominal form, which may be used as a common noun then meaning 'the place X', or may differ in meaning slightly from other similar forms of the adverb, e.g. *katama* (nominal form) and *katśa* are both translated as 'outside', but *katama* means 'outdoors' (i.e. no specific location, then functioning as an adverb) while *katśa* means outside (of something) and the nominal form in a locative case, e.g. *katakkia* 'in the space outside of X'. The nominal form can stand on its own as a noun or a postposition, then meaning something like 'the place behind/above/etc.', e.g., *loalla* 'behind' becomes *soakka loalakia* 'in the place behind the house'.

Most special adverbs exist in three forms for direction to and from, as well as a static form. The three forms are simple movement (to for direction to, and from for direction from), an approximate movement (towards) and a movement along. Only the adverbs 'up' and 'down' have a destinal forms. All other adverbs have one general form (directional).

Postpositions are found after nouns in the genitive or a locative case, but when a personal pronoun is found with a postposition, either the recipient personal endings or the hyphened personal endings are found as clitics to the noun (see §9.3.2). Possessive personal pronouns are more complete, and for that reason sometimes preferred over recipient personal endings.

		recipient	possessive
1P.	SG.	·ki	-go
	PL. INCL	·bi	-ura
	PL. EXCL		-uri
2P.	SG.	·s(i)	-so
	PL.	·hi	-si
3P.	SG. ANI	·ti or ·tsi	-ho
	SG. INA		-ha
	PL.		-hi
	OBV.	·s(i)	-hon
4P.		·n(i)	-nen

ilta·ki	or	*ilta-go*	'to(wards) me'
ilta·bi	or	*ilta-uri*	'to(wards) us'
kika·ti	or	*kika-hi*	'over it/them'
ůrja·si	or	*ůrja-so*	'close to you'

Poetic language and the more conservative dialects allow special postpositional forms. These forms distinguish fewer persons, lacking a clear distinction between the first and second person singular[1], and having only one form for the third person (no obviative or plural distinction). Postpositions ending in -a often combine with the i- of these endings to simply form -e-.

1P.SG	-is/-iṡ
1P.PL	-iu/-iŭ
2P.SG	-is
2P.PL	-i
3P.	-id
4P.	-in

ilta·is	'to(wards) me/you'	(also **iltes**)
ilta·iu	'to(wards) us'	(also **ilteu**)
kika·i	'over you (pl)'	(also **kike**)
ůrja·id	'close to it/them'	(also **ůrjed**)
gala·in	'with oneself'	(also **galen**)

The forms for the third and fourth person are more common in normal speech than the other markers.

§6.5.1 Cardinal Directions

Adverbs indicating cardinal directions in Siwa exist for 8 directions (all 4 main directions and 4 compound directions). Adverbs of cardinal direction have special compound forms used when the direction is integrated into another word. Like the other spacial adverbs, cardinal directions are found in 8 other forms;

nominal
static
movement to
movement towards
movement from
movement along

The dialects of the east have an additional form, the combination of the 'from' form as the stem and the ending -ri of the 'towards' form, meaning then 'from roughly X'. Cardinal directions are fairly irregular in their patterns, especially in the formation of the noun nominal and locative forms and the compound form.

---

[1] The lack of distinction between the first and second person is a typical trait of older or higher language registers in Siwa.

	noun	static	to	towards	along	from
north	sibema (GEN. sibekka)	biekkia	biehta	biehteri	bentsi	biehka
south	siseri (GEN. sisehdi)	siehdia	siehta	siehteri	siehtsi	siehka
east	takęna (GEN. takekka)	kękia	keuhta	keuhteri	keuhtsi	keuhka
west	tona (GEN. tomma)	jikia	jihta	jihteri	jihtsi	jihka
north-east	benka (GEN. benkari)	benkaśa	benkahta	benkahteri	benkahtsi	benkahka
south-east	sehka (GEN. sehkari)	sehkaśa	sehkahta	sehkahteri	sehkahtsi	sehkahka
north-west	bůgji (GEN. bůjima)	bůimi	bůinda	bůinderi	bůintsi	bůinka
south-west	siarji (GEN. siarjid)	siarja	siarjata	siarjateri	siarjatsi	siarjaka

The western dialects have jè- where other dialects have ji- for 'west'.

    The nominal form of cardinal directions are used quite a lot in daily life to refer to various locations. Siwa speakers rely heavily on them for spacial orientation. Most dialects use the **sehka** 'south-east' to mean 'left' and the **siarji** 'south-west' to mean 'right' – unlike in western culture, Siwa people see the world as facing south, from the north. **Siseri** 'south' is thus often used to mean 'front/ahead' or 'down', and **sibema** 'north' is used to mean 'back' or 'behind/up'. People on the eastern dialects generally adhere to the east-left, west-right, south-ahead and north-back format, but western dialects also sometimes use *siseri* 'south' to mean 'left' and *tona* 'west' to mean 'right', as well as *sehka* 'south-west' to mean 'front/ahead' or 'down', and *benka* 'north-east' to mean 'back' or 'behind/up'.

Here is the Siwa compass:

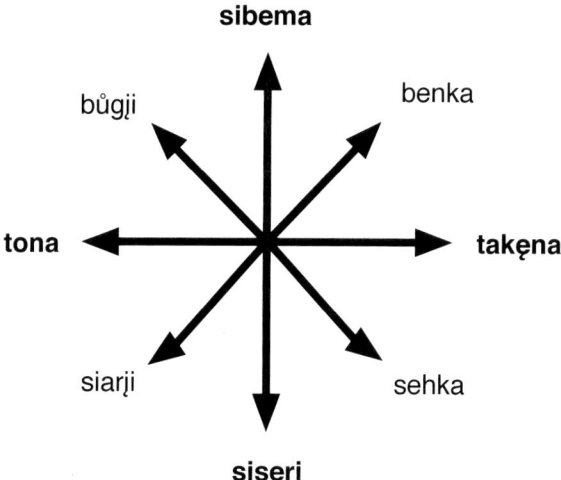

And here are the eastern and western cardinal orientations;

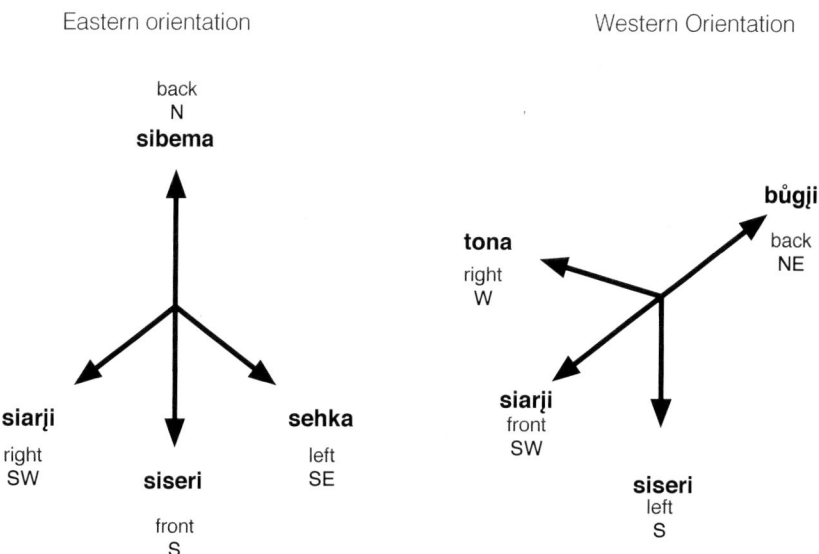

The actual locative forms of cardinal directions are used to refer to literal cardinal directions, while the nominal forms are used for orientation. Compare the following phrases;

> *kodiri siehteri*
> [ˈkʰɔdiri ˈsɪɛhteri]
> ko<d>-i-ri sieht=eri
> walk.PAST-ASS.CONCL.ITR-3P.AG.PL south-TOWARDS
> 'they walked southwards'

> *tuvviri sisehdita*
> [ˈtʰuwːiri ˈsisɛhdʑida]
> tu<vv>-i-ri siser-di=ta
> turn.PAST-ASS.CONCL.TR-3P.AG.PL south-ILLAT
> 'they turned left' (western dialect)

The words for the cardinal directions seem to have originally been descriptive of the movement or location of the sun. The north-south axis has the prefix **si-** (perhaps related to the negation particle *se/set/sem* and -si-, as the sun does not set in the north or the south) while the east-west axis has the prefix **t-** (perhaps originally related to the illative **-ta-**).

The stem for 'north' (**be-/bie-**) can also be seen in the adjective *biehna* 'highest' (not an actual superlative). Similarly, the stem for 'south' (**ser-**) can be seen in the verb *sisi* 'X lies low' and *sianta* 'horizon'. The stem for 'east' (**kek-**) is related to the verb (*o*)*keui* 'X rises', while the stem for 'west' (**jik-**) is related to the verb (*o*)*gjahtsi* 'X lies down'.

§6.5.2 Up and Down

Siwa has two pairs of adverbs to show location up or down - they are the destinal and directional forms. Destinal forms point to a specific destination, whereas direction simply point to a direction. Thus, if the adverb *up* has a specific destination, for example *up on the table*, it will be found in its destinal form, but if *up* is used to mean *upward* or simply *up* without any specific destination, it will be found in its directional form. Destinal forms acting as postpositions usually agree in their locative cases with the head noun, and require the ditransitive with verbs.

Another way of describing the difference between destinal and direction is to imagine that directional adverbs are seen from a static position that only shows where something is headed, whereas destinal adverbs not only show the direction, but also where the movement ends, or reaches its destination.

Compare the following examples:

> *ihàbmui boikibma tvunda hemi*
> [iˈhæːʔpmui ˈbɔiɟɪʔpma ˈtʰvʊnda ˈhemi]
> i-hàbm-u-i bo<Ø>i-k=ibma tvun=da hemi-Ø
> DIT-fly.PAST-ASS.CONCL.ITR branch-ALLAT down.to.DEST bird-AGT
> 'the bird flew down onto the branch' (destinal)

hȧbmui tvǔda hemi
[hæ:ʔpmui 'tʰvøda 'hemi]
hȧbm-u-i tvǔ=da hemi-Ø
fly.PAST-ASS.CONCL.ITR down.to.DIR bird-AGT
'the bird flew down' (directional)

The table bellow illustrates agreement between postposition and noun;

	static	to	towards	along	from
interior	inessive	illative / elative	genitive		elative
surface	adessive	allative / ablative			ablative

Like cardinal directions and other spacial adverbs and/or postpositions, 'up' and 'down' are found in the nominal and compound forms as well as forms for static location, movement to, movement along and movement from. Nominal forms do not differentiate between destinal and directional, and neither do the compound forms.

	noun	compound	static	to	towards	along	from
up destinal	*hemma*	*he-*	*heni*	*henda*	Ø	Ø	*henga*
up directional			*hey*	*heyta*	*heytari*	*heytsti*	*heyka*
down destinal	*tvǔmma*	*tvu-*	*tvuni*	*tvunda*	Ø	Ø	*tvunga*
down directional			*tvǔ*	*tvǔda*	*tvǔdari*	*tvǔtsti*	*tvǔga*

The directional **from** forms have come to mean 'up above' and 'down below'.

heni	'up in/on'	*tahhia heni*	'up in the tree'
henda	'up (to)'	*tahhita henda*	'up into the tree'
henga	'from up in/on'	*tahhika henga*	'from up in the tree'
heyta	'up (to)'	*tahhi heyta*	'up the tree'
heyka	'up above'	*tahhi heyka*	'up above the tree'
tvuni	'down in/on'	*tahhia tvuni*	'down in the tree'
tvunda	'down (to)'	*tahhita tvunda*	'down into the tree'

tvŭnga	'from down'	tahhika tvŭnga	'from down in the tree'
tvŭda	'down (to)'	tahhi tvŭda	'down the tree'
tvŭga	'down below'	tahhi tvŭga	'down below the trees'

The destinal forms for static, movement to and from here can be taken to mean 'up on' (i.e. up on a surface) and 'under' (i.e. under a surface).

peymmibma henda
['pʰɛœm:ʔpma hɛnda]
peyma-mi=bma henda
table-ALLAT up.to.DEST
'up onto the table'

hoahkima tvuni
['hɔahcima 'tʰvuni]
hoari-k=ima tvuni
hull-ADESS down.DEST
'under the hull' (i.e. on the outside of the hull)

Similarly, the directional forms simply mean 'up (in the air)' and 'below (the surface)':

hȧbmui heyta 'X flew up'[1]

The directional static form *hey* is restricted in use and commonly appears in:

rekkes hey	'(up) in the sky)'
oimmo hey	'up in smoke' (vanished, disappeared)
hŭbŭ hey	'up in vapour' (id.)

The towards form are quite straight-forward. Directional forms *tvŭdari* and *heytari* mean 'downward' and 'upward'.

Note that *tvŭdari* (sometimes *tvŭari*) is used to mean 'out to sea/away from land' and *heytari* mean 'landward, up land'. The special form *tvŭdairi* is used to mean 'on board', or to ask if everyone is safe in a boat before leaving show, hence the verb *o·tvŭd·i* (tvŭd-)'X embarks' and the use of *tvŭmamoja* (inessive of *tvŭmma*) to mean 'safe' or 'in a secure position/state/place'.

Similarly, the special form *heytairi* means 'on land' (as in 'out of a boat/canoe' or 'home from fishing'), the verb *o·heyt·i* (heyt-) means to 'disembark' or 'come to land' and *hęmaria* means 'on land/at home/come back from fishing'. Some dialects also use *hęmaria* to mean 'at home from hunting'. For this reason, Siwa people nearly

---

[1] The forms *hȧbmui heyta* and *hęhȧbmui* are nearly identical in meaning. The independent directional adverb *heyta* is more emphatic.

always refer to going out to fish or hunt as going 'down to fish or hunt' (*sitkista tvǔda/ mahhanta tvǔda*), and coming home or coming back is come 'up home' (*oakibma heyta*).

The nominal forms are used to mean 'the space up/down' and may be equivalent to English 'the upper/lower part/space/etc.', e.g. *da hẹmaria tahhi hemi*, lit. 'the bird is in the up of the tree' meaning 'the bird is in the upper part of the tree' or possibly 'the bird is in the safety of the tree'.

Below are more examples:

hẹmarika tvǔmimoibma
[ˈhæmɑriga ˈtʰvømimːɔɪʔpma]
hẹ<m>a-r=ika tvǔmi-mo=ibma
up-ELAT down-ALLAT
'from top to bottom'

tvǔmimoima
[ˈtʰvømimɔima]
tvǔmi-mo=ima
down-ADESS
'at the bottom'

tahhia hẹni
[ˈtʰɑhːia ˈhæni]
tahh-i=a hẹni
tree-INESS up.DEST
'up in a tree'

kamjokima tvuni
[ˈkʰɑmjɔɟima ˈtʰvuni]
ka<m>jo-k=ima tvuni
frozen.lake-ADESS down.DEST
'down on a frozen lake'

tahhita henda
[ˈtʰɑhːida ˈhɛnda]
tahh-i=ta henda
tree-ILLAT up.to.DEST
'up into the tree'

risoita tvunda
[ˈrisɔida ˈtʰvʊnda]
riso-i=ta tvun=da
sandy.ground-ILLAT down.to.DEST
'down onto the ground/ sand'

rjaubba heytari
[ˈrjɑupːa ˈhɛœdɑri]
rja<ubba>- heytari
hips-ILLAT up.towards
'(water/sand/dirt) up to the hips'

hois tvǔdari
[ˈhɔis ˈtʰvødɑri]
ho<Ø>e-s= tvǔdari
groin-ILLAT down.towards.DEST
'down towards the groin'

kolmo heytsti
[ˈkʰɔlmɔ ˈhɛœtstːi]
kola-mo heytsti
esker-GEN up.along.DEST
'up along the esker'

gekkos tvǔtsti
[ˈɟɛʔkɔs ˈtʰvœtstːi]
gekko-s tvǔtsti
slope-GEN down.along.DEST
'down along the slope'

tahhika henga
[ˈtʰɑːhːiga ˈhɛŋːa]
tahh-i=ka henga
tree-ELAT up.from.DEST
'from up in the tree'

ġolkoibma tvunga
[ˈxɔlkɔɪʔpma ˈtʰvuŋːa]
ġoli-ko=ibma tvunga
hill-ALLAT down.from.DEST
'from down on the hill'

rekkes hey
[ˈrɛʔces ˈhɛœ]
rekke-s hey
sky-GEN up.DIRECT
'up in the sky'

gekkos tvů
[ˈɟɛʔkɔs ˈtʰvø]
gekko-s tvů
slope-GEN down.DIRECT
'down in the slope'

tahhi heyta
[ˈtʰɑhːi ˈhɛœda]
tahh-i heyta
tree-GEN up.to.DIRECT
'up the tree'

ehhakka tvůda
[ˈehːaʔka ˈtʰvøda]
ehham-ka tvůda
seam-GEN down.to.DIRECT
'down the seam'

jaśid heytari
[ˈjaɕiːdʑ ˈhɛœdari]
jaśi<Ø>i-d heytari
old.age-GEN up.towards.DIRECT
'up to/until senility'

hůśmo tvůdari
[ˈhœsmɔ ˈtʰvødari]
hůhhj-mo tvůdari
heron-GEN down.towards.DIRECT
'down to the heron'

baletta heytsti
[ˈbalɛʔta ˈhɛœtstːi]
balet-ta heytsti
flank-GEN up.along
'up along the flank'

jeigeri tvůtsti
[ˈjeiɣeri ˈtʰvœtstːi]
jei<g>e-ri tvůtsti
snow.trench-GEN down.along
'down along the snow trench'

tahhi heyka
[ˈtʰɑhːi ˈhɛœga]
tahh-i heyka
tree-GEN up.from.DIRECT
'up above the tree'

ġolko tvůga
[ˈxɔlkɔ ˈtʰvøga]
ġoli-ko tvůga
hill-GEN down.from.DIRECT
'down (below) the hill'

§6.5.3 Over and Under

The words for 'over' and 'under' in Siwa only exist in one form – destinal and directional are not distinguished in this case.

Like cardinal directions and other spacial adverbs and/or postpositions, 'over' and 'under' are found in the nominal forms as well as forms for static location, movement to, movement along and movement from.

	noun	static	to	towards	along	from
over	kikama	kika	kihta	kihtairi	kihtsi	kikka
under	umna	unnja	unta	untairi	untsi	unka

Neither word especially distinguishes between contact or lack thereof. Thus, *uki kika* may mean 'over the lake (i.e. on the water)' or 'over the lake (up in the air)'.

tokoma kikandia
[ˈtʰɔkɔma ˈcʰikandʑia]
to<k>o-ma kikam-di=a
tree.trunk-GEN over-INESS
'(in the) upper part of the trunk'

voamma umnamima
[ˈvɔɑmːa ˈʊmnːɑmima]
v<oav>-ma umna-m=ima
lake-GEN under-ADESS
'on the lower part of the lake'

todatta-so kika
[ˈtʰɔdaʔtasɔ ˈcʰika]
to<da>-tta–so kika
head-GEN=2P.POSS.SG over
'over your head'

tobo unnja
[ˈtʰɔbɔ ˈuɲːa]
t<obo> unnja
rock-GEN under
'under a rock'

soakka kihta
[ˈsɔaʔka ˈcʰɪhta]
soaki-ka kihta
house-GEN over.to
'over the house'

kůimpa mihu unta
[ˈcʰœɪmpa ˈmiːʔu ˈʊnta]
kůimpa mi=hu unta
boots-AGT feet-GEN under.to
'a pair of boots for (lit. under) feet'

The *towards* form are more general in meaning, used especially abstractly. The form *kihtairi*, for example, is often used to mean 'over, too much, too far/high, passed a set goal/location':

maskigge kihtairi   'we went over (i.e. too far)'

Similarly, **untairi** means 'under, not enough, not far enough, too low':

siksui untairi   'you shot your arrow too close'
          or   'you missed you target when you shot your arrow'.

| | kōkko kihtairi | 'over the mind (i.e. over the head/not noticed) |
| | iksui måhraka untairi | 'X did not shot far enough to hit the bear' (lit. X shot under the bear) |

The along forms mean 'along the top/surface' for *kihtsi* and 'along the underside/back' for *untsi*:

	da bjenne kihtsi nidagan	'there is a stripe along the top of X's back'.
	ġŭtġŭt keppie kihtsi	'a crest along the top of the head'
	aki moukkiko untsi	'X will cut under along the underside of the belly'

The *from* form of 'under', *unka*, is used to mean 'from under one's feet' or 'without permission' or 'unexpectedly'

| | gidlkui imedi unka | 'the ice broke (through)' (lit. 'from under') |
| | tanantu gogi unka | 'it snapped/broke (in my hands, unexpectedly)'. |

The nominal forms are used to mean 'the space above/below' and may be equivalent to English 'the upper/lower part/space/etc.':

| | kikandia | 'in the sky/heaven' |
| | umnamia | 'in the bowels of the earth/in the part below something'. |

§6.5.4 In, On and Out

The words for 'in', 'on' and 'out' in Siwa only exist in one form – destinal and directional are not distinguished in this case.

Like cardinal directions and other spacial adverbs and/or postpositions, 'in', 'on' and 'out' are found in the nominal form as well as forms for static location, movement to, movement along and movement from.

	noun	static	to	towards	along	from
in	tatama	tatsa/tatśa	tadda	taddairi	tatsti	tatka
on	tamima	tamja	tanta	tantairi	tantsi	tanka
out	katama	katsa/katśa	kadda	kaddairi	katsti	katka

The from form *tatka* means 'out (of the inside of something)' but differs from the forms for 'out' *katama* in that *katama* refers to something being out/outside, and thus *katka* '(from) out' implies movement from the outside of something (into or onto something).

soakka tatśa
['sɔaʔka 'tʰatɕa]
soaki-ka tatśa
house-GEN in
'inside the house'

ila tadda
['ila 'tʰɑt:a]
i-la tadda
dark-GEN in.to
'into the dark'

śines tamja
['ɕinɛs 'tʰamja]
śi<n>e-s tamja
lake-GEN on
'on the lake'

miuhdi tanta
['mɪʊhdʑi 'tʰanta]
miuki-di tanta
bog-GEN on.to
'on(to) the bog'

soakka katśa
['sɔaʔka 'kʰatɕa]
soaki-ka katśa
house-GEN out
'outside the house'

hůnamo kadda
['hu:namɔ 'kʰɑt:a]
hů<n>a-mo kadda
steam.hut-GEN out.to
'out of the steam hut'

The *towards* form are more general in meaning, used especially in an abstract meaning. The form *tantairi*, for example, is often used to describe a movement headed onto something without necessarily reaching a destination or may also describe a downward movement towards a surface:

tůśilbui ůki tantairi sieḍbi   'the eagle glided down over the lake (without touching it)'.

Similarly, *taddairi* means 'towards the inside (without however reaching the destination):

aiga koruri taddairi   'X threw Y at the pot (aiming inside the pot)'

The word *kaddairi* has a similar meaning, but with aim towards the outside.
The *along* forms mean 'along the inside/surface/outside'. The form *tantsi* is often synonymous with the form *kihtsi* given above. While *kihtsi* emphasizes that something is over the top surface, the form *tantsi* emphasizes contact on the surface and may thus be somewhat more common with things 'stuck' to each other:

tsġiamie hoahka tantsi   'cedar strips along the surface of the hull'

Similarly, the form *katsti* means 'on the outer/outside surface' but *untsi* means 'on the lower/bottom surface'.

The *from* form is straightforward. The form *tatka* means 'from the inside (out)', *tanka* means 'off of something' and *katka* means 'from the outside (in)'.

The nominal forms are used to mean 'the space in/on/out' and may be equivalent to English 'the inner/surface part/outer/etc.':

katakkia/katakkima	'on the outside of'
tatakkia	'in inside/guts'
tamikkima	'on the surface of'

§6.5.5 Before, Behind, In The Middle and Through

il-	'before, forward, against'
loal-	'behind, back, in secret'
manj-	'in the middle'
irr-	'through'.

These do not distinguish between destinal or directional. They are found in the nominal form as well as forms for static location, movement to, movement along and movement from.

	noun	static	to	towards	along	from
before	*ilama*	*il*	*ilta*	*iltairi*	*ilsi*	*ilka*
behind	*loalla*	*loagja/ loalja*	*loalta*	*loaltairi*	*loalsi*	*loalka*
middle	*manima/ mamna*	*mannja*	*mantsa*	*mantsairi*	*mantsi/ mantsi*	*mankja*
through	*irrima*	*issa*	*irta*	*irtairi*	*irsi*	*irka*

The static form *il* usually means 'before' (someone/something) or 'in front'. Similarly, *loagja* or *loalja* means 'behind' or 'at the back' and *mannja* simply means 'in the middle', while *issa* means 'through' as in 'having gone through something' (usually implies breaking/piercing through).

soakka il
['sɔaʔka iːl]
soaki-ka il
house-GEN before
'in front of the house'

tokoma loagja
['tʰɔkɔma 'lɔɑjːa]
to<ko>-ma loagja
tree.drunk-GEN behind
'behind the tree trunk'

śines mannja
['ɕinɛs 'mɑɲːa]
śine-s mannja
lake-GEN middle
'in the middle of the lake'
(or 'between the lakes')

jasukka iśśa
['jɑsʊʔka 'iɕːa]
jasum-ka iśśa
skin-GEN through
'through the skin'

The *movement to* forms may have a slightly broader meaning – *ilta* means 'before' or 'in front' but also 'forward' or even 'to' (as in presenting/offering/showing something to someone). The form *loalta* can be taken to mean 'to the back of' or 'behind' and *mantśa* means 'to the middle', especially used to show that something or someone has come somewhere where they shouldn't be, i.e. it may give the sentence a sense of meddling. In this case, it may also have a static meaning:

    gaggani mantśaki   'X will examine my things (without my permission, when X shouldn't)'

The form **irta** can mean 'through' (something) or may also give a sense of trying to complete something (difficult), quite like English:

    śivi irta   'X will remain (through a trial/difficult situation)'
        or   'X will pull through'

If the action has successfully been completed already, the form **irka** is preferred:

    akvi irka   'X remained (through a trial/difficult situation)'
        or   'X pulled through'

The *towards* form are more general in meaning, used especially in an abstract meaning. The form *iltairi*, for example, is often used to describe a movement headed forward necessarily reaching a destination or may also be used to show encouragement:

    iltairi benho   'go/that's it/good dog!'

The form *loaltairi* means 'backwards' both in space and time:

    loaltairi tabmosġen   'thinking back'

The word *loaltairi* may also convey a sense of doing something in the wrong way:

    loaltairi bùntiami śośśi   'I weaved everything wrong'

The word *mantśairi* can mean 'towards the middle' or it may also be used to mean 'roughly half-and-half':

> *gigagge ippŭ mantśairi*   'we shared the **ippŭ** (berries and tallows) equally'.

The form **irtairi** shows a movement through a hole or a passage which is already there, i.e. requires no piercing or creation of space to get through:

> *iddi sorohma atra irtairi*   'the piece fell out (lit. through) of X's mouth (because it was open)'

Similarly, the form *irtairi* may be used to imply that something was done for nothing, was unheard or did not create any reactions:

> *koki irtairi*   'X spoke (but no one listened/heard)'

The along forms mean 'along the front/back/middle':

> *suvvi suingamo ilsi niansodi*   'a creek runs along the front of the ground (we chose to build a house onto)'

The form *irsi* however is fairly restricted and normally applies to sewing, i.e. the line along which one sews:

> *ōde voallami keḍma irsi*   'I still have (to sew) along the shoulders'.

The *from* form is straightforward. The form *ilka* means 'from the front', *loalka* means 'from behind' and *mankja* means 'from the middle'. The form *mankja* also has the meaning of 'barely' or 'by very little'. It can also convey a meaning of something being interrupted:

> *iddi tahhi mankja*   'a tree fell (in the middle of something else happening)'

As it was mentioned above, the form *irka* is used with verbs to show that something difficult was completed successfully. It may also be used to mean 'through' while talking about the other side of thing:

> *so lykie-a irka?*   'did X pierce through? (asking people on the other side of the surface)'.

The nominal forms are used to mean 'the space in front/behind/in the middle/through'. The form *manikkia* may also mean 'stuck between':

> *nama pèuma manikkia*   'I am (stuck) between two logs'

The form *loalkita* can be used to mean 'left behind' or 'left alone' or 'abandoned':

  ubodjaka loalkita   'I was forgotten and left behind/I was abandoned'

The form *irrindia* can also be used to mean 'stuck', but in relation to a passage or a hole:

  natsta irrindia   'X (a needle) is stuck (in leather, for example)'

§6.5.6 At, Near, Away

The Siwa adverbs and/or postpositions in **půh-**, **ůrů-** and **suṡ-** can respectively mean 'at (specific place/level)', 'near/towards' and 'far/away'. They do not distinguish between destinal or directional. They are found in the nominal form as well as forms for static location, movement to, movement along and movement from.

	noun	static	to	towards	along	from
at	půbma	půhja	půtta	půttairi	půtsti	půkka
near	ůrůma	ůrja	ůhta	ůhtairi	ůhtsi	ůhka
far	suṡma	suhhja	suṡta	suṡtairi	suṡṡi	suṡka

The static form *půhja* usually means 'at (a certain point/level/place)'. It can also be found as an adverb meaning 'at the point of/at the moment of/just about':

  půhja middi   'I was just about to fall'

Similarly, *ůrja* means 'near' or 'close to' and *suhhja* means 'away (somewhere)' or '(in the) far away'. It can be used adverbially to mean 'passed away':

  suhhja lolli   'X passed away'.

  sogjudle půhja
  [ˈsoːutɬe ˈpʰø̞ʔja]
  sogj-u-dle půhja
  break-TRANSL-INFI.TRANSL.UNAG.GEN at.point
  'on the verge of breaking'

mõkko ůrįa
['mõʔkɔ 'ørja]
moni-ko ůrįa
path-GEN near
'close to the path'

tśomma suhhįa
['tɕɔm:a 'suh:ja]
tśo\<m\>-ma suhhįa
finger-GEN far
'not at hand' (lit. far from finger)

The *movement to* forms may are *půtta* for 'to (a certain point/level/place)' or can be found as an adverb with certain translative verbs to mean 'reached the point of':

    půtta tanuḍbuġa   'X reached the point of becoming angry'
                or   'X burst out in anger'

The form *ůhta* can be taken to mean 'near (with movement to)' or 'close (with movement to)' but it can also be taken to mean 'towards (the speaker)':

    mansi ůhtaki   'X came over to me'

The form *suśta* means 'far (with movement to' or 'away (with movement to)':

    suśta hàbmiaki hemri   'the bird flock flew out into the far away'

The *towards* form are more general in meaning, used especially in an abstract meaning. The form *půttairi*, for example, is often used to describe a movement headed for a point/level/place without necessarily reaching a destination, or more abstractly – especially with verbs of change or translative verbs and the particle *mes*, '(X is finally) turning into a (real)':

    mikųista půttairi i mes na   '(now) it's turning into a real feast!'
    pungittasta mes půttairi   'it's starting to really pour'

The form *ůhtairi* can mean 'in the general direction of' or more abstractly and in the diminutive form of the verbs '(X is slowly) growing to be/turning out to be':

    ůhtairi obinen mes jela keḍḍa su ůn maihheka-ůt
    'this hunt is turning out to be quite a success'

The word *suśtairi* can mean 'away (with movement to)' for abstract places and it can also be used with a negative particle and a noun to show that the thing should leave/go away:

suśtairi tei myry	'out with the fly!'

The *along* form *půtsti* has taken the specialized meaning of 'in rotation around X':

můrůsti tadatta půtsti sa or	'X is buzzing around X's head' 'X has a crush on Y'

The form **ůhtsi** means 'in the area' or 'somewhere around here':

da tamosi saisla ůhtsi	'X is the best fellow around here'

Similarly, the form **suśsi** means 'somewhere far away':

suśsi tingi	'X lives somewhere far away'

The *from* form *půkka* means 'from a certain point/level/place' or also as an interjection to wish something away:

půkka myry	'woosh, fly!'

The form **ůhka** means 'from near' or 'from close by'. The form **suśka** also has the meaning of 'from far' or 'from far away':

pednidni suśka	'X will return from being far away'

The nominal forms are used to mean 'a certain point/at a place near/the far away'. The form *půmamia* can mean 'on the verge of', while *ůrůmmia* means 'in the vicinity' and *suśmimia* means 'in the distance'.

§6.5.7 Amongst, Next To and At The Edge Of

The Siwa adverbs and/or postpositions in **mum-**, **aro-** and **oahr-** can respectively mean 'amongst', 'next to, 'beside' or 'on the side of' and 'at the edge/tip/end of'. They do not distinguish between destinal or directional. They are found in the nominal and compound forms as well as forms for static location, movement to, movement along and movement from, though *mumna* lacks forms for towards and along. They are;

	noun	static	to	towards	along	from
amongst	mumna	mumma	mubma	Ø	Ø	munka
next to	aroma	arrui/ arria	arta	artairi	aṡṡi	arka
at edge of	oahtsuma	oahtsia/ oahtsa	oahtsta	oahtstairi	oahtsti	oahtska

The static form *mumma* usually means 'amongst' or also 'in X's protection' or 'in X's fathom/arms'. Similarly, *arrui* or *arria* mean 'next to', 'beside' or 'on the side' while *oahtsia* or *oahtsa* means 'at the edge/tip/end of '.

The movement to forms may are *mubma* for 'amongst (movement to)' or 'into X's protection/fathom/arms'. The form *arta* can be taken to mean 'next to (movement to)' or 'to the side of'. The form *oahtsta* means 'to the edge/tip/end of' or adverbially, can also mean 'to the maximum extend of':

    vibmi kykkyma oahtsta   'X screamed at the top of his/her lungs (lit. to the edge of his/her voice)'

Note that *gekkos arrui* means 'side by side'.

    tahhi mubma
    [ˈtʰɑhːi ˈmʊʔpma]
    tahh-i mubma
    tree-GEN amongst
    'among the trees'

    soakka arrui
    [ˈsɔaʔka ˈarːui]
    soaki-ka arrui
    house-GEN next.to
    'next to the house'

    manya oahtsta
    [ˈmɑnwa ˈɔahtstːa]
    man-ya oahts=ta
    world-GEN edge.to
    'to the edge of the world'

The *towards* form are more general in meaning, used especially in an abstract meaning. The word **mun-** lacks a towards form. The form *artaita*, for example, is generally used to compare two things and thus means 'compared to':

> *artaitaki sisutuana*   'compared to me, you are taller'

The form *oahtsti* means 'towards the edge/tip/end of', especially with time periods:

> *koba oahtstairi*   'towards the end of summer'

The *along* form also lacks from the **mun-** paradigm, but the others forms are: *aśśi* to mean 'along X (while being next to it)'. This can be found adverbially to mean that two things are in movement next to each other:

> *kodistari aśśi*   'X were walking side by side'

The form *oahtsti* means 'along the edge/tip/end of'. It is often used with verbs of cutting or slicing to underline the precision of the cut:

> *aḍgi bienne oahtsti*   'X cut right along the back'

The *from* form *munka* means 'amongst (movement from)' and can also be used with verbs of movement to mean that the doer has left an X group for the purpose of the verb:

> *munka tśandaki*   'X left us to go and find Y'

Similarly, *arka* means 'from the side of' or 'from next to' and *oahtska* means 'from the edge/point/end of'.

The nominal forms are used to mean 'the place amongst/next to/at the edge/tip/end'. The form *mumnimia* can mean 'in the embrace of' or 'secure amongst', while *arokkima* means 'on the side of' and *oahtsukkia* means 'at the very edge/tip/end', while *oahtsukkita* or *oahtsukkika/oahtsugga* means 'to the limit of' or 'to the end of':

> *jekki mieumi oahtsugga*   'X ran until as much as his/her legs could take'

§6.5.8 Across and On The Other Side

The Siwa adverbs and/or postpositions in **jal-/jau-** and **(bal-)jamp-**[1] can respectively mean 'across' and 'on the other side' or simply 'on the side of'. They do not distinguish between destinal or directional. They are found in the nominal and compound forms as well as forms for static location, movement to, movement along and movement from.

---

[1] The prefix **bal·jamp-** is found in many western and far-eastern dialects, where the non-compound form is rare.

	noun	static	to	towards	along	from
across	jalma	jalra	jaudda	jauddairi	jalsi	jaugga
on the other side	jamma	jampo	jabmo	jabmoiri	jamsi	jamga

The static form *jalra* usually means 'across' and is different from the static form *jampo* 'on the other side' in that *jalra* implies having successfully crossed or gone over/waded something, while *jampo* simply implies location on the other side of something and may place more emphasis on the surface of a location.

Similarly, the movement to forms may are *jaudda* for 'across (with movement to)':

    kodimi ùki jaudda   'I walked across the lake'

It also has the meaning of being safe from a danger:

    tiddi on ùkita, lolli ka jaudda   'X fell in the water but lived through it (lit. but left across)'

The form *jabmo* means 'to the other side' and can also be taken more abstractly, sometimes in reference to either a higher state of mind (usually used when talking about trances) or to be particularly distracted, as can be seen in the compound *jabmogamiha* 'absent-minded' (or also possibly 'hypnotized').

The *towards* form are *jauddairi* '(towards) across' and *jabmoiri* 'towards the other side'. The form *jauddairi* is generally used more abstractly to describe an uncontrolled movement into a certain direction:

    tahõhrjupiki jauddairi   '(a fish) jumped out (away and into a certain direction)'

The *along* form are *jalsi* is generally only used as an adverb with a postposition, especially *mantsa* and *mankja* to mean 'diagonally':

    jalsi nodi ùki mantsa   'X swam diagonally across the lake' (i.e. across the middle of the lake)

The form *jamsi* usually means 'along the side of something', especially rivers, lakes and other waterways or paths:

    kehkeigge temme jamsi   'we paddled along the side of the shore'.

The *from* form *jaugga* means 'from across' and the form *jamga* means 'from the other side'. The word *jamga* is sometimes used as an interjection to call someone's attention back to a subject/situation, especially with young children:

   te taju...jamga!   'and then...hey!'

The nominal forms are used to mean 'the place across/on the other side'. The form *jamśia* can be used to mean 'not mentally present', especially of senile people. The form *jalmakia* can be used to mean 'in a safe place' or simply 'at the place across X'.

§6.6 Temporal adverbs

Temporal adverbs indicate time. Many temporal adverbs are set forms of nouns which can be found in the following cases to indicate a set time:

genitive	past	for X	*kenda*	'for a day'
illative	future	for X	*kendaita*	'for a day'
ablative	approx	for ± X	*kendaiska*	'for roughly a day'
adessive	set time	at X	*kendaima*	'on a day'
allative	future	in X	*kendaibma*	'in a day('s time)'
inessive	Ø	in X	*kendaja*	'(with)in a day'
elative	past	since X	*kendaika*	'a day ago'

genitive
for how much time something happened (used for the past)

  tèrrima kenda kildi
  [ˈtʰerːima ˈcʰɛnda ˈcʰɪldʑi]
  <sub><tè<rr>-i-ma ken-da kil-di
  is.sunny.PAST-ASS.ITR-INCONCL day-GEN whole-GEN
  'it was sunny (for) the whole day'

  gaiskka śivvi
  [ˈgaɪskːa ˈɕiwːi]
  gaisġ-ka śi<vv>-i-Ø
  month-GEN stay.PAST-ASS.CONCL.ITR-3P.AG.SG
  'X stayed for a month'

illative
for how much time something is set to happen (used for the future)

> *tèhmo kendaita kildi*
> [ˈtʰeːhmɔ ˈcʰɛndaida ˈcʰɪldʑi]
> tèr-m-o ken-da=ita kil-di
> is.sunny-INCONCL-INFER.ITR day-ILLAT whole-GEN
> 'it will be sunny for the whole day'

> *muongori ylymita*
> [ˈmuɔŋːori ˈylymida]
> muong-o-ri yly-m=ita
> stay.overnight-INFER.CONCL.ITR-3P.AG.PL night-ILLAT
> 'they will stay for the night'

> *kobaita ibaunomi*
> [ˈkʰɔbaida iˈbaunɔmi]
> ko-ba=ita i-baun-o-mi
> summer-illat dit-be.in.time-INFER.CONCL.ITR-1P.AG.SG
> 'I will arrive in time for summer'

ablative
for roughly how much time something happened/is set to happen (used for approximate duration, sometimes also used with distances).

> *sidni teuśirre baskiska tid-hi*
> [ˈsɪʔtni ˈtʰeuɕirːɛska ˈbascɪska ˈtʰiːdʑhi]
> sidn-i teu<ś>ir-re ba-ski=ska t<i>-d–hi
> last-ASS.CONCL.ITR few-GEN day-ABLA mating.period-GEN–3P.POSS.PL
> 'their mating period lasts for a few days'

> *geunumo tèrkimoiska silkehi*
> [ˈɟeunumɔ ˈtʰeːrˈcimɔɪska ˈsiːlcehi]
> geun-um-o tèr=kimo<Ø>-i=ska silke-hi
> diminish-OBLI-INFER.CONCL.ITR hour-ABLA swelling-PAT
> 'the swelling should diminish in a (few/rough) hour'

> *konihhan eumo magjikiska*
> [ˈkʰɔniʔːan ˈeumɔ ˈmajːiɟɪska]
> kon-i-ḥḥa-n eu-mo ma<gj>i-ki=ska
> walk-ITR-PERSI-IMPER.2P.SG few-GEN maidi-ABLAT
> 'keep on walking for a few feet'

adessive
at what time something happens (set point in time)

> *ijama pyhli elepśita eleu estodna*
> [ˈiːjɑmɑ ˈpʰœhɬi ˈelɛpɕːidɑ ˈeleu ˈɛstɔʔtnɑ]
> i<ja>-ma pyhl-i elepś-ita ele-u esto-dna
> early.summer-ADESS bloom-ASS.CONCL.ITR bloom-ILLAT flower-PAT first-PAT
> 'in early summer, the first flowers burst into bloom'

> *mitvoima estodna kebsie goakumajo*
> [ˈmɪtːvɔimɑ ˈɛstɔʔtnɑ ˈcʰɛpsie ˈɡɔɑɡumɑjɔ]
> mitvo-<Ø>=ima esto-dna ke<bs>i-e goak-um-a-jo
> night.frost-ADESS first-GEN mushroom-GEN pick-OBLI-ASS.CONCL.TR-4P.AG
> 'one must pick mushrooms on the first night frost'

> *kendaima tapodna ija*
> [ˈcʰɛndɑimɑ ˈtʰɑpɔʔtnɑ ˈiːjɑ]
> ken-da=ima tapo-dna i-ja
> day-ADESS last-GEN early.summer-GEN
> 'on the last day of early summer (i.e. summer solstice)'

allative
in how much time something is set to happen (used for the future)

> *kendaibma pedno*
> [ˈcʰɛndɑɪʔpmɑ ˈpʰɛʔtnɔ]
> ken-da=ibma pedn-o-Ø
> day-ALLAT arrive-INFER.CONCL.ITR-3P.AG.SG
> 'X will arrive in one day'

> *keulemi kòmibma gjekehi jàlhi*
> [ˈcʰeulemi ˈkʰʊmɪʔpmɑ ˈdʑecehi ˈjæːlhi]
> keul-e-mi k<ò>-mi=bma gjeke-hi jàl-Ø-hi
> observe-INFER.CONCL.TR-1P.AG.SG half-ALLAT year-GEN jàl-DAT-PL
> 'in half a year, I will celebrate jàlhi (male rite of passage)'

> *kimoibma saskeri*
> [ˈcʰimɔɪʔpmɑ ˈsɑsceri]
> kimo-<Ø>i=bma sask-e-ri
> moment-ALLAT wake.up-INFER.ASS.ITR-3P.AG.PL
> 'they will wake up in a short while'

inessive

in how much time something happens or at what time something happens (common with the habitual)

    tèrkimodia tubohis
    [ˈtʰeːrˈcimodʑia tʰubˈɔʔɪs]
    tèr=kimod-ia t-ub-oh-i-s
    hour-INESS 3P.PAT-PASS-smoke-ASS.CONCL.ITR-HAB
    'it is smoked in one hour' (i.e. it takes one hour to smoke)

    jùnaṡimi tehterreja kenda
    [ˈjuːnaɕimi ˈtʰɛhterːeja ˈcʰɛnda]
    jùn-a-ṡi-Ø-mi sehter-re=ia ken-da
    finish-ASS.CONCL.TR-HABI-3P.PAT-1P.AG.SG couple-INESS day-GEN
    'I can finish it in a couple of days'

    oskibis màhraka kadlụa kòmia eṡudna gaiskka
    [ˈɔscibɪs ˈmæːhrɑga ˈkatɬwːa ˈkʰʊːmia ˈeɕʊʔtna ˈgaɪskːa]
    osk-i-bi-s màhra-ka kadl-ụa k<ò>-m=ia eṡu-dna gaisġ-ka
    last-ASS.CONCL.ITR-1P.RECI.PL-HABI bear-PAT whole-PAT half-INESS second-GEN month-GEN
    'a whole bear usually lasts us for two months and a half'

elative

how much time since something happened (similar to English *ago* or *since*)

    kendika   'a day ago'
    gaiskkika   'a month ago'
    sinka   'a long time ago'

In addition, the genitive is used with a number of special postpositions. Some of these may be found in an adjectival phrase. These include:

    ebi   'for X at a time, for many X'

    kenda ebi   'for days at a time'
    biohtsiṡiri tèrkimodi ebi   'they can play for hours at a time'
    mytimo keilgie ebi   'since the dawn of time *or* all the time' (lit. for low and high tides)

    jeḍḍia   'going into X, until X'

    sidne kemṡie jeḍḍia   'X will last until the morning'
    kenda kadlġõ jeḍḍia   '(about to last) the whole day'

igja or nibma   'within X, before X (runs out)'

    jùnumimi atkemehi igja   'I have to finish it before the day after tomorrow'
    nõstetta kenda nibma ṡoṡi   'in one day, everyone had heard about it'

inka or soska   'X ago'

    tammi gjekehi inka   'many years ago'
    kimodi soska   'a moment ago'

inni   'having lasted X, over X'

    tammi gjekehi inni   'over many years'
    kėut tammi gjekehi inni   'war of many years'

ubma (negated with sę/set/sem and past) or tsoska (perfective) '(not) for X time'

    nuhlami hestie tsoska   'I haven't seen X in two weeks'
    set ma kenda ubma   'I haven't eaten for a day'

Common temporal adverbs are as follow.

Declinable adverbs and time expressions:

kendai/kendaita/kendaika	'today (also ûakken~ûakket)
kengi-ni	'today (noun)'
itśa/itita/itika	'late'
it·i·ma	'it is late'
kendia/kendita/kendika	'early'
kend·i·ma	'it is early'
kenka	'tomorrow'
kenehta	'for/to/before tomorrow'
kenes	'tomorrow (noun)'
atkenka	'the day after tomorrow'
kirja	'in the mornings'
kirma/kimra	'in the morning'

kirta	'for/to/before morning'
kisġi	'this morning'
kiras	'morning'
kirį·i·ma	'it is morning'
kįamnia/kįamnita/kįamnika	'at dawn'
kįamnima	'during dawn, at dawn'
kįangi	'today at dawn'
kįamni	'dawn'
kįam·m·i	'it is dawn'
pihi	'for a short time (in the past)'
pitta	'for a short time (in the future)'
pikka	'a moment ago, just now'
sigįa/sigita/sigika	'at dusk'
sigima	'during dusk, at dusk'
singi	'today at dusk'
sigo	'dusk'
sigv·i·ma	'it is dusk'
sindi/sinta/sinka	'for a long time'
sidn·i·ma	'it is long'
sośa/ȯhkįa	'in the evenings'
sohma/ȯhma	'in the evening'
soḍḍa/ȯhta	'for/to/before evening'
so(hh)i/ȯ(hh)i	'this evening'
soḍḍos/ȯhhįi	'evening'
sod·m·i/ȯś·m·i	'it is evening' (**soḍḍ-** and **ȯhhį-**)
ylįa/ulįa or yįa/ẏa	'during the night'
ylma/ulma	'at night'
ylta/ulta	'for/to/before night'
ůgįů	'tonight'
yly/ulu or ẏl	'night'
ul·m·i	'it is night'
mẏtẏ	'yesterday night'

Note that soḍḍos refers to a fixed time, while ȯhhįi refers to the earlier part of twilight (the later part being dusk, or sigo). Thus, ȯhhįi is used earlier during the winter days, and later during summer days. Twilight (both ȯhhįo/**soḍḍos** and sigo) is called teroma (a participle of the verb **terv-**, to twilight).

The difference between the illative (-**ta**) and the inessive (-**ia**) mainly has to do with the time of the action (wether it happens in the present/past or will happen in the future). However, often times there is a correlation between a movement/change of state and the use of the illative. This is especially true of verbs of motion, even though the motion may not be in time but space. For example, one goes to sleep late, with the illative;

    postuimi kendita   'I went to sleep late'.
    (not *kendia)

The form *kendia* can be used in contexts where there is no perceived movement or change of state. Compare the two following sentences:

    kendita pendidna muośi
    [ˈcʰendʑida ˈpʰendʐɪʔtna ˈmuɔɕi]
    kend-ita pe<nd>-i-dna muośi-Ø
    late-ILLAT return.PAST-ASS.CONCL.ITR-REVERS group.of.hunters-AGT
    'the group of hunters arrived late' (i.e. later than expected)

    kendia pendidna muośi
    [ˈcʰendʑia ˈpʰendʐɪʔtna ˈmuɔɕi]
    kend-ia pe<nd>-i-dna muośi-Ø
    late-INESS return.PAST-ASS.CONCL.ITR-REVERS group.of.hunters-AGT
    'the group of hunters arrived late' (i.e. while it was late)

These examples illustrate that the adverb *kendita* refers to a change of state or perceived movement in time relative to the verb, while *kendia* simply refers to a time non-relative to the verb, i.e. 'while it was late'. This distinction is lost with indeclinable adverbs.

§6.7 Indeclinable Adverbs
Below is a list of other adverbs, all of which are fixed and indeclinable. The list includes a few quantitative adverbs and adverbs of manner or attitude.

§6.7.1 Indeclinable Adverbs of Degree
Adverbs of degree describe how much or how little something is.

    auhka or *au(ġ)*   'quite, very'
    eren   'so, very'
    eukken~ŭkken~eukkil~ŭkli   'a little'
    ġai(lli)   'quite, rather'
    hehta   'completely, to death (*hehta vahta* is a commonly used intensifier)'

    hemora/hemua   'extremely'

ihha	'only, just'
isi~iḥḥen	'so, very'
kekken	'too (much)'
kommen	'much, a lot'
kůtvil	'somewhat'
sipi	'just, only, exclusively'
taģien~taģiil	'a lot, much'
uįote	'really'
ugįi	'really, truly'
ůlla	'nearly'
vahta	'completely, entirely'

§6.7.2 Indeclinable Adverbs of Time

The following temporal adverbs do not decline:

ihko, higgo	'sometimes'
ihkyai, higvai	'soon'
jogįu	'once, formally, in the past'
ju	'then (X, then Y)'
kůssů	'suddenly'
kilbi	'usually, normally'
kidl·i	'to be customary to'
kinoni, kinoḥḥi	'immediately'
kosti, gassen	'soon'
kitġ-	'to be soon, to be about to'
kitġõ	'soon'
killįu	'always'
kilpp·i	'to happen all the time'
mitka	'yesterday'
mitabe	'yesterday (noun)'
moannil	'regularly'
moanta	'every X'
haihkįu	'at the time'
ůhkįu	'at this time'
oa/voa	'already/yet'
svoa/sẏ	'not yet'
ȯdni~ėudni, nįa, ey	'now'
ȯnitka	'from now on'
orirra, orril, oarril	'always, without exception'
õde	'still (now)'
õsi, õtsi, ůntsi	'no longer (now)'
õska	'often'
õska·i	'to happen often'

ośia	'in time'
ośkju	'once (one time, also *migju*)'
ośi nildita	'ahead of time, in advance'
sadnu	'no longer'
sġůgju	'never'
taju	'then'
taite	'still (then)'
tatka	'from then on'
teuko	'ever (before), ever'
tevu nildita	'earlier than expected, before time'
tsalbi	'rarely'
tsaupr·i	'to happen rarely'
toġa/totska	'suddenly'
tohkju	'at that time'

§6.7.3 Other Indeclinable Adverbs

The following adverbs are also indeclinable.

aiho~aiḥho~aiḥḥen	'wrong (cf. **aih-** to be incorrect)'
aihůhta(iri)	'in the wrong direction (**aihůhka**(iri) from the wrong direction)'
aimra	'wrong, in the wrong way'
gemi	'with pleasure'
gemmoba/gemba	'preferably'
genne/genni	'rather (than)'
hymmi	'quietly (cf. *homora* quiet and **homott-** to be quiet)'
inta/ihna	'certainly, 'yes'
kůkja	'amongst other things'
maddja	'out hunting, away'
medde	'even'
nunne	'namely, you see'
neksura	'by surprise, unexpectedly'
nenna	'of course'
netra	'really'
nette	'to be sure, certainly'
ohia~oḥḥia	'suddenly'
onnanka/onnika	'at least'
salla	'well'
sene	'probably'
sġehta	'maybe, perhaps'
sůppi	'badly'
tahlanka/tahlika	'at most'
tatkatka	'inside out, confused'

tetteri	'upside down, the wrong way'
ùhkari	'on the contrary'
ujora	'right (cf. **ujo-** to be right)'

§6.8 Negation Adverbs

Negation is expressed mainly by the main negative adverb, which exists in three forms, *sę/set/sem* (clustering, non-clustering or vocalic) or alternatively by other types of negation, like pronouns or negative conjunctions (the negation morpheme is **si-** or sometimes **sġ-**). The negative adverb also has the emphatic form *hjayt*.

The form *set* is used before m- n- l- t- and k- and forms the clusters [sɛʔpm- sɛʔtn- sɛtɬ:- sɛʔt- sɛʔk-], and alternatively also before s- ṡ- and more rarely v-. It is also possible to write negation as a clitic, though the orthography is not recommended.

The form *sę* occurs before all other consonants, and *sem* before vowels. Note that the sequence *sę on* [sæɔ̃] is more common than *sem on*.

CLUSTERING		NON-CLUSTERING	VOCALIC
set m-	set s-	sę C-	sem V-
set n-	set ṡ-	sę on	
set l-	set v-		
set t-			
set k-			

oittami	'I looked at it'
sem oittami	'I did not look at it'
maki	'X will go'
set maki	'X won't go'
	(pron. [sɛˈʔpmɑci], also *sebmaki*)
netami	'I know'
set netami	'I don't know'
	(pron. [sɛˈʔtnetɑmi], also *sednetami*)
lemnika	'I am thirsty'
set lemnika	'I am not thirsty'
	(pron. [sɛˈtɬɛmnːigɑ], also *sedlemnika*)
hjayt ahtami	'I did *not* do it'
sę rakmehmi	'I will not rely on you'

§7 Conjunctions

Siwa uses three different types of conjunctions to join phrases together. One of them are used in so called link constructions, which are described in section *§9.16.1.3.5*. The other two types of conjunctions will be described here. They are the proper conjunctions and the coordinated conjunctions, called coordinating particles. The difference between proper and coordinated conjunctions is whether they are dependent on the order of the phrases or not. Coordinating particles appear in pairs and join phrases by appearing in both of them. Proper conjunctions have no such limitations and may appear in one phrase only, independently of the conjunctions in the other phrase.

§7.1 Proper Conjunctions

Proper conjunctions may appear at the beginning of a clause or between two clauses. There are three types of proper conjunctions; coordinators (not to be confused with coordinating particles), subordinating conjunctions and correlative conjunctions.

§7.1.1 Coordinators

Coordinators can join two words or phrases. Generally, coordinating particles are preferred to coordinators in Siwa, and coordinators have a limited use, for example at the beginning of a phrase that is understood to be the continuation of a longer, interrupted sentence. Siwa has the following coordinators:

ba 'but' (usually only used at the beginning of a new sentence)
siba 'but not'

   ...ba jottaja sġůdni
   [ˈba ˈjɔʔtɑja ˈsxœʔtni]
   ba jotta=ia sġůdni-Ø
   but that.DIST.INESS nothing-AGT
   '...but it doesn't matter' (lit. nothing in this)

egi~ġyo 'or'
egsen~sġyo 'or not'

   ůat egi hait?
   [ˈœæʔæ ˈeɟi ˈhaɪʔɪ]
   ůat-Ø egi hait-Ø
   this.PROXI-AGT or that.MEDI-AGT
   'this or that?'

ko/kon/kõ/kõkõ is used at the beginning of emphatic or explanatory statements

> *ko hanni ukitumajo-ḥa!*
> [ˈkʰɔ ˈhanːi uˈcʰitumajɔʔa]
> ko hanni u-kit-um-a-Ø-jo–ḥa
> EXPL.PART this.MEDI.way PASS-do-OBLI-ASS.CONCL.TR-3P.PAT-4P.AG–ASS.PART
> 'now that's how one does it!'

mega   'thus, so' (starting a new phrase)

> *mega sę gusseigge sohhjinebma*
> [ˈmega sæ ˈgusːɛɪcːe ˈsɔhːjinɛʔpma]
> mega sę guss-e-i-gge sohhji-ne-bma
> thus not ITR-travel-PAST-ASS.CONCL.ITR-1P.AG.PL.EXCL far-COMP.ADV-ALLAT
> 'thus, we travelled no further'

taga~toga~toġa   'and so, thus, and' (to continue a phrase or thought,
doġ~daġ   in enumerations or to show the consequence of a
                      conditional irrealis statement)
           or   'then also' (in phrases of the type *da*-X, *taga* Y 'if
                      X, then also /then it follows that Y, too')

> *jotta na aska ednantia nokkiu Tatasen taga*
> [ˈjɔʔta na ˈaska ɛʔtˈnantɕia ˈnɔʔciu ˈtʰatɑsɛn ˈtʰaga]
> jo=tta na aska ed-nant-i-a nokk-i-u-Ø tatasen taga
> that.DIST.GEN ASS.PART because 1P.ACT.UNAG.SG-receive-PAST-ASS.CONCL.TR name-PAST
> PAT.PART-DAT tatasen thus
> 'and thus, because of that, I received the name **Tatasen**'

te [de] or *-t* [ʔ]   'and' (used especially to link two or more things
                      of the same type, not verbal phrases)
sete/sede/sè/hjaydde   'and not'

> *tamosi te njelli*
> [ˈtʰamɔsi de ˈɲelːi]
> tamosi-Ø te njelli-Ø
> hunter-AGT and chief-AGT
> 'a hunter and a chief'

sigju~siu   'rather than, instead' (often with negative)

> *jeḍḍisen sigju konin*[1]
> ['jeð:isɛn 'ɕij:u 'kʰɔnɪn]
> jeḍḍ-i-sen sigju Ø-kon-i-n
> run-ITR-IMPER.NEG.2P.SG rather.than ITR-walk-ITR-IMPER.2P.SG
> 'walk instead of running!' (lit. don't run rather, walk!)

ednet~ednůt[2]   'and (+GEN)'

> *megi son ednet*
> ['meʝi sɔn 'ɛʔtnɛʔ]
> megi-Ø son ednet
> 1P.PRON.SG-AGT 2P.PRON.SG-GEN and
> 'you and me'

§7.1.2 Subordinating Conjunctions

Subordinating conjunctions only join two clauses together and in Siwa, they are found at the beginning of the dependent clause.

bata(vvi)   'otherwise than, unlike, but (in fact)'

> *noai ahtote, batavvi sem ahta*
> ['nɔai 'ahtɔde 'bataw:i sɛm 'ahta]
> n=oa-i-Ø a<ht>-ot-e-Ø-Ø, batavvi sem a<ht>-a-Ø-Ø
> say.PAST-ASS.CONCL.ITR do.PAST-COMPLE-INFER.CONCL.TR-3P.PAT-3P.AG.SG, otherwise.than not do.PAST-ASS.CONCL.TR-3P.PAT-3P.AG.SG
> 'X said X did Y, but in fact X did not do Y'

geska   'as far as, concerning, considering, since ' (also postposition, +ELAT)

> *kyminai geska sihri-ma*
> ['cʰyminai 'ʝɛska 'sɪhri]
> kymina-i geska si<hr>-i-ma
> pleasant-cop.past.ass considering rain.past-ass.itr-inconcl
> 'it was fun, considering it rained (or: as far as the fact that it rained, it was still fun)'

---

[1] Note that both phrases are imperative!

[2] Many variations exist including *eneḥe, enḥe, eiḥe, eiḥḥe* or *enůḥů, enḥů, eiḥů* and *eiḥḥů*

ṡemimattaikami geska...
[ˈɕemimaʔtaigami ˈɟɛska]
ṡem-i-m-a-tta=ika-mi geska
believe-ITR-INCONCL-AGT.PART.UNAG-ELAT-1P.AG.SG as.far.as
'as far as what I believe/as for my beliefs/as far as I'm concerned...'

ihhyo   'as, as if, like, similar to'

ihhyo sadjeṡijo amokvelu
[ˈih:wɔ ˈsadʑeɕijo ˈamɔˈkʰvelu]
ihhyo sa<dj>-e-ṡi-jo amokvel-u
as.if hear.PAST-INFER.CONCL.TR-HABIL-4P.AG northern.lights-GEN
'it was as though one could hear the northern lights'

inte (Ø-ḥa)   'although, however, but, on the other hand'[1]

inte heji̯a-ḥa...
[ˈɪnte ˈhejiaʔa]
inte heje-a–ḥa
although cold-COP.ASS–ASS.PART
'although, it *is* cold...'

komo   an explicative subordinating particle, may also be (con)sequential

komo muhkia atsiokia batsġviaḥḥen kjamnutta nita somigi
[ˈkʰomo ˈmʊhcia ˈatsiɔɟia ˈbatsxwːiaʔːɛn ˈcʰamnʊʔta ˈniːda ˈsɔmiɟi]
komo mur=kia atsio-kia batsġv-i-a-ḥḥen kjamn-u-tta nita somi-gi-Ø
EXPL.PART thick-INESS glade-INESS TR-search-PAST-ASS.CONCL.TR-PERSIS dawn-PAT.PART GEN into man-PL-AGT
'so, you see, the men kept on searching wide and large into dawn' (lit. in thick, in glade)

komo-ḥa sipi maba màra
[ˈkʰomɔʔa ˈsipi ˈmaba ˈmæːra]
komo sipi m-a-ba màra-Ø
EXPL.PART-ASS.PART just COP.PAST-ASS-1P.AG.DUAL 1P.PRON.PL-AGT
'so, as you know, there were only us two'

---

[1] This coordinator is often used to show that the speaker concedes that some statement may, in fact, be true, perhaps after having opposed it before.

sahra   'that is to say, in other words, well'

> *euka on kůnůma sauma, da on tingima salama, sahra dari mosġi te solra*
> ['eugã͂ 'cʰɵnɵma 'sauma dã͂ 'tʰiŋːima 'salama 'sahra 'dari 'mɔsxi de 'sɔlra]
> euk-a on kůnů-ma sauma-Ø d-a on tingi-ma salama-Ø sahra d-a-ri mosġi-Ø te solra
> produce-ASS.CONCL.TR PART. milk-GEN caribou-AGT COP-ASS PART 3P.PRON.PL-ADESS antler-AGT, in.other.words COP-ASS-3P.AG.PL mammal-AGT and cervidae-AGT
> 'caribous both produce milk and have antlers - that is to say they are mammals and *cervidae*'

siġa~sviġa   'except, besides (+ELAT)'

> *usotsi iskidita hami soroko ġůsti mahtsiska, sindika siġa*
> [uˈsɔtsi iːscidʑida 'hami 'sɔrɔgɔ 'xœsti 'mahtsɪska 'ɕɪndʑiga 'sixa]
> u-sot-s-i iski-d=ita h-a-mi soroko-Ø ġů-sti mah-tsi=ska śim-di=ka siġa
> PASS-give-HAB-ASS.CONCL.ITR-woman-ILLAT eat-TR-infi.AG.TR part-DAT any.INA DAT bear-ABLAT bear.head-ELAT except
> 'women are allowed to eat any part of the bear, except the head'

tavvi   'than, as'

> *tata tavvi duhma*
> [ˈtʰata ˈtʰawːi ˈdʊhma]
> ta-ta tavvi duhma
> much.COMP than previously
> 'more than before'

tonta(vvi)   'in the same way as, just as' (+ILLAT, pre- or postposition)

> *taniḋgi tontavvi gastaita-ho*
> [tʰaˈnɪðɟi ˈtʰɔntawːi ˈgastaidahɔ]
> ta-ni<ḋg>-i tontavvi <gasta>=ita-ho
> 3P.ACT.UNAG-die.PAST-ASS.CONCL.ITR just.like older.brother-ILLAT-3P.POSS.ANI.SG
> 'X died in the same way as X's older brother'

tvaḥḥo~daḥḥo~dat [1]   'as though'

> *ihko tvaḥḥo mohigjenoġa*
> ['ɪhkɔ 'tʰvɑʔːɔ mɔ'hijːenɔxa]
> ihko tvaḥḥo m-o-higjen-o-ġa
> sometimes as though 1P.ACT.UNAG.SG-SUBJ-feel.cold-INFER.CONCL.ITR-SEMELF
> 'sometimes it's as though I get the chills' (lit. I feel cold once)

tvori~dori[2]   'as, like' (used as a hesitation particle)

> *taju noai tvori....*
> ['tʰaju 'nɔai 'tʰvɔri]
> taju n=oa-i-Ø tvori
> then say.PAST-ASS.CONCL.ITR-3P.AG.SG like
> 'then X said like...'

§7.1.2 Correlative Conjunctions

kuppi...kippi[3]	'either...or'
sikuppi~sġuppi~sġůppi...sippi	'neither...nor'
kuppi...sippi	'either...or not'

> *kuppi hantui neta kippi njosuimi*
> ['kʊʔpi 'hantui neta 'cʰɪʔpi 'ɲɔsuimi]
> kuppi hanto-i n-e-ta kippi njoso-e-mi
> either lie-ITR COP.INCONCL-INFER-3P.AG.SG or deaf-COP.INFER-1P.AG.SG
> 'either X is lying, or I am deaf'

---

[1] Also exists as the clitic **-dat** used with many sensive verbs or phrases, e.g. *himi-dat* 'it is hot, it seems'.

[2] May also be found hyphened as *-dori*.

[3] There is great variation in the form of these words, including:
    kuppi kippi
    kuppi kuppi-ne
    keppi keppi-ne
    minni minni-ne
    mi-ůt mi-ut
    bemoni behanni
    bemo behha~beġa

sedde...Ø te/medde   'not only...but also'

> *sedde ireluata medde tygyhua*
> [ˈsetːe ˈireluɑda ˈmetːe ˈtʰygyhua]
> sedde irela-a-ta medde tygyha-a
> not.only beautiful-COP.ASS-3P.AG.SG but.also poisonous-COP.ASS
> 'not only is it beautiful, it's also poisonous'

Ø-te tavvi da...Ø-te tainne da   'the more....the more...'
                                      coordinates two link phrases

> *kòite tavvi gakita, gjosite tainne maka*
> [ˈkʰʊːide ˈtʰawːi ˈgɑcida ˈjoside ˈtʰainːe ˈmɑka]
> kò-i-te tavvi g-a-ki-ta gjos-i-te tainne m-a-ka
> speak-ASS.ITR PART COP.PASS-ASS-1P.RECI.SG-3P.AG.SG be.tired-ASS.ITR PART COP.INCONCL.PAST-ASS.TR-1P.PAT.SG
> 'the more X spoke, the more tired I was'

ġuo...Ø ġuodde   'whether...or'

> *ġuo sarvata ġuodde hosġona, haundamō*
> [ˈxuɔ ˈsarwːɑda ˈxuɔtːe ˈhɔsxɔnɑda ˈhaʊndɑmō]
> ġuo sarv-a-ta ġuodde hosġon-a h-a-unda-mō
> whether good-COP.ASS-3P.AG.SG or inedible-COP.ASS eat-ASS.CONCL.TR-DIMI-OBLI.IMP.2P.SG
> 'whether it's good or disgusting, you will have to eat a little'

§7.2 Coordinating Particles

Coordinating particles are particles that coordinate two phrases as pairs, with one particle in each phrase. Generally, a phrase will be introduced with the particle *on* or the more contrastive *onta*, and the second phrase will contain another particle. Coordinating particles are placed directly before the verb if the verb is not the first word of the phrase. They may intersect between nouns and adjectives.

> **VERB** → COORDINATING PARTICLE → Ø
> Ø → COORDINATING PARTICLE → **VERB**

If the verb is the first word of the phrase, the coordinating particle follows the verb, without however coming in between a verb and link construction particles.

Coordinating particles have two positions; first (in the first sentence), second (in subsequent sentences). First position particle may mix with second position particle, so long as their order is respected. Some particles can be present in the opposite order that is shown here.

Some coordinating particles show a more adverbial relationship between two phrases (**mi/avvi**). A set of four pairs of particles are called dramatic particles – positive or negative. They are used to underline either a positive or negative aspect of the phrase.

Coordinating particles are used extensively in Siwa and are ubiquitous in most texts, stories and narration.

on...	*ka...*	and, but, while
		weakly contrastive or non-contrastive

umaġamsi on gone tśibe sara, voavvimi ka kůtůhma-ne
[uˈmɑxamsiɔ̃ ˈgɔne ˈtɕibe ˈsɑra ˈvɔawːimi ka ˈcʰøtɕehmːane]
u-<agam>-s-i on tśibe-Ø sara d-o-i-m-a-Ø voa<vv>-i-mi ka kůtůh-ma–ne
PASS-believe.PAST-HAB-ASS.CONCL.ITR PART COP.CONCL.PAST-COMPLE-INFER.TR ACT.PART-AGT sign-AGT good-AGT be.afraid.PAST-ASS.ITR-INCONCL PART some.UNKNOWN.-PAT.PL–ne
'while it was believed to be a good omen, others were afraid'

onta...	*katta...*	but, yet, whereas, and
		strongly contrastive, counter to expecations

soarri onta enebemni, set katta oni ladjo teboatsita-ne
[ˈsɔɑrːi ˈɔnta ˈenebɛmnːi sɛʔ ˈkʰaʔta ˈɔni ˈlɑdʐo ˈtʰebɔɑtsidane]
soa<rr>-i onta ene-be=mni set katta oni a<dj>-o t-eb-oats-ita
survive.PAST-ASS.CONCL.ITR PART some.OUT.OF.TWO-AGT not PART so happen.to-INFER.CONCL.TRANSL some.OUT.OF.TWO-ILLAT-other
'one survived, yet the other would not be so lucky (lit. it apparently didn't appear to be so for the other one)'

on...	*bė...*	although, while PHRASE.1, PHRASE.2 also
		contrastive additional information

tygyhua on to kepsi-ůt, komuoyiekkabmisa bė
[ˈtʰygyhuɑ̃ɔ̃ tʰɔ ˈcʰɛpsːɪœʔ ˈkʰɔmuˈowɪɛʔkaʔpmisa beː]
tygyha-a on to kepsi-Ø–ni komu=oyiekk-a=bmis-a bė
poisonous-COP.ASS PART this.ANI.AGT mushroom-AGT-DET.PROXI mind-make.feel.wider-PART.ADJ-COP.ASS
'while this mushroom is poisonous, it is also psychoactive (lit. mind-widening)'

on...	*ġyo...*	or
		alternative

sapru on pikśotoma, sapru ġyo pikśontoma
[ˈsapxuɔ̃ ˈpʰɪkɕɔdɔma ˈsapxuxwɔ ˈpʰɪkɕɔndɔma]
sapr-u on pikś-ot-o-ma sapr-u ġyo pikś-ont-o-ma
may.be-ASS.CONCL.TRANS PART hurt-that-INFER.ITR-INCONCL may.be-ASS.CONCL.TRANSL PART hurt-that.not-INFER.INTR-INCONCL

'it may hurt or it may not hurt'

on…   ne(tta)   but (of course), then (surely)
contrastive, expected information
often anaphoric to conditional irrealis phrase

vahta eruljoila, nette eruluiata taga
[ˈvahta ˈeruljɔila ˈnɛʔte ˈeruluiɑda ˈtʰɑga]
vahta er<u>l-joi-la-Ø nette er<u>l-u-ia-ta taga
completely work.PAST-COND.IRR.INFER-PERF-3P.AG.SG surely work.PAST-   PAT.PART.AGT
COP.COND.IRR.ASS-3P.AG.SG PART
'if X would have worked to completion, then surely (it follows that) Y would be done'

on…   on…   both PHRASE.1 and PHRASE.2
equal statements

euka kŭnŭma on sauma, on simṡi
[ˈeuga ˈcʰønøma ɔ̃ ˈsɑuma ɔ̃ ˈsɪmɕi]
euk-a kŭnŭ-ma sauma-Ø on on simṡi-Ø
produce-ASS.CONCL.TR. milk-GEN PART caribou-AGT PART human-AGT
'both caribou and humans produce milk'

on…   de(bmi)…   so, thus, because
consequential information

sę on nega, set de nemantia nonkiuma mansodlot
[ˈsæɔ̃ ˈnega sɛʔde neˈmantɕia ˈnɔŋciuma ˈmansɔtɬɔʔ]
sę on n<eg>-a-Ø-Ø set de ne-mant-i-a nonkiu-ma ma=ns-ot-l-o-t
not PART. see.PAST-ASS.CONCL.TR-3P.PAT-3P.AG.SG not PART 3P.PROXI.ACT.UNAG-get-PAST-
ASS.CONCL.TR rumor-GEN come.PAST-COMPLE-PERF-INFER.CONCL.ITR-3P.OBVI.AG.SG
'X did not see Y, so X didn't find out that Y had come' (lit. get the rumor)

on…   komo…   because, as, since

ednantia on savvu, leurrimi komo sajukibma luvveima
[ɛʔtˈnantɕiɑ̃ɔ̃ ˈsɑw:u ˈleur:imi ˈkʰɔmɔ ˈsɑjuɟʔpma ˈluw:eima]
ed-nant-i-a on savvu-Ø leu<rr>-i-mi komo sai<Ø>u-k=ibma luvvei-ma
1P.ACT.UNAG.SG-receive.PAST-ASS.CONCL.TR PART burn-DAT touch.PAST
ASS.CONCL.ITR-1P.AG.SG PART pot-ALLAT very.hot-GEN
'I got a burn because I touched the scolding hot pot'

on(ta)... kade(bmi)...   even though, despite
contrastive, counterfactual

oa on mahhikis, hanni-ḥa kade iśia
[ɔãɔ̃ ˈmɑhːɑɟʂ ˈhɑnːiʔa ˈkʰɑde ˈiɕia]
oa on mahh-i-ki-s-Ø hani-ḥa kade iśi-a
still PART hunt-ASS.CONCL.ITR-TRANSLO-HAB-3P.AG.SG SO.MEDI–ASS.PART PART old-COP.ASS
'X still goes hunting, despite being so/this old'

on... ju...   then, so, after
successive

lungittia on, heirihta ju
[ˈluŋːɪʔtiãɔ̃ ˈheirɨhta ju]
lungit-tia on heirih=ta ju
steam-INESS PART cool.down-ILLAT PART
'first steam, then cooling down'

on... [(te)₂...]te...taga/toġa   as well as, and
then (anaphoric to conditional)
enumerative

iuditagi gielsuajo on kolkonta, kolsotta, mihnadi, hiamis te ippůdi taga
[ˈiudʑidɑji ˈɟɛlsuɑjɔː ˈkʰɔlkɔnta ˈkʰɔlsɔʔta ˈmiːhnɑdʑi ˈhiɑmɪs de ˈɪʔpødʑi ˈtʰɑga]
iu-di=ta-gi giels-u-a-jo on kolko-s kolsot-ta mihna-di hiami-s te ippů-di taga
winter.solstice-ILLAT-PL prepare-PAST-ASS.CONCL.TR-4P.AG PART bread-GEN cheese-GEN
mihna-GEN hiamin-GEN and ippů-GEN PART.
'for the in winter solstice celebration, we prepared bread, cheese, **mihna** (pemmican), **hiamin** (honey and milk brew) and **ippů** (tallow and berries)'

katta... de(bmi)...   seeing as, since
consequential, contrastive information

nantia katta isto kośi, nantia debmi karsa te
[ˈnantɕia ˈkʰaʔta ˈiːstɔ ˈkʰɔɕi ˈnantɕia ˈdɛʔpmi ˈkarsa de]
nant-i-a katta isto-Ø kośi-Ø, nant-i-a debmi karsa-Ø te
receive-PAST-ASS.CONCL.TR PART. gift-DAT older.brother-AGT, receive-PAST-ASS.CONCL.TR PART. younger.brother-AGT and
'seeing as the older brother received a gift, so did the younger brother too'

mi/avvi...   on...   (by) PHRASE.1, (then) PHRASE.2
                                adverbial, consequential

pakkima-nen kedahta avvi poannoṡmomia derrotuvven neka sȯka, oa on ojagjiela tsamġa mema
[ˈpʰaʔcimanɛn ˈcʰedahta ˈawːi ˈpʰɔanːˈɔɕmomia ˈderːɔduwːɛn ˈneka ˈsʊːga ˈɔãɔ̃ ɔˈjɑjːiela ˈtsamxa ˈmema]
pa<kk>=ima–ha ked-aht-a avvi poav=noṡmo-mia de<rr>-ot-u-vven n-e-ka sȯ-Ø=ka oa on o-jagjiel-a   tsa<m>-ġa m-e-ma
back-ADESS–POSS.4P bear-aht-TR ADV.PART seal=pouch-INESS wrap.PAST-COMPLE-PAT.PART.AG-ADV COP.PAST-INFER-1P.PAT.SG mother-AGT=1P.PAT.AG already PART SUBJ-get.to.know-TR forest-GEN COP.INCONCL.PAST-INFER-1P.UNAG.ACT.SG
'as my mother was carrying me wrapped in a sealskin pouch on her back, I was already getting to know the forest'

tei/tẹrẹ...   ari...   unfortunately, alas, dramatic negative
                                weakly contrastive
                                weakly consequential

tamara tei omuki atkanokkamo, kekken ari ymyra nikimi
[ˈtʰamara ˈtʰei ˈɔmuʃi ˈatkaˈnɔʔkamɔ ˈcʰɛʔcɛn ˈari ˈymyra ˈnicimi]
tama-ra tei o-m-u-ki-Ø atka=nokka-mo, kekk-en ari ymy-ra nik-i-m-i-Ø
many-COP.PERF.ASS PART. attack-PAST-PAT.PART-PL-AGT tail=call-GEN too-GEN ARI terrible-COP.PERF.ASS die-ITR-INCONCL-AGT.PART.UNAG.PL-AGT
'alas, the wolf attacks have been many and the deaths too terrible'

mes/meġi...   gi~ġi~ġvi...   fortunately, praise, dramatic positive

soprei sikvihidohaita mes, kiḏba-ho ġi itiujai
[ˈsɔpxei ˈsɪkːviˈhidɔhaida mɛs ˈcʰɪ̈baho ˈxi ˈitiˈujai]
sopr<e>-i sikvi=hidoha-i-ta mes, kiḏba-Ø–ho ġi iti=uja-Ø-i
golden-ADV shiny=haired-COP.PAST.ASS-3P.AG.SG PART. eye.DUAL-AGT–3P.POSS.SG.ANI PART. ice=water-AGT-COP.PAST.ASS
'X was blonde haired, the eyes like ice-water' (lit. goldenly shiny-haired)

Dramatic particles can also be contrasted together or stand alone

nata ġi tamosi ata-errobmot – růtůmmai ari te
[ˈnata xi ˈtʰamɔsi ˈataˈerːɔʔpmɔʔ ˈrɔtømːai ˈari de]
n-a-ta ġi tamosi-Ø ata=erro=bmot-Ø, růtůmma-i ari te
COP.PAST-ASS-3P.AG.SG PART hunter-AGT hard=working-AGT, fool-COP.PAST.ASS PART and
'he was a hardworking man/hunter – unfortunately, he was also a fool'

růtůmmaita – na ġi tamosi ata-errobmot
[ˈrøtømːɑida ˈna xi ˈtʰɑmɔsi ˈɑtaˈerːɔʔpmɔʔ]
růtůmma-i-ta n-a ġi tamosi-Ø ata=erro=bmot-Ø
fool-COP.PAST.ASS-3P.AG.SG COP.PAST-ASS PART hunter-AGT hard=working-AGT
'he was a fool – fortunately, he was a hardworking man/hunter'

tśandagge meġi suikna!
[ˈtɕandacːe ˈmiɟi ˈsʊɪʔŋa]
tśa<nd>-a-gge migi suikna-Ø
find.PAST-ASS.CONCL.TR-1P.AG.PL.EXCL PART. suitable.gound-DAT
'finally, we found suitable ground for a house!'

tęrę tanikli
[ˈtʰæræ tʰɑˈnɪkːli]
tęrę ta-nik-l-i
PART. 3P.ACT.UNAG-die-PERF-ASS.CONCL.ITR
'alas, X has died'

§8 Postpositions

Siwa makes use of postpositions. Postpositions have their head noun in either the genitive or a locative case – the locative or genitive cases are used for destinal postpositions (those which show a movement to a destination) and the genitive is used for directional postpositions (those which show a movement to a general direction). Postpositions may be found before their head noun (then becoming prepositions), but this is unusual.

Postpositions can be found in a variety of forms. Usually, a single postposition will have at least three forms (static, movement to and movement from). Certain postpositions exist in both the internal locative cases (inessive, illative and elative) and the surface locative cases (adessive, allative and ablative). Another set of special cases only found with postpositions and adverbs exist, showing movement towards and along, both with movement to and from.

Most spacial postpositions are also used as adverbs. They are listed in **§7.3**. Conjunctions are also used as postpositions (see **§8.1**) Other postpositions include:

 ahha[1]   'after' +GEN.

  kůlda ahha sindi salla besġi ma
  [ˈcʰœlda ˈɑhːa ˈsiːndʑi ˈsɑlːa ˈbɛsxi ma]
  ků-lda ahha sindi sa=lla besġ-i m-a
  war-GEN after long-GEN good-ADV peace-ITR COP.PAST.INCONCL-ASS
  'after the war, there was a long period of peace'

 aska   'because' +ELAT/GEN

  nonisentseka aska otůrůdgi
  [ˈnɔniɕɛntsega ˈaska ɔˈtʰɔrœðɟi]
  non-i-sen-t=se=ka aska o-t-ůrů<ḍg>-i
  swim-ITR-HAB.NEG-INFI.ITR.AG-ELAT because
  SUBJ-3P.ACT.UNAG-
  drown.past-ASS.CONCL.ITR
  'X drowned because of his/her not being able to swim'

 dů or *tevu, tvo* 'before' +GEN

  koba tevu
  [ˈkʰɔba ˈtʰevu]
  ko-ba tevu
  summer-GEN before
  'before summer'

---

[1] Also commonly found as *aġga, eġġa, aġa, ayġa, eġe*.

gala[1]   'with' (instrumental meaning)

misahi gala hůtvia
[misɑhi ˈgɑla ˈhœtwːia]
misa-hi gala hůtv-i-a-Ø-Ø
rock-GEN with hit-PAST-ASS.CONCL.TR-3P.PAT-3P.AG.SG
'X hit Y with a rock' (also *misahigla*)

gagi   'with' (comitative meaning) +GEN

ikid gagi boinnia koni mata
[ˈicɪdʑ ˈgaɟi ˈbɔinːia ˈkɔni ˈmɑta]
iki-d gagi boi‹nn›=ia kon-i m-a-ta
axe-GEN with belt-INESS walk-ITR COP.PAST.INCONCL-ASS-3P.AG.SG
'X was walking with his/her axe in his/her belt'

gari   'instead of X' +GEN
garita   'id.' (movement to)
garika   'id.' (movement from)

iltottaja sihdi sitkabme gari
[ilːˈtɔʔtaja ˈsɪhdʑi ˈsɪtkaʔpme ˈgɑri]
il-tott-aj-a-Ø sir-di sitk-at=me gari
forward-trade-PAST-ASS.CONCL.TR-3P.AG.SG fish-GEN fish-INFI.TR.AG-GEN instead
'X bought fish instead of fishing for it'

gatta   'along, with, as well' +GEN

iskutsai gatta
[ˈiːskutɕai ˈgaʔta]
isku-tśa-i gatta
womenfolk-GEN-PL ALONG
'with the womenfolk' or 'the womenfolk as well'

gattia   'in the presence of, when X is present, in X case, in the situation of X' +GEN

iśuyagi gattia sejumi
[ˈiɕuwaji ˈgaʔtia ˈsejumi]
iśu-ya-gi gattia sej-um-i

---

[1] Also found as a clitic -ġla, -ġil, -ġġeli or -gla, see section §4.5.5.4

elders-GEN-PL in.the.presence listen-OBLI-ASS.CONCL.ITR
'in the presence of elders, one must listen'

genna/gedna	'at X's place, in (of area), in the area of, on the subject of' +GEN
genta	'id.' (movement to)
genka	'id.' (movement from)
geska	'as far as X is concerned, concerning X, as for X, with respect to X' +ELAT

pirrabme genna sohluata
[ˈpʰiːraʔpme ˈɟenːa ˈsɔɬːuada]
pirr-a-t=me genna soh=la-a-ta
heal-ASS.TR-INFI.TR.AG-GEN in best-COP.ASS-3P.AG.SG
'in the field of healing, X is the best'

śemitsekami geska...
[ˈɕemitsegami ˈɟɛska]
śem-i-t=sa=ika-mi geska
believe-ITR-INFI.ITR.AG-GEN-ELAT-1P.AG.SG as.far.as
'as far as me believing it, ...'

haljia~hallja	'in the wake of, as a result of, because, following, after' +GEN

longamo haljia nekettagga kolja
[ˈlɔŋːamɔ ˈhaljia ˈnecɛʔtakːa ˈkʰɔlja]
lo<ng>a-mo haljia neke<tt>-a-gga kolja-Ø
intense.cold-GEN in.wake lose.PAST-ASS.CONCL.TR-1P.AG.PL.INCL crops-DAT
'as a reseult of the intense cold, we lost our crops'

hokvi	'all the way to X and back'
hokoma	'back and forth'

kodi temme tvŭdari hokvi
[ˈkʰɔdi ˈtʰemːe ˈtʰvødari ˈhɔkwːi]
ko<d>-i-Ø te<mm>=e tvŭd=airi hokvi
walk.PAST-ASS.CONCL.ITR-3P.AG.SG shore-GEN down.DIRECT.ALONG to.and.back
'X went all the day down to the shore and back'

iska   'thanks to' +ELAT

oapigga iska irriṡinkeimi
[ˈɔɑbɪkːa ˈiːska irːiˈɕiːŋceimi]
oapi-ka=ka iska irri-ṡink-e-i-mi
help-ELAT thanks.to through-be.able-past-ASS.CONCL.ITR-1P.AG.SG
'thanks to (your) help, I was able to make it through'

kehhịa   'in the form/shape of, as, in X's skin/position/point of view' +GEN

keḍḍa   'id.' (movement to)

keḍga   'id.' (movement from)

obimi tatȧtta keḍḍa
[ɔbˈiːmi ˈtʰɑtaʔta ˈcʰeðːa]
o-i‹m›-i-Ø tata-tta keḍḍa
SUBJ-change.PAST-ASS.CONCL.ITR-3P.AG wolf-GEN in.form.ILLAT
'X turned into a wolf'

kėhịa   'within X's reach' +GEN

so da-a sosia kėhịa kịoknen?
[s(ɔ) daː ˈsɔsia ˈcʰeːʔja ˈcʰɔʔŋɛn]
so d-a–a sosi=a kėhịa kịoknen-Ø
INTERROG COP-ASS–INTERROG 2P.SG.INESS at.hand kịoknen-AGT
'do you have a **kịoknen** (cedar strip basket) within reach?'

keṡa   'for' (directed at someone's/something's memory/honor/person) +GEN

geimuo kịalka keṡa
[ˈʝeimuɔ ˈcʰalːka ˈcʰeɕa]
geimo-o-Ø kịala-ka keṡa
feeling-PL-AGT land-GEN for
'(the) feelings for the land'

ketsġo   'according to, due to, because' (usually implies a tradition or a custom) +GEN

sġouma ṡeimue ketsġo kịeggaska kolottaika

['sxɔuma 'ɕeimue 'cʰɛtsxɔ 'cʰjɛkːaska 'kʰɔlɔʔtaiga]
sġo-um-a-Ø śeimo-e ketsġo kjeggas-Ø-ka kolo-tta=ika
feed-OBLI-ASS.CONCL.TR-IMP belief-GEN due.to foetus-DAT-PL womb-ELAT
'according to our believes, we must feed the foetuses (when taking them) out of the womb (of a killed animal)'

   keu or ġye   'together, with, as well' (sometimes pronounced [-kʷ] or [-xʷ]) +GEN

      sankiami kottaka keu
      ['saŋciami 'kʰɔʔtaga 'cʰeu] or ['kʰɔʔtagakʷ] or ['kʰɔʔtagaxʷ]
      sank-i-a-Ø-mi ko=tta-ka keu
      build-past-ASS.CONCL.TR-3P.PAT-1P.AG.SG older.brother-GEN-1P.PAT.SG with
      'I built X with my older brother'

   kimi   'for' (for a purpose) +ILLAT

      eskujekkuma tsehmeitagi kimi mjaha
      ['ɛskujɛʔkuma 'tsɛhmeidaji 'cʰimi 'mjaʔa]
      eskujekk-um-a-Ø tseru-me=ita-gi kimi mjaha-Ø
      empty-OBLI-ASS.CONCL.TR-IMP steam.hut.ceremony-ILLAT-PL for stomach-DAT
      '(we) must empty our stomachs for the **tserugi** (steam hut ceremony)'

   kiśa   'away' (static) +GEN
   kiśta   'id.' (movement to)
   kiśka   'id.' (movement from)

      katotsůġjin oahka kiśka
      [kʰatɔ'tsøjːɪn 'ɔahka 'cʰɪɕka]
      kat-o-tsůġj-i-n oari-ka kiśka
      from-SUBJ-move-ASS.CONCL.ITR-IMPER.2P.SG edge-GEN away-ELAT
      'move away from the edge!'

   kiḋḋja   'within X's sight' +GEN

      tahopsei śośton kiḋḋja
      [tʰa'hɔpːsei 'ɕɔɕton 'cʰið:ja]
      ta-hops-e-i soś=ton kiḋḋja
      3P.ACT.UNAG-vomit-PAST-ASS.CONCL.ITR every-GEN in.sight
      'X vomited in front of everybody/while everyone saw'

ki̇uṡka 'because of, on the basis of, based on' +ELAT

sekueika ki̇uṡka
['sekueiga 'cʰʊɕka]
seko-e=ika ki̇uṡka
law-ELAT because
'because of the law/on account of the law'

kolo 'around (here/there), close to (here), in the vicinity of' +GEN
kolta 'id.' (movement to)
kolka 'id.' (movement from)

ụara unahi kolo tiogi
['wɑrɑ 'unɑhi 'kʰɔlɔ 't'iɔji]
ụar-a u<n>a-hi kolo tiogi-Ø
there.is.somewhere-ASS.CONL.TR widening-GEN around dam-AGT
'there is a dam somewhere around where (the river) widens'

kõuja 'in X's distance, at a distance of X' +GEN
kõita 'id.' (movement to)
kõika 'id.' (movement from)

kengukoamo kõuja denarika
['cʰɛŋ:u'kʰɔamɔ 'kʰɔ̃:ja 'denariga]
kengu=ko<Ø>a-mo kõuja de<n>a-ri=ka
day=half-GEN at.distance village-ELAT
'at half a day's distance from the village'

kõuma 'with X number of people, in a group of X' +GEN
kõbma 'id.' (movement to)
kõska 'id.' (movement from)

tahrikiri hangụa kõuma
['tʰahriɟiri 'haŋ:wa 'kʰɔ̃:ma]
ta<hr>-i-ki-ri hang=ụa kõuma
leave.PAST-ASS.CONCL.ITR-TRANSLO-3P.AG.PL five-GEN.ANI in.number
'they left as a group of 5'

maggja	'in the case of X, in the event of X, should X be' +GEN	

> *màhruomatta maggja set netiemi niġu-ḥa kitami*
> ['mæːhruˈɔmaʔta ˈmaɟːia sɛʔ ˈnetiemi ˈniːxuʔa ˈcʰitami]
> màhru-o-m-a-tta maggja set Ø-net-ie-mi ni-ġu–ḥa kita-a-mi
> bear-attack-INCONCL-AGT.PART.UNAG-GEN what.INA-GEN–REL NEG
> know-COND.IRR.INFER-1P.AG.SG what-GEN do-TR-INFI.AG.TR
> 'I wouldn't know what to do in the case of a bear attack'

maiḥai	'the whole X through, the entire X' +GEN

> *kòi viskitse maiḥai mata*
> [ˈkʰʊːi ˈviːscitse ˈmaiʔai ˈmata]
> kò-i visk-i-t=se maiḥai m-a-ta
> talk-ITR travel-ITR-INFI.ITR.AG-GEN through.out COP.PAST-ASS-3P.AG.SG
> 'X was talking the whole trip through'

mihja	'with the help of, with the power of' +GEN

> *hùnamo mihja piagjuasa*
> [ˈhuːnamɔ ˈmiːʔja ˈpʰiɑjːuɑsa]
> hù\<n\>a-mo mihja piagju-a-sa-Ø
> steam.hut-GEN with.help heal-ASS.CONCL.TR-2P.PAT-3P.AG.SG
> 'with the help/power of the steam hut, X will heal you'

negůa	'in the light of, since, because' +GEN

> *ōdlumatta negůa*
> [ˈɔ̄tɬumaʔta ˈneɟœa]
> ōdl-u-m-a-tta negůa
> be.a.certain.way-ASS.CONCL.TRANSL-INCONCL-AGT.PART.UNAG-GEN in.light
> 'in light of the situation'

nogja	'at the end of, depending on' (usually implies something hanging) +GEN
nogjita	'id.' (movement to)
nogjika	'id.' (movement from) (most commonly used)

> *tśilippen sviladi nogjika na kves*
> [ˈtɕilɻʔpɛn ˈsviladʑi ˈnɔjːiga na ˈkʰvɛs]
> tśil-i-ppen svi\<l\>a-di nogji=ka n-a kve-s
> HANG-FREQ BRAID-GEN AT.END.ELAT COP.INCONCL-ASS FEATHER-PAT
> 'a feather is hanging from the end of X's braid'

harka nogja
['harka 'nɔjːa]
ha<r>a-ka nogja
weather-GEN depending.on
'depending on the weather'

nonga/nõ(gu)   'in X language, in X's word' +GEN

sẏdi nõ(gu)
['syːdʑi 'nõ(gu)]
s<ẏ>-di nõ(gu)
Siұa-GEN in
'in Siwa'

ortta or *ohta*   'for, because' (on the occasion of - usually implies some event or time) +GEN

mauhheka tohtamha ortta moġigga
['mɑuhːega 't̪ʰɔhtamha 'ɔrtːa 'mɔxikːa]
mau<hh>e-ka tohta=m=ha ortta moġ-i-gga
hunt-GEN fruitful-GEN for drink-ASS.CONCL.ITR-1P.AG.PL.INCL
'because/for the fruitful hunt, we will drink'

(ni)raima   'against, in front of, before, to (someone's face)' +GEN
(ni)raibma   'id.' (movement to)
(ni)raiska   'id.' (movement from)

raima-ṡi hantojeṡemmi
['rɑimaɕi 'hantɔjeɕemːi]
raima–ṡi Ø-hanto-ie-ṡ=en-mi
before-2P.POSS.PL ITR-lie-COND.IRR-NEG.HABIL-1P.AG.SG
'I would not lie to you (lit I would not be able to lie before you)'

riki   'at X's house, in X's opinion' +GEN
riehta   'id.' (movement to)
riehka or *rikka*   'id.' (movement from)

iṡivikimi lilda riehta
[iˈɕiviʝimi ˈlɪlda ˈrɪɛhta]
i-ṡiv-i-ki-mi lil-da rieh=ta
DITR-stay-ASS.CONCL.ITR-TRANSLO-1P.AG.SG paternal.uncle-GEN to=house
'I'm going to stay at my paternal uncle's house'

roġo	'in the way' +GEN
roṡta	'id., to someone' (movement to, implies an event happening to someone)
roṡka	'id.' (movement from)

katotsůġjin roṡka
[kʰatoˈtsøjːɪn ˈroɕka]
kat-o-tsůġj-i-n roṡ-ka
from-SUBJ-move-ASS.CONCL.ITR-IMPER.2P.SG in.the.wat-ELAT
'move out of the way'

saḍḍja	'within X's earshot' +GEN

loaltsġovisen ġůġjů sikengōdi saḍḍja
[lɔalˈtsxɔvisɛn ˈxøjːø ˈsicɛŋːōdi ˈsɑðːja]
loal-tsġov-i-sen ġů=gjů sike<ng>-un-di saḍḍja
secret-say.about-ASS.CONCL.ITR-2P.IMP.NEG any.TEMPO enemy-GEN within.earshot
'never talk behind your enemy's back'

sesta	'X's turn' +GEN

iṡkutṡai sesta ėudni
[ˈiːskutɕai ˈsɛsta ˈøːʔtni]
iṡku-tṡa-i sesta ėudni
womenfolk-GEN-PL turn now
'it's the women's turn now'

siġa~sviġa	'except' +ELAT

negagge sġůt iṡihka sviġa
[ˈnegacːe ˈsxœʔ ˈiɕɪhka ˈsvixa]
n<eg>-a-gge sġů=t i<ṡ>i-Ø-ka sviġa
see.PAST-ASS.CONCL.TR-1P.AG.PL.EXCL nothing-GEN bark-ELAT except
'we didn't see a single thing (lit. we saw nothing except bark)'

samna   'during' +GEN

    śindi katanotsabme samna mǔgjilumi
    ['ɕɪndʑi kʰata'nɔtsaʔpme 'samnːa 'møjːilumi]
    śimi-di kata-nots-a-t=me samna mǔgjil-i-mu
    bear.head-GEN from-take-ASS.TR-INFI.AG.TR-GEN while be.silent-OBLI-ASS.CONCL.ITR
    'while taking the bear head, one must be silent'

sẏsġi   'past, by, close to (over there), at' +GEN
sẏsġita   'id.' (movement to)
sẏsġika   'id.' (movement from)

    konin seskosta sẏsġita
    ['kʰɔnɪn 'sɛskɔsta 'syːsxida]
    kon-i-n sesko-sta sẏsġi-ta
    walk-ASS.CONCL.ITR-2P.IMPER seskora-GEN past-ILLAT
    'walk past the **seskora** (tree used to find one's way)'

sygja or *sǔi* 'by (X amount of time/quantity), by X measure (comparative)' +GEN

    todatta sǔi sisotuana savi megi
    ['tʰɔdaʔta 'sœi 'sisɔduana 'savi 'meʝi]
    toda-tta sǔi sis-ota-a-na savi megi-Ø
    head-GEN by tall-COMPAR-COP.ASS-2P.AG.SG than 1p.PRON.AGT
    'you are taller than me by a head'

śilju   'X time ago' (usually found with a subordinate or relative clause) +ELAT

    taba sinka śilju konkonimi
    ['tʰaba 'sɪŋka 'ɕilju 'kɔŋkɔnimi]
    ta-ba sin=ka śilju konk-on-i-mi
    much-GEN long-ELAT ago be.young.boy-REL-COP.PAST.ASS-1P.AG.SG
    'a long time ago, when I was a young boy'

tevu....nildita   'before X's time, earlier than expected' +GEN

>*tanidgi tevu iṡula nildita*
>[tʰɑˈnɪðɟi ˈtʰevu ˈiɕula ˈniːldʑida]
>ta-ni<dg>-i tevu iṡu-la ni<ld>-ita
>3P.ACT.UNAG-die.PAST-ASS.CONCL.ITR before age-GEN face-ILLAT
>'X died before its age'

tatsŭi   'in addition to, plus' +GEN

>*tatsŭi-so*
>[ˈtʰatsœisɔ]
>tatsŭi–so
>in.addition-2P.SG.POSS
>'in addition to you' or 'plus you' +GEN

tonta   'as, in the same way as' +ILLAT

>*kȯi attṡaita tonta*
>[ˈkʰʊːi ˈɑtɕːɑida ˈtɔnta]
>kȯ-i-Ø a-ttṡa=ita tonta
>speak-ASS.CONCL.ITR-3P.AG.SG father-ILLAT same.way
>'X speak's in the same way as his/her father'

tsodlo   'through' (usually implies a complicated path) +GEN

>*riebmiṡi siajakadi tsodlo*
>[ˈɹɛʔpmiɕi ˈsiɑjɑɡɑdʑi ˈtsɔtɬɔ]
>riebm-i-ṡi-Ø sia<j>aka-di tsodlo
>navigate-ASS.CONCL.ITR-HABIL-3P.AG.SG river.system-GEN through
>'X knows how to navigate through (the maze of) the river system/ waterways'

tsẏhma   'at the point of, at, on the verge of' +GEN
tsẏhpa   'id.' (movement to)
tsẏska   'id.' (movement from)

>*rarpiri tsẏhma*
>[ˈrarpiri ˈtsyːhma]
>rarpi-ri tsŭih=ma
>madness-GEN on.verge
>'at the edge of madness'

tsůků   'per, every' +GEN

    mi todatta tsůků
    [mì: 'tʰɔda?ta 'tsøcø]
    mi-Ø toda-tta tsůků
    one-AGT head-GEN per
    'one per person/head'

tukśa   'despite' +ELAT

    butamika tukśa
    ['butɑmiga 'tʰʊk:ɕa]
    bu<t>a-mi=ka tukśa
    bad.weather-ELAT despite
    'despite the bad weather'

tśita   'not until' +ILLAT

    jehrů tahsa deitabi kjamnikita tśita
    ['jɛhrø 'tʰahsa 'deidɑbi 'cʰamniɟida 'tɕita]
    jehr-ů tahh-sa d-e-ita-bi kjamni-ki=ta tśita
    possible-ASST.CONCL.TRANSL leave-INFI.AG.ITR COP-INFER-ILLAT-1P.PL.RECI dawn-ILLAT not.until
    'it won't be possible for us to leave until dawn'

ubukka   'for X's part, on X's behalf' +GEN

    set-ḥa usotisi kòsa ubukka-go
    [sɛʔ:a u'sɔtisi 'kʰʊ:sa 'ubʊ?kagɔ]
    sem u-sot-i-si kò-sa ubukka–go
    NEG–ASS.PART PASS-give-ASS.CONCL.ITR-2P.SG.RECI speak-INFI.AG.ITR on.behalf-1P.POSS.SG
    'you may not speak on my behalf'

vitġe   'for' (the honor of, for the benefit of - usually implies some sacrifice) +GEN

    tatantůsůkihi vitġe
    ['tʰatan'tøsøɟihi 'vɪt:xe]
    tatan=tůsůki-hi vitġe
    wolf=guardian-GEN for
    'in honor of/for the wolves' *tůsůkis* (parent spirit)'

vevi/vevvi 'after, around, in the direction of' (when two things are in movement) +GEN
vůita/veita 'id.' (movement to)
vůika/veika 'id.' (movement from)

lomi mimŭkihi vevvi na garis
[ˈlɔmi ˈmimøɟihi ˈvewːi na ˈgɑrɪs]
lom-i mimŭki-hi vevvi n-a garis-Ø
chase-ITR butterfly-GEN after COP.INCONCL-ASS little.boy-AGT
'the little boy is chasing after the butterfly'

oakibma vůita
[ˈɔaɟɪʔbma ˈvœida]
oak=ibma vů-ita
home.ALLAT after.ILLAT
'homeward, towards home'

voagja 'for fear of' +GEN

set ma tykkidne voagja
[sɛʔ ma ˈtʰœʔcɪʔtne ˈvɔɑjːa]
set m-a-Ø-Ø tykk-i-t=ne voagja
NEG eat.PAST-ASS.CONCL.TR-3P.PAT-3P.AG.SG poison-ASS.ITR-INFI.SUBJ.UNAG-GEN for.fear
'X didn't eat Y for fear of getting poisoned'

§9 Verbs

Verbs are by far the most complex part of the Siwa grammar – a verb stem can be modified to take on a wide variety of meanings, aspects, moods, persons, etc. Many Siwa verbs correspond to English adjectives. A verbal root can be taken from nouns or adjectives and may require very little modification, such that verbs are extremely productive and an open class. A large set of derivative endings also allow for the creation of many types of verbs from many word categories.

Both prefixes and suffixes are part of Siwa verbal conjugation. Suffixes are much more common and there can sometimes be seven or more, whereas the most prefixes there can be on a verb is four. The most basic form a verb can have in any tense, mood, aspect or otherwise is equivalent to the English 'X will VERB' or 'X will V', where V stands for the action. For simplicity's sake, these forms will be translated as 'X will VERB Y' when there is an object. Verbs are most often listed in this form in dictionaries, as it shows in most cases the bare stem of the verb, and the addition of -a (for transitive verbs) and -i (for intransitive verbs) and preverbal vowels, for example:

keg·a	v.at	'X will hide Y'
o·keg·i	v.asubj	'X will hide (him/herself)'
nen·i	v.ai	'X will sit'

This shows the reader that the stems of the verb are **keg-** 'to hide' and **nen-** 'to sit'.

§9.1 Verb morphology

Verbs can be marked for:

transitivity
  transitive
  intransitive
  translative
  subjective
  ditransitive
  passive

tense
  non-past
  past

agentivity
  agentive
  unagentive

evidentiality
  assertive
  inferential

<table>
<tr><td>aspect</td><td>mood</td></tr>
</table>

aspect
- conclusive
- inconclusive
- habitual
- perfective [1]

secondary aspects
- reversive
- semelfactive
- persistive
- frequentative
- inchoative
- subitive
- habilitive
- diminutive

location and manner
- cislocative
- translocative
- locative markers
- preverbal adverbs
- agentive descriptive

mood
- indicative
- optative
- conditional realis
- conditional irrealis
- obligative
- imperative
- imperative obviative

person
- first
- second
- third animate
- third inanimate
- third person obviative
- fourth person

number
- singular
- plural
- inclusive
- exclusive

In addition, Siwa has nine absolutive descriptives which can be added to the stem of verbs. Not all these markings can be present at all times, but transitivity marking as well as person/number is required for all verb forms. In addition, all pronouns are marked for agentivity (agentive or unagentive) and role (subject [agent], direct object [patient] or indirect object [recipient]) in addition to number. Thus, the underlying form of *kega* 'X will hide Y' and *neni* 'X will sit'

> *kega*
> ['cʰega]
> keg-a-Ø-Ø
> hide-ASS.CONCL.TR-3P.PAT-3P.AG.SG
> 'X will hide Y'

---

[1] The word perfective here does not refer to an actual perfective aspect (which is marked by conclusivity), but rather a perfect tense marker, which in Siwa behaves morphologically like an aspect marker but semantically like a tense marker. The actual marker is called the perfective (aspectual marker), but the result is simply called the perfect.

neni
['neni]
nen-i-Ø
hide-ASS.CONCL.ITR-3P.AG.SG
'X will sit'

Siwa is a VOS language with a strict word order. The verb is generally only preceded by adverbs and coordination particles, and is followed by temporal and locative adverbs, recipients, objects and finally subjects.

ADV	**VERB**	TEMPORAL	LOCATIVE	RECIPIENT	OBJECT	SUBJECT

Consider the phrase below:

ōska iluhha kendia kemra karttaita ùki to kośi
['ōska i'luh:a 'cʰɛndʑia 'cʰɛmra 'kʰart:aida 'u:ʝi tʰɔ 'kʰɔɕi]
ōska i-luhh-a kend-ia kem=ra kar-tta=ita ù=ki to-Ø kośi-Ø
often DIT-boil-ASS.CONCL.TR early-INESS in.the.morning younger.brother-ILLAT water-GEN 3PRON.ANI.AGT.SG older.brother-AGT
'The older brother often boils water for his younger brother early in the morning'

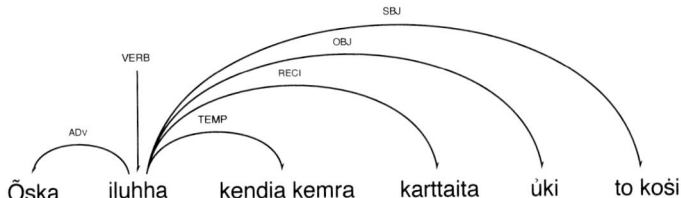

Take a look at the following similar sentences, both VOS but showing independent and incorporated subjects and objects.

nokkianija
['nɔʔcianija]
nokk-i-a-ni-ja-Ø
call-PAST-ASS.CONCL.TR-CISLO-3P.PAT.PL-3P.AG.SG
'X called them over'

nokkiani tśegmua to kesġamo
['nɔʔciani 'tɕegmua tʰɔ 'cʰɛsxamɔ]
nokk-i-a-ni tśegma-Ø-a to kesġamo-Ø
call-PAST-ASS.CONCL.TR-CISLO child-DAT-PL 3P.PRON.ANI.AGT.SG teacher-AGT
'The teacher called the children over'

§9.2 Verb Structure

The structure of Siwa verbs can be divided in two types; independent verbs and copular constructions. Verbs can assume both forms, depending on their syntactical role and the phrase construction. Independent verbs carry all the information, where as copular verbs have both the copula and the verb carrying parts of the information, separated amongst themselves according to specific rules.

Verbs are copular in relative clauses and subclauses as well as in the inconclusive, except impersonal verbs, which have a special inconclusive marker. A few verbs, such as **tat-** 'to think' (*tabmimi* or *tabmami* 'I think/I am thinking') and **det-** 'to feel like, want' (*debmami* 'I feel like X') are inconclusive but are not impersonal. Verbal adjectives also use the independent inconclusive.

§9.2.1 Independent Verbs

Independent verbs are so called because they are not cleaved like the copular verbs. Independent verbs are made up of a stem, which is surrounded by affixes, which are housed in specific slots. Each slot is numbered from the stem, and each slot houses affixes or classes of endings. The minimal form of the verb always has at least one used slot (the post verbal vowel is always present) – the root is never bare.

The three slots that precede the stem, termed prefix slots, are regular. However, the same cannot be said of the 9 suffix slots. While the majority are fixed and regular, two slots may switch places with one another according to the ending of the verbal stem.

Below is a description of each slot's function in the verb.

§9.2.1.1 Prefix slots

Prefix slots are those which come before the stem. There are three such slots, numbered -3, -2 and -1. Note that prefix slots are always unstressed, and thus follow the same orthography rules as unstressed prefixes.

preverbal adverbs	unagentive pronouns	preverbal vowel	**stem**
-3	-2	-1	0

§9.2.1.1.1 Slot -3

Slot -3 houses all preverbal adverbs. These prefixes are a kind of incorporated form of spacial, temporal or manner adverbs, which may significantly change the meaning of the original verb. They resemble prepositional verbs in English, e.g. *give in* vs. *give up*. Compare the verb *kon·i* 'X will walk' with *uta·kon·a* 'X will disobey Y' and *aro·kon·a* 'X will be loyal to Y'.

See *§9.14* on preverbal adverbs

§9.2.1.1.2 Slot -2

Slot -2 houses unagentive pronouns. Unagentive pronouns are pronouns used to show that the doer of an action is not in control, or acts unwillingly or by accident. For example, the verb stem **sahhi̱**- 'to speak' may combine with the preverbal adverb **aiẖ**- in slot -3 and the unagentive pronoun **ent**- (first person singular).

See *§9.3.5* on unagentive pronouns

aiẖ-	-ent-	-Ø-	sast·i
-3	-2	-1	0

aiẖentsasti
[ai?ɛnt'sasti]
aiẖ-ent-sa<st>-i
wrong-1P.UNAG.SG-speak.PAST-ASS.CONCL.ITR
'I misspoke'

§9.2.1.1.3 Slot -1

Slot -1 houses all preverbal vowels. Preverbal vowels include **a**- for translative verbs made from adjectives, **o**- for subjective verbs and **d-/da**- or **r-/ro**- for conditional realis. The conditional realis prefix always precedes other preverbal vowels. For example, the verb 'to break' has both slot -2 and -1 filled, and slot -1 can have two morphemes (conditional realis and subjective preverbal vowel).

a-	agentive (translative from adjectives)
o-	subjective
i-	ditransitive
u-	passive
d(a)-, ro-	conditional realis

See *§9.5.2, §9.5.4* and *§9.5.6* on preverbal vowels.

Ø-	-en-	d-o-	sogi̱·a
-3	-2	-1	0

endosogi̱a tiema
[ɛndɔ'sɔjːa 't^hiema]
en-d-o-sogi̱-a tiema-Ø
1P.UNAG.SG-COND.REAL-SUBJ-break-
ASS.CONCL.TR hand-DAT
'if I break my hand'

§9.2.1.2 Verb Stem

The verb stem is core of the verbal phrase. The stem is the bare verb, as it is given in dictionaries, but lacking both prefixes and suffixes. The form of the verb stem is an important factor for the order of slots 3 and 4. Verb stems also carry stress.

Certain verb stems contain only consonants and are called consonantal roots. These verbs are usually preceded by a preverbal vowel. Their number is very small and include:

-r-	'to bite'	found as i·r-
-t-	'to unite'	found as o·t-
-tk-	'to train'	found as o·tk-
-h-	'to eat'	found as h-
-ht-	'do (past)'	found as a·ht-

Verb stems may also be vocalic, containing only a vowel. These are often irregular, and not as common as consonantal stems. They are usually augmented either in the present or the past form (commonly with **an-** or **n-** in the past) or mark their past by diphthong coalescence (see *§3.1.5.1* on diphthong coalescence or *§9.10.1.1.3* on diphthong-final verbs).

			present	past
AUGMENTED				
	-e-	'to bathe'	gi·i·a	an·e·vva
	-i-	'to throw'	b·i·a	an·i·a
	-i-	'to change'	i	i·m·i
	-o-	'to attack'	j·o·a	an·o·a
	-oa-	'to say'	oa·i	n·oa·i
	-ů-	'to lie'	j·ů·i	an·ů·i
COALESCING				
	ią-	'to raise'	ią·	ięi·a
	ę-	'to be disgusted'	t·ęb·ů	t·ęmi·ů
	ay-	'to feel sick'	aym·i	ęmam·i
	paį-	'to disappear'	ta·paį·u	ta·pe·y

§9.2.1.2.1 Slot 1

Slot 1 houses absolutive descriptives, which are attached directly onto the bare stem. Absolutive descriptives are not necessary, but they add information about the shape or appearance of the absolutive participant, which is the subject of an intransitive verb or the object of a transitive verb. There are nine such descriptives.

Absolutive descriptives begin with a vowel, which is deleted if the stem of a verb ends in the same vowel. For example, the form of the verb *sarkk·ia* 'X broke Y' can be modified by the absolutive descriptive ·**ahp**·, which describes something long or pointy, to *sarkk·ahp·ia* 'X broke Y into a point'. See *§9.15* on absolutive descriptives.

§9.2.1.2.2 Slot 2
Slot 2 houses the complementizer (most commonly -ot- or -tot-), which is a subordination conjunction, equivalent to the English *that*, as in 'I know that you saw me', or in Siwa: *netami neg·ot·a·nga*. See *§9.16* on complementization.

<pre>
       neg-   -Ø-   -ot-   -a·nga

         0   1   2   ...
</pre>

negotanga
['nɛgɔdɑŋ:a]
n<eg>-ot-a-n=ga
see.PAST-COMPLE-
ASS.CONCL.TR-1.PAT.SG=2P.AG.SG
'that you saw me'

§9.2.1.2.3 Slot 3 and 4
Slot 3 and 4 are sometimes found in the reverse order **4-3** rather. Their order depends on how the post verbal vowel and the endings housed in the two slots combine.

Slot 3 contains the markers for the obligative (-**um**-), the perfective (-**l**- or -**la**-) and habitual aspects (-**s**- or -**sa**-). Slot 4 contains the postverbal vowel, which shows :

mood
    indicative
    optative
    conditional irrealis
evidentiality
    assertive
    inferential
transitivity
    transitive
    intransitive
    translative

There are two rules that determine the order of slots 3 and 4. The order **3-4** is called rule 1, while the order **4-3** is called rule 2. These rules do not apply to the obligative -**um**-, as it always uses the 3-4 slot order.

There are three main criteria that determine which rule applies. The normal **3-4** order (rule 1) is changed to **4-3** (rule 2) if:

- The verb does *not* end in one of the consonant clusters given in the table below.

- The verb is is in the **third person singular, first and second person plural** and in the **habitual aspect**.
    -a·s
    -a·s·kka
    -a·s·kke
    -a·s·ta

- The verb is in the **first and second person plural** and the **perfective aspect**.
    -a·l·kka
    -a·l·kke
    -a·l·tta

- There are **no overtly used slots** between slot 4 and the subject pronouns (slot 9).

When there is no personal pronoun used at all, such as in passives, rule 1 is preferred.

Rule 1 (3-4)
(-s·a-, -l·a-)

keg·s·a ·mi
'I usually hide Y'
(ends in rule 1 consonant)

keg·s·a·ri
'they usually hide Y'
(3P.PL habitual)

keg·l·a·mi
'I have hidden Y'
(1P.SG and perfective)

keg·l·a·sa·gge
'we have hidden you'
(slot used between 4 and 9)

umaġamsi
'it was onced believed'
(no pronoun)

Rule 2 (4-3)
(-a·s-, -a·l-)

ketk·a·s·mi
'I usually hid Y'
(does not end in rule 1 consonant)

keg·a·s
'X usually hides Y'
(3P.SG habitual)

keg·a·l·kka
'we have hidden Y'
(1P.PL and perfective)

keg·a·l·kka
'we have hidden Y'
(1P.PL and perfective)

aġamis
'X used to believe'
(3P.SG habitual)

All other forms of verbs (the endings not provided in the table below) follow the rule 1, with the slot order **3-4**.

	Rule 1 Slot 3-4	
Verb stem	habitual aspect marker	examples
-m-	-mh-	*nemami* 'I will pile Y up' → *nemhami* 'I usually pile Y up'
-bb- -pp- -p-	-ps-	*vappana* 'you will praise Y' → *vapsana* 'you usually praise Y'
-b-	-bs-	*oboibina* 'you will arm yourself' → *oboibsina* 'you usually arm yourself'
-n-	-nt- or -ōt- (or -ōr-)	*nonina* 'you will swim' → *nōtina* 'you usually swim' *munina* 'you will rest' → *mōtina* 'you usually rest' *nayinana* 'you will use Y' → *nayintana* 'you usually use Y'
-nt-	-nts- or -ōts-	*buntami* 'I will weave Y' → *buntsami* 'I usually weave Y' (also *bōutsami*)
-t-	-ts-	*eitari* 'they will build Y' → *eitsari* 'they usually build Y'
-s-	-ss-	*saisami* 'I will warn Y' → *saissami* 'I usually warn Y'
-r-	-rh-	*mjorana* 'you will grind Y' → *mjorhana* 'you usually grind Y'
-lt- -ltt- -ld-	-lts-	*suikildiri* 'they will live together' → *suikiltsiri* 'they usually live together'
-l-	-ls- *or* -lh-	*vielami* 'I will snare Y' → *vielsami* or *vielhami* 'I usually snare Y'
-gg- -kk- -k-	-ks-	*ġuikkami* 'I will jump over Y' → *ġuiksami* 'I usually jump over Y'

Rule 1
Slot 3-4

-g-	-gs-	*kegami* 'I will hide Y' → *kegsami* 'I usually hide Y'
-h- -hh- -ġ-	-hs-	*dohhari* 'they will say goodbye to Y' → *dohsari* 'they usually say goodbye to Y'
-hhi̯-	-ṡṡ-	*pohhi̯imi* 'I will sleep' → *poṡṡimi* 'I usually sleep'
Verb stem	perfective aspect marker	examples
-t- -tt- -d- -dd-	-dl-	*pittami* 'I will pay attention to Y' → *pidlami* 'I have paid attention to Y'
-s-	-sl-	*kesana* 'you will pay learn Y' → *keslana* 'you have paid learned Y'
-l-	-ll-	*setulari* 'they will push Y' → *setullari* 'they have pushed Y'
-n-	-ndl-	*manimi* 'I will come' → *mandlimi* 'I have come'
-gg- -kk- -k-	-kl-	*tsuoggami* 'I will hope for Y' → *tsuoklami* 'I have hoped for Y'
-g-	-gl-	*geigana* 'you will share Y' → *geiglana* 'you have shared Y'
-h- -hh-	-hl-	*nyhha* 'you will bend Y' → *nyhla* 'you have bent Y'
-ġ- -ḥ-	-ġl-	*kiaha* 'there is something big' → *kiaġla* 'there have been something big'

Because of the form of the obligative marker -um-, it always requires the order **3-4**. Notice that the inconclusive and perfective markers have the following behaviour (PV is the postverbal vowel):

```
-C-  +  -m-
 →      -C-m-PV      where -Cm- is allowed
 →      -C-PV-ma     where -Cm- is not allowed
```

	→	-C-PV-m-mi	with first person -mi

-C- + -l-
→	-C-l-PV	where -Cl- is allowed
→	-C-PV-la	where -Cl- is not allowed

Compare the following paradigms for the habitual form of the verb **mjor-** 'to grind' (predominantly rule 1) and **nots-** 'to take' (exclusively rule 2):

1P.SG	mjorhami	'I usually grind Y'	(rule 1)
2P.SG	mjorhana	'you usually grind Y'	(rule 1)
3P.SG	mjoras	'X usually grinds Y'	**(rule 2)**
1P.PL.INCL	mjoraskka	'we usually grind Y'	**(rule 2)**
1P.PL.EXCL	mjoraskke	'we usually grind Y'	**(rule 2)**
2P.PL	mjorasta	'you usually grind Y'	**(rule 2)**
3P.PL	mjorhari	'they usually grind Y'	(rule 1)
3P.OBV	mjorhat	'X usually grinds Y'	(rule 1)
4P.	mjorhajo	'one usually grinds Y'	(rule 1)

1P.SG	notsasami	'I usually take Y'	(rule 2)
2P.SG	notsasana	'you usually take Y'	(rule 2)
3P.SG	notsas	'X usually takes Y'	(rule 2)
1P.PL.INCL	notsaskka	'we usually take Y'	(rule 2)
1P.PL.EXCL	notsaskke	'we usually take Y'	(rule 2)
2P.PL	notsasta	'you usually take Y'	(rule 2)
3P.PL	notsasari	'they usually take Y'	(rule 2)
3P.OBV	notsasat	'X usually takes Y'	(rule 2)
4P.	notsasajo	'one usually takes Y'	(rule 2)

Compare the paradigm with perfective aspect marker and the verb **pitt-** 'to pay attention' (predominantly rule 1) and **saykl-** 'to protect' (exclusively rule 2):

1P.SG	pidlami	'I have paid attention to Y'	(rule 1)
2P.SG	pidlana	'you have paid attention to Y'	(rule 1)
3P.SG	pidla	'X have paid attention to Y'	(rule 1)
1P.PL.INCL	pittalkka	'we have paid attention to Y'	**(rule 2)**
1P.PL.EXCL	pittalkke	'we have paid attention to Y'	**(rule 2)**
2P.PL	pittaltta	'you have paid attention to Y'	**(rule 2)**
3P.PL	pidlari	'they have paid attention to Y'	(rule 1)
3P.OBV	pidlat	'X has paid attention to Y'	(rule 1)
4P.	pidlajo	'they have paid attention to Y'	(rule 1)

1P.SG	*sayklalami*	'I have protected Y'	(rule 2)
2P.SG	*sayklalana*	'you have protected Y'	(rule 2)
3P.SG	*sayklala*[1]	'X has protected Y'	(rule 2)
1P.PL.INCL	*sayklalkka*	'we have protected Y'	(rule 2)
1P.PL.EXCL	*sayklalkke*	'we have protected Y'	(rule 2)
2P.PL	*sayklaltta*	'you have protected Y'	(rule 2)
3P.PL	*sayklalari*	'you have protected Y'	(rule 2)
3P.OBV	*sayklalat*	'X has protected Y'	(rule 2)
4P.	*sayklalaįo*	'one has protected Y'	(rule 2)

If the verb does not fulfill the fourth criterion (the verb **does not** contain a used slot between slot 4 and 9), the paradigm reverts to rule 1:

1P.SG	*pidlahmi*	'I have paid attention to you'	(rule 1)
2P.SG	*pidlanga*	'you have paid attention to me'	(rule 1)
3P.SG	*pidlaka*	'X has paid attention to me'	(rule 1)
1P.PL.INCL	*pidlasagga*	'we have paid attention to you'	(rule 1)
1P.PL.EXCL	*pidlasagge*	'we have paid attention to you'	(rule 1)
2P.PL	*pidlakadda*	'you have paid attention to me'	(rule 1)
3P.PL	*pidlakari*	'they have paid attention to me'	(rule 1)
3P.OBV	*pidlakat*	'X has paid attention to me'	(rule 1)
4P.	*pidlakaįo*	'one has paid attention to me'	(rule 1)

This means that when no other slot between 4 and 9 is used, the form *pittaltta* is used (pitt-a-l-tta), but should the segment -ltta- be intercepted, then the verb reverts to rule 1, i.e. *pidlakatta* (pitt-l-a-<ka>-tta).

Certain verbs can govern both rule 2 for the perfective aspect but rule 1 for the habitual aspect, as both endings do not behave in the same way. For example, the verb **num-** 'to pick' uses rule 1 with the habitual, but rule 2 with the perfective:

	numhana	'you usually pick Y'	(-h·a-)	(rule 1)
but				
	numalna	'you have picked Y'	(-a·l-)	(rule 2)

§9.2.1.2.4 Impersonal Verbs and Verbal Adjectives

Impersonal verbs, verbal adjectives and a very few other verbs also including **tat-** 'to think' (*tabmimi* 'I am thinking') and **det-** 'to feel like, want' (*debmami* 'I feel like X') use slot 3 for the markers of the inconclusive (-m- or -ma-). See section *§9.9.1.1* for a list of such verbs. It governs the first rule in all cases if verb stems (augmented or bare) end in the following consonants:

---

[1] The combination -lala- is commonly changed to -lola-.

Rule 1 Slot 3-4	If the verb stem ends in the following consonants		
Verb stem	inconclusive	examples	
-p- -bb-	-bm-	sġàt- 'to be dark'→ sġàbmi 'it is dark'	
-t- -d- -dd-		nup- 'to be angry'→ nubmi 'X is angry'	
-m-	-mm-	kęm- 'to be happy'→ kęmmi 'X is happy'	
-v- -ų-		tyv- 'to be heavy'→ tymmi 'it is heavy'	
-l-	-lm-	ul- 'to be night'→ ulmi 'it is night'	
-n-	-mn-	len- 'to be thirsty'→ lemni 'X is thirsty'	
-tt-	-tm-	mott- 'to go downhill'→ motmi 'X goes downhill'	
-ḍḍ-	-ḍm-	soḍḍ- 'to be evening'→ soḍmi 'it is evening'	
-r-	-hm- or -mr-	her- 'to be cold'→ hehmi 'it is cold'	
-s-	-sm-	kùs- 'for light to change'→ kùsmi 'the light is changing'	
-ṡ-	-ṡm-	oṡ- 'to be strong'→ oṡ·mi 'X is strong'	
-gg- -k-	-km-	huok- 'to be quite'→ huokmi 'it is quite X'	
-g- -ng-	-gm-	hing- 'to be dying'→ higmi 'X is dying'	
-ġ-	-ġm-	saġ- 'to be alright'→ saġmi 'X is alright'	
-hh-	-hm-	tůhh- 'to be anxious'→ tůhmi 'X is anxious'	

In all other cases, the ending will be -ma-. Compare the verbs sìut- 'to be hungry' and njoltt- 'to be sick'.

1P.SG	sìubmika	'I am hungry	(rule 1)
2P.SG	sìubmisa	'you are hungry'	(rule 1)
3P.SG	sìubmi	'X is hungry'	(rule 1)

1P.PL.INCL	*siubmiba*	'we are hungry'	(rule 1)
1P.PL.EXCL	*siubmibe*	'we are hungry'	(rule 1)
2P.PL	*siubmiha*	'you are hungry'	(rule 1)
3P.PL	*siubmija*	'they are hungry'	(rule 1)
3P.OBV	*siubmin*	'X is hungry'	(rule 1)
4P.	*siubmija*	'one is hungry'	(rule 1)
1P.SG	*njolttimaka*	'I am sick'	(rule 2)
2P.SG	*njolttimasa*	'you are sick'	(rule 2)
3P.SG	*njolttima*	'X is sick'	(rule 2)
1P.PL.INCL	*njolttimaba*	'we are sick'	(rule 2)
1P.PL.EXCL	*njolttimabe*	'we are sick'	(rule 2)
2P.PL	*njolttimaha*	'you are sick'	(rule 2)
3P.PL	*njolttimaja*	'they are sick'	(rule 2)
3P.OBV	*njolttiman*	'they are sick'	(rule 2)
4P.	*njolttimai*	'they are sick'	(rule 2)

Note that in the eastern dialects, the endings for rule 2 are sometimes found combined with the inconclusive marker in older speakers or higher registers, if no other slot is used between them:

1p. singular	-mġa
2p. singular	-mha
1p. plural incl.	-mpa
1p. plural excl.	-mpe
2p. plural	-mha

For example:

njolttimġa	'I am sick'	(rule 2)
njolttimha	'you are sick'	(rule 2)
njolttimpa	'we (incl.) are sick'	(rule 2)
njolttimpe	'we (excl.) are sick'	(rule 2)
njolttimha	'you (pl.) are sick'	(rule 2)

§9.2.1.2.5 Slot 5

Slot 5 houses locative markers. These locative markers are most commonly -**ni** for the cislocative (towards the speaker) and -**ki** for the translocative (away from the speaker). Other locative markers also exist, as well as relative locative markers. See *§9.12* on locative markers.

Note that -**ni** and -**ki** usually combine with the perfective and habitual markers in rule 2 to form the following clusters.

HAB + CISLO	-sa-ni-	-hni-	*kẏegviasami* 'I usually called Y' → *kẏegviahnimi* 'I usually called Y over here'
HAB + TRANSLO	-sa-ki-	-ski-	*kůkůasari* 'they usually bring Y' → *kůkůaskiri* 'they usually bring Y away'
PERF + CISLO	-la-ni-	-lni-	*lehkalagga* 'we have floated Y' → *lehkalnigga* 'we have floated Y to us'
PERF + TRANSLO	-la-ki-	-lki-	*meniẏalami* 'I have lured Y' → *meniẏalkimi* 'I have lured Y away'

Rule 1

svùk-	-Ø-	-Ø-	-l-	-a-	-ki-	-dda
0	1	2	3	4	5	...

svùklakidda
[ˈsvuːklːɑɟitːa]
svùk-l-a-ki-Ø-dda
throw-PERF-ASS.CONCL.TR-TRANSLO-3P.PAT-2.AG.PL
'you (pl.) have thrown Y away'

Rule 2

hůtv-	-Ø-	-Ø-	-a-	-l-	-ni-	-ka-Ø
0	1	2	4	3	5	...

hůtvalnika
[ˈhœtwːalciga]
hůtv-a-l-ni-ka-Ø
hit-ASS.CONCL.TR-PERF-CISLO-1P.PAT.SG-3P.AG.SG
'X has hit me here'

§9.2.1.2.6 Slot 6

Slot 6 contains all the secondary aspect markers; reversive, semelfactive, persistive, frequentative, inchoative, subitive, habilitive and diminutive. They appear in this particular row and can be combined. See *§9.9.4* on secondary aspectual markers.

kidg-	-∅-	-∅-	-a-	-sa-	-∅-	-ḥḥen-	-∅
0	1	2	4	3	5	6	...

kidgasaḥḥen pèuma
[ˈcʰɪ̀gasaʔːɛn ˈpʰøːma]
kidg-a-sa-ḥḥen-∅ pŭ<∅>ŭ-ma
pick-ASS.CONCL.TR-HAB-PERS-3P.AG.SG log-GEN
'X is always picking up logs (off the ground)'

§9.2.1.2.7 Slot 7

Slot 7 houses all patientive pronouns, which are equivalent to the objects of verbs. See *§9.3.4* on patientive pronouns.

sedj-	-∅-	-∅-	-a-	-∅-	-∅-	-∅-	-ja-	-mi
0	1	2	4	3	5	6	7	...

sedjajami
[ˈsedʑajami]
se<dj>-a-ja-mi
hear.PAST-ASS.CONCL.TR-3P.PAT.PL-1P.AG.SG
'I heard them'

§9.2.1.2.8 Slot 8

Slot 8 houses recipient pronouns, which have two functions; they may work as indirect objects (then with ditransitive verbs) or may simply show the beneficiary of the action (without ditransitive markers). See *§9.3.3* on recipient pronouns.

i-	-soatsk-	-ot-	-∅-	-a-	-∅-	-∅-	-∅-	-ja-	-hi-	-gge
-1	0	1	2	4	3	5	6	7	8	...

...isoatskotajahigge
[iˈsɔatskːɔdajahiːe]
i-soatsk-ot-a-ja-hi-gge
DIT-offer-ASS.CONCL.TR-COMPLE-3P.PAT.PL-2P.RECI.PL-1P.AG.PL.EXCL
'...that we will offer them to you'

§9.2.1.2.9 Slot 9

The last slot houses agentive pronouns. Thus, these are always the very last thing to be added to the verb. Any subsequent clitic is attached to the verb with a hyphen. Note that slot 9 also holds the imperative markers, and for that reason they can be considered to be forms of the agentive pronoun endings. See *§9.3.2* on agentive pronouns.

i-	-st-	-Ø-	-Ø-	-a-	-Ø-	-Ø-	-Ø-	-ja-	-si-	-mi
-1	0	1	2	4	3	5	6	7	8	9

istajasimi
[ˈɪstajasimi]
i-s<Ø>t-a-ja-si-mi
DIT-give.PAST-ASS.CONCL.TR-3P.PAT.PL-2P.RECI.SG-1P.AG.SG
'I gave them to you'

With the imperative:

i-	-sot-	-Ø-	-Ø-	-a-	-Ø-	-Ø-	-Ø-	-ja-	-bi-	-uri
-1	0	1	2	4	3	5	6	7	8	9

isotajabiuri
[ˈisɔtajabiuri]
i-sot-a-ja-bi-uri
DIT-give-ASS.CONCL.TR-3P.PAT.PL-1P.RECI.PL-IMPER.2P.PL
'give them to us!'

§9.2.2 Split Stems

Copular verbs, called split stem verbs, are those which require an auxiliary copula in order to be grammatical. Various things can cause a verb to split, and the vast majority of verbs can become copular. The inconclusive aspect (but not of impersonal verbs), relative clauses, certain fixed expressions and other types of sentences require the verb to be copular. See *§9.17* on the copula for a more in-depth description.

Copular verbs are composed of two parts – the verbal stem with certain slots, called a split-stem, and the copula, with the rest of the slots.

The split-stem has 3 prefix slots and 1 or 2 (in the case of the obligative only) suffix slots, while the copula has one extra prefix slot and the rest of the normal slots.

Slot 4 follows the split-stem immediately, but the slots 1 2 3 and 4^2 5 6 7 8 9 are attached onto the copula. The copula is placed at the end of the verbal phrase, usually only followed by the agent of the phrase. The copula adds a 10th slot, which is actually a prefix (o-), used to form relative clauses. It is called slot -1COP.

The slot 4 is actually marked twice in the sentence, as it is both found at the split-stem slot 4 and the copula slot 4. The copula slot is termed slot 4^2. The functions of slot 4 are thus split into two:

Slot 4 (Split-stem):
    transitivity
        transitive   (-a)
        intransitive   (-i)
        ditransitive   (i-Ø-i or i-Ø-a)
        objective   (o-Ø-i or o-Ø-a)
        translative   (-u/-ů)
        passive   (u-Ø-i or u-Ø-a)

mood
    obligative

Slot 4² (Copula):
    mood
        indicative
        optative
        conditional irrealis
    evidentiality
        assertive
        inferential

This means that when a verb is split for a copular construction, the stem only retains markers for transitivity, while everything else is marked onto the copula, which is always transitive[1].

The rest of the verbal phrase is unaffected by this copular split. Adverbs still precede the verb and the verbal phrase continues within the boundaries of the

Split-stem slots

kat-	-Ø-	-o-	-rinta-	-um-	-i
-3	-2	-1	0	[3]	4

Copular slots

-Ø-	n-	-ohk-	-Ø-	-on	-e-	-Ø-	-Ø-	-Ø-	-Ø-	-Ø-
-1COP	COP	1	2	3	4²	5	6	7	8	9

---

[1] In reality, the copula can be transitive or translative, but because the translative is already marked in slot 4, it is not necessary in slot 4².

... katorintaumi sevvue unnja nohkone to kinagi
[kʰatoˈriːntaumi ˈsewːue ˈuɲːa ˈnɔhkɔnˈe tʰɔ ˈcʰinaji]
kat-o-rinta-um-i sevvo-e unnja n-ohk-on-e to kinagi-Ø
from-SUBJ-scratch-OBLI-ITR shirt-GEN under COP.INCONCL-ohk-COMPLE-INFER 3P.SG.ANI.AG stranger-AGT
'...that the stranger must be scratching himself under his shirt'

Split-stem slots

ah-	-Ø-	-Ø-	-kid̪g-		-um-	-i
-3	-2	-1	0		[3]	4

Copular slots

-Ø-	m-	-Ø-	-Ø-	-Ø-	-e-	-jo-	-Ø-	-Ø-	-ni-	-Ø-
-1COP	COP	1	2	3	4²	5	6	7	8	9

tatė, ahkid̪gumi mitabe mejoni peggů
[ˈtʰate: ahˈcɪd̪gumi ˈmiːdabe ˈmejɔnˈe pʰecːø]
tatė-Ø, ah-kid̪g-um-i mitabe me-jo-ni peggů-Ø
room-AGT after-clean.up-OBLI-ITR yesterday COP.PAST.INCONCL-REL.INESS-4P.RECI girl-AGT
'...the room, (in) which the girl was supposed to clean up after herself'

§9.2.2.1 Split Stem Concord

The copula and the split stem verbs in certain cases must concord in either valency or conclusivity. Passive and translative verbs require the copula to be in the translative valency (which can also be considered an aspect in Siwa), while all inconclusive verbs transfer their inconclusivity onto the copula.

Passive:
utki   'it was done'
ukitauts guta   'when it was done'

ukvigji   'it can be felt'
ukviuts guta   'when it can be felt'

Translative:
mahatru   'I ought to'
hatrùts guma   'when I ought to'

ijomu   'it is possible'
ijomùts mel o   'as soon as possible'

Inconclusive:
sihmi   'it is raining'

sihhiuts na	'when it is raining'
tabmimi	'I think'
tatauts nami	'when I think'
logmi	'it is freezing'
longiuts ma	'when it was freezing'

§9.3 Verbal Personal Pronouns

Pronouns can be attached to the verb. There are 4 types of personal pronouns – agentive, unagentive, patientive and recipient pronouns. Note that the eastern and western dialects differ somewhat in the form of their personal pronouns.

Agentive pronouns occupy slot 9 and are used with conscious and/or willing agents, i.e. acting of their own accord or purposefully. Unagentive pronouns, which occupy slot -2, are used with unconscious and/or unwilling agents, i.e. acting by accident or driven by an exterior force. Patientive pronouns are used with the objects of verbs and occupy slot 7, while recipient pronouns serve two roles – the indirect object (to whom) or the beneficiary (for whom), and occupy slot 8.

Siwa pronouns exist for the following persons, found in their four types or roles:

I	1p. singular
you	2p. singular
he/she/it	3p. (animate and inanimate) singular
we	1p. plural inclusive (1p. plural + 2p. person singular/plural)
we	1p. plural exclusive (1p. plural)
you	2p. plural
they	3p. (animate and inanimate) plural
he/she/it	3p. obviative (no number distinction)
they/one/we	4p. (no number distinction)

The third person pronouns are not concerned with animacy, only number and proximity (obviative vs. proximate).

§9.3.1.1 Inclusive vs. Exclusive

The inclusive vs. exclusive distinction is always made in Siwa – an inclusive **we** assumes the second person, whether singular or plural, to be included, while an exclusive **we** assumes that the second person is not part of the group to which the pronoun refers. Compare the following examples:

makigge taskkita Talgo
['mɑciːe 'tʰascːida 'tʰalgɔ]
mak-i-gge task-ki=ta Talgo-Ø
go-ASS.CONCL.ITR-1P.AG.PL.EXCL woods-ILLAT Talgo-AGT
'Talgo and I/us will go into the woods'

makigga taskkita Talgo
['mɑcikːa 'tʰascːida 'tʰalgɔ]
mak-i-gga taskk-ki=ta Talgo-Ø
go-ASS.CONCL.ITR-1P.AG.PL.INCL woods-ILLAT Talgo-AGT
'we (you and me) will go into the woods with Talgo'

Very formal Siwa sometimes requires that the speaker who wishes to be humble avoid the second person all together and simply use the first person plural inclusive:

sytùegga nedġitseta
['sytuːekːa 'nɛðxitseda]
syty-ue-gga nedġ-i-t=se=ita
wish-INFER.CONCL.OBT-1P.AG.PL.INCL sit.down-ITR-INFI=ILLAT
'please sit down! (lit. may we wish to sit down)'

In fact, the form *sytùegga* is a very common polite form for asking someone to do something, or to ask someone to accompany one. It exists in various shortened form, such as *sytka*, *tỳi* and *sytvi*, which can commonly found in utterances in order to make them more like a polite request:

deladnauri sytka/tỳi/sytvi	'please take off your coat'
katomolkiuri sytùegga	'please move out of the way'
hagjenaunni tỳi, ot…	'you will/must notice that…'
siopuadnakimi sytka	'please help me (a little)'

§9.3.1.2 Obviative vs. Proximate

The third person has two forms – a normal form, called proximate, and an obviative form. The proximate form is the default form of the third person, and it distinguishes between singular and plural. The obviative form however, lacks a number distinction and has a much more restricted use.

The third person obviative is used when more than one third person is involved in a sentence. The third person obviative is generally found in a subsequent phrase to an initial statement – the obviative is thus cataphoric, referring to an antecedent.. The proximate in contrast is anaphoric, meaning it refers to a precedent. The rules as to when the obviative is used are as follow, illustrated in the table below and described here:

1. If a subject¹ in phrase¹ is also subject¹ in phrase², it is found in its regular proximate form. *Anaphoric subject.*

2. If subject¹ in phrase² is not the same as in phrase¹, subject² is in the obviative. *Cataphoric subject.*

3. If phrase¹ has both subject¹ and a recipient, and phrase² has subject² and an object which is not the same as the recipient, the subject² is in the obviative and the object² is found as a proximate independent pronoun.

4. If a subject¹ in phrase¹ is the object **or** not longer the subject in phrase², the subject² will be in the obviative, and the object of phrase² (subject¹) will be found in the fourth person.

	phrase¹		phrase²	
1	subject¹		subject¹	
	proximate			
2	subject¹		subject²	
	proximate		obviative	
3	subject¹	recipient¹	subject²	object²
	proximate		obviative	independent proximate pronoun
4	subject¹	object¹	subject²	subject¹ → object²
	proximate		obviative	4p.

1.
>
> *neta negota*
> ['neta 'negɔda]
> net-a-Ø n<eg>-ot-a-Ø-Ø
> know-ASS.CONCL.TR-3P.AG.SG see.PAST-COMPLE-
> ASS.CONCL.TR-3P.PAT-3P.AG.SG
> 'X¹ knows that X¹ saw Y'

2.
>
> *neta negotat*
> ['neta 'negɔda?]
> net-a-Ø n<eg>-ot-a-Ø-t
> know-ASS.CONCL.TR-3P.AG.SG see.PAST-COMPLE-
> ASS.CONCL.TR-3P.PAT-3P.OBV.AG
> 'X¹ knows that X² saw Y'

3.
>
> *nonati negotat otta*
> ['nɔnatɕi 'negɔda? 'ɔ?ta]
> n=on-a-ti-Ø n<eg>-ot-a-t o=tta
> tell.PAST-ASS.CONCL.TR-3P.RECI-3P.AG.SG see.PAST-COMPL
> ASS.CONCL.TR-3P.OBV.AG 3P.PRON.ANI.SG.PAT
> 'X¹ told Y¹ that X² saw Y²'

4.
>
> *neta negotait*
> ['neta 'negɔdaɪ?]
> net-a-Ø n<eg>-ot-a-i-t
> know-ASS.CONCL.TR-3P.AG.PL see.PAST-COMPLE-
> ASS.CONCL.TR-4P.PAT-3P.OBV.AG
> 'X¹ knows that X² saw X¹'

§9.3.1.3 Fourth Person

The fourth person in Siwa serves three main purposes.

1. With a plural subject, the fourth person may serve as a reciprocality and/or reflexivity marker, to indicate that the plural subjects act on each other.

negairi	'they saw each other'
jedlairi	'they killed each other'

2. The fourth person serves as an impersonal pronoun referring to an unnamed agent. It can be equivalent to a first person plural without associating oneself to the group (compared the inclusive and exclusive first persons, this would be an excluded first person). It can also be used in a similar fashion to English *one*. Forms in *-gjen/-jen* are most common for this in the agentive.

pendigjen	'we/one arrived'

ujovoammįja   'we/one was very afraid'

3. The fourth person refers back to the subject of a previous phrase when a new subject has been introduced.

ikigutta ipednidna oakibma deika śini-nen
'X couldn't wait for his/her daughter to come back home'

idadga kůlita te ihůtvia kepieita-ho kaimka-nen gala
'he₁ attacked him₂ and hit him₂ on his₂ head with his₁ stick'

When a third person acts upon itself, the fourth or third person is used. When a third person, similarly, uses the third person proximate (i.e. non-obviative) in a non-verbal form (usually in the genitive or with double case marking), it carries a simple reflexive meaning, whereas using the fourth person usually implies one's own:

ha ůnsi~tůmůsi   'X eats his/hers'
ha nihõsi   'X eats his/her own'

The fourth person can be used as a patientive pronoun (-i or -ja) to show reflexivity. It can also be used as an agentive pronoun (-jen or -gjen), coalesced with the appropriate plural agentive pronoun, to show reciprocality.

Reciprocal

A reciprocal verb has plural subjects acting upon each other.
Uses -jen- or -gjen- coalesced with the appropriate plural agentive pronoun:

1P.PL.INCL	-jen·ka	'you and me VERB each other'
1P.PL.EXCL	-jen·ke	'X and I VERB each other'
2P.PL	-jen·da	'you VERB each other'
3P.PL	-jenri	'they VERB each other'

rutrajenri   'they hate each other'
oittagajenri   'the quickly glanced at each other'
màra ilajenka   'we know each other'

negajenri katvèumemia didagi[1]
['negajɛn(d)ri kʰat'vø:memia 'didaji]
n<eg>-a-jen=ri kat=vèume-m=ia dida-Ø-gi
see.PAST-ASS.CONCL.TR-RECIPRO.3P.PL.AG reflection-INESS girl-AGT-PL
'the girls saw each other in the reflection' (X and Y saw X and Y)

Another way of marking reciprocality is with the pronoun nin- (see §10.1.5):

negari katvèumemia nigeni didagi
'the girls saw each other in the reflection'

imairi nika ţiegmagi
'the children laughed at each other' (*i·mairo- Ø-ika* 'laugh at X')

Reflexive

A reflexive verb has a subject acting upon itself.
Uses -i- or -ja- as patientive pronouns.

onegairi katvèumemia didagi
[ɔ'negairi kʰat'vø:memia 'didaji]
o-n<eg>-a-i-ri kat=vèume-m=ia dida-Ø-gi
SUBJ-see.pAST-ASS.CONCL.TR-4P.PAT-3P.AG.PL reflection-INESS girl-AGT-PL
'The girls saw themselves in the reflection' (X saw X, Y saw Y)[2]

Verbs whose object arguments are not verbal pronouns (like verbs involving nin- 'oneself') use a special set of object forms of the nin- pronouns. For the second and first person, the former pronoun (normally *nigen*) may instead be the personal pronoun (*megi, negi*).

patientive	nigennin, nigennin, niennin
genitive	niġõ nin, niġonnin, nihõ nin, nihonnin
dative	nitsi nin, nitsinin, nitsnin (nihnin)
locative	ni-Ø–nin, ni-Ø nin

	imairi nikanin~nika nin ţiegmagi	'the children laughed at themselves' (X laughed at X, Y laughed at Y)
	ihenni nitanin~nita nin roami	'each is responsible for himself'
	sailumana nigen ninta	'you have to trust in yourself'
or	*sailumana neidġi ninta*	'you have to trust in yourself'

---

[1] These types of sentences sometimes trigger the subjective preverbal vowel o- to appear, such that the phrase can also be found as *onegajenri katvèumemia didagi*.

[2] The use of reflexives will often trigger the subjunctive preverbal vowel o-.

Reciprocality is generally *not* expressed by use of the patientive 4th person -i- or -ja- if verbs have an inherently reciprocal meaning, such as verbs in o-Ø-ld- (see §14.2.2).

dohrajenri
[ˈdɔhrɑjɛn(d)ri]
do<hr>-a-jen=ri
say.goodbye.PAST-ASS.CONCL.TR-REIPCRO.3P.AG.PL
'they said goodbye to each other'

ojagjelejenka
[ɔˈjɑjːelejɛŋka]
o-jagjel-e-jen=gga
SUBJ-get.to.know-INFER.CONCL.TR-RECIPRO.1P.AG.PL.INCL
'we will/should get to know each other'

ogjikkiajenri
[ˈɔjːɪʔciɑjɛn(d)ri]
ogjikk-i-a-jen=ri
be.enamored-PAST-ASS.CONCL.TR-RECIPRO.3P.AG.PL
'they were enamored with each other'

saibba daumi-nen lugjudneka
[ˈsɑipːɑ ˈdɑuminɛn ˈlujːʊʔtnega]
saibb-a <daumi>-nen lugju-t=ne=ika
must.not-ASS.CONCL.TR older.sister.GEN–4P.PRON.POSS love-INFI.AG.TR=ELAT
'one must not love one's *own* (older) sister'

oneigjenri
[ɔˈneijːɛn(d)ri]
o-n=e-i-gjen=ri
SUBJ-bathe.PAST-ASS.CONCL.ITR-RECIPRO.3P.AG.PL
'they washed each other'

oneijari
[ɔˈneijɑri]
o-n=e-i-ja=ri
SUBJ-bathe.PAST-ASS.CONCL.ITR-4P.PAT-.3P.AG.PL
'they washed themselves'

oveibmigjenri daḍḍaita-nen[1]
[ɔˈvɛɪʔpmijːɛn(d)ri ˈdaðːɑidanɛn]
o-vei<bm>-i-gjen=ri da<ḍḍa>-ita–nen
SUBJ-marry.PAST-ASS.CONCL.ITR-RECIPRO.3P.AG.PL younger.sister-ILLAT–4P.POSS
'they married each other's younger sisters'

§9.3.2 Agentive Pronouns

Agentive pronouns are the last thing to be added to the verb stem, and they occupy slot 9. They are used for conscious, willing agents. The third person has a special form found with the copula. The first person is sometimes found as -b, especially in poetry. The fourth person -gjen ending is used after -i-, whereas -jen is used elsewhere.

person		agentive pronoun	example
1P.	SG.	-mi/-b (-u̯(i) WEST)	*makimi~makib~makiu̯i* 'I will go'
	PL. INCL	-gga (-ko WEST)	*makigga~makiko* 'we will go'
	PL. EXCL	-gge (-ků WEST)	*makigge~makiků* 'we will go'
2P.	SG.	-na	*makina* 'you will go'
	PL.	-dda (-d WEST)	*makidda~makid* 'you will go'
3P.	SG.	-Ø (-ta/-ra with the copula)	*maki* 'X will go'
	PL.	-ri (-ts WEST) (-tari/-ddari with the copular)	*makiri~makits* 'they will go'
	OBV.	-t	*makit* 'X will go'
4P.		-jo / -jen / -gjen	*makijo~makigjen* 'one will go'

§9.3.3 Recipient Pronouns

Recipient pronouns precede agentive pronouns directly. They are used to show that the person is the recipient of something, i.e. is the indirect object. Its other role is to show who benefits from the action. When the recipient pronoun's function is that of an indirect object, the verb is generally found in the ditransitive. However, transitivity is not a factor when a beneficiary is marked onto the verb by the recipient pronouns. This means that even intransitive verbs may have a recipient pronoun.

---

[1] The 4th person possessive -nen here is prefered to the 3rd person animate -ho because the subject of the phrase (they) is considered as a single person.

| | | RECIPIENT | i-Ø-a-ti | 'X will VERB **to** Y' |
| | | BENEFICIARY | Ø-a-ti | 'X will VERB **for** Y' |

The recipient pronouns do not distinguish between the first person inclusive or exclusive, and similarly between the third person plural or singular. The example below is the verb **i·sot-** 'to give (to)'

person		recipient pronoun	example
1P.	SG.	-ki-	*isotaki* 'X will give Y to me'
	PL. INCL	-bi-	*isotabi* 'X will give Y to us'
	PL. EXCL		
2P.	SG.	-si-	*isotasi* 'X will give Y to you'
	PL.	-hi-	*isotahi* 'X will give Y to you'
3P.	SG.	-ti- (-tsi WEST)	*isotati* 'X will give Y to Z'
	PL.		
	OBV.	-ṡi-	*isotaṡi* 'X will give Y to Z'
4P.		-ni-	*isotani* 'X will give Y to one'

Third person recipient pronouns are also commonly found as locative markers (see §4.5.5.3), especially with ditransitive verbs.

§9.3.4 Patientive Pronouns

Patientive pronouns are found in slot 6 and they are used for objects, whether their nominal counterpart is in the dative or the genitive. All object pronouns have a single form, the patientive form. When the nuance, which normally is expressed through the object case (genitive vs. dative), is not expressed saliently enough for the speaker's intention, it may be represented both by a verbal pronoun and an independent pronoun in the appropriate case. The example below is the verb **neg-** 'saw' (past of **nuj-**).

Personal pronouns exist both in the dative and the patientive. The distinction between dative and patientive however is not realized with verbal pronouns, and the independent pronouns thus have two corresponding cases to a single set of verbal pronouns. Telicity is thus only shown through independent pronouns.

VERBAL PRONOUNS   CORRESPONDING INDEPENDENT PRONOUNS patientive → dative or genitive

adlmiaka gogi   'X raised *me* (to be something)'
adlma gogi maka   'X was raising *me*'

person		patientive pronoun	example
1P.	SG.	-ka-	*negaka* 'X saw me'
	PL. INCL	-ba-	*negaba* 'X saw us'
	PL. EXCL	-be-	*negabe* 'X saw us'
2P.	SG.	-sa-	*negasa* 'X saw you'
	PL.	-ha-	*negaha* 'X saw you'
3P.	SG.	-Ø-	*nega* 'X saw Y'
	PL.	-ja-	*negaja* 'X saw them' (also 'one saw Y')
	OBV.	-no- or -u	*negau* 'X saw Y'
4P.		-i or -ja	*negai* 'X saw itself'

Should slot 8 be empty, certain patientive pronouns coalesce with the agentive pronouns:

2P.PAT.SG + 1P.AG.SG	-sa-mi	→	-hmi
arkiasami	'I used to babysit Y'		
arkiasahmi	'I used to babysit you'		
2P.PAT.SG + 1P.PL.EXCL	-sa-gge	→	-skka
dohhagga	'we will say goodbye to X'		
dohhaskka	'we will say goodbye to you'		
1P.PAT.SG + 2P.AG.SG	-ka-na	→	-nga or -kna
goskkana	'you will betray Y'		
goskkanga	'you will betray me'		

§9.3.5 Unagentive Pronouns
Unagentive pronouns are those which describe an agent acting as the subject of the verb, but which acts unwillingly, unconsciously, against his or her will, by accident, or

with various verbs which require an unagentive pronoun. Unlike the three other types of pronouns, unagentive pronouns are prefixes to the verb and are housed in prefix slot -2.

However, when unagentive pronouns are found attached to the copula (in copular constructions), the pronoun is found as a suffix in slot 9. The examples below are with the verb id- 'to fall' in its verbal form and in a past relative copular clause.

The third person singular pronoun attached directly to verbs to form clusters when possible:

    t-v-
    d-l-
    t-s-
    t-sv-
    t-sġ-
    t-sġv-
    t-ṡ-
    t-ṡv-

Dialects that allow complex initial clusters also allow:
    t-m- (sometimes s-m-)
    t-k-

The first person has the following forms:

    en- before
        en-t-
        en-d-
        en-ts-
        en-tṡ-
        en-dị-
        en-k-
        en-g-
  em- before
        em-b-
        em-p-
  ed- before
        ed-n-
  ent- before
        ent-s-
        ent-ṡ-
        ent-ġ-
ma- elsewhere

There is quite a lot of variation between dialects in the exact forms of the first person (perhaps due to the convergence of the singular and plural forms). One common form is simply eC-C or ẹC-C where the initial consonant is geminated according to the same rules as approbation (see *§4.4.1*), **ei-**, **m(a)-** in all cases (mostly older western dialect speakers) or even **meC-** (far eastern dialects). Forms in **eC-** are slowly becoming favored over **en-**.

> *en·gidlki*   'I surrender'
> *eg·gidlki*
> *ęg·gidlki*
> *ei·gidlki*
> *ma·gidlki*
> *meg·gidlki*

Not all dialects use **en-/em-/ent-**. Forms in **ei-** are also common, and some western dialects use the pattern **e·C-C-** or **eḥ-** with gemination of the initial vowel (same rules as pejorative, see *§4.4.3*)[1]. Forms in **e·C-C** or **eḥ-** are common amongst younger speakers and males.

person		unagentive pronoun		example	
		verb	copula		
1P.	SG.	m(a)-	-ma	*middi* 'I/we fell'	*idi gaitoma* 'in which I fell'
	PL. INCL	or en(t)-/ed-	-mari		*idi gaitomari* 'in which we fell'
	PL. EXCL	m(e)- or en(t)-	-meri (-můri WEST)		*idi gaitomeri* 'in which we fell'
2P.	SG.	s(a)-	-sa	*siddi* 'you fell'	*idi gaitosa* 'in which you fell'
	PL.	sġ(a)-	-sari (-sġi WEST)	*sġiddi* 'you fell'	*idi gaitosari* 'in which you fell'
	SG.	t(a)-	-ta	*tiddi* 'X fell'	*idi gaitota* 'in which X fell'

---

[1] Examples: 'I fall asleep' can be *mapiagi*, *empiagi*, *eipiagi* or *ebbiagi*.

person		unagentive pronoun		example	
		verb	copula		
3P.	PL.	ts(e)-	-tari (-dġi WEST)	*tsiddi* 'they fell'	*idi gaitotari* 'in which they fell'
	OBV.	n(e)-	-ne	*niddi* 'X fell'	*idi gaitone* 'in which X fell'
4P.		j̨(a)-	-j̨a	*j̨iddi* 'one fell'	*idi gaitoj̨a* 'in which one fell'

§9.3.6 Overview

person		agentive	unagentive		patientive	recipient
			verbal	copular		
1P.	SG.	-mi	m(a)- en-	-ma	-ka	-ki
	PL. INCL	-gga	m(a)- en-	-mari	-ba	-bi
	PL. EXCL	-gge	m(e)- en-	-meri	-be	
2P.	SG.	-na	s(a)-	-sa	-sa	-si
	PL.	-dda	sġ(a)-	-sari	-ha	-hi
3P.	SG.	-Ø	t(a)-	-ta	-Ø	-ti
	PL.	-ri	ts(e)-	-tari	-j̨a	
	OBV.	-t	n(e)-	-ne	-no/-u	-ṡi
4P.		-j̨o/-j̨en	j̨(a)-	-j̨a	-i/-j̨a	-ni

314

§9.4 Agentivity

All verbs with an agent in Siwa are found in one of two possible agentivities – the agentive and the unagentive.

Verbs may only allow one or the other, or both agentivities, usually with changes in meaning. How a verb's agentivity behaves can be difficult to predict, but in the majority of cases, it reflects the Siwa speakers' understanding of agentivity or may simply be the result of the verb's assigned agentivity.

Agentivity describes whether the doer of an action, the agent, is conscious or not. An agentive verb involves a doer who is perceived to be conscious, willing or personified inanimate nouns. An unagentive verb on the other hand, is the opposite – the agent is perceived to be unconscious, unwilling or a depersonified animate noun.

AGENTIVE	UNAGENTIVE
I eat	I vomit
I walk	I stumble
I go to sleep	I fall asleep

Conscious and/or willing or unconscious and/or unwilling agents are not so much determined by the actual consciousness or willingness but rather by whether or not their action is the result of the agent's own decision. For example, the form *middi* 'I fell' is in its unagentive form, while if it is put in the agentive, *iddimi*, the meaning becomes 'I willingly fell/I made myself fall/I pretended to fall'.

Certain verbs have assigned agentivity which may or may not reflect the actual semantic agentivity of the verb. For example, while the verb *to like* might actually involve a conscious decision on the agent's half, the Siwa verb **kokk-** 'to like, to please' is always unagentive. In fact, the English subject of the verb is found in the patientive in Siwa, and the English object is found in the unagentive. Verbs where the logical topic of the phrase is not the agent are called patientive verbs (see *§9.4.1.1*)

sakokkaka
[saˈkʰɔʔkaga]
sa-kokk-a-ka
2P.UNAG.SG-please-ASS.CONCL.TR-1P.PAT.SG
'I like you' (lit. you please me)

§9.4.1 Unagentive Verbs

Unagentive verbs are vast class. Semantically agentive verbs that behave as unagentive verbs are more common than semantically unagentive verbs that behave as agentive verbs. For that reason, unagentive verbs may appear slightly more counterintuitive.

Unagentive verbs are easy to recognize as use prefixes for pronouns (in slot -3), unlike agentive verbs. Common unagentive classes include:

1. Verbs denoting an involuntary state:

m·aihi	'I will be wrong'
m·aiteili	'I will be severely sick'
ma·mendui	'I will dream'
em·punkųi	'I will feel remorse'

Verbs denoting an involuntary/accidental action:

ma·hejoli	'I will shiver'
m·aiha	'I will do something (wrong)'
ed·nekeni	'I will lose'
ta·roahtś·i	'X will chafe'
t·eli	'X will grow'

3. All verbs in -eni and -uni with a meaning of 'to seem Y' or 'to feel Y' and most other verbs denoting senses:

em·pialjeni	'I will seem red/I will flush'
ent·serjeni	'I will feel good'
ent·śauttuni	'I will seem hungry'
gjosi̇ engeki	'I seem tired'
mohjeimeni	'I am hot'
mohigjeni	'I am cold'

4. Certain causative verbs:

t·atujukka	'X will make Y sick'
ta·higjekka	'X will make Y cold'

5. All translative verbs (in -u or -ů):

ma·hingů	'I will die (in combat)'
ma·jaśku	'I will grow older'
m·amagju	'I will fade'
ta·njanku	'X will pile up, accumulate'
t·sadlu	'X will burn (in a pot)'
t·silků	'X will swell up'

A great number of auxiliary verbs (which are also often translative):

ma·hatru	'I ought to'
ma·hjoma	'I had better do Y'
m·jahhju	'I can do Y (because I have enough endurance)'

en·kaha	'I need to (do Y)'
m·ijomu	'I can do Y (because I have enough time/conditions are favourable)'

7. A small number of semantically ambiguous or agentive verbs (often in their negative form):

m·ingi	'I will live'
m·iljili	'I will be alive'
ma·hirkurui	'I will shriek'
m·ib·oaki	'I will come from'
m·orpi	'I will misbehave'
em·pirru	'I will recover'
en·gimia	'I will look forward to Y' (cf. *gimiaka* 'I am anxious')
set m·alla	'I will not have time for Y' (cf. *allami* 'I will have time for Y')

§9.4.1.1 Patientive Verbs

A small group of verbs, often considered to be a subset of unagentive verbs, are called the patientive verbs. They also have an unagentive subject, but rather than using unagentive pronouns and have the agent be the subject, patientive verbs have the subject in the patientive. The actual object is usually an unagentive subject. Verbal adjectives are also patientive verbs, and many true verbs semantically similar to adjectival verbs belong to this group:

gimmi·ka	'I am excited' (cf. *ta·gimmi·ka* 'X exites me')
ta·hammjua·ka	'I love X'
ta·kokka·ka	'I like X'
(ta)·koaibma·ka	'X is enough for me'

§9.4.2 Agentive Verbs

Agentive verbs include the majority of verbs whose agent is perceived to be in control or to be acting willingly. Opposite to unagentive verbs, agentive verbs use suffixes to mark pronouns in slot 4.

Because agentive verbs require self-awareness, will, intent or control, they will most commonly involve human or personified agents. Because of this, they are more restricted than unagentive verbs, but include more of the most common verbs.

nega·mi	'I will see Y'
kita·mi	'I will do Y'
poṡki·mi	'I will go to sleep'
arka·mi	'I will babysit Y'
askila·mi	'I will control/govern Y'
eita·mi	'I will build Y'

geiga·mi	'I will share Y'
gika·mi	'I will glance at Y'
eri·mi	'I will be careful'
hiddjuja·mi	'I will stack Y up'
gagema·mi	'I will feel compassion for Y' (as an act of solidarity)

§9.4.3 Ambiguous Agentivity

Verbs whose agentivity is ambiguous may sometimes be found in the unagentive or in the agentive, and this difference may subtly or greatly affect the verb's meaning or possible interpretations. A change of assigned agentivity may be used for personification or depersonification of an agent.

Personification is taking a generally inanimate action and conferring it the qualities of an animate action, thus giving the inanimate agent life, a will and/or a consciousness – this is especially common in storytelling and more poetic language.

> *keyi tèrhi*
> '(the) Sun will rise'
> personified – the sun is a deity acting consciously

> *keyi tèhtsa*
> 'the sun will rise'
> not personified – the sun is simply a natural phenomenon

Depersonification is making a generally agentive verb unagentive. This is usually used:

1. With pejorative nouns:

> *nanta eteri-go oddolba*
> ['nanta 'eterigɔ ɔ'tːɔlba]
> na<nt>-a eteri-Ø–go od-t<olba>
> break.PAST-ASS.CONCL.TR spear-DAT–1P.POSS.SG PEJ-son-PAT
> 'your (worthless/damn) son broke my spear'

2. To belittle the agent of the verb (especially with rhetoric questions in **so-** Ø**-ahte**):

> *medde vuihlina*
> ['metːe 'vʊɪhɬina]
> medde vuihl-i-na
> even whistle-ASS.CONCL.ITR-2P.AG.SG
> 'you even whistle'

so medde sviuhlo-ahte
[s(ɔ)'metːe sˈvʊɪhɬɔahte]
so medde sa-vuihl-o–ahte
INTERRO even 2P.UNAG.SG-whistle-INFER.CONCL.ITR–INTERRO.RHETO
'heh, so you even whistle!' (said to intimidate/bully)

3. To diminish the agent's worth:

tṡandana revvagegna
[tɕandɑna ˈrewːaˈɟɛŋnːa]
tṡa<nd>-a-na revva=gegna-Ø
find.PAST-ASS.CONCL.TR-2P.AG.SG fox=den-DAT
'you found a fox hole' (agentive)

ihha satṡanda revvagegna
[ˈihːa sɑˈtɕanda ˈrewːaˈɟɛŋnːa]
ihha sa-tṡa<nd>-a revva=gegna-Ø
just 2p.UNAG.SG-find.PAST-ASS.CONCL.TR-2P.AG.SG fox=den-DAT
'you merely found a fox hole (and you were just lucky)' (unagentive)

Ambiguous agentivity may also simply result from actions that may be performed as conscious acts (generally by humans) or by other animals or factors.

euksami detkenůjůma   'I produce quality knives' (agentive)
euka geletsta sirůkůdi   'spiders produce silk' (unagentive)

§9.4.4 Double Agentivity

Double agentivity refers to a grammatical construction where two sets of pronouns are added onto a verb – when both the unagentive and agentive pronoun sets are present. Such constructions occur with certain verbs, commonly in the obligative or the optative, and always with the reversive aspect marker (-**dna**-/-**adn**-):

INTRANSITIVE	TRANSITIVE	
sa-Ø-um-i-dna-mi	sa-Ø-um-a-dna-mi	I need you to VERB
ma-Ø-um-i-dna-na	ma-Ø-um-a-dna-na	you need me to VERB
ta-Ø-um-i-dna-Ø	ta-Ø-um-a-dna-Ø	X needs Y to VERB
sa-Ø-vi-dna-mi	sa-Ø-ua-dna-mi	I want you to VERB
ma-Ø-vi-dna-na	ma-Ø-ua-dna-na	you want me to VERB
ta-Ø-vi-dna-Ø	ta-Ø-ua-dna-Ø	X wants Y to VERB

These constructions correspond to English phrases of the type *X wants/needs Y to Z*. The agentive pronoun always refers to the agent acting on the verb (X wants/needs), while the unagentive pronouns refer to the actor of the obligation or the wish (in the optative). Double agentivity does not affect a verb's valency.

> I need you to go
> *sa·mak·um·i·adna·**mi***

Consider the following phrases:
keknumami sasame
[ˈcʰɛʔŋunami ˈsasame]
kekn-um-a-mi sasame-Ø
put.together-OBLI-ASS.CONCL.TR-1P.AG.SG tipi-DAT
'I must to put the tipi together'

sakeknumadnami sasame
[saˈcʰɛʔŋunaʔtnami ˈsasame]
sa-kekn-um-a-dna-mi sasame-Ø
2P.UNAG.SG-put.together-OBLI-ASS.CONCL.TR-REVERS-1P.AG.SG tipi-DAT
'I need you to put the tipi together'

makyimi
[ˈmakwimi]
mak-yi-mi
go-ASS.CONCL.ITR.OPT-1P.AG.SG
'I want to go'

samakyidnami
[saˈmakwɪʔtnami]
sa-mak-yi-dna-mi
2P.UNAG.SG-go-ASS.CONCL.ITR.OPT-REVERS-1P.AG.SG
'I want you to go'

Such constructions can sometimes contain a pronominal object, which is then found as a recipient. This type of double agentivity construction *does* affect valency, placing verbs in the ditransitive:

s-i-Ø-ua-dna-ki-mi	'I want you to VERB me'
m-i-Ø-ua-dna-si-na	'you want me to VERB you'
t-i-Ø-ua-dna-ti-Ø	'X wants Y to VERB X'
t_z-i-Ø-ua-dna-ni$_y$-Ø$_x$	'X wants Y to VERB Z'

sinokkuadnakimi Sappa
[siˈnɔʔkʊaʔtnajimi ˈsaʔpa]
s-i-nokk-ua-dna-ki-mi Sappa-Ø
2P.PAT-DIT-call-ASS.CONCL.TR.OPT-REVERS-1P.PAT-1P.AG.SG **Sappa**-AGT
'I want you to call me **Sappa**' (i.e. my name is **Sappa**)

There is an important distinction to be made between the object of the double agentivity and the object of the verb. If a doubly agentive verb is intransitive, then the object of the double agentivity is in the unagentive. If the verb is transitive, the object of the verb is in the unagentive, and the object of the double agentivity is instead found in the recipient. Nouns that are objects of doubly agentive verbs are usually not found in the expected illative but instead in the ablative.

INTRANSITIVE	SUBJECT	OBJECT OF DOUBLE AGENTIVITY	OBJECT OF VERB
	agentive	unagentive	Ø

ta$_y$·man·ua·dna·ri$_x$
'they$_x$ what him$_y$ to come'

TRANSITIVE	SUBJECT	OBJECT OF DOUBLE AGENTIVITY	OBJECT OF VERB
	agentive	recipient	unagentive

t$_z$·i·non·ęll·adn·a·si$_y$·ri$_x$
'they$_x$ made you$_y$ say it$_z$'

i·non·ęll·adn·a kohkoika$_y$ uini$_z$ svattaita-hõ ki sġotrage$_x$.
'the enemies$_x$ made the boy$_y$ say the truth$_z$ to his mother'

§9.4.4.1 Causative Double Agentivity

A special form of doubly agentive verbs has the infix -ęll- or -ęgj- added directly after the stem and has a causative meaning. It is not widely used, but it is still productive to a certain degree. Like the other doubly agentive verbs, it also uses the reversive -dna-/-adn-. Such causative constructions require an agentive subject. When both the object of the double agentivity and the original object of the verb are nouns, the object is always in the dative.

kilona	'X repeats it'
kiltatonęlladna	'X makes Y repeat it'

kilibonęlladna tamottaika-nen oanika to kori
'the boy makes his friend repeat the story'

ha	'X eats it'
tahęlladna	'X makes Y eat it'

tahopsai	'X vomits'
tahopsęięgjadna	'X makes Y vomit'

§9.5 Valency

Siwa verbs differ greatly depending on their valency, i.e. how and which arguments of verbs are involved. Siwa has 7 main types of valencies, with three types having both transitive and intransitive distinctions. Included in this are impersonal verbs, which are always intransitive. Each valency type has its own infinitive form and post- and preverbal vowel qualities.

    transitive
    intransitive
        (impersonal verbs)
    translative
    subjective
        transitive
        intransitive
    ditransitive
        transitive
        intransitive (also called destinal ditransitive)
    passive
        transitive (also called agentive)
        intransitive

§9.5.1 Transitive

Transitive verbs are verbs whose agent acts upon a patient or object. They are a very large class or verbs whose only specific common trait is having an object.

The transitive agentive infinitive marker is -**mi** and its unagentive form is -**mu/-mů**, which deletes the preceding postverbal vowel if a consonant cluster can be formed, behaving exactly like the inconclusive marker (see *§9.2.1.8.1*).

infinitive marker	agentive	unagentive
unmarked	-mi	-mu/-mů
marked	-bme or -nta	

ala
['ɑla]
al-a-Ø-Ø
tan-ASS.CONCL.TR-3P.PAT-3P.AG.SG
'X will tan Y'
(inf. *almi* 'to tan')

alla
['ɑlːa]
all-a-Ø-Ø
have.time-ASS.CONCL.TR-3P.PAT-3P.AG.SG
'X will have time for Y'
(inf. *allami* 'to have time')

teukiula
[ˈtʰeuɟiula]
t-euk-iul-a-Ø
3P.UNAG-produce-ABS.DESC-ASS.CONCL.TR-3P.PAT
'X will secrete Y'
(inf. *eukiulmu* 'to secret')

ha
[ˈha]
h-a-Ø-Ø
eat-ASS.CONCL.TR-3P.PAT-3P.AG.SG
'X will eat Y'
(inf. *hami* 'to eat')

tandida
[tʰandˈida]
tama-t-id-a-Ø
upon-3P.UNAG-fall-ASS.CONCL.TR-3P.PAT
'X will stumble upon Y'
(inf. *tamibmu* 'to stumble upon')

iskua
[ˈɪskʊa]
isko-a-Ø-Ø
clean-ASS.CONCL.TR-3P.PAT-3P.AG.SG
'X will clean Y'
(inf. *iskomi* 'to clean')

luhha
[ˈluhːa]
luhh-a-Ø-Ø
boil-ASS.CONCL.TR-3P.PAT-3P.AG.SG
'X will boil Y'
(inf. *luhmi* 'to boil')

nuja
[ˈnuja]
nuj-a-Ø-Ø
see-ASS.CONCL.TR-3P.PAT-3P.AG.SG
'X will see Y'
(inf. *nuimi~nugmi* 'to see')

tsipra
[ˈtɕɪpxa]
tsipr-a-Ø-Ø
write-ASS.CONCL.TR-3P.PAT-3P.AG.SG
'X will write Y'
(inf. *tsiprami* 'to write')

taheskva
[tʰaˈhɛskwːa]
ta-heskv-a-Ø
3P.UNAG-receive-ASS.CONCL.TR-3P.PAT
'X will receive Y' (something bad)
(inf. *heskvamu* 'to receive')

ihhja
[ˈihːja]
ihhj-a-Ø-Ø
thank-ASS.CONCL.TR-3P.PAT-3P.AG.SG
'X will thank Y'
(inf. *iśmi* 'to thank')

tigjukka
[ˈtʰiːjːʊʔka]
t-igjukk-a-Ø
3P.UNAG-rejuvenate-ASS.CONCL.TR-3P.PAT
'X will rejuvenate Y'
(inf. *igjukkamu* 'to rejuvenate')

keda
[ˈcʰeda]
ked-a-Ø-Ø
carry-ASS.CONCL.TR-3P.PAT-3P.AG.SG
'X will carry Y'
(inf. *kebmi* 'to carry')

mahha
[ˈmɑhːa]
mahh-a-Ø-Ø
follow-ASS.CONCL.TR-3P.PAT-3P.AG.SG
'X will hunt/follow Y'
(inf. *mahmi* 'to hunt')

tatsasga
[tʰaˈtsasxa]
ta-tsasġ-a-Ø
3p.unag-forget-ass.concl.tr-3p.pat.sg
'X will forget Y'
(inf. *tsasġamu* 'to forget')

sanka
[ˈsaŋka]
sank-a-Ø-Ø
scratch-ASS.CONCL.TR-3P.PAT-3P.AG.SG
'X will scratch Y'
(inf. *sankami* 'to scratch')

tatśiba
[tʰɑˈtɕiba]
ta-tśb-a-Ø
3P.UNAG-signify-ASS.CONCL.TR-3P.PAT
'X will signify/mean Y'
(inf. *tśibmu* 'to signify/mean')

tvaika
[ˈtʰvɑiga]
t-vaik-a-Ø
3P.UNAG-be.ashamed-ASS.CONCL.TR-3P.PAT
'X will be ashamed of Y'
(inf. *vaikmu* 'to be ashamed')

§9.5.1.1 Non-Valent Triggers of Transitivity

Many verbs may be required to be transitive even though their valency does not reflect any transitive object. So called non-valent triggers of transitivity force a verb into a transitive state without being a participant in the verbal phrase (not an object, recipient or subject). Non-valent triggers include a complementized phrase (§9.15), and adverbial forms of non-numeral quantifiers (§6.3). Although adverbial non-numeral quantifiers may not differ much from their non-adverbial counterparts in meaning, syntactically they are more likely to come before the verb, and are non-objects.

Complementized phrases:

sedjami   'I heard it'
sedjami, itita pednotori   'I heard that they would arrive early'

nonaka   'X told me (Y)'
nonaka, kitote   'X told me that X would do Y'

s-negana-a ůdda?   'did you see this?'
s-negana-a, ihõhrotita?   'did you see that X jumped into it?'

Adverbial non-numeral quantifiers:

mami   'I ate X'
kommen mami   'I ate a lot'

nuhlami taba   'I've seen many things'
tagjil nuhlami   'I've seen a lot'

§9.5.2 Intransitive

Intransitive verbs are verbs which only involve one agent, the subject. Intransitive verbs cannot have an object, but may also be found with a beneficiary pronoun.

The transitive agentive infinitive marker is -**sa** and its unagentive form is -**su**, which deletes the preceding postverbal vowel if a consonant cluster can be formed, behaving similarly like the habitual marker (see *§9.2.1.2.3*).

	infinitive marker	agentive	unagentive
	unmarked	-sa	-su/-sǔ
	marked		-tse or -sta

di
['di:]
di-i-Ø
step-ASS.ITR.CONCL-3P.AG.SG
'X will step'
(inf. *disa* 'to step')

jairi
['jaɪri]
jair-i-Ø
row-ASS.ITR.CONCL-3P.AG.SG
'X will row'
(inf. *jairha* 'to row')

hõhhi
['hõh:i]
hõhh-i-Ø
jump-ASS.ITR.CONCL-3P.AG.SG
'X will jump'
(inf. *hõhsa* 'to jump')

tagihli
[tʰa'ɪhɬi]
ta-gihl-i
3P.UNAG-hang-ASS.ITR.CONCL
'X will hang'
(inf. *gihlisu* 'to hang')

takylki
[tʰa'cœlci]
ta-kylk-i
3P.UNAG-slip-ASS.ITR.CONCL
'X will slip'
(inf. *kylkisǔ* 'to slip')

maki
['maci]
mak-i-Ø
go-ASS.ITR.CONCL-3P.AG.SG
'X will go'
(inf. *maksa* 'to go')

eri
['eri]
er-i-Ø
be.careful-ASS.ITR.CONCL-3P.AG.SG
'X will be careful'
(inf. *erha* 'to be careful')

keụi
['cʰewi]
keụ-i-Ø
rise-ASS.ITR.CONCL-3P.AG.SG
'X will stand up/rise'
(inf. *keụisa* 'to rise')

tagjàli
[tʰa'dzæ:li]
ta-gjàl-i
3P.UNAG-spin-ASS.ITR.CONCL
'X will spin'
(inf. *gjàlsu* 'to spin')

tagogantsi
[tʰa'gɔgantsi]
ta-gogants-i
3P.UNAG-limp-ASS.ITR.CONCL
'X will limp'
(inf. *gogantsisu* 'to limp')

mani
['mani]
man-i-Ø
come-ASS.ITR.CONCL-3P.AG.SG
'X will come'
(inf. *manta* 'to come')

tamendui
[tʰa'mɛndui]
ta-mendo-i
3P.UNAG-dream-ASS.ITR.CONCL
'X will dream'
(inf. *mendosu* 'to limp')

saśi or *sahhji*
['saɕ:i] or ['sah:ji]
saś/sahhj-i-Ø
talk-ASS.ITR.CONCL-3P.AG.SG
'X will talk'
(inf. *saśsa* 'to talk')

tahhi
['tʰah:i]
tahh-i-Ø
leave-ASS.ITR.CONCL-3P.AG.SG
'X will leave'
(inf. *tahsa* 'to leave')

tuvi
['tʰuvi]
tuv-i-Ø
turn-ASS.ITR.CONCL-3P.AG.SG
'X will turn'
(inf. *tussa* 'to turn')

pośki
['pʰɔɕci]
pohhj=k-i-Ø
sleep=TRANSLO-ASS.ITR.CONCL-3P.AG.SG
'X will go to sleep'
(inf. *pośkisa* 'to go to sleep')

§9.5.2.1 Intransitive Syncope

Intransitive verbs are unique in regularly going through syncope, or the loss of the assertive marker -i- which characterizes all intransitive verbs. Syncope is most common in specific situations, but it is never required.

Syncope of the -i- vowel occurs mostly with the first person plural agentive markers -gga/-gge, and a handful of verbs may also be found in the singular of the first and second person singular. The general rule is that a verb of the form -Ci·gga will become -C(k)ka, although a few geminated clusters also allow for syncope (-ḍḍ- and -hts-).

However, these are less common possibly due to confusing with infinitive endings (-mi and -na). For that reason, the syncoped forms are more common in the past than the present, or in the subjective (which are distinct from their infinitive counterparts). Most commonly, the syncope will be -CCi-na/-mi to -Cna/-Cmi.
For a complete description of the sound changes, see the section on allophony of consonants (*§3.4.1.1*).

	Non-syncoped	Syncoped	
1P.PL.AG			
	sġaumigga	sġaumkka	'we will breathe'
	iltśemigga	iltśemkka	'we will come crawling'
	otigga	otka	'we will unite'
	tśotigga	tśotka	'we will cooperate'
	biohtsigga	biohtska	'we will play'
	norigga[1]	noḍka~norkka	'we will sing'
	jeḍḍigga	jeḍka	'we will run'

---

[1] The verb 'to sing' has the underlying form **nod-** but the -d- commonly becomes -r- before vowels.

tsoairigga	tsoarkka	'we will go by ski'
erigga	erkka	'we will be careful'
otśiligga	otśilkka	'we will dry ourselves'

1P.SG.AG
    omingimi   omigmi   'I will get ready'
    odjikkimi   odjikmi   'I will show off'

2P.SG.AG
    siddina   sitna   'you understood'
    toaddina   toatna   'you came along'

§9.5.3 Translative

Translative verbs involve only one participant, an unagentive subject. All translative verbs are unagentive, and they typically depict a change of state, although the translative is also used with a great number of auxiliary verbs. Impersonal verbs, as will be explained below, have no translative form and instead use the conclusive aspect to express this distinction.

The translative verbs are unique in that many adjectives can be made into a translative verb by using the preverbal marker **a-** to create verbs with a meaning of 'to become (more) ADJ':

kjuomon	'bent'	→	t·a·kjuom·u	'X will become (more) bent'
magja	'white'	→	t·a·magj·u	'X will become white(r)'
ljekna	'snowless'	→	a·ljekn·ů	'it will become snowless'
minga	'ready'	→	t·a·ming·ů	'X will become ready'

The transitive infinitive marker is **-lu/-lů**, which deletes the preceding postverbal vowel if a consonant cluster can be formed, behaving exactly like the perfective marker (see *§9.2.1.2.3*). If a cluster cannot be formed, the ending becomes **-oru** or in certain dialects **-ol, -ȯ, -ul**.

infinitive marker	agentive	unagentive
unmarked	∅	-oru(-ol)/-ůrů or -lu/-lů
marked		-dle or -olta/-ůlta

entů
['ɛntø]
ent-ů
be.unlikely-ASS.TRANSL.CONCL
'it is unlikely'
(inf. *entůrů* 'to be unlikely')

mjahhju
['mjɑh:ju]
m-jahhj-u
1p.UNAG-endure-ASS.TRANSL.CONCL
'I will be able to endure Y'
(inf. *jahhjoru~jahhjol* 'to be able to endure')

titků
['tʰi:tkø]
t-itk-ů
3P.UNAG-melt-ASS.TRANSL.CONCL
'X will melt'
(inf. *itkoru~itkol* 'to melt')

tanjalu
[tʰɑ'ɲɑlu]
ta-njal-u
3P.UNAG-taste-ASS.TRANSL.CONCL
'X will taste (like…)'
(inf. *njallu* 'to taste')

tohku
['tʰɔhku]
t-ohk-u
3P.UNAG-fit-ASS.TRANSL.CONCL
'X will fit'
(inf. *ohkoru~ohkol* 'to fit')

tsadlu
['tsɑtɬu]
t-sadl-u
3P.UNAG-burn-ASS.TRANSL.CONCL
'X will get burnt (in a pot)'
(inf. *sadloru~sadlol* 'to burn')

teuvvu
['tʰeuw:u]
t-euvv-u
3p.UNAG-reach-ASS.TRANSL.CONCL
'X will be able to reach Y'
(inf. *euvvoru~euvvol* 'to be able to reach')

takyu
['tʰɑkwu]
taky-u
be.worth-ASS.TRANSL.CONCL
'it is worth it'
(inf. *takyoru~takyol* 'to be worth')

tamoahnu
[tʰɑ'mɔahnu]
ta-moahn-u
3P.UNAG-get.damaged-ASS.TRANSL.CONCL
'X will get damaged'
(inf. *moahnoru~moahnol* 'to get damaged')

manjoapsu
[mɑ'ɲ:ɔaps:u]
ma-njoaps-u
1P.UNAG-grow.a.beard-ASS.TRANSL.CONCL
'I will grow a beard'
(inf. *njoapsoru~njoapsol* 'to grow a beard')

tapẏhhů
[tʰɑ'pʰy:h:ø]
ta-pẏhh-ů
3P.UNAG-menstruate-ASS.TRANSL.CONCL
'X will become menstruated'
(inf. *pẏhlů* 'to become menstruated')

tatèulů
[tʰɑ'tø:lø]
ta-tèul-ů
3P.UNAG-subside-ASS.TRANSL.CONCL
'X will subside'
(inf. *tèullů* 'to subside')

tatśoairu
[tʰaˈtsɔairu]
ta-tśoair-u
3P.UNAG-rot-ASS.TRANSL.CONCL
'X will rot'
(inf. *tśoairoru~tśoairol* 'to rot')

tvoavvu
[ˈtʰvɔawːu]
t-voavv-u
3P.UNAG-get.scared-ASS.TRANSL.CONCL
'X will get scared'
(inf. *voavvoru~vòavvol* 'to get scared')

§9.5.4 Subjective

Subjective verbs are marked by the preverbal vowel **o-**, and can be found as agentive, unagentive, transitive or intransitive verbs. Subjective agentive verbs are verbs whose subject and object are the same *or* closely related, unalienable possessions. Subjective agentive verbs are used, for example, when the subject acts upon itself or its body, for its own benefit or by itself. When the subject and object are the same, the subjective verb is marked as intransitive. If the object of the verb is a noun, then the verb will be transitive.

Many transitive verbs may be found as subjective, and only a few verbs are only found as subjective. Usually, transitive subjective verbs will change to ditransitive if the object is no longer the same as or related to the subject. However, ditransitivity yields to subjectivity, such that a verb having both a ditransitive and subjective meaning will only show the subjective markings. Verbs can freely accept preverbal vowels for the subjective and ditransitive.

SUBJECTIVE

ometami hide
[ɔmˈetami ˈhide]
o-et-a-mi hide-Ø
SUBJ-cut-ASS.CONCL.TR-1P.AG.SG hair-DAT
'I will cut my hair'

obolluhhimi
[ɔbɔˈlːuhːimi]
o-ol=luhh-i-mi
SUBJ-leaf=boil-ASS.CONCL.ITR-1P.AG.SG
'I will boil tea for myself'

DITRANSITIVE

jetasimi hide
[jˈetisimi ˈhide]
i-et-a-si-mi hide-Ø
DITR-cut-ASS.CONCL.TR-2P.PAT.SG-1P.AG.SG hair-DAT
'I will cut your hair'
(lit. I will cut you the hair)

ibolluhhasimi
[ibɔˈlːuhːasimi]
i-ol=luhh-a-si-mi
DIT-leaf=boil-ASS.CONCL.TR-2P.RECI.SG-1P.AG.SG
'I will boil tea for you'

The subjective's infinitive markers are the same regardless of their transitivity, but they have a distinction for agentivity; **-(e)na** marks subjective agentive and **-(e)nu** marks subjective unagentive. Infinitive subjective verbs usually lack the preverbal **o-**, but some keep it even in the infinitive.

infinitive marker	agentive	unagentive
unmarked	-na	-nu/-nů
marked	-dne or -nda	

The subjective agentive verbs may also denote a rough, impolite or rude action, usually denoting selfishness, greed or a rough action (especially with the semelfactive):

oma siehhõdi
[ɔˈma ˈsiehːɔ̃dʑi]
o-m-a-Ø siehhum-di
SUBJ-eat.PAST-ASS.CONCL.TR-3P.AG.SG dried.meat- GEN
'X ate him/her/itself some dried meat'

ma siehhõdi
[ˈma ˈsiehːɔ̃dʑi]
m-a-Ø siehhum-di
eat.PAST-ASS.CONCL.TR-3P.AG.SG dried.meat-GEN
'X ate some dried meat'

mobiddiġa
[mɔˈbiːtːixa]
m-o-i<dd>-i-ġa
1P.UNAG.SG-SUBJ-fall.PAST-ASS.CONCL.ITR-SEMELF
'I took a bad fall'

middi
[ˈmitːi]
m-Ø-i<dd>-i
1P.UNAG.SG-ITR-fall.PAST-ASS.CONCL.ITR
'I fell'

More examples:

osyśki
[ɔˈsœɕci]
o-syśk-i-Ø
SUBJ-move.away-ASS.CONCL.ITR-3P.AG.SG
'X will move away'
(inf. *syśkena* 'to move away')

otiri
[ɔˈtiri]
o-t-i-ri
SUBJ-unite-ASS.CONCL.ITR-3P.AG.PL
'they will unite'
(inf. *otena~odna* 'to unite')

otkimi
[ɔˈtcimi]
o-tk-i-mi
SUBJ-train-ASS.CONCL.ITR-1P.AG.SG
'I will train myself'
(inf. *otkena* 'to train')

otsġovi
[ɔˈtsxɔvi]
o-tsġov-i-Ø
SUBJ-introduce-ASS.CONCL.ITR-3P.AG.SG
'X will introduce itself'
(inf. *tsġonna* 'to introduce oneself')

motṡipri
[mɔˈtɕɪpxi]
m-o-tṡip<r>-i
1P.UNAG.SG-SUBJ-cut.PAST-ASS.CONCL.ITR
'I cut myself'
(inf. *tṡimnṹ* 'to cut oneself')

mosavvi
[mɔˈsawːi]
m-o-sa<vv>-i
1P.UNAG.SG-SUBJ-burn.PAST-ASS.CONCL.ITR
'I burnt myself'
(inf. *sahnu* 'to burn oneself')

ogauldari
[ɔˈgaʊldɑri]
o-gauld-a-Ø-ri
SUBJ-discuss-ASS.CONCL.TR-3P.PAT-3P.AG.PL
'they will discuss Y together'
(inf. *gauldena* 'to discuss')

ogetildiri
[ɔˈɟetɪldʑiri]
o-getild-i-ri
SUBJ-meet-ASS.CONCL.ITR-3P.AG.PL
'they will meet each other'
(inf. *getildena* 'to meet')

tsobṹbi
[tsɔbˈøbi]
ts-o-ṹb-i
3P.UNAG.PL-SUBJ-multiply-ASS.CONCL.ITR
'they will multiply'
(inf. *ṹmnṹ* 'to multiply')

obṹkkṹiri
[ɔbˈœʔcœiri]
o-ṹkkṹ-i-ri
SUBJ-fight-ASS.CONCL.ITR-3P.AG.PL
'they will fight'
(inf. *ṹkkṹna* 'to fight, quarrel')

soketsodji
[sɔˈcʰeˈtsodʑi]
s-o-ket=so<dj>-i
2P.UNAG.SG-SUBJ-arm=break.PAST-
ASS.CONCL.ITR
'you broke your arm'
(inf. *ketsogjenu* 'to break one's arm')

torettuvvi
[tʰɔrɛˈʔtuwːi]
t-o-rev=tu<vv>-i
3P.UNAG-SUBJ-ankle=turn.PAST-ASS.CONCL.ITR
'X twisted his/her/its ankle'
(inf. *rettunnu* 'to twist one's ankle')

When a subjective verb becomes ditransitive, it may retain its subjective preverbal vowel and simply have a recipient in a locative case, or it may become ditransitive and have the subjective marker instead as a reflexive or 'self' pronoun. Reflexive pronouns and ditransitive pronouns may be perceived to be impolite. Certain speakers allow subjective verbs to also be ditransitive, though this is not common.

otsġovimi — 'I introduce myself'
otsġavimi sosita — 'I introduce myself to you'
itsġovasimi nitsika — lit. 'I introduce you myself' (impolite, lower register)
otsġovisimi — 'I introduce myself to you' (uncommon)

§9.5.5 Ditransitive

Ditransitive verbs are marked by the preverbal vowel i-, which yields to the passive marker u- and the subjective marker o-, and can be transitive or intransitive, agentive or unagentive. Ditransitive verbs are verbs with a patient and a recipient. Ditransitive verbs are also those of motion with a set destination (with postpositions *henda* 'up' and *tvunda* 'down' and their other destinal forms and with the use of the movement locative cases).

The recipient in Siwa can be the indirect object but also the beneficiary of an action. A recipient can also be an agent which stands to gain something from the action. Siwa has special recipient pronouns, but when the direct object is a noun or an independent pronoun, it is found in the illative. Benefactive ditransitive verbs are only commonly made from otherwise transitive verbs, *not* if the verb is intransitive or translative.

The ditransitive infinitive is -(i)**nin** when agentive and -(i)**non** when unagentive. Unagentive intransitive verbs are rather rare.

infinitive marker	agentive	unagentive
unmarked	-nin	-non/-nůn
marked	-nidne/-nõdne or -nita/-nõta	

The ditransitive is used:
1. When a verb has a precise destination, especially with locative markers in verbs such as -**ita**-/-**ibma**- and -**ika**/-**iska**

> *imuojaitasa*
> [i'muɔjaidɑsa]
> i-muoj-a-ita-sa-Ø
> DIT-dress-ASS.CONCL.TR-ILLAT-2P.PAT.SG-3P.AG.SG
> 'X will dress you in it'
> (inf. *muojinin~muoinin* 'to dress in')

> *isetġaibmamõ*
> [i'sɛt:xaɪʔpmamõ]
> i-setġ-a-ibma-Ø-mu=n
> DIT-place-ASS.CONCL.TR-ALLAT-3P.PAT-OBLI=IMPER.2P.SG
> 'you will have to place X onto Y'
> (inf. *setġinin* 'to place')

> *s-aniaitana-a?*
> [s'aniɑidɑna:]
> s-an=i-a-ita-Ø-na–a
> INTERRO-PAST=throw.-ASS.CONCL.TR-ILLAT-3P.PAT-2P.AG.SG
> 'did you throw X into Y?'

(inf. *binin* 'to throw', irr.)

middita
['miːtːida]
m-i-i<dd>-i-ta
1P.UNAG.SG-DIT-fall.PAST-ASS.CONCL.ITR-ILLAT
'I fell into it'
(inf. *idnin* 'to fall [into])

2. With the postposition sets of *henda* 'up' and *tvunda* 'down':

isetġamō pėumibma henda
[iˈsɛtːxamɔ̃ ˈpʰøːmɪʔpma ˈhɛnda]
i-seġ-a-Ø-mu=n pŭ<Ø>ŭ-ma=ibma henda
DIT-place-ASS.CONCL.TR-3P.PAT-OBLI=IMPER.2P.SG log-ALLAT up.to.DESTI
'you will have to place Y up on the log'

3. With other movements having a specific end point or destination:

irehraka kalahkika
[iˈrɛhraga ˈkʰalahciga]
i-re<hr>-a-ka-Ø kalari-k=ika
DIT-pull.PAST-ASS.CONCL.TR-1P.PAT.SG-3P.AG.SG pit-ELAT
'X pulled me out of the hole'
(inf. *rehnin* 'to pull')

4. When a verb has:
4.a A recipient:

isyvvasimi sindu-go
[iˈsywːasimi ˈsɪndugɔ]
i-syvv-a-si-mi sindu-Ø-go
DIT-show-ASS.CONCL.TR-2P.RECI.SG-1P.AG.SG
'I will show you my catch'
(inf. *synnin* 'to show')

4.b A beneficiary (**only** if the verb is generally transitive or translative):

ikosġasimi
[iˈkɔsxasimi]
i-kosġ-a-Ø-si-mi

DIT-carve-ASS.CONCL.TR-3P.RECI-2P.RECI.SG-1P.AG.SG
'I will carve Y for you'
(inf. *kosġinin* 'to carve [for someone]')

ikosġami kohkita
[iˈkɔsxɑmi ˈkʰɔhcida]
i-kosġ-a-Ø-mi kori-ko=ita
DIT-carve-ASS.CONCL.TR-3P.RECI-1P.AG.SG boy-ILLAT
'I will carve Y for the boy'

but

set toskibi
[sɛʔˈtɔscibi]
set t-osk-i-bi
NEG 3P.UNAG.SG-last-ASS.CONCL.ITR-2P.RECI.PL
'X won't last us'

ijomubi
[ˈijɔmubi]
ijom-u-bi
be.possible-ASS.CONCL.TRANSL-2P.RECI.PL
'it will be possible for us (because of good conditions/enough time)'

Notice the use of the verb *i·digg·a* or *i·digg·i* which is commonly used with nouns denoting actions or changes of states (in the illative, sometimes allative).

idigga kŭlita	'X will attack Y'
idigga oaḍgita	'X will come to Y's help'
t·idigga kepieita	'X will go to Y's head'
idaḍgi rereggeita	'X changed his/her mind'
t·idaḍgi keggeita	'X was boastful, arrogant'
t·idaḍgi meulleita	'X became blue (from not breathing/cold)'
t·idaḍgi torõrita	'X got into danger (lit. into big bear)'
t·idaḍgi sinisibma	'X caught a big fish'

§9.5.5.1 Subjective Directional

Some subjective verbs also have a sense of movement or directionality, and the preverbals o- and i- would thus both be appropriate. In older speakers or higher register or poetic language, they may unite as a single preverbal vowel e- (or ɥe- or vi-), conferring the verb both a subjective and essentially ditransitive meaning, although it can be ambiguous whether there is a beneficiary or movement/direction. The ambiguity is caused by the subjective directional being always found in its transitive form (e-Ø-a). The intransitive form does not exist (*e-Ø-i)

SUBJ	*oketki hokonta loalta*		'X hid behind a boulder'
DIT	*iketka hokonta loalta*		'X hid Y behind a boulder'
SUBJ.DIT	*eketka hokonta loalta*		'X hid itself behind a boulder'
		or	'X hid Y for itself behind a boulder'

§9.5.6 Passive

Passive verbs are those whose topic (i.e. that which would normally be the subject or agent of the phrase) is treated like a patient. They have the preverbal vowel **u-**. Passive verbs are generally intransitive (then with no syntactical agent), or they may be transitive when the agent of the verb is expressed, which is either agentive or unagentive. Most verbs can be found in the passive, which Siwa treats as a valency type more than a voice. For that reason, passive verbs are very similar to patientive verbs.

The passive has the infinitive endings **-mon** or **-můn**.

infinitive marker	agentive	unagentive
unmarked	∅	-mon -můn
marked	-modne/-můdne or -mōta/-můta	

uhůtvuika
[uˈhœtwːuiga]
u-hůtv-u-i-ka
PASS-hit.PAST-ASS.CONCL.ITR-1P.PAT.SG
'I was hit'
(inf. *hůtvimůn* 'to be hit')

uhůtviakana
[uˈhœtwːiagana]
u-hůtv-i-a-ka-na
PASS-hit.PAST-ASS.CONCL.ITR-1P.PAT.SG-2P.AG.SG
'I was hit by you'

utitkika
[uˈtɪtciga]
u-ti<tk>-i-ka
PASS-cured.PAST-ASS.CONCL.ITR-1P.PAT.SG
'I was cured'
(inf. *tigmůn* 'to be cured')

utitkakana
[uˈtɪtkagana]
u-ti<tk>-a-ka-na
PASS-cured.PAST-ASS.CONCL.TR-1P.PAT.SG-2P.AG.SG
'I was cured by you'

ujuiẹgjisa
[uju'jæj:isa]
uj-u-j<eġj>-i-sa
rightly-PASS-raise.PAST-ASS.CONCL.ITR-2P.PAT.SG
'you were raised well'
(inf. *ujojàmon* 'to be well raised')

ujuiẹjahmi
[uju'jæjahmi]
uj-u-j<ẹj>-e-sa=mi
rightly-PASS-raise.PAST-
ASS.CONCL.TR-2P.PAT.SG-1P.AG.SG
'you were raised well by me'

cf.
ujojẹjahmi
[ujo'jæjahmi]
ujo-j<ẹj>-a-sa=mi
rightly-raise.PAST-ASS.CONCL.TR-2P.PAT.SG-1P.AG.SG
'I raised you well'
(inf. *ujojàmi* 'to raise well')

§9.5.7 Impersonal Verbs

Impersonal verbs form a class of their own. They have zero valency, though they may incorporate recipient pronouns. Impersonal verbs are made up of two groups: inconclusive impersonal verbs (generally verbs for natural phenomena) and conclusive (which simply lack valency but otherwise behave like normal verbs). Inconclusive impersonal verbs in the conclusive form usually translate as inchoatives, and inconclusive forms are their default form.

Inconclusive verbs generally refer to weather or geographical phenomena:

sihmi		'it rains'	(sihh-)
	siġva	'rain'	
sisġi		'it thunders' (**conclusive**)	(sisġ-)
	sisi	'thunder'	
kůilmi		'it is drizzly'	(kůil-)
	kuilva	'drizzle'	
daimmi		'it is humid'	(daim-)
	daiye	'humid'	
	daiggi	'humid weather'	
sůimi		'it is dry'	(sůi-)
	sůiggi	'dry weather'	
auhmi		'it is cool/crisp weather'	(aur-)
	aurin	'cool'	
himmi		'it is hot/warm'	(him-)
	himi	'warm'	

loḍmi		'it is sweltering'	(loḍḍ-)
	loḍva	'sweltering heat'	
hehmi		'it is cold'	(her-)
	heje	'cold'	
logmi		'it is freezing'	(long-)
	lokna	'intense cold'	
pugmi		'it is pouring'	(pung-)
	pungẏa	'pouring rain'	
vimmi		'it is snowing'	(vim-)
	omi	'snow'	
vadlmi		'there is a snow storm'	(vadl-)
	odlna	'snow storm'	
gi̯ylybmi		'it is snowing (wet snow)'	(gi̯ylyp-)
	gi̯ylppi	'wet snow'	
huhmi		'(the sun) shines, it is sunny'	(huhh-)
	hu̯eġgi	'shiny weather'	
kvelmi		'it is cloudy'	(kvel-)
	kolo	'cloud'	
	kvelgi	'cloudy weather'	
ġu̯emmi		'it is windy'	(ġu̯en-)
	ġu̯eni	'wind'	
	ġu̯etta	'windy weather'	
utubmi		'it is still'	(utut-)
	ututa	'still'	
	vetġi	'still weather'	
nuśkvemi		'it is hailing'	(nuśkve-)
	nuśkva	'hail'	
ni̯eyhmi		'it is misty'	(ni̯eyg-)
	ni̯eygi	'mist'	
rummi		'it is foggy'	(rum-)
	rumu	'fog'	
	rõtta	'foggy weather'	

hoimmi	'it is flooding (of rivers)'	(hoivv-)
hoivva	'flooding'	

§9.5.8 Prefix Coalescence

The ditransitive, subjective and passive preverbal vowels (i- o- u-) coalesce in a specific way with the stem they are prefixed to. The changes are generally the addition of -b- before o u ů y, -m- before a e and j- (for i-) before a e i.

	a-, e-	i-	o-, u-, ů-, y-
SUBJECTIVE	om-	obi-	ob-
DITRANSITIVE	j-	i-, iddj-	ib-
PASSIVE	um-	ubi-	ub-

ůkk-	'fight'
ob·ůkkůi	'X will fight' (o-)
ekkj-	'bear'
um·ekkjuika	'I was born' (u-)
utṡo-	'pack'
ib·utṡiasimi	'I packed X for you' (i-)

§9.6 Evidentiality

The postverbal vowel, present in all non-finite forms of the verb shows, along with valency and transitivity, evidentiality. Evidentiality refers to the source of the information given by the verb. Siwa distinguishes two types of evidentiality.

The assertive is the default type of evidentiality, and its role is to show that the information given by the verb is known to be true, real or to be a first-hand account.
The inferential is the second type of evidentiality, which shows the information given by the verb to be uncertain, within the realm of possibilities, unconfirmed or from sensory information.

In other words, an assertive verb relays certain information, while an inferential verb relays less certain information. There are many nuances that can come about from using either evidentiality marker.

Evidentiality must be marked onto verbs, but it also exists as free particles that follow any phrase element, called evidential particles. They are:

Assertive	na or -ḥa
Inferential	ne or -ḥe

§9.6.1 Assertive
The most basic definition of the assertive is a marking that shows that a statement is real or certain, often equivalent to the English indicative mood. However, Siwa speakers use the assertive to show a variety of nuances between certainty and uncertainty. Generally, if the speaker has acquired the information shared in the statement first-hand, then it will be in the assertive. The assertive particle may also be used to underline an agreement or assumed knowledge of the other speaker or to counter an assumption or to underline the speaker's belief in a statement even thought he information is not first-hand. The assertive is also used in gnomic statements.

atemi
['atemi]
ate-m-i-Ø
sick-INCONCL-ASS.ITR-3P.PAT
'X is sick (because speaker saw)'

negami kita ome
['negami 'cʰita ɔ'me]
n<eg>-a-Ø-mi kita-a o-m-e
see.PAST-ASS.CONCL.TR-3P.PAT-1P.AG.SG
do.ASS.TR COMPLE-COP.INCONCL.PAST-INFER.INDIC
'I saw X do Y'

netami monina jogjia
['netami 'monina 'jɔj:ia]
net-a-mi m<on>-i-na jogj-ia
know-ASS.CONCL.TR-1P.AG.SG
COP.PAST.INCONCL.COMPLE-ASS.ITR-2P.AG.SG
there.DISTAL.APROX.INESS
'I know that you were over there'

negahmi seja omeina
['negahmi 'seja ɔ'meina]
Ø-n<eg>-a-sa=mi sej-a o-m-e-i-na
see.PAST.ASS.CONCL.TR-2P.PAT.SG-1P.AG.SG
listen.ASS.TR COMPLE-COP.INCONCL.PAST-INFER.INDIC-3P.PAT.PL-2P.AG.SG
'I saw you listening to them'

§9.6.2 Inferential
Inferential in its simplest definition is an evidentiality marker that denotes uncertainty, indirect information, information acquired through senses or that shows hypothetical or subjunctival statements. However, the inferential serves many other purposes, namely one analogical to the subjunctive of many European languages. The inferential is used in the following cases:

1. When the information the speaker is giving has been acquired through a second or indirect source
2. When the speaker acquires uncertain information through senses (with unagentive active pronoun and generally genitive object)

3. When the speaker wants to show that the information is not a fact but a possibility (in relative clauses)
4. When asking questions with intent to verify the verity or validity of information
5. In many fixed expressions or in story telling and narrative speech.

A verb marked with inferential may appear with an assertive particle, in which case the speaker wishes to show his belief (or in jocular or ironic language his disbelief) in indirectly acquired information.

1. *kisġi itahkieni sùḍbi*
['cʰɪsxi i'tʰahcieni 'suːðbi]
kisġi i-tahk-i-e-ni suḍbi-Ø
this.morning DIT-leave-PAST-INFER.CONCL.TR-3P.AG.PL winter.camp-DAT
'they apparently left camp this morning'
(i.e. speaker did not see them leave)

nonakiri keiddodlot
['nɔnaɟiri cʰɛɪtːɔtɬɔʔ]
n<non>-a-ki-ri-Ø kei<dd>-ot-l-o-t
tell.PAST-ASS.CONCL.TR-1P.RECI.SG-3P.AG.PL 3P.AG.SG-OBV.TR-start.fire.PAST-COMPLE-PERF-INFER.CONCL.ITR-3P.AG.OBV
'they¹ told me that they² had started the fire.

2. *ednege oskos*
[ɛʔtˈnːeɟe ɔskɔs]
ed-n<eg>-e osko-s
1P.UNAG.SG-see.PAST-INFER.CONCL.TR male.moose-GEN
'I think I saw a male moose'

entsame kykkyma
[ɛntsˈsame cʰœʔcyma]
ent-sa<m>-e kykky-ma
1P.UNAG.SG-hear.PAST-INFER.CONCL.TR voice- GEN
'I think I heard a voice'

3. *tabmami atetotomġa*
['tʰaʔpmami 'atedɔdɔmxa]
tat-m-a-mi ate-tot-o-ma=ka
think-INCONCL-ASS.TR-1P.AG.SG sick-COMPLE-INFER.ITR-INCONCL-1P.PAT.SG
'I think I could/might be sick'

noairi gone retro atana sira
['nɔairi 'gone 'rɛtxɔ 'atana sira]
n=oa-i-ri-Ø g-on-e retro-Ø atana-Ø sira-Ø
say.PAST-ASS.CONCL.TR-3P.AG.PL-3P.PAT COP.PAST-COMPLE-INFER northern.pike-AGT big-AGT fish-AGT
'they said that the fish was a big northern pike'

4. *õ neǥena-a amokvelu*
[õ 'neɟenaː 'amɔˈkʰvelu]
õ n<eg>-e-na-a amokvel-u
well see.PAST-INFER.CONCL.TR-2P.AG.SG–INTERR northern.lights-GEN
'so you saw the northern lights, eh'

ge-de retro atana sira
['ɟede 'rɛtxɔ 'atana sira]
g-e-de retr-o-s-Ø-atar-m-u-Ø na sira-Ø
COP.PAST-INFER–INTERR northern.pike-AGT BIG-AGT fish-AGT
'The fish was a big northern pike, you say'

ubme retro atana sira
['ʊʔpme 'rɛtxɔ 'atana sira]
ubm-e retro-Ø atana-Ø sira-Ø
COP.OBLI.PAST-INFER northern.pike-AGT big-AGT fish-AGT
'The fish must have been a big northern pike (right?)'

5. *isohhje momśitsita mone somi...*
   [iˈsoh:je ˈmomɕitsida ˈmone ˈsomi]
   i-sohhj-e-Ø momśi-tsita m<on>-e somi-Ø
   DIT-is.far-INFER.CONCL.ITR
   1P.GEN.PL.INCL-2ND.ILLAT COP.PAST.TEMP-
   COMPLE-INFER.INDIC man-ACT
   'a long time ago/once upon a time, there was a man...'
   (lit. it is far away to our's that there was a man)

   atanauta te ohhjú
   [ˈatɑnɑuda de ˈoh:ju:]
   atana-o-ta te ohhjo-o
   big-COP.PAST.INFER-3P.AG.SG and strong-
   COP.PAST.INFER
   'X was (said to be) big and (said to be) strong'

§9.7 Mood

Siwa verbs are marked for mood. They are the indicative, optative, conditional realis, conditional irrealis, obligative, imperative and imperative obviative. Indicative, optative and conditional irrealis are shown through postverbal vowels, which means that they also coalesce with transitivity and evidentiality. In addition, the conditional realis uses both a postverbal vowel and a verbal prefix. The imperative is always the very last marking on a verb, and so it is not marked through a postverbal vowel. The imperative obviative is a combination of the obligative and imperative markings. The obligative is marked through a verbal infix, which follows the postverbal vowel.

The moods in Siwa are organized in two groups – coalescing moods (indicative, conditional irrealis and optative) and non-coalescing moods (conditional realis, obligative, imperative and imperative obviative).

Because of the way mood coalesces with evidentiality and valency, a system of three postverbal vowel emerges: the transitive postverbal vowel, the intransitive postverbal vowel and the passive postverbal vowel. Each of these three vowels represent the various valency markers as well as evidentiality, and as it will be introduced here, mood.

transitive postverbal vowel
    transitive   Ø-a
    subjective transitive   o-Ø-a
    ditransitive transitive   i-Ø-a
    passive transitive   u-Ø-a

intransitive postverbal vowel
    intransitive   Ø-i
    subjective intransitive   o-Ø-i
    ditransitive intransitive   i-Ø-i
    passive intransitive   u-Ø-i

translative postverbal vowel
    translative   Ø-u, Ø-ů

§9.7.1 Indicative

transitive postverbal vowel		intransitive postverbal vowel		translative postverbal vowel	
assertive	inferential	assertive	inferential	assertive	inferential
-a-	-e-	-i-	-o-	-u-/-ů-	-o-

The indicative is the default mood. It shows that an action is within the realm of the real world (be the verb in assertive or inferential). It is the most common mood. The obligative usually uses the indicative mood. Note that the indicative is not glossed here in verbs, only in with the copula. The translative assertive ending is -ů if directly preceded by -e- -i- -y- and -ů-, but not by -ai- -oai- -ui- or -oi-.

> *śykami*
> 'I will take care of Y'
>
> *tȧimi*
> 'I will stand'
>
> *mavahsu*
> 'I will grow stronger'

§9.7.2 Conditional Realis

transitive postverbal vowel		intransitive postverbal vowel		translative postverbal vowel	
assertive	inferential	assertive	inferential	assertive	inferential
da-Ø-a-	da-Ø-e-	da-Ø-i-	da-Ø-o-	da-Ø-u- da-Ø-ů-	da-Ø-o-

The conditional realis shows that the verb is in a possible but conditional reality. If used by itself, it is equivalent to the English conjunction *if* in realistic statements. In certain cases, the conditional may be used where English would use *when* or *although* (especially with an evidentiality particle). Conditional realis and irrealis clauses are often linked together with the conjunction ju.

There is considerable variation in the form of the conditional realis marker. The most widespread and standard for is **da-** or **d-**, but other forms exist:

ro-/r-	*Ėdnu* and *Riekka* dialects
aḥḥ(a)-	*Sorhi* and *Neyihesko* dialects (old *Aingo* dialect)
eġġ(a)-	Most midwestern dialects

The conditional realis does not affect the postverbal vowel, such that it is the only mood not to be reflected in the vowel. For this reason, the conditional realis shares its postverbal vowel with the indicative.

man·i·mi
'I will come'

da·man·i·mi
'if I come'

m·id·i
'I will fall'

en·d·id·i
'if I fall'

van·a·mi
'I will stretch Y'

da·van·a·mi
'if I stretch Y'

It is not uncommon for the **da-** to form a consonant cluster with the verb's initial consonant if possible if is preceded by a pronoun. This is especially common of verbs beginning in **m- n- l- ġ-** (then becoming **-bm- -dn- -dl-** and **-dġ-** respectively) and less commonly with verbs in **p- b-** and **k- g-** (then becoming **-ḍb-** and **-ḍg-** respectively). This is called conditional contraction, and it is mostly a trait of relaxed speech:

-da-m-	→	-bm-
-da-n-	→	-dn-
-da-l-	→	-dl-
-da-ġ-	→	-dġ-
-da-p-/-b-	→	-ḍb-
-da-k-/-g-	→	-ḍg-
-da-v-	→	-ḍv-

mavoavvu
'I will get scared'

endavoavvu ~ maḍvoavvu
'if I get scared'

ednekeni ~ manekeni 'I will lose'	*madnekeni ~ endanekeni* 'if I lose'
mamyhybmui ~ emmyhybmui 'I will moan'	*mabmyhybmui ~ endamyhybmui* 'if I moan'
malodni ~ edlodni 'I will sink'	*madlodni ~ endalodni* 'if I sink'
entġemi ~ maġemi 'I will tremble'	*madġemi ~ endaġemi* 'if I tremble'
empialjeni ~ mapieljeni 'I will flush'	*madbialjeni ~ endapialjeni* 'if I flush'

Certain speakers have a so-called expended conditional, that includes more forms that are otherwise expressed by other words. These include the forms **daġi-/daġ-** 'if ever' and the more formal **sasa-/sas-** 'if' (much more reserved possibility).

dasihhi, tahhumikigga ju
[ˈdɑˈsihːi ˈtʰɑhːumiɹikːaju]
da-sihh-i tahh-um-i-ki-gga ju
COND.REAL-rain-ASS.CONCL.ITR leave-OBLI-ASS.CONCL.ITR-TRANSLO-1P.AG.PL.INCL |U
'if it rains, we will have to leave'

sę on danjallana, netaśenna ju sareta-ḥa
[ˈsæɔ̃ dɑˈɲalːɑna ˈnetɑɕenːaju ˈsɑredaʔa]
sę on da-njal-l-a-na Ø-net-a-ś=en-na sar-e-ta-ḥa
not ON COND.REAL-taste-PERF-ASS.CONCL.TR-2P.AG.SG know-ASS.CONCL.TR-NEG.HABIL-2P.AG.SG |U good-COP.ASS.INFER-3P.AG.SG-REL.INTERR
'if you haven't tasted it, then you cannot know whether it is good'

daġisihhi, tahhumikigga ju
[ˈdɑxiˈsihːi ˈtʰɑhːumiɹikːaju]
daġi-sihh-i tahh-um-i-ki-gga ju
COND.REAL-rain-ASS.CONCL.ITR leave-OBLI-ASS.CONCL.ITR-TRANSLO-1P.AG.PL.INCL |U
'if ever it rains, we will have to leave'

sastanaknu
[sastɑˈnaʔŋu]
sas-ta-nakn-u
COND.REAL-3P.UNAG.SG-break-ASS.CONCL.TRANSL
'should X ever break'

Conditional realis in indirect clauses is expressed by the verb clitic -**ḥa**:

addata sara   'if it is good'
set negami, sarvata-ḥa   'I don't know if/whether it is good'

§9.7.3 Conditional Irrealis

	transitive postverbal vowel		intransitive postverbal vowel		translative postverbal vowel	
	assertive	inferential	assertive	inferential	assertive	inferential
eastern	-ia-	-ie-	-iu-	-joi-	-ui- -ůi-	-jui-
western	-ę-	-ey-	-iů-	-ėu-	-ẏ-	-jėu-

The conditional irrealis mood shows that the verb is in a impossible or unrealistic but conditional reality. If used by itself, it is equivalent to the English conjunction *if* in irrealis statements (i.e. *if I were, if I came, if you did*). In certain cases, the conditional may be used where English would use *when* or *although* (especially with an evidentiality particle). There are two sets of endings for the conditional irrealis. One is primarily used in the eastern dialects, the other in the western dialects.

naụinami
'I will use Y'

naụiniami~naụinęmi
'if I used Y'

saskimi
'I will wake up'

saskiumi~saskiůmi
'if I woke up'

mahingu
'I will die in combat'

mahingui~mahingẏ
'if I died in combat'

The conditional irrealis inferential generally corresponds to the English subjunctive mood, which Siwa otherwise lacks and generally expressed through the inferential:

naụiniami~naụinęmi
'if I used Y'

naụiniemi~naụineymi
'I would use Y'

saskiumi~saskiůmi
'if I woke up'

saskjoimi~saskėumi
'I would wake up'

mahingui~mahingẏ

mahingjoi~mahingjėu

'if I died in combat' 'I would die in combat'

Unlike the conditional realis, the conditional irrealis is not strictly used in phrases with a clear condition. It may simply be used to show an irrealis situation (then often in the inferential). Thus, a clause whose main verb is in the conditional irrealis and whose conjuncted clause is in the same mood (or in the optative) but in the inferential, it is often equivalent to English *if X were to Y, then X would Y*.

When two phrases are in the conditional irrealis (counterfactual conditional phrases), and the second phrase is considered to be a possible result of the first phrase, the first one (protasis) will be found in the inferential, and the second one in the assertive (apodosis) (see fourth example below).

sihhiu on, tahhumjoikigga ju
[ˈsihːiuõ ˈtʰɑhːumjɔiɟɹkːaju]
sihh-iu on tahh-um-joi-ki-gga ju
rain-ASS.CONCL.COND.IRREAL.ITR ON leave-OBLI-INFER.CONCL.COND.IRREAL.ITR-TRANSLO-1P.AG.PL.INCL JU
'if it were to rain, we would have to leave'

sę on njalliana, netieśenna ju sareta-ḥa
[ˈsæ̃õ ˈɲalːiana ˈnetieɕenːaju ˈsaredaʔa]
sę on njal-l-a-na ju net-ie-ś=en-na sar-e-ta–ḥa
not ON taste-PERF-ASS.CONCL.COND.IRREAL.TR-2P.AG.SG know-INFER.CONCL.COND.IRREAL.TR-NEG.HABIL-2P.AG.SG JU good-COP.ASS.INFER-3P.AG.SG-REL.INTER
'if you wouldn't have tasted it, then you would not know whether it is good'

sariata de, njaluemi ka
[ˈsariade ˈɲaluemika]
sar-ia-ta de Ø-njal-ue-mi ka
good-COP.COND.IRRREAL.ASS-3P.AG.SG DE taste-INFER.CONCL.OPT.TR-1P.AG.SG KA
'If it were good, then I would want to taste it'

vahta eruljoila, nette erulujata taga
[ˈvahta ˈeruljɔila ˈnɛʔte ˈeruljɑda ˈtʰaga]
vahta er<u>l-joi-la-Ø nette er<u>l-u-ia-ta taga
completely work.PAST-COND.IRR.INFER-PERF-3P.AG.SG surely work.PAST-PAT.PART.ACT-COP.COND.IRR.ASS-3P.AG.SG TAGA
'if X would have worked to completion, then surely (it follows that) Y would be done'

Conservative eastern dialects have kept the older versions of the vowels:

transitive postverbal vowel		intransitive postverbal vowel		translative postverbal vowel	
assertive	inferential	assertive	inferential	assertive	inferential

transitive postverbal vowel		intransitive postverbal vowel		translative postverbal vowel	
-iġa-	-iġe-	-iġu-	-joġi-	-uġi- -ůġi-	-juġi-

§9.7.4 Optative

transitive postverbal vowel		intransitive postverbal vowel		translative postverbal vowel	
assertive	inferential	assertive	inferential	assertive	inferential
-ua- -ůa-	-ue- -ůi-	-ųi- -ůi-	-uo-	-ųu- -ųů-	-ue- or -èu-

The optative mood shows wish or will – it is used to show what the subject wishes to do or wants to do. The optative is generally not found in the inconclusive. Note that the endings -ųi- and -ųu- often become -vi- and -vu- (or -vo-) when a consonant cluster is possible. Similarly, -ua-, -ue- and -ųi- can be found as -ůa- and -ůi- if preceded by i e ů y.

sugami
'I will visit Y'

suguami
'I want to visit Y'

sivimi
'I will stay'

siviumi
'I want to stay'

ednjoapsu
'I will grow a beard'

ednjoapsųu
'I want to grow a beard'

kodi
'X walked'

kotvi
'X wanted to walk' (cf. *koni* 'X will walk')

nodi
'X swam'

notvi
'X wanted to swim' (cf. *noni* 'X will swim')

beiddji
'X spent the day'

beitsvi
'X wants to spend the day' (cf. *beiśi* 'X will spend the day')

kůnnjůlimi
'I will settle down'

kůnnjůlůimi
'I want to settle down' (also *kůnnjůlvimi*)

The inferential optative corresponds to a subjunctive form of the optative:

suguami
'I want to visit Y'

suguemi
'I would want to visit Y'

śiviumi
'I want to stay'

śivvimi
'I would want to stay'   (or 'I stayed')

ednjoapsu̧u
'I want to grow a beard'

ednjoapsue
'I would want to grow a beard'

It is also used as a sort of imperative with the third person in the inferential (called the optative imperative). The first or second persons are also used in this construction, which can be translated as *may X Y*, especially if the subjects are unagentive (the imperative used with an unagentive subject is common, but is considered poor language).

Another optative construction involves a copular construction, which may be coupled with **bahtśu ... o-** or (**bà**) **ari -tśu/-uts...o-**, then meaning *if only* (often with dramatic coordinating particles). The postverbal vowel is often absent, unlike in normal -uts/-tśu temporal link constructions. Phrases of this construction commonly have have the form:

Ø-uts/-tśu ari...oduo~oḍvo[1]

tauts ari inina oḍvomi   'if only I were rich'
hàbmuts ari oḍvośimi   'if only I could fly'
bà ari netuts oḍvona   'if only you knew'
pednuts ari oḍvori   'if only they would arrive'

The optative may reflect the subject's wish upon an object, in which case the reversive must be used (see section on reversive §9.9.4.1). This is similar to English *X wants Y to Z*.

---

[1] The form *oḍvo* is a short form used mainly in this type of phrases.

The optative is frequently used with the conclusive despite often carrying a habitual meaning.

otoatŭimi
[ɔˈtʰɔadwimi]
o-toat-ŭi-mi
SUBJ-join-ASS.CONCL.OPT.ITR-1P.AG.SG
'I want to come along/join in'

sotoatuadnami
[sɔˈtʰɔaduaʔtnami]
s-o-toat-ua-dna-Ø-mi
2P.UNAG.SG-SUBJ-join-ASS.CONCL.OPT.TR-REVERS-3P.PAT.SG-1P.AG.SG
'I want you to come along/join X'

sihhi nuo
[ˈsihːi ˈnuɔ]
sihh-i n-uo
rain-ITR COP.INCONCL-INFER.OPT
'if only it would rain...'

tanikuo
[tʰaˈnikuɔ]
ta-nik-uo
3P.UNAG.SG-die-INFER.CONCL.ITR
'may X die'

bà ari imanitśu mubma oduona
[ˈbæː ˈari iˈmanitɕu ˈmʊʔpma ɔˈduɔna]
bà ari i-ma=n-i-tśu mù=bma o-d-uo-na
oh ari DIT-come-ITR-LINK.TEMP among.ALLAT COMPLE-COP-INFER.OPT-2P.AG.SG
'oh if only you could come to me'

kesŭami nori deita
[ˈcʰesøami ˈnɔri ˈdeida]
kes-ŭa-mi nor-i d-e-ita
learn-ASS.CONCL.OPT.TR-1P.AG.SG sing-ITR COP-INFER-ILLAT
'I want to learn to sing'

takessŭadnarimi nori deita
[tʰaˈcʰesːœaʔtnarimi ˈnɔri ˈdeida]
ta-kes-s-ua--dna-ri-mi nor-i d-e-ita
3P.UNAG-learn-HAB-ASS.CONCL.OPT.TR-REVERS-3P.PL-1P.AG.SG sing-ITR COP-INFER-ILLAT
'I want them to learn to sing'

sihhuo
[ˈsihːuɔ]
sihh-uo
rain-INFER.CONCL.ITR.OPT
'may it rain'

hȧbmuośimi
[ˈhæːʔpmuɔɕimi]
hȧbm-uo-śi-mi
fly-INFER.CONCL.ITR.OPT-HABIL-1P.AG.SG
'if only I could fly'

Conservative eastern dialects have kept the older versions of the vowels:

transitive postverbal vowel		intransitive postverbal vowel		translative postverbal vowel	
assertive	inferential	assertive	inferential	assertive	inferential
-uba- -ŭba-	-ube- -ŭbe-	-ŭi- -ŭbi-	-ubo-	-ŭu- -ŭbŭ-	-uboi-

§9.7.5 Obligative

Unlike the indicative, conditional irrealis and optative, the obligative is not expressed through the postverbal vowel. However, it is still considered a mood in Siwa grammar. The obligative marker is -um-, which is found in slot 3. The obligative is generally found in the agentive, although translative verbs remain, as always, unagentive.

The general function of the obligative is to show that the agent of the verb has, must or should (in the inferential) do something. The nature of the obligation or need can range from strong to much lesser necessity.

nuidnami
'I will admit Y'

nuidnumami
'I must admit Y'

ontaimi
'I will dance'

ontaumimi
'I must dance'

entèulŭ
'I will get better'

entèulumu
'I must get better'

Like the optative, the obligative is often found in the conclusive despite having a mostly habitual meaning. In older language, the obligative may also be found with the reversive, as the optative (same construction), equivalent to English **X needs Y to**.

otoatumimi
[ɔˈtʰɔadumimi]
o-toat-um-i-mi
SUBJ-join-OBLI-ASS.CONCL.ITR-1P.AG.SG
'I must come along/join'

kesumami nori deita
[ˈcʰesumami ˈnɔrha ˈdeida]
kes-um-a-mi nor-sa d-e-ita
learn-OBLI-ASS.CONCL.TR--1P.AG.SG sing-ITR COP-INFER-ILLAT
'I must to learn to sing'

sotoatumidnami
[sɔˈtʰɔadumɪʔtnami]
s-o-toat-um-i-dna-mi
2P.UNAG.SG-SUBJ-join-OBLI-ASS.CONCL.TR-REVERS-1P.AG.SG
'I need you to come along/join in'

sihhumi hake sesigga
[ˈsihːumi ˈhace ˈseɕikːa]
sihh-um-i h-a-ke s-e-ɕi-gga
rain-OBLI-ASS.CONCL.ITR eat-TR-LINK.GOAL COP.HAB-INFER.INDIC-HABIL-1P.AG.PL.INCL
'it must rain for us to eat'

§9.7.6 Imperative

The imperative mood shows a direct command. It is the very last morpheme that can be added to a verb, so it appears in slot 9. It is most common with verbs governed by an agentive subject rather than unagentive, in which case the optative imperative is used instead.

Below are the forms of the imperative mood markers. The negative imperative is logically prohibitive. A more direct and sometimes impolite imperative mood can be expressed through the subitive (see §9.9.4.6).

The second and third person plural have two forms – one in -uri and one in -unni. The form in -unni is slightly more polite.

	2p.sg	3p.sg. ani	3p.sg. ina	1p.pl.incl	1p.pl.excl	2p.pl	3p.pl
positive	-n	-t		-oḥa	-oḥe	-uri/-unni	-ġuri/-ġunni
negative	-sen	-set		-soḥa	-soḥe	-suri/-sunni	-sġuri/-sġunni

manina
'you will come'

manin!
'come!'

nonakina
'you will tell me'

nonakin!
'tell me!'

noridda
'you will sing (pl.)'

noriuri!
'sing!'

notsana
'you will take Y'

notsasen!
'don't take Y!'

makigga
'we will go'

makoḥa
'let's go'

nedġigga
'we will sit down'

nedġoḥa
'let's sit down'

otoatin
[ɔˈtʰɔatɕɪn]
o-toat-i-n
SUBJ-join-ASS.CONCL.ITR-IMPER.2P.SG
'come along/join !'

kesauri nori daita
[ˈcʰesɑuri ˈnɔri ˈdɑidɑ]

kes-a-uri nor-i d-a-ita
learn-ASS.CONCL.TR-IMPER.2P.PL sing-ITR COP-ASS-ILLAT
'learn to sing ! (pl.)'

nedġigunni
['nɛðxiɣunːi]
nedġ-i-gunni
sit.down-ASS.CONCL.ITR-IMPER.3P.PL
'let them sit down'

nedġisġuri
['nɛðxɪsxuri]
nedġ-i-sġuri
sit.down-ASS.CONCL.ITR-IMPER.3P.PL.NEG
'let them not sit down'

§9.7.6.1 Imperative Obviative
The imperative obviative mood is a variation of the imperative mood. The command or order of the normal imperative is less urgent and usually refers to something to be done later. The imperative obviative means something like a delayed imperative, and it is marked by using both a modified version of the obligative (-**mu**- instead of -**um**-) and the imperative markings, which can combine with the second person singular imperative ending -**n** to -**mō** if no other slot is taken up between slot 3 and 9. The imperative obviative usually requires the order of slot 3 and 4 to be switched as per rule 1 (see section of slot switch *§9.2.1.8*) It can also have a meaning similar to English phrases such as *X ought to*, especially with 3rd person imperatives and the inferential.

The imperative obviative may also be used to convey that the agent of the verb will have to to do something at a later point.

otoatimō
[ɔˈtʰɔatɕimɔ̃]
o-toat-i-mu=n
SUBJ-join-ASS.CONCL.ITR-OBLI-IMPER.2P.SG
'come along/join later on'
or
'you will have to come along (later on)'

kesumet nori deita
[ˈcʰesumɛʔ ˈnɔri ˈdeida]
kes-um-e-t nor-i d-e-ita
learn-OBLI-INFER.CONCL.TR-IMPER.3P.SG.ANI sing-ITR COP-INFER-ILLAT
'X ought to learn to sing'
or
'X will have to learn to sing (later on)'

§9.8 Postverbal Vowel Coalescence
The sections on valency, evidentiality and mood all concern the postverbal vowel. The table below combines all these morphemes and shows the conjugation pattern for the postverbal vowel. Dialectal forms are given in italics.

			postverb vowel		
			transitive	intransitive	translative
			transitive subjective ditransitive passive	intransitive subjective ditransitive passive	
assertive	indicative		-a	-i	-u / -ů
	conditional irrealis		-ia	-iu / -iů	-ui
			-ẹ	-iủ	-ỳ
			-iga	-igu	-ugi / -ůgi
	optative		-ua / -ůa	-ụi / -ůi	-ụu / -ụů
			-uba / -ůba	-ụi / -ůbi	-ụu / -ůbů
inferential	indicative		-e	-o	-o
	conditional irrealis		-ie	-ịoi	-jui
			-ey	-eu	-ẹu
			-ige	-jogi	-jugi
	optative		-ue / -ůi	-uo	-ue or -ẹu
			-ube / -ůbe	-ubo	-uboi

Below is an example of a verb conjugated in all of its mood, valency and evidentiality forms.

oden·a 'look at Y'

assertive		indicative	conditional realis	conditional irrealis	optative
1P.	SG.	*odenami* 'I will look at Y'	*dodenami* 'if I look at Y'	*odeniami* 'if I looked at Y'	*odenůami* 'I want to look at Y'
	PL. INCL	*odenagga* 'we will look at Y'	*dodenagga* 'if we look at Y'	*odeniagga* 'if we looked at Y'	*odenůagga* 'we want to look at Y'
	PL. EXCL	*odenagge* 'we will look at Y'	*dodenagge* 'if we look at Y'	*odeniagge* 'if we looked at Y'	*odenůagge* 'we want to look at Y'
2P.	SG.	*odenana* 'you will look at Y'	*dodenana* 'if you look at Y'	*odeniana* 'if you looked at Y'	*odenůana* 'you want to look at Y'
	PL.	*odenadda* 'you will look at Y'	*dodenadda* 'if you look at Y'	*odeniadda* 'if you looked at Y'	*odenůadda* 'you want to look at Y'
3P.	SG.	*odena* 'X will look at Y'	*dodena* 'if X looks at Y'	*odenia* 'if X looked at Y'	*odenůa* 'X wants to look at Y'
	PL.	*odenari* 'they will look at Y'	*dodenari* 'if they look at Y'	*odeniari* 'if they looked at Y'	*odenůari* 'they want to look at Y'
	OBV.	*odenat* 'X will look at Y'	*dodenat* 'if X looks at Y'	*odeniat* 'if X looked at Y'	*odenůat* 'X wants to look at Y'
4P.		*odenajo* 'one will look at Y'	*dodenajo* 'if one looks at Y'	*odeniajo* 'if one looked at Y'	*odenůajo* 'one wants to look at Y'

inferential		indicative	conditional realis	conditional irrealis	optative
1P.	SG.	*odenemi* 'I will look at Y'	*dodenemi* 'if I look at Y'	*odeniemi* 'I would look at Y'	*odenŭimi* 'I would want to look at Y'
	PL. INCL	*odenegga* 'we will look at Y'	*dodenegga* 'if we look at Y'	*odeniegga* 'we would look at Y'	*odenŭigga* 'we would want to look at Y'
	PL. EXCL	*odenegge* 'we will look at Y'	*dodenegge* 'if we look at Y'	*odeniegge* 'we would look at Y'	*odenŭigge* 'we would want to look at Y'
2P.	SG.	*odenena* 'you will look at Y'	*dodenena* 'if you look at Y'	*odeniena* 'you would look at Y'	*odenŭina* 'you would want to look at Y'
	PL.	*odenedda* 'you will look at Y'	*dodenedda* 'if you look at Y'	*odeniedda* 'you would look at Y'	*odenŭidda* 'you would want to look at Y'
3P.	SG.	*odene* 'X will look at Y'	*dodene* 'if X looks at Y'	*odenie* 'X would look at Y'	*odenŭi* 'X would want to look at Y'
	PL.	*odeneri* 'they will look at Y'	*dodeneri* 'if they look at Y'	*odenieri* 'they would look at Y'	*odenŭiri* 'they would want to look at Y'
	OBV.	*odenet* 'X will look at Y'	*dodenet* 'if X looks at Y'	*odeniet* 'X would look at Y'	*odenŭit* 'X would want to look at Y'
4P.		*odenejo* 'one will look at Y'	*dodenejo* 'if one looks at Y'	*odeniejo* 'one would look at Y'	*odenŭijo* 'one would want to look at Y'

pośk·i   'go to sleep'

assertive		indicative	conditional realis	conditional irrealis	optative
1P.	SG.	*pośkimi* 'I will go to sleep'	*dapośkimi* 'if I go to sleep'	*pośkiumi* 'if I went to sleep'	*pośkvimi* 'I want to go to sleep'
	PL. INCL	*pośkigga* 'we will go to sleep'	*dapośkigga* 'if we go to sleep'	*pośkiugga* 'if we went to sleep'	*pośkvigga* 'we want to go to sleep'
	PL. EXCL	*pośkigge* 'we will go to sleep'	*dapośkigge* 'if we go to sleep'	*pośkiugge* 'if we went to sleep'	*pośkvigge* 'we want to go to sleep'
2P.	SG.	*pośkina* 'you will go to sleep'	*dapośkina* 'if you go to sleep'	*pośkiuna* 'if you went to sleep'	*pośkvina* 'you want to go to sleep'
	PL.	*pośkidda* 'you will go to sleep'	*dapośkidda* 'if you go to sleep'	*pośkiudda* 'if you went to sleep'	*pośkvidda* 'you want to go to sleep'
3P.	SG.	*pośki* 'X will go to sleep'	*dapośki* 'if X goes to sleep'	*pośkiu* 'if X went to sleep'	*pośkvi* 'X wants to go to sleep'
	PL.	*pośkiri* 'they will go to sleep'	*dapośkiri* 'if they go to sleep'	*pośkiuri* 'if they went to sleep'	*pośkviri* 'they want to go to sleep'
	OBV.	*pośkit* 'X will go to sleep'	*dapośkit* 'if X goes to sleep'	*pośkiut* 'if X went to sleep'	*pośkvit* 'X wants to go to sleep'
4P.		*pośkijo* 'one will go to sleep'	*dapośkijo* 'if one goes to sleep'	*pośkiujo* 'if one went to sleep'	*pośkvijo* 'one wants to go to sleep'

		inferential indicative	conditional realis	conditional irrealis	optative
1P.	SG.	*pośkomi* 'I will go to sleep'	*daposkomi* 'if I go to sleep'	*poskjoimi* 'I would go to sleep'	*poskuomi* 'I would want to go to sleep'
	PL. INCL	*poskogga* 'we will go to sleep'	*daposkogga* 'if we go to sleep'	*poskjoigga* 'we would go to sleep'	*poskuogga* 'we would want to go to sleep'
	PL. EXCL	*poskogge* 'we will go to sleep'	*daposkogge* 'if we go to sleep'	*poskjoigge* 'we would go to sleep'	*poskuogge* 'we would want to go to sleep'
2P.	SG.	*poskona* 'you will go to sleep'	*daposkona* 'if you go to sleep'	*poskjoina* 'you would go to sleep'	*poskuona* 'you would want to go to sleep'
	PL.	*poskodda* 'you will go to sleep'	*daposkodda* 'if you go to sleep'	*poskjoidda* 'you would go to sleep'	*poskuodda* 'you would want to go to sleep'
3P.	SG.	*posko* 'X will go to sleep'	*daposko* 'if X goes to sleep'	*poskjoi* 'X would go to sleep'	*poskuo* 'X would want to go to sleep'
	PL.	*poskori* 'they will go to sleep'	*daposkori* 'if they go to sleep'	*poskjoiri* 'they would go to sleep'	*poskuori* 'they would want to go to sleep'
	OBV.	*poskot* 'X will go to sleep'	*daposkot* 'if X goes to sleep'	*poskjoit* 'X would go to sleep'	*poskuot* 'X would want to go to sleep'
4p.		*poskojo* 'one will go to sleep'	*daposkojo* 'if one goes to sleep'	*poskjoijo* 'one would go to sleep'	*poskuojo* 'one would want to go to sleep'

muh·u 'disappear'

		assertive indicative	conditional realis	conditional irrealis	optative
1P.	SG.	*mamuhu* 'I will disappear'	*mabmuhu* 'if I disappear'	*mamuhui* 'if I disappeared'	*mamuhyu* 'I want to disappear'
	PL. INCL	*mamuhu* 'we will disappear'	*mabmuhu* 'if we disappear'	*mamuhui* 'if we disappeared'	*mamuhyu* 'we want to disappear'
	PL. EXCL	*memuhu* 'we will disappear'	*mebmuhu* 'if we disappear'	*memuhui* 'if we disappeared'	*memuhyu* 'we want to disappear'
2P.	SG.	*samuhu* 'you will disappear'	*sabmuhu* 'if you disappear'	*samuhui* 'if you disappeared'	*samuhyu* 'you want to disappear'
	PL.	*sġamuhu* 'you will disappear'	*sġabmuhu* 'if you disappear'	*sġamuhui* 'if you disappeared'	*sġamuhyu* 'you want to disappear'
3P.	SG.	*tamuhu* 'X will disappear'	*tabmuhu* 'if X disappears'	*tamuhui* 'if X disappeared'	*tamuhyu* 'X wants to disappear'
	PL.	*tsemuhu* 'they will disappear'	*tsebmuhu* 'if they disappear'	*tsemuhui* 'if they disappeared'	*tsemuhyu* 'they want to disappear'
	OBV.	*nemuhu* 'X will disappear'	*nebmuhu* 'if X disappears'	*nemuhui* 'if X disappeared'	*nemuhyu* 'X wants to disappear'
4P.		*jamuhu* 'one will disappear'	*jabmuhu* 'if one disappears'	*jamuhui* 'if one disappeared'	*jamuhyu* 'one wants disappear'

inferential		indicative	conditional realis	conditional irrealis	optative
1P.	SG.	*mamuho* 'I will disappear'	*mabmuho* 'if I disappear'	*mamuhjui* 'I would disappear'	*mamuhue* 'I would want to disappear'
	PL. INCL	*mamuho* 'we will disappear'	*mabmuho* 'if we disappear'	*mamuhjui* 'we would disappear'	*mamuhue* 'we would want to disappear'
	PL. EXCL	*memuho* 'we will disappear'	*mebmuho* 'if we disappear'	*memuhjui* 'we would disappear'	*memuhue* 'we would want to disappear'
2P.	SG.	*samuho* 'you will disappear'	*sabmuho* 'if you disappear'	*samuhjui* 'you would disappear'	*samuhue* 'you would want to disappear'
	PL.	*sġamuho* 'you will disappear'	*sġabmuho* 'if you disappear'	*sġamuhjui* 'you would disappear'	*sġamuhue* 'you would want to disappear'
3P.	SG.	*tamuho* 'X will disappear'	*tabmuho* 'if X disappears'	*tamuhjui* 'X would disappear'	*tamuhue* 'X would want to disappear'
	PL.	*tsemuho* 'they will disappear'	*tsebmuho* 'if they disappear'	*tsemuhjui* 'they would disappear'	*tsemuhue* 'they would want to disappear'
	OBV.	*nemuho* 'X will disappear'	*nebmuho* 'if X disappears'	*nemuhjui* 'X would disappear'	*nemuhue* 'X would want to disappear'
4P.		*jamuho* 'one will disappear'	*jabmuho* 'if one disappears'	*jamuhjui* 'one would disappear'	*jamuhue* 'one would want to disappear'

§9.9 Aspect

Siwa has four primary aspects:

> conclusive
> inconclusive
> > verbal
> > copular
>
> habitual
> perfective (the perfect tense)

Moreover, it has 8 secondarily aspects:

> reversive
> semelfactive
> persistive
> frequentative
> inchoative
> subitive
> habilitive
> diminutive

Primary and secondary aspectual markers behave differently. Namely, primary markers are found in slot 3, while secondary markers are found in slot 6. Both primary and secondary markers can be combined, and they are found in the order in which they appear above.

Note that the order in which primary aspect markers appear in the verb depends on the verb's stem. See *§9.2.1.8*.

§9.9.1 Conclusivity

Conclusivity is an aspect of every conjugated verb in Siwa. A verb is either conclusive or inconclusive. While the conclusive has no overt marking, the inconclusive has two. Within the verb, it is found as either -ma- or -m- depending on whether the -m- can form a cluster with the preceding consonant (see *§9.2.1.2.4*):

> rule 1   -C-m-PV-   and   -V-m-PV
> rule 2   -C-PV-ma-   and   -PV-ma-C or -PV-m-mi

Only impersonal verbs, participles, a handful of other verbs and verbal adjectives are found with this inconclusive marker called verbal inconclusive. In fact, the verbal inconclusive is the most characterizing feature of impersonal verbs and verbal adjectives, which behave differently than regular verbs in other ways.

The second way to show the inconclusive is through the copular construction, whereby the main verb and the copula are used within the phrase. Impersonal verbs cannot be found in this form, though they may form split stems.

What conclusivity actually shows is whether the verb is perceived to have reached an end, goal or conclusion. While very similar to the perfect or the telic aspects found in many other languages, conclusivity has a broader function – whether the goal of the action was achieved or not.

The conclusive marking (or rather lack thereof) also carries another important function. Whereas the inconclusive clearly shows an ongoing action, the conclusive form is not so limited. The conclusive form is often used for gnomic statement, i.e. general truths or facts. It is also found with the habilitive, and certain verbs have a tendency to use the conclusive form rather than the inconclusive, despite having a rather inconclusive aspect, including verbs such as **nuj**- 'to see' and **net**- 'to know'. These verbs include those which cannot or usually do not have a set goal - verbs with no clear duration, or an inherently short or limited duration. For example, the verb **saj**- 'to hear X' is more often in the conclusive, without taking a particularly conclusive aspect. Thus, while the inconclusive always carries a meaning of *X is doing Y*, the conclusive can carry a meaning of *X will do Y* or *X does Y*.

§9.9.1.1 Verbal Inconclusive

The verbal inconclusive is a marker that is found within the fully conjugated verb. It is primarily found in verbal adjectives, a number of impersonal verbs (whose conclusive meaning is actually an inchoative one) and an even smaller number of other verbs.

The marker for the verbal inconclusive is -**m**- or -**ma**- and is found in slot 3. It often merges with the verb, causing various sound changes. See section *§9.2.1.8.1* on impersonal verbs and verbal adjectives for a detailed description of this.

The number of regular verbs that are or can be found in the verbal inconclusive aspect is small, but varies the eastern and western dialects as a recent development. However, most of the verbs that do appear in the verbal inconclusive usually involve some kind of mental or non-concrete action. Below is a non-exhaustive list of the these verbs.

WESTERN	EASTERN
tab·m·i·mi	
(tat-)	
'I am thinking/I think'	
deb·m·a·mi	
(det-)	
'I feel like Y/I want Y'	
ryts̀·a·ma·mi	*ma·ryts̀·a*
(ryts̀-)	(ryts̀-)
'I am anxious about Y'	'I am anxious about Y'

WESTERN	EASTERN
top·m·a·mi	*en·tobb·a(·ġa)*
(tobb-)	(tobb-)
'I have a feeling (that)'	'I have a feeling (that)'

	kerrj·a·mi
Ø	(kerrj-)
	'I suspect (that)'

koanta·mi	*koanta·m·mi*
(koanta-)	(koanta-)
'I assume'	'I assume'

vi·ma·mi	*ma·vi*
(vi-)	(vi-)
'I seem to remember (that)'	'I seem to remember (that)'

iskjel·m·i·mi or *iskjel·i·m·mi*	*iskjel·mi* or *m·iskjeli*
(iskjel-)	(iskjel-)
'I wonder'	'I wonder'

kuimnami	*tsuogg·a·mi*
(kuin-)	(tsuogg-)
'I hope'	'I hope'

§9.9.1.2 Copular Inconclusive

The copular inconclusive is a construction which can be used with all verbs other than impersonal verbs, verbal adjectives and the few verbs given above.

Its construction is explained in *§9.2.2*. Copular inconclusive verbs are split into a split-stem and the copula, each bearing their respective markers. Compare the following example:

slots -1 -3	split-stem	slot 4	phrase	copula	slot 4²	slots 2 5 6 7 8 9	subject
o·b-	-muoj-	-a	kendai	d-	-a-	-ja	peggŭ

domuoja kendai daja peggŭ
[dɔˈmuɔja ˈcʰɛndaɪ ˈdaja ˈpʰecːø]
d-o-muoj-a kenda=i d-a-ja peggŭ-Ø
COND.REAL-SUBJ-wear-TR today COP-ASS-3P.PAT.PL girl-AGT
'if the girl is wearing them today'

Below are examples of the copular inconclusive compared to the regular conclusive forms.

conclusive independent	inconclusive copular
nenimi ůhhįa ['nenimi 'øh:ja] nen-i-mi ůhh=ja sit-ASS.ITR.CONCL-1P.AG.SG here 'I (will) sit here'	*neni ůhhįa nami* ['neni 'øh:ja 'nami] nen-i ůhh=ja n-a-mi sit-ITR here COP-ASS-1P.AG.SG 'I am sitting here'
mottu tėhtśa ['mɔʔtu 'tʰeːhtɕa] mott-u tėr=tśa set-ASS.TRANSL.CONCL sun.PAT 'the sun (will) set(s)'	*mottu tėhtśa na* ['mɔʔtu 'tʰeːhtɕa na] mott-u tėr=tśa n-a set-ASS.TRANSL.INCONCL sun.PAT COP.INCONCL-ASS 'the sun is setting'
soaksa tiogi kįuhkua ['sɔaksa 'tʰiɔji 'cʰʊhkua] soak-s-a tiogi-Ø kįuhko-a-Ø build-HAB-ASS.CONCL.TR dam-DAT beaver-PL-AGT 'beavers build dams'	*soaka tiouid ma kįuhkua* ['sɔaga 'tʰiɔwɪdʑ ma 'cʰʊhkua] soak-a tśo<Ø>i-d m-a-kįuhko-a build-ASS.TR.INCONCL dam-GEN COP.PAST.INCONCL-ASS beaver-PL-AGT 'the beavers were building a dam'
mahhakini kenka koaddjeri saroska ['mɑh:aɟini 'cʰɛŋka 'kʰɔadʑːeri 'sarɔska] mahh-a-ki-ni kenka koaddjeri saro-s-ka hunt-ASS.CONCL.TR-TRANSLO-3P.AG.PL tomorrow south.east=towards deer-GEN-PL 'tomorrow they are going towards the south-east to hunt deer'	*mahha kenka koasġia saroska nani* ['mɑh:ɑ 'cʰɛŋka 'kʰɔasxia 'sarɔska 'neni] Ø-mahh-a kenka koasġia-ia saro-s-ka n-e-ki-ni hunt-ASS.TR.INCONCL tomorrow south.east=INESS deer-GEN-PL COP.INCONCL-INFER-3P.AG.PL 'tomorrow they are going to be in the south-east hunting deer'

§9.9.1.3 Telicity

Conclusivity, in addition to being overtly marked by an infix or through a copular construction, is also marked through the cases of the objects of a verb. This is called telicity in the context of Siwa grammar to distinguish it from verbal conclusivity. The conclusive is equivalent to the telic aspect while the inconclusive corresponds to the atelic aspect. A dative object shows a telic aspect and a genitive object shows an atelic aspect. A verb can have a conclusive aspect but still have an atelic object. In the context of telicity, an genitive object is atelic and the genitive case may be referred to as the partitive (the action only affects part of the object), and a dative object is telic and the case may be referred to as the translative (the action changes the state of the object). This leads to a complex combination of verb-marked conclusivity and object-marked telicity.

> **conclusivity** (verbs)
>   inconclusive   -m-   'X is doing Y'
>   conclusive   -Ø-   'X does/will do Y'
> **telicity** (nouns)
>   atelic   genitive (*partitive*)   'some Y'
>   telic   dative (*translative*)   'all Y, the whole Y'

Telicity effects the definiteness of the object. The translative nearly always adds definiteness to the object (often translated with a definite article in English or *all of* or *a whole*, etc. especially with an inconclusive verb). The partitive may indicate lack of definiteness of the object (often translated with an indefinite article for countable nouns or *some* for uncountable nouns). However, in the future inconclusive, the partitive may indicate both definiteness or lack thereof. Compare the table below (a more complete version of this table is found in the section *§9.11* on tense-aspect coalescence).

marked conclusivity		telicity	non-past	past
conclusive	+	genitive (partitive)	*hami kelhobi* 'I (will) eat (some) dried meat'	*mami kelhobi* 'I ate (some) dried meat'
		dative (translative)	*hami kelho* 'I (will) eat (the whole) dried meat'	*mama kelho* 'I ate (the whole) dried meat'
inconclusive	+	genitive (partitive)	*ha kelhobi nami* 'I am eating (some) dried meat'	*ha kelhobi mami* 'I was eating (some) dried meat'
		dative (translative)	*ha kelho nami* 'I am eating (the whole) dried meat'	*ha kelho mami* 'I was eating (the whole) dried meat'

§9.9.2 Habitual

The habitual aspect shows that an action happens repeatedly or is reoccurring, familiar, or customary. It is also used in gnomic statements, although the conclusive also suffices for that function in many cases as well.

The habitual aspect marker has the form **-s-** or **-sa-**, but because of the way it attaches directly to certain verb types, its actual shape varies in accordance to the slot order of the verbal vowel (VP):

RULE 1	RULE 2
-V-s-VP-	C-VP-sa-
-C-s-VP-	
-C-t-VP-	
-C-h-VP-	
-ś-ś-VP-	

For how the habitual and verb stems combine, see *§9.2.1.8*.

Below are examples of the use of the habitual aspect:

killju jajaśkus
[ˈcʰiːlju jaˈjaɕkʊs]
killju ja-jaśk-u-s
always 4P.ACT.UNAG-age-ASS.CONCL.TRANSL-HAB
'one always gets older'

tagjil imnis õki
[ˈtʰɑjːɪl ˈɪmnːɪs ˈõki]
tagjil imnⱼ-i-s o<n>-ki
MUCH.ADV MAKE.SMOKE-ITR.ASS-HAB TINDER.MOSS-PAT
'tinder moss (dried moss) makes a lot of smoke'

nõtśi ukia yhhůa
[ˈnõtɕi ˈuːɹia ˈyhːœa]
non-s-i <ùk>-ia yhhy-Ø-a
swim-HAB-ASS.ITR water-INESS salmon-AGT-PL
'the salmons swim in the water'

kendita saskisami
[ˈcʰɛndʑida ˈsascisami]
kend=ita sask-i-sa-mi
early wake.up-ASS.CONCL.ITR-HAB-1P.AG.SG
'I (usually) wake up early'

temġis gujaja nolbagi
[ˈtʰɛmxɪs ˈgujaja ˈnɔlbaji]
temġ-i-s gu-ja=ia nolba-Ø-gi
lay.egg-ASS.CONCL.ITR-HAB late.fall-INESS eel-AGT-PL
'eels lay their eggs in the late autumn'

elulis įająa tahpa eleu
['elulɪs 'iːjaja 'tʰahpa 'eleu]
elul-i-s i-ja=ia ta=hpa ele-u
bloom-ASS.CONCL.ITR-HAB early.summer-INESS most-PAT flower-PAT
'most flowers bloom in early summer

§9.9.3 Perfective

The perfective aspect shows that an action is over or completed by the time of the utterance. In the non-past, it corresponds to the perfect tense in English (*I have eaten*) and in the past to the pluperfect tense (*I had eaten*). However, it is less commonly used in Siwa than the perfect and pluperfect tenses, because it usually implies a *before* or *already*.

The perfective marker occurs in slot 3 and has the shape -l- or -la-.

```
        RULE 1          RULE 2
        -V-l-VP         -C-VP-la
        -C-l-VP
```

For how the perfective and verb stems combine, see *§9.2.1.8*.
The perfective and habitual can appear together as -ls-/-lsa- (then equivalent to *has had/had had the habit of X*, i.e. perfective habitual) or as -hl-/-hla- (the equivalent to *has usually X*, i.e. a habitual perfective):

-l-sa
kendita kirha saskilsari
'they have had the habit
of waking up early in the morning'

-h-la
kendita kirha saskihlari
'they have usually awoken early in
the morning'

More examples:

keslana jola tsęmme daita
['cʰɛslana 'jola 'tsæmːe 'daida]
kes-la-na jol-a tsęmme-Ø d-a-ita
learn-PERF-ASS.CONCL.TR -2P.AG.SG read-TR
animal.trace-DAT COP.CONCL-ASS-ILLAT
'you have learned to read animal traces (already/before)'

s-njallana-a mihnadi?
[sʲɲalːanaː 'miːhnadʑi]
s-njal-l-a-na–a mihna-di
INTERR–taste-PERF-ASS.CONCL.TR-2P.AG.SG-INTERR mihna-GEN
'have you tasted **mihna** (before/ever)?'

keġlana jola tsęmme daita
['cʰɛxlana 'jola 'tsæmːe 'daida]
ke<h>-l-a-na jol-a tsęmme-Ø d-a-ita
learn.PAST-PERF-ASS.CONCL.TR-2P.AG.SG read-TR
animal.trace-DAT COP.CONCL-ASS-ILLAT
'you had learned to read animal traces (already/before)'

òdni itkůla õkko
['ʊʔtni 'iːtcøla 'ɔ̃ʔko]
òdna itk-ů-la om-ko
NOW MELT-ASS.TRANSL-PERF SNOW-PAT
'now the snow has melted'

soa jüdlari sitru pednitśu gana?
['sɔa 'juːtɬari 'sɪtxu 'pʰɛʔtnitɕu 'gana]
s-oa jü<tt>-l-a-ri sitru-Ø pedn-i-tśu g-a-na
INTERR-already finish.PAST-PERF-ASS.CONCL.TR-3P.AG.PL soup-DAT arrive-ITR-LINK.TEMP COP.PAST-ASS-2P.AG.SG
'had they already finished the soup when you arrived (back)?'

oa ipendlina oakibma sihhitśu tevu gatta
[ɔa iˈpʰɛntɬina 'ɔaɪʔpma 'sihːitɕu 'tʰevuː gaʔta]
oa i-pe<nd>-l-i-na oa-k=ibma sihh-i-tśu tevu d-a- tta
already DIT-return.PAST-PERF-ASS.ITR-2P.AG.SG home-ALLAT rain-ITR-TEMP.LINK before COP.PAST-ASS-SUBIT
'you had already returned home before it started raining'

śivi mid hejerre mumma-uri ora himha
['ɕivi 'miːdʑ 'hejerːe 'mumːaʊri 'ɔra 'hiːmha]
śiv-i mi-d hejer-re mu=mma-uri or-a himha-Ø
stay-TR one.INA.GEN winter-GEN fathom.INESS-1P.POSS.PL.EXCL COP.PERF.INCONCL-ASS 3P.PRON.FEM
'she/the woman has been staying with us for one winter'

tėrkeуarita saskihlami
['tʰeːrcewarida 'sascɪhlami]
tėr=ke<ɥ>a-ri-ta sask-i-h=la-mi
sunrise-ILLAT wake.up-ASS.CONCL.ITR-HAB=PERF-1P.AG.SG
'I have usually awakened by sunrise'

tėrkeуarita saskilsami
['tʰeːrcewarida 'sascɪlsami]
tėr=ke<ɥ>a-ri-ta sask-i-l=sa-mi
sunrise-ILLAT wake.up-ASS.CONCL.ITR-PERF=HAB-1P.AG.SG
'I have had the habit of waking up before sunrise'

§9.9.4 Secondary Aspectual Markers

Secondary aspectual markers are found in slot 6. They do not coalesce with primary aspectual markers and are not necessary for a verb to be complete. Secondary aspectual markers also differ from primary markers in that they are found on the split-stem in copular constructions.

They are reversive, semelfactive, persistive, frequentative, inchoative, subitive, habilitive and diminutive. They can be stringed one after the other, although using even three consecutive aspectual markers is highly unusual.

reversive	semelfactive	persistive	frequentive	inchoative	subitve	habilitive	diminutive
-dna-	-ġa-	-ḥḥa- -ḥḥen	-ppa- -ppen	-dla-	-tta-	-śi- (neg. -śen-)	-nun-

§9.9.4.1 Reversive

The reversive is a secondary aspectual marker with the form **-dna-**. The reversive plays two important syntactic roles. Its most common role is to reverse the action of the verb, similar the English prefix de- (*derail, deflate, decapitate*, etc.) and un- (*undo, unravel, unstick*, etc.). It is, by semantic extrapolation, also used to show movement down or off things with verbs which normally show the opposite movement. The reversive comes first after the other primary aspectual markers.

    itśidla śimi tahhita henda
    [iˈtɕitɬa ɕimi ˈtɑhːida ˈhɛnda]
    i-tśi<dl>-a-Ø śimi-Ø tahh-ita hen=da
    DIT-hang.PAST-ASS.TR-3P.AG.SG bear.head-DAT tree-ILLAT Up=ILLAT.DESTI
    'X hung the bearhead up in the tree'

cf. *itśidladna śimi tahhika henga*
    [iˈtɕitɬaʔtna ɕimi ˈtɑhːiga ˈhɛnːa]
    i-tśi<dl>-a-dna-Ø śimi-Ø tahh-ika hen=ga
    DIT-hang.PAST-ASS.TR-REVERS-3P.AG.SG bear.head-DAT tree-ELAT UP=ELAT.DESTI
    'X took the bearhead down from the tree'

    ikki misahibma henda
    [ˈiːʔci ˈmisɑhɪʔpma ˈhɛnda]
    i-i<kk>-i-Ø misa-hi=ibma hen=da
    DIT-get.PAST-ASS.ITR-3P.AG.SG stone-ILLAT up=ILLAT.DESTI
    'X got up on the stone'

cf. *sem iḍḍuadna misahiska henga*
    [sem iːðːuaʔtna ˈmisɑhɪska ˈhɛnːa]
    sem i-iḍḍ-ua-dna-Ø misa-h=iska hen=ga
    not DIT-get-ASS.ITR.OPT-REVERS-3P..AG.SG stone-ABLA up=ELAT.DESTI
    'X does not want to get off the stone'

Reversive may also be used to confer a negative aspect to a verb.

    vappa   'X praises/adores Y' (cf. ***vappi*** 'X kneels')
    vappadna   'X insults Y'

    koni   'X walks'
    konidna   'X limps' or 'X walks (with difficulty)'

It can also confer a more vulgar or violent meaning to verbs.

    nakna   'X breaks Y'
    naknadna   'X breaks Y (vulgar)'

tsyka	'X hits Y'
tsykadna	'X hits Y (violently/vulgar)'

The reversive is used with the movement verbs **man-** and **mak-** 'come' and 'go' as well as **tahh-, pedn-** 'leave' and 'arrive' and other similar verbs to mean 'back', e.g. **manidna-** 'come back', **makidna-** 'go back', **tahhidna-** 'leave (to go back)' and **pednidna-** 'arrive (back)'.

Finally, the reversive is used in double agentivity verbs (see *§9.4.4*).

§9.9.4.2 Semelfactive

The semelfactive is a secondary aspectual marker with the form -ġa which comes after the reversive. It denotes that an action takes place quickly and/or only once; a momentary or punctual action. It is also commonly used to show that the verb happens suddenly, unexpectedly, with much force or violently.

    joddi
    ['jɔt:i]
    jo<dd>-i-Ø
    scream.PAST-ASS.CONCL.ITR-3P.AG.SG
    'X screamed'

 cf. *joddiġa*
    ['jɔ:tixa]
    jo<dd>-i-Ø-ġa
    scream.PAST-ASS.CONCL.ITR-3P.AG.SG-SEMELF
    'X let out a scream'
    (also *jodġui*)

    mavuoddu
    [mɑˈvuɔð:u]
    ma-vuo<dd>-u
    1P.PAT.SG-get.scared.PAST-ASS.CONCL.TRANSL
    'I got scared'

 cf. *mavuodduġa*
    [mɑˈvuɔð:uxa]
    ma-vuo<dd>-u-ġa
    1P.PAT.SG-get.scared.PAST-ASS.CONCL.TRANSL-SEMELF
    'I (suddenly) got scared'

    udli
    ['utɬi]
    u<dl>-i
    night.PAST-ASS.CONCL.ITR
    'night was falling'

cf. *udliġa*
['utɬixa]
u<dl>-i-ġa
night.PAST-ASS.CONCL.ITR-SEMELF
'night fell all of a sudden/quickly (also *udlġuî*)'

tatsġatskohki
[tʰa'tsxatskːɔhci]
ta-tsġa<tsk>-ohk-i
3P.UNAG.SG-tear.PAST-OHK-ASS.CONCL.ITR
'(the rope/leather) tore'

cf. *tatsġatskohkiġa*
[tʰa'tsxatskːɔhcixa]
ta-tsġa<tsk>-ohk-i-ġa
3P.UNAG.SG-tear.PAST-OHK-ASS.CONCL.ITR-SEMELF
'(the rope/leather) tore (violently, suddenly)'

Some verbs cannot exist in the semelfactive, but they can be found with an inherent semelfactive meaning, having a root-bound ending which is historically the same as -ġa but may appear as -r-, -k- or -g-. For example, the verb jod- 'to scream' exists in the semelfactive *jodiġa* 'X will [suddenly/violently] scream' but also has the root-bound semelfactive form *jodġi* 'X will let out a scream'.

Opposite to this, the verb *tatsům(i)ġa*[1] 'X will sneeze' is always found in the semelfactive (the form *tatsůmi* is not found).

The semelfactive is not usually found in the inconclusive, as it carries a perfective aspect which is incompatible with an inconclusive aspect. The semelfactive can transform the meaning of the verb and is sometimes unpredictably equivalent to a separate English expression:

tśoda or *tioda*
['tɕɔda] or ['tʰioða]
tśod/tiod-a-∅-∅
contain/close-ASS.CONCL.TR-3P.PAT-3P.AG.SG
'X contains Y/holds Y closed'

tśodaġa or *tiodaġa*
['tɕɔdɑxa] or ['tʰioðɑxa]
tśod-a-ġa-∅-∅
contain/close-ASS.CONCL.TR-SEMELF-3P.PAT-3P.AG.SG
'X closes Y'

---

[1] The form *tatsůmġa* is common in the present, but the vowel-final stem reappears in the past as *tatsůmuiġa*.

Note that the form *tśotra* 'X slams Y closed' is another example of the root-bound semelfactive.

An other use of the semelfactive, with usually inherently perfective verbs, is to underline how sudden and/or violent the action is:

middi
[mit:i]
m-i<dd>-i
1P.UNAG.SG-fall.PAST-ASS.CONCL.ITR
'I fell'

mobiddiġa
[mɔˈbit:ixa]
m-o-i<dd>-i-ġa
1P.UNAG.SG-SUBJ-fall.past-ASS.CONCL.ITR-SEMELF
'I took a bad fall' (with SUBJ)

ma siehhõdi
[ˈma ˈsieh:ɔ̃dʑi]
<m>-a-Ø siehhum-di
eat.PAST-ASS.CONCL.TR-3P.AG.SG dried.meat-GEN
'X had himself a small piece of dried meat'

omaġa siehhõdi
[ɔˈmaxa ˈsieh:ɔ̃dʑi]
o-<m>-a-ġa-Ø siehhum-di
SUBJ-eat.PAST-ASS.CONCL.TR-SEMELF-3P.AG.SG dried.meat-GEN
'X ate/devoured him/her/itself a piece of dried meat' (with SUBJ)

The semelfactive may also be used to emphasize a verb or to make it more intense:

hõhri giandid kihta
[ˈhɔ̃hri ˈɟandʑɪdʑ ˈcʰɪhta]
hõ<hr>-i-Ø giandi-d kih=ta
jump.past-ASS.CONCL.ITR-3P.AG.SG fallen.tree-GEN over-ILLAT
'X jumped over the fallen tree'

hõhriġa giandid kihta
[ˈhɔ̃hrixa ˈɟandʑɪdʑ ˈcʰɪhta]
hõ<hr>-i-Ø-ġa giandi-d kih=ta
jump.PAST-ASS.CONCL.ITR-3P.AG.SG fallen.tree-GEN over-ILLAT
'X leaped over the fallen tree'

Finally, the semelfactive is used with verbs such as *neni* 'X will sit', *tài* 'X will stand' and *jŭi* 'X will lie' to form the verbs 'to sit down', 'to stand up' and 'to lie down'. The verbs have two forms in free variation - one with an analyzed root-bound semelfactive and the other with a normal semelfactive marker.

	no semelfactive		free semelfactive		root-bound semelfactive	
	present	past	present	past	present	past
stand	tá·i 'stand'	tẹgi·i 'stood'	tá·i·ġa 'stand up'	tẹgi·i·ġa 'stood up'	tàġ·i 'stand up'	tàst·i 'stood up'
sit	nen·i 'sit'	ed·i 'sat'	nen·i·ġa 'sit down'	ed·i·ġa 'sat down'	nedġ·i 'sit down'	edġ·i 'sat down'
lie	jů·i 'lie'	anů·i 'lay'	jů·i·ġa 'lie down'	anů·i·ġa 'lay down'	jůġġ·i 'lie down'	anůġġ·i 'lay down'

§9.9.4.3 Persistive

The persistive is a secondary aspectual marker that denotes an action which goes on for a long time or is repeated over and over again. It has the form -ḥḥa- or -ḥḥen word-finally and comes after the reversive and the semelfactive. It is often translated in English by phrases such as *over and over again* and *keep on*.

    cf. *sihrima*
        ['sɪhrima]
        si‹hr›-i-ma
        rain.PAST-ASS.ITR-INCONCL
        'it was raining'

        sihrimaḥḥen
        ['sɪhrimaʔ:ɛn]
        si‹hr›-i-ma-ḥḥen
        rain.PAST-ASS.ITR-INCONCL-PERSIST
        'it kept on raining (over and over again)'

    cf. *kòi nata*
        [ˈkʰʊːi nata]
        kò-i n-a-ta
        talk-ITR COP.INCONCL-ASS-3P.AG.SG
        'X was talking'

        kòi naḥḥata
        [ˈkʰʊːi naʔːada]
        kò-i n-a-ḥḥa-ta
        talk-ITR- COP.INCONCL-ASS-PERSIS-3P.AG.SG
        'X kept on talking (on and on)'

atymmůḥḥen tva tśid-het!
[ɑˈtymːø?ːɛn ˈtʰva ˈtɕiːdʑhɛ?]
a-tyv-m-ů-ḥḥen tva tśi<Ø>i-d–het
TRANSL-fat-INCONL-ASS.TRANSL-PERS this.PAT baby.PAT–DET.MEDI
'this baby just keeps on getting fatter!'

§9.9.4.4 Frequentative

The frequentative is a secondary aspectual marker that denotes that an action happens a few times or frequently/often. Its form is **-ppa-**/**-ppen** and is added after the reversive, semelfactive and the persistive. It is a a very common aspectual marker with certain verbs of motion, to the point where certain verbs show a root-bound suffix which is then part of the root, e.g. *tiappa* [ˈtʰiːa?pa] 'X shakes Y a few times' cf. *tia* [ˈtʰiːa] 'X takes Y in X's hand'. In certain cases, especially with intransitive verbs, the frequentative may be translated as 'a little'. Sometimes, especially with the inconclusive, it translates as 'again' or 'often'.

moġippan
[ˈmɔxɪ?pan]
moġ-i-ppa-n
drink-ASS.CONCL.ITR-FREQ-IMPER.2P.SG
'have a few sips'
(lit. drink a few times)

oa nuhlappami ůn màhraka-ut
[ɔɑ ˈnuɬːa?pami ˈœn ˈmæːhrɑgaʊ?]
oa n<uhl>-a-ppa-mi ůn màhra-ka-ut
already see.PERF-ASS.CONCL.TR-FREQ-1P.AG.SG this.ANI.GEN bear-GEN–DET.DIST
'I have already seen that bear a couple of times'

kodippaki vęja aśśi
[ˈkʰɔdɪ?paɟi ˈvæja ˈɑɕːi]
Ø-ko<d>-i-ppa-ki-Ø v<ęja> av=śi
walk.PAST-ASS.CONCL.ITR-FREQ-TRANSLOC-3P.AG.SG LAKE.GEN next.to-along
'X went for a little walk along the lake (shore)'
(lit. walked a few times)

huhmippen tèhtśa
[ˈhʊhmɪ?pɛn ˈtʰehtɕa]
huh-m-i-ppen tèr-tśa
shine-INCONCL.ASS.TR-FREQ sun-PAT
'the sun is shining again'

§9.9.4.5 Inchoative

The inchoative is a secondary aspectual marker with the form -**dla**- that denotes an action which is about to happen or begin. It is *only* used with unagentive subjects, as it cannot apply to agentive subjects. Impersonal verbs already have an inchoative-like form in the conclusive, such that they are never found in the inchoative. The inchoative cannot be used with the copula, as it too already has a translative form. The inchoative comes after the frequentative, persistive, semelfactive and reversive.

verbal inchoative	*tśaśkajudla*	'X started to get old'
copular inchoative	*iśijata*	'X got/became old'
impersonal inchoative	*sihhi*	'it is about to rain'

When used with animate unagentive subjects and adjectival verbs denoting temporary states, the inchoative shows that the action is not temporary but gradual.

tśaśkudla
['tɕaɕkʊtɬa]
t-jaśk-u-dla
3P.PAT.SG-get.old-ASS.CONCL.TRANSL-INCHOA
'X is starting to get old'

entsibmidla
[ɛnt'sɪʔpmɪtɬa]
ent-sid-m-i-dla
1P.PAT.SG-grab-INCONCL-ASS.ITR-INCHOA
'I am beginning to understand'

horhajidla benhue
['hɔrhajɪtɬa 'bɛnhue]
horh-ai-i-dla benho-e
bark-PAST-ASS.CONCL.ITR-INCHOA dog-PAT
'the dog started barking'

agjosmudla njuhmo
[a'ɟɔsmʊtɬa ɲʊhmo]
a-gjos-m-u-dla njuhhi-mo
TRANSL-tired-INCONCL-ASS.TRANSL-INCHOA old.woman-PAT
'the old woman is beginning to be tired (in general)'
[animate unagentive subject - gradual inchoative]

gjosù ta onga-ůt
['ɟɔsuː tʰa 'ɔŋːæœʔ]
gjoso-u ta onga-Ø–ůt
tired-COP.TRANSL.PRES this.INA.AGT bridge-AGT–DET.PROXI
'this bridge is starting to be/get old (lit. tired)'
[copular – no inchoative marker]

§9.9.4.6 Subitive

The subitive is a secondary aspectual marker with he form -**tta**- (usually -**tto**- in the west) that serves two purposes. Its primary purpose it to show that an action takes place suddenly or rapidly. Its second purpose is to form imperatives or interjections based on nouns, adjectives, adverbs or postpositions. These are often more informal than regular imperatives. The subitive marker is added after the inchoative, frequentative, persistive, semelfactive and reversive. The subitive ending -**tta**- can even be attached to titles or names to form a sort of familiar or rude vocative.

uhustitta tahhi hõttamo
[uˈhʊstɪʔta ˈtʰɑhːi ˈhɔ̃ʔtamɔ]
u-hu<st>-i-tta tahh-i hõtta-mo
PASS-blow.down.PAST-ASS.CONCL.ITR-SUBIT tree-GEN gust.PAT
'the tree was suddenly blown down/over by a gust of wind'

kokitta
[ˈkʰɔcɪʔta]
<kok>-i-tta-Ø
speak.PAST-ASS.CONCL.ITR-SUBIT-3P.AG.SG
'suddenly, X spoke'

sihritta
[ˈsihrɪʔta]
Ø-si<hr>-i-tta
rain.PAST-ASS.CONCL.ITR-SUBIT
'it suddenly started raining'

kȯitta !
[ˈkʰʊːɪʔta]
kȯ-i-tta
speak-ASS.CONCL.ITR-SUBIT
'speak !!'

Sappatta !
[ˈsaʔpaʔta]
Sappa-Ø-tta
Sappa-AGT-SUBIT
Sappa ! / Hey **Sappa**!

The interjections that use the subitive endings can be formed from all classes of words. They are very productive, and when attached to something else than a verb, they are not considered overly impolite but simply informal. Below are some common subitive interjections/imperatives:

katta	'go outside ! / outside !' (cf. **-ika** 'elative')
karakatta	'close the door !' (cf. **karaka** 'door')
matta	'come on ! / hop on !' (cf. **-ibma** 'allative')
màtta	'come ! / come on ! / let's go ! / go ! / please !' (cf. **manin** 'come here')
gosutta	'calm down !' (cf. **gosulhita** 'more calm')
ràtta, ratta	'stop it !' (cf. **rada** 'X will stop Y')
tsetsotta	'quickly !' (cf. **tsetsot** 'quick')
sitatta	'ahead ! / let's go ! / continue ! / yes ! (cf. **sita** 'ahead')
sitta	'of course ! / yes ! / eureka !' (cf. **sidi/si** 'X will understand Y')

siehhutta	'get up ! / get on your feet !'
suhuinetta	'more quietly !' (cf. *suhuine* 'more quietly')
tatta	'come inside ! / inside !' (cf. *-ita* 'illative')
tṡutta	'come on ! (to group) / let's go ! (to group) / keep on going ! (to a group) (cf. *tṡoutigge* 'we are working together')
nu̇tta	'look ! / look out ! / be careful ! / ahead !' (cf. *nuja* 'X sees Y')

§9.9.4.7 Habilitive

The habilitive is a secondary aspectual with the for -ṡi- marker that shows that the subject of the verb is able, can or has the knowledge required to perform the action or simply implies a possibility. It follows the subitive, inchoative, frequentative, persistive, semelfactive and reversive. It often requires an agentive subject, even with otherwise unagentive verbs and in its negative form.

It can be added to the stem of certain nouns to form verbs which are otherwise defunct. The habilitive is the only aspectual marker that incorporates negation, in which case the habilitive (sometimes called habilitive negative) has the form -ṡen(i)- (assimilated to -m- and -n- as -ṡemm- and -ṡenn-) or -siṡi- (sometimes also -ddji-) and also requires an agentive subject, despite the verb having an unagentive meaning:

nonimi	'I will swim'
noniṡimi	'I can swim'
noniṡemmi	'I can't swim'
noniṡenigga	'we can't swim'

The habilitive is most often found in the present or imperfect tense. It is usually not found in the habitual. In a few instances, the habilitive may delete the postverbal vowel -i-, in which case it attaches directly to the stem, if the resulting cluster is allowed.

Siya̞ṡimi
['siwa̞ɕimi]
Siya-ṡi-mi
Siwa-HABI-1P.AG.SG
'I know how to/can speak Siwa'
(defunct verb)

saṡṡimi Sẏdi
['sɑɕ:imi 'sy:dʐi]
sahhj-<Ø>-ṡi-mi S<ẏ>-di
speak-ASS.CONCL.ITR-HABI-1P.AG.SG Siwa-GEN
'I know how to/can speak Siwa'

nonisemmi
['nɔniɕem:i]
non-i-ṡ=en-mi
swim-ASS.CONCL-ITR-HABI=NEG-1P.AG.SG
'I don't know how to swim / can't swim'
(also *nõtsiṡimi*)

ṡemaddjimi
['ɕemadʑ:imi]
ṡem-a-ddji-Ø-mi
believe-ASS.CONCL-TR-HABI=NEG-3P.PAT-1P.AG.SG
'I can't believe it' (also *ṡemaṡemmi*)

gjykyniṡi
['dʑycyniɕi]
gjykyn-i-ṡi-Ø
snow.shoes-ASS.CONCL.ITR-HABI-3P.AG.SG
'X knows (how to make) snowshoes'

bùntaṡi gjykyn
['bu:ntaɕi 'dʑycœn]
bu:nt-a-ṡ-Ø gjyky-n
weave-ASS.CONCL.TR-HABI-3P.AG.SG snow.shoe-DAT
'X knows how to make/weave snowshoes'

§9.9.4.8 Diminutive

The diminutive is the last of the secondary aspectual markers and is thus added at the very end of the chain of aspectual markers. Its form is **-nun-** (usually pronounced [n:] [nʔn], [n̩:] or [ʔn:]. not closing the preceding syllable) or **-(n)unda-** if followed by something.

Only personal pronouns, location markers and certain evidential markers follow the diminutive. Its function is varied and can be hard to pinpoint. The most common use of the diminutive is to make the verb softer or to show that the action happened *only a little* or *so*.

tìspianun
['tʰi:spian:]
t-isp=i-a-nun-Ø
3P.UNAG.SG-pinch-PAST-ASS.CONCL.TR-DIMIN-3P.PAT
'X pinched Y a little/slightly'

kyeilminun
['cʰwɛɪlmin:]
kyeil-m-i-nun
drizzle-INCONCL-ASS.ITR-DIMI
'it is drizzling a little' (also *geilminun*)

haundan
['haʊn:dan]
ha-unda-n
eat-DIMI-IMP.2P.SG
'eat a little!'

tsġovvaundagga
['tsxɔw:aʊndak:a]
tsġo<vv>-a-Ø-unda-gga
discuss.PAST-ASS.TR-3P.PAT-DIMI-1P.AG.PL.EXCL
'we talked about X a little'

§9.10 Tense

Siwa verbs have two real tenses: non-past and past. Only the past tense is overtly marked. The combination of tense and aspect yields 12 primary tenses;

future~present
present (non-past)
        present inconclusive   (copular)
        present habitual conclusive
        present habitual inconclusive   (copular)
        prefect conclusive
        prefect inconclusive in the non-past (copular)

past
        past conclusive
        past inconclusive   (copular)
        past habitual conclusive
        past habitual inconclusive   (copular)
        past pluperfect conclusive
        past pluperfect inconclusive   (copular)

In addition to these 12 primary tenses, the copula combines with the perfect and inconclusive to form the perfect inconclusive non-past or past. Copular constructions are also used to show an immediate past by using the subitive on the non-finite verb, and a distant past which is used in certain narrative styles, realized by using the habitual on the non-finite verb.

    The chart below shows how tense and aspect combine to produce the 14 verb-marked tenses of Siwa.

	non-past	past
	future~present	past conclusive
conclusive	*keda* ['cʰeda] ked-a-Ø-Ø carry- ASS.CONCL.TR-3P.PAT-3P.AG.SG 'X will carry/carries Y'	*kedda* ['cʰet:a] ke\<dd\>-a-Ø-Ø carry.PAST-ASS.CONCL.TR-3P.PAT-3P.AG.SG 'X carried Y'
	present inconclusive	past inconclusive

	non-past	past
inconclusive	*keda nata* ['cʰeda 'nata] ked-a n-a-Ø-ta carry-TR COP.INCCONCL-ASS-INDIC-3P.PAT-3P.AG.SG 'X is carrying Y'	*keda mata* ['cʰeda 'mata] ked-a m-a-Ø-ta carry-TR COP.PAST.INCCONCL-ASS-INDIC-3P.PAT-3P.AG.SG 'X was carrying Y'
	present habitual conclusive	past habitual conclusive
habitual conclusive	*ketas* ['cʰetas] ked-a-Ø-Ø-s carry-ASS.TR-3P.PAT-3P.AG.SG-HAB 'X (usually) carries Y'	*keddas* ['cʰet:as] ke<dd>-a-Ø-Ø-s carry.PAST-ASS.TR.-3P.PAT-3P.AG.SG-HAB 'X (usually) carried Y'
	present habitual inconclusive	past habitual inconclusive
habitual inconclusive	*keda sata* ['cʰeda 'sata] ked-a s-a-Ø-ta carry-TR COP.HAB.INCCONCL-ASS-INDIC-3P.PAT-3P.AG.SG 'X is (usually) carrying Y'	*keda sġata* ['cʰeda 'sxata] ked-a sġ-a-Ø-ta carry-TR COP.PAST.HAB.INCCONCL-ASS-INDIC-3P.PAT-3P.AG.SG 'X was (usually) carrying Y'
	perfect conclusive	pluperfect conclusive
perfect conclusive	*kedla* ['cʰetɬa] ked-l-a-Ø-Ø carry-PERF-ASS.TR-3P.PAT-3P.AG.SG 'X has carried Y'	*keddala* ['cʰɛt:ɑla] ke<dd>-a-la-Ø-Ø carry.PAST-ASS.TR.-PERF-3P.PAT-3P.AG.SG 'X had carried Y'
	perfect inconclusive	pluperfect inconclusive
perfect inconclusive	*keda orata* ['cʰeda 'ɔrada] ked-a or-a-Ø-ta carry-TR COP.PERF.INCCONCL-ASS-INDIC-3P.PAT-3P.AG.SG 'X has been carrying Y'	*keda odlata* ['cʰeda 'ɔtɬada] ked-a odl-a-Ø-ta carry-TR COP.PAST.PERF.INCCONCL-ASS-INDIC-3P.PAT-3P.AG.SG 'X had been carrying Y'
	past	
immediate	*kedatta gata* ['cʰeda?ta 'gata] ked-a-tta g-a-Ø-ta carry-TR-SUBIT COP.PAST.CONCL-ASS-INDIC-3P.PAT-3P.AG.SG 'X just carried Y'	

	non-past	past
distant		*kedas gata* [ˈcʰedas ˈgɑta] ked-a-s g-a-Ø-ta carry-TR-HAB COP.PAST.CONCL-ASS-INDIC-3P.PAT-3P.AG.SG 'X carried Y (a long time ago)'

§9.10.1 Past Form

The past form is the only overtly marked tense. Its marking separates all verbs into three categories:

> vowel-final
> strong consonant-final
> weak consonant-final

Vowel-final verbs are verbs whose final root-bound vowel changes in the past. Similarly, verbs whose roots end in a consonant which is changed in the past are called strong consonant-final verbs. Weak consonant-final verbs are those whose roots end in a consonant which *cannot* change in the past, and instead are augmented by a suffix.

present
- vowel-final — *onta·i* — 'X will dance'
- strong consonant-final — *ets·a* — 'X will start Y'
- weak consonant-final — *radlv·a* — 'X will disturb Y'

past
- vowel-final — *onte·i* — 'X danced'
  onta- → onte-
- strong consonant-final — *etst·a* — 'X startedY'
  ets- → etst-
- weak consonant-final — *radlv·i·a* — 'X disturbed Y'
  radlv- → -radlv·i-

§9.10.1.1 Past Marking on Vowel-Final Verbs

Vowel-Final verbs are those whose stem ends in a vowel and those whose stem ends in a consonant not part of the strong past consonants.

When the final vowel of a vowel-final verb happens to be identical to the postverbal vowel (most commonly -a- or -i-), only the postverbal vowel appears, deleting the identical preceding vowel[1]. This means that a number of verbs whose stems are not obviously vowel-final in the present, or the past in the case of vowel polarization resulting in two identical vowels. Only when the conditions change does the stem vowel appear (sometimes not in its true form). For example:

stem	ivi-	'to increase'
present	tivi	'X will increase' (< *t·ivi·i)
past	tivui	'X increased' (appears after polarization)

This makes knowing whether a verb has a vowel-final or consonant-final past form more difficult. Such verbs are called weak vowel-final verbs (as their vowel only appear in certain cases, whether in the present, past or otherwise). Weak vowel-final verbs are not common.

The past is marked by applying vowel polarization to the last vowel of the stem. Although the underlying form of the vowel is polarized, its surface form may be different due to impossible diphthongs being altered, e.g. verbs in -o- have the polarized version -y-, but because -y- cannot form a diphthong with any other vowels, it will change to -ů- or -u-, or the whole diphthong may change to -ẏ-, -ů- or -uo-, depending on the following sound. The table below shows polarization:

final vowel	polarized
-a	-i- -e-
-e	-u-
-i	-u- -y- (-ůV-)
-o	-i- -y- (-ůV-)
-u	-e- -ai- / -aj-
-y	-oi- / -oj- -ů-
-ů	-i- -ei- / -ej-

---

[1] Note however that **di-** 'to step' has the form *di*.

Verbs ending in -a- have the vowel -e- in the past before -i- or -i̯-, but have -i- elsewhere. Those ending in -e- always have -u-, never -o- (as -e- can sometimes be polarized to -o-).

The vowels -i-, -o- and -y- have a front-rounded and unrounded polarized version for the past. The front-rounded version is only used in a verb with a stressed front-rounded vowel:

    nůria   'X will load Y'
    nůrůa   'X loaded Y'   (-i- → -ů-)

but

    tulpia   'X will turn Y over'
    tulpua   'X turned Y over'   (-i- → -u-)

Vowel-Final verbs are few in number. In *§9.10.1.1.2* are some of the most common verbs (with their present and past forms). The vowel-final verbs in -i- or -a- (past-vowel-final) are listed separately.

§9.10.1.1.1 Vowel-final Stem Coalescence

Because verbs whose stems end in a vowel must also receive the postverbal vowel, these two will coalesce in sometimes irregular ways.

As it was mentioned above, if the stem-final vowel is a single vowel identical to the postverbal vowel, only the postverbal vowel appears.

Verbs whose stems end in a different vowel than the postverbal vowel behave to avoid triphthongs and tetraphthongs by usually lengthening one of the component of the following diphthong. See section *§3.1.5.1* on diphthong coalescence.

-a-
    -a·ua- > -avva-   *nèunavva*   'X wants to close Y'
    -a·ue- > -avve-   *nèunavve*   'X would want to close Y'

-e-
    -e·ua- > -evva-   *saiskevva*   'X wants to cause Y'
    -e·ue- > -evve-   *deri̯evve*   'X would want to rotate Y'
    -e·ui- > -evvi-   *gi̯evvi*   'if X reached its peak'
    -e·uo- > -evvo-   *ni̯oksevvo*   'X would want to sneak'

-i-
    -i·ia- > -igi̯a-   *riekigi̯a*   'if X relaxed Y'
    -i·ie- > -igi̯e-   *riekigi̯e*   'X would relax Y'
    -i·iu- > -igi̯u-   *oriekigi̯u*   'if X relaxed'

-o-
    -o·ua- > -ùa-, -ovva-   *iskùa*   'X wants to clean Y'

-o·ue-	> -u̇e-, -ovve-	*ketu̇e*	'X would want to look for Y'
-o·uo-	> -u̇o-, -ovvo-	*hantu̇o*	'X would want to lie'

-u-

-u·ua-	> -u̇a-	*nuppu̇a*	'X wants to snatch Y'
-u·ue-	> -u̇e-	*nuppu̇e*	'X would want to snatch Y'
-u·uo-	> -u̇o-	*belmu̇o*	'X would have wanted to work'

-ů- (includes -y-)

-ů·ua-	> -ůvva-, -ėua-	*kůkůvva*	'X wants to bring Y'
-ů·e-	> -ůme-, -ůi-	*kůkůme*	'X will bring Y'
-ů·ue-	> -ůbůi-	*sytůbůi*	'X would want to thank Y'
-ů·u-	> -ẏ-	*tsyrẏ*	'X will blister'
-ů·uo-	> -ůvvo-	*obůkkůvvo*	'X would want to quarrel'
-ů·ui-	> -ůbůi-	*tsyrůbůi*	'if X would blister'
-ů·o-	> -ůvvo-	*tsyrůvvo*	'X will blister'

-ai-/-ei-/-oi-

-Vi·ia-	> -Vddjia-	*lugjaddjia*	'if X had loved Y'
-Vi·ua-	> -Vjua-	*sytojua*	'X wanted to thank Y'
-Vi·ie-	> -Vddjie-	*lugjaddjie*	'X would have loved Y'
-Vi·ue-	> -Vjue-	*nuppajue*	'X would have wanted to snatch Y'
-Vi·i-	> -Vgji-	*upiagjagji*	'X was treated'
-Vi·iu-	> -Vddjiu-	*ukůkeddjiu*	'if X had been brought'
-Vi·joi-	> -Vgjoi-	*takyhhjogjoi*	'X would have gotten torn'
-Vi·uo-	> -Vjuo-	*obůkkejuo*	'X would have wanted to quarrel'
-Vi·ui-	> -Vjui-	*tagalmajui*	'if X had gotten pregnant'
-Vi·jui-	> -Vgjui-	*tagalmagjui*	'X would have gotten pregnant'

§9.10.1.1.2 Vowel-Final Verbs

Most verbs describing sounds share the ending -ro-/-ġo (infinitive -h·su). These verbs have nominal counterparts ending in -us (GEN. -uhi):

	t·agvirui	'X will make sound in liquid/wet grass'
→	*t·agviri*	'X made sound in liquid/wet grass'
	geggurui	'X will quack'
→	*gegguri*	'X quacked'

→	*gekvorrui*	'X will croak'
	gekvorri	'X croaked'
	goglurui	'X will gibber/ramble/mumble'
→	*gogluri*	'X gibbered/rambled/mumbled'
	guġġui	'X will growl/bark'
→	*guġġi*	'X growled/barked'
	hirkurui	'X will squawk/shriek'
→	*hirkuri*	'X squawked/shrieked'
	ta·hi̧u̇htsġui	'X will whizz/squeal'
→	*ta·hi̧u̇htsġi*	'X whizzed/squealed'
	hi̧unrui	'X will snort'
→	*hi̧unri*	'X snorted'
	hi̧yhhi̧yrui	'X will mumble'
→	*hi̧yhhi̧yrůi*	'X mumbled'
	hoġorui	'X will roar/howl'
→	*hoġori*	'X roared/howled'
	(ta·)homorui	'X will hum/purr/vibrate'
→	*(ta·)homori*	'X hummed/purred/vibrated'
	kipri̧rui	'X will chirp/tweet'
→	*kipri̧ri*	'X chirped/tweeted'
	koairui	'X will howl/shout'
→	*koairi*	'X howled/shouted'
	(ta·)kohurui	'X will snap/rupture/fracture/get angry'
→	*(ta·)kohuri*	'X snapped/ruptured/fractured/got angry'
	ta·koklorui	'X will click/pop/tick' (also *tapoklorui*)
→	*ta·koklori*	'X clicked/popped/ticked' (also *tapoklori*)
	ta·kůsġirui	'X will cough dryly'
→	*ta·kůsġirůi*	'X coughed dryly'
	ta·lepserui	'X will drip/leak/dribble/trickle'
→	*ta·lepseri*	'X dripped/leaked/dribbled/trickled'

	ta·mairui	'X will laugh'
→	*ta·mairi*	'X laughed'
	ta·moġorui	'X will rumble/thunder/echo/be very hungry'
→	*ta·moġori*	'X rumbled/thundered/echoed/was very hungry'
	motrui	'X will moo (of caribou)'
→	*motri*	'X mooed'
	nehnui	'X will murmur/whisper'
→	*nehni*	'X murmured/whispered'
	ta·njohrui	'X will grunt/complain'
→	*ta·njohri*	'X grunted/complained'
	ta·njuonui	'X will creak'
→	*ta·njuoni*	'X creaked'
	t·sinrui	'X will buzz/drone/be deep inside'
→	*t·sinri*	'X buzzed/droned/was deep inside'
	t·sihkurui	'X will make a dry sound'
→	*t·sihkuri*	'X made a dry sound'
	syrrui	'X will gnaw/chew/munch/crunch'
→	*syrrůi*	'X gnawed/chewed/munched/crunched'
	tś·ůdġui	'X will hiss/froth/fizz' (*śůdġo-*)
→	*tś·ůdġi*	'X hissed/frothed/fizzed'
	tś·uśui	'X will purl/swirl/stream/smart' (*śuśo-*)
→	*tś·uśi*	'X purled/swirled/streamed/smarted'
	tsentsġui	'X will murmur/mutter' (usually groups)
→	*tsentsġi*	'X murmured/muttered'

Similarly, vowel-final verbs include many verbs descriptive of movement in -je, -kle, -kne, -kse, -lse, -dlo, -bmo, -pso and -pre:

	bůbmua	'X will pound/beat Y'
→	*bůbmia*	'X pound/beat Y'

→	ta·dodlui ta·dodlia	'X will hobble/hesitate/be clumsy' 'X hobbled/hesitated/was clumsy'
→	gaksei gaksui	'X will gallop/do something assuredly' 'X galloped/did something assuredly'
→	ta·hauksei ta·hauksui	'X will explode/burst/go through pollination' 'X exploded/burst/went through pollination'
→	huoibmui huoibmi	'X will lurk/hide/lie low' 'X lurked/hid/lay low'
→	ta·holjei ta·holjui	'X will loom/appear' 'X loomed/appeared'
→	kaiksia kaiksua	'X will dodge/escape Y' 'X dodged/escaped Y'
→	ta·kiedlei ta·kiedlui	'X will shatter/break' 'X shattered/broke'
→	ta·kjuknei ta·kjuknui	'X will coil/not work/fail/curl up' 'X coiled/did not work/failed/curled up'
→	ta·kiruprei ta·kiruprui	'X will shiver' 'X shivered'
→	kȯpsia kȯpsua	'X will thump/strike/batter Y' 'X thumped/stroke/battered Y'
→	kȯksei kȯksui	'X will stride/march/do something with ease' 'X strode/marched/did something with ease'
→	d·lalsei d·lalsui	'X will drift/leave/pass' 'X drifted/left/passed'
→	mingipsui mingipsi	'X will tiptoe/sneak/make its way' 'X tiptoed/snuck/made its way'
→	můabmui můabmůi	'X will moan' 'X moaned'
→	ta·muodlui ta·muodli	'X will slide/trickle/sink/drop' 'X slid/trickled/sank/dropped'

	ta·noklei	'X will stagger/stumble'
→	ta·noklui	'X staggered/stumbled'
	(ta·)njaklia	'X will knock Y out/bump into/smash Y'
→	(ta·)njaklua	'X knocked Y out/bumped into/smashed Y'
	njojei	'X will sneak/move silently'
→	njojua	'X snuck/moved silently'
	ta·noprei	'X will crumple/crush/be too much for Y'
→	ta·noprui	'X crumpled/crushed/was too much for Y'
	nohabmui	'X will haul/pull'
→	nohabmi	'X hauled/pulled'
	ta·pėbmui	'X will bounce/spring/reflect/echo'
→	ta·pėbmi	'X bounced/sprang/reflected/echoed'
	ta·ruoiknei	'X will wake up a little'
→	ta·ruoiknui	'X woke up a little'
	t·sipsui	'X will spurt/surge/eject'
→	t·sipsi	'X spurt/surged/ejected'
	t·siuksei	'X will dribble/ooze/seep/go very slowly'
→	t·siuksua	'X dribbled/oozed/seeped/went very slowly'
	t·sijei	'X will flash/gleam/glint/blink'
→	t·sijui	'X flashed/gleamed/glinted/blinked'
	soklia	'X will hoist/raise/winch Y'
→	soklua	'X hoisted/raised/winched Y'
	tś·ihhjiksei	'X will whistle/whizz' (stem śihhjikse-)
→	tś·ihhjiksui	'X whistled/whizzed'
	tś·ugjei	'X will swoop/swoosh/dive/plunge' (stem śugje-)
→	tś·ugjui	'X swooped/swooshes/dove/plunged'
	tsġipsei	'X will tap/knock'
→	tsġipsui	'X tapped/knocked'
	ta·tyklei	'X will twirl/swivel/rotate'
→	ta·tyklui	'X twirled/swiveled/rotated'

→	ta·tujulsei ta·tujulsui	'X will twinkle/sparkle/glimmer' 'X twinkled/sparkled/glimmered'
→	tsuoknia tsuoknua	'X will snatch/grab/pluck/steal Y' 'X snatched/grabbed/plucked/stole Y'
→	t·vipsui t·vipsi	'X will flinch/react' 'X flinched/reacted'

Other vowel-final verbs:

→ →	gielsia gielsua gielsủ	'X will prepare Y' 'X prepared Y' 'prepared'
→	hantui hanti	'X will lie' (stem hanto-) 'X lied '
→ →	hjalvua hjalvia hjalviu	'X will forge/melt Y' (stem hjalvo-) 'X forged/melted Y' 'forged/melted'
→ →	iskua iskia iskiu	'X will clean Y' (stem isko-) 'X cleaned Y' 'cleaned'
→ →	kekia kekua kekủ	'X will place Y' 'X placed Y' 'placed'
→ →	ketua ketủa/ketia ketiu	'X will look for Y' (stem keto-) 'X looked for Y' 'looked for'
→	ta·kikṡui ta·kikṡei	'X will jerk/move' 'X jerked/moved'
→ →	kyegvia kyegvua kyegvủ	'X will call Y (animal)' 'X called y' 'called'
	nuppua	'X will snatch/steal/grab Y'

→	*nuppaįa*	'X snatched/stole/grabbed Y'
→	*nuppaįu*	'snatched/stolen/grabbed'
	nŭria	'X will load/pack/stuff Y'
→	*nŭrŭa*	'X loaded/packed/stuffed Y'
→	*nŭrŭ*	'loaded/packed/stuffed'
	ontai	'X will dance'
→	*onti/ōtśi*	'X danced'
	pugįua	'X will pour/share Y' (stem **pugįo-**)
→	*pugįia*	'X poured/shared Y'
→	*pugįiu*	'poured/shared'
	puoḥḥua	'X will squeeze/hold Y' (stem **puoḥḥo-**)
→	*puoḥḥia*	'X squeezed/held Y'
→	*puoḥḥiu*	'squeezed/held'
	t·saiskia	'X will cause/lead to Y' (stem **saiske-**)
→	*t·saiskua*	'X caused/lead to Y'
→	*saiskù*	'caused'
	t·seiskia	'X will follow/come after Y'
→	*t·seiskua*	'X followed/came after Y'
→	*seiskù*	'followed'
	seitua	'X will threaten Y'
→	*seitaia*	'X threatened Y'
→	*seitaiu*	'threatened'
	sepsei	'X will flap its wings'
→	*sepsui*	'X flapped its wings'
	sġoa	'X will feed Y' (stem **sġo-**)
→	*sġia*	'X fed Y'
→	*sġiu*	'fed'
	śviua, śvivva	'X will sever/amputate Y' (stem **śvio-**)
→	*śvia*	'X severed/amputated Y'
→	*śviu*	'severed/amputated'
	tvelpia	'X will turn Y over/flip Y' (stem **tvelpe-**)
→	*tvelpua*	'X turned Y over/flipped Y'
→	*tvelpù*	'overturned/flipped'

	utśua	'X will pack for/prepare for Y' (stem utśo-)
→	utśia	'X packed for/prepared for Y'
→	utśiu	'packed for/prepared for'

	o·vuksui	'X comb his/her hair' (stem vukso-)
→	o·vuksia	'X combed his/her hair'
→	vuksiu	'combed'

The most common weak vowel-final verbs:

	om·eini	'X will propel itself (using a long stick on logs)' (stem eini-)
→	om·einui	'X propelled itself'
→	einù	'propelled'

	t·ioka	'X will surround Y' (stem ioka-)
→	t·iokia	'X surrounded Y'
→	iokiu	'surrounded'

	t·ivi	'X will increase' (stem ivi-)
→	t·ivui	'X increased'

	meha	'X smear/paint/decorate Y' (stem meha-)
→	mehia	'X smeared/painted/decorated Y' (also mesta)
→	mehiu	'smeared/painted/decorated' (also mestu)

	nèuna	'X will close Y' (stem nèuna-)
→	nèunia	'X closed Y'
→	nèuniu	'closed'

	sèuma	'X will cover Y' (stem sèuma-)
→	sèumia	'X covered Y'
→	sèumiu	'covered'

	oaiga	'X will hook Y' (stem oaiga[1]-)
→	oaigia	'X hooked Y'
→	oaigiu	'hooked'

	o·rieki	'X will relax' (stem rieki-)
→	o·riekui	'X relaxed'
→	riekù	'relaxed'

---

[1] Found as vaiġġa- in western dialects.

§9.10.1.1.3 Diphthong-Final Verbs

A small number of verb roots end in diphthongs or long vowels. The past of such verbs is formed by using the rules of diphthong coalescence in *§3.1.5.1* for the past form. There are only a handful of such verbs:

	ta·i	'X will stand'
→	tẹgi·i	'X stood'
	ja̍	'X will raise Y'
→	i̯ẹi·a	'X raised Y'
→	i̯ẹi·u	'raised'
	ay·m·i	'X is feel sick, be nauseous'
→	ẹma·m·i	'X felt sick/nauseous'
	ta·pai̯·u	'X will disappear'
→	ta·pe·y	'X disappeared'
	ġa̍	'X will fuck Y'
→	ġẹi̯a	'X fucked Y'
→	ġẹi·u	'fucked'

§9.10.1.2 Past Marking on Consonant-Final Verbs

Consonant-Final verbs are those whose roots end in a specific consonant or consonant cluster. A set number of final consonants and consonant clusters change unpredictably and form the strong consonant-final verbs. Verbs whose roots end in other consonants or more commonly consonant clusters cannot change like their strong counterparts and are thus called the weak consonant-final verbs.

§9.10.1.2.1 Strong Consonant-Final Verbs

Strong consonant-final verbs are those whose roots end in one of the 44 consonants or consonant clusters listed in the table below.

The exact form of the consonant or consonant cluster is often changed when the postverbal vowel is -i̯oi-/-i̯ui- (conditional irrealis intransitive inferential/conditional irrealis translative inferential) and -u̯i-/-u̯u- (optative intransitive assertive/optative translative assertive). See *§9.7.2* and *§9.7.4*. Special forms are given in the tables below.

Originally, the strong verb form was the result of a suffix added to the stem of verbs (thought to have been *-θ-). This was an infix, sometimes coming before the last consonant, sometimes attaching itself as a suffix to the stem.

This is most apparent when comparing verbs whose stems end in -k-, which have their past form in -dg- (originally *-θk-), and those ending in -rr-, which have the past form -rt- (originally *-rθ-):

	ta·pirru	'X will recover'
→	ta·pirtu	'X recovered'
	aka	'X will cut Y'
→	adga	'X cut Y'

Here are the consonants affected by the consonant-final past marker (in consonant groups). Some verbs in ivv- uvv- and evv- may have a rounded vowel in the past in some dialects, to become ydd-, ůdd- and èudd-.

	-a/-e/-o/-u/-ů/-y	-i	-ų	-į
-m-	-bm-		-mm- or -mų-	-mmį-
-p- and -b-	-db-		-bb-	-bbį-
-pp- and -bb-	-pr-	-psi-		
-v- and -ų-	-vv-		-ddų-	-ddį-
-vv-	-dd-			
-n-	-tt-	-di- or -ri-	-tv-	-ddį-
-dn- and -bm-	-nd-			-nnį-
-nį-	-ddį-		-tsv-	-ddį-
-ng-	-nd-		-ndų-	-ndį-
-nk-	-ht-		-htv-	-hdį-
-kn-	-nt-		-tv-	-ntś-
-t- and -d-	-dd- or -tt-		-tv-	-ddį-
-ts- and -hts-	-(h)tst-		-(h)tstų-	-(h)tstś-
-tsġ- and -htsġ-	-(h)tsk-		-(h)tskv-	-(h)tskį-
-s-	-ḥ-		-ḥų-	-ḥį-
-sġ-	-skk-		-skv-	-skkį-

	-a/-e/-o/-u/-ů/-y	-i	-ų	-į
-ṡ-	-ddį-	-ddi- or -tsi-	-tsv-	-ddį-
-tṡ-				
-dį-				
-r-	-rr- or -hr- or -dd-		-rv-	-rrį-
-rr-	-rt		-rtv-	-rd-
-l- and -dl-	-dl- or -ll-		-lv-	-llį-
-lį-	-llį-	-llji- or -gji-	-lv-	-gį-
-k-	-ḍg-		-ḍgų-	-dgį-
-g- and -gg-	-tk-		-tkv-	-tkį-
-gį- and -į-	-dį- or -ts-	-gji- or -ts-	-tsv-	-ddį-
-ġ- and -ḥ-	-st- (or -dġ-)		-htų- or -dġų-	-htṡ- or -ddį-
-h- and -hh-	-hr-/-ḍḍ- or -vv(u)-	**-vvi-** or **-hri-**	-hų-	-hį-
-hį-	-st-/-ṡt-	-sti-/-ṡṡi-	-stų- / -ṡv-	-ṡṡ-
-ḍb-	-kk-		-kv-	-kkį-
-ḍḍ-	-kk- or -tġ-		-gv- or -tkv-	-ggį- or -tkį-
-ḍg-	-tġ-		-bbų-	-bbį-

→	numa nubma	'X will pick Y' 'X picked Y'	(-m- → -bm-)
→	o·tṡomi o·tṡobmi o·tṡommi	'X will unite' 'X united' 'X wanted to unite'	(-m- → -bm-) (-m-ų- → -mm-)
→	tṡiba tṡiḍba	'X will mean Y' 'X meant Y'	(-b- → -ḍb-)

	kẹmmi	'X is happy'	
→	kebmima	'X was happy'	(-m- → -bm-)
→	kẹmmima	'X wanted to be happy'	(-m-ụ- → -mm-)
	teupa	'X will predict Y'	
→	teuḍba	'X predicted Y'	(-p- → -ḍb-)
	ta·nyppi	'X will stand out' (stem **nypp-**)	
→	ta·nypsi	'X stood out'	(-p- → -psi-)
→	nybbi	'X wanted to stand out'	(-p-ụ- → -bb-)
	ivva	'X will climb Y'	
→	iḍḍa	'X climbed Y' (also **yḍḍa**)	(-vv- → -ḍḍ-)
	śivi	'X will stay'	
→	śivvi	'X stayed'	(-v- → -vv-)
→	śiḍḍụi	'X wanted to stay' (also **śyḍḍụi**)	(-v-ụ- → -ḍḍụ-)
	keụi	'X will rise'	
→	kevvi	'X rose'	(-ụ- → -vv-)
→	keḍḍụi	'X wanted to rise' (also **kėụḍḍụi**)	(-ụ-ụ- → -ḍḍụ-)
	t·suvvi	'X will flow'	
→	t·suḍḍi	'X flowed' (also **t·sůḍḍi**)	(-vv- → -ḍḍ-)
→	suḍḍụi	'X wanted to flow' (also **sůḍḍụi**)	(-vv-ụ- → -ḍḍụ-)
	tśini	'X will leave traces'	
→	tśidi	'X left traces'	(-n- → -di-)
→	tśitvi	'X wanted to leave traces'	(-n-ụ- → -tv-)
	gaggana	'X will examine Y'	
→	gaggatta	'X examined Y'	(-n- → -tta-)
	koni	'X will walk'	
→	kodi~kori	'X walked'	(-n- → -di-/-ri-)
	hȧbmi	'X will fly'	
→	hȧndi	'X flew' (less commonly **hȧbmui**)	(-bm- → -nd-)
→	hȧtvi	'X wanted to fly' (less commonly **hȧbmụi**)	(-bm-ụ- → -tv-)
	hůmmi	'it is windy' (stem **hůn-**)	
→	hůbmi	'it was windy' (from < *hůd-m-i)	(-n- → -d-)

	nuidna	'X will identify Y'	
→	*nuinda*	'X identified Y'	(-dn- → -nd-)
→	*o·nuitvi*	'X wanted to identify himself/herself'	(-dn-ų- → -tv-)
	inįi	'X will sneak'	
→	*iddįi*	'X snuck'	(-nį- → -ddį-)
→	*itsvi*	'X wanted to sneak'	(-nį-ų- → -tsv-)
	o·mingi	'X will get ready'	
→	*o·mindi*	'X got ready'	(-ng- → -nd-)
→	*o·mindųi*	'X wanted to get ready'	(-ng-ų- → -ndų-)
	nįanka	'X will pile Y up'	
→	*nįahta*	'X piled Y up'	(-nk- → -ht-)
	kekna	'X will organize/be responsible for Y'	
→	*kenta*	'X organized/was responsible for Y'	(-kn- → -nt-)
	ta·djati	'X will mourn'	
→	*ta·djaddi*	'X mourned'	(-t- → -dd-)
→	*djatvi*	'X wanted to mourn'	(-t-ų- → -tv-)
	keda	'X will carry Y'	
→	*kedda/ketta*	'X carried Y'	(-d- → -dd-/-tt-)
	etsa	'X will begin Y'	
→	*etsta*	'X began Y'	(-ts- → -tst-)
	t·suodu	'X will bloom'	
→	*t·suoddu*	'X bloomed'	(-d- → -dd-)
→	*suotvi*	'X wants to bloom'	(-d-ų- → -tv-)
	kautsġa	'X will make jam out of Y'	
→	*kautska*	'X made jam out of Y'	
	t·o·lįasi	'X will cut itself deeply'	
→	*t·o·lįahi*	'X cut itself deeply'	(-s- → -h-)
	sisġi	'there is thunder'	
→	*siskki*	'there was thunder'	(-sġ- → -skk-)
	kyṡa	'X will try Y'	
→	*kyha*	'X tried Y'	(-ṡ- → -h-)
	nitṡa	'X will teach Y'	

→	*niḍdja*	'X taught Y'	(-tś- → -ddj-)
	jairi	'X will row'	
→	*jaihri*	'X rowed'	(-r- → -hr-)
→	*jairvi*	'X wants/wanted to row'	(-r-u̧- → -rv-)
	ta·pirru	'X will recover'	
→	*ta·pirtu*	'X recovered'	(-rr- → -rt-)
→	*ta·pirvu*	'X wants/wanted to recover'	(-rr-u̧- → -rv-)
	kidli	'it is customary'	
→	*killi*	'it was customary'	(-dl- → -ll-)
	ila	'X will know Y'	
→	*idla*	'X knew Y'	(-l- → -dl-)
	ilja	'X will grow Y'	
→	*illja*	'X grew Y'	(-lj- → -llj-)
	giki	'X will glance'	
→	*giḍgi*	'X glanced'	(-k- → -ḍg-)
→	*giḍgu̧i*	'X wanted to glance'	(-k-u̧- → -ḍgu̧-)
	kega	'X will hide Y'	
→	*ketka*	'X hid Y'	(-g- → -tk-)
	ta·piagi	'X will fall asleep'	
→	*ta·piatki*	'X fell asleep'	(-g- → -tk-)
→	*piatkvi*	'X wanted to fall asleep'	(-g-u̧- → -tkv-)
	ruikima	'X will be anxious'	
→	*ruiḍgima*	'X was anxious'	(-k- → -ḍg-)
	ogja	'X will remember Y'	
→	*odja/otsa*	'X remembered Y'	(-gj- → -dj-/-ts-)
	o·meġi	'X will shake itself'	
→	*o·medġi*	'X shook itself'	(-ġ- → -dġ-)
→	*o·medġu̧i*	'X wanted to shake itself'	(-ġ-u̧- → -dġu̧-)
	pùha	'X will scold Y'	
→	*pùsta*	'X scolded Y'	(-h- → -st-)
	sahha	'X will burn Y'	

→	sahra	'X burnt Y'	(-hh- → -hr-)
→	u·savvi	'X was burnt'	(-hh- → -vvi-)
→	savv·u	'burnt'	(-hh- → -vvu-)
	d·luhhi	'X will boil'	
→	d·luvvi	'X boiled'	(-hh- → -vvi-)
	sahhi̯i	'X will speak'	
→	saśśi	'X spoke'	(-hhi̯- → -śś-)
→	saśvi	'X wanted to speak'	(-hhi̯-u̯- → -śv-)
	ihhi̯a	'X will thank Y'	
→	ista	'X thanked Y'	(-hhi̯- → -st-)
	i̯ed̯d̯i	'X will run'	
→	i̯ekki	'X ran'	(-d̯d̯- → -kk-)
→	i̯ekvi	'X wanted to run'	(-d̯d̯-u̯- → -kv-)
	dad̯d̯a	'X will ask Y'	
→	dakka	'X asked Y'	(-d̯d̯- → -kk-)
	kid̯ga	'X will pick Y up'	
→	kigga/kitġa	'X picked Y up'	(-d̯g- → -gg-/-tġ-)
	dad̯bi	'X will drum'	
→	dabbi/datvi	'X drummed'	(-d̯b- → -bb-/-tv-)

§9.10.1.2.2 Weak Consonant-Final Verbs

Weak consonant-final verbs are those whose roots end in consonants or consonant clusters other than those listed above. The markings for these verbs are valency dependent – the root is augmented by an ending which depends on whether ther verb is transitive (including subjective, passive and ditransitive), intransitive (including subjective, passive and ditransitive) or translative. In other words, the past of weak consonant-final verbs depends on which postverbal vowel it will precede.

	ASSERTIVE	INFERENTIAL
transitive	-a	-e
intransitive	-i	-o
translative	-u/-ů	-o

The ending for such verbs is the polarized version of the valency vowel preceding the correct postverbal vowel:

	PRESENT	PAST
transitive	-a	-i-
intransitive	-i	-u-
translative	-u/-ů	-ai-/-ei-

		postverb vowel					
		transitive		intransitive		translative	
		transitive subjective ditransitive passive		intransitive subjective ditransitive passive			
		Present	**Past**	Present	**Past**	Present	**Past**
ASS.	indicative	-a	-i·a	-i	-u·i	-u / -ů	-aj·u / -ej·ů
	conditional irrealis	-ia	-i·gja	-iu / -iů	-u·ju	-ui	-aj·ui
	optative	-ua / -ůa	-i·vva	-ųi / -ůi	-u·vvi	-ųu / -ůů	-ai·ųu
INF.	indicative	-e	-i·e	-o	-ů	-o	-aj·o
	conditional irrealis	-ie	-i·gje	-joi	-u·joi	-jui	-a·gjo
	optative	-ue / -ůi	-i·vve	-uo	-ůo	-ue or -ėu	-aj·ue / -ej·ęu
	PASS	-i·u		∅		-aj·u	

When confusion may arise due to the merging of the past indicative and present conditional irrealis for transitive verbs (both -ia-), the older forms of the conditional may be used instead (-iga-). The same goes for the inferential, where they merge as -ie- but may be found as -ige- for clarity.

Common consonant clusters for such verbs include -sk- -ld- and -kk-:

			stem
	aiska	'X will fix/sew Y'	aisk-
→	*aiskia*	'X fixed/sewed Y'	aisk·i-
→	*aiskiu*	'fixed/sewn'	aisk·i-

	belmi	'X will work'	belm-
→	*belmui*	'X worked'	belm·u-
	o·gaulda	'X will discuss Y together'	gauld-
→	*o·gauldia*	'X discussed Y together'	gauld·i-
→	*gauldiu*	'discussed'	gauld·i-
	o·gauldi	'X will discuss'	gauld·i
→	*o·gauldui*	'X discussed'	gauld·u-
	gaykka	'X will satisfy Y'	gaykk-
→	*gaykkia*	'X satisfied Y'	gaykk·i-
→	*gaykkiu*	'satisfied'	gaykk·i-
	ġoppa	'X will knock on Y'	ġopp-
→	*ġoppia*	'X knocked on Y'	ġopp·i-
→	*ġoppiu*	'knocked, exhausted'	ġopp·i-
	uġoppi	'X is knocked (on)'	u·ġopp·i
→	*uġoppui*	'X was knocked (on)'	u·ġopp·u-
	jesta	'X will succeed at Y'	jest-
→	*jestia*	'X succeeded at Y'	jest·i-
→	*jestiu*	'succeeded/successful'	jest·i-
	piegjukka	'X will greet Y'	piegjukk-
→	*piegjukkia*	'X greeted Y'	piegjukk·i-
→	*piegjukkiu*	'greeted'	piegjukk·i-
	ta·tůreisků	'X will shed fur'	tůreisk-
→	*ta·tůreiskejů*	'X shed Y'	tůreisk·ej-
	ta·bjeulusku	'X will lose weight'	bjeulusk-
→	*ta·bjeuluskaju*	'X lost weight'	bjeulusk·aj-
	ta·neinnu	'X will get dirty'	neinn-
→	*ta·neinnaju*	'X gort dirty'	neinn·aj-

§9.10.1.3 Irregular verbs

A number of verbs in Siwa follow no regular pattern to form their past. There are four types of irregular verbs; present augmented verbs, past augmented verbs, irregular verbs and syncopic verbs. Present and past augmented verbs are those which either gain or lose an augment (vowel or consonant). Present augments have their augments in the present, and past augmented verbs in the past. Proper irregular verbs are those that simply do not follow any pattern, and syncopic verbs are those that lose a vowel in the past (or with a handful of verbs, gain a vowel in the past). Sometimes, having or losing an augment is enough to mark the past, such that actual past markings are not present.

§9.10.1.3.1 Augmented Verbs

Augmented verbs are verbs whose present form has an extra prefix which disappears or changes in the past. Another subclass is that of vowel-final verbs ending in diphthongs. The diphthongs have their complex form in the present, but a simple (past marked) form in the past (for the special behavior of monosyllabic words ending in diphthongs, see *§3.1.5.1*). There is a handful of verbs who have the pattern j-/n- or b-/n- for present/past.

Present augment: stem

	Present	Gloss	Stem
	j·oa	'X will attack Y'	o-
→	*an·oa, h·oa*	'X attacked Y'	
	j·û·i	'X will lie'	û-
→	*(a)n·û·i*	'X lay'	
	gi·ia, j·eh·a	'X will bathe Y'	e(h)-
→	*eh·a*	'X bathed Y'	
	o·j·ei, o·j·eh·i	'X will bathe itself'	e(h)-
→	*o·m·ehi*	'X bathed itself'	
	m·uni	'X will rest'	un-
→	*udi~uri*	'X rested'	
	n·eni	'X will sit'	en-
→	*edi~eri*	'X sat'	
	n·eska	'X will ask about Y'	esk-
→	*a·iska*	'X asked about Y'	
	v·ana	'X will stretch Y'	an-
→	*(a)n·adda*	'X stretched Y'	
	om·ana	'X will stretch itself'	an-
→	*o·n·adda*	'X stretched itself'	
	s·eta/s·etġa	'X will put Y (somewhere)'	et-, etġ-

→	t·eta/t·etġa	'X put Y (somewhere)'	
	s·aila	'X will trust Y'	ail-
→	t·aila	'X trusted Y'	
	b·ia	'X will throw Y'	i-
→	(a)n·ia	'X threw Y'	
	b·eḥḥi	'there is a path '	eḥḥ-
→	(a)n·eḥḥi	'there was a path'	

§9.10.1.3.2 Syncoped Verbs

Syncoped verbs are those whose present or past form goes through syncope, i.e. loses a vowel between two consonants, thus creating a consonant cluster. The following verbs are examples of this type of irregular verbs:

	Past Syncope			Present Syncope	
	setula	'X will push Y'		erri	'X will work'
→	sedla	'X pushed Y'	→	eruli	'X worked'
	moġa	'X will drink Y'		t·ûdli	'X will sweat'
→	a·mġa	'X drank Y'	→	t·ûheli	'X sweated'
	geiga	'X will share Y'			
→	giga	'X shared Y'			

§9.10.1.3.3 Proper Irregular Verbs

Proper irregular verbs are those whose stem changes in unpredictable ways from non-past to past. Many of them involve the addition of -ḍ- or -d- in the past or go through stem suppletion. The following verbs are examples of this type of irregular verbs:

			stem
	ira	'X will kill Y'	ir-
→	jahra, jẹdla	'X killed Y'	jahr-, jẹdl-
	nodi/nori	'X will sing'	nod-
→	nenodi	'X sang'	nenod-
	oai	'X will say'	oa-
→	noai	'X said'	noa-

	ona	'X will tell Y'	on-
→	*nona*	'X told Y'	non-
	maki	'X will go'	mak-
→	*maski, maḍgi*	'X went'	mask-, maḍg-
	mani	'X will come'	man-
→	*mansi, mandi*	'X came'	mans-, mand-
	dieggi, diggi	'X will go (and come back)'	diegg-, digg-
→	*daḍgi,*	'X went (and came back)'	daḍg-
	geḍḍa	'X will dig (for) Y'	geḍḍ-
→	*gaḍba*	'X dug (for) Y'	gaḍb-
	i	'X will change'	i-
→	*imi*	'X changed'	im-
	sota[1]	'X will give Y'	sot-
→	*i·sotati*	'X give Y to Z'	i·sot-
→	*sodda*	'X gave Y'	sodd-
→	*i·stati*	'X gave Y to Z'	i·st-
	dolla	'X will hold Y'	doll-
→	*dalda*	'X held Y'	dald-
	riddja	'X will propose to Y'	riddj-
→	*reḍḍa*	'X proposed to Y'	reḍḍ-
	tśalli	'X will run (of animals)'	tśall-
→	*tśvedli*	'X ran (of animals)'	tśvedl-
	njaba	'X will use Y'	njab-
→	*niḍba*	'X used Y'	niḍb-
	rehmi	'X will go by boat'	rehm-
→	*raḍmi*	'X went by boat'	raḍm-
	ha	'X will eat Y'	h-
→	*ma*	'X ate Y'	m-

---

[1] Compare to the declension for **u·sot-** 'allow':

	u·sot·i	'X is allowed'
→	*u·sodd·i*	'X was allowed'

	peva	'X will eat[1] Y'	pev-
→	*bůa*	'X ate Y'	bů-
	kita	'X will do/make Y'	kit-
→	*a·hta, tka*	'X did/made Y'	a·ht-, tk-
	kjoka	'X will weave Y'	kjok-
→	*kėuhka, keygga*	'X wove Y'	kėuhk-, keygg-
	komi	'it is summer'	ko-
→	*koabmi/gabmi*	'it was summer'	koab-, gab-
	miedda	'X will want Y'	miedd-
→	*medba*	'X wanted Y'	medb-
	roahtśi	'X will chafe, irritate, annoy (-a)'	roahtś-
→	*růddji*	'X chafed'	růddj-
	mjora	'X will grind Y'	mjor-
→	*myrra*	'X ground Y'	myrr-
	nuja	'X will see Y'	nuj-
→	*nega*	'X saw Y'	neg-
→	*nuhla*	'X has seen Y'	nuhl[2]-
	notsa	'X will take Y'	nots-
→	*oġa*	'X took Y'	oġ-
	śema	'X will believe Y'	śem-
→	*aġama/oġma*	'X believed Y'	aġam-, oġm-
	tata	'X will think about Y'	tat-
→	*taidda, daidda*	'X thought about Y'	taidd-, daidd-
	uora/ůra/vora	'X will worship/serve Y'	uor-, ůr-, vor-
→	*ȯdla*	'X worshiped/served Y'	ȯdl-
	o·kaiki	'X will kneel'	kaik-
→	*o·kȧdgi*	'X kneeled Y'	kȧdg-

---

[1] The verb *pev·a* used to be more commonly used about animals, while *h·a* was restricted to humans. The distinction is not as rigorously held as before.

[2] This form is nearly always pronounced [nuɫ:-] rather than [nʊhl-].

§9.11 Tense-Aspect Coalescence

The results of combining tense, verbal conclusivity (conclusive vs. inconclusive) and telicity (genitive vs. dative) is illustrated in the table below.

		telic	atelic
conclusive	present	future~present telic *ikeda oakibma kili* [iˈcʰeda ˈɔɑɹʔpma ˈcʰili] i-ked-a-Ø oak=ibma kili-Ø DIT-carry-ASS.CONCL.TR-3P.AG.SG home-ALLAT wood-DAT 'X will carry the wood home' or 'X carries the wood home'	future~present atelic *ikeda oakibma kidli* [iˈcʰeda ˈɔɑɹʔpma ˈcʰɪtɬi] i-ked-a-Ø oak=ibma ki<d>li DIT-carry-ASS.CONCL.TR-3P.AG.SG home-ALLAT wood.GEN 'X will carry (some) wood home' or 'X carries (some of the) wood home'
	past	past telic *ikedda oakibma kili* [iˈcʰetːa ˈɔɑɹʔpma ˈcʰili] i-ke<dd>-a-Ø oak=ibma kili-Ø DIT-carry.PAST-ASS.CONCL.TR-3P.AG.SG home-ALLAT wood-DAT 'X carried the wood home'	past atelic *ikedda oakibma kidli* [iˈcʰetːa ˈɔɑɹʔpma ˈcʰɪtɬi] i-ke<dd>-a-Ø oak=ibma ki<d>li DIT-carry.PAST-ASS.CONCL.TR-3P.AG.SG home-ALLAT wood.GEN 'X carried (some of the) wood home'

		telic	atelic
inconclusive	present	present telic inconclusive *ikeda oakibma kili nata* [iˈcʰeda ˈɔɑɹʔpma ˈcʰili ˈnata] i-ked-a- oak=ibma kili n-a-ta DIT-carry-TR home-ALLAT wood-GEN COP.INCONCL-ASS-3P.AG.SG 'X is carrying (the/all the) wood home'	present atelic inconclusive *ikeda oakibma kidli nata* [iˈcʰeda ˈɔɑɹʔpma ˈcʰɪtɬi ˈnata] i-ked-a- oak=ibma ki<d>li n-a-ta DIT-carry-TR home-ALLAT wood.GEN COP.INCONCL-ASS-3P.AG.SG 'X is carrying (some) wood home'
		past telic inconclusive	past atelic inconclusive

		telic	atelic
past		ikeda oakibma kili mata [iˈcʰeda ˈɔɑɟɪʔpma ˈcʰili mɑtɑ] i-ked-a- oak=ibma kili m-a-ta DIT-carry-TR home-ALLAT wood-GEN COP.PAST.INCONCL-ASS-3P.AG.SG 'X was carrying (all) the wood home'	ikeda oakibma kidli mata [iˈcʰeda ˈɔɑɟɪʔpma ˈcʰɪtɬi mɑtɑ] i-ked-a- oak=ibma ki<d>li m-a-ta DIT-carry-TR home-ALLAT wood.GEN COP.PAST.INCONCL-ASS-3P.AG.SG 'X was carrying (some) wood home'

§9.12 Location and Movement

Siwa verbs can house markers that relate information about the location or movement of its constituents, called locative markers. These markers are all housed in slot 5. Locative markers are separated into two groups: primary and secondary locative markers. The primary markers are the cislocative and translocative, which respectively show movement toward the speaker and away from the speaker.

The secondary markers are identical to the locative markers for nouns – inessive, illative, elative, adessive, allative and ablative. These exist in two sets - definite and relative. The definite markers refer to a 3rd person object, while relative markers are used to form locative and genitive relative phrases (..*in which/whose X*). Definite markers generally require the ditransitive.

The primary markers coalesce, when possible, with the habitual and perfect markers (see section *§9.2.1.9*).

primary markers		
cislocative	-ni-	
translocative	-ki-	
secondary markers	**definite**	**relative**
inessive	-ja- or -igja-	-jo- or -igjo-
illative	-ita-	-ito-
elative	-ika-	-iko-
adessive	-ima-	-imo-
allative	-ibma-	-ibmo-
ablative	-iska-	-isko-

§9.12.1 Primary Locative Markers

The primary locative markers are simply used to show motion away or towards the agent of the verb.

The translocative shows movement away from the speaker, or simply movement towards something. It is very commonly used to mean *go and X*, e.g.;

    mahhami   'I will hunt Y'
    mahhakimi   'I will go and hunt Y'

The cislocative shows the opposite, or movement towards the speaker, or often also *come and X*.

    opanikan   'come and help me'
    dohhanikan   'come and say good bye to me'

Their use is fairly loose and quite common. In copular constructions, the primary locative markers may be marked onto the verb instead of the copula. Newer generations tend to group all markers onto the copula, such that having the locative markers on the main verb may be considered older or more formal language. Note that combining the translocative and cislocative (-kini- or sometimes -kni-) shows a movement without any particular destination, similar to English Ø-ing around/about. It can also be used with verbs not denoting movement, then placing emphasis on the idleness of the action.

biakin
['biɑɟɪn]
bi-a-ki-n
throw-ASS.CONCL.TR-TRANSLO-IMP.2P.SG
'throw it away/there'

bianin
['biɑnɪn]
bi-a-ni-n
throw-ASS.CONCL.TR-CISLO-IMP.2P.SG
'throw it here/over here'

koni maknita
['kʰɔni 'maʔŋida]
kon-i m-a-ki=ni-ta
walk-ITR COP.PAST.INCONCL-ASS-TRANSLO=CISLO-3P.AG.SG
'X was walking about'

tàiknisen
['tʰæːɪʔŋisɛn]
tà-i-ki=ni-se=n
stand-ITR-TRANSLO=CISLO-IMPER.2P.SG.NEG
'don't just stand there'

usìdliki ohkihi-go
[uˈsiːtɬiɟi ˈɔhcihigɔ]
u-si<dl>-i-ki ohki=hi–go
PASS-blow.PAST-ASS.CONCL.ITR-TRANSLO birch.bark.box-PAT–1P.POSS.SG
'my **ohkis** (birch bark box) got blown away'

sem usìdlinika ylihma
[sɛm uˈsiːtɬiniga ˈylɪhma]
sem u-si<dl>-i-ni-ka yli-hi=ma
not PASS-blow.PAST-ASS.CONCL.ITR-CISLO-1P.PAT.SG little.leaf-ADESS
'I wasn't blown here on a leaflet (i.e. I wasn't born yesterday)'

§9.12.2 Definite Secondary Locative Markers
The definite secondary locative markers are used to show location in (inessive) or on (adessive), motion into (illative) or onto (allative) or out of (elative) and off of (ablative) a third person object. This triggers the verb to be in the ditransitive. Secondary locative markers are also used with destinal locative adverbs *up* and *down* (see *§6.5.2*).

tinodigja
['tʰi'nɔdijːa]
t-i-no<d>-i-ia
3P.UNAG-DIT-swim.PAST-ASS.CONCL.ITR-INESS
'X swam/floated into Y'

tinodika
['tʰi'nɔdiga]
t-i-no<d>-i-ka
3P.UNAG-DIT-swim.PAST-ASS.CONCL.ITR-ELAT
'X swam/floated out of Y'

henda isetaibman
['hɛnda i'setaɪman]
hen=da i-set>-a-ibma-n
up.ILLAT.DESTI DIT-place-ASS.CONCL.TR-ALLAT-1P.AG.SG
'put X up on Y'

henga inotsaiskan
['hɛŋːa i'nɔtsaɪskan]
hen=ga i-not-a-iska-n
up.ELAT.DESTI DIT-take-ASS.CONCL.TR-ALLAT-IMPER.2P.SG
'take X off of Y'

ipugjuaitappatta
[i'puj:uɑida?pa?ta]
i-pugjo-a-ita-pp-tta
DIT-pour-ASS.CONCL.TR-ILLAT-FREQ-SUBIT
'poor some into it'

ibutśuaitami
[ib'utɕuɑidami]
i-utśo-a-ita-Ø-mi
DIT-pack-ASS.CONCL.TR-ILLAT-3P.PAT-1P.AG.SG
'I will pack Y into Z'

Mahhjuts sà ha sappiskua deiskogge
['mɑhːjʊtːsæː ha 'sa?pɪskua 'deɪskɔcːe]
mahhj=uts-Ø sà h-a sappiska-Ø-a d-e-isko-gge
fallenbear.VOC-AGT VOC.PART eat-TR paw-DAT-PL COP-INFER-ABLAT.REL-1P.AG.PL.EXCL
'oh Bear, whose paws we will eat'

The secondary locative markers can be exchanged for primary locative markers if the person is no longer a third person:

gag·i·totra·ita	'X is related to Y'
gag·i·totra·ki	'X is related to me'
gag·o·totri·ri	'they are related to each other'

§9.12.3 Relative Secondary Locative Markers
Relative secondary locative markers are used to form locative relative clauses. In addition, the elative and ablative are used to form genitive relative clauses. This triggers the copular construction. The markers are always and only found inside the copula, which then lacks the regular relative prefix *o-*. Just like definite locative markers, relative ones also trigger the ditransitive when possible.

sėu, ida gaitori
['sø: i'iða 'gɑidori]
sėu-Ø ij-id-a g-a-ito-ri
river-AGT DIT-fall-TR COP.PAST.CONCL-ASS-ILLAT.REL-3P.AG.PL
'the river into which they fell'

nidna, iu̯avva bengomu gaibmogga
['nɪʔtna i'wɑw:a 'bɛŋ:omu 'gɑɪʔpmɔk:a]
nidna-Ø i-u̯avv-a bengomu-Ø g-a-ibmo-ka
hut-AGT DIT-spread.out-TR roof-DAT COP.PAST.CONCL-ASS-ALLAT.REL-1P.AG.PL.EXCL
'the hut over which we spread (i.e. placed) a roof (of leather)'

seumi, ukedi gaitoka
['seumi u'cʰedi 'gɑidɔga]
seumi-Ø u-ked-i g-a-ito-ka
land-ACT PASS-bear-ITR COP.PAST-ASS-ILLAT.REL-1P.PAT.SG
'the land in(to) which I was born'

toḓgo, ikosġa toaḓḓi gaitomi
['tʰɔðgo i'kʰɔsxa 'tʰɔaðːi 'gɑidɔmi]
toḓgo-Ø i-kosġ-a toa-ḓḓi g-a-ito-mi
tree.trunk-AGT DIT-engrave-TR some.INA-DAT COP.PAST-ASS-ILLAT.REL-1P.AG.SG
'the tree trunk into which I engraved something'

makidnan, ioka sġaikona
['mɑcɪʔtnan i'ɔka 'sxɑigɔna]
ma=k-i-dna-n i-oka-a sġ-a-iko-na
go-ASS.CONCL.ITR-REVERS-IMP.2P.SG DIT-originate-TR COP.HAB.PAST-ASS-ELAT.REL-2P.AG.SG
'go back to where you came from'

genitive relative

somi, ila kohko saikomi
['sɔmi 'iːla 'kʰohkɔ 'sɑigɔmi]
somi-Ø il-a kori-ko s-a-iko-mi
man-AGT know-TR boy-GEN COP.HAB.CONCL-ASS-ELAT.REL-1P.AG.SG
'the man whose boy I know'

nidna, gaikomi eiddu bengomu
['nɪʔtna 'gɑigɔmi 'eitːu 'bɛŋ:omu]
nidna-Ø g-a-iko-mi ei<dd>-u bengomu-Ø
hut-AGT COP.PAST-ASS.CONCL.TR-ELAT.REL-1P.AG.SG build.PAST-PAT.PART roof-AGT
'the hut whose roof I built/was built by me'

maski, kesa sauhhjaha naikomi
['masci 'cʰesa 'sɑuh:jaha 'nɑigɔmi]
maski-Ø kes-a sauhhja-ha n-a-iko-mi
people-AGT learn-TR language-GEN COP.INCONCL-ASS-ELAT.REL-1P.AG.SG
'the people whose language I am learning'

§9.13 Preverbal Adverbs
Certain verbs may be found with an adverbial clitic showing space, time or manner. Preverbal adverbs can be separated into two groups – concrete and abstract.

The preverbal adverbs hę- 'up', tů- 'down', tat- 'into', tam- 'onto' and kat- 'from/about' are more abstract than the other preverbal adverbs, and although they are more common, they generally change the meaning of the verb they modify significantly. In their more concrete meaning, these adverbs are rarer and usually found with regular adverbs instead.

The other preverbal adverbs are more freely used and have a more concrete function than abstract adverbs.

Each preverbal adverb has a vowel-final and consonant-final form. Preverbal spacial adverbs are always the very first element of the verb and are housed in slot -3 (see *§9.2.1.2*).

§9.13.1 Locative Preverbal Adverbs
Locative preverbal adverbs correspond to both an existing free-standing adverb *and* three forms corresponding to the six locative cases. However, as clitics, these adverbs only distinguish between location in/into, on/onto and off/from:

inessive and illative	**tat-**
adessive and allative	**tam-**
elative and ablative	**kat-**

In addition to these three prefixes, locative preverbal adverbs also include hę- 'up' and tů- 'down'.

Locative preverbal adverbs serve three main functions:

1. They are found with transitive verbs which cannot have an object in a locative case.
2. They are found with semantically passive verbs whose topic (subject) would normally be found in a locative case.
3. They are found with patientive and agentive participles.

In addition to these three functions, locative preverbal adverbs can also modify the meaning of a verb entirely.

The locative preverbal adverbs sometimes appear with verbs which already carry a preverbal adverb in slot -3. Locative preverbal adverbs are found after the pre-existing preverbal adverb.

gag·i·syvva·ita	'X will show explain Y to Z'
ga·tat·u·syḍḍi	'Y was explained (to Z)'

§9.13.1.1 With Transitive Verbs

Preverbal adverbs are commonly found with transitive verbs which *cannot* be found with an object in any of the locative cases or with postpositions/adverbs. Typically, these verbs have an underlying movement into, onto or out of something, which is generally left out of the phrase.

Thus, this function of preverbal adverbs is to allow a dropped locative in the verb phrase of transitive verbs. These verbs typically contain only one object. This creates two ways for verbs to behave and express the same idea in two different ways, sometimes allowing for similar constructions to those found in English. The preverbal adverbs are similar in their evolution to the incorporating verbs – something known or unimportant (because easily inferred) is more likely to be found with a preverbal adverb.

In other words, the difference between secondary locative markers (after the stem) and locative preverbal adverbs (before the stem) is whether the location refers to a specific third person (movement in relation to a thing) or if only the movement is specified:

Secondary locative markers (movement in relation to a specific object)
Ø-ia	'VERB in X'
Ø-ita	'VERB into X'
Ø-ika	'VERB out of X'

Locative preverbal adverbs (movement without specific object)
tat-Ø	'VERB in/into'
tam-Ø	'VERB on/onto'
kat-Ø	'VERB out/off'

Consider the examples below:

eskujekkami pęles	'I will empty the stomach'
eskujekka·ika·mi utśudas	'I will empty the content out of Y'
kat·eskujekkami utśudas	'I will empty the content out'
ġaispa jata	'X will rinse the bowl'
ġaispa·ika lůri	'X will rinse the dirt out of Y'
kata·ġaispa lůri	'X will rinse the dirt out'
o·setġa·ibma	'X will put X on (itself)'
tam·o·setġan liabmis!	'put your tuque on!'
isetġan liabmis osibma!	'put your tuque on yourself!'

§9.13.1.2 With Semantically Passive Verbs

When a verb which usually has an argument in a locative case is found in the passive, preverbal adverbs are used.

i·gik·ibma	'X will glance at Y' (**gik·**)
tam·u·giḍgi	'X was glanced at' (lit. was at-glanced)
iddj·iks·ita	'X will shoot it' (lit. into it)
tat·ub·iksui	'X was shot' (lit. in-shot)
i·mŭiggibma	'X will infect Y' (lit. onto Y)
tam·u·mŭiggui	'X was infected'
i·r·ita	'X will bite into Y' (**r·**)
tat·u·rui	'X was bit into' (lit. was into-bit)
i·muoja·ita	'X will dress Y into Z'
tat·u·muots·i	'used'
i·gaihtsa·ki·na	'you owe me X'
tat·u·gaihtsti·ki	'owed to me, in debt to me'

§9.13.1.3 With Paritciples

Verbs whose argument is found in a locative case will also be found with a preverbal adverb in their patientive participal forms. This includes a number of verbs which commonly govern an infinitive clause with the copula in a locative case. The resulting participles may be difficult to translate into English.

i·mŭiggibma	'X will infect Y' (lit. onto Y)
tam·u·mŭiggui	'X was infected'
tama·mŭiggù	'(the) infected'
i·kaha·ika	'X will need Y (lit. of Y)'
kat·u·kahi	'X is needed'
kata·kastu	'(the) needed'
kastu	'needed, necessary'

§9.13.1.4 Modifying the Verb
A number of verbs are found with preverbal adverbs which modify their meaning.

TAT-   'in(to)'
This preverb has the form **tat-/tata-** (sometimes merging as **tad-** or **tatṡ-**, **tata·ta** merge as **tadda·/tadd·**) and has the meaning 'in' on 'into'. It also modifies a number of verbs by changing their meaning:

t·idi	'X will fall'
tadd·idi	'X will happened to'
keyi	'X will rise'
tat·o·keyi	'X will join/participate/grow/mature'
kůkůa	'X will bring Y'
tat·kůkůa	'X will involve'
manta	'X will accept Y'
tat·u·manti	'X will be accepted'
nuja	'X will see Y'
tad·nuja	'X will guess Y'
piegjukka	'X will greet Y'
tata·piegjukka	'X will welcome/host Y'
pugjua	'X will pour Y'
tata·pugjomi	'it is flooding'
suga	'X will visit Y'
tat·suga	'X will interfere with/obstruct/block/disrupt Y'
o·toati	'X will join Y'
tata·toata	'X will include/integrate/assimilate/blend/mix/mingle with Y'
ůrůi	'X will approach'
tat·ůrůmi	'it is imminent/near/impending/approaching'
om·ani	'X will stretch'
tat·om·ana	'X will get used to X/be enough for X'
t·vietku	'X will cave/slant'
tata·t·vietku	'X will cave in/collapse/give in'

TAM- 'on(to)'

This preverb has the form **tam-/tama-** (sometimes merging as **tav-/taC-**, **tama-ta-** merge as **tanda-/tand-** or **tamda-/tamd-**) and has the meaning 'on' on 'onto'. It also modifies a number of verbs by changing their meaning:

o·gahhi	'X will lean'
tam·o·gahha	'X will tend to/be prone to/prefer/favour Y'
t·idi	'X will fall'
tand·idi	'X will stumble upon/find out (by accident)'
jeḍḍi	'X will run/flow/go'
tand·jeḍḍi	'X will turn out to/be found to/happen to'
t·igiri	'X will seep'
tand·igira	'X will affect Y'
joa	'X will attack Y'
tam·joa[1]	'X will confront/tackle/oppress Y'
o·kaiki	'X will kneel'
tam·o·kaiki	'X will swear'
tama·kjuśa	'X will trespass/infringe upon/threaten'[2]
kůkůa	'X will bring'
tanda·kůkůa	'X will cause Y (to happen)'
d·laugji	'X will hesitate'
tama·lauja	'X will stall/distract/hinder/stop Y'
d·lodni	'X will sink'
tama·d·lodni	'X will sink to the bottom/become forgotten/go into oblivion'
manta	'X will receive Y'
tam·manta	'X will take it upon itself to/take responsibility/assume/play the role of Y'
raja	'X will push Y'
tama·raja	'X will emphasize/accentuate/focus on Y'

---

[1] The form **tam·o·a** also exists, usually meaning exclusively 'to confront'.

[2] (*kjuśa does not exist)

tam·o·ragji	'X will flow/advance (of tide)'
tama·rajō	'especially'
sèuma	'X will cover Y'
tam(a)·sèuma	'X will give shelter to/preserve/shield Y'

KAT- 'out/from'

This preverb has the form **kat-/kata-** (sometimes merging as **kad-/kadj-**) and has the meaning 'out', 'off' 'form' or 'about'. It also modifies a number of verbs by changing their meaning:

daḍḍa	'X will answer Y'
kata·daḍḍa	'X will turn Y down/decline/dismiss/reject Y'
geḍḍa	'X will dig (for) Y'
kata·geḍḍa	'X will empty Y (by scooping out water from a boat), dig out'
t·eli	'X will grow'
kata·t·eli	'X will mature (grow into an adult)'
hid·eti	'X will cut one's hair'
kata·(hid)·eti	'X will shave one's head'
ta·gedli	'X will function'
kata·gedla	'X will work/figure Y out, know how to Y'
ta·gimia	'X will look forward to Y'
kata·gimia	'X will expect/presume/figure Y'
kata·goa	'X will push (on) Y' (cf. *teki·goa* 'X will pull (on) Y')
hagjena	'X will notice Y'
kat·i·hagjena	'X will point Y out to Z'
iġa	'X will receive Y'
kat·iġa	'X will inherit Y'
jola	'X will read Y'
kat·jola	'X will interprete/assume Y'
kekia	'X will place Y'
kata·kekia	'X will displace/elliminate/destroy/ruin Y'

kosġa	'X will engrave Y'
kata·kosġa	'X will scrape Y off'
kuoġni	'X will ague'
kata·kuoġna	'X will claim/maintain Y'
mitia	'X will explain Y'
kata·mitia	'X will clarify/reason for/define Y'
molka	'X will slide Y'
kat·o·molki	'X will move out of the way/make way/yield/submit'
neska	'X will ask Y'
kata·neska	'X will beg Y'
notsa	'X will take Y'
kata·notsa	'X will capture/abduct/run off with/be influenced by/look like (relative) Y'
ogja	'X will remember Y'
kat·ob·ogja	'X will reminisce/recall/reflect (on) Y'
kat·ib·ogji	'X will correspond/be similar (to) Y'
raja	'X will move'
kata·raja	'X will put Y aside (for later)/retract'
kat·o·ragji	'X will withdraw/retreat/recede/ebb (of tide)'
kat·o·rintai	'X will scratch (an itch)' (*rintai* does not exist)
śivi	'X will stay'
kata·śivi	'X will stay behind'
tatska	'X will consider/think about Y'
kata·tatstka	'X will reject Y'
tsasġa	'X will forget Y'
kata·tsaskku	'desolate/deserted/forgotten/abandonned'
tsġova	'X will discuss Y'
kata·tsġova	'X will describe Y'

§9.13.2 Simlpe Preverbal Adverbs

Simple preverbal adverbs have a simpler function than their locative counterparts. They can be freely added to almost any verb, or can also modify the verb's meaning. This is especially true of the prefixes hę- 'up' and tǔ- 'down'.

Like their locative counterparts, simple preverbal adverbs give extra information about the movement or manner of the verb, often refering to a dropped argument.

HĘ-   'up'

This preverb has the form hę-/hi- or hen- and has the general meaning 'up'.

hęsuvvis sǔma
[hæˈsuwːɪs ˈsøma]
hę-suvv-i-s se<Ø>i-hhi
up-flow-ASS.CONCL.ITR-HAB river-PAT
'the river flows up'

heniḍḍa segme
[henˈiðːa ˈsɛŋmːe]
hen-i<ḍḍ>-a-Ø seky-me
up-climb.PAST-ASS.CONCL.ITR cliff-GEN
'X climbed up the cliff'

It also modifies a number of verbs by changing their meaning:

auḍga	'X will tie Y into a knot'
hen·auḍga	'X will trick/deceit/catch Y (doing something)'
baulla	'X will wade Y'
hę·baulla	'X will face/encounter Y'
bùnta	'X will weave Y'
hę·bùnta	'X will charm/fascinate Y'
geḍḍa	'X will dig for Y'
hę·geḍḍa	'X will dig Y up/discover/uncover Y'
delpia	'X will flip Y over'
hę·delpia	'X will expose Y'
dì	'X will step'
hę·dia	'X will count Y'

etsa	'X will start Y'
hi·etsi	'X will take to the air (of birds)'
gogįa	'X will adze Y'
hę·gogįa	'X will excite/stimulate Y'
įairi	'X will row'
hen·įairi	'X will resist'
t·idi	'X will fall'
hę·t·idi	'X will realize/wake up suddenly'
įehtsgi	'X will walk (slowly)'
hen·įehtsga	'X will stalk Y'
t·įeḍḍi	'X will run/flow/go'
hę·t·įeḍḍi	'X will run/flow/go up, become excited/upset/enflamed'
t·igiri	'X will seep'
hę·t·igiri	'X will slowly happen/(X) little by little' (especially *hętigirō*)
ihha	'X will climb Y'
hen·ihha	'X will climb Y/conquer Y'
iksi	'X will shoot (an arrow)'
hen·iksi	'X will concede/admit (defeat)/grant/accept'
ila	'X will know Y'
hen·ila	'X will recognize Y'
ilka	'X will present/offer Y'
hen·ilka	'X will sacrifice Y'
iḍḍi	'X will get (somewhere)'
hen·iḍḍi	'X will get up'
įola	'X will read Y'
hen·įoli	'X will conclude/judge/assess (that)'
kaikni	'X will stare'
hę·kaikna	'X will contemplate/consider/imagine Y'
kekna	'X will organize Y'
hę·kekni	'X will set up camp/settle down'

komi	'it is summer'
hę·komi	'it is (the first part of) summer'
munta	'X will tread Y'
hę·munti	'X will walk/go up hill'
ta·nyppi	'X will stand out'
hę·nypmi	'it is obvious'
rehha	'X will pull Y'
hę·rehha	'X will find/invent/lie/come up with/say/claim Y'
ruodla	'X will fold Y'
hę·t·ruodla	'X will shrink/wrinkle/contract/react'
t·sadlu	'X will burn (in a pot)'
hę·t·sadlu	'X will burn up/consume/use up'
saiskia	'X will lead to Y'
hę·t·saiskia	'X will influence Y'
sidi	'X will understand'
hę·sida	'X will recognize/admit Y'
sivi	'X will stay'
hę·siva	'X will win/be superior/better than Y'

TŮ- 'down'

This preverb has the form **tů-/tym-** and has the meaning 'down'.

tůsomnui tůppůma
[tø'sɔmnːui 'tʰœʔpøma]
tů-somn-u-i tůppů-ma
down-fall-PAST-ASS.CONCL.ITR cone-PAT
'the cone fell down (something)'

tymukillji kehhya
[tymu'cilːji 'cʰehːwa]
tym-u-ki<ll>j-i kehh-ya
down-PASS-cut.PAST-ASS.CONCL.ITR pine.tree-PAT
'the pine tree was cut down (somewhere)'

It also modifies a number of verbs by changing their meaning:

aka	'X will cut Y'
tym·aka	'X will cut Y down/eliminate Y'
daḍbi	'X will drum'
tů·ta·daḍbi	'X will subside/ease up'
maivvi	'X will smile'
tů·maivvi	'X will frown'
jeḍḍi	'X will run/flow/go'
tym·jeḍḍi	'X will run smoothly/go well/go according to plan'
luhha	'X will boil Y'
tů·luhha	'X will make a broth/soup (out of Y)'
moġa	'X will drink Y'
tym·o·moġa	'X will gorge itself on/absorb Y'
ogja	'X will remember Y'
tym·ogja	'X will make note/inscribe/write down/record Y'
utśua	'X will pack Y'
tym·utśua	'X will compact/compress/press Y'

AH-   'after'

This preverb has the form **ah-/ahha-** and shows that something is done after or late(r).

kiḍga	'X will pick Y up'
ah·kiḍga	'X will clean Y up'
kita	'X will do Y'
ah·kita	'X will put Y off/back/postpone Y'
koairui	'X will howl'
ah·ta·koairui	'X will 'jump the gun'/react prematurely'
si	'X will understand'
ah·t·si	'X will grasp/realize Y'

AUR- 'mis-'

This preverb has the form **aur-/auh-** and shows that something fails, goes by or is side-by-side. This prefix is also found as **aiḥ-/aiḥo-** in certain dialects.

di	'X will step'
auh·ta·di	'X will misstep/make a mistake'
jeḍḍi	'X will run/go/flow'
aur·jeḍḍa	'X will miss out on/pass up/reject/refuse Y'
iksi	'X will shoot (an arrow)'
auh·t·iksi	'X will fail/backfire/misfire/miss'
neni	'X will sit'
auh·neni	'X will sit side-by-side'
sahhji	'X will speak'
auh·t·sahhji	'X will misspeak'
setġa	'X will place Y'
aur·setġa	'X will compare Y'
auh·t·seta	'X will misplace Y'
si	'X will understand'
auh·t·si	'X will misunderstand' (also commonly *aiḥotsi*)

GA- 'with'

This preverb has the form **ga-/gag-** and shows that something is done with someone else. It has a reciprocally comitative meaning ('with each other').

ga·gemi	'X will feel compassion/grief (with someone)'
jeḍḍi	'X will run/go/flow'
ga·t·jeḍḍi	'X will converge/meet/unite'
joa	'X will attack Y'
ga·joa [1]	'X will combat Y'
syvva	'X will show Y'
ga·syvva	'X will explain Y'
ga·temna	'X will be congratulate Y'

---

[1] Also exists as *gag·o·a*.

GAT- 'along'

This preverb has the form **gat-/gata-** and means 'along'. It is an accompanying comitative. It may also have a meaning of doing something 'accordingly' or as a reaction to something (thus often equivalent to the adverb 'back' in English).

askila	'X will control Y'
gat·askila	'X will handle Y'
gedli	'X will behave'
gata·gedli	'X will react'
keda	'X will carry Y'
gat·keda	'X will bring Y along'
koni	'X will walk'
gat·koni	'X will follow along/obey'
kosu	'X will be carried (sound)'
gat·kosu	'X will resound/echo (sound)'
saṡi	'X will speak'
gat·saṡi	'X will reply/talk back'
ob·ůkkůi	'X will fight'
gat·ob·ůkkůi	'X will fight back'

İL- 'forward'

This preverb has the form **il-/ila-** and shows that something goes forward, ahead, or that something is done/given/offered to someone.

di	'X will step'
il·di	'X will step forward/volunteer'
il·ta·nẏ	'X will unwind/develop'
oai	'X will say'
il·oai	'X will claim'
syvva	'X will show Y'
il·syvva	'X will present/offer Y'

il·o·tsieki	'X will crawl forward'

İRR- 'through'

This preverb has the form ir(r)-/irra- and shows that something goes through something or that is done with great success. Some dialects have jer- or jeh- instead of irr-.

kohhja	'X will rip Y'
ir·kohhja	'X will rip apart Y'
lukka	'X will pierce Y'
irra·lukka	'X will succeed at Y'

KEM- 'with'

This preverb has the form keu-/kem- (sometimes merging as ků-) and shows that something is done 'together' or as a group. It is generally found with plural subjects.

belmi	'X will work'
keu·belmiri	'they will cooperate'
neni	'X will sit'
keu·neni	'X will be correct/will compare/contrast'
nodi	'X will sing'
keu·nodiri	'they will sing together'
notsa	'X will take Y'
keu·notsari	'they will agree on Y'

KİL- 'again'

This preverb has the form kil-/kild(a)- and shows that something is done again or one more time.

t·eluli	'X will bloom'
kil·t·eluli	'X will recover/get revitalized'

iksi	'X will shoot'	
kil·iksi	'X will give another try'	
ona	'X will tell Y'	
kil·ona	'X will repeat Y'	
tsadna	'X will find Y'	
kil·tsadna	'X will recover Y'	

LOL- 'back'

This preverb has the form **lol-/lola-** and shows that something is goes back, behind or happens secretly or hidden from view.

mahha	'X will hunt Y'
lol·mahha	'X will stalk Y'
medga	'X will respect Y'
lol·medga·dna	'X will betray/be unfaithful to Y'
noski	'X will get somewhere'
lol·noski	'X will escape'
ogja	'X will remember Y'
lol·ogja	'X will regret Y'
tahhi	'X will leave'
lol·tahhi	'X will flee'

RAH- 'against'

This preverb has the form **rah-/rog(a)-** and shows that something is done against someone's will or in the opposite direction.

gjuki	'X will stride'
rag·gjuk·i	'X will persevere/continue'
jairi	'X will row'
rog·jairi	'X will row (at the opposite rhythm as someone else)'
joa	'X will attack Y'

rag·joa[1]	'X will counter attack'
neni	'X will sit'
rah·neni	'X will sit against each other/be parallel'
rah·nenõ	'in a row, consecutively'
notsa	'X will take Y'
rah·notsa	'X will rape/steal/rob Y'
oai	'X will say'
rog·oai[2]	'X will reply'
raja	'X will push Y'
rah·raja	'X will resist/protest/endure Y'
belmi	'X will work'
rah·belmi	'X will work in shifts'

TEKI- 'towards'

This preverb has the form **tek-**/**teki-** (sometimes merging as **teg-**) and has the meaning 'towards' or 'closer'. It tends to form transitive verbs from intransitive ones. It can also be used to mean 'roughly' or 'imprecisely'.

teki·goa	'X will pull (on) Y' (cf. *kata·goa* 'X will push (on) Y')
koni	'X will walk'
teki·kona	'X will approach Y'
oai	'X will say'
tek·oai	'X will continue (to say), to estimate'
saimni	'X will run'
tek·saimna	'X will charge at Y'
o·sali	'X will head (to)'
tek·sala	'X will aim for Y'
tapakva	'X will use a knife on Y'

---

[1] Also found as *rah·o·a*.

[2] Also found as *rog·vai* in the present.

teki·tapakva	'X will (roughly/imprecisely) use a knife on Y'

TEM- 'before'
This preverb has the form **tem-/teu-** (sometimes also **tŭ-**) and shows that something is done before or in advance.

aiska	'X will sew Y'
tem·aiska	'X will prevent Y'
pedni	'X will arrive'
teu·(ta)·pedni	'X will precede'
tŭ·pednotima	'preceding'
nuja	'X will see Y'
teu·nuja	'X will predict Y'
saisa	'X will warn Y'
tem·saisa	'X will forewarn Y'
t·vipsui	'X will flinch'
tŭ·t·vipsui	'X will anticipate/preempt Y'

TVE- 'in disorder'
This preverb has the form **tv-/tve-** and shows that something is done in the wrong order, in disorder, loosely, clumsily or with a certain level of freedom or at random.

goaka	'X will choose Y'
tve·goaka	'X will choose Y at random'
ta·koasga	'X will do Y regularly'
tve·ta·koasga	'X will be unpredictable/will happen unpredictably'
lola	'X will leave Y'
tve·lola	'X will leave Y in disorder'
losta	'X will take care of Y'
tve·losta	'X will neglect Y'
ogja	'X will remember Y'
tv·ogja	'X will remember Y incorrectly/confuse Y'

UNG- 'very/well'

This preverb has the form **ung-/ujo-** (sometimes also found as as **un-**) and shows that something is done in the right, correct way or may simply be translated as 'very'.

gaggana	'X will look at Y'	
ujo·gaggana	'X will examine/scrutiny Y'	
kyśa	'X will try Y'	
ung·o·kyśi	'X will make an effort/apply itself'	
sahhji	'X will speak'	
ujo·sahhja	'X will pronounce/enunciate Y'	
tayhha	'X will beat Y (at something)'	
ujo·tayhha	'X will vanquish/defeat Y'	
tegji	'X will be able to see'	
ung·i·tegji·bma	'X will (be able to) distinguish Y'	
ta·tihhjeni	'X will seem fresh'	
ujo·ta·tihhjeni	'X will seem very fresh'	

UT- 'around'

This preverb has the form **ut-/uta-** (sometimes merging as **ud-**) and gives a meaning of going 'around' or 'about'. It also implies a circumvention or acting without permission or not according to the rules.

audga	'X will tie Y into a knot'
ut·audga	'X will noose Y, have Y under control'
ut·autġu	'OK, yes, alright'
di	'X will step'
uta·di	'X will ignore Y'
kidga	'X will pick Y up'
uta·kidga	'X will be busy with Y'
koni	'X will walk'
uta·kona	'X will disobey/avoid Y'
noski	'X will get somewhere'
ud·noski	'X will use another way/way around'

ŮL-   'nearly'

This preverb has the form ůl-/ůlů- (sometimes also found as as ėu-) and shows something nearly or just about happens. In negative verbs, it may also mean 'hardly'. In some dialects, namely **Ėdnu** and **Riekka**, the negation and preverb merge as *semůlů* og *sůmůlů/sůmůrů* meaning 'hardly'.

t·idi	'X will fall'
ůl·t·idi	'X will nearly fall'
sem ikahaika	'X will not need Y'
sem ůl·ikahaika	'X will hardly need Y'
set kvìa	'X will not feel Y'
sem ůlů·kvia	'X will hardly feel Y'

Some less common preverbal adverbs include:

KEŚ-   'helping'

This preverb has the form **keś-/keśo-** and shows that someone is doing something in order to help, as a favor or replacing something else.

aiska	'X will sew Y'
keś·aiska	'X will assist at sewing Y'
koni	'X will walk'
keś·kona	'X will help Y walk'

SOŚ-   'from a distance'

This preverb has the form **soś-/soh-** and shows that someone is doing something from afar. It is most commonly used with the following verbs:

t·j·ėhhjeni·ka	'X will smell like Y'
soh·t·j·ėhhjeni·ka	'X will smell like Y from far away'
gag·i·totru·ita	'X is related to Y'
sośa·gag·i·totru·ita	'X is loosely related to Y'
tegji	'X will be able to see'
soś·tegja	'X will be able to see Y from a distance'
seja	'X will hear Y'
soh·seja	'X will hear Y from afar'

t·ůrůi   'X will approach'
soṡ·t·ůrůi   'X will approach from afar'

oina   'X will look at Y'
soṡ·oina   'X will spy on Y'

ŮR-   'from up close'

This preverb has the form **ůr-/ůh-** and shows that someone is doing something from up close. It is most commonly used with the following verbs:

kjoka   'X will weave Y'
ůr·kėuhku   'involved/related'
ůr·kjokō   'speaking of which, à propos'

koni   'X will walk'
ůr·kona   'X will be close/closely tied to Y'

oina   'X will look at Y'
ůr·oina   'X will examine/wonder about/reflect upon Y'

VŮ-   'after'

This preverb has the form **vů-/vůvv-** and shows that something is happening following something else, as a result. It is also found as **ve-/vevv-**.

lomi   'X will run around'
vů·loma   'X will pursue/chase Y'

rehha   'X will drag Y'
vůvv·u·rehhō   'as a result'

§9.14 Absolutive Descriptives

Absolutive descriptives are infixes which can be added directly to the root of verbs and the copula. They are housed in the slot 1 of verbs (directly onto the root)[1]. They are called absolutive descriptives because their main function is to describe the shape, state, form or nature of absolutive arguments, that is to say the subjects of intransitive verbs and the objects of transitive verbs. There are nine such markers and each describes a category of characteristics, usually descriptive of the shape or form of the arguments. Absolutive descriptives have four main functions.

They describe the shape/state/form/nature of:

1. The subject of an intransitive verb

2. The object of a transitive verb

3. The change of state of the subject of translative or passive intransitive verbs or the object of causal transitive verbs

They can also act as adverbs, generally describing the way in which the action is performed. Some descriptives may combine to form a more specific derivative and some extra descriptives exist but are very restricted in use (dialectally or in certain fixed expressions).

Absolutive descriptives are attached directly to the verb stem. Verb stems ending in a consonant see no change, whereas verb stems ending in a vowel have vowel coalescence. The absolutive descriptive markers lose their initial vowel if they precede an identical vowel.

For the formation of the past, the stem vowel is re-used after the absolutive descriptive. Consonant-final verbs use regular postverbal vowels:

sokli·a
['sɔkl:ia]
sokl=i-a-Ø-Ø
hoist-ASS.CONCL.TR-3P.PAT-3P.AG.SG
'X will hoist Y'

sokl·u·a
['sɔkl:ua]
sokl-u-a-Ø-Ø
hoist-past-ASS.CONCL.TR-3P.PAT-3P.AG.SG
'X hoisted Y'

---

[1] Siwa verbs can be preceded by three *preverbal* slots and followed by nine *postverbal* slots.

sokl·ohk·u·a
[ˈsɔklːɔhkua]
sokl-ohk-u-a-Ø-Ø
hoist-**ohk**-PAST-ASS.CONCL.TR-3P.PAT-3P.AG.SG
'X hoisted (a heavy thing/container)'

ked·a
[ˈcʰeda]
ked-a-Ø-Ø
carry-ASS.CONCL.TR-3P.PAT-3P.AG.SG
'X will carry Y'

kedd·a
[ˈcʰetːa]
ke<dd>-a-Ø-Ø
carry.PAST-ASS.CONCL.TR-3P.PAT-3P.AG.SG
'X carried Y'

kedd·ohk·a
[ˈcʰetːɔhka]
ke<dd>-ohk-a-Ø-Ø
carry.PAST-**ohk**-ASS.CONCL.TR-3P.PAT-3P.AG.SG
'X carried (something heavy)'

Absolutive Descriptives are not required for any verb, but are common in story telling and more vivid or expressive speech. They may also be found with the copula of there-existential sentences (or other there-existential verbs). In this case, the absolutive descriptives refer to the argument of the copula.

Siwa allows its speaker to state where or what something is by referring to it indirectly, only giving information about the shape or nature of the argument.

Syntactically, absolutive descriptives often occur once the object of the verb has already been mentioned, in which case they function as a descriptive of the argument. New objects however can be introduced with a descriptive whose function is then adverbial. And as stated above, the descriptives may also give information about the state of the argument as induced by the verb:

nubm·aht·a elepri
[ˈnʊʔpmahta ˈelɛpxi]
nu<bm>-aht-a-Ø eleba-ri
catch.PAST-**aht**-ASS.CONCL.TR-3P.AG.SG flower-PAT
'X gathered flowers (into a bouquet)'

sarkk·ahp·i·a
['sark:ahpia]
sarkk-ahp-i-a-Ø-Ø
break-ahp-PAST-ASS.CONCL.TR-3P.PAT-3P.AG.SG
'X broke Y into a point or a flake'

Compare the basic verb form *iruita* 'X bit into Y' when used with absolutive descriptive:

    iribuita
    [i'ribuida]
    i-r-ib-u-i-ta-Ø
    DIT-bite-ib-PAST-ASS.CONCL.ITR-into-3P.AG.SG
    'X bit into (something small)'
or   'a child/boy/girl bit into it'

    iriuluita
    [i'riuluida]
    i-r-iul-u-i-ta-Ø
    DIT-bite-iul-PAST-ASS.CONCL.ITR-into-3P.AG.SG
    'X bit into (something ripe)'

    irebuita~irjubuita
    [i'rebuida ~ i'rjubuida]
    i-r-eb/jub-u-i-ta-Ø
    DIT-bite-eb/jub-PAST-ASS.CONCL.ITR-into-3P.AG.SG
    'X bit into (something fresh/new)'

    irohnuita
    [i'rohnuida]
    i-r-ohn-u-i-ta-Ø
    DIT-bite-ohn-PAST-ASS.CONCL.ITR-into-3P.AG.SG
    'X bit into (something dry)'

    irohkuita
    [i'rohkuida]
    i-r-ohk-u-i-ta-Ø
    DIT-bite-ohk-PAST-ASS.CONCL.ITR-into-3P.AG.SG
    'X bit into (something big)'
or   'X took a big bite of X'

Compare these examples to the same verb but lacking a patientive argument (changing the verb from locative ditransitive to intransitive). The absolutive descriptive then describes the subject of the verb (the active agent).

ribui
['ribui]
r-ib-u-i-Ø
bite-ib-PAST.ASS.CONCL.ITR-3P.AG.SG
'a child/small animal bit'

§9.14.1 -AHP-

This absolutive descriptive is generally associated with long, flat, pointy or sharp objects, although large open spaces (skies, rivers, fields) may also be found with -ahp- then accentuating the openness, flatness or emptiness of the space. Below are examples of words which may trigger the use of absolutive descriptive -ahp- or may be referred to implicitly by it.

pointy / sharp / horned / hoofed / hard

ihpi	'arrow head, point'
usġas	'flake'
eteri	'spear'
ennju	'pole'
irri	'arrow'
tapaki	'knife'
nůjů	'knife'
sira	'fish'
aihha	'needle, thorn' (and by extension all thorny plants)
okęhi	'pine needle' (and by extension all trees with needles)
ridni	'itch' (and by extension most pains)
ri	'tooth'
salama	'antler/caribou' (and by extension all livestock)
goi	'point, edge'
nyly	'nose, snout'
tàs	'nose'
mokkuo	'beak'

gikkahpuma
['ɟi:ʔkahpuma]
gikk-ahp-um-a-Ø-Ø
sharpen-ahp-OBLI-ASS.CONCL.TR-3P.PAT-3P.AG.SG
'X must sharpen (a knife/spear)'

usarkkahpui
[uˈsarkːahpui]
u-sarkk-ahp-u-i-Ø
PASS-break-ahp-PAST-ASS.CONCL.ITR-3P.AG.SG
'X was broken into an arrow/point'

tsuoknahpua to hemi
[ˈtsʊɔʔŋahpua tʰɔ ˈhemi]
tsuokn-ahp-u-a-Ø to hemi-Ø
snatch-ahp-PAST-ASS.CONCL.TR-3P.PAT 3P.ACT.SG.ANI bird-ACT
'the bird snatched (a fish/bone)'

jahrahpa tṡeddjet
[ˈjahrahpa ˈtɕedʑːɛʔe]
<jahr>-ahp-a-Ø tṡeddjet-Ø
kill.PAST-ahp-ASS.CONCL.TR-3P.PAT old.man-ACT
'the old man killed (a caribou/fish)'

nantahpu ritṡa
[ˈnantahpu ˈritɕa]
na<nt>-ahp-u ri-tṡa
break.PAST-ahp-ASS.CONCL.TRANSL tooth-PAT
'a (sharp/pointy) tooth broke'

knirahpippen ma benho
[ˈkʰnirahpɪʔpɛn ma ˈbɛnhɔ]
knir-ahp-i-ppen m-a benho-Ø
smell-ahp-ASS.INCONCL.ITR-FREQU COP.PAST.INCONCL-ASS.TR dog-ACT
'the dog was sniffing around with its (long) snout'

long / flat / open / straight

gjaukama	'down, feathers'
kven	'feather'
alahra	'floating log'
birgo	'beam, log'
kili	'wood'
tini	'fire wood' (by extension also fires)
givo	'nail'
ehrana	'stick to hunt fish'
nomono	'fang'
deumu	'bone (tissue)'
demo	'(single) bone'

nìdla 'face, surface'
sèu 'river'
dìn 'barren field'
eulhi 'grassy field'
atsio 'glade' (and by extension other landscape features)

buikkahpuma tsi hemi
[ˈbʊɪʔkahpuma tsi ˈhemi]
buikk-ahp-um-a-Ø tsi hemi-Ø
pluck-**ahp**-OBLI-ASS.CONCL.TR-3P.AG.SG 3P.DAT.SG bird-DAT
'one needs to pluck the bird (of its feathers)'

tileḍḍahpini ůvvita
[tʰiˈleð:ahpini ˈowːida]
t-i-le<ḍḍ>-ahp-i-ni ůvv-ita
3P.UNAG-float-**ahp**-ASS.CONCL.ITR-CISLOC here-ILLAT
'a log/beam floated over here'

setġahpan ůaddja
[ˈsɛtːxahpan ˈøædʑːa]
setġ-ahp-a-Ø-n ůa-ddja
put-**ahp**-ASS.CONCL.TR-3P.PAT-2P.IMP right.here
'put it (wood, logs) right here'

so solukkahpui-a?
[ˈsːɔlʊʔkahpuja]
so s-o-lukk-ahp-u-i–a
INTERR 2P.UNAG.SG-SUBJ-prick-**ahp**-PAST-ASS.CONCL.ITR-INTERR
'did you prick yourself (with something sharp)?'

suḍḍahpi sůbů
[ˈsuðːahpi ˈsøbø]
su<ḍḍ>-ahp-i s<ůbů>
flow-**ahp**-ASS.CONCL.ITR river-PAT
'the river (narrowly, flatly) flowed'

idedlahpabi (nomono)
[iˈdetɬahpabi (ˈnɔmɔnɔ)]
i-de<dl>-ahp-a-bi-Ø (nomono-Ø)
DIT-show-**ahp**-ASS.CONCL.TR-1P.PL.RECI-3P.AG.SG (fangs-DAT)
'X showed us its (pointy fangs)'

tatśilahpippen
[tʰaˈtɕilahpɪʔpɛn]
ta-tśil-ahp-i-ppen-Ø
3P.PAT-hang-**ahp**-ASS.CONCL.TR-FREQU
'(bone, knife) hangs'

neynůrahpi ġyenneja eutśagi
[ˈneønørahpi ˈxwenːeja ˈeutɕaji]
neynůr-ahp-i ġye<nne>-ja eu-tśa-gi
billow-**ahp**-ASS.CONCL.ITR wind-INESS grassy.field-PAT-PL
'the (flat, long) grassy fields are billowing in the wind'

rekkahpaju rekkes
[ˈrɛʔkahpɑju ˈrɛʔcɛs]
rekk-ahp-aj-u rekke-s
open-**ahp**-PAST-ASS.CONCL.ITR sky-PAT
'the sky opened (widely) up'

or 'the sky opened up (in a narrow band)'

nenahpin!
[ˈnenahpɪn]
nen-ahp-i-n
sit-**ahp**-ASS.CONCL.ITR-2P.SG.IMP
'sit straight'

oġa on misas, sarkkahpia ju
[ˈɔxãõ ˈmisas ˈsarkːahpiaju]
<oġ>-a-Ø on misas-Ø, sarkk-ahp-i-a-Ø-Ø ju
take.PAST-ASS.CONCL.TR-3P.AG.SG ON rock-DAT, break-**ahp**-PAST-ASS.CONCL.TR-3P.PAT-3P.AG.SG JU
'X took the rock and broke it (into a point or flake)'

tśanda on demo, djiḍgahpia ju
[ˈtɕandãõ ˈdemɔ, ˈdʑɪðgahpiaju]
tśa<nd>-a-Ø on demo-Ø, dji<dg>-ahp-i-a-Ø-Ø ju
find.PAST-ASS.CONCL.TR-3P.AG.SG ON bone-DAT, carve-**ahp**-PAST-ASS.CONCL.TR-3P.PAT-3P.SG JU
'X found a bone and carved it (into something long and sharp)'

§9.14.2 -AHT-

This absolutive descriptive is used for things bound, packed or contained but also for things that are scattered around or large and/or formless (skins, things that have to be spread out). The words below are likely to trigger or be found with the absolutive descriptive -aht-. It may also confer an idea of 'tight' or 'full' to verbs such as *utśua* 'pack', *seta/setġa* 'put', *nůria* 'load, stuff' and *hiddjuja* 'stack' and *ha* 'to eat' (especially *o·h·aht·i* 'to eat oneself full').

large / formless / scattered / stuffed / packed

nośmo   'bag, pouch'
bename   'pouch, leather pouch'
pęles   'stuffed stomach, belly'
keggas   'baby, foetus'
bengomu   'roof, skins'
damu   'skin with fur'
jasuma   'animal skin'
iri   'skin, bark'
kehma   '(human) skin'
rihko   '(human) skin'
nuobmo   'stretched skin, window'
puna   'deer skin' (and by extension living deer)
pẏbme   'seal skin' (and by extension living seals)

isetġahtaitan
[i'sɛt:xahtɑidan]
i-setġ-aht-a-ita-Ø-n
DIT-put-aht-ASS.CONCL.TR-into-3p.pat-2P.SG.IMP
'put X into y (by stuffing it, pushing it, packing it)'

tymutśuahtan õkki
[tym'utɕʋahtan 'ɔʔci]
tym-utśu-aht-a-n omi-ki
down-press-aht-ASS.CONCL.TR-2P.SG.IMP snow-GEN
'compress the snow (tightly together)'

omahtimi
[ɔ'mahtɕimi]
o-<m>-aht-i-mi
subj-eat.PAST-aht-ASS.CONCL.ITR-1P.AG.SG
'I ate too much/until I was full'

kedahti na
['cʰedahtɕina]
ked-aht-i n-a-Ø
carry-aht-ASS.TR COP.INCONCL-3P.AG.SG
'she is with child'

iүavvahtumagga
[i'wɑw:ahtumɑk:a]
i-үavv-aht-um-a-Ø-gga
DIT-spread-aht-OBLI-ASS.CONCL.TR-3P.PAT-1P.AG.PL.INCL
'we have to spread (the skin, something that was packed) out'

vanahta nuomoma
['vɑnahta 'nuɔmɔma]
van-aht-a-Ø nuo<m>o-ma
stretch-aht-ASS.CONCL.TR-3P.AG.SG skin-GEN
'X will stretch the skin out (after having been packed)'

The absolutive descriptive -aht- is also used with things after falling to the ground and scattering or to allude to complex/complicated objects/tasks.

enclosed / contained / bound / dead

nęnnu	'box, container'
ohkis	'birch bark box'
saiyu	'pot, safe place'
kolra	'large container/pot/tub'
korù	'pot'
ailme	'tanned skin'
tulmu	'clothing' (and by extention all clothes)
amoi	'blood' (inside the body)
horet	'body, torso'
amora	'vein'
tȧhma	'heart'
bilin	'liver'
tśoadjun	'intestines, guts'
sȧhpa	'lungs'
mahhji	'fallen bear'
helba	'[pregnant] female moose' (and by extension *liota* 'female bear')
ipro	'carcass'
rohtot	'hollow tree' (by extension, old/abandoned/long dead structures/animals)
jata	'bowl'
tsgůli	'skull' (and by extension, all animal heads)
nję̀ut	'package, parcel, bundle'
hide	'hair' (when tied)
vebo	'knot'

utśodahti
[u'tɕɔdahtɕi]
u-tśod-aht-i-Ø
PASS-hold-aht-ASS.CONCL.ITR-3P.PAT
'X is held (in a box)'

luhhahti nata
[ˈluhːahtɕi ˈnɑta]
luhh-aht-i na-ta
boil-aht-ASS.ITR COP.INCONCL-3P.PAT
'(a pot) is boiling'

iruollahtaki tulmuma tobika
[iˈruɔlːahtɑɟi ˈtʰʊlmuma ˈtʰɔbiga]
i-ruo<ll>-aht-a-ki tulmu-ma tobi-Ø-ka
DIT-roll.PAST-aht-ASS.CONCL..TR-1P.RECI.SG clothes-GEN sister-ACT-1P.PAT.SG
'my older sister folded me clothes (into a container)'

bùbmuahti tàhma
[ˈbuːʔpmʊahtɕi ˈtʰæːhma]
bùbmo-aht-i tàhma-Ø
beat-aht-ASS.CONCL.ITR heart-ACT
'the heart beats (in the chest)'

njerterahtaka
[ˈnjɛrterahtɑga]
njerter-aht-a-ka
smart-aht-ASS.CONCL.TR-1P.PAT.SG
'I have chest pains'

konahti ma helba
[ˈkʰɔnahtɕi ma ˈhɛlba]
kon-aht-i m-a helba-Ø
walk-aht-ASS.ITR COP.INCONCL-ASS.TR pregnant.female.moose-ACT
'the female moose was walking (heavily due to pregnancy)'

śośia rihnahtui iprua
[ˈɕɔɕia ˈrɯhnahtui ˈɯpxua]
śoś-ia rihn-aht-u-i ipro-a-Ø
every-INESS is.scattered-aht-PAST-ASS.CONCL.ITR carcass-PL-ACT
'there were carcasses scattered on the ground everywhere'

medġahta tsġůldi
[ˈmɛðxahta ˈtsxœldʑi]
me<dġ>-aht-a-Ø tsġůli-di
shake.PAST-aht-ASS.CONCL.TR-3P.AG.SG skull-GEN
'X shook the (empty) skull'

omauḑgahtas hide
[ɔˈmaʊðgahtas ˈhide]
om-auḑg-aht-a-Ø-s hide-Ø
SUBJ-tie-aht-ASS.CONCL.TR-3P.AG.SG-HABT hair-DAT
'X usually ties her hair into a bun'

kiggahtaja on, tûtatiellia de suvo
[ˈcʰikːahtajãõ tʰɵtaˈtielːia de ˈsuvɔ]
ki<gg>-aht-a-ja-Ø on tû-ta-tiell-i-a-Ø de suvo-Ø
pick.up.PAST-ahta-ASS.CONCL.TR-3P.PAT.PL-3P.AG.SG ON down-3P.ACT.UNAG-miss PAST-ASS.COCNL.TR DE berry-DAT
'X missed the berries down and picked them up (from being scattered/into a container/gathered together)'

jasuma kedahta kepsi-ho gajo
[ˈjɑsuma ˈcʰedahta ˈcʰɛpsːihɔ ˈgajɔ]
jasuma-Ø ked-aht-a kepsi-Ø–ho g-a-io-Ø
tanned.skin-AGT carry-aht-TR mushroom-DAT-3P.ANI.POSS COP.PAST-ASS-INESS.REL-3P.AG.SG
'the skin in which X carried mushrooms (as a bag)'

§9.14.3 -ATST- or -ADDI̧-

This absolutive descriptive is similar to -ahp- but usually also entails some sort of fragility, breakability or flexibility which -ahp- lacks. In opposition to -aht-, -atst- can also imply loose, not bound. -atst- is also sometimes used when talking about women and children to underline their fragility. The difference between -ahp- and -atst- is that the former refers to long, solid or hard things (like a spear, large branch, pole, big stick) while the latter refers to long, fragile or thin things (like a branch, blade, a stick).

thin / long / narrow / fragile

hide	'hair' (when loose)
hiri	'hair' (on body)
kèppa	'arm' (of women or children)
miebi	'leg'
nayi	'waist'
tsġiame	'cedar strip'
nidagan	'stripe'
aihha	'needle' (for sewing)
aihhabi	'coniferous branch'
baja	'branch'
letse	'stick/pole'

kaibmu	'stick, walking stick, support'
tvela	'blade'
holi	'stem'
jeigge	'path' (in snow)
moni	'path, way'
mykyt	'way along a river'
rodlot	'wrinkle' (and by extension old faces)

suḍḍatsti hiedi
['suð:atst:i 'hiedʐi]
su<ḍḍ>-atst-i hi<Ø>e-di
flow.PAST-**atst**-ASS.CONCL.ITR hair-PAT
'X's hair flowed (unbound)'

isyvvatstakin tieka
[i'syw:atst:ɑɟ̞n 'tiega]
i-syvv-atst-a-ki-n tie-ka
DIT-show-**atst**-ASS.CONCL.TR-1P.RECI.SG-2P.SG.IMP hand-GEN
'show me your hand (to a child/woman)'

de ju sopratstajagjen
[deju 'sɔpxatst:ɑjɑj:ɛn]
de ju sopr-atst-a-ja-gjen
so then split-**atst**-ASS.CONCL.TR-3P.PAT.PL-4P.AG
'then we split them (into long thin strips)'

nantatstu aihka
['nantatst:u 'ɑɪhka]
na<nt>-atst-u aihha-ka
break.PAST-**atst**-ASS.CONCL.TRANSL needle-PAT
'the (thin) sewing needle broke'

aḍgatstami letsġeita
['aðgatst:ɑmi 'lɛtsxeida]
a<ḍg>-atst-a-Ø-mi le<tsġe>-ita
cut-**atst**-ASS.CONCL.TR-3P.PAT-1P.AG.SG stick-ILLAT
'I cut X into sticks'

katamakatsti rihta
[kʰɑtɑ'mɑkatst:i 'ri:hta]
kata-mak-atst-i ri=h-ta
from-goes-**atst**-ASS.CONCL.ITR skin-PAT
'the skin is peeling off in flakes'

oahkurtatsti
[ˈɔahkʊrtatstːi]
oahkur-t-atst-i-Ø
test-PAST-atst-ASS.CONCL.ITR-3P.AG.SG
'X tested the snow's depth (with a blade, stick)'

cf. *oahkurrahpi*
[ˈɔahkurːahpːi]
oahkurr-ahp-i-Ø
test-ahp-ASS.CONCL.ITR-3P.AG.SG
'X tested the snow's depth (with a long branch, spear)

konatsti nata
[ˈkɔnatstːi ˈnɑta]
kon-atst-i n-a-ta
walk-atst-ASS.ITR COP.INCONCL.TR-3P.AG.SG
'X is walking (with a walking stick/cane)'

kataḍgatsta
[kʰatˈaðgatstːa]
kat-a<dg>-atst-a-Ø-Ø
from-cut.PAST-atst-ASS.CONCL.TR-3P.PAT-3P.AG.SG
'X cut (a branch/stem/strip) off'

gakodatstiri
[gɑˈkɔdatstːiri]
ga-ko<d>-atst-i-ri
along-walk.PAST-atst-ASS.CONCL.ITR-3P.AG.PL
'they walked in a queue/path'

nėuntaddjia kiḍba
[ˈnø:ntadʑːia ˈcʰɪðba]
nėunt-addj-i-a-Ø ki=ḍba
close-atst-PAST-ASS.CONCL.TR-3P.AG.SG eyes-DAT
'X closed its (wrinkly/thin) eyes'

mahhaddjoḥa
[ˈmɑ:hadʑːɔʔa]
mahh-addj-oḥa
follow-atst-1P.PL.IMP
'let's follow (the river, path)'

akatstake omi deiko oġami tsġiauhdi
[ˈakatstːaɟe ˈomi deigɔ ˈɔxami ˈtsxɪaʊhdʑi]
ak-atst-a-ke omi d-e-iko <oġ>-a-mi tsġiaug-di
cut-atst-TR-LINK.GOAL for COP-INFER-ELAT.REL take.PAST-ASS.CONCL.TR-1P.AG.SG cedar.wood-GEN
'I took cedar wood in order to cut out of it (*tsġiame* 'cedar stripes')'

tetatsta sviladi nogjita
[ˈtʰetatstːa ˈsviladʑi ˈnɔjːida]
<tet>-a-atst-a-Ø-Ø svi<l>a-di nogj-ita
place.PAST-atst-ASS.CONCL.TR-3P.PAT-3P.AG.SG braid-GEN at.end.ILLAT
'X placed Y (a hair needle) at the end of X's braid'

§9.14.4 -IB- or -IḎB-

This absolutive descriptive is generally descriptive is small and young things and can carry a diminutive connotation as well. It is commonly used in speech with children. The form -iḏb- is especially common for round things or things that roll. Unlike other absolutive descriptives, it is often used to describe the subject of verbs whether they are transitive or intransitive, especially if the subject is a child.

round / fat / little / small / fine / young / ripe

hogi	'ball, pearl'
bieli	'fat'
tśibi	'baby, toddler'
eno	'little bay'
hylys	'little/thin person'
kydly	'bell, little girl'
kori	'boy'
dida	'girl'
tśegma	'child'
kigjini	'youngest child'
njunni	'little child'
suvo	'berry' (and by extension all berries and fruits)
pivi	'cheek' (and by extension young/healthy faces)

manibin
['manibɪn]
man-ib-i-n
come-ib-ASS.CONCL.ITR-2P.SG.IMP
'come here (to a child)'

mairibi
['mairibi]
mair-ib-<i>-Ø
laugh-ib-PAST.ASS.CONCL.ITR-3P.AG.SG
'X giggled, X laughed (of something small, cutely)'

tśitśibi
['tɕitɕibi]
tśitś-ib-i-Ø
crawl-ib-ASS.CONCL.ITR-3P.AG.SG
'X crawls around (of a child)'

tiddid̦bi
['tidːɪðbi]
t-i<dd>-id̦b-i
3P.PAT-fall-id̦b-ASS.CONCL.ITR
'X fell (and rolled around)'

biaid̦bakin
['bɪaɪðbaɟɪn]
bia-id̦b-a-Ø-ki-n
throw-id̦b-ASS.CONCL.TR-3P.PAT-1P.RECI.SG-2P.SG.IMP
'throw X at me (by rolling it on the ground)'

edġibi
['ɛðxibi]
e<dġ>-ib-i-Ø
sit.down.PAST-ib-ASS.CONCL.ITR-3P.AG.SG
'the boy/girl/child sat down'

hid̦baundan
['hɪdbaʊndan]
h-id̦b-a-unda-n
eat-id̦b-ASS.CONCL.TR-DIM-2P.SG.IMP
'eat a few (berries)'

or   'eat a few (to a child)'

nëuntiban
[ˈnøːntɕiban]
nëunt-ib-a-Ø-n
close-ib-ASS.CONCL.TR-3P.PAT-2P.SG.IMP
'close (your eyes)'

kediba nata
[ˈcʰediba ˈnata]
ked-ib-a n-a-Ø-ta
carry-ib-TR COP.INCONCL-ASS-3P.PAT-3P.AG.SG
'X is carrying a baby/is pregnant'

sġittiba śośia njunnie
[ˈsxɪʔtiba ˈɕoɕia ˈɲunːie]
sġi<tt>-ib-a śoś=ia njunni-Ø-e
there.is.little.PAST-ib-ASS every.INESS child-AGT-PL
'there were little children everywhere'

§9.14.5 -IKS-

This absolutive descriptive is often used in pair with the pejorative or things perceived to be old, broken, no good or bad. It can also be found to refer to tools and stones. In combination with the pejorative, the preverb **aiḥ-** 'wrongly', **-iks-** can be added to verbs to confer a sense of performing the action in a completely wrong way:

gikka nŭjŭma nana
[ˈɟiːʔka ˈnøjøma ˈnana]
gikk-a nŭjŭ-ma n-a-na
sharpen-ASS.TR knife-GEN COP.INCONCL-TR-2P.AG.SG
'you are sharpening your knife'

aiḥeggikkiksa nŭjŭma nana
[aiʔeˈɟiːʔka ˈnøjøma ˈnana]
aiḥe-gikk-a nŭjŭ-ma n-a-na
wrong-sharpen-ASS.TR knife-GEN COP.INCONCL-TR-2P.AG.SG
'you are sharpening your knife all wrong'.

crooked / broken / cold / old / tools / pieces / arrows / projectiles

boġi	'deciduous branch'
njuhhi	'old woman'
tśeddjet	'old man'

iu	'older relative'
davva	'past, old times'
śeśo	'old tree'
kene	'broken/dead tree'
kvispi	'scraper'
eidbi	'cutter, carving tool'
eirpi	'tool'
soroko	'piece'
kidjut	'part, room' (and by extension most rooms)
irri	'arrow'
tȯ	'stone'

mansiksi tśeddjet
['mansɪks:i 'tɕedʑ:ɛʔɛ]
ma\<ns\>-iks-i tśeddjet-Ø
come.PAST-**iks**-ASS.CONCL.ITR old.man-ACT
'the old man came'

kodiksiḥḥen
['kɔdɪks:iʔɛn]
ko\<d\>-iks-i-ḥḥen-Ø
walk.PAST-**iks**-ASS.CONCL.ITR-FREQU-3P.AG.SG
'(an old person) kept on talking'

iddiksi śeśue
['i:t:ɪks:i 'ɕeɕue]
i\<dd\>-iks-i śeśo-e
fall.PAST-**iks**-ASS.CONCL.ITR old.tree-PAT
'an old tree fell'

delpiksumagga kene
['dɛlpɪks:umɑk:a 'cʰene]
delp-iks-um-a-gga kene-Ø
flip.over-**iks**-OBL-ASS.CONCL.TR-1P.AG.PL dead.tree-DAT
'we must flip the (old) dead tree over'

gikkiksa nami
['ɟi:ʔcɪks:a 'nami]
gikk-iks-a n-a-Ø-mi
sharpen-**iks**-ASS.TR COP.INCONCL-TR-3P.PAT-1P.AG.SG
'I am sharpening (the tool)'

aniksia
[a'nɪks:ia]
a=n-isk-i-a-Ø-Ø

```
PAST.throw-iks-PAST-ASS.CONCL.TR-3P.PAT-3P.AG.SG
```
'X threw (a stone)'

rostiksa oddjobmua-ho
[ˈrɔstɪkːsa ˈɔˈdʑːɔʔpmuahɔ]
ro<st>-iks-a odj=tsobmu-Ø-a–ho
lies.there.PAST-iks-TR PEJ-finger-AGT-PL–3P.POSS.ANI
'X's old (crooked) fingers were lying there'

katakostiksa hõttamo
[kʰatakɔstɪkːsa ˈhɔ̃ʔtamɔ]
kata-ko<st>-iks-a-Ø hõtta-mo
from-rip.PAST-iks-ASS.CONCL.TR-3P.PAT gust.of.wind-PAT
'the gust of wind ripped it away (branch/arrow/piece of wood)'

§9.14.6 -IPR-/-IBĠ- or -IUL-

These absolutive descriptives refer to things that are alive, moving, wet and may confer vigour to an absolutive argument or the verb. The -iul- is especially common with liquids and wet things. Certain speakers add -ibġ- to underline the animacy of the absolutive argument. The verb *siv·ibġ·i* or *siv·ipr·i* is often used with bad weather (patientive).

lively / living / fresh / pretty / vivid / spry / plants / happy / bright / coloured / intense / warm / clear

ȯlma	'leaf' (and by extension all leaves or vegetation)
eleba	'flower' (and by extension all flowers)
ė	'plant' (and by extension all plants)
kepsi	'mushroom' (and by extension all fungi)
homot	'insect' (and by extension all insects)
tsammi	'forest'
tasko	'woods'
elet	'meadow'
miuki	'bog'
njelsi	'sprig'
pihba	'sapling'
idlu	'sprout'
gilra	'drizzly weather'
igmo	'rapidly changing/unpredictable weather'
butta	'bad weather'
rõtta	'foggy weather'
ujo	'(fresh/clear) water' (and by extension all fresh water bodies)
omġautsaka	'fall colors'

śabśibġui ġyenneja òlkagi
[ˈɕabɕɪbxui ˈxwenːeja ˈʊːɬkɑji]
śabś-ibġ-u-i ġye<nne>-ja òl-ka-gi
sway-ibġ-PAST-ASS.CONCL.ITR wind-INESS leaf-PAT-PL
'the leaves swayed spryly in the wind'

edlibġi iludi
[ˈetɬɪbxi ˈiːludʑi]
e<dl>-ibġ-i i<l>u-di
grow.PAST-ibġ-ASS.CONCL.ITR sprout-PAT
'a sprout grew'

negipra tśekśigi
[ˈneɟpxa ˈtɕɛkɕːiji]
n<eg>-ipr-a-Ø tśek-śi-gi
see.PAST-ipr-ASS.CONCL.TR-3P.AG.SG child-GEN-PL
'X saw children (moving, playing)'

homottibġuima tsamśia
[ˈhɔmɔʔtɪbxuima ˈtsamɕia]
homott-ibġ-u-i-ma tsa<mś>-ia
is.quiet-ibġ-PAST-ASS.TR-INCONCL forest-INESS
'it was quiet (but teeming with life) in the forest'

kodiuligga irta
[ˈkʰɔdiulikːa ˈɪrta]
ko<d>-iul-i-gga irta
walk.PAST-iul-ASS.CONCL.ITR-1P.AG.PL.INCL through
'we walked through (a bog, a wet place)'

śivvibġi gilradi
[ˈɕiwːɪbxi ˈɟɪlrɑdʑi]
śi<vv>-ibġ-i gilra-di
stay-ibġ-ASS.CONCL.ITR wet.weather-PAT
'there was (lit. stayed) wet weather'

amġibġi
[amˈxɪbxi]
a=mġ-ibġ-i-Ø
drink.PAST-ib-ASS.CONCL.ITR-3P.AG.SG
'X drank (fresh water)'

nubmipra sù
['nʊʔpmɪpxa 'suː]
nu\<bm\>-ipr-a-Ø su\<v\>o
pick.PAST-ipr-ASS.CONCL.TR-3P.AG.SG ON berry-GEN
'X picked (brightly colored/ripe) berries'

rekkiulu nata
['rɛʔciulu 'nɑta]
rekk-iul-u n-a-ta
open.up-iul-ASS.CONCL.TRANSL COP.INCONCL-ASS-3P.AG.SG
'(a flower) is opening up'

iriuliaita
[i'riuliɑida]
i-r-iul-i-a-ita-Ø
DIT-bite-iul-PAST-ASS.CONCL.TR-ILLAT-3P.AG.SG
'X bit into (something ripe)'

§9.14.7 -JUP-/-YP-/-EB-

Similar to -ipr-/-ibġ-/-iul-, this absolute descriptive is used to infer a sense of something wet, humid or fresh. However, -jup- is also used heavily with smells. While the previous descriptive denoted a certain vitality, this descriptive also invokes freshness or the idea of something ephemeral. Thicker liquids also usually appear with -jup-, such as honey, resin, sap. The descriptive can be found as -jup- or -jub-, -yp- or -yb- or -ůb- after rounded vowels, and -eb- in other cases.

Compare the two examples contrasting the idea of 'wet' or 'living' with -ibġ- and the idea of 'fresh' (previously unexposed) or 'wet (but not alive)' with -jup-.

rekkjubia giandid
['rɛʔcjubia 'ɟɑndʑɪdʑ]
rekk-jub-i-a-Ø giandi-d
open-jup-PAST-ASS.CONCL.TR-3P.AG.SG rotten.fallen.tree-GEN
'X opened up the rotten fallen tree (which had not been exposed before)'

rekkibġia giandid
['rɛʔcɪbxia 'ɟɑndʑɪdʑ]
rekk-jub-i-a-Ø giandi-d
open-ibġ-PAST-ASS.CONCL.TR-3P.AG.SG rotten.fallen.tree-GEN
'X opened up the rotten fallen tree (which was wet or teeming with life)'

iddibġi òlkagi
['itːɪbxi 'ʊːɬkɑji]
i\<dd\>-ibġ-i òl-ka-gi
fall.PAST-ibġ-ASS.CONCL.ITR leaf-PAT-PL
'the (wet/living) leaves fell off' (animate)

iddjupi òlmamo
['idʑ:ubi ʊ:lmamɔ]
i<dd>-jup-i òlma-mo
fall.PAST-jup-ASS.CONCL.ITR leaf-PAT
'the (wet) leaves fell off' (inanimate)

wet / humid / fresh / new(ly born) / smells

siġva	'rain'
nieugi	'mist'
õut	'newly fallen snow'
sira	'fish' (and by extension all fish)
sitru	'soup'
kikin	'soup, meal'
sivi	'honey'
ljò	'resin'
ijuri	'pitch' (and by extension glues and sticky things)
maudli	'maple sap'
paġlis	'urine'
tsemmi	'animal tracks'
akna	'traces'
ėmsi	'smell' (and by extension all smells)
mieri	'moss'
kjori	'rotten wood'
kelta	'ground'
seuma	'soil'
ůmů	'earth'

sasleba meihhie ma màhra
['sastɬeba 'meih:iema 'mæ:hra]
sasl-eb-a meihhi-e m-a màhra-Ø
lick-eb-ASS.TR honeycomb-GEN COP.INCONCL-TR bear-ACT
'the bear was licking (the honey out of) the honeycomb'

ykjůbis njuhhi-go
['ycjøbɪs 'ɲuh:igɔ]
ykj-ůb-i-s njuhhi-Ø–go
collect-ůb-ASS.CONCL.ITR-HABT old.woman-ACT-1P.SG.POSS
'my grandma usually goes around collecting (resin/honey/pitch)'

katabiebuma (paġlihi)
[kʰɑtɑˈbiebuma (ˈpʰaxlihi)]
kata-b=i-eb-um-a-Ø (paġli-hi)
from-throw-eb-OBL-ASS.CONCL.TR-3P.AG.SG urine-GEN
'X must go (urinate)'

tśandjupagga tśemme
[ˈtɕandʑubɑkːa ˈtɕemːe]
tśa<nd>-jup-a-gga tśemmi-e
find.PAST-jup-ASS.CONCL.TR-1P.AG.PL.INCL animal.tracks-GEN
'we found (fresh) animal tracks'

hętśadnjupeba
[hæˈtɕaʔtɲubeba]
hę-tśadn-jup-e-ba-Ø
up-find-jup-INF.CONCL.TR-1P.PAT.PL.INCL-3P.AG.SG
'X will find us out (by our smell)'

hękeyebi keltariska ma niûbid
[hæˈcʰewebi ˈcʰɛɫtɑrɪskama ˈniøbɪdʑ]
hę-key-eb-i ke<lt>a-ri=ska m-a nieugi-d
up-rise-eb-ASS.ITR ground-ABLA COP.INCONCL.PAST-TR ground.mist-PAT
'ground mist was rising up from the (fresh/wet) ground'

jekkjupi õuttaita bidjiska
[ˈjɛʔcjubi ˈõːʔtɑida ˈbidʑɪska]
je<kk>-jup-i õutta-ita bidjis-Ø-ka
run.PAST-jup-ASS.CONCL.ITR new.snow-ILLAT puppy-ACT-PL
'the puppies ran into the newly fallen snow'

knirreba ůmůma
[ˈkʰnirːeba ˈømøma]
kni<rr>-eb-a-Ø ůmů-ma
smell.PAST-eb-ASS.CONCL.TR-3P.AG.SG earth-GEN
'X smelled (the fresh) earth'

sinda on retro, miaddjupa ju
[ˈsɪndɑ̃õ ˈrɛtxɔ ˈmɪadʑːubaju]
si<nd>-a-Ø on retro-Ø mia<att>-jub-a-Ø ju
catch.PAST-ASS.CONCL.TR-3P.AG.SG ON northern.pike-DAT, gut.PAST-jub-ASS.CONCL.TR-3P.PAT-3P.AG.SG
'X caught a northern pike and then gutted it (still fresh)'

kvigjupake on kimi atseba oskon, keidigga ka
['kʰviːjːubɑɟẽ 'cʰimi ɑˈtseba 'ɔskɔn 'cʰeidʑikːaka]
kvi-jup-a-ke on kimi at=s-e-ba oskon-Ø keid-i-gga ka
feel-jup-TR-LINK.ADV ON for NEG=COP-INFER-1P.PAT.PL male.moose-AGT, light.fire-ASS.CONCL.ITR-1P.AG.PL.INCL KA
'so the moose does not feel us (our smell), we will light a fire'

iddjupi òlmamo
['idʑːubi 'ʊːlmamɔ]
i<dd>-jub-i òlma-mo
fall.PAST-jub-ASS.CONCL.ITR leaf-PAT
'the (wet) leaves fell'

§9.14.8 -OHN/-ÕHN-

This absolutive descriptive is opposite to -ibġ- and -jup- in that it invokes something dry, powdery and also refers to dry smells and fire.

powder / dirt / sand smells (dry/fire/wood)

neyri	'powder, dust'
vihi	'dust, dirt'
lůri	'dirt, scum'
lagjas	'flour'
rento	'grain, seed'
kelho	'hung meat'
siehhumi	'dried meat'
sẏkẹhi	'dried needle bed'
oni	'dried moss, tinder' (and by extension inflammable things)
tinin	'fire wood'
sogjì	'drought'

ġillohni noimmika
['xiːlːɔhni 'nɔimːiga]
ġi<ll>-ohn-i nobem-m=ika
crackle-ohn-ASS.CONCL.ITR fire-ELAT
'the fire was cracking (dryly)'

isidlohniki
[iˈsiːtɬohniɟi]
i-si<dl>-ohn-i-ki
DIT-blow.PAST-ohn-ASS.CONCL.ITR-1P.RECI.SG
'I got dirt/sand/smoke (in my eyes)'

sarkkohnia tinis
['sark:ɔhnia 'tinɪs]
sarkk-ohn-i-a-Ø tini-s
break-**ohn**-PAST-ASS.CONCL.TR-3P.AG.SG firewood-GEN
'X broke (dry) firewood'

tamaduohni
[tʰama'dʊɔhni]
tama-d=u-ohn-i-Ø
on-step.PAST-**ohn**-ASS.CONCL.ITR-3P.AG.SG
'X stepped (on something dry)'

irohnuita
[i'rɔhnuida]
i-r-ohn-u-i-ta-Ø
DIT-bite-**ohn**-PAST-ASS.CONCL.ITR-into-3P.AG.SG
'X bit into (something dry)'

tsaundohni
['tsaʊndɔhni]
t-sau<nd>-ohn-i
3p.unag-catch.on.fire.PAST-**ohn**-ASS.CONCL.ITR
'X caught on fire (from being too dry)'

myrrohna pini
['myr:ɔhna 'pʰi:ni]
m<yrr>-ohn-a-Ø pini-Ø
grind.PAST-**ohn**-ASS.CONCL.TR-3P.AG.SG corn-DAT
'X ground the corn (into a flour)'

tsahhōhni
['tsɑh:ōhni]
t-sahh-ōhn-i
3P.UNAG-burn-**ōhn**-ASS.CONCL.ITR
'(dry wood/tinder) will burn'

hepohni na nûnamo
['hepɔhni na 'nʊnamɔ]
hep-ohn-i n-a nṹ<n>a-mo
break-**ohn**-ITR COP.INCONCL-ass wave-PAT
'the waves are breaking (on the sand)'

luhhōhna
['luh:ōhna]
luhh-ōhn-a-Ø-Ø
boil-**ōhn**-ASS.CONCL.TR-3P.PAT-3P.AG.SG
'X will boil (a tea/treatment/grounded leaves)'

iyavvohnaibma
[iˈwɑwːɔhnaɪʔpma]
i-ɥavv-ohn-a-ibma-Ø
DIT-spread-ohn-ASS.CONCL.TR-ALLAT-3P.AG.SG
'X spread/add (flour/sand/dirt/dried ingredients) on it'

§9.14.9 -OHK-

The absolutive descriptive -ohk- generally refers to large, heavy, male or difficult things. It is also used with the verbs *seja* 'listen', *odena* 'look', *kyśa* 'try', *pitta* 'pay attention to' in the imperative to make a more emphatic demand:

sejohkan
[ˈsejɔhkan]
sej-ohk-a-Ø-n
listen-OHK-ASS.CONCL.TR-3P.PAT-2P.SG.IMP
'listen well!'

odnohkan~oinohkan   'look well!'
[ˈɔʔtnɔhkan~ˈɔinɔhkan]
odn~oin-ohk-a-Ø-n
look-OHK-ASS.CONCL.TR-3P.PAT-2P.SG.IMP

kyśohkan
[ˈcʰyɕɔhkan]
kyś-ohk-a-Ø-n
try-OHK-ASS.CONCL.TR-3P.PAT-2P.SG.IMP
'try (your best)'

pittohkan
[ˈpʰɪʔtɔhkan]
sej-ohk-a-Ø-n
pay.attention-OHK-ASS.CONCL.TR-3P.PAT-2P.SG.IMP
'pay all your attention to X'

In addition, it also refers to long things such as neck/throat/tongue, heads, geese and swans and even canoes.

large / round / cylindrical / long / heavy / male / big / difficult

tahha	'tree' (and by extension all large trees)
sukno	'large conifer'
půdů	'log'

sikvut	'bonfire'
tŭmkki	'boulder'
hokon	'big rock'
oskon	'male moose' (and by extension all [large] male animals)
okon	'big man'
toron	'big bear/guy'
peilini	'eldest'
ņjelli	'chief'
sappiska	'paw, big hand'
selo	'large river'
sinin	'big fish'
ata	'(open) mouth'
gegin	'(animal) mouth'
kvoga	'throat'
oadi	'tongue'
niman	'neck'
totami	'head'
giga	'goose' (and by extension all long-necked birds)
gŭme	'rope'
tonkua	'sinew'
kehkjo	'canoe'
mavvu	'meat'

iddohki śeśue
['iːtɔhci 'ɕeɕue]
i<dd>-ohk-i śeśo-e
fall.PAST-**ohk**-ASS.CONCL.ITR old.tree-PAT
'the big old tree fell (heavily)'

kedohkan ŭat
['cʰedɔhkan 'œææ?æ]
ked-ohk-a-n ŭat-Ø
carr-**ohk**-ASS.CONCL.TR-3P.PAT-2P.SG.IMP this-DAT
'carry this (heavy thing)'

mairiohki
['mairɔhci]
mair=i-ohk-i-Ø
laugh.PAST-**ohk**-ASS.CONCL.ITR-3P.AG.SG
'X laughed (loudly)

or   '(a large man) laughed'

maiḍḍohki
[ˈmaiðːɔhci]
mai<ḍḍ>-ohk-i-Ø
smile.PAST-**ohk**-ASS.CONCL.ITR-3P.AG.SG
'X smiled from ear to ear'

nẏh sindohkami keppi
[ˈnyːh ˈsɪndɔhkami ˈcʰɛʔpi]
nẏh si<nd>-ohk-a-mi keppi-Ø
wow catch.PAST-**ohk**-ASS.CONCL.TR-1P.AG.SG head-DAT
'wow, I caught a big one'

rekkohkin
[ˈrɛʔkɔhcɪn]
rekk-ohk-i-n
open-**ohk**-ASS.CONCL.TR-2P.SG.IMP
'open wide (your mouth)'

sarkkohkia mekvi
[ˈsarkːɔhcia ˈmɛkːvi]
sarkk-ohk-i-a-Ø mekvi
break-**ohk**-PAST-ASS.CONCL.TR-3P.AG.SG swan-DAT
'X broke the swan('s neck)'

katagiohka kohdaika
[kʰataˈɟɪɔhka ˈkʰɔhdaiga]
kata-g=i-ohk-a-Ø koh=da-ika
from-push.PAST-**ohk**-ASS.CONCL.TR-3P.AG.SG anchorage.on.beach-ELAT
'X pushed (the canoe) from the its anchor on the shore'

tamokevvohki toron
[tʰamɔˈcewːɔhci ˈtɔrɔn]
tam-o-kevv-ohk-i toron-Ø
on-SUBJ-rise-**ohk**-ASS.CONCL.ITR big.bear-AGT
'the big bear (heavily) stood up (on its two legs)'

tatsġatskohki
[tʰaˈtsxatskːɔhci]
ta-tsġa<tsk>-ohk-i
3P.UNAG.SG-tear.PAST-**OHK**-ASS.CONCL.ITR
'(the rope/leather) tore'

katśaḍgohkaika soroko
[kʰatɕˈaðgɔhkaiga ˈsɔrɔgɔ]
kat-i-a<ḍg>-ohk-a-ika-Ø soroko-Ø
from-DIT-cut.PAST-**ohk**-ASS.CONCL.TR-ELAT-3P.AG.SG piece-DAT
'X cut (a large) piece from it'

hohkas
['hɔhkas]
h-ohk-a-Ø-Ø-s
eat-**ohk**-ASS.CONCL.TR-3P.PAT-3P.AG.SG-HAB
'X eats (meat/a lot)'

Absolutive descriptives in Siwa are a useful way of implying something about the subject of intransitive verbs or the object of transitive verbs. Each descriptive covers a certain number of qualities, often shapes (long, sharp, straight, large, etc.), qualities (hard, bundled, dead, fragile, fat, young, odorant, etc.) or allude to the doer's gender, age or physical status. This allows speakers of Siwa to use contextual information in order to avoid directly naming participants. Because Siwa's third person has no overt form, either as a subject (agentive) or an object, it is possible that absolutive descriptives emerged as a disambiguative device, similar to the distinction between the proximate and obviative third person and the fourth person found in Siwa pronouns.

§9.15 Complementization

To form subordinate conjunctions, Siwa uses an infixed complementizer, hosted in slot 2. The complementizer's function is that of the English word *that* as in *I know that you saw me* – the complementizer, or subordination conjunction, relates a main clause to a subordinate clause. It is added directly after the root of a verb, but following absolutive descriptives. In addition, the complementizer carries negation, such that negative subordinate phrases are not negated by the regular *sę/set/sem* particle. The complementizer differs slightly when used with the copula, whether dependent or independent. Some speakers do not make use of the dependent complementization infix but rather use the independent copula instead (some have a special short form in Ø-ų-. The use of complementization on adjectives with the dependent copular is very much disappearing from common use.

Another role of the complementizer is to act as a relative marker for participles. Below are the different forms of the complementizer, which vary according to whether it is added to a vowel-final or consonant-final stem of a copula or a verb.

The vowel-final forms -**tot**- and -**tont**- are also found as -**rot**- and -**ront**-, and a shorter form of the complementizer exists for verbs. Alternative negative forms in -**ents**- also exist, typically used in the western dialects.

	positive	negative	
vowel-final	-tot- -rot-	-tont- -ront-	-rents-

	positive	negative	
consonant-final	-ot-	-ont-	-ents-
copular vowel-final	-non-	-nont-	-nents-
copular consonant-final	-on-	-ont-	-ents-

In addition to negative forms in -ont-, forms in -ōtġ- or -ōtsġ- also exist, but may be considered more emphatic. Negative copular forms are not as common as using the negative copula (si-), or may be found doubly negated with both the negative copula si- and the negative complementizer -(n)ont-.

	makimi	'I will come'
	mak·ot·imi	'...that I will come'
	mak·ont·imi	'...that I won't come'
	mak·ōtsġ·imi	'that I will *not* come'
	utśua	'X will pack Y'
	utśo·tot·a	'...that X will pack Y'
	nuppuami	'I will snatch Y'
	nuppu·ront·ami	'...that I won't snatch Y'
	daḍb·ahti nata	'(the heart) is beating'
	daḍb·ahti n·on·ata	'...that (the heart) is beating'
	uinuata	'X is true'
	dona uino	'...that X is true'
	uino·nont·ata	'...that X isn't true' (rare, often ungrammatical!)
rather:	dontata uino	'...that X isn't true'
	sinonata uino	'...that X isn't true (singly negated)'
	sinontata uino	'...that X isn't true (doubly negated)'

noairi sihrotśoi
['nɔɑiri 'sɪhrotɕɔi]
<n>oa-i-ri si<hr>-ot-joi
PAST.say-ASS.CONCL.ITR-3P.AG.PL rain.PAST-COMPLE-INFER.ITR.COND.IRREAL
'they said that it would rain'

ogjan herenonas komyly
['ɔj:an 'herenɔnas 'kʰɔm'yly]
ogj-a-n here-non-a-s kom=yly-Ø
remember-TR-IMP.2P.SG cold-COMPLE-COP.ASS-HAB summer=night-AGT
'remember that summer nights are cold'

tabmami gonteta negi
[ˈtʰaʔpmami ˈgonteda ˈneɟi]
tat-m-a-Ø-mi g-ont-e-ta negi-Ø
think-INCONL-ASS.TR-3P.PAT-1P.AG.SG COP.PAST.CONCL-COMPL.NEG-INFER-3P.PAT 2P.SG.PRON-AGT 3P.INA-AGT
'I think that it wasn't you'

nonaki hunimo orpotiohna
[ˈnɔnaɟi ˈhunimɔ ˈɔrpɔtɕɪɔhna]
n-on-a-ki hun-i-mo-Ø orp-ot-i-o-h-na
PAST-tell-ASS.CONCL.TR-1P.RECI.SG wind-ITR-ACT.PART.AG-AGT misbehave-COMPLE-PAST-INFER.ITR-HAB-2P.AG.SG
'the wind told me you are misbehaving yourself' (i.e. a little someone told me…)

§9.15.1 Short Forms

The complementizer for verbs has short forms sometimes found in attributive forms of adjectival verbs. They are more common with nouns with a certain familiarity, and for that reason are more epithetic than the regular forms (used in titles).

	positive	negative
vowel-final	-t-	-ts-
consonant-final	-o- / -ų- / -v-	-ō(t)s-

Short forms are also typically found with participles. The most common forms are as follow. Note that short forms lack the distinction between agentive and unagentive forms. These doubly short forms (both the complementizer and the participle are shortened) are common in the eastern dialects.

	long	short
singular	-ot·i·ma	-ųen/-ven
	-ot·i·mo	-ųen/-ven
plural	-ot·i·mi	-ųin/-vin

	ośmi	'strong'
	somi oś·v·ima	'(the) strong man' (also *ohhjotima*)
or	*somi ośven*	
	somi ohhį·ōts·ima	'(the) man who is not strong' (also *ohhjontima*)
	tośmi	'young'
	kori toś·v·ima	'(the) young boy' (also *tohhjotima*)
or	*kori tośven*	
	kori tohhį·ōs·ima	'(the) boy that is not young' (also *tohhjontima*)

	pigjima	'healthy'
	dida pigj·o·mi	'(the) healthy young girl' (also *pigjotima*)
	atemi	'sick'
	njuhhi ate·v·ima	'(the) sick old woman' (also *atetotima*)
or	*njuhhi ateųen*	

§9.15.1.1 Short Forms in Direct Speech

Short forms are very commonly found after a quote or direct speech. This is especially true of the Siwa narrative style. The most common forms are:

dakkųa	'...X asked' (cf. *dakka* 'X asked Y')
noati	'...X said' (also *noavvi*, cf. *noai* 'X said Y')
bialtta	'...X said' (*bialla* 'X said Y')
aiskųa	'...X answered' (cf. **aiska** 'X answered Y')
mjaguḍḍųa	'...X exclaimed' (also *mjagutva*, cf. *mjaguḍḍa* 'X exclaimed Y')
joddųi	'...X screamed' (also *jotvi*, cf. *joddi* 'X screamed')
daddųi	'...X thought' (also *datva*, cf. *dadda* 'X thought Y')

§9.16 Copula

Siwa has a copula whose infinitive is *ta·mi* 'to be' (split stem has many dialectal forms including *tà, tẹ, dà, dẹ,* most commonly *tà* then identical to *tàsa* 'to stand'). The They behave differently and perform various functions in the phrase, namely to form copular constructions, which are used to form relative and infinitive clauses and more. The copula has two forms – the independent copula and the clitical copula. The independent copula stands on its own and serves many purposes, whereas the clitical copula is only found as the verb 'to be' with adjectives. The copula has most of the regular constituents of a verb but behaves different. Both copulas' conjugations are irregular.

The copula can be found in three main roles:

Independent copula
       the verb 'to be' with nouns
       copular constructions

Clitical copula
       As a clitical form of the verb 'to be' with adjectives

§9.16.1 Independent Copula

The independent copula is used for the following purposes:

1. To form there-existential phrases
2. As the verb *ta·mi* 'to be' whose argument is not an adjective
3. To form the inconclusive of all verbs except adjectival and impersonal verbs
4. To form relative clauses
5. In various other constructions (link constructions)

The independent copula consists of a root, augmented by a postverbal vowel. As such, it behaves exactly like regular verbs, having the same number of slots with the addition of the slot COP -1 (see *§9.2.2*). This extra slot houses the relative marker o-/on- (in non-locative relative phrases).

The copula has 9 distinct stems.

non-past
    indicative
        conclusive   *d·a* (or short form *Ø·a*)
        inconclusive   *n·a* (or short form -n)
    habitual   *s·a* (or short form -s)
    perfective   *ol·a* (or also *or·a*)

past
    indicative
        conclusive   *g·a*
        inconclusive   *m·a*
    habitual   *sġ·a*
    perfective   *odl·a*
imperative   *nent·a*

The copula is negated internally. These are it's negative forms:

non-past
    indicative
        conclusive   *at·sa*
        inconclusive   *ant·a*
    habitual   *ass·a*
    perfective   *olt·a*

    past
        indicative
            conclusive   *aks·a*
            inconclusive   *ahm·a*

habitual	askk·a
perfective	ots·a, olts·a
imperative	neist·a

When in the indicative optative assertive (-ua-) or inferential (-ue-) and the translative conditional realis assertive (-ui-) and optative inferential (-ue-), certain forms of the copula may have a v- instead of a diphthong, which in turn may modify the copula (sometimes only with the relative prefix):

o·dua	or	(o)·tva
o·due	or	(o)·tve
o·dui	or	(o)·tvi
sua	or	sva
sue	or	sve
sui	or	svi
olua/orua	or	olva/orva
olue/orue	or	olve/orve
olui/orui	or	olvi/orvi
o·gua	or	(o)·kva
o·gue	or	(o)·kve
o·gui	or	(o)·kvi

These forms are more formal than the regular ones.

In copular constructions, the split-stem is much less commonly preceded by adverbial phrases, unlike regular constructions which may favour adverbs appearing before the verb. Adverbs preceding split-stems are very emphatic:

õska neniehmi tamiemi
'I often want to sit alone'

netasa, neni õska tamiemi osuami
'you know that I often want to sit alone'

netasa, õska neni tamiemi osuami
'you know that I often want to sit alone'

§9.16.1.1 There-Existential Phrases

There-existential phrases state that something is or exists. All there-existential phrases have an agentive subject and a transitive (or possibly translative) form. The most basic there-existential verb is the copula, *da*. The inconclusive forms *na* and *ma* are usually only used with clearly temporary phenomena.

da tahha	'there is a tree'
dohka tahha	'there is a (big) tree' (with **-ohk-** absolutive descriptive)
da soakkia kekila	'there is a hearth in the house'
sġa soakkia kekila	'there used to be a hearth in the house'
sġe somi	'there once was a man'
sġe somigi	'there once were men'
nenta siġva	'let there be rain!'
neista sogji!	'let there not be drought!'
na siġva	'there is rain (right now)'
ma taja omi	'there was a lot of snow (at that moment)'
ora iyo	'there's been trouble'
oltsa suikildas	'there hasn't been inhabitation'
atsa havva	'there is no such thing'
sa moni	'there is usually a way'

assa miola sahhontama
[ˈasːa ˈmiɔla ˈsahːɔntama]
as=s-a miola-Ø sahh-ont-a-ma
NEG=COP.HAB-ASS flame-AGT burn-COMPLE.NEG-ASS.CONCL.TR-HAB-ACT.PART.UNAG
'there is no flame that does not burn'

da tsamśia tahha
[da ˈtsamɕia ˈtʰahha]
d-a tsa\<m\>-ś=ia tahha-Ø
COP.-ASS forest-INESS tree-AGT
'there is a tree in the forest'

na bengommeima kekki ōkko
[na ˈbeŋːɔmːeima ˈcʰɛʔci ˈɔ̃ʔkɔ]
n-a bengo\<mme\>-ima kekki-Ø omi-ko
COP.INCONCL-ASS roof-ADESS too-AGT snow-GEN
'there is too much snow on the roof'

However, even the copula can be found in a reduced form, especially in the present, then simply *a* (sometimes this short version has a more aoristic meaning)

da tahha	'there is a tree'
a tȯ	'there's a rock' (in general)

In fact, the copula can be replaced in specific cases with other copula-like verbs. They are used in specific cases and often say something about their arguments' size or distribution. A few of these verbs have a stronger form, more or less created through reduplication. They behave much like the copula, even in relative clauses.

ind·a	'there are a few (scattered around)'
inind·a	'there are very few (scattered everywhere)'
tsekl·a	'there are many/is much'
tsehil·a	'there are very many/is very much'
repp·a, rapp·a	'there is (in water)'
ɥar·a, ar·a	'there is' (often used with locatives)
kiah·a	'there is (something big/large number)'
kiahaḥ·a	'there is something (huge/very large number)'
sġin·a, sigg·a	'there are few/is little/is (something little)'
sġikin·a	'there are very few/is very little/is (something tiny)'
tůmpů·a	'there is (something formless, disgusting or scary)'
rohhi̯·a, rihn·a	'there is (something lying/resting/stuck)'

inda jogjia utra
['ɪnda 'jɔj:ia 'ʊtxa]
ind-a jogj=ia utra-Ø
is.few-ASS.CONCL.ITR there-DIST.INESS.APROX crowberry-AGT
'there are a few scattered (bunches of) crowberries over there'

ininda hiedia-so ėu
['ɪnɪnda 'hiedʑiasɔ ø:]
inind-a hi<Ø>e-d=ia–so ėu-Ø
is.very.few-ASS.CONCL.ITR hair-INESS-2P.POSS.SG sand-AGT
'there is sand (everywhere) in your hair'

tsekla tahhia saimnenka
['tɕɛk:la 'tʰɑh:ia 'saɪmn:ɛŋka]
tsekla-a tahh-ia saimnen-Ø-ka
is.many-ASS.CONCL.ITR tree-INESS starling-AGT-PL
'there are many starlings in the tree'

reppa nęnumeja kuiliska
['rɛʔpa 'nænumeja 'kʰuilɪska]
reppa-a nę<n>u-me=ia kuilis-Ø-ka
is.in.water-ASS.CONCL.ITR container-INESS tadpole-AGT-PL
'there are tadpoles (swimming) in the container (filled with water)'

yara rapuka arrui sirůků
['wɑra 'rɑpuga 'arːui 'siːrø̞ɟø]
yar-a rapu-ka arrui sirůků-Ø
is.somewhere.-ASS.CONCL.ITR door-GEN next.to.STATIC spider-AGT
'there is a spider somewhere by the door'

sġina sirůků
['sxina 'siːrø̞ɟø]
sġin-a sirůků-Ø
is.small-ASS.CONCL.ITR spider-AGT
'there is a small (number of) spider'

kiaha sirůků
['cʰiaʔa 'siːrø̞ɟø]
kiah-a sirůků-Ø
there.is.big-ASS.CONCL.ITR spider-AGT
'there is a big (number of) spider'

tůmpůa hiedia-go toadni
['tʰœmpœa 'hiedʑiagɔ 'tʰɔaʔtni]
tůmpů-a hi<Ø>e-d=ia–go toa-dni
is.formless-ASS.CONCL.ITR hair-INESS-1P.SG.POSS some.INA-AGT
'there is something in my hair'

rosta kvohmia nokos
['rɔsta 'kʰvɔhmia 'nɔkɔs]
ro<st>-a kvog-m=ia nokos-Ø
is.resting.PAST-ASS.CONCL.TR throat-INESS stick-AGT
'there was a stick (stuck) in the throat'

§9.16.1.2 To Be

The independent copula *ta·mi* serves as the verb *to be* in cases where the argument of the verb is a noun or a pronoun. For inherent qualities and aorist statements, the conclusive is used rather than the habitual. The case of both the object and subject of the copula is normally the agentive, although the partitive-genitive is allowed for uncountable nouns. It is also very common to use a relative construction, usually leaving out the main copula to form such phrases. In relaxed speech, the relative marker o- may also be dropped all together. This is perhaps due to the fact that the copula is often found after its argument (in all copular constructions), unlike regular verbs.

1P.SG	d·a·mi	'I am'
2P.SG	d·a·na	'you are'
3P.SG	d·a·ta	'X is'
1P.PL.INCL	d·a·gga	'we are'
1P.PL.EXCL	d·a·gge	'we are'
2P.PL	d·a·dda	'you are'
3P.PL	d·a·ri	'they are'
3P.OBV	d·a·t	'X is'
4P.	d·a·jo	'one is'

The third person singular has the ending -ta with the copula, which differs from the normal -Ø ending found in verbs. This happens to be identical to the unagentive and patientive endings of the third person. Thus, one can have the following form:

    datata   'X is Y'

However, to avoid this redundancy, Siwa speakers will generally replace the sequence -ta-ta- by - -det- or -jet- or -ret-.

    dadet or dajet or daret   'X is Y' or 'yes'

Another unique feature of the copula is the so-called short relative form in the present oa or alternatively ya/va/ra instead of the regular oda. The inferential and the relative form combine as ue to form a more polite or modest statement.

    nalbi ue ůat   'this is (my) husband'
    soaki ue ůat   'this is (my) house'

In addition, the form ueta is a more polite 'yes'.
    In copular constructions, the copula is commonly found in a locative case (deita, deika, gaika). These forms have corresponding shorter forms which do not distinguish evidentiality. Short forms are more common in younger males. They vary greatly across dialects:

LONG	SHORT
-eita, -aita	-et, -eḍ
-eika, -aika	-eġ, -et

kesůami nori deita	'I want to learn to sing' (standard)
kesůab nori det	'id.' (relaxed, familiar)

The copula can only be found in the transitive or translative. The translative form of the copula is common with passive verbs in copular constructions. It is not, however, found with translative verbs (the translative is either marked exclusively on the split-stem or the copula, but not both).

or
    u·kiekvui   'X was stolen'
    u·kiekvi o·g·u   '(X) which was (got) stolen' (lit. became stolen)
    u·kiekvi o·g·a   '(X) which was stolen' (already)

Below are more examples of the verb *ta·mi* 'to be':

    da ojula to tahha-ůt
    [da ˈɔjula tʰɔ ˈtʰɑhːæœʔ]
    d-a ojula-Ø to tahha-Ø–ůt
    COP-ASS birch.tree-AGT this.ANI.AGT tree-AGT–DET.PROXI
    'this tree is a birch'

    ojula oa to tahha-ůt
    [ˈɔjula oɑ tʰɔ ˈtʰɑhːæœʔ]
    ojula-Ø o-d-a to tahha-Ø–ůt
    birch.tree-AGT (REL)-COP-ASS this.ANI.AGT tree-AGT–DET.PROXI
    'this tree is a birch' (lit. [it is] a birch that this tree is)

    gata ojula
    [ˈgɑta ˈɔjula]
    g-a-ta ojula-Ø
    COP.PAST-ASS-3P.AG.SG birch-AGT
    'it was a birch'

    dami somi
    [ˈdɑmi ˈsɔmi]
    d-a-mi somi-Ø
    COP-ASS-1P.AG.SG man-AGT
    'I am a man'
    (or *somi oami / y̨ami / rami*)

    da somi megi
    [ˈda ˈsɔmi ˈmeɟi]
    d-a somi-Ø megi-Ø
    COP-ASS man-AGT 1P.PRON.SG.AGT
    'me, I am a man'

§9.16.1.3 Relative Clauses
The copula is necessary to create relative clauses. There are various types of relative clauses:

> subjective
> Subject in main clause is subject in relative clause

> objective
> Argument in the main clause is a patientive or recipient object in the relative clause

> possessive relative clause
> Argument in the main clause possesses the argument in the relative clause

> locative relative clauses
> Relative clause argument is in a locative case

In all of these cases, relative clauses are formed by splitting the verb into the split-stem and the copula. The details of this split are found in *§9.2.2*.

All relative causes, unless they contain a relative locative marker (see section *§9.12.2*), are found with the relative marker **o-** (or **on-** before a vowel) prefixed to slot COP -1.

The copula is found in the following forms with the relative prefix.

>   **non-past**
>   indicative
>   conclusive   *o·d·a* (or short form *o·a*)
>   inconclusive   *o·n·a*
>   habitual   *o·s·a*
>   perfective   *on·or·a*
>
>   **past**
>   indicative
>   conclusive   *o·g·a*
>   inconclusive   *o·m·a*
>   habitual   *o·sġ·a*
>   perfective   *on·odl·a*
>   imperative   *o·nent·a*

Similarly, the negated forms are:

non-past
    indicative
        conclusive   o·t·sa
        inconclusive   o·nt·a
    habitual   o·ss·a
    perfective   on·olt·a

past
    indicative
        conclusive   o·ks·a
        inconclusive   o·hm·a
    habitual   o·skk·a
    perfective   on·ots·a
imperative   o·neist·a

When the copula itself is the main verb of the relative clause, it is found in its normal first position with the appropriate relative marker (this includes the copula-like there-existential verbs, though not in all dialects).

    *selga, koni sẏsġita-go **oga***   'the young woman who walked past me'
    *selga, **oga** hjŭdja*   'the young woman who was pregnant'

More examples:

    nalbi, oda tairsi elusara
    [ˈnalbi ɔˈda ˈtʰaɪrsi ˈeluˈsara]
    nalbi-Ø o-d-a tairsi-Ø elu=sara-Ø
    husband-AGT, REL-COP-ASS worker-AGT excellent-AGT
    'a husband who is an excellent worker'

    riehpi, osġa suosa isi hjoaikna
    [ˈrɪɛhpi ɔˈsxa ˈsuɔsa ˈisi ˈhjɔaɪʔŋa]
    riehpi-Ø, o-sġ-a suosa-Ø isi hjoaikna-Ø
    wife-AGT, REL-COP.PAST.HAB mother-AGT so caring-AGT
    'a wife who used to be/was once such a caring mother'

    soaki, odo kitġō lolsoka
    [ˈsɔɑɟi ɔˈdo ˈcʰɪtxō ˈlɔlsɔga]
    soaki-Ø, o-d-o kitġ=ō lolsoka-Ø
    house-AGT, REL-COP.INFER.TRANSL soon abandoned.house-AGT
    'a house which will soon become abandoned (lit. a *lolsoka*)'

    kistamo, odo kesġamo

['cʰɪstamɔ ɔˈdɔ ˈcʰɛsxamɔ]
kista=mo-Ø o-d-o kesġa=mo-Ø
student-AGT REL-COP.INFER.TRANSL teacher-AGT
'a student who will become a teacher'

garoko, ohma takeulmo
[ˈgarɔgɔ ɔhˈma ˈtʰacɛʊlmɔ]
garoko-Ø o=s=m-a takeulmo-Ø
boy-AGT REL-COP.NEG.INCONCL righteous=man-AGT
'the little boy who was being naughty' (lit. not a righteous man)

opo, oa iu
[ˈɔpɔ ɔˈa ˈiu]
opo-Ø o-a iu-Ø
person-AGT REL-COP.ASS older=relative-AGT
'a person who is an older relative'

tahha, otsa piġo
[ˈtʰɑh:a ɔˈtsa ˈpʰixɔ]
tahha-Ø o=t=s-a piġo-Ø
tree-AGT REL-COP.NEG.ASS conifer-AGT
'a tree which is not an conifer'

ėu, onininda kygjuaja
[ˈø: ɔnˈinɪnda ˈcʰyj:uɑja]
ėu-Ø on-inind-a ky=jua=ja
sand-AGT REL-be.scattered-ASS boots-INESS
'sand which is (scattered around) in (my) boots'

kuiliska, orappa śintadia
[ˈkʰuilɪska ɔˈraʔpa ˈɕɪntadʑia]
kuilis-Ø-ka o-rapp-a śinta-d=ia
tadpole-PL-AGT REL-be.in.water-ASS pond-INESS
'the tadpoles which (swim) in the pond'

The imperative is used in relative clauses in a way which has no equivalent in English, often similar to vocative expressions.

viekna, onenta viekke!
[ˈvɪɛʔŋa ɔˈnenta ˈvɪɛʔce]
viekna-Ø o-nent-a viekke-Ø
thief-AGT REL-COP.IMPER-ASS bruised-AGT
'(you) thief, curse you! (lit. thief, which may be a bruised person)'

tarilni-go, oneistu njuhhi!
[ˈtʰarɪlnigɔ ɔˈnɛɪstu ˈɲuh:i]
tarilni-Ø–go o-neist-u njuhhi-Ø

beautiful.person-AGT-1P.POSS.SG REL-COP.IMPER.NEG-ASS old.woman-AGT

'my beauty, may you not turn into an old woman! (lit. my beautiful woman, which may not become an old woman !)'

Below are more examples of phrases and equivalent relative clauses:

PHRASE	RELATIVE CLAUSE
INDEPENDENT	COPULAR

śivis nìndia somi
['ɕivɪs 'niːndʑia 'sɔmi]
śiv-i-s n<i>n=di=a somi-Ø
stay-ASS.ITR.CONCL-HAB hut=INESS man-AGT
'the man stays in a hut'

somi, śivi nìndia osa
['sɔmi 'ɕivi 'niːndʑia ɔ'sa]
somi-Ø śiv-i n<i>n=di=a o-s-a
man-AGT stay-ITR hut=INESS REL-COP.HAB-ASS
'the man who stays in a hut'

ukeddika nonia nìndia-ůt
[u'cʰetːiga 'nɔnia 'niːndʑiæœ?]
u-ke<dd>-i-ka non=ia n<i>n=di=a–ůt
PASS-bear.PAST-ITR-1P.PAT.SG this.INA.INESS hut=INESS–DET.PROXI
'I was born in this hut'

nidna, ukedi gajoka
['nɪʔtna u'cʰedi 'gajɔga]
nidna-Ø u-ket-i g-a-jo-ka
hut-AGT PASS-bear-ITR COP.PAST.CONCL-ASS-INESS.REL-1P.PAT.SG
'the hut I was born in'

sunnumi sakkia na iski
['sunːumi 'saʔcia na 'iːsci]
suv=num-i sa<kk>=ia n-a iski-Ø
berry=gather-INCONCL.ITR berry.field-INESS COP.INCONCL-ASS woman-AGT
'the woman is gathering berries in the field '

iski, sunnumi ona
['iːsci 'sunːumi ɔ'na]
iski-Ø sun=num-i o-n-a
woman-AGT berry=gather-ITR COMPLE-COP.INCONCL-ASS
'the woman gathering berries'
or
'the woman who is gathering berries'

numi sakkia sù pildi ma iski
['numi 'saʔcːia 'suː 'pʰɪldʑi ma 'iːsci]
num-i sa<kk>=ia s=ù pil-di m-a iski-Ø
gather-ITR.INCONCL berry.field-INESS berry.gen red.gen COP.PAST.INCONCL-ASS woman-AGT
'the woman was gathering red berries in the field'

iski, kautsġa suvuo pila gaikomi
['iːsci 'kʰaʊtsha 'suvuɔ 'pʰila 'gaigɔmi]
iski-Ø kautsġ-a suvo-Ø-o pila-Ø g-a-iko-mi
woman-AGT make.jam-TR berry-DAT-PL red-DAT COP.PAST.CONCL-ASS-ELAT.REL-1P.ACT.AG.SG
'the woman whose red berries I turned into jam'

§9.16.1.3.1 Subjective Relative Clauses

The subject relative clause construction has the subject or argument of the main clause as the subject of the relative clause.

main clause	relative clause			main clause
	main verb	verbal phrase		copula
somi ['sɔmi] somi-Ø man-AGT	soaka ['sɔaga] soak-a build-TR	dappen dauśka ['daʔpɛn 'dauɕka] dappen dauś=ka alone last.year-GEN	atsi sùḍbi-ůt ['atsi 'suːðbɪœʔ] at=si sùḍbi-Ø–ni this.INA.DAT winter.camp-DAT–DET.PROXI	oga [ɔ'ga] o-g-a REL-COP.PAST.CON CL-ASS
somi, soaka dappen dauśka atsi sùḍbi-ůt oga 'the man who build this camp by himself last year'				

Siwa allows reduction of relative clauses in certain cases. The whole of the relative clause may be moved before the noun and using a participle with a relative marker (which, in participles, is the same as a complementizer) instead. This is usually only found with subject relative clauses.

relative clause		main clause
verbal phrase	main verb	
dappen dauśka atsi sùḍbi-ůt ['daʔpɛn 'dauɕka 'atsi 'suːðbɪœʔ] dappen dauś-ka at=si sùḍbi-Ø–ni alone last.year-GEN this.INA.DAT winter.camp-DAT–DET.PROXI	soaḍgotamo ['sɔaðgɔdamɔ] soaḍg-ot-a-mo build.PAST-COMPLE-ASS.CONCL.TR-PRES.PART.AG	somi ['sɔmi] somi-Ø man-AGT
dappen dauśka atsi sùḍbi-ůt soaḍgotamo somi 'the man who build this camp'		

More examples:

suvo, njalu osven oda
['suvɔ 'ɲalu 'ɔsvɛn ɔ'da]
suvo-Ø njal-u os=ven o-d-a
berry-AGT taste-TRANSL sour-ADV REL-COP-ASS
'a berry which tastes sour'

tòmo, ikòi hemtaitagi odeṡi
['tʰʊːmɔ i'kʊːi 'hɛmtaidaji ɔ'deɕi]
tòmo-Ø i-kò-i hem-ta=ida-gi o-d-e-ṡi
tribe-AGT DIT-speak-ITR bird-ILLAT-PL REL-COP-INFER-HABIL
'a tribe who can apparently speak with birds'

maihhi oa ta tahha, eukiula maulika oda
['maihːi ɔ'a tʰa 'tʰɑhːa 'euɟiula 'mauliga ɔ'da]
maihhi-Ø o-a ta tahha-Ø euk-iul-a mau<I>i-ka o-d-a
mapple-AGT REL-(COP)-ASS 3P.PRON.INA.AGT tree-AGT produce-IUL-TR maple.sap-GEN REL-COP-ASS
'the tree which produces **maudli** (maple sap) is the maple'

lolkůkiami malma, oahrjukka ogaka
[lɔl'cœciami 'malma 'ɔahrjʊʔka ɔ'gaka]
lol=kůk-i-a-mi malma-Ø oahrjukk-a o-g-a-ka
back=bring-PAST-ASS.CONCL.TR-1P.AG.SG jelly.fish-DAT sting-TR REL-COP.PAST-ASS-1P.PAT.SG
'I brought back the jelly fish that stung me'

eu, amagju sǵůgju osibma ode
['eu a'majːu 'sxøjːu 'ɔsɪʔpma ɔ'de]
eu-Ø a-magj-u sǵůgju os-ibma o-d-e
scar-AGT TRANSL-white-TRANSL never 2P.PRON.SG-ABLA REL-COP-INFER
'a scar which will never fade (from you[r face])'

isyvvakin gobi, mụihnu saidgia onora
[i'sywːaɟɪn 'gɔbi 'mwɪhnu 'saɪðɟia ɔn'ɔra]
i-syvv-a-ki-n gobi-Ø mụihn-u saip-k=ia on-or-a
DIT-show-ASS.CONCL.TR-1P.RECI.SG-IMP.2P.SG oar-DAT damage-TRANSL race-INESS REL-COP.PERF-ASS
'show me the oar which has been damaged in the race'

sẏkęhi, oninda keingaria
['syːɟæhi ɔn'ɪnda 'cʰeiŋːaria]
sẏkęhi-Ø on-ind-a kei<ng>a-r=ia
needle.bed-AGT REL-be.scattered-TR floor-INESS
'the dried needle bed, which lies scattered around the floor'

§9.16.1.3.2 Objective Relative Clauses

The objective relative clause construction is when the subject or argument of a main clause is the object of the relative clause. Pronouns are not repeated in the relative copula.

There are two types of object relative clauses: patientive and recipient. Patientive agents are more similar to normal subject relative clauses, in that the object marker is left out. Recipient relative clauses mark their ditransitivity on the main verb and use the illative relative marker in the copula, which lacks its normal relative marker o-.

main clause	relative clause		copula
	main verb	verbal phrase	copula
OBJECTIVE RELATIVE CLAUSE			
somi ['sɔmi] somi-Ø man-AGT	*nuja* ['nuja] nuj-a see-TR	Ø	*ogami* [ɔ'gami] o-g-a-mi REL-COP.PAST.CONCL-ASS-1P.AG.SG
somi, nuja ogami 'the man I saw'			
RECIPIENT RELATIVE CLAUSE			
somi ['sɔmi] somi-Ø man-AGT	*isota* ['sɔta] i-sot-a DIT-give-TR	*istu* ['iːstu] istu-Ø gift-DAT	*gaitomi* ['gaidɔmi] g-a-ito-mi COP.PAST.CONCL-ASS-ILLAT.REL-1P.AG.SG
somi, isota istu gaitomi 'the man to whom I gave a gift'			

More examples:

eusko, peha neskami ogana
['ɛʊskɔ 'pʰeʔa 'nɛskami ɔ'gana]
eusko-Ø peh-a nesk-a=mi o-g-a-na
question-AGT dare-TR ask-TR-INFI.AG.TR REL-COP.PAST-ASS-2P.AG.SG
'the question which you dared to ask'

vihla, mjosta ona somigi
['viɬːa 'mjɔsta ɔ'na 'sɔmiji]
vihla-Ø mjost-a o-n-a somi-Ø-gi
meat-AGT chew-TR REL-COP.INCONCL-ass man-AGT-PL
'the meat that the men are chewing'

sauhhjas, kista onami
[ˈsɑuhːjas ˈcʰɪsta ɔˈnɑmi]
sauhhjas-Ø kist-a o-n-a-mi
language-AGT learn-TR REL-COP.INCLONCL-ASS-1P.AG.SG
'the language I am learning'

iu, ila otsa tyry-go
[ˈiu ˈiːla ɔˈtsa ˈtʰyrygɔ]
iu-Ø il-a o-t=s-a tyry-Ø-go
relative-AGT know-TR REL-COP.NEG-ASS son-AGT-1P.POSS.SG
'a relative that my son does not know'

kůira, ahma tůgjů osatari
[ˈcʰøira ˈahma ˈtʰøjːø ɔˈsatɑri]
kůira-Ø ahm-a tůgjů o-s-a-tari
thing-AGT want-TR strong=ly REL-COP.HAB-ASS-3P.AG.PL
'the thing that they yearn for'

lunju, aiska mitka ogaki sòka
[ˈluɲu ˈaɪska ˈmiːtka ɔˈgɑci ˈsʊːga]
lunju-Ø aisk-a mitka o-g-a-ki sò-Ø-ka
winter.dress-AGT sew-TR yesterday REL-COP.PAST-ASS-1P.RECI.SG mother-AGT-1P.PAT.SG
'the winter dress that my mother fixed/sewed for me yesterday'

půdů, svůkaġa iltaki ogana
[ˈpʰødø ˈsvuːgɑxa ˈiːltɑɟi ɔˈgɑna]
půdů-Ø svůk-a-ġa il=ta-ki o-g-a-na
log-AGT throw-TR-SEMELF towards-1P.RECI.SG REL-COP.PAST-ASS-2P.AG.SG
'the log you threw at me'

Objective relative clauses can also be reduced, with the whole of the relative clause being moved after the noun. However, unlike subjective relative clauses, the verb in this construction is a patientive participle, with the agent of the passive found as an agentive or unagentive pronoun, or in the case of a noun, in the genitive:

kůira tůgjů meḍbutari
[ˈcʰøira ˈtʰøjːø ˈmɛðbudɑri]
kůira-Ø tůgjů me<ḍb>-u-Ø-tari
thing-AGT strong=ly want.PAST-PAT.PART-AGT-3P.AG.PL
'the thing that they yearn for' (lit. their yearned-for thing)

lunju mitka aiskiuki sòmaka
[ˈluɲu ˈmiːtka ˈaɪsciuɟi ˈsʊːmaga]
lunju-Ø mitka aisk-i-u-Ø-ki sò=ma-ka
winter.dress-AGT yesterday sew-PAST-PAT.PART-AGT-1P.RECI.SG mother.GEN–1P.PAT.SG

'the winter dress that my mother fixed/sewed for me yesterday'

pŭdŭ iltaki svủdguna
['pʰødø 'iːltaɟi 'svuːðguna]
pŭdŭ-Ø il-ta-ki svủ<dg>-u-Ø-na
log-AGT towards-ILLAT-1P.RECI.SG throw.PAST-PAT.PART-AGT-2P.AG.SG
'the log you threw at me'

§9.16.1.3.3 Possessive Relative Clauses

The possessive relative clause construction is used when the argument of a main clause is the possessor of either the subject or the object of the relative clause. There are two ways of marking possession and both involve the relative locative markers.

Unalienable possessions are usually marked with the ablative relative marker in the copula (-**isko**-). Alienable possessions are usually marked with the elative (-**iko**-).

The relative marker **o**- is not used onto the copula, as it is already present in the relative elative or ablative markers.

main clause	relative clause		copula
	main verb	verbal phrase	copula
possessive relative clause			
himha ['hiːmha] himha-Ø she-AGT	*ila* ['iːla] il-a know-TR	*śiśi njeltśa* ['ɕiɕi 'ɲɛltɕa] śi-śi njel-tśa daughter-GEN chief-GEN	*daiko toabi* ['daigɔ 'tʰɔabi] d-a-iko toabi-Ø COP-ASS-ELAT.REL older.sister-AGT
himha, ila śiśi njeltśa daiko toabi 'she, whose older sister knows the chief's daughter'			

More examples:

mŭjŭmi, svoa tōkka daiko helva
['møjømi 'svɔa 'tʰɔ̄ʔka 'daigɔ 'hɛlva]
mŭjŭmi-Ø sv=oa tōkk-a d-a-iko helva-Ø
herder-AGT not=yet give.birth-TR COP-ASS-ILLAT.REL female.caribou-AGT
'the herder whose female caribou hasn't given birth yet'

kori, idaḍḍi euskueita aksaikomi
[ˈkʰɔri iˈdaðːi ˈɛʊskueida akˈsːaigɔmi]
kori-Ø i-daḍḍ-i eusko-e=ita ak=s-a-iko-mi
boy-AGT DIT-answer-ITR question-ILLAT NEG.COP.PAST-ASS-ELAT.REL-1P.AG.SG
'the boy, whose question I did not answer'

hialkko, gelja śildi atseiskośi ihmi
[ˈhɪalkːɔ ˈjelja ˈɕɪldʑi aˈtsɛiskɔɕi ˈiːhmi]
hialkko-Ø gelj-a śi‹l›-di at=s-e-isko-śi ih-mi
wound-AGT soothe-TR pain-GEN NEG.COP.HAB-INFER-ABLA.REL-HABI nothing.INA-AGT
'a wound, whose pain nothing can soothe'

saumie, heja tśekśitagi kůnůma saiskojo
[ˈsaumie ˈheja ˈtɕɛkɕːidaji ˈcʰønøma ˈsaɪskɔjɔ]
saumi-e-Ø hej-a tśek-śi=ta-gi kůnů-ma s-a-isko-jo
caribou-PL-AGT feed-TR child-ILLAT-PL milk-GEN COP.HAB-ASS-ABLA.REL-4P.AG
'the caribous, whose milk we feed to our children'

davvetamosi, katiġa moḍbi gai(s)kot
[ˈdawːeˈtamɔsi kʰatˈixa ˈmɔðbi ˈgaigɔʔ/ ˈgaɪskɔʔ]
davve=tamosi-Ø kat-iġ-a moḍbi-Ø g-a-isko/iko-t
former=hunter-AGT from-inherit-TR hunting.territory-DAT COP.PAST-ASS-ELAT/ABLA.REL-3P.OBV.AG
'an ex-hunter, whose hunting territory X inherited'

dedna, ujoi ęngatśagi goiko
[ˈdɛʔtna uˈjɔi ˈæŋːatɕaji ˈgɔigɔ]
dedna-Ø u-j=o-i ęnga-tśa-gi g-o-iko
village-AGT PASS-attack-ITR inhabitant-PAT-PL COP.PAST.TRANSL.INFER-ELAT.REL
'a village whose inhabitants were apparently attacked'

maski, kista sauhhjahi sġaiskomi
[ˈmasci ˈcʰɪsta ˈsauhːjahi ˈsxaɪskɔmi]
maski-Ø kist-a sauhhja-hi sġ-a-isko-mi
people-AGT learn-TR language-GEN COP.PAST.HAB-ASS-ABLA.REL-1P.AG.SG
'the people whose language I used to learn'

§9.16.1.3.4 Locative Relative Clauses
The locative relative clause construction is used when the argument of a main clause is referred to with a locative case in a relative clause, or is the recipient in the relative clause. Two types of locative relative clauses exist - simple and complex.

Simple locative relative clauses use only locative cases, whereas complex use postpositions. Postpositions usually come before the verb, but may precede it immediately. The argument of the postposition is either found as the recipient of the relative clause (copularly relative), or sometimes in the elative or ablative (intracopularly relative) or with the relative marker on the preposition at the head of the relative phrase (postpositionally relative).

The postpositions do tend to become affixed to the verb, if they are allowed as preverbal adverbs (copularly relative), in which case the relative clause marker o- is used. Postpositionally relative clauses are common with more complex postpositional phrases (with postpositions found in one of the locative cases) in all dialects – it can be considered clearer and more concise. Copularly relative clauses are often considered to be bad language.

This allows for three different markings for a phrase like *the girl with whom I used to play in the summer*:

1. *kydly, gagi biohtsi kobia sġaitomi*   intracopularly relative
2. *kydly, gabiohtsi kobia osġami*   copularly relative
3. *kydly, ogagi biohtsi kobia sġami*   postpositionally relative

main clause	relative clause		copula
	main verb	verbal phrase	copula
	simple locative relative clause		
můjůmi ['møjømi] můjůmi-Ø herder-AGT	*igaihtsa* [i'gaɪhtsa] i-gaihts-a DIT-owe-TR	*salśun* ['salɕʊn] salśun-Ø caribou.head-DAT	*sġaitomi* ['sxɑidɔmi] sġ-a-ito-mi COP.PAST.HAB-ASS-ILLAT.REL-1P.AG.SG

můjůmi, igaihtsa salśun sġaitomi
'the herder to whom I used to owe a caribou head'

main clause	relative clause		copula
	main verb	verbal phrase	copula
	postpositional locative relative clause		
kydly ['cʰytɨy] kydly-Ø little.girl-AGT	*gagi biohtsi* ['gɑɟi 'bɪɔhtsi] gagi biohts-i with play-ITR	*jogju kobia* ['jɔjːu 'kʰɔbia] jogju k<ob>-ia once summer-INESS	*sġaitomi* ['sxɑidɔmi] sġ-a-ito-mi COP.PAST.HAB-ASS-ILLAT.REL-1P.AG.SG

kydly, gagi biohtsi kobia sġaitomi
'the little girl with whom I once used to play in the summer'
(also *kydly, gabiohtsi jogju kobia osġami*
or *kydly, ogagi biohtsi kobia sġami*)

More examples:

selo, kidli sitkotuimi atkasa gagi sġaiko
['sɛlɔ 'cʰitɬi 'sɪtkɔduimi 'atkɑsa 'gɑɟi 'sxɑigɔ]
selo-Ø kidl-i sitk-ot-u-i-mi at-ka-sa gagi sġ-a-iko
river-AGT use-ITR fish-COMP-PAST-ASS.ITR-1P.AG.SG father-GEN-2P.PAT.SG with COP.PAST.HAB ASS-ELAT.REL
'the river from which I used to fish with your father'

also
selo, kidli sġaiko sitkotuimi atkasa gagi
['sɛlɔ 'cʰitɬi 'sxɑigɔ 'sɪtkɔduimi 'atkɑsa 'gɑɟi]
selo-Ø kidl-i sġ-a-iko sitk-ot-u-i-mi at-ka-sa gagi
river-AGT use-ITR COP.PAST.HAB ASS-ELAT.REL fish-COMP-PAST-ASS.ITR-1P.AG.SG father-GEN-2P.PAT.SG with
'id.'

sitġobi, gala sibmjupa otsi sinin-ůt ogami
['sɪtːxɔbi 'gɑla 'sɪʔpmjuba 'ɔtsi 'sininœʔ ɔ'gami]
sitġobi-Ø gala sibm-jup-a ot=si sinin-Ø-ůt o-g-a-mi
fishing.rod-AGT with catch-JUP-TR this.ANI.DAT big.fish-DAT-DET.PROXI REL-COP.PAST-ASS-1P.AG.SG
'the fishing rod with which I caught this big fish'

or
sitġobi, ogala sibmjupa otsi sinin-ůt gami
['sɪtːxɔbi ɔ'gɑla 'sɪʔpmjuba 'ɔtsi 'sininœʔ 'gami]
sitġobi-Ø gala sibm-jup-a ot=si sinin-Ø-ůt o-g-a-mi
fishing.rod-AGT REL-with catch-JUP-TR this.ANI.DAT big.fish-DAT-DET.PROXI COP.PAST-ASS-1P.AG.SG
'id.'

tsviro, unnja ingi ode Guokvinilmi
['tsvirɔ 'uɲːa 'iːɲːi ɔ'de 'gʊɔkwːinɪlmi]
tsviro-Ø unnja ing-i o-d-e guokvinilmi-Ø
under.water.fallen.tree-AGT under live-ITR REL-COP-INFER guokvinilmi-AGT
'the fallen tree in water under which the King Frog **Guokvinilmi** supposedly lives'

or
tsviro, onunnja ingi de Guokvinilmi
['tsvirɔ ɔn'uɲːa 'iːɲːi de 'gʊɔkwːinɪlmi]
tsviro-Ø on-unnja ing-i o-d-e guokvinilmi-Ø
under.water.fallen.tree-AGT REL-under live-ITR COP-INFER guokvinilmi-AGT
'id.'

tśegjobi tśemi, onogjika ikeiditta uohmita gana
[ˈtɕejːɔbi ˈtɕemi ɔˈnɔjːiga iˈceidʑɪʔta ˈʊɔhmida ˈgɑna]
tśegjobi-Ø tśemi-Ø o-nogj=ika i-keid-i-tta u<Ø>ok-m=ita g-a-na
little.ligher-AGT little-AGT REL-from.the.end.of DIT-light-ITR-SUBIT pipe-ILLAT
COP.PAST- ASS-2P.AG.SG
'the little lighter from which you just lit your pipe'
(less commonly *tśegjobi tśemi, nogjika ikeiditta uohmita gaikona*)

daḍbiḥḥen talkiska na, onildiska ůalda půtsti-hon nabe nytsġyma
[ˈdaðbiʔːɛn ˈtʰalcɪska na ɔˈniːldʑɪska ˈœalda ˈpʰœtstːihɔ̃ ˈnɑbe ˈnœtsxyma]
daḍb-i-ḥḥen ta<l>-k=iska n-a o-ni<l>-d=iska ůald-a půtsti-hon n-a-be nytsġy-ma
beat-ITR-P drum-ABLA COP.INCONCL-ASS REL-surface-ABLA entrance-TR around-3P.OBV-POSS
COP.INCONCL-ASS-2P.PAT.EXCL music-PAT
'the drum beats, from whose surface the music puts us in a trance around it'
(less commonly *daḍbista talkiska na, nildiska ůalda půtsti-hon naikobe nytsġyma*)

taulhi, ilisyvvahta eleugi sytėu kvaitogge
[ˈtʰaʊlhi iːliˈsywːahta ˈeleuji ˈsytø ˈkʰvaidɔcːe]
taur̀-gi il-i-syvv-aht-a ele-u-gi syt=ėu g-ua-ito-gge
soldier-AGT.PL to-DIT-offer-AHT-TR flower-GEN-PL thank=ESS COP.PAST-OPT-
ILLAT.REL-1P.AG.PL.EXCL
'the soldiers, to whom we wanted to present (a bouquet of) flowers as thanks'
(more commonly *taulhi, onilta isyvvahta eleugi sytėu kvagge*)

§9.16.1.3.5 Link Constructions

Link constructions are copular phrases triggered by the addition of a so-called link clitic to the verb. This clitic is added to the split-stem after the postverbal vowel.

These link clitics can be used to form temporal subordinating clauses (*when X...*), clauses showing goal (*in order to X...*) and adverbial subordinating clauses (*by X...*). They can be combined with various conjunctions, some of which are only found with link clitics. Link phrases are contained within the verb and the copula, and generally do not take coordinating particles. Link constructions are nearly always at the beginning of clauses. Generally, link constructions are separated from the main sentence by a comma, but when the link construction appears as the subject of a phrase, it may be found after the main clause. Link constructions and conjunctions can be intersect by adverbs.

sihhitśu da, imakihmi oakibma
[ˈsihːitɕuda iˈmɑcɪhmi ˈɔɑɟɪʔpma]
sihh-i-tśu d-a i-mak-i-s-mi oak=ibma
rain-ITR-LINK.TEMP COP-ASS DIT-go-ASS.CONCL.ITR-HAB-1P.AG.SG home=ALLAT
'when/if it rains, I go home'

> *kemjekkaka sihhitṡu atsa*
> [ˈcʰemjɛʔkaga ˈsihːitɕu ɑˈtsa]
> kemjekk-a-ka sihh-i-tṡu at=s-a
> make.happy-ASS.CONCL.TR-1P.PAT.SG rain-ITR-LINK.TEMP COP.NEG-ASS
> 'it makes me happy when it does not rain'

Link constructions may also be found attached directly to the marked form of the infinitive of a verb:

> *sihhitsetṡu manidnan*
> [ˈsihːitsetɕu ˈmanɪʔtnan]
> sihh-i-t=se-tṡu man-i-dna-n
> rain-ITR-INFI.UNAG.ITR=GEN-LINK.TEMP come-ITR-REVERS-IMP.2P.SG
> 'come back when it rains' (lit. when raining)

The copula in link constructions tends to be found in its short form (*a* or *e*) especially with longer phrases.

It is important to note that link constructions do **not** have a visible third person patientive form like the copula.

Link constructions can be used with verbal adjectives by using the inconclusive copula.

> *siubmika*   'I am hungry'
> *siututs nami*   'when I am hungry'
> *iṡiuts orona*   'when you will have gotten old'

§9.16.1.3.5.1 Temporal Link Constructions

The temporal linking suffix is **-tṡu** (or also commonly in eastern dialects **-ju** or even **-u**) or **-uts** (slightly higher register) and is used with temporal conjunctions (see *§6.6*). The inferential is especially common with such temporal conjunctions because many of them have an inherently non-present meaning. Without conjunction, **-tṡu/-uts** means 'when'. It can be added directly to verbal adjectives (without a postverbal vowel).

> *kokkaka sihhitṡu a*
> [ˈkʰɔʔkaga ˈsihːitɕua]
> kokk-a-ka sihh-i-tṡu Ø-a
> like-ASS.CONCL.TR-1P.PAT.SG rain-ITR-LINK.TEMP COP-ASS
> 'I like it when it rains'

siututs nami
'when I'm hungry'

tevu, dù, tvo 'before'[1]

makiuts tevu dena
['mɑcɪʊts 'tʰevu 'dena]
mak-i-uts tevu d-e-na
go-ITR-LINK.TEMP before COP-INFER-2P.AG.SG
'before you go'

umekkitśu tvo gusa
[uˈmɛʔcitɕu 'tʰvɔ 'gusa]
u-ekk-i-tśu tvo g-u-sa
PASS-be.born-ITR-LINK.TEMP before COP.PAST-TRANSL-2P.PAT.SG
'before you were born'

pośkiju dù sasakkita demi
['pʰɔɕciju duː 'sɑsaʔcida 'demi]
pośk-i-ju dù sasam-k=ita d-e-mi
go.to.sleep-ITR-LINK.TEMP before tent-ILLAT COP-INFER-1P.AG.SG
'before I go to sleep in the tent'

ahha, aġġa, eġġa, àġa, ayġa 'after'

ipendidnatśu ahha oakibma gagga
[iˈpɛndʑɪʔtnɑtɕu 'ɑhːa 'ɔɑɟʔpma 'gakːa]
i-pe<nd>-i-dna-tśu ahha oak=ibma g-a-gga
DIT-return.PAST-ITR-REVERSE-LINK.TEMP after home=ALLAT COP.PAST-ASS-1P.AG.PL.INCL
'after we came back home'

luhhauts ahha mavvu deta
['luhːaʊts 'ɑhːa 'mɑwːu 'deta]
luhh-a-uts ahha mavvu-Ø d-e-ta
boil-TR-LINK.TEMP after meat-DAT COP-INFER-3P.AG.SG
'after X boils the meat'

iratśu kinoni ahha e, mianumajo
['irɑtɕu 'cʰinɔni 'ɑhːae 'mianumajɔ]
ir-a-tśu kinoni ahha Ø-e mian-um-a-Ø-jo
kill-TR-LINK.TEMP immediately after COP-INFER gut-OBLI-ASS.CONCL.TR-3P.PAT.SG-4P.AG
'immediately after killing it, one must gut it'

---

[1] Many speakers have -uts and **tevu/dù/tvo** merge to -uddeu, -uddù, -utvo, e.g. *makiuddù dena* 'before you go'

maja, mai 'while'

> *tatśu maja maḍḍja sa somigi, tulmaiskis iskigi*
> [ˈtʰatɕu ˈmaja ˈmaðːjasa ˈsɔmiji ˈtʰʊlmaɪscɪs ˈiːsciji]
> ta-tśu maja maḍḍ=ja s-a somi-Ø-gi tulm=aisk-i-s iski-Ø-gi
> be-LINK.TEMP while out=hunting COP.HAB-ASS man-AGT-PL,
> clothes=sew-ASS.CONCL.ITR-HAB woman-AGT-PL
> 'while the men are out hunting, the women sew clothes'

> *sihhitśu maja anta, allami erritseta*
> [ˈsihːitɕu ˈmaja anˈta ˈaːlami ˈerːitseda]
> sihh-i-tśu maja an=t-a all-a-mi err-i-t-se=ita
> rain-ITR-LINK.TEMP while COP=NEG.INCONCL-ASS have.time-ASS.CONCL.TR-1P.AG.SG
> work.outside-ITR-INFI.AG.ITR-ILLAT
> 'while it is not raining, I have time to work outside'

> *itskiuts mai ůrůddjia-nen mumma na, kessajo komma*
> [ˈɪtscːɪʊts ˈmai ˈørødʑːianɛn ˈmumːana ˈcʰesːajɔ ˈkʰɔmːa]
> itsk-i-uts mai ůrů-ddj=ia-nen mumma n-a kes-s-a-jo ko=mma
> spend.time-ITR-LINK.TEMP while nature-INESS–4P.POSS among COP.INCONCL-ASS
> learn-HAB-ASS.CONCL.TR-4P.AG much-GEN
> 'while one spends time in nature, one learns a lot'

soska 'since' (sometimes 'after')

> *tahhiuts soska munka-uri gana, orami mytymia*
> [ˈtʰahːɪʊts ˈsɔska ˈmʊŋkawri ˈgana ˈɔrami ˈmytymia]
> tahh-i-uts soska mu=nka-uri g-a-na or-a-mi mytym=ia
> leave-ITR-LINK.TEMP since among=from–1P.POSS.PL COP.PAST-ASS-2P.AG.SG
> COP.PERF-ASS-1P.AG.SG sad=INESS
> 'since you've left us, I have been sad'

> *nikiuts soska ga svottaki, nelis sġůbma*
> [ˈnicɪʊts ˈsɔskaga ˈsvɔʔtaɟi ˈnelɪs ˈsxœʔpma]
> nik-i-uts soska g-a svo=tta-ki nel-i-s sġů-bma
> die-ITR-LINK.TEMP since COP.PAST-ASS mother-PAT-1P.RECI.SG bud-ITR-HAB nothing-PAT
> 'since my mother died, nothing "buds"'

> *sůppi besġiuts soska kjalkiaba ma, umekkjuis ohtanna tśegmari*
> [ˈsœʔpi ˈbesxɪʊts ˈsɔska ˈcʰalciabama umˈɛʔcʊɪs ˈɔhtanːa ˈtɕɛŋmːari]
> sůppi besġ-i-uts soska kjak-k=ia-ba m-a u-ekkj-u-i-s oh-ta-nna tśegma-ri
> bad-adv be.peace-ITR-LINK.TEMP while land-INESS-1P.PAT.PL COP.INCONCL-ASS
> PASS-be.born-PAST-ASS.CONCL.ITR-HAB less-PAT child-PAT
> 'since/after the wartime, fewer children were born'

mehdil, mehhil, mehhen 'once'

> *kesatśu mehdil da, tsasġaśenjo*
> [ˈcʰesatɕu ˈmɛhdʑɪl da ˈtsasxaɕenjɔ]
> kes-a-tśu mehdil d-a-Ø tsasġ-a-ś=en-Ø-jo
> learn-TR-LINK.TEMP once COP-ASS-3P.PAT forget-ASS.CONCL.TR-HABI=NEG-3P.PAT-4P.AG
> 'once you learn Y, you can't forget'

> *mjahkihitśu mehdil ore, numejo ysġitsta ukatsġahta*
> [ˈmjahcihitɕu ˈmɛhdʑɪl ˈɔre ˈnumejɔ ˈœsxɪtstːa ˈukatsxahta]
> mjahkih-i-tśu mehdil or-e num-e-jo ysġit-sta ukahtsġa-h=ita
> is.frost-ITR-LINK.TEMP once COP.PERF-INFER pick-INFER.CONCL.TR-4P.AG sour.berry-GEN jam-ILLAT
> 'once there will have been frost, we will pick the sour-berries for jam'

> *nujatśu mehdil dena, nuidnena*
> [ˈnujatɕu mˈɛhdʑɪl ˈdena ˈnʊɪʔtnena]
> nuj-a-tśu mehdil d-e-Ø-na nuidn-e-Ø-na
> see-TR-LINK.TEMP once COP-INFER-3P.PAT-2P.AG.SG recognize-INFER.CONCL.TR-3P.PAT-2P.AG
> 'once you will see Y, you will recognize Y'

meddil, mel, medden 'as soon as'

> *onakin, nujaju meddil dena*
> [ˈɔnaɟɪn ˈnujaju ˈmetːɪl ˈdena]
> on-a-ki-n nuj-a-ju meddil d-e-Ø-na
> tell-TR-1P.RECI.SG-IMP.2P.SG see-TR-LINK.TEMP as.soon.as COP-INFER-3P.PAT-2P.AG.SG
> 'tell me as soon as you see it'

> *vimiuts mel do, tśemme tśegjejo*
> [ˈvimɪʊtsmɛldɔ ˈtɕemːe ˈtɕejːejɔ]
> vim-i-uts mel d-o tśem-me tśegj-e-jo
> snow-ITR-LINK.TEMP as.soon.as COP-TRANSL.INFER track-GEN can.see-INFER.CONCL.TR-4P.AG.SG
> 'as soon as it starts to snow, you will be able to see the tracks'

> *jehrŭju mel o*
> [ˈjɛhrøjumɛlɔ]
> jehr-ŭ-ju mel Ø-o
> is.possible-TRANSL-LINK.TEMP as.soon.as COP-TRANSL.INFER
> 'as soon as possible'

sinnil, sidnen 'as long as'

> *iljiliuts sinnil dema*
> [ˈiljilɯts sinːɪl ˈdema]
> iljil-i-uts sinnil d-e-ma
> live-ITR-LINK.TEMP as.long.as COP-INFER-1P.UNAG.SG
> 'for as long as I will live'

> *huhiju sinnil e hõtta*
> [ˈhuʔiju sinːɪl ˈhɔ̃ʔta]
> huh-i-ju sinnil Ø-e hõtta-Ø
> blow-ITR-LINK.TEMP as.long.as COP-INFER wind-AGT
> 'as long as the wind blows' (i.e. for ever)

> *ujokòitśu sinnil dena, śemeśihmi*
> [ujɔˈkʊːitɕu sinːɪl ˈdena ˈɕemeɕɪhmi]
> ujo=kò-i-tśu sinnil d-e-na śem-e-śi-h=mi
> right=speak-ITR-LINK.TEMP as.long.as COP-INFER-2P.AG.SG believe-ASS.CONCL.IFER-HABI-2P.PAT.SG=1P.AG.SG
> 'as long as you say the truth, I will [able to] believe you'

ůddjen, djen 'now that'

> *pednitśu ůddjen oradda, ijomu etsi deitagga*
> [ˈpʰɛʔtnitɕu ødʑːɛn ˈɔratːa ˈijɔmu ˈetsi ˈdeidɑkːa]
> pedn-i-tśu ůddjen or-a-dda ijom-u ets-i d-e-ita-gga
> come-ITR-LINK.TEMP now.that COP.PERF-ASS-2P.AG.PL be.possible-ASS.CONCL.TRANSL begin-ITR COP-INFER-ILLAT-1P.AG.PL.INCL
> 'now that you have arrived, we may begin'

> *ikesġatśu ůddjen orasimi, nidluma nivva-ḥa, śinkena*
> [iˈcɛsxatɕu ødʑːɛn ˈɔrasimi ˈnitɬuma ˈniːwaʔa ˈɕiːŋcena]
> i-kesġ-a-tśu ůddjen or-a-si-mi nidl-um-a-Ø nivva–ḥa śink-e-Ø-na
> DIT-teach-TR-LINK.TEMP now.that COP.PERF-ASS-2P.RECI.SG-1P.AG.SG do.thus-OBLI-ASS.CONCL.TR-3P.PAT how–REL.INTERRO know-ASS.CONCL.INFER-3P.PAT-2P.AG.SG
> 'now that I have shown you how to do it properly, you will know how'

> *sihhiju djen na, kadda makiśemmi*
> [ˈsihːijudʑɛn na ˈkʰatːa ˈmɑɕiɕemːi]
> sihh-i-ju djen n-a ka=dda mak-i-śen-mi
> rain-ITR-LINK.TEMP now.that COP.INCONCL-ASS out-ILLAT go-ITR-HABIL=NEG-1P.AG.SG
> 'now that it's raining, I can't go outside'

daġe 'if ever, in the case' (also *taġe, tẹġẹ*[1])

sėuskėuts daġe desa, ogjamõ ikosġi seskotokomita deita
[ˈsøːskøːts ˈdɑxe ˈdesa ˈɔjːɑmõ iˈkʰɔsxi ˈsɛskɔˈtɔkɔmida ˈdeida]
sėusk-ů-uts daġe d-e-sa ogj-a-mu=n i-kosġ-i sesko=to<k>o-m=ita d-e-ita
lost-TRANSL-LINK.TEMP if.ever COP-INFER-2P.UNAG.SG remember-ASS.CONCL.TR-OBLI=IMP.2P.SG DIT-cut.into-ITR landmark=tree.trunk-ILLAT COP-INFER-ILLAT
'if you ever get lost, remember to cut into the trunk of landmark trees'

oljasitśu daġe desa, dųihmeigla tśevvukkahtamõ otski ljausva
[ɔˈljɑsitɕu ˈdɑxe ˈdesa ˈdwɪmɛɪkla ˈtɕewːʊʔkahtɑmõ ˈɔtscːi ˈljɑʊsva]
o-ljas-i-tśu daġe d-e-sa dųihme<Ø>-i=gla tśevvukk-aht-a-mu=n otski ljausva-Ø
SUB-cut-ITR-LINK.TEMP if.ever COP-INFER-2P.UNAG.SG cloth-INSTRU bind-AHT-TR-OBLI=IMP.2P.SG tightly cut-DAT
'if you ever cut yourself, you must bind the laceration with soft bark (cloth)'

gedliju daġe atseta, tei tẹġẹ
[ˈɟetɬiju ˈdɑxe ɑˈtseda tʰei ˈtʰæxæ]
gedl-i-ju daġe at=s-e-ta tei tẹġẹ
work-ITR-LINK.TEMP if.ever COP=NEG-INFER-3P.UNAG.SG, TEI if=ever
'if ever it does not work, tough luck'

ġeyl, ġůhdil, ġůddjen 'whenever' (also 'every time')

ėhhatśu ġeyl kitkadi dami, mitvaġasa
[ˈeːhːɑtɕuxɛœl ˈcʰiːtkɑdʑi ˈdɑmi ˈmiːtwːɑxɑsa]
ėhh-a-tśu ġeyl kitka-di d-a-mi m-itv-a-ġa-sa
smell-TR-LINK.TEMP whenever pitch.smell-GEN COP-ASS-1P.AG.SG 1P.UNAG.SG-think.of-SEMELF-2P.PAT.SG
'whenever I smell the smell of pitch/perfume, I think of you'

nyġatśu ġůhdil kůtůt tśehtsotima dasa, saisakan
[ˈnyxɑtɕu xœhdʑɪl ˈcʰøtœʔ ˈtɕɛhtsɔtɕima ˈdɑsa ˈsɑisɑgan]
nyġ-a-tśu ġůhdil kůtů=t tśehts-ot-i-ma d-a-sa sais-a-ka-n
catch.glimps-TR-LINK.TEMP whenever something.UNKNOWN-GEN move-COMPLE-ITR-ACT.PART.UNAG COP-ASS-2P.UNAG.sg warn-TR-1P.PAT.SG-IMP.2P.SG
'every time you see catch a glimpse of something moving, tell me'

---

[1] The form *tẹġẹ* is nearly exclusively used phrases with a negative conotation, e.g. *oseintiuts tẹġẹ desa* 'if you (are) ever (so unlucky as to) hurt yourself'

>
> *maivvitśu ġŭddjen dakina, entsasġa, onuami nit-ḥa*
> [ˈmaiwːitɕu xødʑːɛn ˈdɑcina ɛnˈtsasxa ˈɔnuami ˈniːʔːa]
> maivv-i-tśu ġŭddjen d-a-ki-na en-tsasġ-a on-ua-mi ni=t–ḥa
> smile-ITR-LINK.TEMP when.ever COP-ASS-1P.RECI.SG-2P.AG.SG 1P.UNAG.SG-forget-ASS.CONCL.TR say-ASS.CONCL.TR.OPT what-GEN–REL.INTERRO
> 'whenever you smile to me, I forget what I wanted to say.

meihtsa, meuta, meuḍḍa 'until'

> *nikiuts meihtsa dema, lugjuehmi*
> [ˈnicɪʊts mɛɪhtsa ˈdema ˈlujːʊɛhmi]
> nik-i-uts meihtsa d-e-ma lugju-e-h=mi
> die-ITR-LINK.TEMP until COP-INFER-1P.UNAG.SG love-INFER.CONCL.TR-2P.PAT.SG=1P.AG.SG
> 'I will love you until I die'

> *raditśu meuta dena, sę̇ radumi*
> [ˈraditɕumeuda ˈdena sæ ˈradumi]
> rad-i-tśu meuta d-e-na sę̇ rad-u-mi
> stop-ITR-LINK.TEMP until COP-INFER-2P.UNAG.SG NEG stop-INFER.CONCL.ITR.1P.AG.SG
> 'I won't stop until you stop'

> *śidumajo kilkotśu meuḍḍa ne*
> [ˈɕidumajɔ ˈcʰiːlkɔtɕumeuðːa ne]
> śid-um-a-jo kil-ko-tśu meuḍḍa n-e
> wait-OBLI-ASS.CONCL.TR-4P.AG again=be.summer-LINK.TEMP until COP.INCONCL-INFER
> 'one has to wait until summer again'

§9.16.1.3.5.2 Goal Link Constructions

The linking suffix is *-ke* and is used to show a goal. It may be found with the conjunction *kimi* 'so that' and *ome* 'in order to, for'. On its own, *-ke* simply means 'to' or 'for', indicating that the link construction is the aim of the main verb. The conjunctions *kimi* and *ome* are used rather simply and may be quite synonymous, although *ome* may have a slightly more inferential meaning. The ending *-ke* and *kimi* sometimes combine as *-kkimi*. Some dialects only have *-kkęmmę*, *-kkáma* or *-kkámę* instead of *-ke kimi* and *-ke ome*.

> *dohhake desa mansimi*
> [ˈdɔhkaɟe ˈdesa ˈmansimi]
> dohk-a-ke d-e-sa ma<ns>-i-mi
> say.goodbye-ITR-LINK.GOAL COP-INFER-2P.PAT.AG come.PAST-ASS.CONCL.ITR-1P.AG.SG
> 'I came to say goodbye'

kimi 'so that'

> *tůreiskůke kimi deta, damu tymiśugjiajo lůlkimoita*
> [ˈtʰɵrɛɪscɵɟe ˈkʰimi ˈdeta ˈdamu tymiˈɕujːiajo ˈluːlcimɔida]
> tůreisk-ů-ke kimi d-e-ta damu-Ø tym-i-śugje-a-Ø-jo lůl<k>i-mo=ita
> lose.fur-TRANSL-LINK.GOAL so.that COP-INFER-3P.UNAG.SG skin-DAT down-DIT-submerge-ASS.CONCL.TR-4P.AG hot.water-ILLAT
> 'we submerge the skin in hot water so that it will lose its fur'

> *nupukkimi atsesa, set nonasimi*
> [ˈnupʊʔcimi aˈtsesa sɛʔtˈnɔnasimi]
> nup-u-k=imi at=s-e-sa set <non>-a-si-mi
> get.angry-TRANSL-LINK.GOAL=so.that COP=NEG-INFER-2P.PAT.SG NEG tell.PAST-ASS.CONCL.TR-2P.RECI.1P.AG.SG
> 'I didn't tell you so you wouldn't get angry'

> *jůnake kimi ośia de, okjasumigga*
> [ˈjuːnaɟe ˈcʰimi ˈɔɕia de ɔˈcʰasumɪkːa]
> jůn-a-ke kimi ośia d-e o-kjas-um-i-gga
> finish-TR-LINK.GOAL in.order in.time COP-INFER.INDIC SUBJ-hurry-OBLI ASS.CONCL.ITR-1P.AG.PL.INCL
> 'in order to finish in time, we must hurry up'

ome 'in order to'

> *oaigake ome mjeutskes de, sem bedna eterre*
> [ˈɔaiɣaɟe ˈɔme ˈmjɛʊtscːɛs de sɛm ˈbɛʔtna ˈeterːe]
> oaig-a-ke ome mjeutske-s d-e sem bedn-a ete<rr>-e
> catch-TR-LINK.GOAL in.order.to slug-GEN COP-INFER NEG need-ASS.CONCL.TR spear-GEN
> 'in order to catch slugs, you don't need a spear'

> *eukake ome haja dejo, tśadnuma ljó te ohna*
> [ˈeugaɟe ˈɔme ˈhaja ˈdejo ˈtɕaʔtnuma ˈljʊːde ˈɔhna]
> euk-a-ke ome haj-a d-e-jo, tśadn-um-a ljó-Ø te ohna-Ø
> produce-TR-LINK.GOAL in.order.to glue.GEN COP-INFER-4P.AG find-OBLI-ASS.CONCL.TR resin-DAT and ash-DAT
> 'to make glue, you need to find (the) resin and (the) ash'

> *śibike ome kenehta de, sapohhjumi*
> [ˈɕibiɟe ˈɔme ˈcʰemɛhta de saˈpʰɔhːjumi]
> śib-i-ke ome kemeh=ta d-e sa-pohhj-um-i
> have.energy-ITR-LINK.GOAL for tomorrow=ILLAT COP.INFER 2P.UNAG.SG-sleep-OBLI-ASS.CONCL.ITR
> 'if you want to have energy for tomorrow, you must sleep'

§9.16.1.3.5.3 Adverbial Link Constructions

The adverbial linking suffix is -**te** and is used with a variety of conjunctions. Used alone, -**te** shows the means by which something is done. Conjunctions used with -**te** include: *aska* 'because (negative)', *ḱiuṡka* 'because (neutral)' *iska* 'thanks to', *eppi* '(so) that/nothing but (without adverbial link)' and *osġe* 'unless'.

>   *munite sa opiagjuku*
>   ['munidesa ɔ'piɑj:ugu]
>   mun-i-te s-a o-piagjuk-u
>   rest-ITR-LINK.ADV COP.HAB-ASS SUBJ-recover-ASS.CONCL.TRANSL
>   'one gets better by resting'

aska 'because' (usually implies something negative)

>   *herite aska ga, palvaiu kebsie*
>   ['heride 'askaga 'pʰalvaiu 'cʰepsie]
>   her-i-te aska g-a palv-ai-u ke<bs>i-e
>   cold-ITR-LINK.ADV because COP.PAST-ASS be.ruined-PAST-ASS.CONCL.TRANSL mushroom-PAT
>   'because it was cold, the mushrooms were ruined'

>   *derite aska tsġiandika ga, set mallia ḱjonges jùnanteta*
>   ['deride 'aska 'tsxɪandʑiga ga sɛʔ 'mɑl:ia 'cʰɔŋ:ɛs 'ju:nanteda]
>   der-i-te aska tsġiam-di=ka g-a set m-all-i-a kjo<ng>-e-s jùn-a-m=ta-ita
>   roll-ITR-ADV.LINK because cedar-strip-ELAT COP.PAST-ASS.CONCL not 1P.ACT.UNAG-have.time-PAST-ASS.CONCL.TR kjoknen.GEN finish-TR-infi.TR.AG-ILLAT
>   'I didn't have time to finish the **kjoknen** (cedar strip basket) because we ran out of cedar strips' (lit. it rolled out of cedar strips)

>   *atujukkate aska gakata, ōsi huami mìskodi*
>   ['ɑtujʊʔkade 'aska 'gakɑda 'ōsi 'huami 'mi:skɔdʑi]
>   atujukk-a-te aska g-a-ka-ta ōsi h-ua-mi misko-di
>   make.sick-TR-LINK.ADV because COP.PAST-ASS-1P.PAT.SG-3P.UNAG.SG no.longer eat-ASS.CONCL.OPT.TR-1P.AG.SG beaver.meat-GEN
>   'because it made me sick, I no longer want to eat beaver meat'

iska	'thanks to/because' (introducing a generally positive reason)
sigjiska	'not thanks to/not because' (used with the -**te** linking particle)

ivůte iska ůkibma ga, ijobmubi kisine jalrisa
['ivøde 'i:ska 'u:ɲ?pma ga 'ijɔ?pmubi 'cʰisine 'jalrisa]
iv-ů-te iska ůki=bma g-a ijo<bm>-u-bi kisi-i=ne jalr-i-sa
freeze-TRANSL-ADV.LINK thanks.to water-ALLAT COP.PAST-ASS
possible.PAST-TRANSL-1P.PL.RECI quick-ADV.COMP cross-ITR-INFI.ITR.AG
'thanks to the water freezing over, we were able to cross more quickly'

kjuṡka 'because' (fairly neutral)

allate kjuṡka kiltůrhůsůdleta mopiko tvadnajagga, loalkita ulolhija
['al:ade 'cʰʊɕka cʰi:l'tœrhøsœtɬeda 'mɔpigɔ 'tʰva?tnɑjɑk:a 'lɔalcıda u'lɔlhija]
all-a-te kjuska kil=tůrhůs-ů-t=le=ita mo<p>i-ko d-ua-dna-ja-gga loal-k=ita u-lol-h-i-ja
have.time-TR-LINK.ADV because again=grow-TRANSL-INFI.TRANSL.UNAG-ILLAT
hunting.territory-GEN COP-ASS.OPT-REVERS-3P.PAT.PL-1P.AG.PL.INCL abandon-ILLAT
PASS-leave-HAB-ASS.CONCL.ITR-3P.PAT.PL
'because we want our hunting territory to have time to recover, it is left abandoned'

tṡadnate kjuṡka oṡotta sohtanna de, tamamiddi kjuṡpa-ṡi
['tɕa?tnade 'cʰʊɕka 'ɔɕɔ?ta 'sɔhtɑn:a de tʰamɑ'mit:i 'cʰʊɕpaɕi]
tṡadn-a-te kjuṡka oṡot-ta s=oht-anna d-e tama-m-i<dd>-i kjus=pa-ṡi
find-TR-ADV.LINK because fish.stock-GEN good.COMP-GEN COP-INFER
onto-1P.ACT.UNAG-fall.PAST-ASS.CONCL.ITR territory=ALLAT-2P.POSS.PL
'we stumbled onto your territory in order to find better fish stock'

miůt, miůdda, mio, meu 'because' (fairly neutral)

neskate miůdda gaka to njuhhi, oḍbami
['nɛskade miøt:a 'gaka tʰɔ 'ɲuh:i 'ɔðbami]
neks-a-te miůdda g-a-ka to-Ø njuhhi-Ø, o<ḍb>-a-Ø-mi
ask-TR-LINK.ADV because COP.PAST-ASS-1P.PAT.SG 3P.PRON.ANI.AGT old.woman-AGT
help.PAST-ASS.CONCL.TR-3P.PAT-1P.AG.SG
'because the old woman asked me, I helped her'

iska, itska 'thanks to'

merite iska eteria na, tsaupribi ůakkia savengaṡġejetṡagi
['meridei:ska 'eteria na 'tsaʊpxibi 'œa?cia 'sɑvɛɲ'gasˣxejetɕaji]
mer-i-te iska eter=ia n-a tsaupr-i-bi ůakk=ia saven=gas-heje-tṡa-gi
be.mild-ITR-LINK.ADV thanks.to air-INESS COP.INCONCL-ASS
be.rare-ASS.CONCL.ITR-1P.RECI.PL around.here ear.lobe=frostbite=winter-PAT-PL

'thanks to the air being milder, we rarely get harsh winters around here (lit. earlobe-frostbite winters)'

salla sejate iska gaṡita, kvu̇aṡi haljukkotiai ku̇tu̇mni
[ˈsalːa ˈsejɑdeiːska ˈɡɑɕida ˈkʰvuːɑɕi ˈhaljʊʔkɔtɕiaɪ ˈkʰɵtœmnːi]
sa=lla sej-a-te iska g-a-ṡi-Ø kv-u̇-a-ṡi haljukk-ot-i-a-i ku̇tu̇mni-Ø
well hear-TR-LINK.ADV thanks.to COP.PAST-ASS-HABIL-3P.AG.SG feel-PAST-ASS.CONCL.TR-HABIL follow-COMPLE-PAST-ASS.CONCL.ITR-4P.PAT someone.UNKNOWN-AGT
'thanks to X's good hearing, X could feel that someone was following him/her'

eppi 'so X (that), nothing but X'

vimite eppi ōkko ga, hokjimi katvėumema
[ˈvimideːʔpi ˈɔ̄ʔkɔga ˈhɔcimi kʰatˈvøːmema]
vim-i-te eppi omi-ko ga hokj-i-m-i katvėume-ma
snow-ITR-LINK.ADV so COP.PASS-ASS blind-PAST-INCONCL-ASS.ITR reflection-PAT
'it snowed so much that the reflection (off the snow) was blinding'

lugjuate eppi dahmi, ednikjoiṡi
[ˈlujːuadeːʔpi ˈdahmi ɛʔtˈnicjɔiɕi]
lugju-a-te eppi d-a-h=mi ed-nik-joi-ṡi
love-TR-LINK.ADV so COP-ASS-2P.PAT=1P.AG.SG 1P.UNAG.SG-die-INFER.CONCL.COND.IRR.ITR-HABIL
'I love you so much I could die'

allate eppi a allami
[ˈalːade ˈɛʔpia ˈalːami]
all-a-te eppi a all-a-Ø-mi
have.time-TR-LINK.ADV eppi COP.ASS have.time-ASS.CONCL.TR-3P.PAT-1P.AG.SG
'I have nothing but time'

osg̣e, heḍven, siḍven 'unless'

tȧte heḍven somi dana, tatadiṡenna
[ˈtʰæːde ˈhɛðwːɛn ˈsɔmi ˈdana tʰatɑˈdiːɕenːa]
tȧ-te heḍven somi-Ø d-a-na tata-di-i-ṡ=en-na
be-LINK.ADV unless man-ACT COP-ASS-2P.AG.SG into-step-ASS.CONCL.ITR-HABIL.NEG-2P.AG.SG
'you cannot step in here unless you are a man'

oaite osġe kŭtõtsita dena, meylumi
[ˈɔɑide ˈɔsxe ˈkʰɵtõtsida ˈdena ˈmɛœlumi]
oa-i-te osġe kŭtŭn-ts=ita d-e-na meyl-u-mi
tell-ITR-LINK.ADV unless any.ANI-ILLAT COP-INFER-2P.AG.SG be.silent-INFER.CONCL.ITR-1P.AG.SG
'I will keep silent unless you tell anyone'

§9.16.1.3.5.4 Copular Link Constructions
Certain fixed expressions contain the link constructions attached directly onto the copula without any split stem verb. The most common such construction involves the temporal link clitic **-uts**.

tsegma gauts	'as a child (while X was a child)'
njelli dauts	'as the chief (since X is the chief…)'
oni dauts	'being so, in that case'
addauts	'if so'
siaddauts	'if not, otherwise'
dŭntauts	'if need be'
voḍḍauts	'hopefully'

§9.16.2 Dependent Copula

The dependent copula is a defective verb found as a clitic used with adjectives and sometimes other parts of speech. The clitic is either attached directly to the adjective or it can be found attached to a number of defective copular stems (originally all variants of tà- 'to be/stand').

negative defective copular verb	si- or hjed-
conditional realis copular verb	add-[1] (neg. siadd-)
optative copular verb	voḍḍ- (neg. svoḍḍ-)
obligative copular verb	ùnt- (neg. siùnt-)

The negative, optative and obligative also have an additional conditional realis form:

	tsi-, dahjed-	'if X is not'
	tvoḍḍ-	'if X wants'
neg.	sitvoḍḍ-	'if X does not want'
	dùnt-	'if X must'
neg.	sidùnt-	'if X must not'

The dependent copula lacks many constituents that the independent copula has, for example conclusivity (inconclusive adjectives are found in their verbal adjective form). Both the defective copular verbs and the adjective clitic form may take personal pronouns (generally agentive), using the copular set. However, the clitical form of the dependent copula is also commonly found with independent pronouns:

1P.SG	iśiami	or	iśia megi	'I am old'
2P.SG	iśiana	or	iśia negi	'you are old'
3P.SG	iśiata	or	iśia to/ta	'X is old'
1P.PL.INCL	iśiagga	or	iśia màra	'we are old'
1P.PL.EXCL	iśiagge	or	iśia màri	'we are old'
2P.PL	iśiadda	or	iśia nàri	'you are old'
3P.PL	iśiatari	or	iśia ki	'they are old'
3P.OBV	iśiat	or	iśia onto	'X is old'
4P.	iśiajo	or	iśia nin	'one is old'

siata iśi	'X is not old'
addita iśi	'if X was old'
voḍḍeta iśi	'X would want to be old'
tvoḍḍuna iśi	'if you want to become old'
sitvoḍḍuna iśi	'if you do not want to become old'
siùnturena iśi	'you must not have been old (I imagine)'

---

[1] Dialectal versions of the conditional realis are somewhat reflected in the copula – the forms aḥḥ- and eġġ- also exist.

but   *iśijaita*   'if X were old'

The dependent copula, whether as a clitic to a defective copular verb or directly attached to an adjective, behaves like any other verb and is thus usually found at the beginning of the phrase.

killju iśirita okon-go   'my old man had always been old'

The copular endings can also take all the secondary aspect markers found in regular verbs.

iśijata	'X grew old'
iśijaġata	'X suddenly grew old'
iśijanundata	'X grew a little old'
sitvoḍḍuḥḥana iśi	'if you do not want to keep getting older'

The dependent copula and defective copular verbs cannot be found in link constructions – instead, the copular verb *ta·mi* is used (split stem is *tä-*).

The dependent copula is *not* used with complementized phrases, in which case the independent copula is used, except with the conditional realis dependent copula (add-) in certain speakers, but a corresponding independent form (da-da) is much more common.

siata iśi		'X is not old'
	atsonata iśi	'that X is not old'
addita iśi		'if X was old'
	dagonata iśi	'that X was old'
rarely:	*addonita iśi*	'that X was old'
voḍḍeta iśi		'X would want to be old'
	donueta iśi	'that X would want to be old'
or:	*tvoneta iśi*[1]	
tvoḍḍuna iśi		'if you want to become old'
	dadonuana iśi	'that if you want to become old'
commonly:	*tvoddonuna iśi*	
rarely:	*addonuana iśi*	

---

[1] The special obviative forms of the independent copula in **tv-** are sometimes reanalyzed and suppleted for the normal form in *d·on·ua* or *d·on·ue*, to give *tvon·a* and *tvon·e* in the present.

sitvoḍḍuna iṡi		'if you do not want to become old'
	atsonuana iṡi	'that if you do not want to become old'
	sitvoḍḍonuna iṡi	
siùnturena iṡi		'you must not have have been old (I imagine)'
	siùntonurena iṡi	'that you must not been old (I imagine)'

The dependent copula is most commonly attached onto adjectives, but it can sometimes be added onto deictic words, although this is nearly entirely restricted to simple present or past forms (-a/-i or -e/-o). It should be noted that the dependent copula never occurs as a clitic to patientive participles (in -u) in standard Siwa, but the Sorhi dialect and some younger speakers sometimes use it.

	data ůvvia	ůvviuata	'it is here'
	oni ga	onì	'it was like this'
	ůdda oata	ůdduata	'this is it'
	da mimi	mimia	'this is why'
but	data nantu		'it is broken'

The dependent copula is a clitic that attaches different to adjectives ending in **a- o- u-** (-u-Ø) or -i -e (-i-Ø) and -y -ů (-ů-Ø). Below is an illustration of this the adjective *iṡi* 'old' and *atana* 'large, big'.

I E

TRANSITIVE				
-ia	*isia*	'is old'	-ie	*isie*	–
-ias	*isias*	'is usually old'	-ies	*isies*	–
-ra, ra	*isira*	'has been old'	-re	*isire*	–
-jai	*isijai*	'if X were old'	-jei	*isijei*	'would be old'

PAST				
-į, -ę̃	*isį*	'was old'	-io	*isio*	–
-įs, -ęs	*isįs*	'used to be old'	-ios	*isios*	–
-ri	*isiri*	'had been old'	-ro	*isiro*	–
-ųį	*isiųį*	'if X would have been old'	-ųų̃, (-ey)	*isiųų̃*	'would have been old'

IMPERATIVE				
-iunta	*isiunta*	'may X be old'	-iunte	*isiunte*	'(hopefully) is old'

TRANSLATIVE				
-iū̃, -ey	*isiū̃*	'becomes old'	-ivo, -eu	*isivo*	–
-iū̃s, -eys	*isiū̃s*	'usually becomes old'	-ius	*isius*	–
-rū̃	*isirū̃*	'has become old'	-rvo	*isirvo*	–
-jūi	*isijūi*	'if X became old'	-juo	*isijuo*	'would become old'

PAST				
-ija	*isija*	'became old'	-ųa	*isiųa*	–
-ijas	*isijas*	'used to become old'	-ųas	*isiųas*	–
-rja	*isirja*	'had become old'	-irva	*isirva*	–
-jau	*isijau*	'if X would have become old'	-jeu	*isijeu*	'would have become old'

A O U

TRANSITIVE

-ua	atanua	'is big'	-ai, -ui	atanai	–
-uas	atanuas	'is usually big'	-ais, -uis	atanais	–
-ra	atanara	'has been big'	-re	atanare	–
-jai	atanajai	'if X were big'	-jei	atanajei	'would be big'

PAST

-ai, -ui	atanai	'was big'	-au, -ů	atanau	–
-ais, -uis	atanais	'used to be big'	-aus, -ůs	atanaus	–
-ri	atanari	'had been big'	-ro	atanaro	–
-ųi	atanaųi	'if X would have been big'	-ųů, -(ay)	atanaųů, atanay	'would have been big'

IMPERATIVE

-aunta, -ůnta	atanaunta	'may X be big'	-aunte, -ůnte	atanaunte	'(hopefully) is big'

TRANSLATIVE

-au, -ů	atanau	'becomes big'	-avvo, -ůo	atanavvo	–
-aus, -ůs	atanaus	'usually becomes big'	-avvos, -ůos	atanavvos	–
-ru	atanaru	'has become big'	-rvo	atanarvo	–
-jui	atanajui	'if X became big'	-juo	atanajuo	'would become big'

PAST

-ja	atanaja	'became big'	-ųa	atanaųa	–
-jas	atanajas	'used to become big'	-ųas	atanaųas	–
-rja	atanarja	'had become big'	-rvo	atanarvo	–
-jau	atanajau	'if X would have become big'	-jeu	atanajeu	'would have become big'

§9.16.2.1 Copular Endings
Below are all the forms of the dependent copula:

TRANSITIVE

non-past		assertive	inferential
	indicative	*-a*	*-e*
	habitual	*-as(a)*	*-es(e)*
	perfective	*-(u)la*	*-(u)le*
	conditional irrealis	*-įai*	*-įei*
past			
	indicative	*-i*	*-o*
	habitual	*-is*	*-os*
	perfective	*-(u)li*	*-(u)lo*
	conditional irrealis	*-ųi*	*-ųui* or *-ųů*
imperative		*-unta*	*-unte*

TRANSLATIVE

non-past		assertive	inferential
	indicative	*-u/-ů*	*-uo/-vo*
	habitual	*-us/-ůs*	*-us(vo)*
	perfective	*-(u)lu/-(ů)lů*	*-(u)lvo, -(u)dlvo*
	conditional irrealis	*-įui/-įůi*	*-įuo*
past			
	indicative	*-įa*	*-ųa/-va*
	habitual	*-įas*	*-ųas/-vas*
	perfective	*-(u)lįa*	*-(u)lva, -(u)dlva*
	conditional irrealis	*-įau*	*-įeu*
imperative		*-įanta*	*-ųanto*

The past conditional irrealis inferential ending -ųů is generally found after -u- -o- -e- and -y-, with -ųui elsewhere. Some dialects, especially eastern dialects have -l- where the perfective has -r-. The habitual endings in -s- when preceded by the complementizer in -on-/-non- forms the fused ending -onh-/-nonh- or alternatively -ōh-/-nōh-.

>   *netami, tyhhynonhata*
>   [ˈnetɑmi ˈtʰyh:ynɔnhɑda]
>   net-a-mi tyhhy-non-h-a-ta
>   know-ASS.CONCL.TR-1P.AG.SG green-COMPLE-HAB-3P.AG.SG
>   'I know that it is usually green'

§9.16.2.2 Defective Copular Verbs

The defective forms of the dependent copular verb are as follow.
The negative copular verb in **si-** 'is not' and **hjed-** 'is not at all':

TRANSITIVE

non-past   assertive   inferential
    indicative   *sia / hjeda*   *sie / hjede*
    habitual   *sias / hjedas*   *sies / hjės*
    perfective   *sila / hjedla*   *sile / hjedle*
    conditional irrealis   *sijai / hjeddjai*   *sijei / hjeddjei*

past
    indicative   *sì / hjei*   *sio / hjedo*
    habitual   *sis / hjeis*   *sios / hjeus*
    perfective   *sili / hjedli*   *silo / hjedlo*
    conditional irrealis   *siui / hjedvi*   *siuui / hjedvů*
imperative   *siunta / hjeunta*   *siunte / hjeunte*

TRANSLATIVE

non-past   assertive   inferential
    indicative   *siů / hjedů*   *sivvo / hjevvo*
    habitual   *siůs / hjeus*   *sius / hjeus*
    perfective   *sirů / hjedgu*   *sirvo / hjervo*[1]
    conditional irrealis   *sijůi / hjeddjůi*   *sijuo / hjeddjuo*

past
    indicative   *sigja / hjeddja*   *sivva / hjevva*
    habitual   *sigjas / hjeddjas*   *sivvas / hjevvas*
    perfective   *sirja / hjerja*[2]   *sirvo / hjerva*[3]
    conditional irrealis   *sijau / hjeddjau*   *sijeu / hjeddjeu*
imperative   *sigjanta / hjeddjanta* *sivvanto/ hjevvanto*

Dialects have a lot of variation on the forms in *hjeda* and its other forms, such as *hjela, hjala, śala, śola* and *śora*.

The conditional realis copular verb in **add-** 'if it is' and the conditional irrealis copular verb in **sġadd-** 'if it were':

---

[1] The older form *hjedlvo* also exists.

[2] The older form *hjedlja* also exists.

[3] The older form *hjedlva* also exists.

TRANSITIVE

		assertive	inferential
non-past			
	indicative	*adda*	*adde*
	habitual	*addas*	*addes*
	perfective	*adla*	*adle*
past			
	indicative	*addi*	*addo*
	habitual	*addis*	*addos*
	perfective	*adli*	*adlo*

TRANSLATIVE

		assertive	inferential
non-past			
	indicative	*addu*	*atvo*
	habitual	*addus*	*addusvo*
	perfective	*adlu*	*atvolo~adlvo*
past			
	indicative	*addja*	*atva*
	habitual	*addjas*	*atvaso*
	perfective	*adlja~adlia*	*atvalo~adlva*

The optative copular verb in **voḍḍ-** 'it wants to be' and **u̇nt-** 'if has to be':

TRANSITIVE

		assertive	inferential
non-past			
	indicative	*voḍḍa / u̇nta*	*voḍḍe / u̇nte*
	habitual	*voḍḍas / u̇ntas*	*voḍḍes / u̇ntes*
	perfective	*vodla / u̇ntula*	*vodle / u̇ntule*
	conditional irrealis	*voḍḍjai / u̇ntśai*	*voḍḍjei / u̇ntśei*
past			
	indicative	*voḍḍi / u̇nti*	*voḍḍo / u̇nto*
	habitual	*voḍḍis / u̇ntis*	*voḍḍos / u̇ntos*
	perfective	*vodli / u̇ntuli*	*vodlu / u̇ntulo*
	conditional irrealis	*voḍvi / u̇ntu̇i*	*voḍvů / u̇ntů*
imperative		*- / u̇ntunta*	*- / u̇ntunte*

TRANSLATIVE

		assertive	inferential
non-past			
	indicative	voḍḍu / u̇ntu	voḍvo / u̇ntuo
	habitual	voḍḍus / u̇ntus	voḍḍus/u̇ntus
	perfective	vodġu / u̇nturu	voḍvoro / u̇ntuoro
	conditional irrealis	voḍḍjui / u̇ntśui	voḍḍjuo / u̇ntśuo
past			
	indicative	voḍḍja / u̇ntśa	voḍva / u̇ntya
	habitual	voḍḍjas / u̇ntśas	voḍvas / u̇ntyas
	perfective	voḍḍurja / u̇nturja	voḍḍurvo / u̇nturvo
	conditional irrealis	voḍḍjau / u̇ntśau	voḍḍjeu / u̇ntśeu
	imperative	- / u̇ntśanta	- / u̇ntyanto

§9.16.2.3 Coalescence

The dependent copula is found as a clitic to adjectives which causes the final syllable of to undergo a change. The most noticeable feature of this special coalescence is that adjectives ending in -a- and -o- and -u- marge before back and rounded vowels (not -u-), but not before front vowels. Similarly, adjectives in -e- and -i- merge completely for all copula endings.

The coalescence of adjectives and dependent copula result in the formation of two main groups of adjectives, those ending in -i or -e (and -y, -ů) and those ending in -a -o -u. A third group (-y and -ů) exists in certain dialects.

copula → adjective ↓		-a-	-o-	-u-	-e-	-i-	-y-	-ů-
back	-a	-ua-	-au-		-ai-		-ůa-	
	-o		-u̇-		-ui-		-ėu- or -ůvvů-	
	-u							
front	-e	-ia- / -ja-	-io- / -jo-	-iu- / -ju-	-ė-		-ůi- or -ẏ-	
	-i				-i̇-			
rounded	-y/-ů	-ėu-*			-ẏ-		-ẏ- or -ėu-	

Because so few adjectives end in -y or -ů, they usually behave as -i when cliticized by the copula.

The result of this coalescence pattern is that adjectives in -a -o -u do not distinguish between inferential present (*apparently is*) and assertive past (*was*), between inferential past (*apparently was*) and assertive transitive present (*becomes*):

atanauta	'it was apparently big' or 'it becomes big' (underlying **atana-o-** and **atana-u-**)
atanaita	'it was big' or 'it is apparently big' (underlying **atana-i-** and **atana-e-**)

The distinction is kept with adjectives in -e or -i.

iṡiota	'it was apparently old'
iṡiůta	'it becomes old'
iṡita	'it was old'
iṡieta	'it is apparently old'

§9.16.2.4 Use
More examples of the dependent copula:

atanua tahha
['atɑnua 'tʰɑh:a]
atana-a tahha-Ø
large-COP.ASS tree-AGT
'the tree is big'

tyhhèu òlmua
['tʰyh:ø: ʊ:lmua]
tyhhy-a òlma-a
green-COP.ASS leaf.AGT-Pl
'the leaves are green'

sia atana tahha
['sia 'atana 'tʰah:a]
si-a atana tahha-Ø
NEG.COP.ASS large tree-AGT
'the tree is not big'

sia tyhhy òlmua
[sia 'tʰyhy ʊ:lmua]
si-a tyhhy òlma-a
NEG.COP.ASS green leaf.AGT-Pl
'the leaves are not green'

aypua ta ikos-ůt
['æœbua tʰa 'ikɔsœʔ]
aypo-a ta ikos-Ø–ůt
unusable-COP.ASS this.INA.AGT axe-AGT-DET.PROXI
'this axe is no good'

irelai bauvvo
['irelai 'bauw:ɔ]
irela-i bauvvo-Ø
beautiful-COP.PAST.ASS sky-AGT
'the sky was beautiful'

herias kobyly
['herɪas 'kʰɔb'yly]
here-as kob=yly-Ø
cold-COP.HAB.ASS summer=night-AGT
'summer nights are cold'

himi mitabe
['hi:mi: 'mi:dabe]
himi-i mitabe-Ø
warm-COP.PAST.ASS yesterday-AGT
'yesterday was warm'

aihhiè mitabuoḍḍo
['aih:ie: 'mi:dabu'ɔð:ɔ]
aihhie-i mitabu=oḍḍo-Ø
starry-COP.PAST yesterday=night.sky-AGT
'yesterday's sky was starry'

kulù yly
['kʰulu: 'yly]
kulu-u yly-Ø
cloudy-COP.TRANSLO.ASS night-AGT
'the night is getting cloudy'

tammi gjekehi ebi eskile ta sùḍbi-ůt
['tʰam:i 'dzecehi 'ebi 'ɛscile tʰa 'su:ðbɪœʔ]
ta-mmi gjeke-hi ebi eski-le ta sùḍbi-Ø–ůt
many-GEN year-GEN for empty-COP.PRES.PERF.INFER this.INA.AGT winter.camp-AGT-DET.PROXI
'this winter camp has apparently been empty for many years'

soprai hide nenika
['sɔpxai 'hide 'neniga]
sopra-i hide-Ø nen-ika
golden-COP.PAST.ASS hair-AGT 3P.ANI.PRON-ELAT
'X's hair was golden'

sari mahhakimi
['sari 'mah:aɟimi]
sar-i mahh-a-ki-mi-Ø
good-COP.PAST.ASS hunt-TR-TRANSLO-INFI.AG.TR-AGT
'the (going) hunting was good'

ehhabmisus osi koštet dobmibma tapakka
['eh:aʔpmisʊs 'ɔsi 'kʰɔɕtɛʔ 'dɔʔpmɪʔpma 'tʰapaʔka]
ehhabmis-us osi koštet-Ø dob=m-ibma tapak-ka
detailed-COP.HAB.TRANSL.ASS 2P.SG.PRON-LOC carving-AGT handle-ALLAT knife-GEN
'your carvings onto the handle of the blade are becoming detailed'

§9.16.2.5 Miscellaneous

The dependent copula can be found with certain other words than adjectives, namely pronouns and quantifiers, or even as a hyphened clitic (-a or -e/-ů, sometimes -ḥa and -ḥe/-ḥů) to reinforce the evidentiality of the verb, sometimes triggering a relative clause.

When added directly to pronouns, the copula creates a strong declarative sentence focusing the pronoun as the topic of the phrase. This triggers a relative clause.

megi	'I'
dami kistamo	'I am a student'
megia oa kistamo	'I am the student'
gogitua saṡi oana	'it's to *me* you're talking'

With quantifiers, the dependent copula serves as the verb 'to be', as opposed to the dependent copula which usually makes there-existential phrases:

ga taja omi	'there was a lot of snow'
tajai omi	'(lit.) the snow was much'
ga euma siġva	'there was a little bit of rain'
eumai siġva	'(lit.) the rain was little'

§9.17 Participles

Participles are the forms of a verb which can behave as nouns or adjectives while still keeping elements of verbal morphology. There are two forms of participles, called active participles and patientive participles. All participles show tense and aspect, case and number. Unlike adjectives, participles cannot be found with the dependent copula – instead, they use the independent copula:

	sogjon·ata	'X is dry' (*sogjon* 'dry' is an adjective and takes the dep. cop.)
but	*da·ta tśillu*	'X is dried' (*tśillu* is the pat. part. of *tśil·a* 'X will dry Y')

Active participles show some transitivity and thus have pre- and postverbal vowels., although virtually all attributive active participles only have the intransitive postverbal vowel. Patientive participles do not have any pre- or postverbal vowels. Active participles always have their postverbal vowel come before the aspect marker:

	man·i	'X comes'
	man·i·mo	'coming'
	kengi man·ot·i·ma	'coming day'
	kengi derodlima	'passed day (i.e. a day which has already passed)'
or	*kengi dehrotima*	'past day (i.e. a day which passed [long ago])'
	o·kjas·i	'X hurries'
	o·kjas·i·mo	'hurrying'
	tottamo o·kjas·ven	'a merchant in a hurry'
	iodi kjas·a·ma	'time saving' (lit. task-hurrying)
but	*kjah·u*	'worked in a hurry, botched' (no postverbal vowel)

While active participles may be both agentive or unagentive, patientive participles are only found in one form. Participles may also show both the conclusive and inconclusive aspect (marked by an consonant-final -m-, identical to the adjective and impersonal inconclusive marker).

Although participles may both be found as nouns and adjectives, they behave like neither. When they function as nouns, they differ from true nouns in that they may have a fixed plural ending and their declension differs from that of true nouns.

When they function as adjectives, participles may form long and complex "participial phrases" which precede the adjective-like word. Unlike true adjectives, participles are always marked for number and are only found with the complementizer as a relative clause if the participle is attributive. The complementizer is very commonly found in its short form (see, and active participles also exhibit a short form found in combination with the short complementizer (see *§9.15.1*).

Patientive participles may take personal pronouns – participles allow participants. If a noun is used instead of a pronoun, it is found in the genitive in the participial phrase (i.e. between the noun and the adjective).

Below is a table illustrating the active and patientive participles.

	active		patientive
	agentive	unagentive	
	-o	-a	-u
agentive singular	kòimo ['kʰʊ:imɔ] kò-i-m-o talk-ASS.ITR-INCONCL-ACT.PART.AG.AGT '(X which is) talking' or 'speaker'	pohhjima ['pʰɔh:jima] pohhj-i-m-a sleep-ASS.ITR-INCONCL-ACT.PART.AG.AGT '(X which is) sleeping' or 'sleeper'	sindu ['sɪndu] si<nd>-u catch.PAST-PAT.PART.AGT '(X which was) caught' or 'a catch'
	-e/-i		-uki
agentive plural	tàime ['tʰæ:ime] tà-i-m-e stand-ASS.ITR-INCONCL-ACT.PART.AG.AGT.PL '(X who will be) standing' or 'the winners/victors'		jahruki ['jahruʝi] <jahr>-u-ki kill.PAST-PAT.PART.AGT.PL '(X which have been) killed' or 'the kills'
	-otta	-atta	-utta
patientive/ genitive singular	kòimotta ['kʰʊ:imɔʔta] kò-i-m-o-tta talk-ASS.ITR-INCONCL-ACT.PART.AG.PAT '(X which is) talking' or 'speaker'	pohhjimatta ['pʰɔh:jimaʔta] pohhj-i-m-a-tta sleep-ASS.ITR-INCONCL-ACT.PART.UNAG.PAT '(X which is) sleeping' or 'sleeper'	sindutta ['sɪndʊʔta] si<nd>-u-tta catch.PAST-PAT.PART-PAT '(X which was) caught' or 'a catch'
	-itta or -ottai and -attai		-ukitta or -uttai

	active		patientive
	agentive	unagentive	
patientive/ genitive plural	tàimitta ['tʰæːimɪʔta] tà-i-m-itta stand-ASS.ITR-INCONCL-ACT.PART.AG.PAT.PL '(X who will be) standing' or 'the winners/ victors'		jahrukitta or jahruttai ['jahruɪʔta] or ['jahrʊʔtai] <jahr>-u-(ki)-tta-(i) kill.PAST-PAT.PART.(PL).PAT.(PL) '(X which have been) killed' or 'the kills'

The plural forms -ottai and -attai exist but are restricted in use, especially in the east and in older language. The form -uttai is common in all dialects, as is the form -ukitta. The active plural form -e and -i are used fairly freely, but in correct language, -i tends to be used for inanimate nouns while -e is used for animate nouns. In the locative cases, the final -a in -otta/-atta/-itta is not lost, e.g. *sinduttaita* '(in)to a catch'.

§9.17.1 Active Participles

Active participles are extremely common and serve a variety of purposes. They are derived from verbs, impersonal verbs and verbal adjectives. Compare the form of the three classes:

verb	*ta·hokja*	'X will blind Y'
impersonal verb	*hokja·m·i*	'it is blinding'
verbal adjective	*hokja·m·i·ka*	'I am blinded'
active participle	*hokja·m·a*	'blinding (light)'
attr. active participle	*hudde hokja·tot·i·m·a*	'a blinding light'

The active participle, here *hokjama* may function as a noun. For example, one might say:

tśeklas notśommima omudnamo hokjama
['tɕɛklːas 'notɕɔmːima 'ɔmʊʔtnamo 'hɔcama]
tśekl-a-s notśon-m=ima omudna-mo hokja-m-a-Ø
there.is.a.lot-ASS.CONCL.TR-HAB valley-ADESS snowy-GEN to.blind-INCONCL-ACT.PART.UNAG-AGT
'in snowy valleys, there is quite a lot of reflected sunlight (blinding)'

However, if the participle becomes attributive to a noun, the phrase changes:

tśeklas notśommima omudnamo huḍḍe hokjatotima
[ˈtɕɜklːas ˈnɔtɕɔmːima ˈɔmʊʔtnamo ˈhuðːe ˈhɔcadɔtɕima]
tśekl-a-s notśon-m=ima omudna-mo huḍḍe-Ø hokja-tot-i-m-a
there.is.a.lot-ASS.CONCL.TR-HAB valley-ADESS snowy-GEN light-ACT to.blind-COMPLE-ITR-INCONCL-ACT.PART.UNAG
'in snowy valleys, there is quite a lot of blinding light'

Active participles may be marked for time, mood, aspect and any other markings found in regular verbs. They are also nearly always in the inconclusive. Past participles are most commonly in the perfective (-**odlimo**, -**odlima**, -**odlime**), although past participles also exist – they generally refer to a more distant past.

somi vuihl·ot·i·mo	'the whistling man'
somi vuihl·ot·u·mo	'the man who whistled (i.e. long ago, no longer)'
somi vuihl·od·l·i·mo	'the man who whistled (general, more common)'
o·tarv·od·l·i·mo	'specialized'

Very many active participles may function as nouns entirely - for example, the participle *sah·m·a* means literally '(that which is) burning' but it may very well be used as a noun to mean 'a burn'. Furthermore, it may also show personal suffixes - a patientive pronoun is attached to a patientive participle. This also applies to patientive participles.

	sah·m·a·ka	'my burn' or '(that which is) burning me'
cf.	*sah·m·i·ka*	'I am burning, I feel very hot'
	sind·u	'a catch'
	sind·u·mi	'my catch'

A few nouns behave like participles (marked form in -**tta**) but may lack other verbal markings (such as postverbal vowels) and are called nominal participles. They are include:

ġyadlmi	'rainbow'
keukonhimo	'a (walking) group'
nikima	'death'
ulnuma	'the Milky Way' (originally probably 'that is seen at night)
miasma	'peace' (cognate to **besġ-** 'to be at peace/war')
monokonama	'will-o'-the-wisp' or 'foxfires' (ghost-swamp-ing)
jyryma	'period when migrating birds leave or arrive' (from *njorga* 'duck')
tahama	'world'
seuma	'soil, land'
sitrima	'fish head'

ůma	'a lot of'
ůtůma	'rough, porous, harsh' (from a defunct verb *ůt-, cf. ůdvů 'whetstone')
mosoma	'wolf, beast'

Many impersonal verbs have corresponding active participles for noun forms. An alternative form is in -en.

õskai	'it happens often'
õskama, õsken	'event'
tėrmi	'it is sunny'
tėrma, tėren	'sunny weather' or 'sunlight'
huhmi	'it is bright'
huhma, huhhen	'brightness, light'
komi	'it is summer'
koma, koben	'summer time'
jedmi	'time passes'
idden	'time'
kilppi	'it is common'
kilppima, kilppen	'norm, expectation, habit'

Generally, attributive active participles are typically found in the intransitive, even though the verb from which it is derived is transitive. Such attributive active participles are commonly found with an extra short form, especially in the eastern dialects. The short form is a combination of a reduced complementizer (usually to -ų- or -v-) and a simplified participial ending:

agentive and unagentive singular:	-en
agentive and unagentive plural:	-in

The form hokjama cannot be found as *hokjaen, but the form hokjatotima is also found as hokjaųen. See §9.14.1 on the short forms.

Participial phrase

Active participles may be preceded by a complete verb phrase – this phrase is ordered differently than regular verb phrases in that the verb comes at the very end of the phrase, i.e. the participle should always be the last element of the phrase. This type of construction, called participial phrase, can become quite long, and longer phrases should preferably be found in relative phrase.

njuhhi kidlimatta jeilli ketsġo kautsġodlimo
[ɲuhːi ˈcʰitɬimaʔta ˈjeilːi ˈcʰɛtsxɔ ˈkʰaʊtsxɔtɬimɔ]
njuhhi-Ø kidl-i-m-a-tta jei<lli> ketsġo kautsġ-ot-l-i-m-o
old.woman-AGT is.tradition-ITR-INCONCL-ACT.PART.UNAG-GEN old-GEN according.to make.jam-COMPLE-PERF-ITR-INCONCL-ACT.PART.AG
'the old woman who has made jam according to an old tradition'

njuhhi tammi gjekehi ebi kautsġodlimo
[ɲuhːi ˈtʰamːi ˈdzecehiebi ˈkʰaʊtsxɔtɬimɔ]
njuhhi-Ø ta=mmi gjeke-hi ebi kautsġ-ot-l-i-m-o
old.woman-AGT many.GEN year-GEN for.many make.jam-COMPLE-PERF-ITR-INCONCL-ACT.PART.AG
'the old woman who has made jam for many years'

njuhhi orirra kidlimatta jeilli ketsġo tammi gjekehi ebi kautsġodlimo
[ɲuhːi ˈɔrirːa ˈcʰitɬimaʔta ˈjeilːi ˈcʰɛtsxɔ ˈtʰamːi ˈdzecehiebi ˈkʰaʊtsxɔtɬimɔ]
njuhhi-Ø kidl-i-m-a-tta jei<lli> orirra ketsġo ta=mmi gjeke-hi ebi kautsġ-ot-l-i-m-o
old.woman-AGT always is.tradition-ITR-INCONCL-ACT.PART.UNAG-GEN old-GEN according.to many.GEN year-GEN for.many make.jam-COMPLE-PERF-ITR-INCONCL-ACT.PART.AG
'the old woman who has always made jam according to an old tradition for many years'

or

njuhhi, orirra kautsġi kidlimatta jeilli ketsġo tammi gjekehi ebi onora
[ɲuhːi ˈɔrirːa kʰaʊtsxi ˈcʰitɬimaʔta ˈjeilːi ˈcʰɛtsxɔ ˈtʰamːi ˈdzecehiebi ɔnˈɔra]
njuhhi-Ø kautsġ-i kidl-i-m-a-tta jei<lli> ketsġo ta=mmi gjeke-hi ebi on-or-a
old.woman-AGT always make.jam-ITR is.tradition-ITR-INCONCL-ACT.PART.UNAG-GEN old-GEN according.to many.GEN year-GEN for.many REL-COP.PERF-ASS
'the old woman who has always made jam according to an old tradition for many years'

cf.

orirra kautsġila kidlimatta jeilli ketsġo tammi gjekehi ebi njuhhi
[ˈɔrirːa ˈkʰaʊtsxila ˈcʰitɬimaʔta ˈjeilːi ˈcʰɛtsxɔ ˈtʰamːi ˈdzecehiebi]
orirra kautsġ-i-la kidl-i-m-a-tta jei<lli> ketsġo ta=mmi gjeke-hi ebi njuhhi-Ø
always make.jam-ASS.CONCL.ITR-PERF is.tradition-ITR-INCONCL- ACT.PART.UNAG-GEN old-GEN according.to many.GEN year-GEN for.many old.woman-AGT
'the old woman has made jam always according to an old tradition for many years'

Compare the participial phrase and normal verbal phrase below:

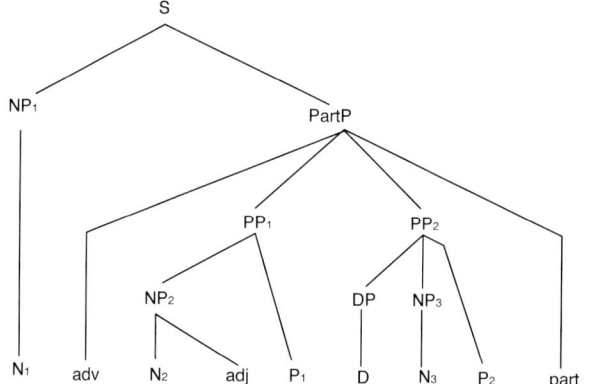

Njuhhi orirra kidlimatta jeilli ketsġo tammi gjekehi ebi kautsġodlimo

The old woman who has always made jam according to an old tradition for many years

Notice how the subject and participle switch places, but adverbs precede verbs whereas they precede participial phrases in the first example.

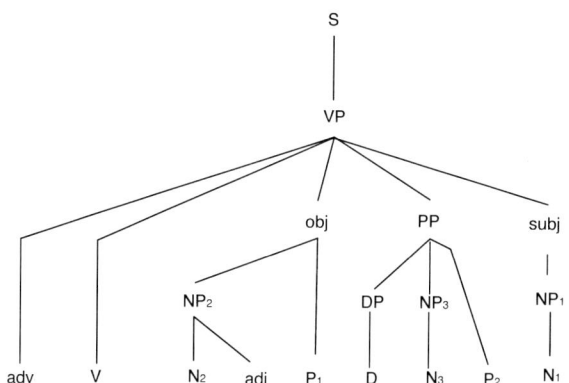

Orirra kautsġila kidlimatta jeilli ketsġo tammi gjekehi ebi njuhhi

The old woman has always made jam according to an old tradition for many years

§9.17.2 Patientive Participles

Patientive participles correspond to passive participles. They end in **-u** and are typically found attached on the past form of the verb. Non-past patientive participles entail a notion that the participles are to be completed in the future:

510

kili savvu	'burnt wood' (past stem **savv-**)
kili sahhu	'wood to be burnt' (non-past stem **sahh-**)

Unlike active participles, patientive participles may stand as attributive adjectives to nouns *without* the complementizer. However, negated participles do take the complementizer, then with the form -ont·u/-nont·u or -ōt·u/-nōt·u:

kili savvontu	'unburnt wood'
kili sahhontu	'wood which is not to be burnt'
tsġavontu	'a taboo' (that which is not to be said)

sem ulolis montu gattia-go milkid
[sɛm uˈlɔlɪs ˈmɔntu ˈgaʔtiagɔ ˈmɪlcːi]
sem u-lol-i-s m-ont-u gattia–go mil<k>i-d
NEG PASS-leave-ASS.CONCL.ITR-HAB eat.PAST-COMPLE-PAT.PART in.presence-1P.POSS.SG fish.scale-PAT
'fish scales are not left uneaten when I'm around'

iriului sihdika peljekkōtiu
[iˈriului ˈsiːhdʑiga ˈpʰeljɛʔkɔ̃tɕiu]
i-r-iul-u-i -Ø sir-di=ka peljekk-ont-i-u
DIT-bite-IUL-PAST-ASS.CONCL.ITR fish-ELAT cook-COMPLE-PAST-PAT.PART
'X took a bit out of the uncooked fish'

lolla tamaleurrontuki eksi ipruo
[ˈlɔlːa tʰamaˈleurːɔntuʝi ˈɛksːi ˈɪpxuo]
lo<ll>l-a-Ø tama-leurr-ont-u-ki eksi ipro-Ø-o
leave.PAST-ASS.CONCL.ITR-3P.AG.SG onto-touch.PAST-COMPLE.NEG-PAT.PART-PL 3P.PRON.PL.DAT carcass-DAT-PL
'X left the carcasses untouched'

Patientive participles allow for pronoun markings. Usually, these will correspond to the agents of the passive form of the phrase. If the agent is a noun, it will be found in the genitive *before* the participle:

usahrami kidli	'the wood was burnt by me'
kili savvu·mi	'wood burnt by me' *or* 'my burnt wood'
kidli savvu·tta·mi	'wood (GEN) burnt by me' *or* 'my burnt wood (GEN)'
kili sōkko savvu	'wood burnt by the man' *or* 'the man's burnt wood'

Other such fixed expressions exist in Siwa:

maistu	'my mistake, my fault, sorry' (cf. *m·aihi* 'I will make a mistake')
ednesku	'please' (cf. *neska·mi* 'I will ask Y')
nõstettumi	'or so I've heard' (cf. *nõstettami* 'I heard Y')

Patientive participles are sometimes found as nouns, though they are not as common as their active counterparts:

tśiḍbu	'meaning, sense' (cf. tśib·a 'X will mean Y')
kesku	'advice'
miedju	'herd, group, collection' (cf. miegi·a 'X will herd Y')
missu	'tobacco' (cf. misu 'X will smove Y')
muontu	'decision' (cf. muont·a 'X will decide Y')
nokkiu	'name' (cf. nokk·a 'X will call Y')
odjuki	'memory' (plural, cf. ogi·a 'X will remember Y')
sindu	'catch' (cf. sibm·a 'X will catch Y')
sotsu	'permission' (cf. u·sot·i 'X will be allowed')
tsimmilsuki	'beliefs, conviction, hope'

Compare more examples of passive participles:

tśadna njorġa	'X will find the duck'
njorġa tśandu	'a/the found duck'
atujukkasa lokna	'the cold will make you sick'
longamo atujukkiu	'sickened by the cold' (also lokne-atujukkiu)

§9.17.3 Temporal Participles

Participles, both active and patientive, may be found in a so-called temporal phrase, equivalent to English temporal relative clauses, or *(after) having Ø-ed* and *(while) Ø-ing*. The temporal phrase contains an agentive participle in the perfective (-l·o, -l·a, -l·i, -l·e), or in patientive participle (-u) both in the inconclusive.

>ẏla soġlolatta, nuskasġivvo selue
>[yːla ˈsɔxlɔlaʔta ˈnʊskɑsxiwːɔ ˈselue]
>ẏ-la soġl-o-l-a-tta, nuskasġivv-o selo-e
>ice-PAT melt-INFER.CONCL.ITR-PERF-ACT.PART.UNAG-PAT become.impassable-INFER.CONCL.TRANSL large.river-PAT
>'when the ice will have thawed, the river will become impassable'

>to tymotuvilo, amġappen ừki
>[tʰɔ ˈtʰymɔˈtuvilɔ ˈamxaʔpɛn ˈuːci]
>to tym-o-tuv-i-l-o to <amġ>-a-ppen-Ø <ừki>
>3P.PRON.AGT.SG down-SUBJ-bend-ASS.CONCL.ITR-PERF-ACT.PART.AG drink.PAST-ASS.CONCL.ITR-FREQU-3P.AG.SG water-GEN
>'having bent down, he drank a little water'

benho bǔalo, maskimi kadda
[ˈbɛnhɔ ˈbœalɔ ˈmɑscimi ˈkʰɑtːa]
benho-Ø <bǔ>-al-o ma<sk>-i-mi ka=dda
dog-AGT eat.PAST-PERF-ACT.PART.AG go.PAST-ASS.CONCL.ITR out-ILLAT
'When the dog had eaten (the dogs having eaten), I went outside'

benhue bǔali, maskimi kadda
[ˈbɛnhue ˈbœali ˈmɑscimi ˈkʰɑtːa]
benho-Ø-e <bǔa>-al-i ma<sk>-i-mi ka=dda
dog-AGT-PL eat.PAST-PERF-ACT.PART.AG.PL go.PAST-ASS.CONCL.ITR out-ILLAT
'When the dogs had eaten (the dogs having eaten), I went outside'

tsġoglita keidu te sasame keʉu, õde na gati taba kitami
[ˈtsxɔklida ˈcʰeiðu de ˈsɑsame ˈcʰewu ˈõde na gɑti ˈtʰɑba cʰitɑmi]
tsġo<gl>i-ta keid-u-Ø te sasame-Ø keʉ-u-Ø õde na g-a-ti ta=ba kita-a-mi-Ø
tsókli-ILLAT start.fire-PAT.PART-ACT and tipi-DAT rise-PAT.PART-ACT still.now ASS.PART COP-ASS-3P.RECi much.GEN do-TR-INFI.AG.TR-ACT
'having yet to light a **tsġokli**-fire and raise the tipi, there was still much to do for them'

kili sahhu, hiddjujahtappajo
[ˈcʰili ˈsɑhːu ˈhidʑujahtaʔpajɔ]
kili-Ø sahh-u-Ø hiddjuj-aht-a-ppa-Ø-jo
wood-AGT burn-PAT.PART-AGT stack.up-AHT-ASS.CONCL.TR-FREQU-3P.PAT-4P.AGT
'the wood having yet to be burned, one will stack it up in a bundle'

§9.18 Infinitives

Siwa has two types of infinitives – copular infinitives and nominal infinitives. Copular infinitives are made up of the main verb with all markings except for pronouns and tense, followed by the infinitive clause (found in ⌐ ⌐ in the examples below.), which itself ends with the copula and the appropriate markings (pronouns):

etsta ⌐nori sengyla jeilli gaita⌐ tanutsigi[1]
[ˈɛtstːa ˈnɔri ˈsɛŋːyla ˈjeilːi ˈɡɑida tʰɑnutsiji]
ets-t-a nor-i sengy-la jei-l-ri g-a-ita tanut-si-gi
start.PAST-ASS.CONCL.TR sing-ITR song-GEN old-GEN COP.PAST-ASS-ILLAT singer-AGT-PL
'the singers started ⌐to sing an old song⌐'

Nominal infinitives are a special class of nouns (verbal nouns) whose objects (provided they are nouns) are found in the genitive before the verbal noun and require no copula:

aksa muontu merana ⌐istodi tatamantami⌐
[ˈakːsa ˈmuɔntu ˈmærɑnɑ ˈiːstɔdʑi tʰɑtɑˈmɑntɑmi]
ak=s-a muontu-Ø merana-Ø isto-di tata-mant-a-mi
COP.PASS=NEG-ASS decision-AGT difficult-AGT gift-GEN into-receive-TR-INFI.AG.TR
'it was not a difficult decision to accept the gift'

aksa muontu merana ⌐tatamantami⌐
[ˈakːsa ˈmuɔntu ˈmærɑnɑ tʰɑtɑˈmɑntɑmi]
ak=s-a muontu-Ø merana-Ø tata-mant-a-Ø-mi
COP.PASS=NEG-ASS decision-AGT difficult-AGT gift-GEN into-receive-TR-3P.PAT-INFI.AG.TR
'it was not a difficult decision to accept it'

Only the infinitive clause of the finite verb is found in the copular form, with all subsequent infinitives being found in the nominal form. Copular infinitives are not in fact true infinitives, as the copula can be found in various tenses, moods, aspects, etc – thus, they can be considered close to a gerund or a participle. Below are the various functions each infinitive form respectively covers:

- An infinitive whose function is that of an adjectival adverbial (*kekken gjosmika ⌐makisteta⌐* 'I am too tired *to go*') is found in the nominal form with appropriate agreement with the verb, noun or adjective (illative or elative). The illative is used with actions which have yet to happen (*gimmika ⌐makisteta⌐* 'I am excited *to go*', i.e. 'I am excited *that I will go*') while the elative is used with actions which have been completed (*gjosmika ⌐noristeka⌐* 'I am tired *of singing*', i.e. 'I am tired *of having sung*') or which have never occurred (*sikkiami ⌐makisteka⌐* 'I refused *to go*').

---

[1] The copula may follow the subject phrase: *etsta tanutsigi nori sengyla jeilli gaita*

- When the infinitive functions as the subject of mostly copular verbs (*ga aimù* ˈmaksaˈ 'it was a mistake to go') or the attribute of an adjective (*męranua* ˈmaksaˈ 'it is hard to go') or noun (the desire to go), as an interrogative (*set netami nit-ḥa* ˈkitamiˈ 'I don't know what to do') or in a infinitive relative clause (*atsa gogia it* ˈkitami/kitabmeˈ 'I don't have anything to do'), it is found as the nominal infinitive in the unmarked form. When in an infinite relative clause, the nominal infinitive may be found in its marked form, then understood to be in the genitive-partitive. It is also found as the subject of impersonal verbs, always unmarked (*voammika* ˈmaksaˈ 'I'm afraid to go'). More complexe relative or interrogative infinitive clauses use the copular infinitive.

- When an infinitive functions as the object of a verb, it is usually found in the nominal form in the illative or elative (*kyhami* ˈmanistetaˈ 'I tried *to go*') or in the copular form if the infinitive clause is more complex, for example if the infinitive itself has an object (*kyhami* ˈsaisa kohko geitaˈ 'I tried *to warn the boy*'). However, the nominal form can be used if the object of the infinitive clause is a verbal pronoun (*kyhami* ˈsaisamiˈ 'I tried *to warn Y*').

- The copular form is used when the infinitive is governed by the indirect or double object of a verb, often in the short form (*nonasimi* ˈmaki oakibma eˈ 'I told you to go home' or *gieliaka* ˈhantui geikaˈ 'he accused me of lying'). This is very often the case with verbs whose subject is not the same as that of the infinitive clause (*ikeskkami benhueita* ˈtsadnaki njorgua deˈ 'I taught the dog to fetch the ducks'). The copular form is also used with various adverbs such as *avvi* or *mi* (ˈjeḍḍi avvi naˈ *mansimi* 'I came running') and with link constructions (see §9.16.1.3.5). Finally, the copular form is also required with many auxiliary verbs.

form		function
nominal	subject (of impersonal verbs)	*ga aimù maksa* [ga ˈɑimùː ˈmaksːa] g-a aimù-Ø maki-sa COP.PAST-ASS mistake-AGT go-INFI.AG.ITR 'it was a mistake to go'
		voammika maksa [ˈvɔamːiga ˈmaksːa] voavv-m-i-ka maki-sa be.afraid-INCONCL-ASS.ITR-1P.PAT.SG go-INFI.AG.ITR 'I'm afraid to go'
	nominal attribute	*muontu maksa* [ˈmuɔntu ˈmaksːa] muontu-Ø maki-sa decision-AGT go-INFI.AG.ITR 'the decision to go'
	adjectival attribute	*męranua maksa* [ˈmæranua ˈmaksːa] męrana-a maki-sa difficult-COP.ASS go-INFI.AG.ITR 'it is difficult to go'
	interrogative	*set netami, nit-ḥa kitami* [sɛʔtˈnetami ˈniːʔːa ˈcʰitami] set net-a-mi ni=t–ḥa kita-a-mi NEG know-ASS.CONCL.TR-1P.AG.SG what.INA.UNKNOWN-GEN do-TR-INFI.AG.TR 'I don't know what to do'
	relative (sometimes marked)	*atsa gogia ihni kitami/kitabme* [ˈatsa ˈgoɟia ˈiːhnĩ ˈcʰitami / ˈcʰitaʔpme] at=s-a gogi-a ih-ni kita-a-mi / kita-a-t=me COP=NEG-ASS 1P.PRON.SG-INESS no.INA.UNKNOWN-AGT do-ASS-INFI.AG.TR / do-ASS-INFI.AG.TR-GEN 'I don't have anything to do'

form		function
nominal + ILLAT/ ELAT	adjectival adverbial	*kekken gjosmika makitseta* ['kʰɛʔkɛn 'ʝɔsmiga 'mɑcitseda] kekk=en gjos-m-i-ka maki-t=se=ita too-ADV tired-INCONCL-ASS.ITR-1P.PAT go-INFI.AG.ITR-ILLAT 'I am too tired to go'
		gjosinami noritseka ['ʝɔsinɑmi 'nɔrɪtsega] gjosin-a-mi nor-i-t=se=ika tired-COP.ASS-1P.ACT.AG.SG sing-ITR-INFI.AG.ITR-ELAT 'I am tired of singing'
	object of verb	*kyhami makitseta* ['cʰyʔami 'mɑcitseda] ky<h>-a-mi maki-t=se=ita try.PAST-ASS.CONCL.TR-1P.AG.SG go-INFI.AG.ITR-ILLAT 'I tried to go'
	indirect object	*nonasimi mani e* ['nɔnɑsimi 'mɑni 'e] n=on-a-si-mi man-i e PAST-tell-ASS.CONCL.TR-2P.RECI-1P.AG.SG go-ITR COP-INFER- 'I told you to come'
	double object	*gieliaka hantui geika* ['ʝieliɑga 'hantui 'ʝeiga] giel-i-a-ka-Ø hanto-i g-e-ika accuse-PAST-ASS.CONCL.TR-1P.PAT.SG-3P.AG.SG lie-ITR COP.PAST-INFER-ELAT 'X accused me of lying'
		ikeskkami benhueita tsadnaki njorġua e [i'cʰɛskːɑmi 'bɛnhueida 'tɕaʔtnɑɟi 'ɲɔrxuae] i-ke<skk>-a-mi benho=eita tsadn-a-ki njorga-Ø-a Ø-e DIT-teach.PAST-ASS.CONCL.TR-1P.AG.SG dog-ILLAT find-ASS-TRANSLO duck-DAT-PL COP-INFER 'I taught the dog to fetch the ducks'

form		function
copular	adverbial	*jeḍḍi avvi na mansi* [ˈjeð:ɪɑwːi na ˈmansi] jeḍḍ-i mi g-a ma<ns>-i-Ø run-ITR ADV.PART COP.PAST-ASS come.PAST-ASS.CONCL.ITR-3P.AG.SG 'X came running'
	link construction	*manike kimi ge jekki* [ˈmanɪje ˈkʰimi ɹe ˈjɛʔci] man-i-ke kimi g-e je<kk>-i-Ø come-ITR-LINK.GOAL for COP.PAST-ASS run.PAST-ASS.CONCL.ITR-3P.AG.SG 'X ran in order to come'
	auxiliary verbs	*tahatru mani oakibma e* [tʰɑˈhatxu ˈmani ˈɔɑcɪʔpma ˈe] ta-hatr-u man-i oak=ibma Ø-e 3P.UNAG-ought-ASS.CONCL.TRANSL come-ITR home-ALLAT COP-INFER 'X ought to come home'
	object of verb (with complex infinitive clause)	*kyhami saisa kohko deita/e* [ˈcʰyʔami ˈsaisa ˈkʰɔhkɔ ˈdeida/e] ky<h>-a-mi sais-a kori-ko d-e-ita/Ø-e try.PAST-ASS.CONCL.TR-1P.AG.SG warn-TR boy-GEN COP-INFER-ILLAT/COP-INFER 'I tried to warn the boy'

While the nominal infinitive can only show relative tense through the use of the illative (imperfect) and elative (perfect), the copular infinitive can use its full conjugation to function as a gerund of a participle. Thus, the copular infinitive is used in Siwa where English uses complex infinitive or participial phrases beyond the scope of the functions introduced above. Complex infinitive or participial phrases are those which include arguments (own subject and/or object), e.g.

ahtami aimù ˹tatamanta ìsto kohko aksaika˺
[ˈahtami ˈaimuː tʰatʰaˈmanta ˈiːstɔ ˈkʰɔhkɔ ˈakːsaiga]
<aht>-a-mi aimù-Ø tata-mant-a isto-Ø kori-ko ak=s-a-ika
do.PAST-ASS.CONCL.TR-1P.AG.SG mistake-DAT into-receive-TR gift-DAT boy-GEN COP.PASS=NEG-ASS-ELAT
'I made the mistake of not accepting the boy's gift'

> *kyhami ⌈saisa kohko ⌈manitseka⌉ ge⌉*
> [ˈcʰyʔami ˈsaisa ˈkʰɔhkɔ ˈmanitsega ɟe]
> ky<h>-a-mi sais-a kori-ko sę mani-t=se=ika g-e
> try.PAST-ASS.CONCL.TR-1P.AG.SG warn-TR boy-GEN go-INFI.AG.ITR-ELAT COP.PAST-INFER
> 'I tried to warn the boy not to go'

Inside an infinitive clause however, there cannot be more than one copula. Infinitives within an infinitive clause, as in the example above, are always in the nominal form. Such nominal infinitives are negatived with *sę/sem/set*, which is generally found before the verbal noun's genitive objects. Infinitive Clause may contain any number of infinitives. Nominal infinitives can also contain pronoun markers, though sometimes independent genitive pronouns may be used, but the distinction between agent and patient becomes blurred can also be used:

> *kyhami ⌈saisa kohko ⌈makitseka ⌈ketojabmeta⌉ ge⌉*
> 'I tried to warn the boy not to go to look them'

or

> *kyhami ⌈saisa kohko ⌈manitseka ⌈kjon ketobmeta⌉ ge⌉*
> 'I tried to warn the boy not to go to look them'

Note that a number of auxiliary verbs may appear with the copular infinitive if the construction is generally impersonal or benefactive, especially with the construction *u·sot·i·ki hanta* 'I am allowed to eat'.

§9.18.1 Nominal Infinitive

The nominal infinitive (also called verbal noun) is composed of the verb and the infinitival ending. It is a noun and can have participants (no agent/patient distinction) which are found *before* the verbal noun. The nominal infinitive may or may not have a postverbal vowel. It is commonly dropped if a cluster can be formed (see *§3.4.7*). It may reappear in the marked form to avoid impossible clusters. Nominal infinitives can house personal pronouns and all other constituents of the normal verb, except for tense. The nominal infinitive endings distinguish agentivity, but not in their marked form. All unagentive infinitive endings in -u also exist in a rounded form -ů used after -y- or -ů-.

| transitive | translative | intransitive | subjective | ditransitive | passive |

		1	2	3	4	5	6
ACTIVE	AGT	-mi		-sa	-na	-nin	
ACTIVE	UNAGT	-mu -mů	-lu -oru -ůrů	-su -sů	-nu -nů	-non -nůn	-monu -můnů
PATIENTIVE GENITIVE		-bme	-dle	-tse	-dne	-nidne/-nōdne	-mōdne
PATIENTIVE GENITIVE		-nta	-lta -olta -ůlta	-sta	-nta	-nita / -nōta	-mōta

The marked form of nominal infinitives exists in two forms, called the -Cta and the -tCe forms. They are both valid and considered correct. Most eastern dialects use the -tCe forms, while the -Cta form is commonly associated with lower or more relaxed language registers and the far western dialects.

When the marked -Cta form is combined with locative endings, its -a- merged with the -i- of the locative endings to -e-, e.g. *maksa* 'to go' becomes *makisteta* 'to go(ing)' (from *maki·s·ta·ita).

Verbal adjectives do not generally have a nominal infinitive, while impersonal verbs simply use their corresponding unagentive nominal infinitive endings:

§9.18.1.2 Verb Stem and Nominal Infinitive Coalescence

The nominal infinitive ending in its unmarked form, when no participants or other endings are found attached to the verb, coalesces in a specific way with the consonant in which verb stems end and drop the postverbal vowel all together. The tables below describes this. All consonants excluded require the postverbal vowel – only the unmarked form of verbs ending in the following consonants or consonant clusters coalesce directly with the nominal infinitive endings.

Only a handful of verbs govern the nominal infinitive in its dative form – most notably, the verb *sot·a*[1] 'X will make Y (do Z)':

> *sodda kori kiḑgami*
> [ˈsɔtːa ˈkʰɔri ˈcʰɪðgami]
> so<dd>-a-Ø kori-Ø kiḑg-a-Ø-mi
> give.PAST-ASS.CONCL.TR-3P.AG.SG boy-DAT PICK.UP-TR-3P.PAT.SG-infi.AG.TR
> 'the boy made X pick it up'

---

[1] The verb **sot·a** having the meaning of 'make X VERB' has the past form **sodd-** as opposed to the past of the same verb with the meaning of 'to give', which has the past form i·st-.

	transitive	translative	intransitive	subjective	ditransitive	passive
-kk- -gg-	-kmi -kmu	-klu	-ksa -ksu	-kna -knu	-knin -knon	-kmon
	peljekmi 'to cook' (*peljekk·a*)	*reklu* 'to open' (*ta·rekk·u*)	*maksu* 'to snow' (*makk·i*)	*djikna* 'to show off' (*o·djikk·i*)	*mŭiknŭn* 'to infect (someone)' (*i·mŭigg·i*)	*gikmon* 'to get sharpened' (*u·gikk·i*)
-ġ-	-ġmi -ġmu	-ġlu	-hsa -hsu	-ġna -ġnu	-ġnin -ġnon	-ġmon
	moġmi 'to drink' (*moġ·a*)	*ljuġlu* 'to rot' (*d·ljuġ·u*)	*tāhsa* 'to stand up' (*taġ·i*)	*gaġna* 'to guess' (*o·gaġ·a*)	*eġnon* 'to remain(somewhere)' (*t·j·eġ·i*)	*iġmon* 'to get accepted' (*ub·iġ·i*)
-h-	-bmi -bmu	Ø	Ø	-dna -dnu	-dnin -dnon	-bmon
	mebmi 'to smear' (*meh·a*)			*ġedna* 'to move' (*o·ġeh·i*)	*ġednin* 'to move(somewhere)' (*i·ġeh·i*)	*obmon* 'to be smoked' (*ub·oh·i*)
-h-	-hmi -hmu	-hlu	-hsa -hsu	-hna -hnu	-hnin -hnon	-hmon
	tayhmi 'to beat' (*tayhh·a*)	*pihlu* 'to be possible' (*pihh·u*)	*sahsu* 'to burn' (*t·sahh·u*)	*gahna* 'to lean' (*o·gahh·i*)	*lehnon* 'to float (somewhere)' (*t·i·lehh·i*)	*nyhmŭn* 'to become bent' (*u·nyhh·i*)

stem ending	transitive	translative	intransitive	subjective	ditransitive	passive
-m-	-mi / -mu / -mü	-lu/-lü, -oru/-ürü	-sa/-su/-sü	-na/-nu/-nü	-nin/-non/-nün	-mon / -mün
	-mmi / -mmu	-mlu	-msa / -msu	-mna / -mnu	-mnin / -mnon	-mmon
	šemmi 'to believe' (šem·a)	ijomlu 'to be possible' (ijom·u)	imsa 'to roam' (im·i)	tsomna 'to unite' (o·tsom·i)	lomnin 'to run (somewhere)' (i·lom·i)	nemmon 'to get piled up' (u·nem·i)
-p- / -b-	-bmi / -bmu	-pru	-bsa / -bsu	-mna / -mnu	-mnin / -mnon	-bmon
	obmi 'to help' (op·a)	liupru 'to die out' (d·liup·u)	semmi 'to believe' (sem·a)	tsimna 'to mean' (tsib·a)	tsemnin 'to have the patience to' (i·sep·i·ta)	nebmon 'to get caught' (u·nep·i)
-pp- / -bb-	-pmi / -pmu	∅	-psa / -psu	∅	∅	-pmon
	vapmi 'to praise' (vapp·a)		ɥepsu 'to slip' (t·ɥebb·i)			vapmon 'to be praised' (u·vapp·i)
-v- / -ɟ- / -vv-	-mmi / -mmu	-llu, -rru	-ssa / -ssu	-nna / -nnu	-nnin / -nnon	-mmon
	voammi 'to scare' (voavv·a)	eullu 'to reach' (t·euvv·u)	kessa 'to rise' (keɥ·a)	tsgonna 'to introduce oneself' (o·tsgov·i)	sunnon 'to flow (somewhere)' (t·i·suvv·i)	menimmon 'to be fooled' (u·meniɥ·i)

	transitive	translative	intransitive	subjective	ditransitive	passive
-n-	-mni / -mnu		-nta / -ntu	-nna / -nnu	-nnin / -nnon	-mnon
	gaggamni 'to examine' (*gaggan·a*)	∅	*konta* 'to walk' (*kon·i*)	*einna* 'to propel oneself' (*om·ein·i*)	*konnin* 'to walk (somewhere)' (*i·kon·i*)	*nayimnon* 'to be used' (*u·nayin·i*)
	-bmi / -bmu	-dlu	-tsa / -tsu	-dna / -dnu	-dnin / -dnon	-bmon
-t- / -d-	*rabmi* 'to stop' (*rad·a*)	*hŭdlŭ* 'to fit, adapt' (*ta·hŭd·ŭ*)	*itsu* 'to fall' (*t·id·i*)	*odna* or *otena* 'to pair up' (*o·t·i*)	*kikudnon* 'not to have patience (for)' (*t·i·kikut·i*)	*tiobmon* 'to be contained' (*u·tiod·i*)
	-tmi / -tmu	-dlu	-tsa / -tsu	-tna / -tnu	-tnin / -tnon	-tmon
-tt- / -dd-	*pitmi* 'to pay attention' (*pitt·a*)	*modlu* 'to go down' (*ta·mott·u*)	*motsa* 'to land' (*mott·a*)	*hetna* 'to scatter' (*o·hett·i*)	*motnin* 'to end up somewhere' (*t·i·mott·i*)	*sautmon* 'to be caught with hands' (*u·saudd·i*)
	-dmi / -dmu	-dlu	-hsa / -hsu	-dna / -dnu	-dnin / -dnon	-dmon
-dd-	*vidmi* 'to steal' (*vidd·a*)	*todlu* 'to turn out, to be the answer' (*ta·todd·u*)	*jehsa* 'to run' (*jedd·i*)	*idna* 'to get somewhere' (*ob·idd·i*)	*jednin* 'to run (somewhere)' (*ig·jedd·i*)	*vidmon* 'to get stolen' (*u·vidd·i*)

	transitive	translative	intransitive	subjective	ditransitive	passive
-l-/-ll-	-lmi -lmu	-llu	-lsa -lsu	-lna -lnu	-lnin -lnon	-lmon
	lolmi 'to leave' (*lol·a*)	*njallu* 'to taste of' (*ta·njal·u*)	*tsoalsu* 'to shimmer' (*ta·tsoal·i*)	*tsilna* 'to dry oneself' (*o·tsil·i*)	*kŭnnjŭlnin* 'to settle (somewhere)' (*i·kŭnnjŭl·i*)	*silmon* 'to get blown away' (*u·sil·i*)
-dl-	-dlmi -dlmu	-dlu	∅	-dlna -dlnu	-dlnin -dlnon	-dlmon
	ruodlmi 'to fold' (*ruodl·a*)	*sadlu* 'to burn' (*t·sadl·u*)		*gedlna* 'to behave oneself' (*o·gedl·i*)	*kadlnon* 'to suffice for (something)' (*i·kadl·i*)	*nidlmon* 'to be done a certain way' (*u·nidl·i*)
-ng-	-gmi -gmu	∅	∅	-gna -gnu	-gnin -gnon	-gmon
	ŭgmŭ 'to excite' (*t·ŭng·a*)			*migna* 'to get read' (*o·ming·i*)	*gjagnin* 'to find shelter (somewhere)' (*i·gjang·i*)	*ŭgmŭn* 'to be excited (by)' (*ub·ŭng·i*)
-k-/-g-	-hmi -hmu	-klu	-ksa -ksu	-hna -hnu	-hnin -hnon	-hmon
	goahmi 'to pick' (*goak·a*)	*bieklu* 'to start to leak' (*ta·biek·u*)	*maksa* 'to go' (*mak·i*)	*inuhna* 'to prosper' (*ob·inuk·i*)	*mahnin* 'to go (somewhere)' (*i·mak·i*)	*oaihmon* 'to get hooked' (*ub·oaig·i*)

	transitive	translative	intransitive	subjective	ditransitive	passive
	-śmi / -śmu	-slu or ∅	-ssa / -ssu	-nta / -ntu	-ntin / -nton	-smon
-s-	*miśmi* 'to smoke' (*miṡ·a*)	*seslu* 'to happen' (*t·ses·u*)	*tissa* 'to laugh' (*tiṡ·i*)	*kjanta* 'to hurry up' (*o·kjas·i*)	*rentin* 'to squeeze (somewhere)' (*i·res·i*)	*saismon* 'to be warned' (*u·sais·i*)
	-tsmi / -tsma			-tsna / -tsnu	-tsnin / -tsnon	-tsmon
-ts-	*vitsmi* 'to fix' (*vits·a*)	∅	∅	*eytsna* 'to nest, to hide' (*t·om·eyts·i*)	*ŭpŭtsnin* 'to slouch (somewhere)' (*t·ib·ŭpŭts·i*)	*miatsmon* 'to get soaked' (*u·miats·i*)
	-śmi / -śmu		-śśa / -śśu			-śmon
-ś-	*kyśmi* 'to try' (*kyṡ·a*)	∅	*saśśa* 'to speak' (*saṡ·i*)	∅	∅	*kyśmon* 'to be tried' (*u·kyṡ·i*)
	-mri / -mru	-rru	-rha / -rhu	-hna / -hnu	-hnin / -hnon	-mron
-r-	*demri* 'to wrap' (*der·a*)	*tsoairru* 'to rot' (*ta·tsoair·u*)	*erha* 'to be careful' (*eri·i*)	*svihnu* 'to consist of' (*o·svir·i*)	*jaihnin* 'to row (somewhere)' (*ig·jair·i*)	*imron* 'to get killed' (*ub·ir·i*)

§9.18.2 Copular Infinitive

Copular infinitives are in fact a copular construction identical to inconclusive copular constructions (*kon·i katsa n·a·mi* 'I am walking outside'). The details of the organization of the copular and verbal stems are explained in *§9.2.2*. The infinitive verb is found as a split-stem, with the normal phrase included between the split-stem and the copula, which is only followed by the agent:

Slot 4 (Split-stem):
    transitivity
        transitive   (-a)
        intransitive   (-i)
        ditransitive   (i-Ø-i or i-Ø-a)
        objective   (o-Ø-i or o-Ø-a)
        translative   (-u/-ů)
        passive   (u-Ø-i or u-Ø-a)

Slot 4² (Copula):
    mood
        indicative
        optative
        conditional irrealis
    evidentiality
        assertive
        inferential

In fact, copular infinitives are not true infinitives at all, because there is agreement between the tense of the phrase governing the infinitive and the copula's tense and evidentiality. A more accurate description of this function of the copula would be that copular verbs act as infinitive-like phrases when the nominal infinitive cannot be used.

    The copular infinitive is used whenever the infinitive verb acts as the object (either direct or indirect) of the matrix verb. In addition, it is used in link constructions (see *§9.16.1.3.5*) and with very many auxiliary verbs.

nonasimi mani deita	'I told you to come'
aiskaka mani geita	'X asked me to go'
kukomi taulhi omingi deita	'to order the soldiers to get ready'

An alternative to this is using the ditransitive and using the nominal infinitive, but it is restricted to a very formal register.

inonasimi manta	'I told you to come' (lit. I told you the coming)
jaiskaki manta	'X asked me to go' (lit. X asked me the going)

> *kukonin tautsaitagi migna*   'to order the soldiers to get ready' (lit. to order to the soldiers the getting ready')

The copular infinitive allows for a different subject of the infinitive clause that that of the matrix verb:

> *tsepumana oheyti deika ki somigi*   'you must wait until the men return home' (lit. 'you must have the patience (that the men) disembark')'

§9.18.2.1 Time And Evidentiality

Copular infinitives agree in tense with the matrix verb – a past matrix verb will have an infinitive copula in the past. Not only is the tense of the matrix verb important, the time-relation of the infinitive clause is also marked through evidentiality on the copula.

Copular infinitive clauses are very commonly found with either illative or elative locative markers on the copula (locative infinitives). The illative is used when the infinitive is a supervenient event to the matrix verb, i.e. has yet to happen in relation to the verb. Because the action has yet to happen, the verb is generally found in the inferential.

> *tsuoggami otoati belmueita deita*
> [ˈtsuɔkːami ɔˈtɔatɕi ˈbɛlmueida ˈdeida]
> tsuogg-a-mi o-toat-i belmo-e=ita d-e-ita
> hope-ASS.CONCL.TR-1P.AG.SG SUBJ-join-ITR work-ILLAT COP-INFER-ILLAT
> 'I hope to join in chore'

The elative is used when the infinitive is a preceding event, i.e. has already happened /begun in relation to the matrix verb. The verbs are more commonly found in the assertive in this case

> *radan nora atsi sengẏ-t daika!*
> [ˈradan ˈnɔra ˈatsi ˈseŋːyː? ˈdaiga]
> rad-a-n nor-a at=si sengẏ-Ø-t d-a-ika
> stop-ASS.CONCL.TR-IMP.2P.SG sing-TR this.INA.DAT song-DAT–DET.MEDI COP-ASS-ELAT
> 'stop singing that (whole) song!'

However, if the infinitive clause is considered to be more closely linked to the main verb, either because the two actions are simultaneous or because they are to be considered as semantically one event, the copula may be left without locative markers. It is often found in its simple form, especially in the present, then simply *a* or *e* (i.e. Ø-a). This is commonly done with the coordinating particles *mi* and *avvi*.

udġyni mi a tàsti	'X stood up, looking around' or 'X stood up and looked around'

It is also used to link two infinitive clauses together, and the infinitive clause containing the copula can be following by a nominal infinitive.

boadni e kyha	'X tried to jump'
hůkka e oskisu	'to salt to preserve'
goaka e obmi	'to pick (someone) to help'
hęgiki a taydiġa	'X stopped and looked up'

§9.18.2.2 Bare Infinitives
A small number of verbs in Siwa allow for the infinitive clause to be found without any additional marking. They typically say something about the likelihood/conditions/ strength of the matrix verb's agent. Note that many speakers use locative markers, or even complementization instead. However, these verbs are more commonly found with a bare infinitive clause.

ent·u	'not to be likely to'
hatr·u	'to ought to'
heskv·a	'to have the bad luck of'
jahhį·u	'to be able to (because of enough endurance/will/strength)'
jest·a	'to succeed to'
ijom·u, ejom·u	'to be possible to (because of sufficient time/good conditions)'
koaibm·a	'to be bored by'
lagj·u	'to happen to'
laugj·i	'to hesitate to'
lůnn·ů	'to be warm enough to'
pes·a	'to have the courage to'
pihh·u	'may be possible to'
sapr·u	'may very well be'
såhk·a	'to have enough courage/to dare to'
sġaht·a	'to be probably (be able to)'
śahhį·u	'not to be able to (because of enough endurance/will/strength)'
śeim·a	'to prevent from'
śink·a	'can, to know how to (because of enough knowledge power)'
takų·u	'to be worth to'
ůt·ů	'not to be able to do something because it is too cold'
vaik·a	'to be ashamed of'

kenka set ento sihsu	'it's not likely to rain tomorrow'
sahatru seimi	'you should listen to X'
heskviami nenita kȯnin	'I made the mistake of speaking to X'
so sahahḥju-a kiḍgami?	'can you lift X?'
jestiami kiḍgami	'I was able to lift it'
s-ijomu-a sugahami?	'is it possible to visit you?'
koaibmaka oakima nenta	'sitting at home bores me'
edladju nuimi	'I happened to see X'
lautsimi manta	'I hesitated to come'
kadda lůnnů sieḍgehhen konta	'it is warm enough outside to walk barefoot'
set pehami aiskami	'I didn't dare to ask'
empihhu suhmi	'it is possible that I may visit X'
tsapru oa niksu	'it may very well be that X died'
so sȧhkana-a maksa	'do you dare to go?'
sġahtami opsa	'I can probably help'
entsahhju kiḍgami	'I am unable to lift X'
sẹ seibmasagge manta	'we did not prevent you from going'
sinka sossi kitami ataka	'my father knows how to make everything'
satakụu-ḥa aiskami	'it is worth that you ask X'
můtů jahhjoru	'I can't do it (because it is too cold)'
vaikasen onakinin	'don't be ashamed to tell me'

§9.18.2.3 Locative Infinitives

Many verbs require locative infinitives. These are usually transitive or translative verbs. Some of the transitive verbs may be found with a nominal object instead of an infinitive clause, in which case they lose their transitivity and become ditransitive, using the same locative case for its object (marked here with *).

With the illative:

all·a Ø-ita	'to have time to/for'
ets·a Ø-ita	'to start to'
euvv·a Ø-ita	'to reach/be able to/to suffice/to be (long/tall/big) enough'
henn·a Ø-ita	'to have the responsibility/be responsible to/for'
jehr·u Ø-ita	'to be possible to (because of favourable conditions)'
kadl·u Ø-ita	'to be enough to/to suffice to'
kyṡ·a Ø-ita	'to try (to)'
ohk·u Ø-ita	'to be possible to (because of space/place/position)'
takụ·u Ø-ita	'to be worth Ø-ing'
tiebb·a Ø-ita	'to have to (because it is the best thing to do)'
tohḥ·a Ø-ita	'to be able/to know how (to) (because of enough skills)'
voall·a Ø-ita	'to have left (to)/to still have left to'

With the elative:

hjom·a Ø-ika	'to ought to'
jahhj·u Ø-ika	'to be able (to) (because of enough will/endurance)/to dare (to)'
*kah·a Ø-ika	'to need (to)'
kigut·a Ø-ika	'not to have enough patience to' (*impersonal verb!*)
saibb·a Ø-ika	'must not/may not/shall not'
*ṡib·a Ø-ika	'to have enough energy to/for/to be able to stand (to)'
*siṡib·a Ø-ika	'not to have enough energy to/for/not to be able to stand (to)'
*tsep·a Ø-ika	'to have enough patience to/for'
ůt·ů Ø-ika	'to be too cold to/for'

Compare the phrases below, showing the transitive form of the verb with an infinitive clause, and the ditransitive form of the verb with a nominal object:

TRANSITIVE + INFINITIVE CLAUSE	DITRANSITIVE + NOMINAL OBJECT
set mallia jùna deitata [sɛʔmˈalːia ˈjuːna ˈdeidɑdɑ] set m-all-i-a jùn-a d-e-ita-ta NEG 1P.UNAG.SG-have.time-PAST-ASS.CONCL.TR finish-TR COP-INFER-ILLAT-3P.PAT.SG 'I didn't have time to finish it'	*set mjallo ningita* [sɛʔmˈjalːɔ ˈninːida] set m-i-all-o ning-ita NEG 1P.UNAG.SG-DIT-have.time-INFER.CONCL.ITR 3p.pl-ILLAT 'I won't have time for them'
euvva sèuma emġet deita gèmme [ˈeuwːa ˈsøːma ˈɛmxɛʔ ˈdeida ˈɟeːmːe] euvv-a sèum-a emġet-Ø d-e-i-ta ge<Ø>-v=me reach-ASS.CONCL.TR cover-TR thighs-DAT COP-INFER-ILLAT hem-PAT 'the hem is long enough to cover the thighs'	*jeuvvi emġetstita gèmme* [ˈjeuwːi ˈɛmxɛtstːida ˈɟeːmːe] i-euvv-i emġet-sti=ta ge<Ø>-v=me DIT-reach-ASS.CONCL.ITR thighs-ILLAT hem-PAT 'the hem reaches to/over the thighs'
hennami kekna sasame deita [ˈhenːami ˈcʰɛʔŋa ˈsasame ˈdeida] henn-a-mi kekn-a sasame-Ø d-e-ita be.responsible-ASS.CONCL.TR-1P.AG.SG put.together-TR tent-DAT COP-INFER-ILLAT 'I am responsible for putting together the tent'	*ihennimi sasakkita* [iˈhenːimi ˈsasaʔcida] i-henn-i-mi sasam-ki=ta DIT-be.responsible-ASS.CONCL.ITR-1P.AG.SG tent-ILLAT 'I am responsible for the tent'

toḥḥa tŭkosġa ipro deita tamosi
['tʰɔʔːa tʰɵ'kɔsxa 'ɪpxɔ 'deida 'tʰamɔsi]
toḥḥ-a tŭ-kosġ-a ipro-Ø d-e-ita tamosi-Ø
know.how-ASS.CONCL.TR down-cut-TR carcass-DAT
cop-infer-ILLAT hunter-AGT
'the hunter knows how to butcher a carcass'

itoḥḥi ḳjongesita tamosi
[i'tʰɔʔːi 'cʰɔŋːesida 'tʰamɔsi]
i-toḥḥ-i kjo<ng>es-ita tamosi-Ø
DIT-know.how-ASS.CONCL.ITR woven.basket-ILLAT
hunter-AGT
'the hunter knows how (to make) woven baskets'

voallami ġjia jasukka deita
['vɔalːami 'dzia 'jasʊʔka 'deida]
voall-a-mi ġj=i-a jasum-ka d-e-ita
have.left-ASS.CONCL.TR-1P.AG.SG wash-TR skin-GEN
COP-INFER-ILLAT
'I still have to wash the skin'

ivoallimi jasukkita
[i'vɔalːimi 'jasʊʔcida]
i-voall-i-mi jasum-k=ita
DIT-have.left-ASS.CONCL.ITR-1P.AG.SG skin-ILLAT
'I still have the skin (as a task)'

kahami taḥḥi deika
['kʰaʔami 'tʰahːi 'deiga]
kah-a-mi taḥḥ-i d-e-ika
need-ASS.CONCL.TR-1P.AG.SG leave-ITR COP-INFER-ELAT
'I need to go'

ikahimi sidika
[i'kʰaʔimi 'siːdʑiga]
i-kah-i-mi si<Ø>i-d=ika
DIT-need-ASS.CONCL.ITR-1P.AG.SG honey-ELAT
'I need honey' (also *kahami/bednami sid*)

kigutaka śivi deika
['cʰigudaga 'ɕivi 'deiga]
kigut-a-ka-Ø śiv-i d-e-ika
can't.stand-ASS.CONCL.TR-1P.PAT.SG-IMP stay-ITR
COP-INFER-ELAT
'I can't stand to stay'

ikigutaka śyjammoika
[i'cʰigudaga 'ɕyjamːɔiga]
i-kikut-a-ka-Ø śy<j>av-mo=ika
DIT-can't.stand-ASS.CONCL.TR-1P.PAT.SG-IMP
summer.camp-ELAT
'I can't wait till summer camp'

so śibana-a erri deika?
[s(ɔ)'ɕibanaː 'erːi 'deiga]
so śib-a-na–a err-i d-e-ika
INTERRO. have.energy-2P.AG.SG–POS.INTERRO
work.outside-ITR COP-INFER-ELAT
'can you stand to/are you good to work outside?'

misiśibi longamoika
[mi'siɕibi 'lɔŋːamɔiga]
m-i-si=śib-a lo<ng>a-mo=ika
1P.UNAG.SG-DIT-not.have.energy-ASS.CONCL.ITR
COLD-ELAT
'I can't stand the cold'

tsepumina oheyti deika somigi
['tsepumina ɔ'hɛœtɕi 'deiga 'sɔmiji]
tsep-um-i-na o-heyt-i d-e-ika somi-Ø-gi
wait-OBLI-ASS.CONCL.TR-2P.AG.SG SUBJ-disembark-
ITR COP-INFER-ELAT man-AGT-PL
'you must wait until the men return home' (lit. 'you must have the patience (that the men disembark')

itsepumina kobika
[i'tsepumina 'kʰɔbiga]
i-tsep-um-i-na ko=b-ika
DIT-wait-OBLI-ASS.CONCL.TR-2P.AG.SG summer-ELAT
'you must be patient until summer'

§9.19 Conjugation Paradigm

ga·man·i 'come along'

PRESENT

Person	ASSERTIVE	INFERENTIAL	CONDITIONAL REALIS ASSERTIVE	CONDITIONAL IRREALIS ASSERTIVE	CONDITIONAL IRREALIS INFERENTIAL	OPTATIVE ASSERTIVE	OPTATIVE INFERENTIAL	IMPERATIVE
1sg	gamanimi *I come along*	gamanomi *I will come along*	gadamanimi *if I came along*	gamanimi *if I came along*	gamanijmi *I'd come along*	gamanujmi *I want to come along*	gamanuomi *I'd want to come along*	
1pl incl	gamanigga *we come along*	gamanogga *we will come along*	gadamanigga *if we came along*	gamanigga *if we came along*	gamanijgga *we'd come along*	gamanujgga *we want to come along*	gamanuogga *we'd want to come along*	
1pl excl	gamanigge *we come along*	gamanogge *we will come along*	gadamanigge *if we came along*	gamanigge *if we came along*	gamanijgge *we'd come along*	gamanujgge *we want to come along*	gamanuogge *we'd want to come along*	
2sg	gamanina *you come along*	gamanona *you will come along*	gadamanina *if you came along*	gamanuna *if you came along*	gamanijna *you'd come along*	gamanujna *you want to come along*	gamanuona *you'd want to come along*	gamanin *come along!*
2pl	gamanidda *you come along*	gamanodda *you will come along*	gadamanidda *if you came along*	gamanudda *if you came along*	gamanijdda *you'd come along*	gamanujdda *you want to come along*	gamanuodda *you'd want to come along*	gamaniun *come along!*
3sg	gamani *X comes along*	gamano *X will come along*	gadamani *if X came along*	gamaniu *if X came along*	gamanji *X would come along*	gamanuj *X wants to come along*	gamanuo *X would want to come along may X come along!*	gamanit *may X come along!*
3pl	gamanin *they come along*	gamanon *they will come along*	gadamanin *if they came along*	gamaniun *if they came along*	gamanjin *they would come along*	gamanujn *they want to come along*	gamanuon *they'd want to come along*	gamanigun *may they come along!*
impers	gamanit *one comes along!*	gamanigen *one will come along*	gadamanigen *if one came along*	gamaniugen *if one came along*	gamanigjen *one would come along*	gamanujgen *one wants to come along*	gamanuogen *one would want to come along*	

PAST

Person	ASSERTIVE	INFERENTIAL	CONDITIONAL REALIS ASSERTIVE	CONDITIONAL IRREALIS ASSERTIVE	CONDITIONAL IRREALIS INFERENTIAL	OPTATIVE ASSERTIVE	OPTATIVE INFERENTIAL	IMPERATIVE
1sg	gamandimi *I came along*	gamandomi *I came along*	gadamandimi *if I had come along*	gamandiumi *if I had come along*	gamandjomi *I'd have come along*	gamandvimi *I wanted to come along*	gamanduomi *I'd have wanted to come along*	
1pl incl	gamandigga *we came along*	gamandogga *we came along*	gadamandigga *if we had come along*	gamandiugga *if we had come along*	gamandjogga *we'd have come along*	gamandvigga *we wanted to come along*	gamanduogga *we'd have wanted to come along*	
1pl excl	gamandigge *we came along*	gamandogge *we came along*	gadamandigge *if we had come along*	gamandiugge *if we had come along*	gamandjogge *we'd have come along*	gamandvigge *we wanted to come along*	gamanduogge *we'd have wanted to come along*	
2sg	gamandina *you came along*	gamandona *you came along*	gadamandina *if you had come along*	gamandiuna *if you had come along*	gamandjona *you'd have come along*	gamandvina *you wanted to come along*	gamanduona *you'd have wanted to come along*	
2pl	gamandidda *you came along*	gamandodda *you came along*	gadamandidda *if you had come along*	gamandiudda *if you had come along*	gamandjodda *you'd have come along*	gamandvidda *you wanted to come along*	gamanduodda *you'd have wanted to come along*	
3sg	gamandi *X came along*	gamando *X came along*	gadamandi *if X had come along*	gamandiu *if X had come along*	gamandjoi *X would have come along*	gamandvi *X wanted to come along*	gamanduo *X would have wanted to come along*	
3pl	gamandin *they came along*	gamandon *they came along*	gadamandin *if they had come along*	gamandiun *if they had come along*	gamandjoin *they would have come along*	gamandvin *they wanted to come along*	gamanduon *they would have wanted to come along*	
impers	gamandit *X came along*	gamandigen *one came along*	gadamandigen *if one had come along*	gamandiugen *if one had come along*	gamandjogen *one'd have come along*	gamandvigen *X wanted to come along one wanted to come along*	gamanduogen *one would have wanted to come along*	

COMPLEMENTIZED
gamanoti
that X comes along
gamanonti
that X doesn't come along

gamanoto
that X will come long
gamanonto
that X won't come along

gamanotiu
that if X came along
gamanontiu
that if X didn't come along

gamanotoi
that X would come along
gamanontoi
that X wouldn't come along

gamanotvi
that X wants to come along
gamanontvi
that X won't come along

gamanotuo
that X would want to come along
gamanontuo
that X wouldn't come along

SPLIT STEM
gamani da
coming along

gamani de
coming along

gamani adda
if coming along

gamani dia
if X were coming along

gamani die
would be coming along

gamani tve
wanting to come along

gamani tva
would want to come along

HABITUAL ASPECT
gamanti
usually comes along
gamantsi
usually came along

gamanto
usually comes along
gamantso
usually came along

gadamanti
if X usually comes along
gadamantsi
if X usually came along

gamantiu
if X used to come along
gamantsiu
if X had used to come along

gamantoi
X would come along
gamantsoi
X would have come along

gamantvi
usually wants to come along
gamantsvi
usually wanted to come along

gamantuo
would usually want to come along
gamantsuo
would usually have wanted to come along

PERFECTIVE ASPECT
gamandli
has come along
or
gamandila

gamandlo
has usually come along

gamandola

gadamandli
if X has usually come along

gadamandoli

gamandliu
if X has used to come along

gamandiula

gamandloi
X would have come along

gamandjoia

gamandlvi
has wanted to come along

gamandjula

gamandluo
would have wanted to come along

gamanduola

DOUBLE AGENTIVITY
gasamanumdnami
I need you to come along

MOODS
gamanumi
has to come along, must come along
gamanidna
comes back along
gamaniga
suddenly comes along
gamanihhen
keeps coming along
gamanippen
comes along every now and then
gatamandia
X starts to come along
gamanitta
suddenly comes along
gamanisi
can come along
gamanisen
can't come along
gamaninun
comes along a little

LOCATIVE
gagimanita
comes along (in)to X
gamanini
comes along (towards speaker)
gamaniki
(goes and) comes along (away)
gamanikni
comes along (here and there)

ABSOLUTIVE DESCRIPTIVES
gamananpi
(tall person) comes along
gamanahti
(fat/dead person) comes along
gamanatsti
(knife) comes along
gamanbi
(child) comes along
gamaniksi
(old) comes along
gamanbgi
(happy person) comes along
gamanupi
(wet person) comes along
gamanohni
(dirty person) comes along
gamanohki
(big person) comes along

PARTICIPLES
gamanimo
coming along, someone who comes along
gamanima
coming along, consequence
gamanime
people who come along, consequences
gamanotimo ~ gamanyen
Ø coming along
gamanotima ~ gamanyen
Ø coming along

INFINITIVES
gamanta, gamantse
to come along, coming alone
gamandva, gamandvaka
coming along

AUXILIARY TENSES
gamanditta_ga
just came along
gamani_ga
came along a long time ago

§10 Pronouns and Determiners

Siwa has various kinds of pronouns and determiners. They can be grouped as follows:

personal	*megi* 'I', *negi* 'you', *nin* 'one'…
demonstrative	*ůat* 'this', *hait* 'that', *ůhhja* 'here', *hahhja* 'there'…
interrogative	*mimni* 'who?', *nidni* 'what?', *nigju* 'when?'…
indefinite	
existential known	*toamni* 'a certain, some', *toadni* 'a certain, some'…
existential unknown	*kůtůmni* 'someone', *kůtůdni* 'something'…
elective	*ġůmni* 'anyone', *ġůdni* 'anything'…
negative known	*sġůmni* 'no one', *sġůdni* 'nothing'…
negative unknown	*set…ihmi* 'not…any', *set…ihni* 'not…any'…
distributive	*roami* 'each', *śośi* 'every'…
universal	*killa/kadlka* 'all, the whole', *killju/kadlkju* 'all the time'…
other -ni determiners	*ůadni* 'such as this', *haidni* 'such as that'…
alternative clitics	
-ne form	*toamni-ne* 'another', *ġůmni-ne* 'any other'…
-uli form	*todni-uli* 'a kind', *ġůdni-uli* 'any kind'…

Personal pronouns are explicitly marked for all the nominal cases, in addition to two other forms called the precedence and possessive forms. Siwa distinguishes between known and unknown for indefinite pronouns.

All other pronouns may be found in many special forms unique to them, which are somewhat regularly derived by function.

All pronouns except demonstrative, distributive and universal pronouns are formed by the infixation of secondary case markers, often causing unpredictable changes in the stem. However, the process is fairly regular and distinguishes between inanimate and animate forms and plural:

	ANIMATE	INANIMATE
agentive	-m·ni	-d·ni
patientive	-m·ma	-b·ma
genitive	-m·ġu/-h·m·ō [1]	-ġu/-t or -h·rō
dative	-s·mi, -ḍ·mi	-s·ti-, -ḍ·ḍi
locative	-tsi-	-tsi-

---

[1] An older form in -hka is found in certain expressions such as *mihka* 'whose (when talking about people)'. Other forms include -m·ron and -n·don.

	PLURAL
agentive	-k·ni
patientive	-h·ma
genitive	-h·k·u/-h·k·ō or -t·k·on
dative	-s·ki, -ḍ·gi
locative	-ksi-

The genitive forms in -mron~-ndon, -hron~-hdon and -tkon are considered higher register.

§10.1 Personal Pronouns

Siwa personal pronouns are generally part of the verb if they are an argument of the verbal phrase. However, personal pronouns also have independent forms. Independent pronouns include proper independent pronouns, possessive pronouns and pronouns of precedence.

meiḍgi te pikśima
[ˈmɛiðɟi ˈde ˈpʰɪkɕima]
meiḍgi te pikś-i-ma
1P.PRON.PAT.SG and hurt-ASS.ITR-INCONCL
'I am hurt as well'

sosi negasari
[ˈsɔsi ˈnegasari]
so=si n<eg>-a-ri
2P.PRON.DAT see.PAST-ASS.CONCL.TR-3P.AG.PL
'they saw *you*'

so sogi-a oata?
[ˈs(ɔ)sɔɟia ɔˈata]
so sogi-a o=<∅>-a-ta
INTERRO 2P.PRON.GEN–INTERRO REL-COP-ASS-3P.AG.SG
'is it yours?'

so siubmisa-a, nůta?
[s(ɔ)ˈsiːʊʔpmisa ˈnøta]
so siut-m-i-sa-∅–sa nůta
INTERRO hungry-INCONCL-ASS.ITR-2P.PAT.SG–INTERRO 2P.PRON.PRECED
'what about you?, are you hungry?'

hat niġōsi roami
[ˈhaʔ ˈnixōsi ˈroamiː]
h-a-t nidin-si roa=mi
eat-TR-3P.IMPER 4P.PRON.GEN-2ND.DAT each-AGT
'may each eat his own (portion)'

da ningia kůimpa-śi
[da ˈninːia ˈcʰœɪmpaɕi]
d-a ning-ia kůimpa-∅–śi
COP-ASS 3P.PRON.PL-INESS boots-AGT–2P.POSS.PL
'they have your boots'

Certain speakers consistently use independent forms for all oblique cases (non-agentive). There is much variation regarding whether these speakers use only independent personal pronouns or also use verbal personal pronouns.

standard:	*set tayḍgaka*	'X did not injure me'
independent:	*set tayḍga meiḍgi*	'X did not injure me'
double:	*set tayḍgaka meiḍgi*	'X did not injure me'

Personal pronouns differ from all other pronouns in having forms of precedence and possession.

Pronouns of precedence are used to to show whose turn it is. Through semantic shift, pronouns of precedence have also come to be used as a sort of interrogative vocative, similar to English 'what about X?'. It can also be said when offering something to someone, similar to 'there you go' in English, in which case the pronoun might be followed by the hyphened interrogative clitic -a. The polite for *eurů* is often used when wanting to show that someone should go ahead or go first.

mŭta moġiundami
[ˈmøta ˈmɔxɪʊndami]
mŭta moġ-i-unda-mi
1P.PRON.PRECE.SG drink-ASS.CONCL.ITR-DIMIN-1P.AG.SG
'it's my turn to have a sip'

nŭtra, so otoatidda-a?
[ˈnœtxa sɔːˈtɔɑtɕitːaː]
nŭtra so o-toat-i-dda–a
2P.PRON.PRECED.PL INTERRO SUBJ-join-ASS.CONCL.ITR-2P.AG.PL–INTERR
'and what about you? Will you join us?'

nŭta-a?
[ˈnøtaː]
nŭta-a
2P.PRON.PRECED–INTERRO
'your turn?, do you want some (when offered something)?'

ėurů kolkon
[ˈøːrø ˈkʰɔlkɔn]
ėurů kolkon-Ø
2P.PRON.PRECED.PL.HONOR bread-AGT
'have some bread'

Possession pronouns are hyphened to the noun they qualify. They can often be dropped. The forms –ho and –ha are both pronounced simply as [w] after vowels, while –hi is often pronouns [j] in the same environment.

iki-go	'my axe'
kamśe-so	'your left hand'
moukkie-hi	'their bellies'
śiśaitta-nen	'to one's (own) daughter'

Note the common expression *nigō-nen* meaning originally 'to each his own' but it has grown into a common interjection showing that one should not try to control the situation, similar to 'oh well' in English:

nanta ikudoamo-so, nigō̃-nen
['nanta ɪku'dɔɑmɔsɔ 'nixɔ̃nɛn]
na<nt>-a iku=do<∅>a-mo-so ni-ġō̃-nen
break.PAST-ASS.CONCL.TR axe=handle-PAT–2P.PRON.POSS.SG 4P.PRON-GEN–4P.PRON.POSS.
'oh well, your axe handle broke'

§10.1.1 First Person
The first person distinguishes between inclusive and exclusive in the plural, but its dative and locative forms do not.

	singular	plural	
		inclusive	exclusive
agentive	*megi*	*màra*	*màri*
patientive	*meiḍgi*	*menra*	*menri*
genitive	*gogi*	*ùra*	*ùri*
dative	*gosi*	*mùsi*	
locative	*gogi-*	*momsi-*	
possessive	*–go*	*–ura*	*–uri*
precedence	*můta*	*můtra*	*můtri*

There is a lot of dialectal variation for the singular forms:

    agentive   *megi, mġegi, mů, mȯ, mġů, mġȯ*
    patientive   *meiḍgi, meihki, metki, medd, madd*
    genitive   *gogi, guoki, guoggi, gueggi, gų̊ůggi*

The forms *mů/mȯ* and *mġů/mġȯ* are characteristic of eastern dialects outside the Sapsi area. The forms *meihki* and *metki* is mostly found in mid-western dialects while **medd** and **madd** are far-western dialectal forms. The genitive forms are found in many different dialects and are not mapped as closely to any area, although *gų̊ůggi* and *gueggi* are mostly heard further east.

§10.1.2 Second Person
The second person has a singular and plural form, and a plural honorific which is only marked through this independent pronoun.

	singular	plural	
		plural	honorific
agentive	negi	nȧri	ıṫ
patientive	neiḑgi	nenri	ibma
genitive	sogi	ṡiron/ṡidon	idġō
dative	sosi	ṡiṡi	ıtsi
locative	sosi-	ṡiṡi-	its-
possessive	–so	–ṡi	–it
precedence	nŭta	nŭtra	idġa / ėurŭ

The second person mirrors the first person in dialects.

§10.1.3 Third Person

The third person distinguishes between animate and inanimate in the singular, has a plural form and an obviative form, which is not marked for number. Note that the forms *to ta* and *ki* can be found as *tot tat* and *kit* in many dialects, especially if the next word begins with a vowel. Many speakers have voiced consonants throughout the paradigm (*do, da, gi, odda*) the dative -si being replaced by -ḑi. This is mostly a trait of younger speakers in the east.

The third person singular has two forms common to both animacies in the patientive (*tva*) and the dative (*tsi*). These forms are short forms of the pronouns and often found before other nouns.

The genitive of the third person singular and plural has a so-called long form and a short form, both of which are equally common:

	singular		plural	obviative
	animate	inanimate		
agentive	to	ta	ki	onto or ōtõ/ōrõ
patientive	otta	tva atta	idgi	ōddo or ōddō
genitive	ůn or tůmů, tomo, tomen	en or taga, taġa, taġen	kjon or kjōhō	ōhō
dative	otsi	tsi atsi	eksi	ōtsi
locative	neni-	noni-	ningi-	teni-
possessive	–ho (pron. [w])	–ha (pron. [w])	–hi (pron. [j])	–hō
precedence	tyta	teta	keta	tōuta

The õ may also be found as a long [ɔ:] (usually spelled <o> or <ō>).

§10.1.3.1 Disambiguative Third Person

The third person pronouns are often required when the object and subject of a verbal phrase appear side by side at the end of the phrase, or when many elements are found between the verb and the nominal arguments of the phrase. Disambiguation is especially common between two nouns in the same form (marked or unmarked), so between dative and active nouns, or between genitive and patientive nouns. Generally, only one disambiguative non-clitical pronoun is necessary, but in more complex phrases they can be repeated before each noun phrase. Non-clitical third person pronouns are also regularly found before personal names. Third person pronouns tend to appear before the last noun only.

> Da soaki temme arrui **nenia** Nillunia. Isygjua on soakkita-nen **tsi** tamosi- nen **tsi** Oihi **to** Nilkka

'Nîlkka has a house next to a lake. Nîlkka invites her friend Oihi to her house.'

se voavva Siusta **tva** tsamġa   'a Siwa is not afraid of the forest'

totkia **tsi** benho   'X bought the dog'
totkia benho **to** kori   'the boy bought the dog'

§10.1.4 Fourth Person
The fourth person only has one form.

	singular
agentive	*nin*
patientive	*nigen*
genitive	*nihõ/nigõ*
dative	*nitsi*
locative	*ni-*
possessive	*–nen*
precedence	*nitra*

The form -nen is often pronounced as a single syllabic [n̩].

§10.1.5 Self
The fourth person found with patientive endings (their copular form) added directly to the declined pronoun correspond to the English construction 'myself' or 'the very'. Locative cases are not used in this case, using instead the genitive *nihõ*.

	'myself'		'ourselves'	'yourself'	'yourself'	'himself/herself/itself/themselves'	
	sg.		pl.	sg.	pl.	sg./pl.	obv.
agentive	*nin·ka*		*nim·ba*	*nin·sa* or *nin·ta*	*nin·ha*	*nin·i*	*nin·no*
patientive	*nigen·ka*		*nigem·ba*	*nigen·sa* or *nigen·ta*	*nigen·ha*	*nigen·i*	*nigen·no*
genitive	*nihõ·ka*		*nihõ·ba*	*nihõ·sa*	*nihõ·ha*	*nihõ·ja*	*nihõ·no*
dative	*nitsi·ka*		*nitsi·ba*	*nitsi·sa*	*nitsi·ha*	*nitsi·ja*	*nitsi·no*

ahtami megi ninka
['ahtɑmi 'meɟi 'nɪŋka]
<aht>-a-Ø-mi megi-Ø nin-ka
do.PAST-ASS.CONCL.TR-3P.PAT-1P.SG.AG 1P.PRON.AG self.AG-1P.SG
'I did it myself (lit. I did it, I myself)'

nonia banśia-ůt nihōja
['nɔnia 'banɕiæœʔ 'niʔɔ̃ja]
non-ia ban-ś=ia–ůt ni-hō-ia
3P.PRON.UNAG-INESS place-INESS-DET.PROXI self-GEN-3P.SG
'in this very place'

neskahmi nigenta
['nɛskahmi 'niɟɛnta]
nesk-a-h=mi ni=gen-ta
ask-ASS.CONCL.TR-2P.PAT=1P.SG.AG self-PAT-2P.SG
'I ask you personally'

§10.2 Demonstrative Pronouns

Siwa demonstrative pronouns can be divided into two different categories – independent and attributive. The independent form is found alone without any noun to qualify. It declines like a noun, with two distinguished forms (marked and unmarked) and exists in the singular and plural.

Independent forms:

da tahha ůdda	'this is a tree'
da tahha hadda	'that is a tree'
da tahha udda	'that over there is a tree'
ůattaja	'in this (one)'
da tahhua eygi	'these are trees'

The attributive demonstrative pronouns qualify a noun (or an adjective). They split into two parts – the first part is a third person pronoun agreeing in case, number and animacy with the noun qualified, while the second part is a hyphened clitic to the noun. This pronoun may be augmented by two special clitics, **ba-** (out of two) and **tsa-** (out of many).

Attributive forms:

to tahha-ůt	'this tree'	(pron. [tʰɑh:æœʔ])

to tahha-t	'that tree'	(pron. ['tʰɑh:aʔ])
to tahha-ut	'that tree over there'	(pron. ['tʰɑh:awʔ])
bata tȯ-ḥůt	'this stone (of two)'	(pron. ['bɑta 'tʰʊ:ʔœʔ])
tsaki henetka-ůt	'these birch shoes (of many)'	

Attributive demonstrative pronouns are found in the genitive before nouns in locative cases – the locative cases are not repeated both on the noun and the pronoun. When used as demonstrative pronouns, the genitive form is nearly always ůn/en (the forms tůmů, tomo, tomen for the animate and taga, taġa, taġen for the inanimate are only found with demonstrative pronouns in higher speech registers or archaic speech).

	SG		PL	
ACT	to tahha-ůt	'this tree'	ki tahhua-ůt	'these trees'
PAT	otta tahhi-ůt	'this tree'	iḍgi tahhi-ůt	'these trees'
GEN	ůn tahhi-ůt	'of this tree'	kjōhō tahhi-ůt	'of these trees'
DAT	otsi tahha-ůt	'this tree'	eksi tahha-ůt	'these trees'
INESS	ůn tahhia-ůt	'in this tree'	kjōhō tahhia-ůt	'in these trees'
ILLAT	ůn tahhita-ůt	'into this tree'	kjōhō tahhita-ůt	'into these trees'
ELAT	ůn tahhiska-ůt	'from this tree'	kjōhō tahhiska-ůt	'from these trees'

Both the attributive and the independent form distinguish three different distances from the speaker – the proximal, medial and distal forms. The proximal and the medial form refer to something closer and further from the speaker, respectively. The third, distal form is used for things that are not within the speaker's sight, or as a more generic pronoun.

> *eidda atsi soaki-ůt kȧmaka, sę hait*
> 'my paternal grandfather build this house (closer to me), not that one (over there)'

> *sùbmua onta to benhi-ůt, magjua katta bidjiska-nen*
> 'while this dog is black, its puppies are white'

> *da on tůpra ůat, da ka pehra hait*
> [dāõ 'tʰœpxa 'œaʔ daka 'pʰɛhra 'haɪʔ]
> d-a on tůpra-Ø ůat-Ø d-a ka pehra-Ø hait-Ø
> COP-ASS ON juniper.berry-AGT this.PROXI-AGT COP-ASS KA yew.berry-AGT that.MEDI-AGT
> 'this is a juniper berry, and that is a yew berry'

da on tuovvumika ta suvèu-t, da ka pihraika ta suvo-t
[dã͂ 'tʰuɔw:umiga tʰa 'suvø:ʔ daka 'pʰi:hrɑiga tʰa 'suvɔʔ]
d-a on tuo<vv>-um=ika ta suvo-Ø–ût d-a ka pih-ra=ika ta suvo-Ø–t
COP-ASS ON juniper-ILLAT this.INA.AGT berry-AGT–DET.PROXI COP-ASS KA yew-ILLAT this.INA.AGT berry-AGT–DET.MEDI

'this berry is from a juniper, and that berry is from a yew'

§10.2.1 Independent Pronouns

The independent pronouns decline as nouns and cannot be found attributively. Each form of the independent pronoun exists in two paired forms called the short and the long form. The medial and proximal merge in their long form. The short form is more common, while the long form is used for emphasis, to elevate the language register, making it more honorific or formal. The final -t common to most pronouns is either pronounced [ʔ] or [h(t)].

The distal form *iot* is generally pronounced ['ɛɔʔ] or ['ɛaʔ] (sometimes spelled *iat/ eat*). There is quite a lot of variation regarding the proximal form *ûat*, including *éut, yt* and *ûvvût*. Similarly, the marked and unmarked form of plural long form *egjit* show a lot of variation: kje-, dje-, hje-.

The short pronouns exist in pairs (ûat~ûdda, hait~hadda, iot~udda). The forms in -dda are more familiar and is slowly replacing the forms in -it.

The form *it* is commonly used in Siwa to refer to a honorific third person.

	singular				plural			
	unmarked		marked		unmarked		marked	
	short	long	short	long	short	long	short	long
proximal	ûat	evvat	ûatta	eyatta	eygi	egjit	eyhta	eihta
	ûdda		ûtten					
medial	hait		haitta		kvagi		kvahta	
	hadda		hatten					
distal	iot	it	iotta	itta	gaugi	gjegji	gauhta	gjehta
	udda		utten					

da sengẏ sara ůat
[da ˈseŋːyː ˈsɑra ˈœæʔ]
d-a sengẏ-Ø sara-Ø ůat-Ø
COP-ASS song-AGT good-AGT this.PROXI-AGT
'this is a good song'

da riehpi evvat
[da ˈrɛhpi ˈewːaʔ]
d-a riehpi-Ø evvat-Ø
COP-ASS wife-AGT this.PROXI-AGT
'this/that is my wife'

da njelba it
[da ˈɲɛlba iːʔ]
d-a njeli-Ø-ba it-Ø
COP-ASS chief-AGT-1P.PAT.PL this.DIST-AGT
'he/(honorific) is our chief'

Many dialects include *out-of-two* and *out-of-many* forms in the declension of independent demonstrative pronouns. These forms are not commonly used by all dialects, but may be more frequent in higher language registers or older speakers.

Out-of-two

	singular				plural			
	unmarked		marked		unmarked		marked	
	short	long	short	long	short	long	short	long
proximal	ůaḍba	evvaḍba	ůappa	eyappa	eyṡpa	egjiḍba	eyhba	eihba
medial	haiḍba		haippa		kvaṡpa		kvahba	
distal	ioḍba	iḍba	joppa	ippa	gauṡpa	gjeiba	gauhba	gjehba

kokkaka ůappa
[ˈkʰɔʔkɑga ˈœæʔpa]
kokk-a-ka ůa=ppa
please-ASS.CONCL.TR-1P.PAT.SG this.PROXI.OUT.OF.TWO.GEN
'I like this (one, of two)'

ûrjŭni ue haiḍba
['ørjøni u'e 'haɪðba]
ûrjŭni-Ø o-Ø-e haiḍba-Ø
female.wolf-AGT REL-COP-INFER this.MED.OUT.OF.TWO-AGT
'the female wolf is that one (out of the pair)'

kŭimpa-go oa eyṡpa
['cœɪmpagɔ ɔ'a 'ɛœɕpa]
kŭimpa-Ø–go o-Ø-a eyṡpa-Ø
boots-AGT–1P.POSS.SG REL-COP-ASS these.PROXI.OUT.OF.TWO.PL-AGT
'these two (shoes) are my pair of boots (of two)'

Out-of-many

	singular				plural			
	unmarked		marked		unmarked		marked	
	short	long	short	long	short	long	short	long
proximal	ůats		ůatsta		eytsġi		eyhtsa	
		evvats		eyatsta		eġits		eihtsa
medial	haits		haitsta		kvatsġi		kvahtsa	
distal	iots	its	iotsta	itsta	gautsġi	ġeits	gauhtsa	ġehtsa

so kuiliska-a oa kvatsġi?
[s(ɔ) 'kʰuilɪska: ɔ'a 'kʰvatsxi]
so kuilis-Ø-ka–a o-Ø-a kvatsġi-Ø
INTERRO tadpole-AGT-PL-INTERRO REL-COP-ASS this.MEDI.OUT.OF.MANY.PL-AGT
'are *those ones* tadpoles?'

da kutkuska nielra eġits
[da 'kʰʊtkʊska 'nɪɛlra 'ej:ɪts]
d-a kutkus-Ø-ka nielra-Ø eġits-Ø
COP-ASS bough-AGT-PL of.fir-AGT this.PROXI.LONG.OUT.OF.MANY.PL-AGT
'these are fir floor boughs'

§10.2.2 Attributive Pronouns

The attributive pronouns consist of the appropriate third person pronoun (*to/ta/ki/ōtõ*), following by the noun phrase, which ends with a hyphenated clitic which only specifies proximity (-ůt, -t and -ut):

to Ø-ůt	to Ø-t	to Ø-ut
ta Ø-ůt	ta Ø-t	ta Ø-ut
ōtõ Ø-ůt	ōtõ Ø-t	ōtõ Ø-ut
ki Ø-ůt	ki Ø-t	ki Ø-ut

The third person pronoun agrees in animacy, case and number – even when the noun itself is not explicitly marked for plural, attributive pronouns may still be found in the plural.

Attributive pronouns often agree with the perceived animacy of the noun rather than its actually grammatical animacy – in fact, these pronouns may be used where English would not to emphasize the perceived animacy contrary to the noun's grammatical animacy.

The proximity marker is usually found at the very end of the nominal phrase:

to/ta kepsi mialha-ůt
[tʰɔ/tʰa ˈcʰɛpsːi ˈmɪalhæœʔ]
to-Ø/ta-Ø kepsi-Ø mialha-Ø–ůt
3P.PRON.ANI.AGT.SG/3P.PRON.INA.AGT.SG mushroom-AGT blue-AGT–DET.PROXI
'this blue mushroom'

mine ůn/en kebsie mialhadi-ůt
[ˈmine œn/ɛn ˈcʰɛpsie ˈmɪalhɑʤɪœʔ]
mine-Ø ůn/ten kepsi-e mialha-di–ůt
flesh-AGT 3P.PRON.ANI.GEN.SG/3P.PRON.INA.GEN.SG mushroom-GEN blue-GEN–DET.PROXI
'this blue mushroom's flesh'

Attributive pronouns are commonly found augmented by either of two special clitics, **ba-** (out of two) and **tsa-** (out of many). The out-of-two form is used when the demonstrative pronoun applies to one of two things, and the out-of-many form identifies one from a group which is often only implied. The out-of-many form is sometimes considered to belong to a more formal and archaic Siwa.

third person pronoun		noun phrase	clitic		
			form	short	long
animate	to / ki	...∅...	proximal	-ŭt	-eɥat
inanimate	ta / ki		medial	-t or -het	
out of two	ba(u)-		distal	-ut [w?]	-jet
out of many	tsa(u)-	-to/-ta/-ki			

The out-of-two and out-of-many forms behave like the passive preverbal vowel **u-** and avoids the formation of a triphthong by following the rules given in section *§9.5.8*:

    bam-a- tsam-a-
    bam-e- tsam-e-
    bab-i-   tsab-i-
    bab-o- tsab-o-
    bab-ů- bab-ů-

	singular				plural	
	animate		inanimate			
	out-of-two	out-of-many	out-of-two	out-of-many	out-of-two	out-of-many
agentive	bato	tsato	bata	tsata	baki	tsaki
patientive	babotta	tsabotta	bamatta	tsamatta	babiḍgi	tsabiḍgi
genitive	bamůn or batůmů	tsamůn or tsatůmů	bamen or bataga	tsamen or tsataga	bakjon or bakjōhō	tsakjon or tsakjōhō
dative	babotsi	tsabotsi	bamatsi	tsamatsi	bameksi	tsameksi
locative	baneni-	tsaneni-	banoni-	tsanoni-	baningi-	tsaningi-
possessive	–hoba	–hotsa	–haba	–hatsa	–hiba	–hitsa
precedence	batyta	tsatyta	bateta	tsateta	baketa	tsaketa

The hyphened clitics coalesce with certain final vowels, sometimes changing significantly. It may cause the medial proximity no longer to be distinguished. This renders distinguishing between proximal and distal difficult.

	hyphened attributive demonstrative coalescence	
-a	·a-ůt [æœʔ] (as -ayt)	·a-ut [awʔ]
-e	·e-ůt [ɛœʔ] (as -eyt)	·e-ut [ɛwʔ]
-i	·i-ůt [ɪœʔ] or ·ẏ-t [y:ʔ]	·i-ut [ɪwʔ]
-o		·o-ut [ɔwʔ] or ·ȯ-t [ʊ:ʔ]
-u	·ėu-t [ø:ʔ]	·u-ut [uwʔ] or ·ů-t [u:ʔ]
-ů		·e-ut [ɛw:ʔ] or ·ėut [ø:ʔ]
-y	·y-ůt [yœʔ] or ·ėu-t [ø:ʔ]	··i-ut [ɪwʔ] or ·ẏ-t [y:ʔ]

ta nidla-ůt
[tʰa ˈniːtɬæœʔ]
'this face'

ta nidla-ut
[tʰa ˈniːtɬawʔ]
'that face'

tsata pẏbme-ůt / pẏbmėu-t
[tsɑta ˈpʰy:ʔpmɛœʔ/ pʰy:ʔpmø:ʔ]
'this seal skin (of many)'
(cf. **pẏbme** 'sealskin')

tsata pẏbme-ut
[ˈtsɑta ˈpʰy:ʔpmɛwʔ]
'that sealskin (of many)'

to saigi-ůt / saigẏ-t
[tʰɔ ˈsɑijɪœʔ/ sɑijy:ʔ]
'this moose'
(cf. **saigi** 'moose')

ta saigi-ut
[tʰa ˈsɑijɪwʔ]
'that moose'

ta selėu-t
[tʰa ˈsɛlø:ʔ]
'this big river'
(cf. **selo** 'big river')

ta selȯ-t / selo-ut
[tʰa ˈsɛlʊ:ʔ/ sɛlɔwʔ]
'that big river'

bata sitrėu-t
[ˈbɑta ˈsɪtxø:ʔ]

bata sitrȯ-t / sitro-ut
[ˈbɑta ˈsɪtxʊ:ʔ/ sɪtxɔwʔ]

  'this soup (of two)'   'that soup (of two)'
  (cf. **sitru** 'fish soup')

  ta lŭkkèu-t   *ta lŭkke-ut / lŭkkèu-t*
  [tʰa ˈlœʔcø:ʔ]   [tʰa ˈlœʔcewʔ/lœʔcø:ʔ]
  'this cascade'   'that cascade'
  (cf. **lŭkkŭ** 'cascade')

  to lygẏ-t   *to lygy-ut / lygẏ-t*
  [tʰɔ ˈlyɟy:ʔ]   [tʰa ˈlyɟywʔ/lyɟy:ʔ]
  'this disease'   'that disease'
  (cf. **lygy** 'disease')

Words ending in the diphthongs (often due to pluralization of inanimate nouns) change the endings -ůt and -ut to -ḥůt and -ḥut. However, to avoid this, the noun may be left in the singular.

  ki elebua-ḥůt   *ki elebua-ḥut*
  [cʰi ˈelebuaʔœʔ]   [cʰi ˈelebuaʔʊʔ]
  'these flowers'   'those flowers'

  or

  ki eleba-ůt   *ki eleba-ut*
  [cʰi ˈelebæœʔ]   [cʰi ˈelebawʔ]
  'these flowers'   'those flowers'

§10.3 Adverbial Pronouns or 'Pro-Adverbs'

Demonstrative pronouns form the basis for so-called 'pro-adverbs', or adverbs that are derived from pronouns. Adverbial pronouns show place, time and manner as well as reason. There are three levels of locative pro-adverbs – the precise form (right here, right there, etc.), the approximate form (around here, around there, etc.) and the general form (here, there, etc.). The approximate forms are also used for paths (by here, by there) or ways (this way, that way).

  Pro-adverbs can become adjectives (in -vva with a special marked form in -ḍḍa and locative in -ḍḍ-) – they follow the noun they qualify and do not take the locative case markings attributively, e.g.:

  tsẏhmoima oḍḍa   'in such a place (as this)'
  sōkkita haḍḍa   'to such a man (as that)'
  joḍḍa gattia   'in such a case (as that)'

A subclass of pro-adverbs is also found preceding nouns. This use is common to show hesitation or as a filler word before an actual noun. Pro-adverbs preceding nouns take locative cases. They are formed by the same endings as normal pro-adverbs but use third person pronouns. They are extremely common in relaxed speech.

UNMARKED	MARKED	
tovva	toḍḍa	'a (sort of) (animate)'
tavva	taḍḍa	'a (sort of) (inanimate)'
kivva	kiḍḍa	'(a sort of) (plural)'

ყahrata toḍḍia soakkia ġvivid — 'X was in a (kind of) big house'
negami kiḍḍa kigedi tśebi — 'I saw (a sort of) little sparks'

The table below shows the various forms such pro-adverbs exist in:

		proximate	medial	distal
locative	precise	ůaddja 'right here'	haiddja 'right there'	ioddja 'right there'
		ůadda 'to right here'	haidda 'to right there'	iodda 'to right there'
		ůatka 'from right here'	haitka 'from right there'	iotka 'from right there'
	approx.	ůvvia 'around/by here'	hagjia 'around/by there'	jogjia 'over/by there'
		ůvvita '(to) around/by here'	hagjita '(to) around/by there'	jogjita '(to) over/by there'
		ůvvika 'from around/by here'	hagjika 'from around/by there'	jogjika 'from over/by there'
	general	ůhhja 'here'	hahhja 'there'	iohhja 'there'
		ůhba 'to here'	hahba 'to there'	iohba 'to there'
		ůhka 'from here'	hahka 'from there'	iohka 'from there'

		proximate	medial	distal
temporal		*ódni~éudni* or *éugia* 'now'	*hagia* 'then, at that moment'	*jogia* 'then, at that moment'
manner		*oni* or *ůnnů* 'like this, thus, hereby'	*hanni* 'like that, thus, thereby'	*joni* 'like that, thus, thereby'
adj.	nom.	*ovva* or *éuvva* 'such (as this)'	*havva* 'such (as that)'	*jovva* 'such (as that)'
	gen.	*oḍḍa* or *éuḍḍa*	*haḍḍa*	*joḍḍa*
reason		*mimi* 'for this reason'	*iomi* 'for that reason'	

tygimua kepsi havva
[ˈtʰyɟimua ˈcʰɛpːsi ˈhɑwːa]
tygima-a kepsi-Ø havva-Ø
poisonous-COP.ASS mushroom-AGT such.MEDI-AGT
'a mushroom like that is poisonous' *or*
'that kind of mushroom is poisonous'

sę jahatru sailmi iskid joḍḍa
[sæ jɑˈhatxu ˈsaɪlmi ˈiːscɪʥ ˈjoðːa]
sę ja-hatr-u s=ail-mi iski-d jo-ḍḍa
not 4P.UNAG-ought-ASS.CONCL.TRANSL trust-INF.AG.TR woman-GEN such.DIST-GEN
'one should not trust a woman like that'

The locative adverbial pronouns have some more specific forms. They can be found in the comparative and the superlative.

ůaddęgiita	'closer here'
hagiikęgiita	'from further that way'
iohka iohkęgiita	'from far far over there'
osyśkin haiddęgiita	'move further over there'

§10.4 Question Words

Siwa question words exist as pronouns, adverbs and quantifiers. Interrogative pronouns show animacy and number. They decline for case and can be found with an infixed -ets- or -eb- to form out-of-many and out-of-two forms like those of the attributive demonstrative pronouns (*to kori-ůt* 'this boy', *bato kori-ůt* 'this boy (of the two)')

Interrogation in general causes no syntactical change, unlike English where question words are usually moved to the beginning of the phrase. In Siwa, question words stand where the part of speech they replace (noun, adjective, quantifier or adverb) would be in a non-interrogative sentence, and they precede nouns. If a pronoun is found with a noun, it does not take locative markers.

	interrogative pronouns	+	noun/adjective
	mimni dida?		'what girl?'
	nonatina nisti ġeugot?		'what kind of lies did you tell X?'
	rento nit ela?		'the seed of what plant?'
	herha mihmon ůdda?		'whose hat is this?'

	interrogative adverbs	+	verb/adjective
	nigju pendidda?		
or	*pendidda nigju?*		'when did you arrive?'
	maskina nidda?		'where did you go?'
	ninni singi?		'how are you?'

	noun/adjective	+	interrogative quantifiers
	da somi nitsva to?		'what kind of man is he?'
	nitsvuata?		'what kind (of person) is X?'
	hisků inniot!		'such bad luck!'
	ge imisi niot to?		'what kind of animal was X?'
	niųi atanaita?		'how big was X?'
or	*niųiata atana?*[1]		'how big was X'
	ni somi-uli oga?		'what kind of man was he'?'

All interrogative pronouns are followed by the clitic -ḥa in relative and subclauses.

set netami, kitami nit-ḥa	'I don't know what to do'
set negami, nigju-ḥa pendi	'I didn't see when they arrived'
s-onaṡikina-a, masko nidda-ḥa?	'can you tell me where X went?'

If followed by -ḥa, a question word in a normal clause refers to a dropped matrix clause (*miskjeli* 'I wonder', *oneskami* 'I ask myself', etc.):

---

[1] Interrogative phrases of the type niųi-COP ADJ are not very common and may be unacceptable in many eastern dialects.

masko niḍḍa-ḥa?	or	'where could X have gone'
		'I wonder where X went'

Interrogative pronouns decline like other -ni pronouns.

	animate	inanimate	plural
agentive	*mimni* 'who?'	*nidni* 'what?'	*mikni* 'who?'
patientive	*mimma*	*nibma*	*mihma*
genitive	*mihmō / mimġu*	*nit / niġu / nihrō*	*mihkō*
dative	*mismi, miḍmi*	*nisti, niḍḍi*	*miski, miḍgi*
locative	**mitsi-**	**nintsi-**	**miks-**

mani mimni?	'who is there?'
da mihmon ůdda	'whose is this?'
nidni oa ůdda?	'what is this?'
otoatebi mikni?	'who wants to join us?'
negana miḍgi?	'whom did you see?'
bůana nit?	'what did you eat?'
niddjana miḍgi?	'whom did you inform?'
da mihka to iu-so?	'(of what people) is this relative of yours?'

The out-of-two pronouns are formed by infixing **-eb-** to the normal pronouns. The plural forms are used with dual nouns.

	animate	inanimate	plural
agentive	*mebimni* 'which one? (of two)'	*nebidni* 'which one? (of two)'	*mebikni* 'which? (of two)'
patientive	*mebimma*	*nebibma*	*mebihma*
genitive	*mebihmō / mebimġu*	*nebit / nebiġu / nebihrō*	*mebihkō*

	animate	inanimate	plural
dative	*mebismi*	*nebisti*	*mebiski, mebiḍgi*
locative	*mebitsi-*	*nebintsi-*	*mebiks-*

oahriasa mebimni?   'which one of the two hurt you?'
iǥuḍgi mebitsi kivvaita rentue?   'in which eye did the grain fly?'
mebikni toaḍba?   'what twins?'

The out-of-many pronouns are formed the same with the infix **-ets-**. The plural forms are used with plural nouns.

	animate	inanimate	plural
agentive	*metsimni* 'which one? (of many)'	*netsidni* 'which one? (of many)'	*metsikni* 'which ones? (of many)'
patientive	*metsimma*	*netsibma*	*metsihma*
genitive	*metsihmō / metsimǥu*	*netsit / netsiǥu / netsihrō*	*metsihkō*
dative	*metsismi*	*netsisti*	*metsiski, metsiḍgi*
locative	*metsitsi-*	*netsintsi-*	*metsiks-*

netsibma bůana?   'what of those did you eat?'
maskiri metsihkō tokkirita?   'in which fish trap(s) did they go?'
luhrana metsiḍgi bytsva?   'which (of these) slime molds did you boil?'
pikśima tẏhhi metsihma   'which joints are hurting?'

§10.5 Interrogative Adverbs

Interrogative adverbs are formed on the stem **ni-**. There is a number of other specialized interrogative forms. The stem **ni-** can occasionally be heard as **nẏ-**. Included here are the adjectival interrogatives.

locative
    adessive   *nivva*   'where?'
    illative   *niḍḍa*   'where to?'

	elative	*niḍga*	'where from? (also 'why')'
	abessive	*nimma*	'where (on)?'
	allative	*nipma*	'where (onto)?'
	ablative	*niskka*	'where (off)?'
time		*nigju*	'when?'
duration		*nigjue, nijuvve*	'in how much time?'
		nigjoga, nigjoġa	'how long ago? (perfect)'
		nigjoda /nigjora	'for how long? (future)'
		nigjoma	'at what time?'
		nigjonta	'how long? (past)'
		nigjonna	'until when?'
reason		*nimi(ta)*	'why?'
		nimuaska	'due to what? how come?'
		ninkomo/ninkõ	'what? why? how come?'
degree		*niui, ni*	'how (X)'
		niui kommen~tagjen	'how much (adv)'
		niui komma~taba	'much much (X)'
manner		*ninni*	'how?'
type (noun)		*ni Ø-uli?*	'what kind of?'
		niui Ø-uli	'what kind of?'
		ni Ø-ne?	'what other?'
adjectival		*nitsva*	'what kind? (GEN. *nitsudda*)'
		niot	'what sort of?'
		inniot	'what sort of? (pejorative)'
		niddjibmis	'like what?'
		nineui	'how manieth?'

makina niḍḍa?	'where are you going?'
siboaki niḍga?	'where are you from?'
iboandi nipma?	'where/what did X jump onto?'
suguabana nigju?	'when do you want to visit us?'
sugebana nigjoma?	'at what time will you visit us?'
negajana nigjoġa?	'how long ago did you visit them?'
sitkuikina nigjonta?	'how long did you go fishingf for?'
sitkokina nigjora?	'for how long will you go fishing?'
jeġvina ůhba nigjonna?	'until what time do you want to stay here?'
hůtviasa nimi?	'why did X hit you?'
nimuaska neta?	'how come X knows about Y?'

	ninkomo tsehu haḍḍa?	'how did such a thing come to happen?'
	niyi atanaita?	'how big was X?'
or	*niyita atana?*	id.
	ga niyi somi-uli atasa?	'what kind of man was your father?'
	ninni obiḍḍona hahba?	'how do you plan on getting there?'
	ninni singi?	'how are you?'
	ga imisi nitsva, nuja ogena?	'what kind of animal did you see?'
	peva bŭbŭ nioddja nana?	'what (kind of) food are you eating?'
	de rŭtŭmmi inniot-ḥe negi?	'what kind of an idiot are you?'
	niddjibmisita?	'how was X?'
	da sinduna nineyi to sira-ŭt?	'this fish is your how manieth catch?'

§10.6 Indefinite Pronouns

Siwa indefinite pronouns all follow the secondary case marking pattern – they all more or less have the following declension pattern:

	animate	inanimate
agentive	-m·ni	-d·ni
patientive	-m·ma	-b·ma
genitive	-m·ġu, -h·m·õ	-t, -ġu or -h·rõ[1]
dative	-s·mi, -ḍ·mi	-s·ti-, -ḍ·ḍi
locative	-tsi-	-tsi-

	plural
agentive	-k·ni
patientive	-h·ma
genitive	-h·k·on, -h·k·õ
dative	-s·ki, -ḍ·gi
locative	-ksi-

The genitive ending has taken over the patientive ending in very many dialects in the case of objects. It is common-place to use patientive endings only in the case of people, and using the genitive with everything else, regardless of the grammatical animacy.

The indefinite pronouns can be subcategorized as such:
      existential

---

[1] The most common form is -hrõ in normal language and the more conserved forms are more formal.

toa-	'some'
toa- Ø-ne	'(some)other, another'
toa- Ø-uli	'some kind of'
ene-	'some, a certain'
ene- Ø-ne	'another'
ene- Ø-uli	'a certain kind of'

existential unknown

kůtů-	'some'
kůtů- Ø-ne	'(some) other, another'
kůtů- Ø-uli	'some kind of'
njoa-	'some (unimportant, unknown)'
njoa- Ø-ne	'(yet) another'
njoa- Ø-uli	'some kind of'

elective

ġů-	'any'
ġů- Ø-ne	'any other'
ġů- Ø-uli	'any kind of'
ůngů-	'any (what so ever/at all)'
ůngů- Ø-ne	'any other (at all)'
ůngů- Ø-uli	'any (kind of) (at all)'

negative

sġů-	'no'
sġů- Ø-ne	'no other'
sġů- Ø-uli	'no (kind of/at all)'
syngy-	'no'
syngy- Ø-ne	'no other'
syngy- Ø-uli	'no (kind of/at all/not a single)'

negative unknown

	set...ih-	'not any'
	set...ih- Ø-ne	'not any other'
	set...ih- Ø-uli	'not any (kind of/at all)'
or	set...mi	'not any'

Note that the unknown negative pronoun ih- only distinguishes animacy and number in the agentive. It's declension is as follows:

	animate	inanimate	plural
agentive	*ihmi*	*ihni*	*ihki*
patientive	*ihma*	Ø	Ø
genitive	*ihrõ~it~iġgu*	Ø	Ø
dative	*ihsi*	Ø	Ø

locative	*ihtsi*	Ø	Ø

Indefinite pronouns can be found with an infixed -ets- or -eb- to form out-of-many and out-of-two forms like those of the attributive demonstrative and question pronouns.

Indefinite pronouns serve 9 main functions. The functions are as follow;

§10.6.1.1 Known To Speaker
(somebody/something, a certain)
This function is used when the pronoun refers to a person, object or group which is known to the speaker. It uses the known existential pronoun series (**to-**, **ene-**).

toamni somi	'some (known) man' or 'some/one of the men'
enemni kengi	'a certain day'
tsandami tetsoahkõ kebsie	'I found some of the mushroom(s)'
so da-a sosia toadni kůnů	'do you have some (of the) milk'

§10.6.1.2 Unknown To Speaker
(someone/something)
This function is used when the pronoun refers to a person, object or group which is not known to the speaker. It uses the unknown existential pronoun series (**kůtů-**, **njoa-**).

kůtůmni růtůmmi	'some idiot'
kůtůkni	'some (people)'
njoamni peggů	'some (unimportant/unknown) girl'
tsandami kůtůdmi kepsi(-uli)	'I found some (kind of) mushroom'
so da-a sosia kůtůdni kůnů	'do you have some (quantity of) milk'

§10.6.1.3 Non-Specific
(someone)
This function is used when the pronoun refers to a person, object or group not defined or specific, or when the pronoun specifically refers to a possible reality. It uses the unknown existential pronoun series (**kůtů-**, **njoa-**).

han kůtůt!	'eat something!'
onan njoat!	'say something (anything)!'

In the case of non-specific phrase types in the negative, the unknown negative pronouns are used, unless the pronoun is found in the locative or adverbial forms, as well as form for reason or there is already a negated pronoun in the phrase.

hasen it!   'don't eat anything!'
set ma ġůt sġůmni! 'nobody ate anything!'

§10.6.1.4 Polar Question
(somebody existential or anyone elective)
There are two possibilities for pronouns: One can use the unknown existential pronoun series (kůtů-, nioa-) or the elective pronoun series (ġů-, ůngů-). The difference is subtle – when using an existential pronoun, emphasis is on the quantity (i.e. 'at least one'), whereas with an elective pronoun, emphasis is on the non-specificity of the pronoun (i.e. 'no matter what/who' or 'any at all').

so yara-a katsa kůtůmni?   'is there someone outside?'
so yara-a katsa ġůmni?   'is anyone outside?'

§10.6.1.5 Conditional
(if somebody/anybody)
This function is used in conditional statements referring to an unknown person, object of group. It uses the elective pronoun series (ġů-, ůngů-).

ronujana ġůt   'if you see anything'
romani ůngůmni   'if anyone at all comes'
datsesu ġůbma   'if anything happens'

§10.6.1.6 Indirection Negation
(not that anyone...)
This function is found in subordinate clause when the main clause is negative. It requires the elective pronoun series (ġů-, ůngů-). This kind of clause usually has a genitive object.

set tabmami negotemi ůngůhma   'I don't think I saw anyone'
set semmi manotu ġůmni   'I don't believe anyone will come'

§10.6.1.7 Direct Negation
(nobody or no one)
This function is used when the pronoun refers to a person, object or group which is negated. There are two possibilities for such pronouns. One can use the unknown negative pronoun series (**set**...ih-) or the known negative pronoun series (**sġů-, syngy-**). When using an unknown pronoun, emphasis is on the quantity (i.e. not any), whereas with a known negative pronoun, emphasis is on the negation (i.e. no one, nothing). The unknown pronoun is usually used with the negation marker **set**, but the known marker is usually the only negated item in the phrase.

mansi sġůmni	'no one came'
biadli syngymni	'no one spoke' or 'not a single person spoke'
set sygjiami ihma	'I didn't invite anyone'

§10.6.1.8 Comparison
(more than anyone)
For phrases of comparison, the elective pronoun series (ġů-, ůngů-) are used to refer to a person, object or group to which something is compared to. The elective pronoun series may be found in a special form only used for this particular function. The form is the stem of the alternative pronoun found as a hyphened (-**ne**) to the noun it describes, then meaning 'anyone/anything else'.

sahne nori tavvi ůngůmni-ne	'X sings better than anyone else'
ůngůt saista	'better than anything'

§10.6.1.9 Free Choice
(anybody)
For free choice phrases with an indefinite pronoun, the elective pronoun series is used (nearly only **ůngů-**), or if the phrase is negative, the known negative pronoun series (**sġů-, syngy-**). In positive phrases, the hyphened clitic -**uli** is commonly attached to the noun or the pronoun itself to add the meaning 'at all'.

hauri ůngůḍḍi soroko-ne	'eat any other piece'
ůnnů norjoisi ůngůmni-uli	'anyone (at all) could sing like this'

§10.6.1 Known Existential Pronouns
The forms of the known existential pronouns are as shown in the table below. The known existential pronouns are inherently less common than their unknown counterparts. They will often best be translated into English as 'a certain' or 'a known (but unspecified)'. The form in **ene-** is closer in meaning to 'a certain' or 'a particular', while **toa-** forms are more neutral. The known existential pronouns have only one 'reason' form.

The -**ne** form is commonly used where English simply has 'another', and the -**uli** form corresponds to 'a type of' or 'a kind of'.

The form **teboa-** means 'either (of two)', 'the other one' or even 'one (of two)'. It is commonly used to refer to one (then unspecified) of a pair:

pikṡimaki teboabma oama	'(one of) my knee is hurting'.

The corresponding **enebe-** form means 'either (no matter which one of two)' or 'which ever (of two)'.

The form **tetso-** and **enetse-** are used when large numbers are involved, often used where English would use 'some of them'. The form **enetse-** also has the specialized meaning of 'a part of (a group)'.

animate	*toamni* 'someone'	*enemni* 'a certain'
inanimate	*toadni* 'something'	*enedni* 'a certain'
plural	*toakni* 'some'	*enekni* 'certain'
out-of-two	*teboamni* 'either, one or the other'	*enebemni* 'either, which ever'
out-of-many	*tetsoamni* 'some of'	*enetsemni* 'some of, which ever of'
time	*toagju* 'sometimes'	*eniu ~ enju* 'sometime'
location	*toavvia* *tovavita* *toavvika* 'somewhere'	*enyia* *enyita* *enyika* 'somewhere'
manner	*toavva* 'in a way'	*enya* 'in a certain way'
reason	*mito* 'for a (certain) reason'	
-ne	*toamni-ne* 'someone else' or '(some) other'	*enemni-ne* 'another'
-uli	*toamni-uli* 'some kind of' or 'a type of'	*enemni-uli* 'a certain kind of'

Note that the word *toavva* is a common hesitation used in speech, similar to English 'hm' or 'uh'. Some speakers pronounce this *doa, tua, tůa, toya, tyà, tyę* or *tùa*.

toavvia ingi somi	'somewhere there lives a man'
eniu onekimi	'I will tell you sometime'
ga toavva geljabmis	'it was comforting in a way'
toagju sisgi	'it sometimes thunders'
so debmana-a toasti-ne	'do you want another one?'
sihi usotisi gatkebmi teboasti	'you can only bring one or the other'
djidgia enet kevvesgela-uli	'X displayed a certain kind of aggressiveness'
da toamni e-uli tygyha ůat	'this is a type of poisonous plant'
tygyhua enetsemni e	'a part of this plant/these plants is/are poisonous'

§10.6.2 Unknown Existential Pronouns

The unknown existential pronouns are more common and have a broader meaning than their known existential counterparts. They exist in two forms, **kůtů-** and **njoa-**. The forms in **njoa-** indicate that the qualified noun is unimportant or even uncertain, but it can also be slightly diminutive, especially with *njoavva*, which can be translated as 'in some (small) way'.

The form *miků* is a common adverb/coordinating particle used to show that the speaker does not understand or is unable to explain his statement, or in negative sentences where it means '(somehow) not even'. The word has diverged into various other forms, such as *migůt*, *můgů* and *ingů*. Certain speakers even use -mġů(t)- as a secondary aspectual marker or even verbal derivative to show that the action is/should be considered unbelievable, or to make the agent seem clumsy, stupid or humorous.

The -**ne** form is commonly used where English simply has 'another', and the -**uli** form corresponds to 'a type of' or 'a kind of'. Note that **njoa-Ø-ne** means both 'some kind of' and 'yet another' (not pejorative).

The form **kebůtů-** (sometimes **kůbůtů-**) means 'either (of two)', 'the other one' or even 'one (of two)'. It is much less commonly used than its known counterpart **teboa-**.

The form **ketsůtů-** (sometimes **kůtsůtů-**)- and **njetsoa-** are used when large numbers are involved, often used where English would use 'some of them'. The form *ketsůtůkni* or alternatively *ketstůkni* is often translated as 'some people'.

animate	*kůtůmni* 'someone'	*njoamni* 'someone'
inanimate	*kůtůdni* 'something'	*njoadni* 'something'
plural	*kůtůkni* 'some'	*njoakni* 'some'

out-of-two	*kebůtůmni* 'either, one or the other'	*njeboamni* 'either, which ever'
out-of-many	*ketsůtůmni* 'some'	*njetsoamni* 'some, which ever'
time	*kůtegju / kůddjů* 'sometimes'	*njoagju* 'at some time'
location	*kůtegja* *kůteita* *kůteika* 'somewhere'	*njoagja* *njoaita* *njoaika* 'somewhere'
manner	*kůtva* 'somehow'	*njoavva* 'in some way'
reason	*miků* 'for some reason'	*minjoa* 'for some reason'
-ne	*kůtůmni-ne* 'someone else' or '(some) other'	*njoamni-ne* 'some other' or 'yet another'
-uli	*kůtůmn-uli* 'some kind of' or 'a type of'	*njoamni-uli* 'some kind of' or 'a type of'

njoagju ylyma mansi	'X came at some point in the night'
kůddjů sesġu	'accidents sometimes happen'
njoagju sesġo	'an accident will happen at some point'
makin kůteita-ne!	'go somewhere else'
kůtva djandiśemmi	'for some reason, I couldn't cry'
miků set tośeintui	'X (somehow) did not (even) get hurt'
tidda on, set můgů ośeintui	'X fell and X unbelievably did not get hurt'
tiddamġů	'X fell clumsily/stupidly/funnily' (notice *mġů-*)
onan kůtůtsita-ne	'tell someone else'
njoadni sindu-ne	'yet another catch'
da njoamni tsieltami-uli to	'X is some kind of an idiot'
da tsieltamie ketstůkni	'some people are idiots'

Both known and unknown existential pronouns in -mni or -dni can be replaced by *mì-uli* or *mi Ø-uli* 'one'. Some dialects replace the stems kůtů- and toa- by mi·ni, with some dialects having both parts decline.

        mansi mì somi-uli   'some man came'
        mansi mini somi   'some man came' (dialectal)

        benho mitśani~mitśarō 'someone's dog'

§10.6.3 Elective Pronouns

The elective pronoun exists in two forms. The standard form is ġů- (sometimes found as ġůġů-) and the emphatic form ůngů- (translated as 'any at all') which is more commonly found in indirectly negated sentences and with comparisons.

The forms ġebů- and ůngebů- (sometimes ġůbů- and ůngůbů-) are used to mean 'either (of two)', while ġetsů- and ůngetsů- (sometimes ġůtsů- and ůngůtsů-) mean 'any (of them)'.

animate	ġůmni 'anyone'	ůngůmni 'anyone'
inanimate	ġůdni 'anything'	ůngůdni 'anything'
plural	ġůkni 'any'	ůngůkni 'any'
out-of-two	ġebůkni 'either'	ůngebůkni 'either'
out-of-many	ġetsůkni 'any of'	ůngetsůkni 'any of'
time	ġůgjů 'anytime'	ůngegju 'anytime'
location	ġůgjia ġůita ġůika 'anywhere'	ůngegja ůngeita ůngeika 'anywhere'
manner	ġůvva 'in any way'	ůngya 'in any way'
reason	miġů 'for any reason'	miůn 'for any reason (at all)'

-ne	ġů̇mni-ne 'any other' or 'anyone else'	ů̇nġů̇mni-ne 'some other' or 'yet another'
-uli	ġů̇mni-uli 'any kind of'	ů̇nġů̇mni-uli 'some kind of' or 'a type of'

lagjui ů̇ngegja tami	'it could be anywhere (at all)'
onakin, ġů̇vva daijomu opotemi	'tell me if I can help in any way'
miů̇n geskkisen	'do not make sound for any reason at all'
usotisi ġů̇ita kegna	'you can hide anywhere'
inguomi ġů̇gjia-ne tavvi jogjia	'I would want to live anywhere else than there'
so-nuidnaṡina-a ġů̇t ela-uli	'can you identify any kind of plant?'
ů̇ngẏa-uli s-opiṡina-a	'can you help in any other way at all?'
hodlan ġebů̇sti	'choose either'
goskkieṡiba ů̇nġů̇tsů̇mni	'anyone of them could betray us'

§10.6.5 Known Negative Pronouns

The known negative pronoun has a normal form in **sġů̇-** (sometimes also **sġẏ-**) and an emphatic form in **syngy-** (in eastern dialects commonly **sôngô-**), which are analogous to electives **ġů̇-** and **ů̇nġů̇-**.

The form *syngymni-uli* means both 'no kind of' and 'not a single'. The ending -uli is sometimes found as -yli if both used with **syngy-** and a word ending in a rounded vowel, for example in the expression *syngydni rymyry-yli* 'no problem, OK' (lit. 'not a single mosquito').

The forms **sġebů̇-** and **syngeby-** (also **sġů̇bů̇-** and **syngyby-**) mean 'neither (of two)', while **sġetsů̇-** and **syngetsy-** (also **sġů̇tsů̇-** and **syngytsy-**) 'none of (a group)'.

animate	sġů̇mni 'no one'	syngymni 'no one'
inanimate	sġů̇dni 'nothing'	syngydni 'nothing'
plural	sġů̇kni 'none'	syngykni 'none'

out-of-two	sġebůmni 'neither'	syngebymni 'neither'
out-of-many	sġetsůmni 'none of'	syngetsymni 'none of'
time	sġůgjů 'never'	syngey 'never'
location	sġůgjia sġůita sġůika 'nowhere'	syngogja syngoita syngoika 'nowhere'
manner	sġůvva 'in no way'	syngųa 'in no way'
reason	misġů 'for no reason'	misůn 'for no reason (at all)'
-ne	sġůmni-ne 'no other' or 'no one else'	syngymni-ne 'no other' or 'no one else'
-uli	sġůmni-uli 'no kind of'	syngymni-uli 'no kind of' or 'not at single'

saibba syngymni nõstenadneka   'no one must hear of X'
sàhkia bialtse sġůhma-ne   'no one else dared to speak up'
syngey edniki   'I'll never ever die'
ga sġůgjia uja   'there was nowhere water'
syngydni rymyry-yli   'not a single mosquito' (i.e. 'no problem')
niḍgi syngytsymma-ne   'none of the others died'

§10.6.6 Unknown Negative Pronouns

The unknown negative pronoun is alone in having only one form, which only distinguishes animacy and number in the agentive case.

animate	set...ihmi 'not any'

inanimate	*set...ihni* 'not any'
plural	*set..ihki* 'not any'
out-of-two	*set...ibehki* 'not...either'
out-of-many	*set...itsehki* 'not...any of'
time	*set...ihhįu* 'not ever'
location	*set...ihhįia* *set...ihta* *set...ihka* 'not anywhere'
manner	*set...ihhųa* 'not in any way'
reason	*set...mihi* 'not for any reason'
-ne	*set...ihmi-ne* 'not any other'
-uli	*set...ihmi-uli* 'not any kind'

set negami it	'I didn't see anyone/anything'
pednisen ihhįu	'don't ever come back'
pednisen itsehhįu-ne	'don't come back any other time'
set tśandami ihka	'I didn't find Y anywhere'
mihi onatisen	'do not for any reason ever tell Y'
set lugįuahmi it-ne	'I won't love any other'

Both known and unknown negative pronouns can be replaced by negative and *mi* 'one' (*set..mi*) or clitically negated *simi*, *sęmi*, *sęmmi*. The emphatic negation particle *hįayt* can also be used, and clitically negated forms also exist: *hįaybmi, hįayhhůmi, hįęmi, hįęmmi*. It is not uncommon for the clitically negated forms to appear in already negated sentences, forming a double negative (which is still negative) which is very emphatic.

set mansi mi ~ sęmmi ~ hįaybmi	'not a soul came'

§10.7 Universal and Distributive Pronouns

Siwa universal and distributive pronouns can be subcategorized as distributive singular (roa-), distributive plural (śoś-) and universal (kil-/kadlk-). Neither distributive nor universal pronouns have the known vs. unknown forms. They do not decline like other -ni pronouns. Below is a table showing their function:

distributive singular each	*manta nůjů roami kori* 'each boy receives a knife' (considered individually)
distributive plural every	*manta nůjů śośi korigi* 'every boy receives a knife' *or* 'all the boys receive a knife' (considered as a group, i.e. all the boys receive knives)
universal countable the whole	*gikkia killa nůjů kori* 'the boy sharpened the whole knife'
universal uncountable all	*amġa killa kůnů kori* 'the boy drank all the milk'

§10.7.1 Distributive Pronouns

The distributive pronouns *roami* and *śośi* differs slightly in its declension. The plural form distinguishes only case – it lacks animacy and number. It is also unique in having no distinction between the agentive and the dative (much like nouns). In some dialects, it is even found as an adjective (though it still usually precedes the noun) with the marked form *śośko*. The singular form *roami* declines like the numeral *mi* 'one' and only has two forms, marked and unmarked, which distinguish animacy.

	animate	
agentive	*roami*	*śośi*
patientive	*roamid~roamitśa*	*śośva, śośko*
genitive	*roamid~roamitśa*	*śośon, śośõ, śośśi, śośko*
dative	*roami*	*śośi*
locative	*roamid~roamitśa*	*śośi-*

Note that the out-of-two form for *śośi* has alternates between *śebś-* and *śeboś-*

	animate
agentive	*śebśi*
patientive	*śebośva* (or *śebośko*)
genitive	*śebśon/śebśõ* (or *śebośko*)
dative	*śebśi*

| | locative | ṡebṡi- |

The form ṡoṡi-uli also has a contracted form in ṡoṡli 'all kinds of' or 'various' which *does not* decline.

Distributive pronouns only have one locative declension in ṡoṡ-. Time expressions using distributive pronouns can often be found int he active form (no case marking).

animate	*roami* 'each'	*ṡoṡi* 'all'
inanimate		
plural		
out-of-two	*reboami* 'each (of two)'	*ṡebṡi* 'both'
out-of-many	*retsoami* 'every (of)'	*ṡetsoṡi* 'all (of)'
time	*ruogju* 'every time'	*ṡoṡṡu* 'all the time'
location	*ṡoṡia* *ṡoṡta* *ṡoṡka* 'everywhere'	
manner	*ruovva* 'in every way'	*ṡoṡva* 'completely'
-ne	*roami-ne* 'every other' or 'everyone else'	*ṡoṡi-ne* 'all other' or 'all else'
-uli	*roami-uli* 'every kind of'	*ṡoṡi-uli* 'all kind of'

niko njoagju roamitṡa	'everyone must die someday'
niḍgi ṡoṡva	'everyone died'
sarkkia retsoami saiyu	'X broke every single pot'
sarkkia ṡetsoṡi saiyu(o)	'X broke all of the pots'
suganika ruogju, saskiuts saka	'X comes to see me every time I wake up'

ɥahrari śośia   'they were everywhere'
ruovva tśvettu   'completely destroyed'
pohḥiuts mai sa roami-ne   'while everyone else is sleeping'
da gogia śośi bẏ-uli   'I have all kinds of food'

§10.7.2 Universal Pronouns

Siwa universal pronouns come in two sets. The first set in **kil-** is the default version, and the second set in **kadlk-** is the more emphatic/poetic version. Their declension diverges significantly from other pronouns, as they lack distinction of animacy, number and various other functions. They do not have a locative form and take instead the genitive form, much like adjectives. Only the **kadlk-** version has a manner form.

	unemphatic	emphatic
agentive	*killa*	*kadlka*
patientive	*kilva*	*kadlɥa*
genitive	*kihlõ/kihlon*	*kadlġõ/kadlġon* or *kadlka*
dative	*killa*	*kadlkis*
locative	Ø	Ø

animate	*killa* 'the whole'	*kadlka* 'the whole'
inanimate		
plural		
out-of-two		
out-of-many		
time	*killju* 'the whole time'	*kadlkju* 'the whole time, all the time'
location	Ø	Ø
manner	Ø	*kadlkɥa, kadlkɥen* 'completely'
reason	Ø	Ø
-ne	*killa-ne* 'the whole other'	*kadlka-ne* 'the whole other'
-uli	*killa-uli* 'the whole kind of'	*kadlka-uli* 'the whole kind of'

bůa killa mavvu to ebbenho	'the damn dog at all the meat'
saposti killju	'you slept the whole time'
sapohhjis kadlkju	'you sleep all the time'
kadlkuen entsaskka	'I completely forgot X'

§10.8 -ni Determiners

So-called -ni determiners are clitics used to create nouns or adjectives from other word classes (often postpositions or adverbs). These adjectives follow the -ni declension of inanimate nouns. The -ni clitic declines in all cases, and is in fact the same declension as secondary case markers (see *§4..6*).

agentive	-ni
patientive	-va/-ua
genitive	-rō/-ġō/-hō or commonly -t
dative	-si, -ḍi
locative	-tsi-

Adjectives can be regularly derived from these words by the ending **-nuha** or **-nha**.

Double case markers can be used with postpositions:

garini	'the one instead, replacement'
cf. *gari*	'instead'
(*ůatta*)*maggjani*	'the one in this case, this particular'
ůatta maggja	'in this case' or 'in the case of this'
roġoni	'the one in the way, obstacle'
roġo	'in the way'
roġonha	'obstructive, counter-productive'
tatsůini	'the additional one'
tatsůi	'in addition'
tatsůinha	'additional, extra'
kiḍḍjani	'the one within sight, witness'
kiḍḍja	'within sight'
koloni	'local, close-by'
kolo	'around here'
samnani	'the one during'
samna	'during'
oapi kelgosamnanha	'war-time help'
tevuni	'the one before, the former, ancestor'
ahhani	'the one after, the latter, descendants'

sia hausġa ė maggjani
['sia 'haʊsxa eː 'mɑcːɑni]
si-a hausġa ė-Ø maggja-ni
COP.NEG-ASS.CONCL edible plant-AGT in.case-SECOND.AG
'the plant in this case is not edible'

sikkui toboita roġotsi
['sɪʔkui 'tʰɔbɔida 'rɔxɔtsi]
sikk-u-i-Ø t<obo>-ita roġo-tsi
kick-PAST-ASS.CONCL.ITR-3P.AG.SG rock-ILLAT in.the.way-SECOND.LOC
'X kicked the rock that was in the way'

mante tatsůisi koḍmi
['mante 'tʰatsøisi 'kʰɔðmːi]
mant-e tatsůi-si koḍmi-Ø
take-INFER.CONCL.TR in.addition-DAT guest-AGT
'the guest shall take the additional one'

tsalbi meḍbubilua kiḍḍjani
['tsalbi 'mɛðbubilua 'cʰiðːjani]
tsalbi me<ḍb>-u-ila-a kiḍḍja-ni
rarely desire.PAST-PAT.PART-SUPER-COP.ASS.CONCL within.sight-SECOND.AG
'the most desired one is rarely the one in sight'

peljekkemi on tevusi, oskemi ka ahhasi
['pʰeljɛʔcemiɔ̃ 'tʰevusi 'ɔscemika 'ɑhːɑsi]
peljekk-e-mi on tevu-si osk-e-mi ka ahha-si
cook-INFER.CONCL.TR-1P.AG.SG on former-SECOND.DAT, smoke-INFER.CONCL.TR-1P.AG.SG ka latter-SECOND.DAT
'While I will cook the former, I will smoke the latter '

§10.8.1 -ni Determiners on Pronouns

The -ni clitic can also be added onto demonstrative pronouns to form adjectives with the meaning 'like this/that one' or 'such as this/that'.

	'like this one'	'like that one'	'like that one'
agentive	ůadni	haidni	iodni
patientive	ůatva	haitva	iotva
genitive	ůadġõ, ůaḍḍa	haidġõ, haiḍḍa	iodġõ, ioḍḍa
dative	ůatsi	haitsi	iotsi
locative	ůatsi-	haitsi-	iotsi-

	'like this one'	'like that one'	'like that one'
agentive	*eygni*	*kvagni*	*gaugni*
patientive	*eyhtva*	*kvahtva*	*gauhtva*
genitive	*eyhtõ, eygḍa*	*kvahtõ, kvagḍa*	*gauhtõ, gaugḍa*
dative	*eyhtsi*	*kvahtsi*	*gauhtsi*
locative	*eyhtsi-*	*kvahtsi-*	*gauhtsi-*

sġůgjů nuhlami it ůadġõ
[ˈsxøjːø ˈnuɬːɑmi ˈiːhrõ ˈœæðxõ]
sġůgjø nuhl-a-mi ihr=õ ůat-rõ
never see.PERF-ASS.CONCL.TR-1P.AG.SG nothing.INA.GEN this.PROXI.GEN
'I've never seen anything like this'

siduma kvahtõ
[ˈsiduma ˈkʰvahtõ]
sid-um-a kvaht=õ
understand-OBLI-ASS.CONCL.TR that.MED.PL.GEN
'one must be understanding of these things'

tsaupri iotva
[ˈtsaʊpxi ˈɪotwːa]
tsaupr-i iot-va
happen.rarely-ASS.CONCL.ITR that.DIST.PAT
'things like that happen rarely'

It can also be added onto other forms of pronouns, such as locative forms of pro-adverbs:

| *ůvvi·ni* | 'the one around here' (from *ůvvia* 'around here') |
| *ůvvih·ni* | 'the one from around here' (from *ůvvika* 'from around here') |

| *hagji·ni* | 'the one around there' (from *hagjia* 'around there') |
| *hagjih·ni* | 'the one from around there' (from *hagjika* 'from around there') |

jogji·ni	'the one over there' (from *jogjia* 'around there')
jogjih·ni	'the one from over there' (from *jogjika* 'from around there')
iksin jogjitsita!	'shoot the one over there!'

Notice also:

ni·ni   'one's own' (derived from the locative form of the fourth person).

§11 Numerals

Siwa's numeral system is decimal, like English – it uses bases of tens. Originally, the numeral system was based on the five fingers of the hand and was thus quinary (using bases of fives). This eventually evolved into the fixed decimal system which is now found in Siwa. Numerals have four main forms; cardinal, ordinal, nominal and collective. Cardinal numerals are those used to count things. Ordinal numerals show order in number (1st, 34th, etc.). Nominal numerals represent the number in itself (number one, number four, etc.) while collective numerals are those describing a group of people of a certain number (a foursome, 8 people). Additionally, collective numerals can be found with absolutive descriptives (see section *§9.14*). Other specializer numerals also exist.

§11.1 Cardinal Numerals

The cardinal numerals are those used to count. Siwa lacks the concept of zero, which can be expressed simply by using a negative circumlocution. However, the neologism *syntů/sůntů* can be used. Each basic numeral (1-9) has three form; one unmarked form, one marked form for inanimate nouns and one marked form for animate nouns. Cardinal numerals agree in animacy with the head noun in marked cases, but do not in the active and the dative forms. They behave like adjectives (the head of the phrase is the noun) and lack locative forms, agreeing in case for active or dative and stative or genitive. Cardinal numerals commonly come before the head noun. If found after the head noun, then they generally mean 'the two X', e.g.

	eśi korigi	'two boys'
but	*korigi eśi(gi)*	'the two boys'

They do not require the head noun to be in the plural, though animate nouns are nearly always found in the plural. Inanimate nouns may have optional plural marking in the active, but marked cases are generally left unmarked for plurality. The numerals from 1-10 are:

	agentive	marked animate	marked inanimate
1	*mi*	*mitśa*	*mid*
2	*eśi*	*ehta*	*etta*
3	*neġvi*	*neġġumi*	*neġůtta*
4	*aits*	*aubmi*	*aiddja*
5	*hakno*	*hangua*	*hangoka*
6	*sudna*	*sutva*	*sunamo*
7	*śvi*	*śumi*	*śvid*
8	*tenga*	*tentsa*	*tengari*
9	*boari*	*boatśa*	*boahka*
10	*nets*	*nedda*	

Thus, one says:

	mi kori	'one boy'
	eśi kori/korigi	'two boys'
but	*eśi půdů~půduo~půdůmů~půdō*	'two logs'
	ehta kohko	'of two boys' (animate genitive)
	etta pèuma	'of two logs' (inanimate genitive).

Numerals from 1-9 can have -gi added to them to mark a plural form used with nouns always in pair or always in the plural, whether animate or inanimate, e.g. *eśigi kůimpa* 'two pairs of boots' but *eśi kůitton* 'two boots'.

Numerals from 11 to 19 are formed by the addition of -**nesta** (a genitive of *nets*) to the stem of the numeral (usually formed by dropping the last syllable of the word). Short forms can also be used, having -**net** instead. The ending *nesta* can take double marking for the genitive, becoming -**netrō** (see section §4.6 on double case marking).

11	*minesta*	or	*minet*
12	*ehnesta*	or	*ehnet*
13	*neġnesta*	or	*neġnet*
14	*aidnesta*	or	*aidnet*
15	*hagnesta*	or	*hagnet*
16	*sunnesta*	or	*sunnet*
17	*śůnesta*	or	*śůnet*
18	*tennesta*	or	*tennet*
19	*boanesta*	or	*boanet*

Numerals from 20 to 90 are formed by the addition of -ra/-ġa/-ka to the lengthened stem of the numerals 2-9. Numerals 1-9 are added after the decimal numerals.

| *iesġa neġvi* | 'twenty three (23)' |
| *boarka boari* | 'ninety nine (99)' |

In most dialects, if *mi* is added to a decimal numeral, it will be preceded by *te* 'and'.

| *hanra te mi* | 'fifty (and) one (51)' |

They have regular declensions of inanimate nouns (in parentheses).

	unmarked	marked
20	*iesġa*	*iesġadi*
30	*neġġa*	*neġari*
40	*aitġa*	*aitġaka*

50	*hanra*	*hanraka*	
60	*suntsġa*	*suntsġamo*	
70	*śura*	*śuhmo, śuramo*	
80	*tenra*	*tenrari*	
90	*boarra*	*boarka*	

The numeral 'hundred' is *giabmi* in the singular, and its genitive form *guoma* or *goma* is consistently used with numerals other than 1, e.g. *giabmi tenra śvi* 'one hundred eighty seven (187)' but *neġvi guoma te mi* 'three hundred and one (301)'.

Numerals from one to nine thousands are expressed with tens of hundreds - teens for 1000-1900 and tens for 2000-9000). Thus, one thousand is *nets guoma*, and *boanesta guoma tenra tenga* is 'nineteen hundred (one thousand nine hundred) eighty eight (1988)'. Similarly, 'two thousand eleven (2011)' is *iesġa guoma minet*. In less conservative dialects, it has merged with the ending -nesta to form -netsġoma, e.g. *minetsġoma* 'one thousand one hundred (eleven hundred) (1100)'. The word *netsġiabmi* can stand on its own, meaning 'one thousand'. It has the genitive form *netsġoma*. This form is more common in the western dialects, but has quickly made its way into the speech of males especially in the eastern dialects.

The tens of thousands, Siwa uses decimal numerals (20-90) and *netsġiabmi* (1000), e.g. 'twenty five thousands five hundred and thirty four (25,534)' is *iesġa hakno netsġuoma hakno guoma neġġa aits* (lit. 25x100 + 534).

The hundreds of thousands are expressed using the word *giamra* (GEN. *guomra*) (100,000) and the right decimal numerals, e.g. 'three hundred and twenty thousand (320,000)' is *neġvi guomra iesġa netsġoma* (lit. 3x100,000 + 20x10,000).

Millions are expressed by using decimals 10-19 or 20-90, e.g. 'one million and two hundred thousand (1,200,000)' is *nets guomra iesġa netsġoma* (lit. 10x100,000+20x10,000) or 'six million and six hundred thousand (6,600,000) *suntsġa guomra suntsġa netsġoma* (lit. 60x100,00+60x1000).

Here to summarize is a comparison of the English and Siwa systems;

	English	Siwa
10	ten	*nets*
100	hundred	*giabmi*
1.000	thousand	*netsġiabmi*
10.000	ten thousand	*nets netsġuoma*
100.000	one hundred thousand	*giamra*
1.000.000	million	*nets guomra*

Cardinal numbers can be made into adverbs by adding -il or -(v)en.

mi	migjil	'once'
eśi	eśven	'twice'
neġvi	neġven	'three times'
aits	aitsven	'four times'
hakno	hanguen	'five times'
sudna	sutven	'six times'
śvi	śvivven, śyvven	'seven times'
tenga	tengen	'eight times'
boari	boaren	'nine times'
nets	neddjil	'ten times'

This is sometimes found also on demonstrative pronouns:

ůattė	'this time'	(also ůattei)
haittė	'that time'	(also haittei)
iottė	'that time'	(also iottei)

§11.2 Ordinal Numerals

Ordinal numerals show position in a series. They are regularly derived by applying vowel polarization to the last vowel of the word and by adding -t. The irregular ordinal form of *mi* 'one' is *estot* 'first'. The genitive ending is fixed (not dependent on the stressed vowel) and is -**dna**, e.g. *neġġet* 'thirtieth' and *neġġedna* 'of the thirtieth'.

	unmarked	marked	
1.	estot	estodna	'first'
2.	eśut	eśudna	'second'
3.	neġvut	neġvudna	'third'
4.	aitset	aitsedna	'fourth'
5.	haknet	haknedna	'fifth'
6.	sudnet	sudnedna	'sixth'
7.	śvoit	śvoidna	'seventh'
8.	tenget	tengedna	'eighth'
9.	boarut	boarudna	'ninth'
10.	neddjut	neddjudna	'tenth'
11.	minestet	minestedna	'eleventh'
12.	ehnestet	ehnestedna	'twelfth'
13.	neġnestet	neġnestedna	'thirteenth'
14.	aidnestet	aidnestetdna	'fourteenth'
15.	hagnestet	hagnestedna	'fifteenth'
16.	sudnestet	sudnestedna	'sixteenth'

17.	śůnestet	śůnestedna	'seventeenth'
18.	tennestet	tennestedna	'eighteenth'
19.	boanestet	boanestedna	'nineteenth'
20.	iasġet	iasġedna	'twentieth'
30.	neġġet	neġġedna	'thirtieth'
40.	aitġet	aitġedna	'fortieth'
50.	anret	anredna	'fiftieth'
60.	suntsġet	suntsġedna	'sixtieth'
70.	śůret	śůredna	'seventieth'
80.	tenret	tenredna	'eightieth'
90.	boarret	boarredna	'ninetieth'
100.	giabmut	giambudna	'hundredth'
1000.	netsġiabmut	netsġiabmudna	'thousandth'

Siwa ordinals behave like adjectives and follow the noun they qualify. Generally, both items of numbers 21-99 are in the ordinal form, but numbers above are found in their cardinal form.

  gjekes aitġet aits   'the 44th year'
  guma neġvi guoma hagnestet 'I became the 315th'

As the last example shows, ordinal numbers are considered to be nouns when in a copular phrase.
  An adverbial form in -ųi can be used to show order of frequency.

  estoųi   'for the first time'
  eśuųi   'for the second time'
  neġnesteųi 'for the 13th time'

The interrogative pronoun for this form is *nineųi* '(for the) how manieth (time)'. Similarly, one can say *ůatteųi*, *haitteųi* and *iotteųi* 'this manieth', 'that manieth' and 'that manieth' (proximal, medial and distal).

  luhhatśu haitteųi orena, tamingo
  'it will be ready when you will have boiled it that many times' (lit. that manieth)'

§11.2.1 Halves and Fractions

Siwa forms fractions by having the numerator as a cardinal number, and the denominator as the (adjectival -**dna**) genitive form of the cardinal form.

  eśi neġvudna 'two thirds'
  neġvi aitsedna 'three fourths'

The genitive form of the numerator is found in the inanimate.

A half is *koho* (GEN. *koamo*). The cardinal form *kohut* (GEN. *kohutta*) is also commonly found, especially qualifying a noun:

	ma kohut sihdi~sihdika
or	*ma koha sihdi~sihdika*
	'X ate half the fish'.

Another word for 'half' is *bialbi*, with the irregular genitive form *bialdi*.

§11.3 Nominal Numerals

Ordinal numerals are called nominal numerals when they behave like nouns, i.e. they decline according to nominal declension patterns, e.g. *niġvut* 'the third' or 'number three' and in the genitive *niġvudna* 'of the third' (as adjective) but *niġvutsta* 'of number three' (as noun). The final syllable (-Vt) can be separated from the stem by an absolutive descriptive. In this case, the nominal numeral may be the head of a noun phrase, with the argument found in the genitive or the elative.

	tsandami sudnohka	'I found six (of the round things)'
	tsandami sudnohka tůme	'I found six (of the) eggs'[1]
cf.	*tsandami sudna tey*	'I found six eggs'

§11.4 Collective Numerals

Collective numerals are a set of fixed nouns that reflect a number of items or people forming a group together. Collective numerals are regularly derived through circumfixes. *ta-* is prefixed to the beginning of the word and *-ri* is suffixed (ta-Ø-ri) to the polarized vowel of the genitive form of the animate numeral, except for the number 1, which has the form *tamiemi*, meaning 'on one's own, alone'. Only numerals 1-4 are found in the collective as well as *giabmi*, which has the form *guomeri*. The noun *guomeri* has the primary meaning of 'an army', as the original meaning of *giabmi* can be seen in the related verb *kalmisa* (or in its older form *kamlisa*) 'to battle' and *kintumi* 'warrior'. For numbers higher than five, the postposition *kōuma* is used with the genitive animate form of the numeral. The word *tahhangyeri* is usually translated as 'a team' or 'a fellowship'. The phrase *eṡi (ta)boaddjeri* means something like 'the whole pack' or 'the whole family', i.e. 'all the members of a large group'. From the form *taubmuri*, the word *aitsġi* 'group of friends' is derived.

---

[1] The form *sudnohka* bears the absolutive descriptive, but it could also be found on the verb, e.g. *tsandohkami sudna tey* 'I found six (round, large) eggs'.

tamiemi	'on one's own, alone'
tehteri	'a pair'
taneġġuri	'a threesome'
taubmuri	'a foursome'

Collective numerals also have an adverbial form created by adding -(v)en. They become *tamiemen* 'alone', *tehteren* 'in pair', *taneġġuren* 'as a threesome' and *taubmuren* 'as a foursome'. When both the collective and adverbial collective forms are side by side, it means 'X by X', e.g. *tehteri tehteren* 'two by two', *taneġġuri taneġġuren* 'three by three'.

Non-numerals are also found with collective markings, e.g. *teuriri* 'a few' (from *eumo* 'few') and *tatammuri* 'many people' (from *tama* 'many') and the derivative *muri-uli* (GEN *muhma-uli* or *muṡid-uli*) 'various' and *murot* 'various' (ADJ).

§12 Interjections

Interjections are words or sounds to communicate specific commands or reactions.

nẏ or nẏa	'wow, woah, oh' (surprise, awe)
mėi	'wow' (amazement, happiness)
hemmėi	'hurray!'
(i)ssėi	'oh, no!' (disbelief')
ġuo	'ugh, huh' (annoyance)
ṡyṡṡ or hi̯yhhi̯	'pfew' (tiredness)
mi̇dl	(sound to get a caribou to move)
tsġebb	(sound to encourage someone)
tṡirri	(sound to make animal go away)
vůvvů	(sound made to calm animals or children)
syll	(sound to tell someone to be silent, pron ['syɬ:])
sytka	'please'
tẏi	'please'
sytvi	'please'
i̇hhi̯ami	'thank you'
i̇hhi̯õ	'thank you'
ista[1]	'thank you, there you go, no problem'
isotveki	'sorry, excuse me'
isotve, sotve	'sorry, excuse me'
kataneskõ	'sorry, excuse me'
i̯amġa	(sound to get someone's attention)
nehḥe	'well, you see, hm...'
puḥhu	'woosh, go away!'
půkka	'woosh, go away!'

See also *§9.9.4.6* on interjections made from the subitive ending -**tta**.

---

[1] The word **ista** is actually the result of two separate words merging into one. The 'thank you' meaning of **ista** simply the past form of the verb root **ihhi̯**- 'to thank', while the meaning of 'there you go, no problem' comes from the verb root -**sot**- 'to give, allow' in the meaning of 'X allowed Y to Z'. This has lead to the word having both the meaning of 'thank you' and it is what is generally said after someone has apologized.

§13 Interrogation

Siwa uses clitics to show that a sentence is a tag question (yes or no question). Positive questions start with **so** (always unstressed, **s-** before vowels, most common simply [s] in all cases). The topic of the question is followed by **-a** (or **-ḥa**) for a basic interrogation and **-de/-re** (or **-ḥe**) for a question expecting a positive answer. If the question is negative, the phrase starts with **si** (which also functions as the negation particle for verbs but not copular constructions) and the enclitic **-i** (or **-ḥi**) when expecting a negative answer. The enclitics are hyphened to the topic of the question, although they also may stand alone. The words **so/si** can be reduced to **s-** and hyphened to the verb. The hyphened enclitic question markers are usually pronounced with a sharp rising tone. They are found at the end of the matrix verb, or in the case of defective copular verbs, hyphened to the adjective.

The prefix **so-** is sometimes found as **sů-**. Both **so-** and **s-** are accepted for words in **p- t- k- ġ- v- m- n-** and **l-**.

	neutral	positive	rhetoric	negative
positive	so... -a 'is X Y?'	so... -de/-re/-r 'X is Y, right/isn't it?'	so ...-ahte/-ahre (+INFER) 'I wonder if XY'	∅
negative	si... -i 'is X not Y?'	∅	∅	so ... -i 'X is not Y, isn't it?'

minguana   'you are ready'
so minguana-a?   'are you ready?'

so minguana-de?   'you are ready, right/aren't you?'
so minguana-ahte?   'I wonder if you are ready'

si siana minga-i   'aren't you ready?'
so siana minga-i   'you're not *ready*, are you?'

The interrogative particle **so/si** must always be at the head of the sentence, but the enclitics may be found at the end of the phrase.

so sasame njeltśa tamotta lilda-go-a saundotu
'was it your paternal uncle's friend's chief's tent that caught on fire?'

§14 Derivation

Siwa uses a large variety of strategies, with various levels of productivity, to create words from other words and roots. Heavily involved in all derivations are three vowel changes called lengthening, fronting and shortening. The combination of these sound changes with derivational endings creates new words.

§14.1 Derivational Phonological Changes

Siwa words may go through various phonological changes caused by derivation processes. These changes are not always fully productive, but they have affected a large number of words, and a good knowledge of these processes is essential to understand how Siwa has developed its vocabulary.

The most important phonological changes in derivational strategies involve changes in the quality of the stressed vowel of a stem, which in term may affect word-initial consonants. There are three important changes: vowel fronting, lengthening and shortening. Various derivational endings trigger various vowel changes. Some can be inferred from the nature of the endings, while most are unpredictable.

Both short and long vowels are affected by these changes, and diphthongs may also be affected. Diphthongs sometimes regress to long monophthongs:

au/ai	→	à/a
ei	→	è/e
ie	→	ì/i
oa/ou/oi/uo	→	ò/o
uo	→	ù/u
eu/ey/ay	→	èu/ů/y

They may lose an initial i- and gain the glide j̦-:

ia	→	j̦a
io	→	j̦o
iu	→	j̦u
iů	→	j̦ů

Or they may lose and initial o-/u- and gain the glide ʉ-:

oa/ůa	→	ʉa
ui/ůi	→	ʉi

Note that the vowel /ō/ reverts to its original <o(n)> or <u(n)> when affected by such changes, and therefore is not included below.

Certain lengthened vowels, specifically those in ʉ- or oa-, may cause preceding <p t k> to become voiced [b d g] <b d g> (usually cause the loss of ʉ-). Similarly, vowels resulting in diphthongs in j̦- may change k to tṡ and t to ts and certain shortened vowels, especially o and a, may change k to h or ġ.

kòi [ˈkʰʊːi] 'X will speak' → goaiġa [ˈgɔɑixa] 'fast-spoken'
puna [ˈpʰuna] 'deer skin' → bename [ˈbenɑme] 'leather bag' (< *pɥename)
kyni [ˈcʰyni] 'nest' → tsůnůni [ˈtɕønøni] 'newborn animal still living in a nest' (< *kjůnůni)

While the particular derivational endings are not discussed in this section, examples will be given for each type of change.

§14.1.1 Fronted Vowels
Vowel fronting is the most common sound change for vowel-initial derivational endings. It is less common than vowel lengthening, but also more regular.

		fronting
a	e	salama [ˈsɑlɑma] 'antlers' → selion [ˈselɪɔn] 'caribou herd' (-ion 'animate aggregate')
ȧ	ei	pȧlli [ˈpʰæːlːi] 'mature male' → peilni [ˈpʰɛɪlni] 'eldest male of a group' (-ɨni 'member of group')
ę	e	nępa [ˈnæpa] 'X catches Y' → nebbi [ˈnepːi] 'trap' (-bi 'tool')
e	i	neyo [ˈnewɔ] 'sand' → niujaka [ˈniujɑga] 'sand dune' (-jaka 'inanimate aggregate')
ė	i	pėsi [ˈpʰeːsi] 'maternal uncle' → pigjon [ˈpʰiːjːɔn] 'maternal uncle's family' (-ion 'animate aggregate')
i	ia/ja	isi [ˈiɕi] 'old' → jaśsi [ˈjaɕːi] 'old age' (-(i)gi 'time period')
i̇	igj-	kì [ˈcʰiː] 'new' → kigjini [ˈcʰijːini] 'youngest child' (-ɨni 'member of group')
o	i/y	obeno [ˈɔbenɔ] 'smoke' → ibengi [ˈibeŋːi] 'smoking period' (-(i)gi 'time period')
ȯ	i/ẏ	ȯlma [ˈʊːlma] 'leaf' → ẏlys [ˈyːlœs] 'leaflet' (-is 'inanimate diminutive')
u	y	muni [ˈmuni] 'X will rest' → myngi [ˈmyŋːi] 'break, pause' (-(i)gi 'time period')

		fronting
ų̊	eu/ẙ	*hju̧* ['hju:] 'sea water' → *hjų̊baka* ['hjøbɑga] 'tidal pool' (-jaka 'inanimate aggregate')
y	jų̊/ey	*kyni* ['cʰyni] 'nest' → *tsų̊nų̊ni* ['tɕønøni] 'newborn animal still living in a nest' (-ɨni 'member of group')
ẏ	ieu	*nẏmi* ['ny:mi] 'it is humid' → *nieugi* ['nieuji] 'ground mist' (-(i)gi 'time period')
ů	e	*půdů* ['pʰødø] 'log' → *peddjaka* ['pʰedʑ:ɑga] 'logs used to build a house' (-jaka 'inanimate aggregate')
eu	ẏ	*seu* ['sø:] 'river' → *sẏgjaka* ['sy:j:ɑga] 'branches of a river' (-jaka 'inanimate aggregate')

§14.1.2 Lengthened Vowels

Vowels change as follow when lengthened. Many lengthened vowels have a front and a back versions, depending on the vowel found in the suffix that causes lengthening. Vowel lengthening is by far the most common of these three vowel changes, but least regular.

		lengthening
a	oa/au/ai	*sarana* ['sɑrɑna] 'narrow' → *soarut* ['sɔɑrʊʔ] 'lower back' (-t 'related to')
		sarana ['sɑrɑna] 'narrow' → *sauhna* ['saʊhna] 'narrowing of a river' (-na 'place')
		sarana ['sɑrɑna] 'narrow' → *saihkena* ['saʊhcena] 'cap' (-kena 'topogaphy/shape')
ȧ	ay/eu/eu	*ràmi* ['ræ:mi] 'rock protruding out of water' → *reumkena/raymkena* ['rɛʊmcena/ræœmcena] 'dangerous spot in a river due to hidden rocks' (-kena 'topography/shape')
		vȧ ['væ:] 'lake' → *vėume* ['vøme] 'reflection' (-me 'surface/material')
ę	ay/ey	*kęrru* ['cʰær:u] 'doubt' → *keyrpa* ['cʰɛœrpa] 'unknown/possibly dangerous plant' (-ba 'plant')

		lengthening
e	eu/ei	*medga* [ˈmɛɖga] 'X respects Y' → *meuḋguna* [ˈmɛʊðguna] 'respectful' (-na 'abundance')
		netro [ˈnɛtxɔ] 'pistil' → *neitrike* [ˈnɛɪtxiɟe] 'proboscis' (-ke 'shape/similarity')
ė	iei/ėu	*ėno* [ˈeːnɔ] 'little bay' → *ėuntsġi* [ˈøːntsxi] 'having many little bays' (-sġi 'abundance')
i	ia/ie	*śiba* [ˈɕiba] 'X has enough energy' → *śiabuna* [ˈɕiabuna] 'energetic, fit' (-na 'abundance')
		hide [ˈhide] 'hair' → *hiebme* [ˈhɪɛʔpmi] 'fur coat' (-me 'material/surface')
į	iai/iei ɉai/ɉei	*iku* [ˈiːgu] 'snow bank' → *ɉeigge* [ˈjeɪɟːe] 'deep path in snow' (-ke 'shape/similarity')
o	oa/ųa/ųi	*kori* [ˈkʰɔri] 'boy' → *garike* [ˈgɑriɟe] 'boyish, childish' (-ke 'shape/similarity')
ȯ	va/vi/ẏ/ oai	*kȯi* [ˈkʰʊːi] 'X will speak' → *goaiġa* [ˈgɔɑixa] 'fast-spoken' (-ġa 'rapidity/facility')
		pȯbi [ˈpʰʊːbi] 'seal' → *pẏbme* [ˈpʰyːʔpme] 'seal skin' (-me 'material/surface')
		ȯ [ˈʊː] 'bruise' → *vike* [ˈvice] 'bruised' (-ke 'shape/similarity')
u	uo/ue/ųe	*puna* [ˈpʰuna] 'deer skin' → *bename* [ˈbenɑme] 'leather bag' (-me 'material/surface')
		kulu [ˈkʰulu] 'cloudy' → *kvolku* [ˈkʰvɔlku] 'cloud cover' (-ku 'inanimate aggregate')
ů	uo/ve	*ɲjů* [ˈɲuː] 'lust' → *ɲjuosġi* [ˈɲʊɔsxi] 'lustful' (-sġi 'abundance')
		uvvů [ˈuwːuː] 'abundance' → *vessu* [ˈvesːu] 'to abound' (-s 'to become more like noun')
y	ůa/ůi/ve	*yśi* [ˈyɕi] 'salmon' → *ůaśků* [ˈœaɕcø] 'salmon migration' (-ků 'inanimate aggregate')
		yly [ˈyly] 'night' → *vellu* [ˈvelːu] 'by night' (-lu 'distributive')

		lengthening
ẏ	eu/veu	ẏ [y:] 'ice' → vėut ['vø:ʔ] 'ices' (-t 'collective/related to')
ů	ey	důnnů ['døn:ø] 'loop' → deydna ['dɛœʔtna] 'whirlpool' (-na 'place')
ėu	evvu/ evva	kèu ['cʰø:] 'attack' → kevvasġa ['cʰew:asxa] 'aggressive, quick-tempered' (-sġa 'rapidity/facility')

§14.1.3 Shortened Vowels

Vowel shortening is the least common vowel change, most commonly caused by circumfixes, or more productively by the adessive ending -skon.

		shortening
a	o/Ø	pila ['pʰila] 'red' → polra [pʰɔlra] 'cranberry' (-ra 'fruit')
a	o/Ø	kalara ['kʰalara] 'hole' → ġouskon ['xɔʊskɔn] 'cover for hunting' (-skon 'abessive')
ȧ	e/ę	ȧli ['æ:li] 'wound' → eluskon [elʊskɔn] 'safe and sound' (-skon 'abessive', also ęluskon)
ę	u/i	kęmes ['cʰæmɛs] 'happy' → ġumeskon ['xumɛskɔn] 'unhappy' (-skon 'abessive')
e	i/Ø	erri ['er:i] 'X will work' → tairsi ['taɪrsi] 'worker' (t-Ø-si 'male agent')
è	e	mėpsei ['me:ps:ei] 'X will repair net' → tamepsusi ['tʰamɛps:usi] 'net repairer/clever man' (t-Ø-si 'male agent')
i	a/Ø	hide ['hide] 'hair' → hatskon ['hatsk:ɔn] 'hairless' (-skon 'abessive')
i̇	ę	mielo ['mielɔ] 'rot' → melki ['mɛlci] 'peat' (-ki 'place')
o	u/i	nori ['nɔri] 'X will sing' → tanutsi ['tʰanutsi] 'singer' (ta-Ø-si 'male agent')
ȯ	o	soalu ['sɔalu] 'perfume' → soluna ['sɔluna] 'fragrant, balmy' (-ɨna 'adjective')
u	a/o/y	uja ['uja] 'water' → ůiki ['œɪɟi] 'marsh' (-ki 'topology')

		shortening
ů	ů	*tuobi* ['tʰuɔbi] 'juniper' → *tůpra* ['tʰœpxa] 'juniper berry' (-ra 'fruit')
y	e	*tygi* ['tʰyɟi] 'poison' → *tekskon* ['tʰɛksk:ɔn] 'not poisonous' (-skon 'abessive')
ẏ	ů/ey	*ẏ* [y:] 'ice' → *eyskon* ['ɛœskɔn] 'iceless, not covered in ice' (-skon 'abessive')
ů	e/Ø	*kůja* ['cʰøja] 'afloat' → *keskon* ['cʰɛskɔn] 'non-buoyant, sinking' (-skon 'abessive')
ėu	ę/e	*tėulů* ['tʰø:lø] 'X will subside' → *tęlaskon* ['tʰælaskɔn] 'not improving, worsening' (-skon 'abessive')

§14.1.4 Overview of Vowel Changes

Below is a table summarizing the various changes vowels can go through;

	fronted	lengthened	shortened	polarized
a	e	oa/au/ai	o/Ø	i/e (o before -i/-e in western dialects)
ȧ	ei	ay/eu/ėu	e	ie/ei
ę	e	ay/ey	u/i	u
e	i	eu/ei	i/Ø	u/o
ė	i	iei/ėu	e	uo/ů(vv)
i	ia/ja	ia/ie	a/Ø	u/y
į	įgį-	iai/iei	ę	uo/ẏ
o	i/y	oa/ya/yi	u/i	i/y
ȯ	i/ẏ	va/vi/ẏ/oai	o	i/ẏ
u	y	uo/ue/ye	a/o/y	e/ai
ů	ėu/ẏ	uo/ve	ů	ę/ey

	fronted	lengthened	shortened	polarized
y	jů/ey	ůa/ůi/ve	e	oi/ů
ẏ	ieu	ėu/vėu	ů/ey	uo/ui
ů	e	ey	e/Ø	i/ei
ėu	ẏ	evvu/evva	ę/e	i̧

§14.2 Derivational Endings

Derivational endings are added to verbs, nouns, adjectives and bare roots to create new words. The form of the ending somewhat dictates what phonological changes, if any, apply to the new word. Derivational endings are grouped by their function. For adjectival derivational endings, see section *§5.5* on adjective formation.

§14.2.1 Nominal Derivational Endings

Endings used to create nouns (and some adjectives) are called nominal derivational endings.

-(i̧)aka — Creates a **noun** for a group/aggregate/assemblage that is either from an inanimate noun or itself inanimate. If -i̧- is included, fronting occurs.

diaka	'collection of bones in a tree' (cf. *demo* 'bone')
euḷiaka	'bouquet of flowers' (cf. *eleba* 'flower')
miriaka	'a cloud of mosquitoes' (cf. *myry* 'fly')
niuiaka	'sand dune' (cf. *neyo* 'sand')
neniaka	'waves' (cf. *nůdna* 'wave')
peddiaka	'logs used to build a house' (cf. *půdů* 'log')
segaka	'burnt embers' (cf. **sahh-** 'to burn')
sesoiaka	'a group of tents' (cf. *sasame* 'tent')

-(i̧)on — Creates a **noun** for a group/aggregate/assemblage that is either from an animate noun or itself animate. If -i̧- is included, fronting occurs.

pigi̧on	'maternal uncle's family' (cf. *pėsi* 'maternal uncle')
selion	'caribou herd' (cf. *salama* 'antler')
mehhi̧on	'maple tree forest' (cf. *maihhi* 'maple tree')
ili̧on	'vegetation' (cf. **el-** 'grow')

	gylkjon	'community' (cf. **golk-** 'to live together')
	iamon	'fauna' (cf. *imisi* 'animal')

-(i)bi — Creates a **noun** for a tool or a diminutive. Causes fronting.

	kysġibi	'carving knife' (cf. **kosġ-** 'to carve')
	kygybi	'horn to call animals' (cf. **kųegvi-** 'to call animal')
	mjambi	'gutting knife' (cf. **mian-** 'to gut')
	nebbi	'trap' (cf. **nęp-** 'to catch')
	riakkabi	'key' (cf. **rikki-** 'to open')
	sitġobi	'fishing rod' (cf. **sitk-** 'to fish')
	toaibi	'cap' (cf. *totami* 'head')
	tśeidobi	'branch used in fire' (cf. *tinin* 'fire wood')

-ɨn (-un/-on/-in/-ůn) — Creates a **noun** for a container/box or organ. It also creates magnitives of words. Causes lengthening

	goamun	'human skull' (cf. *komi* 'mind')
	gůinůn	'little room, small space' (cf. *kyni* 'nest')
	jamnon	'smoke sauna/tent' (cf. **imn-** 'to smoke')
	keynůn	'bucket for milk'
	ljagjin	'nasal cavity' (cf. *lisġi* 'nostrils')
	lůirůn	'resin-filled blister on bark' (cf. *lyra* 'resin GEN.')
	mauvvun	'box to keep meat in' (cf. *mavvu* 'meat')
	tśoadjun	'intestines' (cf. **tiod-** 'to contain')
	toahhun	'big tree' (cf. *tahha* 'tree')
	gausun	'full moon' (cf. *gasi* 'moon')

-(ɨ)ni/-(ɨ)nɨ — Creates a **noun** for member of a group. Causes fronting.

	kigjini	'youngest of a group, runt' (cf. *ki* 'new')
	myśyni	'member of a hunting group' (cf. *muośi* 'group of hunters')
	peilni	'oldest member' (cf. *pàlli* 'mature male')
	pjanni	'harvester, worker' (cf. *pìni* 'corn')
	tinni	'spouse, partner' (cf. **ten-** 'to unite')
	tśůnůni	'animal that has not left its parents/nest' (cf. *kyni* 'nest')
	ydni	'character' (cf. **on-** 'to tell/talk/tell a story')

-gi/-ṡi/(-ġi)		Creates a noun designating a certain time or period. Causes fronting.
	ayrhi	'time while something is still fresh' (cf. *aurin* 'fresh')
	jaṡigi/jaṡṡi	'old age' (cf. *iṡi* 'old')
	ibengi	'time needed to smoke something' (cf. *obeno* 'smoke')
	gymṡi	'period of frost' (cf. *kuima* 'frosty')
	myngi	'pause' (cf. *mun-* 'to rest')
	tingi	'mating period' (cf. *t(en)-* 'to unite')
-(o)ko		Creates a noun for a little part, a diminutive or a small thing part of a greater whole. Causes lengthening.
	bovvoko	'broken branch' (cf. *boja* 'branch')
	deumko	'piece of bone, little finger/toe' (cf. *demo* 'bone')
	geunko	'spore' (cf. *gedna* 'nut')
	saroko	'piece' (cf. *sar-* 'to break')
	toahhoko	'small tree' (cf. *tahha* 'tree')
-ba		Common derivative in nouns for plants and flowers. Can cause lengthening or no change.
	jajalba	'horse tail, *equisetum*' (cf. *ijul-* 'spruce')
	mjaulba	'butterwort, *pinguicula vulgaris* (cf. *mialha* 'blue')
	monoba	'indian pipes, *monotropa uniflora*' (cf. *monona* 'pale')
	soamba	'buttercup' (cf. *somora* 'gold')
	teylba	'cotton grass' (cf. *tůrů* 'fur')
-ġo/-go/-ġo		Creates masculine versions of things, especially animals. Causes polarization.
	kennjego	'male mallard duck' (cf. *kennjut* 'mallard duck')
	nobiego	'male porcupine' (cf. *nobia* 'porcupine')
	tatamġo	'male wolf' (cf. *tatami* 'wolf')

-ha	Creates feminine versions of things, especially animals. Causes polarization. Can sometimes replace -mo.

notsġiha	'shaman woman' (cf. *notsġomo* 'shaman')
njelha	'female leader' (cf. *njelli* 'chief')
kennjeha	'female mallard duck' (cf. *kennjut* 'mallard duck')

-o/-e/-ů/-y	Creates **nouns** from **verbs**. The nouns are usually the result of the verb. Causes lengthening. The ending depends on the stressed vowel:

stressed vowel	ending
a o u	-i
i e ę	-o
y	-y
ů	-ů

The ending may also cause stem-final consonants to become fortified (lenition in the opposite direction). Diphthongs tend to become reduced to monophthongs. No vowel is added to a stem ending in a vowel, though it may change unpredictably.

eiro	'care' (cf. **er-** 'to be careful)
gieko	'glance' (cf. **gik-** 'to glance')
poaśśi	'sleep' (cf. **pohhį-** 'to sleep')
oadni	'look' (cf. **oden-** 'to look')
tama·lagio	'hindrance' (cf. **tama·lauį-** 'to hinder')
muodni	'rest' (cf. **mun-** 'to rest')
noadni	'swim' (cf. **non-** 'to swim')
sieddo	'understanding, intelligence' (cf. **sid-** 'to understand')
tśoati	'cooperation' (cf. **tśot-** 'to work together')
sůitů	'thank' (cf. **syty-** 'to thank')
ůikků	'fight' (cf. **ůkků-** 'to fight')
giegio	'apex, tip, climax' (cf. **gigį-** 'to become pointed')
jaiśke	'senility' (cf. **jaśk-** 'to grow old')
niaki	'death' (cf. **nik-** 'to die')
muihi	'disappearance' (cf. **muh-** 'to disappear')
naukni	'breakage' (cf. **nakn-** 'to break')

	njailli	'taste' (cf. **njal**- 'to taste')
	noksi	'conclusion' (cf. **noaks**- 'to end')
	śailkko	'swelling' (cf. **silk**- 'to swell')
	śatśilo	'starvation' (cf. **śaitśel**- 'to starve')
	tevvulo	'relent, subsiding' (cf. **tėul**- 'to subside')
	vėurhů	'scar, wound healing' (cf. **ẏrh**- 'to scar, to grow')
	oapi	'help' (cf. **op**- 'to help')
	sukli	'protection' (cf. **saykl**- 'to protect')
	seto	'threat' (cf. **seito**- 'to threaten')
	kuoko	'order' (cf. **kuko**- 'to order')
	kůiśśů	'attempt' (cf. **kyś**- 'to try')
	moaldi	'praise' (cf. **malda**- 'to praise')
	moaġi	'drink' (cf. **moġ**- 'to drink')
	mauhho	'a hunt' (cf. **mahh**- 'to hunt')

-lden, -ldon, -ldůn   Creates an **abstract noun**. Causes polarization.

	tamosuldon	'friendship' (cf. *tamosi* 'friend')
	suoselden	'motherhood' (cf. *suosa* 'mother')
	atruldon	'fatherhood' (cf. *atri* 'father')
	ibilden	'seniority' (cf. *iu* 'older relative')
	kinaguldon	'strangeness, unfamiliarity, foreignness (cf. *kinagi* 'foreigner')
	imisuldon	'animality, wildness' (cf. *imisi* 'animal')
	rogilden	'masculinity'
	himhelden	'feminity'
	sibmululdon	'luck at fishing' (cf. *sibmuli* 'lucky at catching')

-ke   Creates **nouns** or **adjectives** similar in shape or appearance. Causes lengthening.

	neitrike	'proboscis' (cf. *netro* 'pistil')
	neuḍge	'dust' (cf. *neyo* 'sand')
	keynke	'sperm' (cf. *kůnů* 'milk')
	paukke	'hole, pit' (cf. *pakvi* 'pit')
	sġoakke	'ghost' (cf. *sġodna* 'shade')
	yahnoke	'dandruff' (cf. *ohna* 'white ash')
	vaukke	'hook' (cf. *ȯu* 'id.')

-kena   Creates a **noun** denoting places characterized by the root word. Causes lengthening. Also creates **adjectives**.

	euḍgena	'sandy forest ground' (cf. *ėu* 'sand')

	geinkena	'oak-forest' (cf. *gedna* 'nut')
	heiggena	'salty marsh' (cf. *hego* 'salt')
	heimkena	'bird nesting area' (cf. *hemi* 'bird')
	hėulkena	'place where melt water pools' (cf. *hjeuli* 'melt water')
	meilkkena	'peat field' (cf. *melki* 'peat')
	naitkena	'precipice' (cf. *nauto* 'vertigo')
	saiḍgena	'spot in a forest where there was a fire' (cf. *saḍḍa* 'a fire')
-ku/-ko/-ků		Creates a **noun** denoting a large aggregate. Causes lengthening.
	kvolku	'cloud cover/layer' (cf. *kulu* 'cloud')
	miasku	'gravel' (cf. *misas* 'stone')
	mjeuhku	'taiga, moss field' (cf. *mieri* 'moss')
	njůalků	'beehive' (cf. *njůadli* 'wasp, bee')
	siaḍgu	'a large group' (cf. *sieḍḍo* 'foot')
	svahku	'skin disease' (cf. *sori* 'blister')
	raunko	'fox/wolf litter' (cf. *raibma* 'tail')
	ůaṡků	'salmon migration' (cf. *yṡi* 'samlon')
-me		Creates **nouns** for materials or surfaces. Causes lengthening.
	gegeme	'hem' (cf. *geg-* 'to be open at one end')
	hiebme	'fur coat (on animal)' (cf. *hide* 'hair')
	kůalme	'inner bark' (cf. *kylk-* 'to slip off, to come off')
	pẏbme	'seal skin' (cf. *pòbi* 'seal')
	roatme	'crust' (cf. *ratta* 'dry, hardened')
	ṡiemme	'bear skin' (cf. *ṡimi* 'bear head')
-na		Creates **nouns** denoting a place. Causes lengthening. Also creates a few adjectives.
	deydna	'whirlpool' (cf. *důnnů* 'loop, repeated pattern')
	geuhna	'mouth of a river' (cf. *geg-* 'to be open at one end')
	keunna	'cape, promontory' (cf. *keu̯-* 'to rise')
	muodna	'grave' (cf. *mun-* 'to rest')
	muogna	'place to stay the night' (cf. *muong-* 'to stay the night')
	sauhna	'narrowing point of a lake/river' (cf. *sarana* 'narrow')

| | śainno | 'courageous' (cf. śavvi 'courage') |

-rV/-ġV/-hV Creates **nouns** depicting species/collective/group. Causes lengthening or no change. See section *§4..3.2.1* on the historical collective plural.

	bi̇rho	'canidae' (cf. *benho* 'dog')
	hoalro	'odonata' (cf. *holokken* 'dragonfly')
	keiġe	'betula (any birch)' (cf. *kehhe* 'birch bark')
	mosġi	'mammal' (cf. *mahhji* 'bear')
	ni̯ylry	'stinging insects (bees and wasps)' (cf. *ni̯ůadli* 'wasp')
	solra	'cervidae' (cf. *salama* 'antler')
	u̇rhu	'bank of fish' (cf. *u̇s* 'young fish')
	vatro	'lichen cover' (cf. *ono* 'lichen')

-t Creates a **noun** related to the stem, sometimes a collective. Causes lengthening or no change. It sometimes reverts long vowels to their short form.

	nangat	'provisions' (cf. **nang-** 'to save up')
	ni̯ertet	'pain, symptoms' (cf. **ni̯ėrtt-** 'to hurt')
	sirit	'fish stock, types/number of fish in a lake' (cf. *sira* 'fish')
	temyt	'moose antlers' (cf. *tėmi* 'moose head')
	tsġeut	'skeleton' (cf. *tsġůli* 'animal skull')
	u̯eit	'quality of water' (cf. *u̯ja* 'water')
	ůrůt	'nature, environment' (cf. *ůrůma* 'vicinity')

-it Creates **nouns** from **passive** verbs. The nouns are usually the result of the verb. Causes shortening and in some cases consonant lenition.

	sutot	'permission' (cf. **u·sot-** 'to be permitted')
	ikket	'birth' (cf. **um·ekk-** 'to be born')
	migit	'respect' (cf. **u·medg-** 'to be respected')
	matot	'explanation' (cf. **u·miti-** 'to be explained')

-(i̇)li̇t Creates **nouns** for an action in which many take place. Causes lengthening.

| | moaġolot | 'a festive occasion' (cf. **moġ-** 'to drink') |

	tśoatolot	'cooperation' (cf. **tśot-** 'to work together')
	hįeidnilit	'a wake' (cf. **heidn-** 'to wake')
	aitilit	'epidemic' (cf. **ate-** 'to be sick')
	nįakolot	'end of the world' (cf. **nik-** 'to die')

-įųe — Creates a **noun** which is 'worth' the action. May also behave as adjectives. Causes no change.

kitaiųe	'(something) worth doing' (cf. **kita-** 'to do')
kyṡyųe	'(something) worth trying' (cf. **kyṡ-** 'to try')
hauųe	'(something) worth eating, appetizing' (cf. **h-** 'to eat')
nauįniųe	'(something) useful' (cf. **nauįn-** 'to use')
onuųe	'(something) worth telling' (cf. **on-** 'to tell')

Agents

-à — Creates an agent who is an expert or experienced at something, or someone who does something often/a lot. If he ending is preceded by a vowel, the vowel is geminated and coalesces with the ending (then -a) as shown in §3.1.5.1.

sitkà	'experienced fisherman' (cf. **sitk-** 'to fish')
iksà	'experienced archer' (cf. **iks-** 'to shoot')
hantoma	'pathological liar' (cf. **hanto-** 'to lie')
belmà	'good/diligent worker' (**belm-** 'to work')
kaiksevva	'coward' (**kaikse-** 'to dodge')
ojuma	'whiner' (cf. **oju-** 'to cry')
siutà	'glutton' (cf. **siut-** 'to be hungry')

-obba/-ebba — Creates an agent who is prone to/known to do something. Causes no change. Adjective form in **beha**.

ůkkůibba	'someone who is prone to quarreling' (cf. **ůkků-** 'to quarrel')
idebba	'a clumsy person' (cf. **id-** 'to fall')
piagebba	'a sleepy person, sleepyhead' (cf. **piag-** 'to fall asleep')
koahlebba	'a noisy person' (cf. **koahl-** 'to be noisy')
listebba	'someone who gives up easily' (cf. **list-** 'to give up')

-uli/-eli		Creates an agent who is able to, good at or has the potential to performing the action. Adjective form in -lha. Causes no change.
	kjaseli	'someone who works quickly' (cf. **kjas-** 'to hurry')
	ogjuli	'someone with a good memory' (cf. **ogj-** 'to remember')
	ogjenuli	'an observant person' (cf. **ogjen-** 'to notice')
	śahhjuli	'someone with low endurance' (cf. **śahhj-** 'not to be able to stand')
	keknuli	'an organized/initiative person' (cf. **kekn-** 'to put together')
	nujuli	'someone who sees well' (cf. **nuj-** 'to see')
	sejuli	'someone who hears well' (cf. **sej-** 'to hear')
	sibmuli	'a lucky/skilled hunter/fisher' (cf. **sibm-** 'to catch')
t(a)-Ø-si		Creates a *male agent*. Causes shortening.
	tamosi	'hunter, friend' (cf. **mahh-** 'to hunt')
	tanutsi	'singer' (cf. **nod-/nor-** 'to sing')
	tagassi	'traveler' (cf. **gus-** 'to travel')
	tōtasi	'dancer' (cf. **onta-** 'to dance')
	tuśkvasi	'murderer' (cf. **uśkva-** 'to murder')
	tśassi	'male guest' (cf. **śiv-** 'to stay')
t(a)-Ø-ni		Creates a *female agent*. Causes shortening.
	tamoni	'female friend' (cf. **mahh-** 'to hunt')
	taiskani	'seamstress' (cf. **aisk-** 'to sew')
	ijutokni	'bough cutter/fetcher' (cf. **iju·ak-** 'to cut boughs')
	tanudni	'singer' (cf. **nod-/nor-** 'to sing')
	tōtani	'dancer' (cf. **onta-** 'to dance')
	tśanni	'female guest' (cf. **śiv-** 'to stay')
t(a)-Ø-ri		Creates a *plural agent*. Causes shortening.
	tamori	'hunters, hunting partners' (cf. **mahh-** 'to hunt')
	tśairri	'row men' (cf. **jair-** 'to row')
	tōtari	'dancers, group of dancers' (cf. **onta-** 'to dance')
	tamoskari	'people, nation, inhabitants, Siwas' (cf. *maski* 'people')
(t)(a)-Ø-ra(gi)		Creates a *people*. Causes shortening.
	Tatimragi	'eastern Siwa' (cf. **temm-** 'lake')
	Aslaragi	'mid-western Siwa' (cf. **sal-** 'caribou')

s(o)-Ø-ge	Creates a *patient*. Causes shortening.
somodġe	'huntee, pray' (cf. **mahh-** 'to hunt')
sġotrage	'enemy' (cf. **rutr-** 'to hate')
saṡkoge	'victim' (cf. **uṡkv-** 'to murder')

§14.2.1.1 Non-Productive Endings

In addition to the endings listed above, Siwa employs a variety of less common endings, which are not productive – they are not generally used to create new words anymore. This includes many endings for various species of animals and insects.

Many insects have endings of the shape **-CCen**.

-kken	'winged insect, *odonata*'
holokken	'dragon fly'
terhekken	'mayfly'
aṡṡekken	'damselfly'

-bben	'winged beetle, *hemiptera*'
olobben	'leafhopper'
tohhobben	'treehopper'

-dlen	'spider, *araneae/arachnida*'
nyggedlen	'wolf spider'
holodlen	'cellar spider'
lehhidlen	'harvestman'
ġyidlen	'jumping spider'

-men	'grasshopper, cricket,
ġyibmen	'grasshopper'
soḍmen	'cricket'
redlmen	'cricket'

-lken	'butterfly'
somolken	'yellow summer butterfly'
kobolken	'monarch'
velken	'moth'

Many birds have endings of the shape **-mi/-in** or **-njut**

biumi	'flycatcher'
jejumi	'shrike'
mialrikkin	'blue jay'
siggini	'sparrow'

itemi	'thrush'
sokmi	'seagull'
mogopimi	'oystercatcher' (also *mȯpimi* or *mȕbmi*)
kikiṡin	'woodpecker'
kennjut	'mallard duck'
jikimainnjut	'eider duck'

§14.2.2 Deverbalizers

Deverbalizers are used to form nouns (names of actions) from verbs. Consonantal roots retain prefixes (-r- 'bite', -t- 'unite' and -tk- 'to train').

    transitive (infinitive -mi/-mu/-mů)
        -on (+lengthening)

mauhhon	'a hunt' (cf. *mahmi* 'to hunt')
nuogjon	'sight' (cf. *nuimi* 'to see')
vagjon	'memory, remembrance' (cf. *ogjami* 'to remember')

    intransitive (infinitive -sa/-su/-sů)
        -va/-ụa (often simplification of diphthongs)

bilva	'speech, talking' (cf. *bialsa* 'to speak')
erva	'toil, hard work' (cf. *errisa* 'to work outside')
gedlva	'function, behaviour, role' (cf. *gedlisu* 'to function')
irva	'bite' (cf. *i·r·inen* 'to bite into')

    subjective (infinitive -na/-nu/-nů)
        o-Ø-en (+shortening; verbs in -ld- get -len)

osoken	'building a house' (cf. *soakna* 'to build a house')
oten	'unit(y)' (cf. *o·t·ena* 'to unite')
otken	'training' (cf. *o·tk·ena* 'to train')
obesġilen	'peace making' (cf. *beisġildena* 'to make peace')
ogalen	'conversation' (cf. *gauldena* 'to speak together')
uŋgokeṡen	'effort' (cf. *uịokyṡina* 'to make an effort')

    ditransitive (infinitive -nin/-non/-nůn)
        (i)-Ø-det~et (often simplification of diphthongs)

jaldet	'free time' (cf. *allnin* 'to have time')
ihendet	'responsibility' (cf. *hennanin* 'to be responsible')
kaddet	'need' (cf. *kadnin* 'to need')
tottet~toḥḥet	'ability, know-how' (cf. *toḥḥanin* 'to know how to')
ivaġlet	'lack' (cf. *vaġlinon* 'to lack')

translative (infinitive -lu/-lŭ or -oru/-ŭrŭ)
    (i)-Ø-et (+shortening; verbs in -sk- get -set)

    soluset   'losing of antlers'
    tegjuset   'losing one's sight, going blind' (cf. *teugjuskoru* 'to go blind')
    soṡet   'venture, migration' (cf. *suṡlu* 'to move away')
    imogjet   'paling, whitening, becoming pale' (cf. *magjoru* 'to become white')
    imanget   'preparation' (cf. *mingoru* 'to get ready')

passive (infinitive **-mon/-mŭn**)
    u-Ø-as (+shortening)

    katubias   'exile' (cf. *katabimon* 'to be thrown out')
    utegjas   'support' (cf. *teigjemon* 'to be supported')
    umedgas   'being wounded' (cf. *aydgimon* 'to be wounded')

§14.2.2.1 Verbal Derivational Endings

Siwa has a rich system of verbal derivational endings. Generally, most verbal derivational endings either cause polarization, lengthening or fronting. Polarization occurs when the derivational ending is added onto a stem ending in a vowel (or which could not form the resulting cluster), while lengthening and fronting occurs if the ending is added to a consonant. The vowel <i> is common, which means verbal endings are heavily harmonized (see *§3.1.1.3*).

Verbalizer   -or-   -er-   -ŭr-

These endings are found attached to all word classes and simply create a verb from the root. They can modify the meaning of the root in various ways. The endings generally cause **lengthening**. It is thought that the -r- is a cliticized form of the copula -d- 'is'.

    mumma   'in X's fathom, amongst'
    muommor·a   'X will hug Y'

    moukki   'belly'
    tama·ta·moaikker·i   'X will fall/lie flat (on its belly)'

    koho   'half'
    koaḥḥor·a   'X will (cut in) half'

    it   'you (honorific)'
    iter·a   'X will use the honorific *it* for Y'

Opportunitive -(ɨ)r- -(ɨ)ġ- -(ɨ)h-

These endings create verbs from any word class with the added meaning that there is enough of a quality for a purpose, that it is the right time for the action or that a period is currently ongoing. The endings generally cause **lengthening**, though less often for nouns.

siubmi	'X is hungry'
t·śautr·i	'X is hungry enough to eat'
śautr·u	'it is time to eat'
misi	'X will smoke'
miasġ·i	'it is (a good) time to smoke/celebrate'
nod·i	'X will sing'
noadġ·i	'it is (a good) time to sing' or 'X wants to sing'
mihki	'rime'
mihkeh·i	'it is cold enough for rime, it is frosty'
moksabi	'ptarmigan'
moksabuh·i	'it is ptarmigan hunting time'
sitk·i	'X will fish'
sitkeh·i	'it is the right time to fish'

Verbal Causative -j- -ju- -je- -jŭ-

The verbal causative endings are found added onto verbal roots and add the meaning of an agent who is made to perform an action, or it may create verbs whose agent causes a patient to change state or perform an action. The endings cause **fronting**. The endings are thought to be a cliticized form of the verb root i- 'to change, to become'.

net·a	'X knows Y'
nitś·a	'X will inform/teach Y'
h·a	'X will eat Y'
hej·a	'X will feed Y'
tà·i	'X will stand'
teigji·a	'X will support/hold up Y'
maivv·i	'X will smile'
meigji·a	'X will make Y smile'

Adjectival Causative   -t-   -ut-   -et-   -ůt-

The adjectival causative endings are added onto adjectives and show that the agent of the verb causes an object to become (more) like the adjective. The endings cause **lengthening**. They are thought to be cognates with the comparative endings.

leyma	'warm'
ljeilt·a	'X will warm Y up'
laippo	'flat'
loait·a	'X will flatten Y'
moton	'sad'
moatut·a	'X will sadden Y'
nivvon	'wet'
njavvut·a	'X will wet Y'
nunna	'angry'
nuont·a	'X will anger Y'
nẏn	'closed, shut'
nėunt·a	'X will shut/close Y'
roko	'hollow'
roaht·a	'X will hollow Y out'

Nominal Causative   -m-   -um-   -em-   -ům-

Thes nominal causative endings are added onto nominal stems and a verb whose agent perform an action related to the noun. It is not associated with any sound change other than deletion of final vowels in some cases.

kėut	'war'
kůlm·a	'X will wage war on Y'
miola	'flame'
miolm·a	'X will set Y on fire/burn Y'
nidagan	'stripe'
nidġem·a	'X will tattoo Y'
njukli	'hook'
njuklum·a	'X will put Y on a hook/catch Y (red-handed)'

Translative   -n-   -un-   -en-   -ůn-

The translative endings create a translative verb whose agent changes state or gains a characteristic. They often cause **lengthening**.

njobba	'beard'
ta·njoabbun·u	'X will grow a beard'
pakvi	'grave'
ta·poakn·u	'X will be(come) very busy/sick/taken'
oḍḍo	'clear night sky'
vadn·u	'the sky clears up'
neyo	'sand'
ta·neinn·u	'X will get sand/dirt on itself'
njůḍḍe	'coil'
ta·njeydn·ů	'X will coil up/retract'
nuobmo	'stretched skin'
ta·nuomn·u	'X will get stretched out/used to (+ELAT)'

Detranslative   -sk-   -usk-   -esk-   -isk-   -ůsk-

The detranslative endings create translative verbs whose agent loses a characteristic, and are opposite to the translative endings. They cause **lengthening**.

tůrů	'fur'
ta·tůreisk·ů	'X will shed its fur'
salama	'antlers'
t·soalusk·u	'X will lose its antlers/be humiliated'
uja	'water'
t·ujeisk·u	'X will become dehydrated'
tegj·a	'X is able to see Y'
ta·teugjusk·u	'X will (slowly) lose its sight/disappear'
bieli	'fat'
ta·bjeulusk·u	'X will lose weight'
kori	'boy'

ta·kvaresk·u	'X will enter adulthood/lose his virginity'
dida	'girl'
ta·diedesk·u	'X will menstruate for the first time'
suosa	'mother'
ta·svesisk·u	'X will miscarry'
tveli	'blood (outside the body)'
ta·tveilosk·u	'X will bleed out'

Reciprocal   -ld-   -uld-   -ild-   -ůld-

The reciprocal forms a verb, often subjective and generally plural, where two agents act toward each other or together. Some eastern dialects use -l- instead of -ld-. The endings cause **lengthening**.

besġima	'there is peace'
o·beisġild·i·ri	'they will make peace with each other'
kò·i	'X will speak'
o·gauld·a·ri	'they will discuss Y together'
gattia	'in X's presence'
o·getild·i·ri	'they will meet/come across each other'
sasame	'tipi'
soasuld·i·ri	'they will share a tipi together'
soaki	'house'
suikild·i·ri	'they will live together/cohabit'
tà·i	'X will stand'
o·teigild·i·ri	'they will face each other off/feud/'
nebbi	'tap'
o·neibbild·i·ri	'they will hunt/try to get/horse around with each other'
nuj·a	'X will see Y'
o·nuojuld·i·ri	'they will see/court/be with each other'

Continual   -jil-   -il-   -kl-

The continual endings create a verb whose action lasts for a long time. It causes lengthening.

siubmi	'X is hungry'
t·saitsel·i	'X will starve'
ta·pohhj·i	'X will sleep'
ta·piskel·i	'X will be in a coma/is dead (euphemism)'
atemi	'X is sick'
t·aitel·i	'X will be severely sick'
il·a	'X will know Y'
jeilgil·a	'X will get to know Y (over time)'
ůt·ů	'it is too cold'
t·eytkůl·i	'X will die of cold'
h·a	'X will eat Y'
haukl·i	'X will eat a meal/feast'
siv·i	'X will stay'
siaggel·i	'X will stay for a while'
nen·i	'X will sit'
neinjel·i	'X will sit for a while'

Sensive   -(j)un-   -(j)en-   -(j)ůn-

The sensive endings create verbs that indicate that the agent 'feels like', 'experiences' or 'seems like' a characteristic. It often causes **fronting** though not always. These verbs are also commonly found in subjective-intransitive pairs, and may also incorporate a beneficiary when placed in the ditransitive:

siubmi	'X is hungry'
m·o·saiteni·	'I feel sick'
ent·saiten·i	'I seem sick'
m·i·saiten·i·si	'I seem sick to you'
atemi	'X is sick'
t·(om)·atojun·i	'X will feel/seem sick'
sara	'good'
t·(o)·serjen·i	'X will feel/seem good'

tohhot	'young'	
ta·tihhjen·i	'X will feel/seem young/fresh'	
heje	'cold'	
t·(o)·higjen·i	'X will feel/seem cold'	
himi	'hot'	
t·(o)·hjeimen·i	'X will feel/seem hot'	
gimha	'pleasant'	
ta·gimjun·i	'X will feel pleasant'	
leyma	'warm'	
d·leiljen·i	'X will feel warm'	
pila	'red'	
ta·pialjen·i	'X will flush/seem red'	

Sensive-Translative Causative   -(j)ɨkk   -ekk

The causative form common to the sensive and translative create verbs where an agent causes an object to appear, feel or gain a characteristic. It often causes **lengthening** or **polarization**, but the sensive ending **-Vn·i** is simply changed to **-Vkk·a**.

eski	'empty'
eskujekk·a	'X will empty Y'
atemi	'X is sick'
t·atojukk·a	'X will make Y (feel/seem/be) sick'
sara	'good'
t·serjekk·a	'X will make Y feel/seem good' or 'X will be enough/too much for (then *t·i·serjekka·ita*)'
heje	'cold'
t·(o)·higjen·i	'X will feel/seem cold'
ta·higjekk·a	'X will make Y (feel) cold'
himi	'hot'
t·(o)·hjeimen·i	'X will feel/seem hot'
ta·hjeimekk·a	'X will make Y (feel) hot/give fever'

gimha	'pleasant'
ta·gimjun·i	'X will feel pleasant'
ta·gimjukk·a	'X will Y feel good/pleasant/intoxicated'

Sensive Excessive   -entsġ-   -untsġ-

The sensive excessive creates verbs generally from adjectives and confers the verb with a meaning of '(far) too much'. It causes **lengthening**. The resulting verbs are commonly without a subject, or ditransitive with a beneficiary.

The form i-Ø-entsġ·a·Ø or i-Ø-untsġ·a·Ø is sometimes found attached on adjectives, though these are not considered verbs because they are only found in this particular form. These forms of adjectives usually mean 'X is too Y for Z' but it can also simply be a very strong emphasizer if the 4th person is the recipient (then i-Ø-entsġani or i-Ø-untsġani). Some speakers reanalyse these forms and decline them like -ni suffixed adjectives and pronouns. The word

sisientsġaki	'you are too old for me'
jatanauntsġani	'the very greatest of all'
itseuntsġa·tsi·ta	'to the very tiniest of all'
himi	'hot'
ta·hjeimentsġ·i	'X will be (far) too hot'
t·i·hjeimentsġ·a·ki	'X will be too hot for me'
heje	'cold'
ta·higjentsġ·i	'X will be (far) too cold'
t·i·higjentsġ·a·ki	'X will be too cold for me'
ihejeuntsġani	'freezing cold'
kendi-	'early'
keindentsġ·i	'it is (far) too early'
idla	'late'
jeidlentsġ·i	'it is (far) too late'

Optative Causative   -ų-   -vv-   -v-

The optative causative creates verbs with an object which is caused to want to perform the verb. The endings cause **lengthening**, though in some cases **fronting**.

net·a	'X knows Y'
ta·neutv·a	'X will interest Y'

h·a	'X will eat Y'
ta·hauvv·a	'X will make Y want to eat/will be appetizing to Y'
vim·i	'X will scream'
ta·viamu̧·a	'X will enrage Y'
man·i	'X will come'
meniu̧·a	'X will lure/fool Y'
ta·pohhi̧·i	'X will sleep'
ta·poaṡv·a	'X will make Y sleepy/bore Y'
saitk·i	'X will disappear'
seitkv·a	'X will put Y to shame/shun Y'
ta·kokk·a	'X will please Y'
gakv·a	'X will (be made to want to) befriend Y'
ob·ůkků·i	'X will fight'
eykv·a	'X will (be made to want to) fight Y'

Comitative   -ul-   -el-   -il-   -ůl-

The comitative endings create verbs, often from adjectives, whose agent is characterized, covered, dressed in or wearing something. Final vowels are **polarized** and sometimes **lenition** also occurs. In some dialects, the resulting verbs have a meaning close to 'X looks Y'. Younger speakers use this more productively.

maiki	'white'
maikùl·i	'X is wearing (all)/looks white'
rybmy	'dress'
rymèul·i	'X is wearing a dress'
sůbma	'black'
sůmùl·i	'X is wearing (all) black/looks black'
tveli	'blood'
tvelèl·i	'X is covered in blood'
rodlot	'folds'
rodlùl·i	'X is wearing beautiful clothes'

Permissive -st- -ust- -est- -ist- -ůst-

The permissive endings create verbs who agent allows an object to perform an action. It causes **lengthening**. It is thought to be a cliticized form of the verb -sot- 'to give, to allow'.

    man·i   'X will come'
    maunust·a   'X will allow Y (in/to come)'

    h·a   'X will eat Y'
    haust·a   'X will allow Y to eat'

    kȯ·i   'X will speak'
    gaist·a   'X will allow Y to speak'

    ta·nik·i   'X will die'
    njakust·a   'X will let Y to die'

Privative -nt- -õt-

The privative creates verbs whose agents take something away of rids something (from some object). It causes **polarization**.

    milki   'scales'
    milkõt·a   'X will remove the scales off Y'

    njelsi   'sprig'
    njelsõt·a   'X will take sprigs from Y'

    damu   'raw hide'
    daument·a   'X will skin Y'

    kehhe   'birch bark'
    kehhõt·a   'X will take bark off (a birch)'

    keppi   'head'
    keppõt·a   'X will decapitate Y'

§15 Syntax

Siwa syntax differs greatly from that of English. Siwa has a fixed word order that offers some variation. Siwa is a VOS, partly head-final language.

§15.1 General Word Order

Siwa is of the rather rare VOS word order, common to only 3% of the world's languages. This means that the verb generally precedes the object and subject of a phrase. The order is commonly switched to SVO by means of relative marker o- in copular sentences.

      Siwa sentences can be broken down into two general types. Both types have the same components which are fixed. They are the adverbial phrase (which does not necessarily only contain adverbs, but also object predicatives and quantifiers), the verb, the locative phrase (which is usually ordered as stative>movement to>movement from and contains indirect objects), the object phrase (contains direct objects and the predicates of copular verbs) and the subject phrase. The copula phrase is only present in certain types of sentence constructions, but it becomes before the subject.

Adverb	Verb	Locative	Object	Subject
	mani			Menho
'Menho will come'				
kenka	*ipendidna*	*oakibma*		Menho
'tomorrow Menho will return home'				
ōska	*irentima*	*hemmita*	rentue	Menho
'Menho often feeds seeds to birds'				
kiloahō	*ista*	*iskita oaḍgika*		Ø
'X thanked the woman for her help repeatedly'				
	da	*nenima*		nalbi
'she has a husband'				
	tŭkillja		tahha	somi
'the man cut down the tree'				
mitka tagjil	*sihri*			
'yesterday it rained a lot'				
	daki		lillu	somi
'the man is my paternal uncle'				

Or more commonly:

	SUBJ,	RELATIVE		SUBJ
	somi,	*oaki*		*lillu*

'the man is my paternal uncle' (SVO copular)

ADV	TEMP.ADV	COP	LOC		SUBJ
ōska	*kobai*	*longiủ*	*ůvvia*		*uja*

'the water is often still freezing cold in the summer around here'

ADV	TEMP.ADV	COP	LOC	OBJ	SUBJ
ōska	*kobai*	*sia*	*ůvvia*	*longiu*	*uja*

'the water is often not freezing cold in the summer around here'

The other type of sentence structure is the copular sentence, which differs by having the copula inserted right before the subject.

Adverb	Verb	Locative/Object	Copula	Subject	Main Clause
neni			*nami*		

'I am sitting'
(inconclusive copular phrase)

sinka	*nauinahpes*	*kysġibmoita kimi ůattaga*	*okabagi*

'our forefathers used to use this as a bark carving knife a long time ago'
(distant past copular phrase)

kori,	*nuja*	*pentsa kaiksitotima*	*oga*

'the boy who saw the wolf cub escape'
(relative clause)

tamosi, kaiksi	*daiko*	*pengi*

'the hunter, whose wolf cub escaped'
(genitive relative clause)

It should be noted that coordination particles are generally found in the adverbial phrase only if is not otherwise empty. If the adverbial phrase is empty, the coordinating particle always directly follows the verb:

...*mitka katta maski*	*denarika*	*muości*

'....however, yesterday the hunters left the village'

...	Ø *maski katta*	*denarika*	*muości*

'....however, the hunters left the village'

§15.2 The Noun Phrase

The Siwa noun phrase contains a head, which may be followed, preceded or surrounded by many components. Here they are listed by where thet stand in the noun phrase.

Preceding the noun:
numerals	*eśi kori*	'two boys'
demonstrative pronouns	*to kori*	'the/that boy'
question pronouns	*mìmni kori*	'what boy?'
indefinite pronouns	*toamni kori*	'some boy'
quantifiers	*tami kori*	'many boys'

Following the noun:
attributive adjectives	*el tygyha*	'a poisonous plant'
pro-adverbial phrases	*el havva*	'a plant like that (one)'
relative clauses	*el, ihhja ogakina*	'the plant you gave me'
locative phrases	*el korulia*	'the plant in the pot'
infinitive phrases	*el iljami*	'a plant to cultivate'
determinate numerals	*el eśi*	'the two plants'
genitive phrase	*el unnjuhmo*	'the witch's plant'

Surrounding the noun:
demonstrative deictic clitics	*to kori-ůt*	'this boy'
-ne 'other' and -uli 'kind of'	*toamni kori-ne*	'another boy'

Below is a syntactic tree for a complex noun phrase.

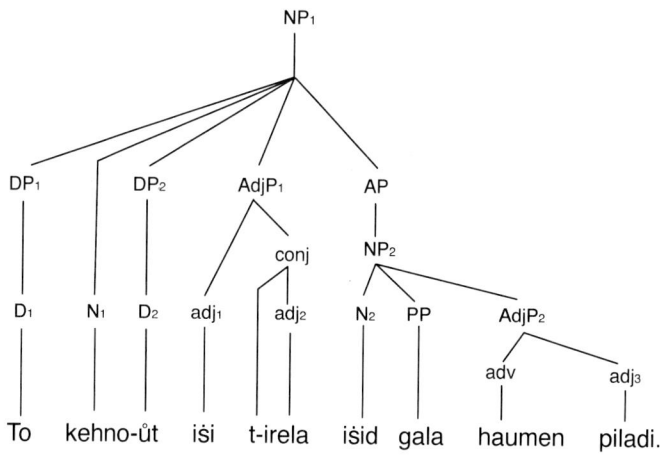

This old and beautiful pine tree with bright red bark.

§15.3 The Adjectival Phrase

The adjectival phrase refers to true adjectives and participal adjectives. The adjectival phrase head may be preceded by adverbs. It can be followed by a locative or postpositional phrase. In other respects, the adjectival phrase behaves like the noun phrase.

adverbial phrase	*seppen tygyha*	'very poisonous'
locative/postp. phrase	*tygyha saumkita*	'poisonous to caribou'
comparative	*tygyhita savi ta*	'more poisonous than it'

The adjective phrase is found before the noun it qualifies only if the adjective is considered to be an object predicate.

mestagga soaki pila	'we painted the red house'
mestagga pila soaki	'we painted the house red'

§15.4 The Adverbial Phrase

The adverbial phrase is exclusively left-branching, meaning the head is preceded by all its modifiers. This reverses the typical order of adjectival phrase from noun-adjective to adjective-noun.

Left Branching

⌐ *tamotta hjȯgjil bettutta nebie aẙdgontuvven* ¬ *lolnoskui jȧlppi*
'the hare escaped unharmed by the hunter's carefully placed trap'
(lit. hunter's carefully placed trap-by unhurtedly escaped hare)

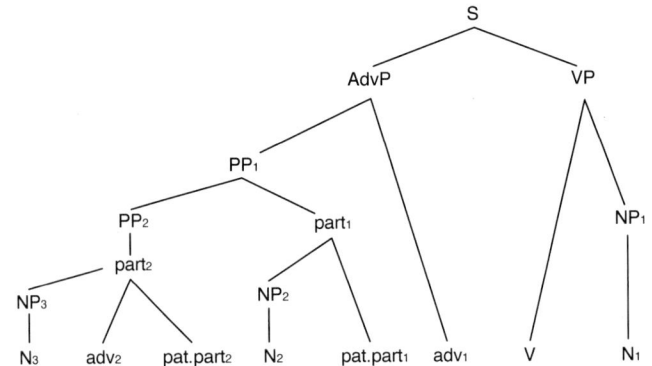

tamotta hjȯgjil bettutta nebbie aẙdgontu·vven lolnoskui jȧlppi.

The hare escaped unharmed by the hunter's carefully placed trap.

The phrase above contains two patientive participles, which are left branching as well with regards to the agents of the participles (in the genitive).

> **tamotta hjȯgjil bettu neppi**   'trap carefully placed by a hunter'
> **nebbie ayḍgontu**   'unharmed by the trap'

The second participial phrase is turned into an adverb, and as an adverbial phrase is left branching, both participial phrases are found before the adverb **auḍgontuvven** 'unharmedly':

> **tamotta hjȯgjil bettutta nebbie ayḍgontuvven**
> 'unharmed by the trap placed carefully by the hunter'

Compare to the same noun phrase outside a larger adverbial phrase:

nebbi ⌜ tamotta hjȯgjil bettu ⌝
'a trap placed carefully by the hunter'

§15.5 Interrogative Phrase

Interrogatives in Siwa do not change the word order of the phrase. Instead, Siwa uses circumfixation for tag questions (see *§13*). The question words are found in their respective slot in the phrase:

Adverb	Verb	Locative	Object	Subject
	so mani-a			Menho?
'will **Menho** come?'				
nìgju	ipendidna	oakibma		Menho?
'when **Menho** will return home?'				
ōska	irentima	nìntsita	rentue	Menho?
'Whom does **Menho** often feed seeds to'				
ōska	irentima	hemmita	nit	Menho?
'What does **Menho** often feed to the birds'				
ōska	irentima	nìntsita	rentue	mìmni?
'Who often feeds seeds to birds?'				

§15.6 Topicalization
Topicalization in Siwa done by moving the topic to the front of the phrase and using the complementizer (especially the short form -ɥ). The topicalized phrase is usually still in the case it would normally be.

>*hemmita ōska irentimɥa rentue Menho*
>'it is to birds that **Menho** is feeding seeds'

>*rentue ōska irentimɥa hemmita Menho*
>'it is seeds that **Menho** is feeding to the birds'

§16 Dialects

Siwa is better described as a continuum of dialects than a single language, although for the purposes of this book, a specific dialect was taken as the standard. There are two main dialects, the eastern and the western dialects. Each contains many smaller dialects, but there are general features which distinguish eastern and western dialects. These will be outlined here.

Western Dialects

Western dialects are divided into far and mid eastern branches. They differ from eastern dialects in being generally less conservative, through many lexical terms and in certain grammatical elements, although syntactically they resemble eastern dialects.

Eastern	Western
Nouns	
Plural of inanimate nouns ending in vowels	
ED have inanimate noun plurals in diphthongs (-ua -ie -uo) and voicing of voiceless stops	WD have inanimate noun plurals in -uma -ime -umo -ůmů or -õ -en -õ -ůn respectively
elebua 'flowers'	*elebuma* or *elebõ* 'flowers'
oarie 'points'	*oarime* or *oaren* 'points'
sekuo or *sego* or *sekůa* 'cliffs'	*sekůmů* or *sekůn* 'cliffs'
tapua or *taba* 'bulbs'	*tapuma* or *tapõ* 'bulbs'
inanimate nouns have undefined plural in -ġ or -ṡ	
siraġ 'a couple of fishes'	
animate plurals in -i are -igi	animate plurals in -i are -ęgi
somigi 'the men'	*somęgi* 'the men'
Inanimate nouns with genitives in -ila and -yla	
ED have agentive form in -il and -yl	WD have agentive form in -i and -ẏ
angil 'seed'	*angi* 'beam'
ymmyl 'good fishing waters'	*ymmẏ* 'good fishing waters'

Eastern	Western
Inanimate words in **-Vut** which have **-Ida** in the patientive	
ED have genitive form in **-Ida**	WD have genitive form in **-utta**
agjėut → agjelda 'marrow'	*agjėut → agjeutta* 'marrow'
baut → balda 'butter'	*baut → bautta* 'butter'
instrumental often clitic: **-gla, -ġla, -ġeli, -ġġeli, -ġil**	instrumental often postposition: **gala**
neniġla 'with him/her'	*neni gala* 'with her'
have equative and semblative	lack equative case, have semblative
iskidiu 'the same as a woman'	Ø
	iskidimi 'like a woman'
Phonology	
ejective pronunciation common	non-ejective pronunciation common
tsġin ['tsʼqʼiːn] 'cedar'	*tsġin* ['tsxiːn] 'cedar'
FE have complex initial clusters t-m- km- kn- sm- tk- mġ-	WD/ED Lack clusters
mġegi 'I'	*megi* 'I'
knes 'beer'	*nes* 'beer'
allow -rg-	allow -rh-
birgo 'beam'	*birho* 'beam'
njorga 'duck'	*njorha* 'duck'
keep -ġi-	have -ṡi-
neuġi 'birch wood'	*neuṡi* 'birch wood'
sevaġi 'burnt embers'	*sevaṡi* 'burnt embers'
have hl [hl], [hɬ] or [ɬː]	have ɬ [ɬ] and gemination
sohla ['sohɬa] 'best'	*sǫła* ['sɔːɬa] 'best'

Eastern	Western
allow word final -ṡ	allow word final -s
seu̯iṡ 'little river'	sevvis 'little river'
some ED have ǒ [ɯ]	have archiphoneme <ɨ>
goamǒn [ˈgɔamɯn] 'human skull'	goamǔn [ˈgɔamʊn] 'human skull'
have closed <ø> [œ]	have closed <ø> is [ɤ]
nǔdna [ˈnœʔtna] 'wave'	nǔdna [ˈnɤʔtna] 'wave'
weakly anaptyctic	strongly anaptyctic
ġertto [ˈxɛrtːɔ] 'threshold'	ġertto [ˈxɛːrɨʔtːɔ] 'threshold'
olkko [ˈɔlkːɔ] 'temple'	olkko [ˈɔːlɨʔkɔ] 'temple'
-u̯- allowed as syllable onset	-u̯- not found as syllable onset
u̯eṡiṡ 'young animal'	veṡis 'young animal'
kl is not preglottalized	kl or ƛ is preglottalized or ejective
reklu [ˈrɛklːu] or [ˈrɛkːlu] 'to open up'	reklu/reƛu [ˈrɛʔtɬu] or [ˈrɛtɬʼu] 'to open up'
-a- polarized to -e- or -i- before -i- or -e-	-a- polarized to -o- before -i- or -e-
elebi̇̇emṡi 'smell of flowers'	eleboėmṡi 'smell of flowers'
-bġ- allowed	-pr- or -pṡi- allowed
sebġi 'bad GEN.'	sepṡi 'bad GEN.'
word initial ṁ- and ṅ- not allowed	word initial ṁ- and ṅ- allowed
mahingu 'I will die in combat'	ṁingu 'I will die in combat'
ED have -ps- and -bs-	WD only have -ps-
kepsi → kebsie 'mushroom'	kepsi → kepsie 'mushroom'
Verbs	
Irregular verbs with vowel prothesis	
have euphonic vowel prothesis	do not have euphonic vowel prothesis

Eastern	Western
amġa 'drank'	*mġa~ma* 'drank(ate)'
Conditional irrealis and optative forms	
have more conservative version	have standard version
sihhubo 'may it rain'	*sihhuo* 'may it rain'
mahingjoġi 'I would die in combat'	*ṁingjoi* 'I would die in combat'
Conditional realis	
da- or d- aḥḥ-	ro- or r- eġġ-
damanimi 'if I come'	*romaniyi* 'if I come'
Verbal adjective rule 1 pronouns	
have coalescing version	have separated version
hoatsimha 'you are surprised'	*hoatsimasa* 'you are surprised'
dappimġa 'I am lonely'	*dappimaka* 'I am lonely'
Negation	
lack negative version of **ůl-**	have negative preverbal adverb **sůmůl-** 'hardly'
Ø	*sůmůlkoki* 'nearly didn't speak'
negative complementizer in **-ont-**	negative complementizer in **-ents-**
montu 'uneaten'	*mentsu* 'uneaten'
Pronouns	
1p.sg agentive **-mi/-m**	1p.sg agentive **-yi**
kȯimi or *kȯim* 'I will talk'	*kȯiyi* 'I will talk'
1p.sg unagentive **en-/em-/ent-/ed-**	1p.sg unagentive **ma-** or **e?-** or **ei-**
engidlki 'I surrender'	*magidlki* 'I surrender'
munimi or *munim* 'I will rest'	*muniyi* 'I will rest'

Eastern	Western
1p.pl agentive inclusive -gga 1p.pl agentive exclusive -gge	1p.pl agentive inclusive -ko 1p.pl agentive exclusive -ků
iljagga 'we will cultivate Y'	*iljako* 'we will cultivate Y'
kaiknigge 'we will look'	*kaikniků* 'we will look'
2p.pl agentive -dda	2p.pl agentive -d
konidda 'you will walk'	*konid* 'you will walk'
3p.pl agentive -ri	3p.pl agentive -(i)ts
keidiri 'they will start a fire'	*keidits* 'they will start a fire'
pedniri 'they will arrive'	*pednits* 'they will arrive'
1p.pl unagentive copular exclusive -meri	1p.pl unagentive copular exclusive -můri
pohhji sajomeri 'in which we sleep'	*pohhji sajomůri* 'in which we sleep'
2p.pl unagentive copular exclusive -sari	2p.pl unagentive copular exclusive -sġi
nekeni ogasari 'which you lost'	*nekeni ogasġi* 'which you lost'
2p.pl unagentive copular exclusive -tari	2p.pl unagentive copular exclusive -dġi
noski gaitotari 'into which they got'	*noski gaitodġi* 'into which they got'
have non-clitical **to/ta** pronouns	have clitical **to/ta** pronouns
to kori te to dida 'the boy and the girl'	*to kori te t-dida* 'the boy and the girl'
Adjectives and Adverbs	
adjectives in -ot	adjectives in -oḥo
tapot 'last'	*tapoḥo* 'last'
adjectives in -on	adjectives in -ō
tausġon 'rigid'	*tausġō* 'rigid'
adverbs in -en, -il	adverbs in -il(i)
sogjen 'dryly'	*sogjil* 'dryly'
tsihen 'slightly'	*tsihil* 'slightly'

Eastern	Western
koken 'lightly'	*kokvil~kokil* 'lightly'
have approximative origin adverbs in -**rika**	only have approximative adverbs
biehterika 'from roughly north'	*biehteri* 'towards the north'
cardinal orientation: south is front	cardinal orientation: south is left
siseri 'forward'	*siseri* 'to the left'
on the other side' without **bal-** (far east)	on the otherside' with **bal-** (some ED too)
sines jampo 'on the other side of the lake'	*sines baljampo* 'on the other side of the lake'

§17 Texts

Nitśaka Siuiko

Kjala

Suikildi tsamnitasia oalmo Siuragi, keuhka jihta. Ipenduni 20 (iesġadi) gjekesġuoma igja en kjalkibma-ůt. Osoaḋgu onta neġůtta śines kolta unokkyi Sipsi okua Kękiesiustagi, siarjupůmamo kolta śines unokkyi Aingo osoaḋgotu katta tabba. Ůmġuolkijo kikarŷhhi 435 (aits guoma neġġa akno) maidġomnihta aśśi Hoklíśes sarakka. Aidlepůmamo śines da gagulka-ne netva Neyihisko, yaraiko śineska benkahteri 135 (giabmi neġġa angoka) maidġuoma kõuja Kjuomśin te Kjevvi ġye, selo sytrotima. Sorhi oa kůadna biekkula Kękiekjalkima, daiko męrarõ siḋva kokket. Inda etta Sipsuśesima rŷhhima unokkyi Rîhri te Kelśin eura dedna. Suśtaśen oa Aingoka siehteri 200 (eśi guoma) maidġuoma kõuja, rů sisella kjalka siyikodi.

Tommitęgjita on sievvi gjekesġuoma est-odna igja ogmo Kękiesiustagi sahra Tatimragi (suikildiri kõ temme aśśi), osoaḋge ju muśid kůanamo-uli. Kękiekjalkaska bůinderi on yara dednuneġvi Sarsirit, Onnju te Okna taga, miullil komo ehmi Tatimstatsita kekkotta-hi. Ůnnů keutsejeibma Suś-kękiekjala sahra kjala Aslastagi, tagjil kõ miegjari salakka, kommil rakma osatari, yara taga Sipsuśeska 215-260 (eśi guoma agnet-eśi guoma suntsġamo) maidġuoma kõuja.

Medde 265 (eśi guoma suntsġa akno) maidġuoma kõutęgjita bůinderi oa Suśjîkiekjala, osviri onta Sůkyisġamoika oda, tśîkka tona takekkita oda, Kolmoika katta te Hadlġogjo. Onokki on Denśigi jogjihni, nokkari ka 'deno' îrid.

Hadlġogjoika tśîkka Suśjîkiekjala ļîkie-kjalkibma selo unokkyi Tsõki, oat eśut kůanamo siyi-kodi. Tymisuvvi Ęnumeita Tsõkmo, oyarat Hadlġo-gjoika 500 (akno guoma) maidġuoma kõuja. Yara Ęnumeika siehteri 65 (suntsġa angoka) maidġuoma kõuja Nenniyauki, medde 65 (suntsġa angoka) maidġuoma kõutęgjita oa Regna, sahra dedna sisella ļîkiekjalkima. Yara Ęnume jampo Riekka, sahra toatnededna ataneila kadlġõ kjalka Siustagi, kemotoatġuli Siuragi te ůrkoloni sajo. Onokki on Heśśigi jogjihni, katibogju de nonuttaika tatimstagi 'hego' nokkiutta-hi, suikildiri kõ vetari aśśi.

Atai on rakma sitkitse te maśmahhabme Tatimragi, otki ka salmiegjabme te Aslaragi te Denśigi, õskai kemunokkotijas mimi Maśmoski. Mahha on ketsġo půumi te sîhhumi Heśśigi, toatġuli on.

Kadlkadlkya, oyavvi Riekunika ļîkia Sohtśa-ita kękia 1835 (netsġiabmi tenga guoma neġġa angoka) maidġuoma kjalka Siustagi, te Suśtaśeska siehdia te Sohtśaita biekkia, 1000 (netsġuoma) maidġuoma ůlla.

Da kõ Siustajagi eśudna nedda inden denari, kůanamo te gaulkka. Tatsaimna on retsotsita muohta-ita mopiko oalmo, kosokkil on piegjista mopi mahrutta. Medde inda 'aġlen' oni-nokkiu, oa ůrůma, usoti sġůppi maśka mahhami sippi kidli akami dujo. Utatski ue bana sytrotima. Uloliuts maja njoabbunolteta a, ikiri tsamśita śośli atoraġ on sara on seba. Piagjuari onta tsamġa, saibba katta radlvajabmeka, teuġġa on sobmate on îlkobmate osġe.

Totōka

Totōka oa suingioten sokuroakkenta Siustagi. Da on attśaita tontavvi kośigi attśa-nen sahra lillu, da on svottaita tontavvi toabigi svotta-nen sahra vilo, utatski kō uetari nůirhi. Sůite utatski, ue kemamomi-nen tymoakimi-hi. Adda attśaja-nen tobori sahra koalgi, egi takeri svattaja-nen sahra pêsi (tveliu), utatski kō ue tveluri ki kvesi sahra tyry koaltsa egi kvena sahra śini koaltsa, sůite pyddji sahra tyry pêta egi pydna sahra śini pêta. Orirra ungitegji epieibma te tůlrimoibma Siuragi.

nůirhi 'parents'			lillu 'father's brother'	ata·ka 'my father'	suo·ka 'my mother'	vilo 'mother's sister'	
tveliu 'aunts ~uncles'	koalgi 'father's sister'			megi 'I'		pêsi 'mother's brother'	
tveluri 'cousins'	kvesi 'cousin (m)'	kvena 'cousin (f)'				pyddji 'cousin (m)'	pydna 'cousin (f)'
kemamo- mi 'siblings'			koso·ka 'my older brother'		toabi·ka 'my older sister'		
			karsa 'younger brother'		dapsa 'younger sister'		

Veimna

Oveimiuts e Siuragi, otis ketsġo totōrita riekumi-nen sahra tatikkita to nalbi. Tobimitta tatsůi onta oti totonta balha sagva-nen somi estoi oveibmu sahra esetvi, oni ju otoatġuloti ki îskigi-ůt. Hanni kō otoatġuli sagna te tobimi boaltta. Sapru tamġusoti eskvarre maggja totonta můbma nalumi-hō, sahra nelimitta ki kosomi, oni ju okoasġulioti ki somigi-ůt. Sidnis kobaika soantśaima ålja jeddja seiskjotima ůatta. Oveimiuts e Siuragi, keulari soangi. Soantśa tevu, saibba boalsagvaita nuja gaiskkita deikoi. Sidniuts mai a ůat, kesa rebomni, toḥḥa nalumi te riekumi halkaita. Atai on miasġi soantśaima sijuikodi, ukvari kō sagva riekumi kedda te umeitvi boaltta nelumi kedda. Kommil on hagjen te moġijen, rodlůli ka śośi. Soantśa ahha, etsa kemîngi deita omna kî. Ketsġo on sytêu ikůkůa tatikkita-nen sindu atana (ōska mahḥji) nalbi kî, îlka nelimittaita-nen rolotta riehpi kî.

Sikkenka

Nînni-ḥa okiokite kiuśka sa totonta-hi, oti on kůsġamita atantanna unokkui sikkenka Siuragi. Sem onta keumahhi heietśai ki sikkenka-ůt, suikildiri katta kobai soakkia totta unokkui okna ki śośi. Jeibma dedna tammi ongamo. Jeibma selue tvomma egi temme aśśi gagulka teuśirre denari. Aingo oa gagulka siuiko tunneila, indaio giabmie ongamo.

Suikiltsa

Suikildi kobai soakkia atakka unokkui okna Siuragi. Soake on ůbůhma totonta, ōskaḥō neġůtta aiddia, da ka okna etta totōrita, unokkui vangoko. Da ieita śiaggelibmis birgira te kehhura oknua. Uara ongamo tatakkia kekila pipid-nen gagi, iokota panraka te liarkodi, opůtsti ogauldō neni sa maski. Oaki on nonutta 'kekila' tontavvi keulmi, orirra de uoli, kiokota iaingoka-nen kekilli aśśi Siuragi.

    Heietśai on eitaio sůpimo, osviri nîdika egi muliomika oda, iśéumaio ka sasakkibma saldamġa otġamo kvekkotsta.

    Sînkate eppi soakna giaungika da Siuragi, tsatsaupri eytkůltse. Eitaśi ůngůsti eiddu-uli Siura. Tśoti avvi sa totōka kadlka ketsġo unidlis osokenta. Kisġilontemġů kukkiuhko tohḥabmolla Siusta neidnobi śigiu nỷlly.

    Ōska udiiki on umehi on ongamo. Sapru on ue kośtet tatamanisbirhoima etta unokkui alppot, karakka ieibmotima, diikmua ka teukue iemiskena. Sůbmil umehi ketsġo sogvilmamo meimeri gala salulkika te asġakika.

    Ongamo siġa, ōska uara nehon, auhneni mi na ogauldi te ogetildi saio tvatå te îśpa. Usotsi ihha sōkkita, kvarruttaita te nåtśaita nios tatimannin. Kidli oa ihha niosia natġa sahra ketġuska keltari akka. Uśemi on, utakona mi keltaribma tamiditse sa, meḋga kō ůrůddia, tsuogga mimi manta hieudi-ha deita Siuragi.

    Nios siġa, gamahha ongamo eltari egi hůnamo, omei, ukedi, utigi te niki saio Siustagi.

Gagolkon

Da tamosi radeddō atśehtsġotuma lolmahhotuma sesveśieika omoḥimo-nen ailit śośi Siuragi. Katiġari sasli enesti kiutśi unokkui moḋbi. Mahhumi onta mopikoima-nen sikken, pihhu katta kůtůt sikkes-ne gakômi. Gatkeitsġa aġmika Siuragi tegionta rumu imisi, lolmahhauts daġe de imisti ola sikken, ialki kiuśpa-ne ogat, usotiti kō ihha en vůlommi. Unokki vůsitas ůatta.

    Tśiba ki gagulkua-ůt atana kemobiġota Siuragi, imůkvi nîdga-ḥa mopiko-nen te inoaksi nîḋḋa-ḥa mopiko enehmō-ne. Kvaulis ketsġo ůrkolot-nen gagi saslusikken. Da komo senni tunna meġie ůrůuen teukeknami. Gaulkkika îska de iiomu tamottaitagi sahne otina, îḋmi mopiko oualtanna, sahne geudluhḥen meġie-hi osatari, netvua ka gagolkon. Kemotoatġuli avvi Siustagi mumma egi kinaubi ġue a on, piusti ka gaulkka atantanna, uara ka somigi te îskigi tohḥeli seppǝn otarvodlimi.

Tvata on gaulkka nielli, ugoaka kō nielta eśmi, somigi on îskigi on. Diehko on ogetildi te ogaulda soġemme te moḋburemme eśmi, lolmahha ka ototġulenta-nen ednet kekna keyulos te moadġula taga svaltonta niaśśitseka. Utatski ue niśka enedni elio nidma. Niaśśiuts daġe de somi, gasůivvi-mi viddenra, irõren egi aykõren, sapru usikkote katubiahta, tśiba oda, sadnu dona ůhõ modbi-ha sě usotsi îngisa îngi sġajota. Pihhu sidnote totta giekehi, etta egi neġůtta giekehi, medde singelote. Unokki "ubiobba" toamma katubiahia. Õska merahmi onta ujobmoita gaulkkita-hi pedninha, sapru tymiġotumari katta topisi-mi seita, oa errimo keśerroti suikilditse toaddjita totonta teġů to topisi. Saupihtsġa on da totõria inintanna topisi, alla debmi omagjelma ekue taukukka eukabmeta seita.

Kůkiket Ůrkolot Keu
Totta ekue kedda jasukka, damġa, nůyetsta, tulmuma, usatahi enetsi mopikoibma te nitśakadi taga mangosvamo balha hemme te omobmo ki Siuragi. Yara ujomaskka mannja ailit śośi ta ototġulen-ůt. Sarai de ůrkona Sigotśagi te Onotśagi ůn Saśkaba, sahne svysġiti gagokŏi e. Totta on ůrkolot-nen keu siarjaka te sehkahka Siuragi, ehmi kõ sauhhjahita, soaġġokita te nîldita kjõhõ, sarai de hjayt ůrkonaja Siustagi hjaydde sarai otoatġuliri. Siarjakva unokkyi Iriragi te Ġůġůragi sehkahkaya. Kůlmalagien medde mopiko, opohmi katta syngyhmõ atarkelgie taddedna samnarõ. Înta on utkagjen enemma kohko kintuttta kedda, îlubiġumi de nalonta. Oveimi on Siura enemni kůtůtsi soaġġokita-ne, oveimi sůite kinagi enemni totõrita siyikodi. Utatski sarone tamosi-ůt kõtotiśi tammi sauhhjahi nonga imisti on tamottagi on.

Tulmu
Euka tulmuma-hi damġa te tůrůma okuhka muśid moskko-uli ki Siuragi. Ketsġo on henna aiska tulmuma aihka gala te tonkamo seita îskigi, da ka kůira tunna tohhanta Siustagi ismet te almi, katibogji daikota saśkaba. Seppen maldota puna nelesita, onome umalatsti tamarajõ holotta kedda dagjen, unokki komo "ġalpot" en jasukka-ůt, nayiniyia katta eukanteta arenta sahra ġarenta damu, tůrů, ůpi te pýbme taga. Atai dela rymyma te herhari ki îskigi. Kobai ko kokkuiba ryměuligjen nelpieja, udeli ra hejetśai lunjuma otġita-jasmiraka. Dela boimmo unokkyi bevvut ki îskigi te somigi, onogjika keśkediksa nůyetsta te elvotsta sahra elepsaśka sari. Da elepri, ela te õska tsġůldi bevvutstia-nen nayinõren lolonnin ta elvot. Tśiba kõkõ bevvutstia-nen etta ġůme, atarotima dailra, tśiba katta jålppuraimaka, oveibmunonte îski. Unayinis on onike kimi vauhkika egi jaingokika enehmõ en elvotsta, dela bě en bevvutsta, oaki nîntsika-ha denarika egi sikkeska.

Nůvvetka

Nauina on euka on muśid nůuetsta-uli ki Siuragi. Naymśa avvi en kolot-n de egi nalonta-nen eirpęįeika mantůtta de, įahhįu on ġůtsia vauhkia-uli iļiilsa neylie[1]. Nůiįa ue nůvvet netveila te tamneiheila keśkediksote ůngůmni somi. Nokka tammi nůįůmįa geilue-hō otarvodlimi ketsġo ki Siuragi, oni kō ta mįambi siehhin te sehi (sehisihin) mianįupake kimi e, ta kysġibi iįurha te otġa kosġohkake kimi e, ta tapaki gigįes te nyġġot akahtake kimi e te ta śesvi taga gîkkiu te gindotima osayklike kimi e. Eukari te gybid kidlita kimi te lygvid damśita otġamo kimi. Bůbůika geska, nauinari lamnaka legįōhka rentue te laįahi e, kosġari įatka, kolraro [2]te koruri kiluhdi, saįuka mesorari, nęnemu te ohkihi kehhorari te kįongenta taga tsġiamuhdi.

Tsaupri itahhotes tsamśita ikiusi egi ôhkousi[3] sahra ůlkůma ůtsů ki somigi. Mahhake tsamśia e keśkediksari ŷgsyma te irid, eterre sahra oroḍgo vetarima, tamasitkaįu a gangaka te sitġobid selueįa.

Norha te Nitkuat

Da kůira tunna soaġġoka siuikodi norha. Kemotihhari on sengyla gigutta îska, opohmi ka oanika-hi. Seppen onta kalvekeudlua norha, daima komo neġvi aidleįeita – ůrkůta saiḍgita estot, onōren nîtkuatsta aidlat-aidlai oneibbildi saįoįa îskigi te somigi – norōren ona rogogoslet sinnena te netsenguesuha to kůsġi tů tanuhtśagi oa įeita eśut norista. Da gontorha sahra gōddorha ta įeita-ůt norista.

Auġmi

Śema Siuragi, imůkvotůi kolmemi sîd ůn manua, idi gaiko diari te tatuhalgui. Sopria neġvita deda en haluka. Iddi on umibma diari estodna, edli įu oįusta keḍda, umekki kehhieika-hō geiko sōkko te imisti. Iddi on vetarita diari eśudna, îmi įu somogalka keḍda, umekki geiko îskid te sîhdi. Mega on iddi eterita diari taḍdedna, îmi įu tĕhtśa te gatta keḍda.

Śema on hingutsta oḍda tatiļįimuadi Siuragi, śema ne ohhistai lîdnitanna tatśoimuhka. Askile enet sorohma manuaika elotima roamî ohra. Da ohra tĕhtśa, unokka Kibo odaįo. Da ohra gatta koḍga iḍgi Eidli te Seidli. Da ohra ośotta sahka, unokka Timuni odaįo. Te da ohra siġġu, unokka Idenga odaįo. Taįu da enekni ohragi-ne te, iśutagi te sayklami kemorre sasatka unokkiuki.

Tśekla on niadlōka siuiko įaingoka gietsġotappima, dįaikekka ka įaingetsapetta tunnamo kįōhō ketsetśagi. Keulumi ketselhi unokkiu įálhi, tatkůkůa nialos naihkuhůnamoįa kokkenda kōuįa odari. Iśuminesta tåuts da korigi, itygluhhitigįen komo te tatatendaįa hůnamoįa terommi

---

[1] neylie dialectal of neylle

[2] kolraro dialectal of kolramo

[3] ôhkousi dialectal of ihkousi

jeḍḍja. Lolumaukustija on hagju ůrůddjita, opiamnumiri ka oakibma te gatkedumari sindu-nen. Saupihtsġa kõ vůvvunokkija sindutta halja.
  Keula on ketselhi didagi te, unokkụino aumulhi, pẙhhůts mehdil duja. Katusokmija on oakiska, îngikiri de sỏtůsůtśagi-nen gagi. Sapru sidnote koggaiskkiska egi kokutta ůat. Urengiti samna-ůt okolva sõkko deikari.
  Ruovva ubůlki gaskia kihlõ tatiddoti aumutśaimagi, ůaḥḥa sõkkika. Sihi neta didari te sỏtůsůnhi, tatiddi nît-ḥa aumutśaimagi.

Sednineros sytrotima keulmi

Unokki kůlůma sytrotimęġjila Siustaitagi sednineron. Kůlů roamitśa Siusta keulumu oa ta sednineron, onnanka on migjil îtstia, keulas ka rogjehki, egi õskęġjita. Da savvů Sednineros ta îlmolkami tayụala, pajůts došį nigen. Utatskis, done kastu sednineron, dụihmorakkęmmę niġõ deśi te tåkkęmmę ningalmoḍḍa došį. Eśisarokihua on njelsavvů sednineros, da komo katahoanumni rumu, okệhja kvîa dagjen utiodote niġõ roamitśa, da komo te kistami kůtůt kîd manụa egi niġõja egi gedlvari balha. Îlmolkakkęmmę kjõhõ sauri-ůt degjen, tatamorenra kebsie nantsġilhaka unokkụi nitmůġla keulhagjen tva sednineros. Ungokeụuma hůnamoja tiskitta gagi enet okangiḥḥenta-uli to, tatamora kebsie oda, sahra to tasednanesi. Yhhjůnů avvi tamageulos, aiskappen tasednanetta to tiski, neta oda opote îlmolka estot savvů sednineros, tsi nantsġj. Õska kîlibonęlladna tasednanettaika kîlononopponta, gasůivvi-mi dami mġegi. Idaḍḍidlaśenuts on mehdil euskueita tiskittaika de tva tasednanetta, katimolkigjen jụ hůnamoika kadda keula sarokka eśudna deita. Hanni nantsġiltayụalia tåinra sipi gakoni tasednanetta gagi to tiskisi te aiskilesta oalenta. Sinnegjil ogaldiri avvi, kendaiska sednineros ahhatsi tagjil kemitski ki tasednanesi te tiskisi.
  Ehmi enetsi kůlmita-ne Siustagi tva Sednineros hanni, keulota tasadnetta, mieḍḍauts ġeyl data. Seppen umauldekki soaġġokia siụikodi kjon nantsġî îlmolkodlimetta te utatski, done neidno ki õska sednineros keulotime, aiska deiko. Umaġami, done pîdna sednineron tekîdna gamġa ůhtairi uinoma ůrůddja. Unoni, done nantsġi latsma tayụalda nigen ůrůddja, imitta, ohhistagi. Da on savvů ta nantsġî, da ka keyśva ta ninhuḍḍe.

17.1 English Version

Territory

The Siwa people inhabit a large belt of forest from East to West. They arrived to this land within the last two thousand years. The ancestors of Eastern Siwa settled around three lakes called **Sipsi**. Most settled around the southwestern point of the lake, called **Aingo** (narrow-lake). The 130km long shores of the narrow **Hokla** lake is sparsely populated. At the other end of the lake, **Neụihisko** is another important community, with **Kjuomṡin** and the sacred river **Kjevvi** about 40km northeast from the lake. The northernmost settlement of Eastern Siwa territory is **Sorhi**, whose dialect is difficult to understand. The two eastern lakes of **Sipsi**, called **Rihri** and **Kelṡin**, are home to a few Siwa villages. About 65km south of **Aingo** is the lake **Suṡtaṡen**, the southern edge of Siwa territory.

Within the first thousand years, the ancestors of Eastern Siwa or **Tatimragi** (they live by lakes, **temmu**) expanded further west and established various villages.

West of the eastern Siwa territory are the three villages of **Sarsirit**, **Onnju** and **Okna**, whose dialect differs slightly from eastern Siwa dialects. Together they form the mid-eastern territory or the **Aslaragi** territory (they herd caribou, **salama**). They rely more heavily on caribou herding and lie about 65-80km west of lakes **Sipsi**.

Still 80km further northwest is the mid-western territory, which consists of **Sùkụisġa** river, which connects the East with the West and **Kola** ('ridge') and **Hadlġoi**. These Siwa call themselves **Denṡigi**, as they call the arrow (**ìrri**) 'deno'.

From **Hadlġoi**, the river **Tsōki** connects the mid-western territory with the western Siwa territory, second largest Siwa population. **Tsōki** flows into **Ėdnu** bay, 150km from **Hadlġoi**. 20km south of **Ėdnu** is **Nenniụauki**, and 20km further is the southernmost village of the western territory, **Regna**. Across the bay from **Ėdnu** is **Riekka**, the biggest trading village of all Siwa territory. There, Siwa trade with their neighbors. These Siwa call themselves **Heṡṡigi**, which corresponds to the Eastern Siwa word hego 'salt', as they live by the sea.

Eastern Siwa or **Tatimragi** rely mostly on fishing and game hunting. Many mid-eastern Siwa, or Aslaragi, and mid-western Siwa, or **Denṡigi**, practice caribou herding and hunt beavers, which is why they are sometimes collectively referred to as **Maṡmoski** 'game-people'. Western Siwa, or **Heṡṡigi**, are known for their seal and whale hunting and trading.

All in all, from **Riekka** in the west to **Sorhi** in the east, the Siwa territory spans about 550km, and from **Suṡtaṡen** lake in the south to **Sorhi** in the north, nearly 300km.

Siwa people live in about two dozen villages, settlements and communities. Each band of hunter receives a vast hunting territory, which is allowed to recover periodically. There are even so-called **aġlen**, which are areas where it is neither allowed to hunt game nor cut wood. It is considered a sacred place. When left to grow back, all kinds of beings come into the forest, some benevolent, some malevolent. They heal the forest, and they must not be disturbed unless one has asked before hand and made a sacrifice.

Family

The basic social unit of the Siwa is a family (**totōka**). The brothers of one's father (**lillu**) and sisters of one's mother (**vilo**) are considered parents, and their children are one's siblings (**kemamomi**). If the father has a sister (**koalgi**), or the mother a brother (**pèsi**), they are considered uncles or aunts (**tveliu**), and their children are cousins (**tveluri**, or **kvesi** for son of father's sister, **kvena** for daughter of father's sister ~ **pyddji** for son of mother's brother, **pydna** for daughter of mother's brother). Siwa always distinguish older siblings from younger siblings.

Generally, when Siwa marry, the husband will join the wife's family. The first man to get married usually unites with his bride's family along with his sisters. If a woman gets married first, her brothers may be sent to her husband's family.

Marriage

Generally, when Siwa marry, the husband (**nalbi**) will join the wife's (**riehpi**) family (**tatriki**). The first man to get married (**esetvi**) usually unites with his bride's family along with his sisters. It is then said that these women 'become sisters' (**o·toabġul·i**), such that the bride and a man's sisters 'become sisters'. If a woman gets married first (**eskvari**), her brothers may be sent to her husband's family (**nelimi**). It is then said that these men 'become brothers' (**o·koasġul·i**). This lasts from the wedding in summer to the following early spring. When Siwa marry, they observe wedding (**soangi**). Before the wedding, bride (**sagna**) and groom (**boalhi**) may not see each other for a month. During that time, each will learn the skills to honour (the title of) wife and husband. Siwa marriage is a big celebration, as the bride is crowned wife (**u·kvar·i** 'to be crowned'), and the groom is knifed husband (**um·eitv·i** 'to be knifed'). People eat and drink a lot, and everyone wears fine clothes. After the wedding, the new married couple (**omna**) begin their life together. It is the tradition that the new husband offers a large catch (often a bear) to his family as a thank, and the new wife offers her husband's family new clothes.

Bands

Because of how their families intertwine, Siwa organize themselves into larger groups they call **sikken**. These bands do not hunt together in the winter time, but in summer, they all live in one long house called **okna**. Many long houses form a village (**dedna**). Two villages or more on the same river/lake form a community (**gagulka**). The largest Siwa community is **Aingo**, where there are hundreds of long houses.

Housing

In the summer, Siwa live in large houses called **okna**. A single **okna** may house several families, usually 3 or 4, though **okna** for two families exist, called **vangoko** (lit. small **okna**). **Okna** are permanant structures, made from logs and bark. Inside the **okna**, there is a hearth (**kekila**) and its smoke hole (**piḍbi**) surrounded by the home-bench (**panra**) and the guestbench (**liarkko**), where people sit and discuss (**kekli** 'to sit around the hearth'). From the word **kekila**, there is also **keula** 'to observe a ceremony', because Siwa people have always centered (lit. 'weaved') their lives around the fire.

In the winter, winter camps (**sùḍbi**) are built, which consist of cabins for keeping (**ni**) or smoking meat (**muljo**). The tents (**sasame**) are covered by thick warm caribou skins (**saldamu**).

Siwa people are so good at building shelters that dying out is nearly unheard of. A Siwa man knows how to build any type of house. Building a house is generally done by whole families cooperating. It is said that even the best beaver cannot outdo a well learned Siwa.

Okna are often decorated and painted. There may be carvings on the two entry beams (**alppot**) which form the door (**karaka**), they often display animal carvings. The front of a house (**sokvilma**) will generally be painted black with paint made from tar or sap and black ashes.

Besides **okna**, there is often a speaking house (**nehon**), where elders and leaders meet and discuss side-by-side. Only men, married women and widows may enter the **nehon**. The **nehon** is traditionally the only building where there is an above ground floor (**natġa**). It is believed that by avoiding to thread on the ground, Siwa show respect to the environment, and therefor hope to gain its favor.

In addition to the **nehon**, **okna** are also accompanied by a steam house (**eltta**) or a steam tent (**hùdna**), where Siwa bathe, are born, are cured and die.

Communities

The majority of Siwa are hunters who must constantly stalk and follow the animals over great distances. Siwa inherit responsibility (**sasli**) for a known territory called **moḍbi**. A band must hunt on their **moḍbi**, but may make deals with other bands. Siwa uphold the belief that animals see no boarders, and if a band has been hunting an animal that crosses into someone else territory, they may pursue it, but only it. This is called **vůsitas**.

These large territories mean that Siwa must agree with each other on where one's territory begins and another's starts. Usually, the band responsible for a land will summer with his neighbours. Thus, summering is an important time for the planning of the coming winter hunting season. Communities are important because they allow hunters to be better organized, have access to larger areas, which renders their hunting more efficient. Larger communities thrive through trading within Siwas and with other non-Siwas and often, one can find able men and women with very specialized skills.

A community is headed by a chief (**njelli**). The chief is chosen by a council of elders (**eṡmi**), women and men alike. The council meet regularly and discuss the economy (**soġemmy**), their territories, keep track of trading relations, organize ceremonies and also maintain order by advocating punishments for crimes. Siwa consider certain offences to be crimes (**niṡka**). If a man commits a **niṡka**, such as stealing, killing or hurting someone, he may be placed in exile (**katubias**, lit. 'being thrown out'), which means his hunting territory is no longer his and he cannot live where he used. This can last one, two or three years, or even be permanent. A person in **katubias** is called **ubiobba**. It is often hard for **ubiobba** to return to their community. They must often resolve to working as helpers (**topisi**). A **topisi** is someone who works for a family in exchange for housing. Generally, wealthier families have a **topisi**, as they can concentrate on producing valuable goods.

Relations With Neighbouring Tribes

Siwa trade goods such as furs and leather, tools, clothes, rights to certain territories and information on the migration of birds and game. The majority of this trading happens within the Alopian tribes (**ujomaski**). Because the Siwa language is closely related to the Sigori and Onori, it is easier for them to communicate together. Siwa trade with their neighbours to the south-west and south-east. Their languages, cultures and faces are different, such that Siwa are not closely tied to them, nor are their trade relations. Siwa call these people **Iriragi** (cf. **iri** 'bark') in the south-west and **Ġuġuragi** in the south-east. There have even been wars fought over territory. No one lives on from the last great war. Some boys are still trained as warriors, because the skills must be passed on. Some Siwa marry into other ethnicities, and some foreigners have been married into Siwa families. It is said that a good hunter will know how to deal the many languages of animals and the hunters.

Material World
Clothing

Siwa make their clothes from the skins and furs of various mammals. Women generally see about sewing clothes with needles and sinew. Leather (**jasuma~jasma**) and tanning (**almi**) are an important part of the Siwa skills, and the language reflects this. The skin of the deer (**puna**) is especially valued for summer clothes (**nellen**), for which it is tanned especially thin, a leather called **ġalpot**, while thick leathers (**damu**) and furs (**tůrů**) or bear skin (**ůpi**), seal skin (**pẏbme**) and caribou skin (**sigme**) are used for winter clothes (**arren~ġarren**).

Women mostly wear a dress (**rybmy**) and a hat (**herha**). In the summer, a lighter dress called **nelppi** is used, while in the winter, a **lunju** made from thicker leather is used. Women and men wear a belt called **bevvut**, which is used to carry tools and **elvot** or flower-code in their **bevvut**. **Elvot** is a code that involves flowers, plants and sometimes animal skulls that are attached to the **bevvut** to signify certain things. For example, two pine cones in a **bevvut** shows that a woman is pregnant (she is a **dailha**). A beaver head means a woman is married to a hunter, and a hare's tail indicates that the woman is not married. While **elvot** is used to state something about the bearer's life or status, the **bevvut** itself usually shows from what village or band one is.

Tools

Siwa use and make a variety of tools (**nůvvet**). A good toolmaker (**neyli**) knows how to survive in any situation by using what is at hand and his skills, which he will have received from a tool master (**eirpà**). The most important and versatile tool any man will have with him is the knife (**nůjů**). Siwa has many ways of calling a knife according to its specialized function, such as **mjambi**, long and thin for gutting fish, **kysġibi**, thick and strong for carving wood, **tapaki**, sharp and curved for cutting skins and bark, **sesvi**, cutting and dangerous for protection. Siwa also make other tools. They also make adzes (**gẏbi**) for wood and awls (**lykvi**) for hard leather.

For food, they use a quern (**lamna**) to crush seeds and make flour, they carve bowls (**jata**), large containers (**kolra**) and smaller ones (**korù**) from wood, bowls from rock (**saiyu**), boxes (**nęnnu**) and bags (**ohkis**) from birch bark, baskets (**kjoknen**) from cedar bark.

Men rarely go into the forest without an axe (**iki**) or a hatchet (**ikos** or **ůlků**). For hunting in the forest, a bow (**ẏksy**) and arrows (**irri**), a spear (**eteri** or **orobi**) at sea, nets (**gakna**) on lakes and fishing rod (**sitġobi**) in rivers

Culture
Singing And Story-telling

Singing is a major part of Siwa culture. Their common songs keep them connected and the stories keep them alive. Singing is highly ritualized and has three main forms. One type of singing is similar to a contest, where men compete against women in telling a story through song (**nitkyat**). Another type of singing is where a single group sings and tells long heroic adventures (**rogogoslet**). This type of singing is called **gontorha** or **gōddorha** (lit. travel-singing).

Religion

Siwa believe the world began as a cloud of honey, from which a drop fell and was struck by lightning. The lightning split the drop of honey in three. One drop fell onto the ground and grew into a birch tree, from whose bark men and animals were born. One drop fell into the ocean and turned into golden row, from which women and fish were born and the last drop fell into the sky and became the sun and the moon.

The Siwa people believe in numerous inhabiting spirits, but they also believe in greater individual deities. Each deity is said to govern certain parts of the living world. There is the sun deity, called **Kibo**. There are the twin deities of the moon, **Eidli** and **Seidli**. There is the deity of good fish stock, called **Timuni**. And there is also the deity of rain, called **Idenga**. Then there are other deities, parents and protectors of animal groups, called the **sasats**.

There are many rituals that punctuate the spiritual life of Siwa people. Rites of passage (**ketselhi**) are ceremonies that represent important moments in one's life. Boys must go through a rite of passage called **jàlhi** that involves a ceremony in a steam hut half a day's walk into the wild, where boys of 11 years of age are intoxicated with a poison and kept in until nightfall. They are released into nature and must find their way back home and bring home an animal that they hunted. They are generally given a name associated with what they bring back.

Girls also observe a rite of passage called **aumulhi**, which is when they first bleed. They are sent away from their homes to alone live with older female relatives (grandmothers or aunts) called **sȯtůsůni** (lit. 'mother-guardian') . This may last a week or more. They are forbidden from interacting with men during this time. What happens during **aumulhi** is kept entirely secret from all, especially men. Only the girls and their mother-guardians know what happens during **aumulhi**.

The Ceremony of the Holy Depersonification

The most holy of all rituals to siwa is called **sednineron** or 'depersonification'. The sednineron is a ritual that all Siwa are required to observe at least once in their lives, though many repeat it every year or more often. The goal of sednineron is to achieve a state of mind where the self disappears.

Depersonification is considered to be necessary in order to soften the ego and become more humble before nature and the world. Depersonification has two main goals – to erase the limits within which each individual perceives himself to be contained, and to learn something new about the world or one's self or one's purpose. To reach these goals, sednineron is observed by ingesting a psychedelic mushroom called **nitmůġla** (mushroom of the self). The person ingesting the mushrooms, **tasednanesi** must engage in a type of meditation in a steam hut with a quest leader (**tiskisi**, lit. asker). As the effects of the mushroom intensify, the tiskisi leads the tasednanesi questions that he knows will help the **tasednanesi** achieve the first goal of sednineron, **nantsġi**. Often the tiskisi will make the tasednanesi repeat mantra-like phrases, such as **dami mġegi** (I am me). Once the tasednanesi becomes unable to answer questions from the tiskisi, the ritual is taken out of the steam hut and the second part begins. In this state of nantsġî or selflessness, the tiskisi simply walks with the tasednanesi and now lets him control the conversation. In the days following the sednineron, the tasednanesi will spend much time with his tiskisi having long discussions.

Sednineron differs from other rituals of the Siwa in being observed at the tasednanesi's will. Siwa culture values people who have achieved nantsġî and those who regularly observe sednineron are often considered wise people from whom to ask advice. Siwa see sednineron as a way of getting closer to the true nature of nature.

Nantsgî is said to be a bridge to the state of mind of nature itself, animals and deities. While the goal is called nantsgî, the experience is called **ninhuḍḍe** (psychedelia).

Mythology and Folklore

Siwa mythology is rich and complex. The core animalistic belief of Siwa people is reflected in the language and consists of a belief of mystical, invisible forces that are personified as a deities. The extensive use of masks in Siwa culture is also a result of the idea that deities are only masks that forces were because humans cannot understand, see or talk to them otherwise.

§18 Lexicon

LEXICON ~ NINJAKA

A a

åhnis, *åhnihi* – (no.ina)
hole/cavity (at the bottom of a tree) used a shelter | hiding place
åli, *ålka* – (no.ina)
wound, injury
ålni, *ålja* – (no.ani)
early spring
abana, *åkka* – (no.ina)
back of canoe
adlm·a, *adlmia* – (v.at. inf. *adlmami*)
to foster, to bring up | to care for, to look after | to nurture (old)
agjelm·a, *agjelmia* – (v.at. inf. *agjelmami*)
to centre, to focus
om·agjeld·i, *omagjeldui* – (v.asubj. inf. *agjeldena*)
to concentrate
agjeut, *ajelda~ajeutta* – (no.ina)
heart, centre, marrow
agjei~agjil – (adv.)
precisely, exactly
aġlen, *aġlenta* – (no.ina)
restricted area (forest not hunted so it may regenerate itself)
ahha – (postp.)
after
ahha·ni – (det.)
after, the latter | descendent(s)
ahtsis, *ahtsihi* – (no.ina)
offspring
aidla, *aidlaka* – (adj.)
in front of each other, opposed | opposing, at odds: *aidlat aidlai~aidlaḥaidlai* : against each other
  aidle– 'proto-, main-, principal'
ajen – (adv.)
clearly, obviously

kat·aigjet·a, *kataigjedda* – (v.at/.ut. inf. *kataigjebmil kataigjebmu*)
to explain, to be due to
aihha, *aihka* – (no.ina)
needle
aihhabi, *aihadga~aihhadga* – (no.ina)
evergreen branch
aihhji, *aiṡka* – (no.ina)
star(s)
aihhjudna, *aihhjudnaka* – (adj.)
starry
aihhot, *aihhotta* – (no.ina)
thorny plant/bush
aih·i, *aisti* – (v.uit. inf. *aihisu*)
to be wrong, to err, to make a mistake
aihmi, *aihmika* – (no.ina)
nesting hole in snow: *maikůli aihmikima* 'like a needle in a haystack' (lit. dressed in white in ~); *tami aihmikia-nen* 'to feel at home/to be in one's element'
aiho – (adv.)
the wrong way, wrongly
aji, *ajika* – (adj.)
clear, transparent
aikla – (adv.)
from all directions, from everywhere, in disorder, in confusion, in disarray: *aikla te aiho* 'completely wrong'
ailit, *ailihka* – (pron.)
one or the other, every other: *ailihka kenda* 'one day or the other' | *ailit śośi* 'the majority, most (people)'
aimra – (adv.)
wrongly, incorrectly, wrong
aingo, *aingoka* – (no.ina)
narrow lake, narrow stretch (of a lake) | canal, channel, passage
ajosi, *ajotta* – (no.ani)
open ocean
aipi·m·i, *aipumi* – (v.adj)
to (feel/be) bloated | to (become/be) vast
aipiot, *aipiotta* – (adj.)
enormous, huge, vast, immense, great, massive

airas, *airhi* – (no.ina)
  penis
airtti, *airtika* – (no.ina)
  large vase, large container | (vulg.) large (penis/ass/breasts/nose)
aisk·a, *aiskia* – (v.at/.ai. inf. *aiskami*))
  to sew
aisl·a, *aislia* – (v.at inf. *aislami*)
  to drag (behind oneself)
aiteil·i, *aiteidli* – (v.ui. inf. *aitelsu*)
  to be severely sick
aitilit, *aitilitsta* – (no.ina)
  epidemic
aits, *aubmi~aiddja* – (num.ani/.ina)
  four
  aidnet 'fourteen'
  aitġa 'forty'
  aitsven 'four times'
  aitset 'fourth'
aitsġemis, *aitsġemhi* – (no.ina)
  Thursday
aitsġi, *aitska* – (no.ina)
  group of friends, circle of friends
ak·a, *aḍga* – (v.at/.ut. inf. *ahmi*)
  to cut
  tym·ak·a 'to cut down (of trees)'
akna, *angaka* – (no.ina)
  traces, remain, sign, mark: *angakia* 'passed away, dead (EAST)' ~ 'sick, with a rash (WEST)'
akṡi, *akohta* – (no.ani)
  death (personification/deity)
akvo, *agvoka* – (no.ina)
  slippery/wet place | (more) difficult alternative
al·a, *adla* – (v.at. inf. *almi*)
  to tan (skin)
  tam·al·a to treat, to tackle, to handle
alahra, *alahraka* – (no.ina)
  floating log
all·a, *allia* – (v.at. inf. *almi~allami*)
  to have time for (+COP +ILLAT)
j·all·i, *jallui* – (v.aditr. inf. *alnin~allinin*)
  to have time for (+ILLAT)
alppot, *alpotta* – (no.ina)
  beam (closest to the entrance) | beam (that runs along the middle part of the roof) | apex, climax
amȧ~amau, *amari* – (no.ina)
  snot
amisaṡmi, *amisaṡmika* – (no.ina)
  hunter speech, masculine pronunciation | *mami~* nonsense, untrue story, bullshit
amoi, *amotṡa* – (no.ani)
  blood (inside the body)
amo·kvelva, *·kvelvari/kvelu* – (no.ina/no.ani)
  northern lights
angi~angiu~angil~angir, *angiri* – (no.ina)
  seed, pit
aroma, *arokka* – (no.ina)
  place next to, side
arroma, *arokka* – (no.ina)
  table side
arru(i)~aṡṡu(i) – (postp.)
  next to
  arta~aṡta 'next to'
  artairi~aṡtairi 'towards the side'
  aṡṡi 'along the side, on the shores of'
  arka~aṡka 'from the side'
artaita~arteta – (postp.)
  compared to
aruka~arkka~erkka, *arukka~arkaka~erkari* – (no.ina)
  branch, fork
asġa, *asġaka* – (no.ina)
  (black) ashes | coal
aska – (conj./postp.)
  because (negative reason) (+ -te / GEN.)
askila, *askidla* – (v.at. inf. *askilmi*)
  to control, to be in charge, to govern, to lead
Aslara(gi), *Aslasta(gi)* – (no.ani)
  mid-western Siwa
aṡṡuta – (postp.)
  compared to
aṡṡekken, *aṡṡekkes~aṡekkes* – (no.ina)
  damselfly
ata-, *atka-* – (act.nom)
  father
ata, *atra* – (no.ina)
  mouth, open mouth
ata-erribmot, *~bmotta* – (adj.)
  hard-working, diligent
atah·m·i, *atarrima* (*atar-*) – (v.adj)
  to be pregnant, to be bloated, to be large(r than usual)
atai – (adv.)

largely, very, verily, mostly
atana, *atakka* – (adj.)
big, large (adv. *atai*)
ataḍga, *atagga* – (no.du)
father and son(s)
ataḍba, *atabba* – (no.du)
father and daughter(s)
ateͅ~ateu~atel, *ateri* – (no.ina)
size, largeness
ate·m·i, *atumi* – (v.adj)
to be sick
atġi, *atġika* – (no.ina)
bass
atkana, *atkavva~atkakka* – (no.ani/.ina)
(bushy) tail | fox('s tail)
atka·nokka, *atka-nokkamo* – (no.ina)
wolf
atkenka – (adv.)
the day after tomorrow
atki, *atkika* – (no.ina)
day after tomorrow
atojukk·a, *atojukkia* – (v.ut. inf. *atojukmu*)
to sicken, to make (feel) sick; *atojukkaka atta soalka-ůt* 'this smell makes me feel sick'
atojun·i, *atojudi* – (v.ui. inf. *atojuntu*)
to feel sick, to seem sick
atora, *atohka* – (no.ina)
being, creature | little man/woman
atri, *attśa* – (no.ani)
father
atsio, *atsioka* – (no.ina)
glade
aubmi, *aumika* – (no.ina)
knot
auhka – (adv.)
quite
auksi, *auhta* – (no.ani)
lumberjack (also *tauksi*)
aumlu, *aumta* – (no.ani)
(smell/taste of) blood
aumul·hi, *aumutśagi* – (no.ani.pl)
first menstruation (ceremony)
aunt·a, *auntia* – (v.at. inf. *auntami*)
to make a knot, to tie
aurin, *aurinta* – (ad.)
crisp, brisk, refreshing | cool, chilly
aurjun·i, *aurjudi* – (v.ui. inf. *aurjuntu*)
to (still) feel/taste/smell fresh

aurko, *aurkka~auruni* – (no.ina/.ani)
lake trout
avoḥi, *auhika* – (no.ina)
membrane, film
ayk·a, *ayḍga* – (v.at/.ut. inf. *aykmi~aykmů*)
to wound, to hurt, to injure
ay·m·i, *ęmami* – (v.adj)
to shudder, to feel sick, to (be/feel) repulsed (see *ęb·ů*)
aypitsġi, *aypitsġika* – (adj.)
huge, substantial, enormous (in number)
ayrhi, *ayrhika* – (no.ina)
time while something is still fresh | prime: *ayrhikia-nen* 'at one's best'
ayųe~ayvve, *ayųeka~ayvveka* – (adj.)
shrill, high-pitched, piercing, sharp

B b

baͅdi, *baͅdga* – (no.ina)
pain (general, non-localized)
baͅhna, *baͅhnaka* – (no.ina)
bed
bahhi, *baski* – (no.ina)
day, 24 hours
bahhjo, *baġa* – (no.ani)
testicle
bahhẏt, *bahhẏtta* – (no.ina)
diary
bahpa, *baġa* – (no.du)
testicles
baja, *baika* – (no.ina)
branch
balet, *baletta* – (no.ina)
flank, side
balha – (postp.)
on(to) the side of | about
balkka 'from the side of'
bamr·i, *bamrui* – (v.ui/.ai inf. *bamrisu/bamrisa*)
to nap, to doze off | to rest (v.ai)
bana, *banka*, *-śi-* – (no.ina)
place, location, site
bansi – (adv.)
today (formal)
batsġv·a, *batsġvia* – (v.at inf. *batsġvami*)

to look for (usually involves leaving one's home to go and look for something)
baulla, *baudla~baullia* – (v.at. inf. *baulmi*)
to cross, to wade
baun·i, *baudi* – (v.ai/.adit. inf. *baunta~baunnin*)
to get somewhere (in time)
baut, *balda~bautta* – (no.ina)
butter
bè~beu~bel, *bela* – (no.ina)
acid
o·beisġild·i, *obeisġildui* – (v.asubj/.at. inf. *beisġildena/ beisġildami*)
to make peace (between each other)
beits·i, *beitsti* – (v.ai inf. beitsisa)
to spend (time/the day)
belha, *belra* – (no.ani)
pregnant lobster/crab
belmå, *belmęie* – (no.ina)
hard worker
belm·i, *belmui* – (v.ai. inf. *belmisa*)
to work, to be busy, to be at work
bename, *benammi* – (no.ina)
leather pouch, bag, purse
bengomu~bengon, *bengomme~bengos* – (no.ina)
roof
benho, *benhue~benra~belra~beddja* – (no.ina/.ani)
dog
benka, *benkari* – (no.ina/.adv)
north-east
benkaśa 'in the north-east'
benkahta 'to the north-east'
benkahteri 'towards the north-east'
benkahtsi 'along the north-east (face/side)'
benkahka 'from the north-east'
besġ·i, *beskki* – (v.imp)
to be peaceful | (*salla* ~) to be in peace
bevvut, *bevvutsta~bevvuddja* – (no.ina)
belt(s) (on a dress/animal) | signal
b·i·a, *ania* – (v.at. inf. *(b)imi*)
to throw
kata·b·i·a 'to throw (into exile), to reject'
bialbi, *bjaldi* – (no.ina.irr)
half
bial·i, *biadli* – (v.ai. inf. *bialsa*)
to talk, to speak | to address, to communicate
bialvuni, *bialvōdi~bialvuja* – (no.ina/.ani)
crustacean
bidjis, *bijihi* – (no.ina)
puppy
biehna, *biehnari* – (adj.)
highest, top, best | superior
biekkia – (adv.)
north
biehta 'northwards, to the north'
biehteri 'towards the north'
bentśi 'along the north(face/side)'
biehka 'from the north'
biekkula 'northernmost'
biele, *bielli* – (adj.)
fat, stout, chubby, thick
bieli, *bielle* – (no.ina)
fat, blubber
bieluha, *bieluhdi* – (adj.)
fat, greasy, oily
bieluhma, *bieluhmari* – (adj.)
quite fat, plump, chubby, stout
bjeni, *bjenne* – (no.ina)
back (of an animal) | (something) facing up
bjeulusk·u, *bjeuluskaju* – (v.utrans. inf. *bjeuluskoru*)
to lose weight
biġġyt, *biġytsta* – (no.ina)
game, play, fun, amusement
bilin, *bȋlis* – (no.ina)
liver: *bȋlisia* 'in luck, at stake, at the right place'
bilitse, *bȋlitsedi* – (adj.)
lucky
birho, *bȋrhodi* – (no.ina)
canidae, dog-like animals
biumi, *bȋundi~bȋutta* – (no.ina/.ani)
flycatcher
billjo, *biljodi* – (no.ina)
hunger, need: *tami biljoja* 'to be hungry'
bilva, *bilvari* – (no.ina)
speech, talking | communication, adress
biohts·i, *biohtsti* – (v.ai inf. biohtsisa)
to play (also bjohtsa)
birġo~birho, *birhodi* – (no.ina)
beam, large round log | tall/big/strong man
boaihhji~boaiśśi, *boaiśka* – (no.ina)
algae

boalhi, *boaltśa~boaltta* – (no.ani)
groom
boari, *boatśa~boahka* – (num.ani/.ina)
nine
boanet 'nineteen'
boarra 'ninety'
boaren 'nine times'
boarut 'ninth'
boġi~boġġi, *bośko~boġġo* – (no.ina)
branch (with leaves)
boja, *boiko* – (no.ina)
branch
boina, *boimmo* – (no.ina)
belt, strap
bovvoko, *bȯkoma* – (no.ina)
broken branch | small branch
bunus, *bunuhi~bunhi~bȯhhi* – (no.ina)
(small) squash
butta, *buttamo* – (no.ina)
bad weather, rainy weather
bu̇bmu·a, *bu̇bmia* (*bu̇bmo-*) – (v.at. inf. *bu̇bmomi*)
to pound (something), to knock
bu̇nt·a, *bu̇ntia* – (v.at. inf. *bu̇ntami*)
to weave (baskets, shoes)
bu̇tni, *bu̇tnȋd* – (no.ina)
cast of bad weather, many days of bad weather in a row
bu̇ġji, *bu̇jima* – (no.ina/.adv)
north-west | back (direction WEST)
bu̇imi 'in the north-west'
bu̇inda 'to the north-west'
bu̇inderi 'towards the north-west'
bu̇intsi 'along the north-west (face/side)'
bu̇inka 'from the north-west'
bu̇lk·a, *bu̇lkia* – (v.at. inf. *bu̇lkami*)
to keep (in fat), to conserve/preserve
bydny, *bynyma* – (no.ina)
squash
bẏ, *bu̇bu̇* – (no.ina)
food

D d

dȧdna, *dȧnaka* – (no.ina)
pillow | pad, stomach | dressing, bandage, plaster
dagis, *daihhi* – (no.ina)
detail, feature, characteristic
dahama, *dåmġa* – (no.ina)
jawbone, jaw line
dahpi, *dahpika* – (no.ina)
clan (3-5 families)
daib·m·i, *daipsima* (*daipp-*) – (v.adj)
to (be/become) wet (of weather) | to be sweaty (from work) | to be hard at work
daiggi, *daigika* – (no.ina)
humid, hot weather
daihha, *daihhaka* – (adj.)
charactestic, typical
dailha, *dailra* – (no.ani)
pregnant woman
dai·m·i, *daumi* – (v.adj)
to be moist, to be damp
daippo, *daippoka* – (adj.)
damp, wet
daiy̨e~daivve, *daiy̨eka~daivveka* – (adj.)
moist, dramp, humid
dament·a, *damentia* – (v.at inf. *damentami*)
to skin (of animal) | to punish (children)
damu, *damġa* – (no.ina)
skin (on living animal/with fur)
dap·m·i, *dapsima* (*dapp-*) – (v.adj)
to be alone/lonely
dappo, *dappoka* – (adj.)
alone, lonely
dapsa, *daḋḋa* – (no.ani)
younger sister
daḋb·i, *dabbi* – (v.ai. inf. *daḋbisa*)
to drum, to beat
daḋḋ·a, *dakka* – (v.at./.adit inf. *daḋmi~dadnin*)
to answer
davva, *dagga* – (no.ina)
past, history | background, setting
deb·m·i, *dettima* – (v.at.inconcl. inf. *debmi*, *det-*)
to want
deda, *diari* – (no.ina)
tear, droplet | drizzle
de̊~deu~del, *dela* – (no.ina)
roll, cylinder, tube
dege, *de̊ri* – (no.ina)
little boat
degga, *degari* – (no.ina)
story, lie

dehruvven – (adv.)
recently
del·a, *dedla* – (v.at. inf. *delmi*)
to wear | to show, to display, to exhibit
delpi·a, *delpua* – (v.at inf. *delpimi*)
to turn over
demo, *deṡi~demme* – (no.ani/.ina)
bone
demy~deġmy, *demme ~deġme–* (no.ina)
mucus, slime, ooze
deno, *denue* – (no.ina)
arrow
der·i, *dehri* – (v.ui. inf. *derhu*)
to roll | to pass (time) | to run out of (+ELAT)
detku~dedġu, *detkume~detume* – (no.ina)
quality, feature, trait, skill
deumko~deunko, *deumkue~deunkue* – (no.ina)
small bone | little finger, little toe | piece of bone
deumu, *deumme* – (no.ina)
bone (dead, of animals)
deusġa, *deusġari* – (adj.)
flexible, bendable, supple, pliable, elastic, stretchy
deusġa·gamiha, *~gamihka* – (adj.)
flexible-minded, open-minded, open, unprejudiced
deusġė~deusġeu~deusġel, *deusġela* – (no.ina)
flexibility, bendability, suppleness, elasticity
deydna, *deynari* – (no.ina)
whirlpool, whirl, spiral
deyri, *deyrre* – (no.ina)
salmon which stays in lake/river over winter
deysġ·i·ma, *dgeysġuima* – (v.adj)
to be flexible, to bend
diaka, *diakadi* – (no.ina)
collection of bones in a tree | symbol
dida, *diadi* – (no.ina)
girl
diedge, *diekedi* – (adj./.no.ina)
girlish, young (female), youthful | little girl
i·digg·a, *idaḍga* – (v.udit. inf. *diknin*)
to happen, to change (of state)
di, *dui* – (v.ai/.ui. inf. *disa/disu*)
to step
dimma, *dı̂ndi* – (no.ina)
treeless mountain

din, *dı̇́s* – (no.ina)
barren land
dirv·a, *dirdi~dihdi* – (no.ina.pl)
gills
diuksi, *diugsid* – (no.ina)
icicle (also *dyksi*)
dle·i, *dloi* – (v.ui inf. *dlesu*)
to itch, to cause itching
dluosta, *dluostamo* – (adj.)
limp, flaccid, soft, flabby
dlùdla, *dlůlmo* – (no.ina)
shank
dlẏ, *dlẏma* – (adj.)
bending, supple | drooping | huge, big, heavy, soft, massive
doba, *doamo* – (no.ina)
handle
dojote, *dojobmo* – (no.ina)
dispute, disagreement | discord, friction
dotsġa, *dotsġamo* – (no.ina)
idea, thought | concept, notion | image
dụihme, *dụihmedi* – (no.ina)
softened bark, cloth
důnnů, *důnnůma* – (no.ina)
loop, pattern
dyra, *dyhmo* – (no.ina)
turn (in a river)

Dį dį

djadlana, *djalakka* – (no.ina)
front of canoe
djadn·i, *djand* – (v.ui. inf. *djadnisu*)
to cry, to shed tears
djat·i, *djaddi* – (v.ui. inf. *djatsu*)
to mourn (sometimes ditr. + INESS)
dje, *djeri* – (adj./.no.ina)
gray | silver
djet, *djetsta~djeddja* – (no.ina)
gray haired man, old man
djik·a, *djiḍga* – (v.at/.ut. inf. *djikmi/djikmu*)
to decorate, to adorn, to garnish | to cut details in, to carve (out) | to (proudly) display (.ut)
djikami, *djikamitta* – (v.act.part.pl)
ornament(s)

o·djikk·i, *odjikkui* – (v.as inf. *djikna*)
  to show off, to boast | *hen~* to aggrandize oneself, to exaggerate
djikma – (adv.)
  on display, obvious, visible
djoki, *djokko* – (no.ina)
  trap (in snow) | hidden danger

E e

ebo, *ivve* – (no.ina)
  small uninhabitable island
edġe, *eteri* – (no.ina)
  air, sky
eddů, *edůme* – (no.ina)
  fungus
  toteddů 'idiot, cretin, moron, imbecile'
ė~el, *ela* – (no.ina)
  plant
ė·gi, *e*
ėhhjen·i, *ȇhhjedi* – (v.ui. inf. *ȇhhjentu*)
  to smell (like, +ADV): *ijeppil tȇhhjeni* 'X smells like sap'
ėhtuma, *ȇhtuka~ȇhtumari* – (no.ani/.ina)
  balsam poplar
ėmśi, *ȇmśie* – (no.ina)
  smell, odor
ėno, *ȇnue~ȇnobi* – (no.ina)
  bay, cove
ėt, *ȇtsta~ȇddja* – (no.ina)
  swampy soil/ground
egjit, *eihta* – (det.)
  these (long/honorific)
  egjidba, eihba 'these (out of two)'
j·eġ·i, *jesti* – (v.adit/.udit inf. **eġnin/eġnon**)
  to remain (somewhere) (+ILLAT)
ehhama, *ehhakka* – (no.ina)
  seam, stitching | vein, streak, strand, stria(tion)
ehhon, *ehhos* – (no.ina)
  nuance, difference, distinction | over-/undertone
ehl·i, *ehlui* – (v.ui. inf. ehlisu)
  to burst, to blow up (of bubbles, arguments, etc.)
eh·m·i, *evvima* – (v.adj)
  to differ (to +ILLAT)

ehrena, *ehrevva~ehredi* – (no.ani/.ina)
  sharpened stick for fishing
eidbi, *eipie* – (no.ina)
  carver, carving knife
eili·a, *eilua* – (v.at/.ut. inf. *eilimi/eilimu*)
  to hurt (someone's feelings), to offend, to upset
eirha, *eirra* – (no.ani)
  female (of animal/plant)
eiro, *eirue* – (no.ina)
  care | accuracy
eirro, *eirue~eirobi* – (no.ina)
  (careful) work
eiskl·a, *eisklia* – (v.at inf. *eisklami*)
  to interview, to interrogate
eiśtis, *eiśtihi* – (no.ina)
  branch, twig (WESTERN)
eit·a, *eidda* – (v.at inf. *eibmi*)
  to build
eitsi, *eitsġi* – (no.ina)
  wall, barrier (also *ȇtsi*)
um·ekk·i, *umekkui* – (v.pass. inf. *ekkimon*)
  to be born
ekni, *engie* – (no.ina)
  way, path (in grass) | route, way
eko, *ekue~ekobi* – (no.ina)
  product, thing, good, item
ekviri, *egvirre~ekvitśa* – (no.ina/.ani)
  walleye
eleba, *elepri -pśi- ~ eleu* – (no.ina/.ani)
  flower
elepśia – (adv.)
  in bloom, blooming
elet, *eletsta~eleddja* – (no.ina)
  open grassland, pasture, meadow
elgi, *elgie* – (no.ina)
  bloom | prime, peak, height
el·i, *edli* – (v.ui. inf. *elhů*)
  to grow | to change
elio, *eliue~eliobi* – (no.ina)
  offense, insult
elki, *elkie* – (no.ina)
  high grasses, reeds
eltta, *eltari* – (no.ina)
  steam house, sauna
eluri, *elurre* – (adj.)
  great, fantastic | important, basic, major
  elul~elů 'great(ly), fantastic(ally) (adv.)
eluskon, *eluskos* – (adj.)

emġet, *emġetsta* – (no.ina)
 thighs
emre, *emreri* – (no.ina)
 skin rash (also **ůre**)
enneu~ennů, *enneume~ennůme* –
 (quant.)
 any number of, some quantity, some number
ennju, *enjume* – (no.ina)
 pole (used to navigate on water)
enśi, *enohta* – (no.ani)
 early winter
ent·u, *entaju* – (v.aux.utrans. inf. *entoru*)
 not to be likely to (+INF)
epri, *epie* – (no.ina)
 older sibling
erho, *erhue* – (adj.)
 careful, prudent
er·i, *ehri* – (v.ai. inf. *erha*)
 to be careful
om·erkkar·i, *omerkkahri* – (v.usubj. inf. *erkkahsu*)
 to diverge, to branch off
err·i, *eruli* – (v.ai. inf. *errisa*)
 to work (outside) | to be outside | to toil
erva, *ervari* – (no.ina)
 toil, work
ervausġi, *ervausġie* – (no.ina)
 weekend
eski, *eskie* – (adj.)
 empty | hollow
eskujekk·a, *eskujekkia* – (v.at. inf. *eskujekmi*)
 to empty, to empty out (**kat·~**)
eskvari, *eskvatśa~eskvarre* – (no.ani/.ina)
 first daughter married
estot, *estodna* – (num.quard)
 first
estoui – (adv.)
 (for) the first time
eśi, *ehta~etta* – (num.ani/.ina)
 two: *eśi (ta)boaddjeri* 'the whole nine years, the whole shabang'
  ehnet 'twelve'
  iesġa 'twenty'
  eśven 'twice'
(om·)eśitġ·i, *(om)eśitġui* – (v.ui/.usubj. inf. *eśitġisul eśitġina*)
 to (get) split (in two) | to separate (.usubj)
eśśemis, *eśśemhi* – (no.ina)
 Tuesday
eśut, *eśudna* – (card.num)
 second
 eśuui '(for) the second time'
ets·a, *etsta* – (v.at. inf. *etsmi*)
 to start, to begin (+ILLAT)
eu, *eme* – (no.ina)
 scab, scar, cicatrix
euk·a, *euḍga* – (v.ut/.at. inf. *eukmu/eukmi*)
 to produce, to yield (.ut) | to supply, to provide (.at) | *euk·iul·a* 'to secrete'
eukken~eukkil~ůkli – (adv.)
 a little (COMP. *ůkne*, SUP. *ůihba*)
eulbi~ėulbi, *eulbie~e̊ulbimo* – (no.ina)
 hoof
euljaka, *euljaġi -śi-* – (no.ina)
 bouquet of flowers | flowery place
euma, *eukka* – (quant.)
 a little (COMP. *onda*, SUP. *olla*, SUP.GEN *uhla*)
eura, *eumo~euhmo* – (quant.)
 few (COMP. *ohta*, SUP. *olra*, SUP.GEN *ouhra*)
euḍgena, *eukedi* – (no.ina)
 sandy forest ground, sandy beach with trees
eul·hi, *eultśagi* – (no.ani.pl)
 (open) field
euvv·a, *euḍḍa* – (v.ut. inf. *eummu*)
 to reach, to be long enough to (+COP +ILLAT)
j·euvv·i, *jeuḍḍi* – (v.uditr. inf. *eunnon*)
 to reach, to be long enough to (+ILLAT)
euot, *ůboddja* – (no.ina)
 unimportant person
ėu, *ůbů* – (no.ina)
 sand(y place)
ėuntsġi, *e̊untsġid* – (adj.)
 having many bays/inlets
evvat, *euatta* – (det.)
 this (long/honorific)
 evvaḍba, euappa 'this (out of two)'
 evvats, euatsta~euaddja 'this (out of many)'
eydnůt·a, *eydnůtta* – (v.at. inf. *eydnůbmi*)
 to modernize, to freshen up, to spruce up
eydvůr·a, *eydvůrr·a* – (v.at.inf. *eydvůhmi*)
 to practice, to perfect, to edge
eygi, *eyhta* – (det.)

safe and sound

these
   eyśpa, eyhba 'these (out of two)'
   eytsği, eyhtsa 'these (out of many)'
eyg·ni   – (det.)
   like these, like such, such
eykv·a, *eykvia*   – (v.at. inf. *eykvami*)
   to want to fight, to look for a fight, to be belligerent
eyskon, *eyskos*   – (adj.)
   iceless, not covered in ice
eytkůl·i, *eytkůdli*   – (v.ui. inf. *eytkůlsů*)
   to die of cold
eyd̯g·a, *eyg̯ga*   – (v.at. inf. *eyd̯gami*)
   to want to fight | to provoke
ẹb·ů, *ẹmiů*   – (v.utrans. inf. *ẹllů*)
   to be(come) disgusted, to feel contempt/aversion/outrage for (+ELAT)

G g

gà·gi, *gẹi̯agi*   – (no.ina.pl)
   summer solstice
gabġas, *gapahi*   – (no.ina)
   larva
gabśi, *gabśika*   – (no.ina)
   fool, moron, idiot
gade, *gaika*   – (no.ina)
   rake
ga·gama, *gagamġa*   – (no.ina)
   condolences, compassion, empathy | pity
gagi   – (postp.)
   with (comitative)
gagulka, *gaulkka*   – (no.ina)
   community, locality, neighborhood
gaist·a, *gaistia*   – (v.at. inf. *gaistami*)
   to allow to speak
gaitsa, *gaitska*   – (no.ina)
   meteor, shooting star
gakna, *gangaka*   – (no.ina)
   net (for fishing)
gakv·a, *gakvia*   – (v.at. inf. *gakvami*)
   to (want to) befriend, to approach in a friendly way
gakvobmot, *-bmotta*   – (adj.)
   friendly
gala~-gla,   – (postp./suff.)
   with (instrumental)

gali, *galka*   – (no.ina)
   (salmon) roe
galmi·m·i, *galmumi*   – (v.adj)
   to be carrying eggs, to be pregnant
galmot, *galmotta*   – (adj.)
   soft, mushy, squishy, spongy | pregnant (with eggs)
gama, *gamġa, -śi-*   – (no.ina)
   character, personality, nature, temper
gapsan, *gabsanta*   – (no.ina)
   placenta
gari   – (postp.)
   instead (+GEN.)
   garita 'instead' (movement to)
   garika 'instead' (movement from
garike, *garikka*   – (adj./no.ina)
   boyish, young (male), youthful | little boy
gasi, *gatta~gaska–* (no.ani/.ina)
   moon: *gaskia* 'during the night, secretly, in secret'
gat·koanta·ḥḥ·a, *-koantia-*   – (v.at. inf. *gatkoantaḥḥami*)
   to take for granted, to neglect
gattia   – (postp. +GEN.)
   in the presence of, in the case of
gaugi, *gauhta*   – (det.)
   those (distal)
   gauśpa, gauhba 'those (out of two)'
   gautsği, gauhtsa 'those (out of many)'
gaug·ni   – (det.)
   like those, like such, such
o·gauld·a, *ogauldia*   – (v.asubj. inf. *gauldena*)
   to discuss (something together)
gausun, *gausunta -ōri-*   – (no.ina)
   full moon
gauta, *gautra*   – (no.ina)
   color, hue, shade
gaykk·a, *gaykkia*   – (v.ut inf. *gaykmi*)
   to satisfy, to fulfill
gedl·i, *gelli~gedlui*   – (v.ai/.ui. inf. *gedlisa/gedlisu*)
   to work (.ai) | to function, to operate, to act, to behave (.ui)
gedlva, *gedlvari~gelvari*   – (no.ina)
   function, behavior, role, task, purpose
gedna, *genari*   – (no.ina)
   nut, kernel
gegeme, *gẽmmi*   – (no.ina)

hem | border | trim, trimming, cut
gegen, *geis* – (no.ina)
 mouth (vulgar)
geggus, *geguhi* – (no.ina)
 quack
geg·i, *getki* – (v.ui. *geksu*)
 to be open (at one end)
gegjin, *gejis* – (no.ina)
 big snout, big nose
gegna, *gegnari* – (no.ina)
 den
gei, *geje* – (no.ina)
 snout, muzzle, nose
geig·a, *giga~gigga* – (v.at. inf. *geihmi*)
 to share
geinkena, *geinkedi* – (no.ina)
 oak-forest
gek·i, *geḑgi* – (v.ui. inf. *geksu*)
 to feel, to seem (+adv): *gjosil engeki* 'I feel tired'
gekkon, *gekkos* – (no.ina)
 slope, hillside
gek·ō – (adv.)
 seemingly, apparently, supposedly
gelj·a, *gedlj·a* – (v.at./.ut. inf. geljami/geljamu)
 to comfort (.at) | to soothe (.ut)
geljabmis, *geljamha* – (adj.)
 comforting, soothing
gendot, *gendotsta~gendoddja* – (adj.)
 tall, high
geskk·i, *geskkui* – (v.ai/.ui. inf. *geskkisa/geskkisu*)
 to make a sound
o·getild·i, *ogetildui* – (v.asubj/.at. inf. *getildena*)
 to come across (each other), to meet (each other)
geudl·u, *geullu* – (v.utrans inf. *geudlolu*)
 to be worth doing, to be possible
geuhna, *geuhnari* – (no.ina)
 mouth of a river
geunko, *geunkue* – (no.ina)
 spore
giabmi, *guoma* – (num.irr)
 hundred
o·gjahts·i, *ogjahtsta* – (v.asubj. inf. *gjahtsina*)
 to lie down

giamra, *giamradi* – (no.ina)
 one hundred thousand (100,000)
gjaukama, *gjaukakka* – (no.ina)
 down (feathers)
giba, *giadi* – (no.ina)
 small problem, little issue
gidlk·i, *gidlkui* – (v.ui. inf. *gidklisu*)
 to break, to crack, to give under, to fracture | to surrender, to give up
gid·u, *giddu* – (v.utrans inf. *gidlu*)
 to dry in the open (also *gid·ů*, *ge·y*)
gieḑbi, *giepid* – (no.ina)
 drying frame | frame(work)
gjegji, *gjehta* – (det.)
 those (long/honorific)
  gjeiba, gjehba 'those (out of two)'
  gjeits, gjehtsa 'those (out of many)'
giegjo, *giejodi* – (no.ina)
 apex, tip, climax
gjekes, *gjekehi~gjehki* – (no.ina)
 year
gjekesġi, *gjekehji~gjekeśśi~gjekśi* – (no.ani)
 birthday
gieko, *giekodi* – (no.ina)
 glance, peek, peep
giga, *giḑḑi/giubi* – (no.ina/.ani)
 goose
gige·moni, *·mōkko* – (no.ina)
 milky way (lit. goose path)
gigjes, *gigjehi* – (adj.)
 sharp
a·gigj·u, *agidju* – (v.ui. inf. *gigjůrů*)
 to become sharp | to improve | to reach a climax | to become dull (~dna- +REVERS)
gikk·a, *gǐkkia* – (v.at. inf. *gǐkmi*)
 to sharpen, to whet, to file | to improve | to climax
girha, *gǐrhadi* – (no.ina)
 flock of geese
gik·a, *giḑga* – (v.at. inf. *gikmi*)
 to glance, peek, peep
gikis, *gikihi* – (no.ina)
 shard, sliver, splinter, chip
gikuni, *gikōdi* – (no.ina)
 cartilage | larynx (often *gikun*)
gilra, *gilradi* – (no.ina)
 wet weather, rain (over many days)
gimha, *gimhadi* – (adj.)
 pleasant, nice

gimjukk·a, *gimjukkia* – (v.ut. inf. *gimjukmu*)
to be pleasing, to make feel nice
gimjukkabmis, *-amhi* – (adj.)
pleasing, appeasing, pleasant
gimjun·i, *gimjudi* – (v.ui. inf. *gimjuntu*)
to feel nice, to feel pleasant, to appear pleasant
ginden, *gindes* – (no.ina)
danger
gind·i·ma, *ginduima* – (v.adj)
dangerous
gjoah·m·i, *gjoarrima* – (v.adj)
to be doubtful, to doubt
gjosin, *gjosis* – (adj.)
tired
gjos·m·i, *gjohima~gjobmi* – (v.adj)
to be tired
gjorha, *gjorhamo* – (adj.)
doubtful, uncertain
gjori, *gjohko* – (no.ina)
doubt, uncertainty, hesitation
giri, *giṡid* – (no.ina)
(leather) pants
gitsin, *gitsis* – (no.ina)
stain, mark, pigment (pl. *gitsinka*)
gjykin, *gjykis* – (no.ina)
snowshoes
gjylppa, *gjylpamo* – (no.ina)
wet snow
hę·goagji, *hę·goajika* – (no.ina)
stimulus, irritant
goaiġa, *goaiġaka* – (adj.)
talkative, who speaks quickly
goakla, *goaglaka* – (no.ina)
mollusca
goamun, *goamunta -ōri-* – (no.ina)
human skull
gogants·i~gogats·i, *gogantsui~gogatski* – (v.ui. inf. *gogantsisu~gogatsisu*)
to limp, to hobble
gogantsuj·a, *gogantsuvva* – (v.ut. inf. *gogantsuimi*)
to make limp | to hurt (in a food)
gogj·a, *godja* – (v.at inf. *gogjami*)
to adze | *hę~* to excite, to exasperate, to agitate
goi, *gogjo* – (no.ina)
edge, point | sting(er)
goka, *gogmo* – (no.ina)
sheath, case, envelope | condom | foreskin
golk·i, *golkui* – (v.ai. *golkisa*)
to live in community, to live together
gonne, *gommo~gomno* – (no.ina)
rind, peel, skin (of food)
goskka, *goskkia* – (v.at. inf. *goskkami*)
to betray
gosulha, *gosulhamo* – (adj.)
calm, quiet, tranquil
gosú~gosul, *gosuri* – (no.ina)
calm, tranquility
gośvari, *gośvahko* – (no.ina)
oak wood
gųesi, *gųesse* – (no.ina)
travel, journey, trip
netsen·gųesi 'adventure'
guni, *guja* – (no.ani)
late fall
guokveid·i, *guokveiddi* – (v.ai inf. *guokveitsa*)
to play hard-to-catch, to fool around
guokvo, *guokouį~guogvoma* – (no.ina)
frog
gus·i, *guhi* – (v.ai. inf. *gussa*)
to travel
tam·ġusi to move/go somewhere (for good)
man·gusi to migrate
guųis, *gẙhhi* – (no.ina)
grape | (vulg.) balls, testicles
gůinůn, *gůinůs* – (no.ina)
little room, little space, small corner: *iketui rotsi gůinůsta* 'to look in every nook and cranny'
gųeklis, *gųeglihi* – (no.ina)
foreskin | placenta
gybi, *gůid* – (no.ina)
horn
gylkjon, *gylkjos* – (no.ina)
community, small village
gymṡi, *gymṡid* – (no.ina)
frost, period of frost
gẏbi, *gybid* – (no.ina)
adze

Ġ ġ

ġaḍbi, *ġapiko* – (no.ina)
vase | puffball | spleen

ġalġa, *ġalġaka* – (no.ina)
callus, hardened skin | pad, cushion

ġarkken, *ġarkenta* – (no.ina)
substance, liquid

ġedlvi, *ġedlvie* – (no.ina)
thick fog: *ha ġedlvie* 'to die'

ġem·i, *ġebmi* – (v.ut inf. *ġemsů*)
to shake, to shiver, to tremble

ġendo, *ġendue~ġendobi* – (no.ina)
small salmon

ġertto, *ġertue* – (no.ina)
threshold | brink, edge

ġėugot~ġėuġot, *ġêuvvotsta* – (no.ina)
lies, fiction, fib

ġey, *ġůbů* – (no.ina)
pine con | child, little child (affectionate)

ġibġi, *ġipid* – (no.ina)
wire, rope

ġidi, *ġîd* – (no.ina)
newborn bird (or other cute animal)

ġi, *ġitśa* – (no.ina)
fall, autumn

ġidl·i, *ġîlli* – (v.ui inf. *ġîdlisů*)
to crackle, to pop

ġiġi, *ġîd* – (no.ina)
kid

ġilka, *ġilkadi* – (adj.)
yellow

ġiltsġa, *ġiltsġadi* – (no.ina)
disgust: *itåiki ůattaika ġiltsġadi* 'is disgusted by this' | nausea

ġiskku, *ġiskudi* – (no.ina)
spark, shock

ġokvali, *ġogvalmo* – (no.ina)
stubborn man

ġoli, *ġolko* – (no.ina)
hill, hilltop

ġopp·a, *ġoppia*– (v.at.inf *ġopmi*)
to hit, to knock, to hurt | to tease

ġotroti, *ġotroika* – (no.ani)
bullfrog

ġouskon, *ġouskonta -ōri-* – (no.ina)p
cover for hunting, hiding spot: *pohhịi ġouskōria-nen* 'to miss out on something'

ġu̯adlmi, *ġu̯adlmitta~ġu̯almika* –
(v.act.part.pl or no.ina)
rainbow

ġu̯ebis, *ġu̯eihhi* – (no.ina)
stick to poke (fire) with | (vulg.) penis

ġu̯euri, *ġu̯eurre~ġu̯eutśa* – (no.ina/.ani)
muskellunge

ġu̯evv·i, *ġu̯eḍḍi~ġu̯êuḍḍi* – (v.ai. inf. *ġu̯essa*)
to bark

ġu̯ibmen, *ġu̯imes* – (no.ina)
grasshopper

ġu̯idlen, *ġu̯iles* – (no.ina)
jumping spider, stressed person, tens

ġu̯ir·i, *ġu̯ihri* – (v.ai/.ui. inf *ġu̯irha/ġu̯irhu*)
to jump (insects)

ġumeskon, *ġumeskonta* – (adj.)
depressed, unhappy, miserable, morose

ġuo – (onom.)
sound to show annoyance

ġupo, *ġubma* – (no.ina)
vine, climbing plant

ġůgị·ia – (adv.)
anywhere
ġůita 'anywhere (movement to)'
ġůika 'anywhere (movement from)'

ġůla, *ġůlamo* – (adj.)
short (length)

ġům·ni, *ġů-* – (pron.)
anyone
ġebůkni 'either'
ġetsůkni 'any (of)'
ġůġịů 'anytime'
ġůvva 'in any way'
miġů 'for any reason'

ġůndl·i, *ġůndlůi~ġůndlỷ* – (v.ai inf. *ġůndlisa*)
to sigh | *hẹ~* to die (v.ui)

ġůtġůt, *ġůtġůtsta~ġůtġůddịa* – (no.ina)
crest, tuft

ġvivi, *ġvivid* – (adj.)
large, big, important

ġylky, *ġylkyma* – (no.ina)
peak, sumit | mountain

ġylkymausi – (adv.)
monotonously, boringly

ġymesk·i·ma, *ġymeskuima* – (v.adj)
to feel depressed, unhappy, miserable, morose

H h

h·a, *ma ~sma* – (v.at/.ut. inf. *hami/hamu*)
to eat

håbm·i, *håbmui~håndi* – (v.ai/.ui. inf. *håbmisa/håbmisu*)
to fly

håppo, *håppoka* – (adj.)
broad, ample, wide, vast

håppo·kelbiha, *~kelbihari* – (adj.)
with broad shoulders

habi, *hapra, -si-* – (no.ina)
nipple

habma, *habmaka* – (adj.)
deep, low (of sound)

hadlna, *hadlnaka* – (no.ina)
sea ice

haga, *håka* – (no.ina)
quill, spike

hagja~hagju – (adv.)
then, at that moment

hagjia – (proadv.)
around there
hagjita 'to ~'
hagjika 'from ~'

hahhja – (proadv.)
there
hahba 'to ~'
hahka 'from ~'

hai, *hagja* – (no.ina)
glue, pitch | spit, liquid | sperm, cum

haibmoki, *haimokka* – (no.ina)
depression

haiddja – (proadv.)
right there
haidda 'to ~'
haitka 'from ~'

haid·ni – (det.)
like that, like such, such

haihpo, *haihpoka* – (adj.)
strong, spicy

haimp·i·ma, *haimpuima* – (v.adj)
to smart, to sting, to burn

haimpo, *haimpoka* – (adj.)
hot, spicy, stinging, smarting, burning

hait, *haitta* – (det.)
that (medial)
haidba, haippa 'that (out of two)'
haits, haitsta~haidja 'that (out of many)'
haitteui 'that manieth'
haittȇ 'that time'

hakno, *hangua~hangoka* – (num.ani/.ina)
five
hagnet 'fifteen'
hanra 'fifty'
hanguen 'five times'
haknet 'fifth'

halge·i, *halgui* – (v.ui inf. **halgesu**)
to be lightning

hallu, *haluka* – (no.ina)
electricity | flash, lightning (also **halgu**)

halma, *halka* – (no.ani)
(honorific title)
halkaita – (postp). 'honorable for'

hamit, *hamitta* – (no.ina)
metal, ore

hammju·a, *hammjaja* – (v.ut.imp inf. *hammjumu*)
to be dear to, to love: *tahammjuaka* 'X is dear to me'

hanna~honna, *hanka~honka* – (adj.)
fair, beautiful, pretty (adv. *hagji~hagjii*)

hanni – (adv.)
thus, like that, thereby

hantoma, *hantokka* – (no.ina)
(pathological) liar

hantu·i, *hanti* – (v.ai. inf. *hantosa*)
to lie (to someone +ALLAT)

hapri, *hapika* – (no.ina)
flock of birds

hartta, *hartaka* – (no.ina)
crown

hatr·u, *hatraju* – (v.aux.utrans. inf. *hatroru*)
ought to, should (+INF)

hatskon, *hatskonta* – (adj.)
hairless, bald

haukl·i, *hauklui* – (v.ai. inf *hauklisa*)
to have a meal, to eat a meal

hauma, *haumka~haumaka* – (adj./.no.ina)
bright (.adj) | brightness, light (.no.ina)

hausġa, *hausġaka* – (adj.)
edible | wholesome

haust·a, *haustia* – (v.at. inf. *haustami*)
to allow to eat, to let be eaten

hauue, *hameka~hauueka* – (no.ina/adj.)

(something) worth eating, appetizing
hauvv·a, *haudda* – (v.ut/.imp. inf. *haummu*)
to make want to eat | to be tempted, to want to (.imp); *so hauvvasa-a gatamani deita?* 'are you tempted to come along?
havva, *hadda* – (adj.)
such, like that, such as that
hėbi, *hėgjie* – (no.ina)
chick (newborn bird)
hegjina, *hejidi* – (no.ina)
restaurant
hegista, *hegistari* – (adj.)
unsalted, sweat (of water)
hego, *hivve~hevvue~hevvobi* – (no.ina)
salt | spice
heh·m·i, *herrima* (*her-*) – (v.adj)
to be cold: *hehmika* 'I am cold'
hehta – (adv.)
completely, entirely
hej·a, *hevva* – (v.at/.ut. inf. *heimi/heimu*)
to feed | to fortify (.ut), to strengthen
heje, *hejeri* – (adj.)
cold
hejeri, *hejetśa* – (no.ani)
winter (also **hjeri**)
heidn·i, *heinti* – (v.ai. inf. *heidnisa*)
to wake, to stay awake
heiggena, *heigedi* – (no.ina)
salty marsh
heih·m·i, *heiddami* – (v.adj)
to be appetizing, to be enticing
heimkena, *heimkedi* – (no.ina)
nesting area
hejoh·m·i, *hejorrima* (*hejor-*) – (v.adj)
to feel weak
hejol·i, *hejodli* – (v.ui. inf. *hejolsu*)
to shiver
hejomi, *hejomme* – (adj.)
winter-like, wintery
hejona, *hejodi* – (adj.)
weak, frail, delicate, feeble
hejù~hejul, *hejula* – (no.ina)
shiver, tremble, quiver
hekken, *hekkes* – (no.ina)
crystal
helon, *helos* – (no.ina)
pregnant mammal
helva, *helvari~helu* – (no.ina/.ani)
female moose, pregnant moose
hemi, *hemta~hemme* – (no.ani/.ina)
bird
hemmė(h)i – (onom.)
hurray! hurrah! huzzah!
henet·ka, *henetsta~heneddja* – (no.ina.pl)
birch shoes
hengy, *hengyme* – (no.ina)
venom, toxin
henn·a, *hennia* – (v.at. inf. *hennami*)
to be responsible for (+COP +ILLAT)
i·henn·i, *ihennui* – (v.aditr. inf. *hennanin*)
to be responsible for (+ILLAT)
hepsa, *hebsari* – (no.ina)
jewel, gem(stone)
hesko, *heskue* – (no.ina)
small bay
heskv·a, *heskvia* – (v.ut. inf. *heskvamu*)
to have the bad luck of (+INF)
hesse, *hesgi~hesseri* – (no.ina)
shovel, spade | paddle, large oar | petal
o·hett·i, *ohettui* – (v.ui inf. *hetnu*)
to scatter, to get caught in the wind
heutsġo, *heutsġue~heutsġobi* – (no.ina)
burbot
hėulkena, *hėulkemmo* – (no.ina)
place where melt water pools | pool
hey, *heyme~hůme* – (no.ina)
swamp
hey – (adv./postp.direct)
up
  heyta 'up (to)'
  heytari 'upward | landward, up (onto) land'
  heytatsti 'up along | along the top'
  heyka 'up above'
(o·)heyt·i, *(o)heytti–* (v.ai/.asubj. inf. *heydna*)
to disembark, to hit land, to land | to stop | to arrive, to return
hękaingil – (adv.)
generally
hęmma, *hęmari* – (no.ina)
(place) up | top
  hęmaria 'on land, at home, back (from fishing/hunting)'
hęni – (adv./postp.desti)
up
  henda 'up (to)'
  henga '(from) up'

hià, *hiala* – (no.ina)
  garden | sheltered spot where a specific plant grows
hi̯a̍hl·i, *hi̯a̍hlui* – (v.ai inf. hi̯a̍hlisa)
  to find shelter, to take shelter | *i·hi̯ahli oke̜tśaita* 'to find a compromise, to take a less desirable decision'
hiamin, *hiamis* – (no.ina)
  milk and honey drink
hiddi̯uj·a, *hiddi̯udi̯a* – (v.at. inf. hiddi̯uima)
  to stack up, to heap up, to pile up
hide, *hieri* – (no.ina)
  hair
hie, *hiddi̯i* – (no.ina)
  pile, mount | a large amount, a lot (.quant)
hiebme, *hiemedi* – (no.ina)
  fur coat (on animal)
hi̯eidnilit, *hi̯einilitsta* – (no.ina)
  wake, funeral
hi̯eimekk·a, *hi̯eimekkia* – (v.ut. inf. hi̯eimekmu)
  to make (feel) hot; *hi̯eimekkaka konitse* 'walking makes me hot'
hi̯eimen·i, *hi̯eimedi* – (v.ui. inf. hi̯einentu)
  to feel hot, to seem hot, to appear hot; *hi̯eimeni kindi-so* 'your hand feels hot'
hi̯eimentsġ·i, *hi̯eimentsġui* – (v.imp)
  to be (far) too hot, there to be a heat wave
hi̯euli, *hi̯eulle* – (no.ina)
  melt water
higi̯ekk·a, *higi̯ekkia* – (v.ut. inf. higi̯ekmu)
  to make (feel) cold; *si higi̯ekkasa-a byltyma* 'isn't the wind making you cold?
higi̯en·i, *higi̯edi* – (v.ui. inf. higi̯entu)
  to feel cold, to appear cold; *higi̯eni kindi-go* 'my hand(s) feel(s) cold'
higi̯entsġ·i, *higi̯entsġui* – (v.imp)
  to be (far) too cold
hihlon, *hihlos* – (no.ina)
  shelter (temporary, from weather)
hi̯ib·m·i, *hi̯istima* (hi̯ih-) – (v.adj)
  to (be/become) slanted/tilted | for there to be a slope, to slope
hi̯ihi, *hi̯ihid* – (adj.)
  slanted, tilted, leaning
himha, *hĩmra* – (no.ani)
  woman, female character, she
himi, *hĩmid* – (adj.)
  hot, warm

hingut, *hingutsta~hinguddi̯a* – (no.ina)
  ghost, spirit
hi̯okot, *hi̯okotta* – (no.ina)
  care, attention, medical care
hi̯om·a, *hi̯obma* – (v.at. inf. hi̯ommi)
  to ought to (+COP +ELAT)
hi̯o̍mno, *hi̯o̍mu̯a* – (no.ani)
  midwife
hi̯o̍nna, *hi̯o̍nnamo* – (adj.)
  careful, precise, meticulous (adv. *hi̯o̍gi̯en~hi̯o̍gi̯il*)
hirh·i·ma, *hirhuima* – (v.adj)
  to be dim | to be drunk
hirhot, *hirhotsta* – (adj.)
  dim | stupid, slow, drunk
hiri, *hiśid~hitśa* – (no.ina/.ani)
  (a single) hair (often animate in the plural)
hisku̍, *hisku̍di* – (no.ina)
  bad luck, curse
hiśkora, *hiśkohdi~hiśkosta* – (no.ina)
  cloudberry
hi̯utu, *hi̯ubma* – (no.ina)
  necklace
hi̯u̍~hi̯ul, *hi̯uri* – (no.ina)
  sea water
hi̯u̍baka, *hi̯u̍ahma* – (no.ina)
  tidal pool | need to pee: *naki hi̯u̍baka* 'I need to pee'
hi̯u̍di̯a – (adv.)
  pregnant
hoadna, *hoadnaka* – (adj.)
  surprised
hoalleri, *hoalehka* – (no.ina)
  court, courting (someone)
hoalra, *hoalraka* – (no.ina)
  odonata (dragonfly-like insects)
hoats·m·i, *hoatskima* – (v.adj)
  taken a back, astonished, amazed
hobbe, *hobmo* – (no.ina)
  (ear)wax
hodl·a, *holla* – (v.at. inf. hodlmi)
  to choose, to select | to decide
hogi, *hokko* – (no.ina)
  pearl, ball, globe, sphere
hogi̯u̍, *hoi̯u̍ma* – (no.ina)
  nonsense, rubbish, gibberish
hoġen, *hois* – (no.ina)
  groin
hohtari – (adv.)

on board, aboard
hoivva, *hoimmo* – (no.ina)
flooding/flooded river/area
hokja·m·i, *hokjimi* – (v.adj)
to be blind(ed)
hokju, *hokjumo* – (adj.)
blind
hokoma – (adv.)
back and forth
hokon, *hokonta -ōri-* – (no.ina)
(large) boulder, rock, stone
holho, *holra* – (no.ani)
nymph, female spirit
holi, *holko* – (no.ina)
stem, stalk, trunk | cane
hol·m·i, *hodlmi* – (v.adj)
to be malnourished/sickly/starving | to (become/be) sparse(ly vegetated)
holodlen, *holodles* – (no.ina)
cellar spider, spider
holokken~horokken, *holokkes~horokkes* – (no.ina)
dragon fly
holot, *holotta* – (adj.)
thin, sparse
holp·i·ma, *holpuima* – (v.adj)
to be muffled: *ōkkia konōra salla holpima* 'walking in the snow muffles (our presence) well | to be bored
holpo, *holpoma* – (adj.)
dull, muffled, faded, washed out
holu, *hoda* – (no.ani)
ghost, spirit, soul
homna, *homnamo* – (no.ina)
quiet spot in a river | calm, peace, serenity
honomi, *honŏkko~honomitta* – (no.ina/.ag.part)
(hot) embers
hȯ, *hobo* – (no.ina)
(hot) embers
hopsa·i, *hopsi* – (v.ui inf. *hopsasu*)
to vomit
hori·m·i, *horumi* – (v.adj)
to feel tender/sore: *horimika oboja* 'the bruise feels sore'
horiot, *horiotta* – (adj.)
tender, sore | fragile
hosġon, *hosġonta* – (adj.)
inedible, disgusting

hoto, *hobma* – (no.ina)
peel, layer, coating, sheet, film
huġuna, *huvvummo* – (no.ina)
ulnus
huhh·i, *huhri* – (v.ui. inf. *huhsu*)
to shine
huh·m·i, *huhrima* (*huhh-*) – (v.adj)
to be bright
hum·mi, *huḍḍima* (*huvv-*) – (v.adj)
to be cool/chilly
huoka, *huohmo* – (qant.)
quite (also *ġuoka*)
huopi, *huobmo* – (no.ina)
scout, spy, mole
hủdna, *hủnamo* – (no.ina)
sweat hut, sweat lodge, Siwa sauna
huḍḍe, *huhhemo~huhmo* – (no.ina)
light, brightness
huųo, *huoma* – (no.ina)
fog
huvvi, *hummo* – (adj/.no.ina)
comfortably/comfortable cold
huvvuhma, *huvvuhmamo* – (adj.)
cool, frisky, chilly, chill, brisk
huvvu·kemśua, *~kemśuari* – (adj.)
(with) a cool morning
hủhhja, *hủśmo* – (no.ina)
heron
hủpśi, *hủppohta* – (no.ani)
purple finch
hųeġġi, *hųeġie* – (no.ina)
sunny weather
hyhhjys, *hyśyhi* – (no.ina)
mumble, sound of people speaking
hylys, *hylhi* – (no.ina)
thin, scrawny person
hynji, *hygjid* – (no.ina)
sponge
hyśi, *hyśmo* – (no.ina)
pregnant salmon
hỷ, *hỷma* – (adj.)
beautiful, gorgeous | bright, brilliant, dazzling

I i

i̯a·, *i̯ei̯a* – (v.at. inf. *i̯åmi*)
to raise, to bring up

i̯ål·hi, *i̯å(l)tśagi* – (no.ani.pl)
male rite of passage

i̯ålppi~jayppi, *i̯alpika~i̯aypika~i̯ållumi* – (no.ina/.ani)
hare

i̯adi̯u·a, *i̯adi̯ia* – (v.at/.ut. inf. *i̯adi̯omi/i̯adi̯omu*)
to make fall, to trip, to trick

i̯ahhi̯·u, *i̯aśtu* – (v.aux.utrans. inf. *i̯ahhi̯oru*)
to be able to (endurance/will) (+ELAT)

i̯ai̯alba, *i̯ai̯albaka~i̯ai̯alu* – (no.ina/ani)
horse tail (*equisetum*): *nielsōta i̯ai̯alu-nen* 'to gather's ones belongings and leave, to pack up and go'

i̯aingo, *i̯aingoka* – (no.ina)
(one's) life

i̯air·i, *i̯airri* – (v.ai. inf. *i̯airha*)
to row

i̯aiśke, *i̯aiśkeka* – (no.ina)
senility

i̯amġa – (interj.)
hey (to get someone's attention)

i̯amma, *i̯amġa* – (no.ina)
the other side

i̯amnon, *i̯amnonta -ōri-* – (no.ina)
smoke tent, sauna tent | confusion, dark (be in the dark): *konikni i̯amnōria* 'to be in the dark, not to know'

i̯ampo – (postp.)
on the other side (stat.)
   i̯abmo   to the other side
   i̯amsi   along the other side
   i̯amġa   from the other side

iamon, *iamos* – (no.ina)
fauna

i̯anna, *i̯anka, -śi-* – (no.ina)
piled-up snow, snow bank, snow (on branches)

i̯asuma~i̯asma, *i̯asukka~i̯askka* – (no.ina)
skin (of dead animal) | leather

i̯aśśi, *i̯aśśid* – (no.ina)
old age, senility

i̯aśk·u, *i̯aśkai̯u* – (v.utrans. inf. *i̯aśkoru*)
to grow older

i̯ata, *i̯atka (-tśi-)* – (no.ina)
carved bowl | open area where people sit, theatre

i̯atkini, *i̯atkii̯a* – (no.ani)
late winter

ibengi, *iengid* – (no.ina)
time needed to smoke meat | time (in the context of waiting): *neni iengid-nen* 'to do one's part, to serve one's time'

ibme, *imedi* – (no.ina)
ice (to walk on)

idebb·a, *iebbadi* – (no.ina)
a clumsy person

id·i, *iddi* – (v.ui. inf. *itsu*)
to fall

idmi, *idda~iddetta~iddutta* – (no.ani)
raven

ie, *iddi̯i* – (no.ina)
crack (where water seeps through), fracture

iedot, *iedotta* – (adj.)
deciduous

i̯e~i̯eu~i̯el, *i̯ela* – (no.ina)
growth, success, increase

i̯ehr·u, *i̯ehrai̯u* – (v.aux.utrans. inf. *i̯ehroru*)
to be possible (favourable conditions) (+ILLAT)

i̯eibm·a, *i̯einda* – (v.at/.ut inf. *i̯eibmami/i̯eibmamu*)
to form, to create, to build, to shape

i̯eidlentsġ·i, *i̯eidlentsġui* – (v.imp)
to be (far) too late (for +ILLAT)

i̯eiddo, *i̯eihhue~i̯eihhobi* – (no.ina)
run, race

i̯eigge, *i̯eigeri* – (no.ina)
snow trench | ditch, furrow (in snow)

i̯eita, *i̯eitri* – (no.ina)
structure, shape, form | system, organization

i̯ei̯umi, *i̯ei̯umme~i̯ei̯utta* – (no.ina/.ani)
shrike

i̯eilgil·a, *i̯eilgidla* – (v.at. inf. *i̯eilgilmi*)
to get to know (someone, over time)

jemr·a, *jemria* – (v.at/.ut inf. *jemrami/jemramu*)
to bore, to pierce, to go through (a surface) | to exasperate, to provoke (.ut)

jenji, *jegjie* – (no.ina)
snake, viper

jest·a, *jestia* – (v.at. inf. *jestami*)
to succeed, to achieve (+ INF.)

jeḍḍ·i, *jekki* – (v.ai. inf. *jehsa*)
to run

jeydna, *jeydnari* – (adj.)
adult (usually male)

jeyġġů, *jeyġůma* – (no.ina)
nap

jeyt·a, *jeydda* – (v.at. inf. *jeybmi*)
to parboil (mushrooms) to remove poison

igjut, *ijutsta~ijuddja* – (no.ina)
personality, humor, mood, temper, disposition

igmo, *igmodi* – (no.ina)
rapidly changing weather, uncertain weather | uncertainty, ambiguity

iġ·a, *ista* – (v.at. inf. *iġmi*)
to accept | to agree | to trust (that something is)
    tym·iġa 'to resolve to, to accept (one's faith)'
    îl·iġa 'to pass on, to give (something as a gift), to entrust'
    kem·iġa 'to agree (with +DIT)

ihko~ihkõ – (adv.)
sometimes, occasionally, from time to time

i·, *îmi* – (v.ui. inf. *îsů*)
to change

i~il~iu~iů~iddji~iddjil~iddjiu~iddjiů~iddjir, *ila~îla* – (no.ina)
darkness, pitch dark | shadow

ini, *îja* – (no.ani)
early summer

ihha – (adv.)
only, just

ihna – (conj./adv.)
of course, yes, certainly

idla, *îdladi* – (adj.)
late

idlu, *îludi* – (no.ina)
sprout, bud, offshoot, sprig

igjůn·a, *îgjůtta* – (v.ut. inf. *îgjůmnů*)
to inspire

ijeb·m·i, *ijepsima* (*ijepp-*) – (v.adj)
to feel sticky, to be sticky/tacky: *ijebmi tśomumia ijuhdi* 'my fingers are sticky because of the sap' (lit. the sap stickies in my fingers)

ijeppi, *ijeppid* – (adj.)
sappy, sticky, gluey, tacky, gummy

ijeppů~ijeppul, *ijeppula* – (no.ina)
stickiness, tackiness

ijeppi·tiekiha, *~tiekihdi* – (adj.)
sticky-handed, with sticky hands

ihhj·a, *ista~išta* – (v.at/.adit. *îšmi/îhhjanin*)
to thank (for +ELAT)

ihhj·ia – (adv.)
(not) anywhere
    îhta '(not) anywhere (movement to)'
    îhka '(not) anywhere (movement from)'
    îhhµa '(not) in any way'

ih·mi, *îh-* – (pron.)
(not) anyone
    îbehki 'not either'
    îtsehki 'not any (of)'
    set îhhju 'not ever'

ihpi, *îhpid* – (no.ina)
arrowhead | penis (*vulg.*)

jikia – (adv.)
west
    jîhta 'westwards, to the west'
    jîhteri 'towards the west'
    jîhtsi 'along the west(face/side)'
    jîhka 'from the west'

jiki·mainnjut, *jki·mainnjutta–* (no.ina)
eider duck

ikså, *îgsęgji* – (no.ina)
experienced archer

iks·i, *îksui* – (v.at/.adit. inf. *îksisa/îksinin*)
to shoot (an arrow) (at/Ø +ILLAT)

iku, *îhdi~îkudi* – (no.ina)
snow bench

il·a, *îdla~îlla~îlda* – (v.at. inf. *îlmi*)
to know (someone)

vův·il·a, *-îdla~-îlla~îlda* – (v.at. inf. *vůvvîlmi*)
to forgive

ilama, *îlakka* – (no.ina)
facade, front, place in front

ilk·a, *îlkia* – (v.at/.adit. inf. *îlkami/îlkanin*)
to present, to offer, to suggest | to give

ilkobm·a, *îlkonda* – (v.dit. inf. *îlkobmanin*)

to make an offering to
ing·i, *ĭndi* – (v.ai. inf. *ĭngisa*)
to live: *nĭnni sĭngi?* 'how are you?'
inta – (adv.)
still
iɟom·u, *iɟobmu* – (v.aux.utrans. inf. *iɟomlu*)
to be possible (time/conditions) (+INF)
irri, *ĭrid* – (no.ina)
arrow
isp·a, *ĭspia* – (v.at/.ut inf. *ĭspami/ĭspamu*)
to pinch, to squeeze
iṡpa, *ĭṡva* – (no.du)
grandparents, elders
it, *ĭtta* – (det.)
that (long/honorific)
ĭdba, *ĭppa* 'that (out of two)'
ĭts, *ĭtsta~ĭddja* 'that (out of many)'
it – (pron.)
you (honorific)
ĭbma PAT.
ĭdġō GEN.
ĭts DAT.
ĭtsi- LOC.
–it POSS.
ĭdġa~ėurŭ PREC
it, *ĭtsta* – (no.ina)
life time, life
iter·a, *ĭtehra* – (v.at. inf. *ĭtehmi*)
to use honorific it
it·i·ma, *ĭddima* – (v.adj)
to be late
itina, *ĭtindi* – (adj.)
late
iki, *ikid* – (no.ina)
axe
ik-, *ikih-* – (act.nom)
axe
ikket, *ikketsta* – (no.ina)
birth
ikos, *ikohi~ihki* – (no.ina)
(small) axe
iljil·i, *iljidli* – (v.ui/.ai inf. *iljilsu/iljilsa*)
to be alive, to live: *jahhju iljilsa~·lsu* 'to survive'
iljon, *iljos* – (no.ina)
vegetation
ilkima, *ilkia* – (no.du)
temples | forehead
ilun, *ilus* – (no.ina)

young (boy/girl)
imanget, *imangetsta* – (no.ina)
preparation | maturation
imisi, *imisti* – (no.ina)
animal
imogjet, *imogjetsta* – (no.ina)
whitening, paling
jobu, *jouma~jobma* – (no.ina)
sheaf, bundle, stack
iskan·hi, *ĭskajagi* – (no.ani.pl)
vernal equinox
iski, *ĭskid* – (no.ina/.ani)
woman
iju·ak·i, *ijuaḍgi* – (v.ai. inf. *ijuaksa*)
to cut boughs
ijurha, *ijurhadi* – (adj.)
vigorous, strong, robust, sturdy | sappy, juicy
ijurhė~ijurheu~ijurhel, *ijurhela* – (no.ina)
vigor, strength, robustness, sturdiness | sappiness, juiciness
ijuri, *ijuhdi* – (no.ina)
sap | juice | life spirit, vigor, strength
ijutokni, *ijutongja* – (no.ani)
bough cutter/fetcher
imkki, *imkid* – (no.ina)
swallow
imn·a, *imnia* – (v.at. inf. *imnami*)
to smoke (meat to preserve it)
imni·i, *imnui* – (v.ui inf. *imnisŭ*)
to produce smoke
ind·a, *india* – (v.cop)
to be scattered around
inden – (postp.)
roughly, about, something like: *eṡudna nedda inden* 'something like twenty, two dozens'
inj·i, *injui* – (v.ai. inf. *injisa*)
to sneak, to creep, to slide | to go unnoticed: *injisa kejemi* 'to go (completely) unnoticed' (lit. to sneak like a lynx)
inina, *inindi* – (adj.)
rich, wealthy, well-off
ob·inuk·i, *obinuḍgi* – (v.as inf. *inukna*)
to become wealthy
inủ~inul, *inula* – (no.ina)
wealth
irela, *ireldi* – (adj.)
beautiful

Irhi, *Ihtśa* – (no.ani)
(female personal name)
irhon, *irhos* – (no.ina)
holiday, leave, work-free period
iri, *iśid* – (no.ina)
bark (usually for writing on) | paper | skin
iruoga, *iruohdi* – (no.ina)
coniferous wood
iruorha, *iruorhadi* – (adj.)
made of coniferous wood
irủ~irul, *irula* – (no.ina)
beauty
irva, *irvadi* – (no.ina)
bite
i·sohhi·e·ita – (fixed)
once upon a time
istoma, *istōdi* – (no.ina)
scalp
iśi, *iśid* – (adj.)
old
iśu-(numeral) – (indecl. adj.)
X years old
iśuminesta 11 year old
iśủ, *iśula* – (no.ina)
age
joairha, *joairhaka* – (adj.)
easy to row in | calm, serene, still, tranquil
jokon, *jokonta -ōri-* – (no.ina)
large caribou herd
ioddja – (proadv.)
right there (distal)
iodda 'to ~'
iotka 'from ~'
jodġ·i, *jodġui* – (v.ai inf. *jodġisa*)
to yelp, to scream
iod·ni – (det.)
like that, like such, such
jogja~jogju – (adv.)
then, at that moment (distal)
jogjia – (proadv.)
over there (distal)
jogjita 'to ~'
jogjika 'from ~'
iohhja – (proadv.)
there (distal)
iohba 'to ~'
iohka 'from ~'
iomi – (adv.)
for that reason, thus, so

joni – (adv.)
thus, like that, thereby (distal)
jorro, *jorma* – (no.ina)
young bull
josli, *josliko* – (no.ina)
complication, knot, problem | lump, clump, shapeless aggregate
iot, *iotta* – (det.)
that (distal)
iodba, ioppa~joppa 'that (out of two)'
iots, iotsta~ioddja 'that (out of many)'
iotteui 'that manieth'
iottẻ 'that time'
jovva, *joḍḍa* – (adj.)
such, like that, such as that (distal)
ipro, *ipodi* – (no.ina)
carcass
ismet, *ismetsta* – (no.ina)
leather work
(i)sse̊(h)i – (onom.)
sound to show disbelief
itemi, *itendi~itetta* – (no.ina/.ani)
thrush
itvi, *itvid* – (adj.)
short (time)
iu, *ibi* – (no.ina)
older relative, superior
iuo, *iodi* – (no.ina)
difficult task, difficulty: *ioila~joila~joira* 'with difficulty, hardly'
juoku, *juohma* – (no.ina)
caribou enclosure
jůn·a, *jůtta* – (v.at. inf. *jůmni*)
to finish, to complete
jůtsuma, *jůtsummo* – (no.ina)
fear, paralysis, terror
jůliha~jůlha, *jůlihma~jůlhama* – (adj.)
sweaty
jůli·lielliha, *~liellihdi* – (adj.)
sweaty-palmed, stressed, anxious
jůlů, *jůlma* – (no.ina)
sweat
iv·i, *ivvi* – (v.ui. inf. *issu*)
to increase
iv·õ – (adv.)
increasingly, more and more
jẏ~jyl, *jyla* – (no.ina)
end, ending, extremity, conclusion

K k

kȧhli~kȧhlil, *kȧhliri* – (no.ina)
height, elevation.

kȧhlo, *kȧhloka* – (adj.)
high, elevated, highest

kȧma-, *kȧmġa-* – (act.nom)
paternal grandfather

kadas, *kȧhhi~kalhi* – *(no.ina)*
helmet

kadlka (pron.ina)
the whole
  AG. *kadlka*
  PAT. *kadlµa*
  GEN. *kadlġō*
  DAT. *kadlkis*
  kadlkju 'the whole time'
  kadlkµa 'completely'

kadl·u, *kallu* – (v.aux.utrans inf. *kadloru*)
to be enough, to suffice to/for (+ILLAT)

kaḍgju, *kakjuka* – (no.ina)
fresh wood (also *gaḍgju* or *geḍgy*)

kah·a, *kadġa* – (v.aditr. inf. *kabmi*)
to need (+COP +ELAT)

i·kah·i, *ikadġi* – (v.aditr. inf. *kadnin*)
to need (+ILAT)

kahi, *kaika* – (no.ina)
shell, husk

kahu̇d·a, *kahůdda* – (v.at inf. *kahůbmi*)
to decorate (with shells, prize)

kaibmu, *kaimka* – (no.ina)
walking stick | support (beam)

kaikseuha, *kaikseuhka* – (adj.)
evasive, elusive, vague, ambiguous

kaiksevva, *kaigsegga* – (no.ina)
coward

kaiksi·a, *kaiksua* – (v.at. inf. *kaiksimi*)
to dodge, to dart, to elude, to evade, to avoid, to escape

kalara, *kalahka* – (no.ina)
hole (dug)

kalm·i, *kalmui* – (v.ai. inf. *kalmisa*)
to (go into) battle, to wage war

kalsa, *kalsaka* – (no.ina)
oven | insides, interior, core, centre

kalu̇~kalul, *kaluri* – (no.ina)
stringency, strictness, firmness, rigidity, rigor, discipline | tightness, pressure, compression

kalve, *kalveka* – (adj.)
stringent, strict, firm, rigid, rigorous, disciplined, harsh | tight | under pressure, pressurized, compressed

kalve·geigabmot, *~bmotta* – (adj.)
cheap, miserly, stingy

kammjo, *kamjoka* – (no.ina)
frozen lake | thick ice

kamśe, *kamśeka* – (no.ina)
left hand

kani, *kanka, kanśi-* – (no.ina)
stink, bad smell

kan·ni, *kan-* – (quest.pron.)
who? (plural)
  keban·ni 'who (out of two)'
  ketsan·ni 'who (out of many)'

kansi, *kanta* – (no.ani)
female moose (young)

karsa, *karta~kartta* – (no.ani)
younger brother

katama, *katakka* – (no.ina)
(place) outside, outdoor, exterior

katśa~katsa – (adv./postp.)
out(side)
  kadda 'out'
  kaddairi 'towards the outside, at (missing)'
  katsti 'along the outside'
  katka 'from the outside'

katsġi, *katska* – (no.ina)
jam

katubias, *katubiahi* – (no.ina)
exile

ked·a, *kedda~ketta* – (v.at/.ut. inf. *kebmi/kebmu*)
to carry, to bear
  keś·ked·iks·a 'to carry X attached to/with Y'
  gat·ked·a 'to bring'

keg·a, *ketka* – (v.at. inf. *kegmi*)
to hide

o·keg·i, *oketki* – (v.asubj. inf. *kegna*)
to hide (oneself)

keggas, *kegahi* – (no.ina)
foetus

keggeki, *kegegge* – (no.ina)

brag, boast; *irehhaika kegegge* 'X will brag about Y'

keheb·m·i, *kehepsima (kehepp-)* – (adj.) to feel sulky, sullen, surly | to mope | to be grumpy, grouchy

keheppi~keheppil, *keheppila* – (no.ina) sulkiness, sullenness, grumpiness

keheppo, *keheppue~keheppobi* – (adj.) sulky, sullen, surly, moping, grumpy

kehhe, *kehhie~keġġi* – (no.ina) birch bark

kehho·kjokabmot, *~bmotta* – (adj.) birch-bark weaving | normal, standard (person), every- day

kehkjo, *kehkjue* – (no.ina) canoe (from birch)

kehmo, *kehka* – (no.ani) skin (human)

kehno, *kehhua~kehnue~kehnobi* – (no.ani/.ina) pine

kehhõt·a, *kehhõtta* – (v.at. inf. *kehhõbmi*) to remove bark (of tree) | to peel off

kehma, *kehka* – (no.ani) (human) skin

kei, *keje* – (no.ina) lynx | person/animal/thing that is difficult to see/spot

keiḍgi, *keiḍḍja~keihtśa* – (no.ani) helmet

keiġe, *keiġġi~keiġie~keiśie* – (no.ina) betula (any birch tree)

keihme, *keihmie* – (no.ina) page

keilba – (adv.) most

keindentsġ·i, *keindentsġui* – (v.imp) to be (far) too early

keingůit·a, *keingůitta* – (v.at. inf. *keingůibmi*) to polish, to smooth out

keisme, *keismie* – (no.ina) course, formation, guide

kekki, *kekkie~kekken~keggen* – (quant.) too (much): *kekken atana* 'too big'

kekn·a, *kenta* – (v.at/.ut. inf. *keknami/ keknamu*) to organize, to put together | to initiate, to spark (.ut)

keknuli, *kengulle~keknultśa* – (no.ina/.ani) organized, structured person, initiator

kelba, *keḍma* – (no.du) shoulders

kelgi~kelki, *kelgie* – (no.ina) war, warfare, conflict

kelhegemis, *kelhegemhi* – (no.ina) Wednesday

kelho, *kelhue~kelhobi* – (no.ina) dried meat, hung meat

kelme~kelne – (adv.) more

kelta~keltta, *keltari* – (no.ina) ground

keltaus, *keltauhi* – (adj.) terristrial, land-

kem·amo·mi, *kemamomitta* – (v.act.part.pl) siblings (sg.

kembo~sambo, *kåmouj~såmouj* – (no.ani) grandfather

kemhù, *kemhula* – (no.ina) happiness, joy

kem·jaingo, *kemjaingoka* – (no.ina) society

kemśi, *kemśie* – (no.ina) morning

kend·ia, *-ita, -ika* – (adv.) early, at an early time

kend·i·ma, *kenduima* – (v.adj) to be early

kenehta – (adv.) tomorrow (for, to, before)

kenes, *kenhi* – (no.ina) tomorrow

kengi, *kenda~kegna* – (no.ani) day: *sare kengi!* 'hello!'

kenho, *kenra* – (no.ani) virgin/prepubescent girl

kenka – (adv.) tomorrow

kennjut, *kennjutsta* – (no.ina) mallard duck
kennjeha 'female'
kennjego 'male'

keppi, *keppie* – (no.ina) head, number, quantity

keppõt·a, *keppõtta* – (v.at. inf. *keppõbmi*)
to behead, decapitate

kepsi, *kebsie~keutta(kepta)* – (no.ina/.ani)
mushroom

kes·a, *keha* – (v.at/.ut. inf. *kesmi/kesmu*)
to learn | to discover (.ut)

kesġ·a, *keskka* – (v.at inf. *kesġami*)
to teach

kesġam·o, *kesġamotta* – (v.ap)
teacher

kesġven, *kesġves* – (no.ina)
chickadee

keskon, *keskos* – (adj.)
non-buoyant, sinking

ketku, *ketkume* – (no.ina)
shoulder(blade)

ketsġo – (adv.)
as per the custom, because of a custom, customarily, usually

keu~ků~ġụe – (postp.)
with (as one, together)

keugo, *kůbue* – (no.ina)
burden, load

keụ·i, *kevvi* – (v.ui/.ai. inf. *kessu/kessa*)
to rise, to go up

keundlu, *keundluma* – (adj.)
daily, by day, day-

keunlė~keunleu~keunlel, *keunlela* – (no.ina)
dailiness, routine

keullu, *keulluma* – (ajd.)
per person | personal, individual

keunna, *keunnari* – (no.ina)
cape, promontory, hill, high point

keḍḍa – (postp.)
as, in the form of | in X's skin/view/opinion
keḍga from (being)

kevvasġa, *kevvasġari* – (adj.)
aggressive, quick-tempered

keu·konsim·o, *keukonsimotta* – (v.ap)
band (of hunters)

kėu, *kůla* – (no.ina)
attack, fight: *idigga kůlita* 'to attack X'

kėut, *kůlda* – (no.ina)
violence, war

keyġġůn, *keyġůs* – (no.ina)
big birch tree | (vulg.) penis

keynke, *keynkie* – (no.ina)
sperm, ejaculation

keynůn, *keynůs* – (no.ina)
milk bucket | (vulgar) breasts, tits

keyrpa, *keyrpari* – (adj.)
unknown, possibly dangerous

kękia – (adv.)
east
keuhta 'eastwards, to the east'
keuhteri 'towards the east'
keuhtsi 'along the east(face/side)'
keuhka 'from the east'

kęmes, *kemhi* – (adj.)
happy, glad (also *kęmis~kęmus~kęmys*)

kęm·m·i, *kebmima* – (v.adj)
to feel happy, to be happy

kęrru, *kęrume* – (no.ina)
doubt, suspicion, distrust

ki – (pron.)
they
idgi PAT.
kjon~kjōhō GEN.
eksi DAT.
ningi- LOC.
–hi POSS.
keta PREC

kjala, *kjalka* – (no.ina)
land, territory

kjal·ba, *kjalkaba* – (act.no)
Siwa land

kjaseli, *kjaselka~kjaseltśa* – (no.ina/.ani)
someone who works quickly

kjas·a, *kjaha* – (v.at inf. *kjasmi*)
to speed up, to accelerate

o·kjas·i, *okjahi* – (v.asubj/.ai. inf. *kjantal kjassa*)
to hurry up | to work quickly (.ai)

kiesk·a, *kieskia* – (v.at. inf. *kieskami*)
to watch, to observe, to view, to look at

kieḍg·a, *kietġi* – (v.at. inf. *kieḍgami*)
to steal

kjennut, *kjenutsta* – (no.ina)
mallard duck

o·kig·i~o·ki, *okitki* – (v.as inf. *kigna*)
to take a break, to pause, to rest

kigjut, *kijutsta* – (no.ina)
room

(i)·kigut·a, *(i)·kigutta* – (v.ui/.uditr. inf. *kigubmi~kigudnon*)

not to be able to wait | not be able to wait for (+ELAT, .uditr.)
kihaḥ·a, *kihasta* – (v.cop)
to be (something very large, a very large number of)
kihli, *kihlid* – (no.ina)
thread
ki, *kȋd* – (adj.)
new
kigge, *kȋgedi* – (no.ina)
spark
kigjini, *kȋgjija~kȋjindi* – (no.ani/no.ina/adj.)
youngest of a group | runt (.ina)
kilda – (adv.)
again
kiloahō – (adv.)
repeatedly, over and over again
kipriru·i, *kȋpriri* – (v.ai inf. *kȋprirosa*)
to chirp
kislo, *kȋslodi* – (no.ina)
noose
kika – (adv./postp.)
over
  kihta 'over (to)'
  kihtairi 'over, too much, too far, too high, passed a goal'
  kihtsi 'along the top/surface'
  kikka '(from) over, from the top/surface'
kikama, *kikandi* – (no.ina)
(place) over, space over | surface area | upper part
kikin, *kikis* – (no.ina)
meal
  kemṡukikin 'breakfast'
  ȏṡkikin~soḏgikin 'supper'
kikiṡin, *kikiṡis* – (no.ina)
woodpecker
kilbi – (adv.)
usually
kilge, *kilgedi* – (no.ina)
blade
kilj·a, *killj·a* – (v.at. inf. *kiljami*)
to cut, to fall (tree)
  tȗ·kilj·a 'to cut down (tree) | (~ohk-) 'to kill a large game'
kili, *kidli* – (no.ina)
wood
killa – (pron.ani)

the whole, all
AG. *killa*
PAT. *kilva*
GEN. *kihlō*
DAT. *killa*
killju 'always'
killju – (adv.)
always
kilura, *kiluhdi* – (adj.)
wooden
kilurė, *kilurela* – (no.ina)
woodenness
kimra – (adv.)
in the morning
kinagi, *kinaḏḏi /kinaubi* – (no.ina/.ani)
foreigner, stranger
kinapoṡmi, *kinapoṡta* – (no.ani)
guest, foreigner | invader, aggressor
kinaubmi, *kinaundi* – (adj.)
foreign, exotic, alien
kinaubmù, *kinaubmula* – (no.ina)
foreignnes, exoticism, alienness
kinji, *kigjid* – (no.ina)
fringes
kinna, *kindi* – (no.ina)
fist, paw | (large) hand
kintumi, *kintutta* – (no.ani)
warrior, hero
kinuba~kinulba, *kinǔ~kinulu~kinuadi~kinuldi* – (no.ani)
thistle
kjoḏma, *kjomamo* – (no.ina)
auk bird
kjoḏmimu, *kjoḏmimma* – (adj.)
auk bird-like, sea bird(like)
kjoḥḥo, *kjoḥḥoma* – (adj.)
rapid, quick, fast | sudden
kjok·a, *kė̇uhka~kė̇ukka* – (v.at. inf. *kjokmi*)
to weave (especially birch bark)
kjori, *kjohko* – (no.ina)
rotten wood
kjorki, *kjorkko* – (no.ina)
mulch
kjoro, *kjohma* – (no.ina)
sea bird
kiras, *kirhi* – (no.ina)
morning
kirkkyt, *kirkytsta* – (no.ina)
pine warbler

kisit, *kisitsta* – (no.ina)
culture
kisġil·i, *kisġidli* – (v.ai. inf. *kisġilsa*)
to work fast, to be fast
kisina, *kisindi* – (adj.)
quick, fast, rapid, swift
kisi·nupubmot, *~bmotta* – (adj.)
quick-tempered
kisú~kisul, *kisula* – (no.ina)
quickness, speed, rapidity, swiftness
kit·a, *ahta* – (v.at. inf. *kibmi*)
to do
kita, *kivva* – (no.ani)
eye
kitaiu̯e, *kitaiu̯edi* – (no.ina/adj.)
(something) worth doing
kju̯hko, *kju̯hhuni* – (no.ani)
beaver
kju̯omon, *kju̯omonta* – (adj.)
bent, twisted, warped, out of shape
Kju̯omśin, *Kju̯onśis* – (no.ina)
(name of a village)
a·kju̯om·u, *akju̯obmu* – (v.utransl. inf. *kju̯omlu*)
to become bent, to bend out of shape
kju̯rppo, *kju̯rppoma* – (adj.)
hollow, empty | pitted, emptied, gutted
kju̯tśi, *kju̯tśimo* – (no.ina)
territory, used land
kiḍg·a, *kitġa* – (v.at. inf. *kiḍgami*)
to pick up | to lift, to hoist
kiḍba, *keubba* – (no.du)
eyes
kiḍḍi̯a – (postp.)
within sight, in sight, with/while X watching/seeing
kiḍḍi̯a·ni – (det.)
the one within sight | witness
kmaitsa, *kmaitta* – (no.ani)
toe | hoof
kmanda, *kmanu̯a* – (no.ani)
student of shaman, type of student priest | apprentice
knabi, *knaumi~knaika* – (no.ani/.ina)
small mushroom | endearment term for child
knes, *knehi* – (no.ina)
sour~fermented drink | beer
ko, *koba* – (no.ina/.ani)
summer
koaḥḥor·a, *koaḥḥohra* – (v.at. inf. *koaḥḥohmi*)
to half, to split in halves
koahi, *koakka* – (quant.)
enough, well (COMP. *koatta*, SUP. *kodla*, SUP.GEN. *kuhla*)
koah·i, *koasti* – (v.ui/.ai. inf. *koahisu~koassu*)
to be enough, to suffice | to fulfill
koahibmis, *-mhi* – (adj.)
sufficient (adv. *koahimui*)
koahimú, *koahimuri* – (no.ina)
sufficiency, abundance
koahlebba, *koahlebbaka* – (no.ina)
a noisy person | a misbehaved child
koahl·i, *koahlui* – (v.ai/.ui. inf. *koahlisa/koahlisu*)
to make noise, to be noisy | to misbehave (.ai)
koaibm·a, *koainda* – (v.ut/at. inf. *koaibmimu/koaibmimi*)
to be bored (of +INF.): *koaindaka neutvamatta* 'I lost interest'
koakken~koakkil – (adv.)
enough, well (COMP. *koakne* SUP. *koaiba*)
koakvi, *koagvika* – (no.ina)
call, address, summon
koalgi, *koaltsa* – (no.ani)
paternal aunt
koat, *koatta* – (no.ina)
(person/animal) born during the summer
kobas, *koahhi* – (no.ina)
freckle, speckle, fleck, dot
kobbomora, *kobomohmo* – (no.ina)
salamander
kobolken, *kôlkes* – (no.ina)
monarch (butterfly)
kode, *koimo* – (no.ina)
shoulder blade
kodlken, *kodlkenta~kolkenta* – (no.ina)
firefly
koḍmi, *koḍḍa* – (no.ani)
guest
koha, *koamo* – (no.ina)
half
kohhi̯·a, *kośta* – (v.at inf. *kośmi*)

to rip, to slit, to gash, to slash | *hẹ~* to destroy, to win | *tama~* to come (suddenly, vulg.)
koho, *kôma* – (no.ina)
half
kohut, *kohutta* – (card.)
half (often used before nouns)
ma kohut~koho~koha sîhdi 'X ate half the fish'
koita~koidḍa, *koibmo~koidmo* – (no.ina)
cocoon | wrap, cloak
kokk·a, *kokkia* – (v.ut. inf. *kokmu*) (patientive)
to like; *takokkaka* 'I like X' | to please
kokket, *kokketta* – (no.ina)
dialect, speech
kokkú, *kokkuri* – (no.ina)
lightness, lightweightness | agility, nimbleness
koklu, *kohda* – (no.ani)
place where boat is lowered into lake
kok·m·i, *kodgima* – (v.adj)
to (be/feel) relieved, glad, reassured
kokve, *kokvemo* – (adj.)
light, lightweight, not heavy | agile, nimble
kola, *kolmo* – (no.ina)
ridge, esker
kolia – (adv.)
strained, tensed, stretched, tight
kolkon, *kolkonta -ōri-* – (no.ina)
bread
kolla, *komma* – (quant.)
much, a lot (COMP. *kvolda*, SUP. *kvobba*, SUP.GEN *kuohba*)
kolo~kulo, *kolma~kulma* – (no.ina)
cloud
kolo·ni – (det.)
the one close by | at hand | local, close-by
kolot, *kolotta* – (no.ina)
womb, placenta
komi, *kōkko* – (no.ina)
mind | memory: *maski kōkko kihtairi* 'it didn't dawn (on me)'
kommen~kommil – (adv.)
much, a lot (COMP. *komne~kelme*, SUP. *keilba~kōuba*)

kon·i, *kodi~koddi* – (v.ai/ui. inf. *konta/kontu*)
to walk
konihta, *konihtamo* – (adj.)
one summer old/long
konkot, *konkotta* – (adj.)
horrible, terrible, awful, dreadful (sometimes *konkoġonkot*)
kò·i, *koki* – (v.ai. inf. *kôsa*)   IRR
to speak, to talk
ga·kôa 'to deal with someone'
kori, *kohko* – (no.ina)
boy
koro, *kohma* – (no.ina)
headwear,
korù~korul, *koruri* – (no.ina)
pot
kosġ·a, *koskka* – (v.at. inf. *kosġami*)
to carve (out)
koso-, *kotta-* – (act.nom)
older brother
koso·m·i, *kosomitta* – (v.act.part.pl)
brothers
kosi, *gasta* – (no.ani)
older brother
kośma, *kośmamo* – (no.ina)
strong wind
kostet, *kostetta* – (no.ina)
woodwork, art, carvings | pattern
kotskven, *kotskventa* – (no.ina)
wooden ring to stretch skin onto | frame, framework | *kû~* skeleton
kotsmi, *kotsmiko* – (no.ina)
walking path
kotson, *kotsonta -ōri-* – (no.ina)
shock, scare, fright | jolt, blow
kodga, *kôgga* – (no.du)
twins (brothers)
kodda, *kôhha* – (no.du)
twins
kodba, *kôbba* – (no.du)
brother(s) and sister(s)
kõhi, *kõkko* – (no.ina)
memory, remembrance
kõdga, *kōkamo* – (no.ina)
bear cub
kụegvi·a, *kụegvua* – (v.at. inf. *kụegvimi*)
to call (an animal)
kuilis, *kuilhi* – (no.ina)

tadpole
kuilva~kůilva, *kuilvamo~kůilvamo* – (no.ina)
drizzle, spray, mist
kuima, *kuimamo* – (no.ina)
frosty
kuki, *kutśa* – (no.ani)
mouth
kuku·a, *kukia* – (v.at. inf. *kukomi*)
to order
kulu~kolu, *kuluma~koluma* – (adj.)
cloudy
Kumho, *Kumtsa* – (no.ani)
(male personal name)
kumora, *kumosta~kumohma* – (no.ani/.ina)
white spruce
kunna, *kunu̯a/kulva* – (no.ani)
oak tree
kuogn·i, *kuognui* – (v.ai inf. *kuognisa*)
to argue, to quibble, to disagree (+ *balha*)
kuohhidna, *kuohhidnamo* – (adj.)
noisy
kuoko, *kuokoma* – (no.ina)
order
kuos, *kuohhi* – (no.ina)
noise
kuspo, *kusou̯i* – (no.ani)
skunk
kutkus·ka~kutġus·ka, *kutkuhi~kutġuhi* – (no.ina.pl)
floor(ing)
kůadna, *kůanamo* – (no.ina)
settlement, community, outpost
kůalme, *kůalmemo* – (no.ina)
inner bark
kůja – (adv.)
afloat, floating
kůimpa, *kyģjua~kẙbba* – (no.du)
(pair of) boots/shoes
kůira, *kůihmo* – (no.ina)
issue, matter, question, point
kůiśůn, *kůiśůs* – (no.ina)
big squirrel | adult squirrel
kůitton, *kůittos* – (no.ina)
shoe, boot
ků·kiket, *kůkiketsta* – (no.ina)
relations
kůiśśů, *kůiśśůma* – (no.ina)

attempt, exam(ination), test
kůků·a, *kůkia* – (v.at. inf. *kůkůmi*)
to bring (along) | to escort, to guide
kůlm·a, *kůlmia* – (v.at. inf. *kůlmami*)
to wage war on, to combat, to battle
o·kůln·i, *okůlnui~okůlnẙ* – (v.as inf. *kůlnina*)
to make a nest, to settle down
kůmkků, *kůmkůma* – (no.ina)
snot
kůmůl·i, *kůmůdli* – (v.uit. inf. *kůmůlsů*)
to be in rut, to be horny
kůngů·i, *kůngei* – (v.at. inf. *kůngůsa*)
to knock
i·kůnnjůl·i, *ikůnnjůdli* – (v.adit. inf. *kůnnjůlnůn*)
to settle (somewhere)
kůnů, *kůnůma* – (no.ina)
milk
kůsġi, *kůsġimo* – (no.ina)
place where many mushrooms are found | group, team
kůtegj·a – (adv.)
somewhere (unknown)
kůteita 'somewhere (movement to)'
kůteika 'somewhere (movement from)'
kůtům·ni, *kůtů-* – (pron.)
someone (unknown)
kebůtůmni 'either, one or the other'
ketsůtůmni 'some'
kůddjů 'sometimes'
kůtva 'somehow'
miků 'for some reason'
kůvůn, *kêus* – (no.ina)
brain
eddůkůvůn 'idiot, fool, halfwit'
kvaul·i, *kvaudli* – (v.ai. inf. *kvaulsa*)
to summer, to spend the summer somewhere
kvagi, *kvahta* – (det.)
those (medial)
kvaśpa, kvahba 'those (out of two)'
kvatsġi, kvahtsa 'those (out of many)'
kvag·ni – (det.)
like those, like such, such
kvavi, *kvaika* – (no.ina)
sleet, hail
kvegjo, *kvejue~kvejobi* – (no.ina)
feeling, perception, sense

kvekkot, *kvekkotsta* – (adj.)
insulating, warm
kvemmet, *kvemetsta* – (no.ina)
heather
kven ~kvon, *kves~kvonta* – (no.ina)
feather
kvena, *kvevva* – (no.ani)
female cousin (father's sister's)
kvesi, *kvetta* – (no.ani)
male cousin (father's sister's)
kvi·a, *kvȋma~kvivva* – (v.at/.ut. inf. *kvȋmi~kvȋmu*)
to feel, to perceive | to sense, to detect (.ut)
o·kvi, *okvivvi* – (v.usubj inf. *kvȋna*)
to feel like (noun+ ELAT or keḍḍa~keḍga, adj + ADV)
kvikvon, *kvigvos* – (no.ina)
riddle, mystery | joke
kvilli, *kvilid* – (no.ina)
sperm
kvisġil – (adv.)
regularly
kvisġot, *kvisġotsta* – (adj.)
regular
sikvisġot 'irregular'
kvolku, *kvolkuma* – (no.ina)
cloud cover, cloudy weather
kvollu, *kvolma* – (no.ina)
cave
kydly, *kylyma* – (no.ina)
bell | little girl
kylys~kvylys 'little flower'
kygybi, *kẏbid* – (no.ina)
calling horn
kyġġa, *kyġmo* – (no.ina)
mouse
kyhhisi, *kyhhitta* – (no.ani)
mink
kykky, *kykkyma* – (no.ina)
voice
kykkymġil – (adv.)
out loud
kylk·ů, *kylkejů* – (v.utrans. inf. *kylkůrů*)
to slip off, to come off (easily)
kymina~kymna, *kymimmo~kymmo* – (adj.)
nice, pleasant, agreeable
kyni, *kyndi* – (no.ina)
nest, lair, den

kysġibi, *kysġibid* – (no.ina)
carving knife
kyś·a, *kyha* – (v.at. inf. *kyśmi*)
to try to (+ILLAT)
kyśi, *kyśti~kyhta* – (no.ina/.ani)
squirrel
ung·o·kyś·i, *ungokyhi* – (v.asubj inf. *ujokyśina*)
to apply oneself, to make an effort
kyśyųe, *kyśyųemo* – (no.ina/adj.)
(something) worth trying | valuable experience
kẏ~kvẏ, *kyby~kvyby* – (no.ina)
grease, fat, oil

L l

laḍḍonga, *lahhongaka~lahhonka* – (no.ina)
root soup, soup made from vegetables
lagjas, *lajahi* – (no.ina)
ingredient | powdered grains, flour
lagjo, *lajoka* – (no.ina)
hesitation, doubt
lagj·u, *ladju* – (v.aux.utrans. inf. *lagjoru*)
to happen (to be) (+INF)
lahton, *lahtos* – (no.ina)
(single) mitten
laib·m·i, *laiḍbima* (*laip-*) – (v.adj)
to (be/become/feel) resentful/jealous
laiḥu, *lajuka* – (no.ina)
straw
laiklo, *laigloka* – (no.ina)
the innermost part of a house/tipi
lainga~laikna, *lainka* – (no.ina)
bait, lure
laipin, *laipinta* – (adj.)
bitter, sour, sharp
laippo, *laippoka* – (adj.)
flat
laipů~laipul, *laipuri* – (no.ina)
bitterness, sourness, sharpness
lammi~lammil, *lamiri* – (no.ina)
boldness, braveness | arrogance
lammon, *lammonta* – (adj.)
bold, brave | arrogant: *gegin lammon* 'big~foul mouth'

latsma, *latsmaka* – (no.ina)
small bridge, log bridge, path that avoids water (by hopping between rocks or on fallen trees, for example)
laugj·i, *lautsi* – (v.ui. inf. *laujisa*)
to hesitate
tama·lauj·a, *~laudja* – (v.at/.ut. inf. tamalaujami/~laujamu)
to hinder
ledba, *ledma* – (no.du)
mittens
legj·a, *ledja* – (v.at inf. leimi)
to crush (seeds, flour, often *legj·õhn·a*) | to win, to beat someone | to hit someone (violently), to strike
lehhidlen, *lehhidles* – (no.ina)
harvestman, daddy long legs
lehra, *lehrari* – (no.ina)
straw, hay
leikva, *leikvari* – (adj.)
slippery, slimey
leilma, *leilmari* – (adj.)
warm
leil·m·i, *leidlmi* – (v.adj)
to (be/become) warm
leilù, *leilula* – (no.ina)
warmth | kindness
leren, *leres* – (no.ina)
pile of straw/moss/boughs
letku, *letkume* – (no.ina)
paddle
letkuika – (adv.)
confused, lost, astray
letse, *letsġi* – (no.ina)
pole, post, pillar
leuvva, *leuuari~lŭmari* – (no.ina)
reindeer moss
ljagjin, *ljajinta -õri-* – (no.ina)
nasal cavity, sinuses
lialse·i, *lialsui* – (v.ui. inf. *lialsesu*)
to drift, to be carried away | to stray
lialse·hõ – (adv.)
adrift | lost, off course
liamis, *liamhi* – (no.ina)
(winter) hat, fur hat
liarkko, *liarkodi* – (no.ina)
guest bench (in house or *sasame*).
ljeilen·i, *ljeiledi* – (v.ui. inf. *ljeilentu*)
to feel warm, to be warm

ljeilt·a, *ljeiltia* – (v.at/.ut. inf. *ljeiltami/ljeiltamu*)
to warm up
ljekna, *ljeknari* – (adj.)
snowless (also noun, *ljengari*)
liello, *liellodi* – (no.ina)
palm
ljemi, *ljemme* – (no.ina)
infection | pus
ljemkk·a, *ljemkkia* – (v.ui inf. *ljemkkamu*)
to infect
lidna, *lîdnadi~lîndi* – (adj.)
great, powerful, famous
likni, *lîngid* – (no.ina)
splinter
lisġi, *lihhjet* – (no.ani)
nostril(s)
likion, *likios* – (adj.)
awful | rude, bad-tempered | bitter (of food)
lillot, *lilotsta* – (no.ina)
paternal uncle's house/family
lillu, *lilda* – (no.ani)
paternal uncle
ljodla, *ljotsta~ljollamo* – (no.ani/.ina)
balsam fir (*abies balsamea*)
ljohma, *ljohmamo* – (adj.)
infection (also *ljohma, ljohmatta*)
liota, *liovva* – (no.ani)
mother (animal)
ljó, *lyra* – (no.ina.irr)
resin, pitch
ljouhe, *ljoubmo* – (no.ina)
fin
list·a, *listia* – (v.at/.ut. inf. *listami/listamu*)
to abandon | to give up (on)
listebba, *listebbadi* – (no.ina)
someone who gives up easily, coward
list·i, *listui* – (v.ai/.ui. inf. *listisa/listisu*)
to give up (on, +ELAT)
loabġis, *loapihi~loahpi* – (no.ina)
shirt
o·loaġ·i, *oloasti* – (v.asubj. inf. *loaġna*)
to masturbate
loait·a, *loaitta* – (v.at/.ut. inf. *loaibmi/loaibmu*)
to flatten, to level | to crush
loalla, *loalaka* – (no.ina)
(place) behind | back, backside
loba, *loamo* – (no.ina)

dregs
lodbo, *lopoma* – (no.ina)
  jelly
lodvot, *lodvotta* – (adj.)
  slow, delayed, long (also *logvot* or *lot*)
loġveli, *loġvelko* – (no.ina)
  a jerk-off, idiot, wanker (insult)
lohhe~loġġe, *lohmo~loġmo* – (no.ina)
  bob | jolt, jerk
loib·m·i, *loipsima* (loipp-) – (v.adj)
  to (be/become) flat | to be bored
loiśi, *loiśko* – (no.ina)
  leech, parasite
loippo, *loippomo* – (adj.)
  flat
lokk·ima – (adv.)
  flat (on one's stomach)
lokl·i, *loklui* – (v.ai. inf. *loklisa*)
  to lie flat (on one's stomach)
lokna, *longamo* – (no.ina)
  (intense) cold
lom·i, *lobmi* – (v.ai. inf. *lomsa*)
  to run: *obůrůrikmaita lomsa* 'to run as fast as one can' (lit. to run into drowning)
longiė~longieu~longiel, *longieri* – (no.ina)
  iciness, coldness
longiu, *longiuma* – (adj.)
  icy, (very) cold
lonis, *lonhi~lōhhi* – (no.ina)
  short walk, short distance
lȯ, *lommo* – (adj.)
  slow
o·lōhk·i, *olōhkui* – (v.st *lōhkina*)
  to go for a short walk, to walk a short distance
lugju·a, *lugjaja* – (v.at. inf. *lugjumi*)
  to love: *lugjuahmi* 'I love you'
luhh·a, *luhra* – (v.at. inf. *luhmi*)
  to boil
luhh·i, *luvvi* – (v.ui. inf. *luhsu*)
  to boil
lui·ka~lůi·ka, *lujukka~lůjůkka* – (act.nom. 1p)
  my love, my darling
lukki, *lukkimo* – (no.ina)
  hole (in the ice)
lungit, *lungitta* – (no.ina)
  steam
lůlkki, *lůlkimo* – (no.ina)

hot water, hot pool of water
luvvů~luvvul, *lůri* – (no.ina)
  (intense) heat | fervor, passion
luvvulden, *lůldenta* – (no.ina)
  heat, passion, lust
lůirůn, *lůirůs* – (no.ina)
  resin-filled blister on bark | pimple
lůkků, *lůkkůma* – (no.ina)
  rapids, turbulent waters | froth, foam
lůnn·ů, *lůnneju* – (v.aux.utrans. inf. *lůnnůrů*)
  to be warm enough to (+INF)
lůri, *lůhdi* – (no.ina)
  scum, filth, dregs
lybby, *lybma* – (no.ina)
  vine
lygy, *lůimo* – (no.ina)
  disease | defect, disability
lẏ, *lůbů* – (no.ina)
  love | *lẏgjia* 'in love'

M m

mȧhra, *mȧhraka* – (no.ina)
  bear
mȧra~mġȧra – (pron.)
  we (inclusive)
  menra~mġenra PAT.
  ůra GEN.
  můsi DAT.
  momśi- LOC.
  -ura POSS.
  můtra~mġůtra PREC
mȧri~mġȧri – (pron.)
  we (exclusive)
  menri~mġenri PAT.
  ůri GEN.
  můsi DAT.
  momśi- LOC.
  -uri POSS.
  můtri~mġůtri PREC.
madu, *mama* – (no.ina)
  pregnancy
maggja – (postp.)
  in the case of, in the event of
maggja·ni – (det.)
  this one, the one in this case

magja, *magjaka* – (adj.)
white
a·magj·u, *amadju* – (v.utransl. inf. *magjoru*)
to become white | to pale
mahh·a, *mahra* – (v.at. inf. *mahmi*)
to hunt | to stalk, to track down
lol·mahha 'to stalk, to keep track of, to recount'
mahhji, *maśka* – (no.ina)
fallen bear, dead bear
maidġiabmi, *-ġuoma* – (no.ina)
measuring unit of length (±300m)
maidi, *magjaka* – (no.ina)
measuring unit of length (±30cm)
maidnet, *mainetta* – (no.ina)
measuring unit of length (±3m)
maihhi, *maitśa~maihka* – (no.ani/.ina)
maple tree
maiki, *maikika* – (adj.)
white
maikjukk·a, *maikjukkia* – (v.at/.ut. inf. *maikjukmi/ maikjukmu*)
to whiten, to bleach
maikůl·i, *maikůdli* – (v.ai/.ui. inf. *maikůlsa/ maikůlsu*)
to be wearing white | to be covered in snow (.ui)
mairu·i, *mairi* – (v.ai/.ui. inf. *mairosa/ mairosu*)
to laugh (also *smairu·i*)
maivv·i, *maiḍḍi* – (v.ai/.ui. inf. *maissa/ maissu*)
to smile
mak·i, *maski* – (v.ai/.ui. inf. *maksa/ maksu*)
to go, to leave, to go there
mald·a, *maldia* – (v.at. inf. *maldami*)
to praise
maldot, *maldotta* – (adj.)
valuable, precious, important
malva, *malvaka* – (no.ina)
sprain
mamma, *mamśi* – (no.ani)
leg (from knee to ankle) | tibia and fibula
mamna, *mamnaka~mammua* – (no.ina/ani)
center
man·gosva, *mangosvamo* – (no.ina)
migration
man·i, *mansi* – (v.ai/.ui. inf. *manta/ mantu*)
to come, to approach, to come here
manji, *magjika* – (no.ina)
broken weapon/tool | idiot
mankobi, *mankoumi* – (no.ani)
red-winged black bird
mant·a, *mantia* – (v.at inf. *mantami*)
to take, to receive, to accept | to host
manta, *mantaka~manua* – (no.ina/.ani)
world, earth, land
marva, *marvaka* – (no.ina)
laughter
maski, *maskka* – (no.ina)
people
matsli, *matslika* – (no.ina)
bastard, fucker
matot, *matotta* – (no.ina)
explanation, reason
maudli, *maulika~maultśa* – (no.ina/ani)
maple sap
mauhhon, *mauhhonta* – (no.ina)
hunt
maukust·a, *maukustia* – (v.at. inf. *maukustami*)
to allow to go, to let go
maunust·a, *maunustia* – (v.at. inf. *maunustami*)
to allow in/to come
mauvvun, *mamunta~mauuunta -ōri-* – (no.ina)
meat box
mavvedna, *mavvednaka* – (adj.)
meaty, beefy | muscular, strong, burly
mavvu, *magga* – (no.ina)
meat, flesh
medde, *mederi* – (no.ina)
corner | angle
medvi, *meḍḍumi* – (no.ani)
eyelid (often includes eyebrows) | thin leather
mėi – (onom.)
wow, sound to show amazement
mėppi, *mėḣḣumi* – (no.ani)
knee(cap)
mėpse·i, *mėpsui* – (v.ai. inf. *mėpsesa*)
to repair nets | to do something boring and tidious

megi~mġegi – (pron.)
I, me
  meiḑgi~mġeiḑgi PAT.
  gogi GEN.
  gosi DAT.
  gogi- LOC.
  -go POSS.
  mǔta~mġǔta PREC
meġi – (coord.part)
fortunately
meh·a, *mesta* – (v.at. inf. *mebmi*)
to paint | to smear, to smudge, to coat
mehhjon, *mehhjos* – (no.ina)
maple tree forest
meigji·a, *meidjia* (*meigje-*) – (v.at/.ut. inf. *meigjemi/meigjemu*)
to make smile, to cheer up
meihhi, *meihhie* – (no.ina)
honeycomb
meilkkena, *meilkedi* – (no.ina)
peat field
meirjisġa, *meirjisġari* – (adj.)
funny, amusing
meitskva, *meitskvari* – (no.ina)
spruce sprout, spruce sapling
mekǔ, *megme* – (no.ina)
river banks (especially raised)
melki, *melkie* – (no.ina)
peat
Menho, *Mentsa* – (no.ani)
(male personal name)
meniu̧·a, *menivva* – (v.ut/.at. inf. *menimmu/menimmi*)
to lure | to fool (.at)
mesora, *mesorari* – (no.ina)
stone, made from stone
mesu, *mesume* – (no.ina)
rock, stone (material)
meuli, *meulle* – (adj.)
dark blue>green
meuḑguna, *meuḑgudi* – (adj.)
respectful, polite
meḑg·a, *metġa* – (v.at. inf. *meḑgami*)
to respect | to esteem, to admire
męrah·m·i, *męrarrima* (*męrar-*) – (v.adj)
to be difficult (to nagivate, of a river)
męrai – (adv.)
with difficulty, hardly
męrana, *męradi* – (adj.)
difficult, hard, complicated | troublesome, tiresome
męrė~męreu~męrel, *męrela~męręla* – (no.ina)
difficulty, complication | trouble
-mi – (hyphened clitic)
as (essive) (also *-imi/-emi/-ebi/-iu/-eu/-ǔ*)
mialha, *mialhadi* – (adj.)
pale blue>gray
mialrikkin, *mialrikkis* – (no.ina)
blue jay (also *mialrikkini* no.ani)
mjambi, *mjambika* – (no.ina)
gutting knife
mian·a, *miatta* – (v.at. inf. *miamni*)
to gut (game)
miasġ·i, *miaskki* – (v.imp/.at. inf. *miasġami*)
to be an occasion to smoke | to celebrate (.at)
miasku, *miaskudi* – (no.ina)
gravel
miasma, *miasmadi~miasmatta* – (no.ina/.vap)
peace
miats·a, *miatsta* – (v.at. inf. *miatsmi*)
to let soak | to neglect
mjaulba, *mjaulbaka~mjaulu* – (no.ina/ani)
butterwort (*pinguicula vulgaris*)
midlkis, *midlkihi* – (no.ina)
crab
miebi, *mieumi* – (no.ani)
leg (from hip to ankle)
miebṡiṡi, *miebṡiṡid* – (no.ina)
old bear, fat bear
miedi·u~mġiedju, *miedjutta~mġiedjutta* – (v.pat.part)
herd (usually *miedjumi~mġiedjumi* 'my herd')
mieḑḑ·a, *meḑba* – (v.at. inf. *mieḑmi*)
to desire, to want, to wish | to lust for
miegj·a~mġiegja, *miedja~mġiedja* – (v.at. inf. *miegjami~mġiejami*)
to herd | to round up, to gather | to guide
mjeuhku, *mjeuhkume* – (no.ina)
taiga, mossy ground
mielo, *mieldi* – (no.ina)
mold, mildew | short/fine hairs
mieri, *miehdi* – (no.ina)
moss

**migji~migjil~migjiu~migjiŭ~middji~middjil
~migjir**, *mijila* – (no.ina)
dew, moisture

migit, *mîtsta* – (no.ina)
respect, honor

miġe, *mied* – (no.ina)
crystall

mihi – (adv.)
(not) for any reason

mihtv·i, *mihtvŭi~mihtvŷ* – (v.ai inf. *mihtvisa~mihtsa*)
to whisper

mihy, *miŭdi* – (no.ina)
monster, beast, giant

mi, *mitśa~mîd* – (num.ani/.ina)
one
minet 'elleven'
migjil 'once'
estot 'first'

mim·ni, *mî-* – (quest.pron.)
who?
mebîm·ni 'who (of two)'
metsîm·ni 'who (of many)'
mîkni 'who (pl.)'

midl – (onom.)
sound to get a caribou to move | let's go!

mihkeh·i, *mîhkehri* – (v.imp)
to be frosty, to be cold enough for rime to form

mihki, *mîhkid* – (no.ina)
rime, frost: *mîhkidia* 'frosty, covered in frost'

mippa, *mîhu* – (no.ani)
(two) feet: *mîhuja* 'winning, superior, ready, steadfast'

misko, *mîskodi* – (no.ina)
beaver meat

mitabe, *mîtaid* – (no.ina)
yesterday

milki, *miltśa~milkid* – (no.ani/.ina)
fish skin | scales (.ina)

milkōt·a, *milkōtta* – (v.at. inf. *milkōbma*)
to remove/collect sprigs (for a beverage)

milla, *mildi* – (no.ina)
soggy spot

milmi, *miltta* – (no.ani)
lip

milttet, *miltetsta* – (no.ina)
little mouth

mimi – (adv.)
for this reason, thus, so

mimŭkis, *mimŭkihi~mimŭhki* – (no.ina)
butterfly (also *mŭmŭkis, mimikis, -ggis, -kŭs, -ggŭs, -kli*)

mine, *mindi* – (no.ina)
flesh (of plant/fruit) | fibers

minhi, *mintśa~minhid* – (no.ani/.ina)
black spruce

miniso, *minihi* – (no.ani)
common snipe

minga, *mingadi* – (adj.)
ready

a·ming·u, *amindu* – (v.utrans. inf. *mingoru*)
to become prepared | to mature

miniso~minso, *minihi~midni* – (no.ani)
common snipe

mjoahna, *mjoahnaka* – (no.ina)
sparsely populated area | difficult time period, poverty

mjoallus, *mjoaluhi~mjoahli* – (no.ina)
particle | fine dust, finely ground

miohhot, *miohhotsta* – (adj.)
slender, slim, lean | scant, sparse

miola, *mioldi* – (no.ina)
flame, fire, warmth

miolm·a, *miolmia* – (v.at/.ut. inf. *miolmami/miolmamu*)
to set on fire, to set fire to | to ignite | to trigger, to cause

mjost·a, *mjostia* – (v.at. inf. **mjostami**)
to chew

miout, *miolda~mioutta* – (no.ina)
warmth, energy

mipsi, *mibsid* – (no.ina)
thief

mirjaka, *mirjakadi~miśakadi* – (no.ina)
cloud of mosquitos

mis·a, *miha* – (v.at. inf. *mismi*)
to smoke

misas, *misahi~misġid* – (no.ina)
stone (also *tmisas*)

misġemis, *misġemhi* – (no.ina)
Friday

miss·u, *missutta* – (v.past.patpart)
tobacco

mite(us), *mitedi~miteuhi* – (no.ina)
reason, cause, grounds

mitejusi~miteuhiusi – (adv.)
unnecessarily, without reason, irratioinal
u·mit·i, *umitui* – (v.pass. inf. *mitimon*)
to be explained
mitsem·a, *mitsebma* – (v.at. inf. *mitsemmi*)
to wash, to soak
mitvo, *mitvodi* – (no.ina)
night frost
miudla, *miuhla* – (adj. sup)
least (most little) (sup. of *mǒs*, *tiuhhen~tyhhyn~tyǵǵyn*)
miudna, *miudnanna~miudnammo* – (adj.comp)
(a little) less (comp. of *mǒs*, *tiuhhen~tyhhyn~tyǵǵyn*)
miuki, *miuhdi* – (no.ina)
bog, marsh (mostly wet, low acidity)
miullen~miullil – (adv.)
a little, slightly (COMP. *mylne~mǔlne* SUP. *mylba~mǔlba*)
mjuti, *mjuika* – (no.ani)
finger tip, palm
miḍbi, *mihhumi* – (no.ani)
gray jay
moadǵul·a, *moadǵudla* – (v.at. inf. *moadǵulmi*)
to keep ordered | to police, to moderate
moaǵi, *moaika* – (no.ina)
drink
moaǵolot, *moavvolotta* – (no.ina)
festive occasion, celebration, party
moaǵundi, *moavvundika* – (no.ina)
sip (sometimes *mǵoaǵundi*)
moahrit, *moahritta* – (no.ina)
water supplies
tama·moaikker·i, *~moaikkehri* – (v.ui. inf. *~moaikkerhu*)
to fall flat (on one's belly), to be knocked out, to pass out
moaksapr·i, *moaksaprui* – (v.ui inf. *moaksaprisu*)
to be time for ptarmigan hunting | for there to be a lot of ptarmigans
moaldi, *moaldika* – (no.ina)
praise
moasi, *moatta~moaska* – (no.ani/.ina)
black bear

moatut·a~moarut·a, *moatutta~moarutta* – (v.at/.ut. inf. *moatubma/moatubmu~moarubma/moarubmu*)
to sadden, to dishearten, to depress
mob·mi, *mostima* (*moh-*) – (v.adj)
not to be able to understand/imagine | for something to slip one's mind, to forget (completely)
modǵori, *motohdi* – (no.ina)
watcher, guard | police
mogopimi, *mogopitta* – (no.ani)
oystercatcher (also *mǒpimi/mǔbmi*)
moǵ·a~mǵoǵ·a, *amǵa* – (v.at. inf. *moǵmi~mǵoǵmi*)
to drink
mohe, *moimo* – (no.ina)
loaf of bread
mohi, *mohiko* – (adj.)
slippery, slimy | elusive, evasive | ambiguous, difficult
mohù~mohul, *mouri* – (no.ina)
slipperiness, sliminess | elusiveness | ambiguity
mokku·o~mokku·mo~mokk·õ, *mokkoma* – (no.ina.pl)
beak
moksabi, *moksaumi* – (no.ani)
ptarmigan (*lagopus muta*)
moksabuh·i, *moksabuhri* – (v.imp)
to be ptarmigan hunting time
molk·a, *molkia* – (v.at/.ut. inf. *molkami/molkamu*)
to slide, to move | to push to the side
îl·molk·a 'to accomplish, to achieve, to realise' (.at)
molki, *molkko* – (no.ina)
erosion, wearing away, abrasion, decay
mome, *mommo* – (no.ina)
slope | angle, gradiant, slant; *mommoimo* 'slanted, tilted, leaning, distorted, drunk'
mongemis, *mongemhi* – (no.ina)
Sunday
moni, *mõkko* – (no.ina)
path, walkway | possibility
monnu, *monnuma* – (no.ina)
damage, harm
monoba, *monou~monobmo* – (no.ani/.ina)
indian pipe

mȯs, *mȯhhi~mȯhko* – (quant.)
slight, little
mori, *mohko* – (quant.)
a little
mosġi, *moskko* – (no.ina)
mammal
moski, *moskko* – (no.ina)
wild copper, ore
motom·m·i, *motobmi* (*moton-*) – (v.adj)
to feel sad, to be sad
moton, *motonta* – (adj.)
sad, unhappy
motona~mġotona,
motovva~mġotovva – (no.ani)
claw
moukki, *moukkiko* – (no.ina)
belly (of animal)
mouị, *mỷko* – (no.ina)
grandpa
moḍbi, *mopiko* – (no.ina)
hunting territory | domain, field, department
moḍḍot, *mohhotta* – (no.ina)
rule, law, command, order
muh·u, *mustu* – (v.utrans. inf. *mubmon*)
to disappear, to vanish
muihi, *mugjid* – (no.ina)
disappearance
Muịhti, *Muịhtśa* – (no.ani)
God, god, deity
mun·i, *mudi~muri* – (v.ai. inf. *munha*)
to rest
muodni, *muonimo* – (no.ina)
rest, pause, break
muogna, *muognamo* – (no.ina)
place to stay the night
muommor·a, *muommohra* – (v.at. inf. *muommohmi*)
to hug, to comfort | to welcome, to host
muong·i, *muondi* – (v.ai. inf. *muongisa*)
to stay the night (also *o·muongi*)
muont·a, *muontia* – (v.at inf. *muontami*)
to decide
muoṡi, *muoṡid* – (no.ina)
group of hunters, band
muri-uli, Ø-uli, *muṡid* – (quant.)
various, a number of, some
murot, *murotta* – (adj.)
various, varied
i·mủigg·i, *imủitki* – (v.ad inf. *mủiknin*)
to hold on to | (.ud) to infect (*-bma*)
mủjủmi~mġủjủmi, *mủjủtta~mġủjủtta* – (no.ani)
herder | owner
mủksủ, *mủgsủma* – (no.ina)
winter down or fur
mủkv·i, *mủkvủi* – (v.ut. inf. *mủkvisủ*)
to begin (somewhere)
myben – (adv.)
silently, in silence
mybi, *mủid* – (no.ina)
silence
mybi, *mybid* – (adj.)
silent
mybi·dibmot, *~bmotta* – (adj.)
sneaky, stealthy
mybm·a, *mynda* – (v.at/.ut. inf. *mybmami/mybmamu*)
to silence, to hush | to muffle (.ut)
myb·m·i, *myḍbima* – (v.adj)
to be silent, still, calm
mykyt, *mykytsta~mykyddja* – (no.ina)
path along a river
myndủ, *myndủma* – (adj.)
muffled, unclear, mumbled
myngi, *myngid* – (no.ina)
pause, calm | calm period
mynnj·a, *myḍdja~mynnjia* – (v.at/.ut. inf. *mynnjami~mynnjamủ*)
to damage, to cause damage, to harm
mynty, *myntyma* – (no.ina)
animal tracks (not in snow)
myry, *myhma* – (no.ina)
fly, bug
myvy, *mỷmo* – (no.ina)
little girl, girl, daughter | honey, darling
mẏhni, *mỷhhja* – (no.ani)
wolverine
mẏṡyni, *mỷṡyja* – (no.ani)
member of a **muoṡi** | member of a group

N n

nȧi, *nȧtśa* – (no.ani)
widow
nȧri – (pron.)
you (pl.)

nenri PAT.
śiron GEN.
śiśi DAT.
śiśi- LOC.
-śi POSS.
nůtra PREC
nàrri, *nẹrẹt* – (no.ani WEST)
nose
nadlõ·ka, *nalonta, -õr-* – (no.ina)
skills, traditions (involving learned skills)
nagit, *naitta* – (no.ina)
dry branch, dry wood
nahkara, *nahkahka* – (no.ina)
louse (also *půa*)
naiġġa, *naiġaka* – (no.ina)
thicket; *ġuḋgi naiġaka* 'X failed' (lit. flew into the thicket)
naihto, *naihhџa* – (no.ani)
infectious disease, virus
naipi, *naipra* – (no.ina)
banks (of a river, usually low)
naitkena, *naitkekka* – (no.ina)
precipice, steep cliff
nakn·u, *nantu~nantsġu* – (v.ui[.semel]. inf. *naknoru*)
to break, to snap
nalbi~nalvi, *nalumi* – (no.ani)
husband
nalppa, *nalpaka* – (no.ina)
snout
nang·a, *nanda* – (v.at. inf. *nagmi*)
to save up, to put aside, to stash | (tama~) to hoard
nangobba, *nangobbaka* – (adj.)
greedy, cheap, niggardly, miserly
natabi, *nataḋga* – (no.ina)
hemlock
Natsu, *Natska* – (no.ina)
(male personal name)
naukni, *naungika* – (no.ina)
breakage, fracture, rupture
nauto, *nautra* – (no.ina)
nausea, vertigo
naџin·a, *naџitta* – (v.at inf. *naџimni*)
to use (also *naym·a* 'to put to use')
naџiniџe, *nainiџeka~naџiniџeka* – (no.ina/adj.)
(something) useful
nay, *nẹma* – (no.ina)
use (also *nåvi*)
nebbi, *nebie* – (no.ina)
trap
nebmia~nebmẏ – (conj.)
perhaps, maybe
nedġ·i, *edġi* – (v.ai. inf. *nedġisa*)
to sit down
negi – (pron.)
you (.sg)
neiḋgi PAT.
sogi GEN.
sosi DAT.
osi- LOC.
–so POSS.
nůta PREC
neġvi, *neġġumi~neġůtta* – (num.ani/.ina)
three
neġnet 'thirteen'
neġġa 'thirty'
neġven 'three times'
neġvut 'third'
nehhe – (interj.)
well, you see, hm
o·neibbild·i, *oneibbildui* – (v.asubj/.at. inf. *neibbildena/ neibbildami*)
to hunt (each other), to try to get (each other) | to compete (against each other)
neidden~neiddil – (adv.)
wisely
neidġeme, *neitemme* – (no.ina)
chair
neidno, *neidnue~neidnobi* – (adj.)
wise, sage, learned, knowledgeable
neinjel·i, *neinjedli* – (v.ai. inf. *neinjelsa*)
to sit for a while, to have a sit-down
neinko, *neinkue~neinkobi* – (no.ina)
care, attention | aid, relief
neinn·u, *neinnaja* – (v.utrans. inf. *neinnoru*)
to get sand/dirt on oneself
neitrike, *neitiġe -śi-* – (no.ina)
proboscis, trunk
neivi, *neirri* – (no.ina)
cone
nekõ·ka, *nekunne* – (no.ina.pl)
crumbs | fragment, morsel, speck
nekõs, *nekõhi* – (no.ina)
bit, piece, grain, particle
nel·i, *nedli* – (v.ui inf. nelhů)

to bud (especially *neliġa~nelġa*)
neli·m·i, *nelimitta* – (v.act.part.pl)
husband's family
nen·i, *edi ~ned* – (v.ai. inf. *nenta*)
to sit
nenjaka, *nenjaġi -śi-* – (no.ina)
waves
nen·i·ga, *ediga~nediga* – (v.ai.semel. inf. *nenihsa/neniksa*)
to sit down (also *nedġ-*)
nenk·a, *neht·a* – (v.at. inf. *nenkami*)
to care for, to attend | to aid, to relief
neno, *nenue~nenobi* – (no.ina)
pollen
nerkke, *nerkie* – (no.ina)
chorus
nesk·a, *eska~aiska* – (v.at/.adit. inf. *neskami/neskanin*)
to ask
nesot, *nesotsta* – (adj.)
green, bright green
net·a, *nedda* – (v.at. inf. *nebmi*)
to know (something)
netra~netġa – (adv.)
really, truly
netro, *netue~netobi* – (no.ina)
pistil, stammen
nets, *nedda* – (num.)
ten
neddjil 'ten times | very often'
neddjut 'tenth'
netsġiabmi, *~ġuoma* – (num.irr)
thousand
netuba, *netupri, -pśi-* – (no.ina)
lilly
netva, *netvari* – (adj.)
important
neudge, *neukie* – (no.ina)
light snow
neuka, *neuġi* – (no.ina)
birch wood (also *nẻuka*)
neulkio~nẻulkio, *neulkiue~neulkiobi~nẻulkioma* – (no.ina)
ant
neutv·a, *neutvia* – (v.ut/.imp. inf. *neutvamu*)
to interest, be interested in; *neutvaka sauhhjahi* 'I am interested in languages
neudge, *neukie* – (no.ina)

dust, dirt | light snow
neuo, *niue, niobi* – (no.ina)
sand
nẻuka, *nẻuhmo* – (no.ina)
birch wood
nẻunt·a, *nẻuntia* – (v.at/.ut. inf. *nẻuntami/ nẻuntamů*)
to close, to shut | to lock
nẻusġ·a, *nẻusġia* – (v.ut inf. *nẻusġamu*)
to deafen, to be extremely loud
nẻut, *nẻutsta~nẻuddja* – (adj.)
wet, dripping
nevala~nůala, *nevalli~nůalmo* – (adj.)
diligent, hard-working
nevẻ, *nẻla* – (no.ina)
diligence, hard work
neyrōt·a, *neyrōtta* – (v.at. inf. *neyrōbmi*)
to dust off
nęp·a, *nedba* – (v.at. inf. *nebmi*)
to catch (with a trap)
nja – (interj.)
now, then, well
njaggis, *njagihi~njahki* – (no.ina)
pond, puddle
njaikka, *njaikuni* – (no.ani)
racoon
njailli, *njailika* – (no.ina)
taste, flavor
niaki, *niakid* – (no.ina)
death
njakolot, *njakolotta* – (no.ina)
end (of the world) | apocalyps | death
njakust·a, *njakustia* – (v.at. inf. *njakustami*)
to allow to die, to let to die | to abandon
njal·a, *njalla* – (v.at. inf. *njalmi*)
to taste
njal·u, *njallu* – (v.utrans inf. *njaloru*)
to taste: *osven ta·njalu* 'X tastes sour'
nianso~nianto, *niansodi~niantodi* – (no.ina)
creek | belt, corridor, passage
njarri, *njaret* – (no.ani/.ina)
nose
njaśś·i, *njaddji* – (v.ai. inf. *njaśśa*)
to commit a crime, to break a law, to commit *niśka*
njavvut·a, *njavvutta* – (v.at/.ut. inf. *njavvubmi/ njavvubmu*)

to wet | to dampen (.ut), to moisten
nidaġan, *nilaġas* – (no.ina)
 stripe, band, strip, belt (also **nidġan**)
nidġan, *nitas* – (no.ina)
 stripe, ridge, groove, furrow, channel
  tsamnidġan 'belt of forest, large territory'
nidġem·a, *nidġebma* – (v.at. inf. *nidġemmi*)
 to tattoo | to furrow
nidġula, *nituldi ~ nidġusta* – (no.ina/.ani)
 elm tree
nidi~nidiu~nidiů~nidil~nidir, *nĩla* – (no.ina)
 craftiness, cunningness, skillfulness
nidl·a, *nilla* – (v.at. inf. *nidlmi*)
 to do something in a certain way (often passive, + *avvi*)
nidlme, *nidlmedi~nilmedi* – (no.ina)
 certificat, confirmation
  kes·nidlme degree (studies)
niḍma, *niḍmadi* – (adj.)
 grave, serious, profound
nidot, *nidotsta~nidoddja* – (adj.)
 crafty, cunning, masterful, expert, skillful
niebini, *nieiġja~niêddja* – (no.ani)
 paternal grandmother
niedas, *nielhi* – (no.ina)
 fir
nj̇ėrtta, *nj̇ėrtari* – (no.ina)
 sharp pain
nj̇ėrtten·i, *nj̇ėrttedi* – (v.ui. inf. nj̇ėrttenhu)
 to be painful, to hurt
nj̇eiku, *nj̇eihme* – (no.ina)
 frown, look of anger/dissatisfaction
nj̇el-, *nj̇eltśa-* – (act.nom)
 chief
nj̇elha, *nj̇elra* – (no.ani)
 female chief
nj̇elli, *nj̇eltśa* – (no.ani)
 chief
nj̇elsi, *nj̇elsie* – (no.ina)
 sprig | child (endearing)
nj̇elsõt·a, *nj̇elsõtta* – (v.at. inf. *nj̇elsõbmi*)
 to take sprigs, to gather (something fresh) from | to harvest
nielra, *nielradi* – (adj.)
 (made of) fir
nielsõt·a, *nielsõtta* – (v.at. inf. *nielsõbmi*)
 to remove/collect sprigs (for a beverage)

nj̇ertet, *nj̇ertetsta* – (no.ina)
 pain, symptoms
nj̇ertten·i, *nj̇erttedi* – (v.ui inf. nj̇erttentů)
 to hurt, to smart
nieugi, *niůbid* – (no.ina)
 ground mist, dew
nieua-, *nieuaś-* – (act.nom)
 paternal grandmother
nieugi~nj̇eygi, *niůbid~nj̇eyhdi* – (no.ina)
 ground mist
nj̇eydn·u, *nj̇eyndu* – (v.utrans. inf. *nj̇eydnůrů*)
 to coil up, to wind up, to twine
nige, *niddji* – (no.ina)
 mud (at the bottom of a lake), silt, clay
nigj̇ehd·i, *nigj̇ehdui~nigj̇ehlui* – (v.ai inf. *nigj̇ehtsa*)
 to do summer work, to be a hired hand | *nigj̇ehdi·pp-* to toil
nibma, *nĩmadi* – (no.ina)
 birch bark (usually for tinder)
nibma – (postp.)
 over (the period of), during
nidli~nidla, *nĩldi* – (no.ina)
 face | expression
nidna, *nĩndi* – (no.ina)
 hut (especially for food) | cabin
nid·ni, *nĩ-* – (quest.pron)
 what?
  nebîd·ni 'what (of two)'
  netsîd·ni 'what (of many)'
nigj̇u – (quest.pron)
 when?
  nĩgj̇ue 'in how much time?'
  nĩgj̇oga 'how long ago? (+PERF)'
  nĩgj̇oda~nĩgj̇ora 'for how long (future)?'
  nĩgj̇oma 'at what time/on what occasion?'
  nĩgj̇onta 'how long (past)?'
  nĩgj̇onna 'until when?'
Nilkka, *Nĩlkuni* – (no.ani)
 (female personal name)
nimi – (quest.pron)
 why?
  nĩmita 'for what reason?'
  nĩmuaska 'for what reason/because of what?'
  nĩnkomo 'why?, how come?'
nineui – (quest.pron)
 how manieth? how many times? how often?

ninni – (quest.pron)
how?
niot, *nı̊otsta~nı̊oddja* – (quest.pron)
what sort of?
 innı̊ot 'what sort of (PEJ.)'
nipi, *nı̊umi~nı̊pid* – (no.ani/.ina)
dwarf birch
nipu·tsammiha, *~tsammihka* – (adj.)
(with) birch forests
nitku̧at, *nı̊tku̧atsta~nı̊tku̧addja* – (no.ina)
gender-based story telling singing
nitsva, *nı̊tsudda* – (quest.pron)
what kind of?
niu̧i – (quest.pron)
how (X)?: *nı̊u̧i iśi* 'how old?'
 nı̊u̧i Ø-uli 'what kind of?'
nivva – (quest.pron)
where?
 nı̊dda '~ to?'
 nı̊dga '~ from?'
 nı̊mma '~ on?'
 nı̊pma '~ onto?'
 nı̊skka '~ off?'
nik·i, *nid̦gi* – (v.ui. inf. *niksu*)
to die, to pass away/on
nim·mi, *nid̦d̦ima* (*nivv-*) – (v.adj)
to (be/become) wet | to be slippery
nin- – (act.nom)
-self
nin – (pron.)
oneself | he/she/it (4p.)
 nigen PAT.
 nihō̧ GEN.
 nitsi DAT.
 ni- LOC.
 –nen POSS.
 nitra PREC
ni·ni – (det.)
(one's) own | self
nioabbun·u, *njoabbuttu* – (v.utrans. inf. *njoabbunoru*)
to grow a beard | to regrow, to recover from (+ELAT)
njoagj·a – (adv.)
somewhere
 njoaita 'somewhere (movement to)'
 njoaika 'somewhere (movement from)'
njoam·ni, *njoa-* – (pron.)
someone (unknown)

njeboamni 'either, which ever'
njetsoamni 'some, which ever'
njoagju 'at some time/point'
njoavva 'in some way'
minjoa 'for some reason'
njobba, *njobmo* – (no.ina)
beard, facial hair
njoltt·i·ma, *njolttuima* – (v.adj)
to be (often) sick | to feel unwell
njo̧dna, *njo̧dnami* – (adj.)
unwell, ill
njo̧t, *njo̧tta* – (no.ina)
illness, sickness
njorġa, *njorġamo* – (no.ina)
duck (also *njorha*)
njosa, *njosma* – (adj.)
deaf
nitski, *nitskid* – (no.ina)
unit (of measurement) | group of 10 men
nitś·a *niddja* – (v.at/.ut. inf. *niitśami/nitśamu*)
to inform, to notify | to alarm (.ut)
niś·ka, *niśid* – (no.ina.pl)
crime, offense, sin
niuba, *nivvadi* – (no.ina)
despair, hopelessness, depression
njuhhi, *njuhmo* – (no.ina)
old woman, granny
njuhhu·rẙhha, *-rẙhhama* – (adj.)
toothless, with teeth like an old woman
niujaka, *niujahdi* – (no.ina)
sand dune
nju̧kli, *nju̧glima* – (no.ina)
hook, finger
nju̧klum·a, *nju̧klubma* – (v.at. inf. *nju̧klummi*)
to put on a hook | to get something over with
njulva, *njulu~njulvamo* – (no.ani/.ina)
muskox
nju̧osġi, *nju̧osġid* – (adj.)
lustful, horny
nju̧~nju̧l, *nju̧ri* – (no.ina)
desire, lust | greed
njů̧adli, *njů̧alid* – (no.ina)
wasp, bee, stinging insect
njů̧alků̧, *njů̧alků̧ma* – (no.ina)
beehive
njů̧d̦d̦e, *njů̧hhema* – (no.ina)

coil, loop, curl | seashell
nj̊ůgůkk·a, *nj̊ůgůkkia* – (v.at inf. *nj̊ůgůkmi*)
  to coil, to wrap around
nivvi~nivviu~nivviů~nivvil~nivvir,
niyila~nỉla – (no.ina)
  wetness, humidity
nivvon, *nivvos* – (adj.)
  wet
nj̊ylry, *nj̊ylryma* – (no.ina)
  stinging insects, bugs, pest
noadġ·i, *noadġui* – (v.ui. inf. *noadġisu*)
  to want to sing, to be ecstatic, to be elated, to be euphoric
noadni, *noanika* – (no.ina)
  swim
noaks·i, *noaksui* – (v.ui./.udit inf. *noaksisu/ noaksinon*)
  to end (somewhere)
noaksõ-ḥa – (adv.)
  finally
noalgi, *noalkka~noalgika* – (no.ina)
  tar kiln
noaltta, *noaltaka* – (no.ina)
  tooth, pike, thorn
noangor·a, *noangohra* – (v.at. inf. *noangohmi*)
  to limit, to restrict, to bind
nobemo, *noimma* – (no.ina)
  fire
nobia, *nojamo* – (no.ina)
  porcupine
  nobiego 'male'
  nobieha 'female'
nohi, *nohiko* – (adj.)
  smart, clever, intelligent
nohů~nohul, *nouri* – (no.ina)
  cleverness, intelligence
nokk·a, *nokkia* – (v.at. inf. *nokmi*)
  to call; *unokkika*... 'I am called…'
nokki·u, *nokkiutta* – (v.pat.part)
  name
nokna, *nongamo* – (no.ina)
  end, limit | side
nokos, *nokohi~nohki* – (no.ina)
  stick, cane, staff, twig
noksi, *nogsimo* – (no.ina)
  end, conclusion | margin, border, edge
nomi, *nomġo* – (no.ina)
  screen

nommo~nȯmmo, *nomsi~nȯmsi~nomoma* – (no.ani/.ina)
  sturgeon
nomono, *nomovva* – (no.ani)
  fang
nongamousi – (adv.)
  endless(ly), for ever
non·i, *nodi* – (v.ai. inf. *nonta*)
  to swim
nȯ-nohhi~noġ/naġ – (conj.)
  or (*nȯ̂* [nu:ʔ])
nor·i~nod·i, *nenodi* – (v.ai/.at. inf. *norha~notsa/ nomri~nobmi*)
  to sing
nośmo, *nośmoma* – (no.ina)
  pouch
notśoko, *notśohma* – (no.ina)
  hollow, cavity
nots·a, *oġa~voġa* – (v.at inf. *notsmi*)
  to take
notsġiha, *notsġira* – (no.ani)
  female shaman
notsġom·o, *notsġomotta* – (v.act.part)
  shaman
nõdln·i, *nõdlnui* – (v.ui)
  to overflow, to flood, to inundate
nõsten·a, *nõstetta* – (v.at. inf. *nõstemni*)
  to hear about, to learn of, to hear news
nubba, *nubmo* – (no.ina)
  eyelid
nub·m·i, *nuḍbima* (*nup-*) – (v.adj)
  to be angry
nyeidno, *nyeinue* – (no.ina)
  difference, nuance, distinguishing trait, characteristic
nugjen·i, *nugjedi* – (v.ui. inf. nugjentu)
  to look (some way +adv)
nuj·a, *nega*, PERF. *nuhla* – (v.at. inf. *nuimi~nugmi*)
  to see
nuidn·a, *nuinda* – (v.at inf. nuidnami)
  to identify, to know (plant/animal), to recognize, to distinguish
nujuli, *nujulma~nujultśa* – (no.ina/.ani)
  someone who sees well, with good sight
nunna, *nunnamo* – (adj.)
  angry, mad
nuobmo, *nuomoma~nuomma* – (no.ina)
  stretched skin | window

nuogi̯on, *nuoi̯onta* – (no.ina)
sight, vision | premonition, intuition
o·nuoi̯uld·i, *onuoi̯uldui* – (v.asubj/.at inf. *nuoi̯uldena*)
to see each other | to frequent each other
nuont·a, *nuontia* – (v.at/.ut. inf. *nuontami/nuontamu*)
to anger
nuppu·a, *nuppai̯a* – (v.at. inf. *nuppumi*)
to snatch, to grab, to seize
nuśkva, *nuśkvamo* – (no.ina)
hail(storm)
nŭkskon, *nŭkskonta* – (adj.)
endless, eternal, infinite
nŭtta – (interj.)
look! look out!
nŭabbŭ, *nŭabŭma* – (no.ina)
bump, lump
nŭbŭ, *nĕuma* – (no.ina)
ring finger
nŭdna, *nŭnamo* – (no.ina)
wave, ripple
nŭi-, *nŭi̯ŭm-* – (act.nom)
knife
nŭir·hi, *nŭitśagi* – (no.ani.pl)
parents, adults
nŭi̯ŭ, *nŭi̯ŭma* – (no.ina)
knife (short)
nŭnamousi – (adv.)
still, calm
nŭvvet, *nŭu̯etsta* – (no.ona)
tool
nydna, *nydnamo* – (adj.)
adult, mature (usually female)
nyggedlen, *nygedles* – (no.ina)
wolf spider, big spider
nygi̯is, *nyi̯ihi~nẏhhi* – (no.ina)
spirit, vigor, enthusiasm, zeal
nygi̯y, *nyi̯yma* – (no.ina)
verse, poem
nyġġot, *nyġġotsta* – (adj.)
curved, bent
nyhh·a, *nyhra* – (v.at/.ut. inf. *nyhmi~nyhmŭ*)
to curl, to bend, to make curl, to make bend: *nyhhō* 'extremely'
nykki, *nyhtśa~nykkid* – (no.ani/.ina)
nail
nyly, *nylyma* – (no.ina)
snout | sharp end, (arrow/axe) head
nynnyly~nynni̯yly~nẏlly – (adv.)
it is said, one would say, as though, as it were
nypp·i, *nypri* – (v.ui inf. *nypsŭ*)
to stick out
nypy, *nypyma* – (no.ina)
anger, rage
nẏ – (onom.)
wow, woah, sound to show surprise/awe
nẏdet, *nymetsta* – (no.ina)
fern
nẏdedni̯ukli – furled frond
nẏ·m·i, *nuo·m·i* – (v.imp)
to be humid (usually at dawn)
nẏmmi, *nẏmdi* – (no.ina)
heap, hill
nẏn, *nẏs* – (adj.)
closed, shut

O o

oa – (adv.)
already, yet
oadi, *vaika* – (no.ina)
palate, tongue
oadni, *oanika* – (no.ina)
story | look, glance
oaḍbi, *vaubbi~vaubba* – (no.du)
gums
oagi̯on, *oai̯onta* – (no.ina)
memory (also *vagi̯on*)
oahkurr·a, *oahkurta* – (v.at. inf. *oahkurmi*)
to test, to edge
oaig·a, *oaitka* – (v.at inf. *oaihmi*)
to hook, to pin (down; *kat~*)
oaki·ma– (adv.)
at home: *oakibma* 'to ~', *oakiska* 'from ~'
oams·u, *oamsai̯u* – (v.utrans inf. *oamsoru*)
to get snowed in
oapi, *oadgo* – (no.ina)
help, assistance
oari, *oahka* – (no.ina)
edge, brim, brink, verge
obena, *oimmo* – (no.ina)
smoke, fumes

obeno, *oimma* – (no.ina)
smoke, fumes
obesġilen, *obesġilenta* – (no.ina)
peace making/keeping, resolution
oddo, *odoma* – (no.ina)
white reindeer
odlebi, *olebmo* – (no.ina)
sorrow, sadness | regret
odlna, *odlnamo~olnamo* – (no.ina)
blizzard, white-out, snow storm (with very low visibility)
ogalen, *ovvalenta* – (no.ina)
conversation, discussion, dialogue
ogj·a, *odja* – (v.at/.ut. inf. *ogjami/ogjamu*)
to remember
ogjen·a, *ogjetta* – (v.at)
to notice
ogjenuli, *ojenulko~ogjenultśa* – (no.ina/.ani)
a perspicacious, observant, alert, sharp-eyed person
ogjuli, *ojulko~ogjultśa* – (no.ina/.ani)
someone with a good memory, a wise person
ohha, *ora~ohmo* – (no.ani/.ina)
female salmon
ohhį·i·ma, *ostima* – (v.adj)
to be strong/powerful
ohhįo, *ohhįoma* – (adj.)
strong
ohhįo·tåhmiha, *~tåhmihka* – (adj.)
strong-hearted, generous
ohkama~ohkana, *ohkammo* – (adj.)
raw, uncooked
ohki, *ohkimo* – (adj.)
deep
ohk·u, *ohkaju* – (v.aux.utrans. inf. *ohkoru*)
to be possible to (space/place/position), to fit (+ILLAT)
ohků~ohkul, *ohkuri* – (no.ina)
depth
ohlu, *ohda* – (no.ani)
death | smell of death
ohna, *ohnamo* – (no.ina)
white ash
ohra, *ohhusta~ȯsta* – (no.ani)
god, deity
oi, *otśa* – (no.ani)
moon light
oin·a, *oitta* – (v.at. inf. *oimni*)
to look at, to glance at (older *oden·a*)
oju·i, *ojei* – (v.ui/.ai. inf. *ojusu/ojusa*)
to cry, to whine | to complain (.ai)
ojula~olula, *ojusta~olusta* – (no.ani)
white birch
ojuma, *ojummo* – (no.ina)
whiner, whinger
oka, *ogmo* – (no.ina)
forefather(s), ancestors
okęhi, *okętśa* – (no.ani)
pine needle(s)
okkomosi, *okkomotta* – (no.ani)
poor fellow
okon, *okonta -ȯri-* – (no.ina)
big old man, old man
okuhka – (postp.)
from (as a source of), of X origin: *tulmu damġa okuhka* 'clothes (made) from animal skins'
oků~okul, *okuri* – (no.ina)
origin, source, ancestry
olkko, *olkoma* – (no.ina)
temple(s)
olobben, *olobbes* – (no.ina)
leafhopper, little bug, bug on a leaf
omi, *ȍkko* – (no.ina)
snow
omna, *ȍbba* – (no.du)
married couple
omsta, *omstamo* – (no.ina)
type of knot (square knot, to tie two strings/ropes together) (also *ȍusta*).
on·a, *nona* – (v.at/.adit. inf. *omna/onnin*)
to tell, to let know
onda – (interj.)
yes (short for *oni da*)
oni~ůnnů – (adv.)
thus, like this, hereby
oni·keltuha, *~keltuhari* – (adj.)
(with) lichen on the ground/bottom
onna – (comp.)
less
ono, *omma* – (no.ina)
lichen
onona, *onommo* – (adj.)
little, small, compact
onśi, *onśiko~onohta* – (no.ina/.ani)
(channel) catfish

onta·i, *ontei* – (v.ai. inf. *ontasa*)
to dance
onto~ōtō~ōddō – (pron.)
he/she/it/they (obv.)
ōḍḍo~ōḍḍō PAT.
ōhō GEN.
ōtsi DAT.
teni- LOC.
–hō POSS.
tōuta PREC
onuye, *onuyemo* – (adj./no.ina)
(something) worth telling
ȯ, *obo~ȯbo* – (no.ina)
bruise, lesion, lump
ȯb·i, *ȯḍbi* – (v.un.itr, inf. *ȯpsu*)
to bruise, to get bruised
ȯdni~ėudni – (adv.)
now
ȯhhji, *ȯṡko* – (no.ina)
evening, late afternoon
ȯliha~ȯlha, *ȯlihmo~ȯlhamo* – (adj.)
leafy
ȯlma, *ȯlka* – (no.ani/.ina)
leaf (also **vulma**)
ȯmin, *ȯminta* – (adj.)
stiff, rigid | painful (of muscles)
ȯm·m·i, *ȯbmima* – (v.adj)
to feel stiff/reluctant, unwilling | to prove difficult to
op·a, *oḍba* – (v.at)
to help, to assist, to support
opo, *obma* – (no.ina)
individual, person, human
opoh·m·i, *oporrima* (*opor-*) – (v.adj)
to be (still) alive, to be (still) safe and sound, unhurt
opona, *opommo* – (adj.)
alive, living, breathing | unhurt, safe and sound
opsi, *obsiko* – (no.ina)
cup | mushroom
orobi, *orobmo* – (no.ina)
forked spear
orp·i, *orpui* – (v.ai inf. *orpisa*)
to misbehave
osk·a, *oskia* – (v.at. inf. *oskami*)
to smoke (to preserve) | to preserve
oskon, *oskonta -ōri-* – (no.ina)
male moose
os·m·i, *obmi~ohima* – (v.adj)
to have heartburn | to feel guilty, ashamed
osmu, *osmuma* – (no.ina)
smell of fire, smell of burning
osoken, *osokenta* – (no.ina)
building a house
osve, *osvemo* – (adj.)
sour, acidic, bitter | rancid, turned
oṡot, *oṡotta* – (no.ina)
quantity of animals/fish in a certain area
oten, *otenta* – (no.ina)
organization, union
otġa, *otġamo* – (adj.)
thick, broad
otken, *otkenta* – (no.ina)
training, formation | education
otski – (inv.)
laced: *seta~katagoa~auḍga~aunta otski* to lace
ouala~oala, *oyalmo~oalmo* – (adj.)
wide, broad, extensive
ougu~ouġu, *oumma~ouhma* – (no.ina)
hook, barb: *oummia~ouhmia* 'to have a problem'
ouis, *ẏhhi* – (no.ina)
turtle
oḍḍo, *ohma* – (no.ina)
(clear) night sky
ovva~ėuvva, *oḍḍa~ėuḍḍa* – (adj.)
such, like this, such as this

Ō õ

ōka, *ōġmo* – (no.ina)
tundra
ōri, *ōrko~ōhko* – (no.ina)
stump, lower part of tree
ōsi – (neg.adv.)
no longer, not (now) anymore
ōska – (adv.)
often
ōska·i, *ōskei* – (v.ui inf. *ōskasu*)
to happen often
ōut, *ōutta* – (no.ina)
newly fallen snow

P p

pålli, *påltśa~pållika* – (no.ani/adj.)
mature male animal | mature (male)
pagi, *paika* – (no.ina)
back, backside
paggemis, *pagemhi* – (no.ina)
Saturday
pahla, *pahlaka* – (adj.)
full, filled
paikki, *paihtśa* – (no.ani)
turtle
pakvi, *pagvika* – (no.ina)
grave, pit, hole | mistake
patskon, *patskonta* – (adj.)
inconsiderate | inattentive | distracted
paukke, *paukkeka* – (no.ina)
hole, pit
peddjaka, *peddjagi -śi-*
logs used to build a house
pedn·i, *pendi* – (v.ai/.ui. inf.[irr]
penha~pedninha/pednisa~pednidnasa)
to arrive | to return (~dna- +REVERS)
pèbmu·i, *pėbmůi* (pèbmo-) – (v.ui. inf.
pèbmosu)
to bounce, to rebound, to spring back
pèsi, *pėta* – (no.ani)
maternal uncle
peidni, *peinie* – (no.ina)
return
peggů, *pegůme* – (no.ina)
girl
peibmus, *peimuhi~peihmi* – (no.ina)
ass
peilki, *peiltśa~peilkie* – (no.ani/.ina)
trout
peilni, *peilja* – (no.ani)
eldest (male of group)
peljekk·a, *peljekkia* – (v.at/.ut. inf.
peljekmi/peljekmu)
to cook (over fire)
pendųa, *pendųari* – (no.ina)
arrival
pengi, *pentsa* – (no.ani)
(young) wolf, wolf cub
Pengo, *pentsa* – (no.ani)
(male personal name)
pes·a, *peha* – (v.at. inf. *pesmi*)
to have the courage to (+INF)
peuiskvi, *peuiskkumi* – (no.ina)
slippery jack (*Suillus luteus*) (also *peųiskvi*,
peyskvi, *půvviskvi*)
pev·a, *bůa* – (v.at./.ai inf. *pemmi~pessa*)
to eat (humans only, polite)
peyma, *peymmi* – (no.ina)
table, bench, counter, work bench |
working area
pęles, *pęlehi~pelhi* – (no.ina)
stuffed stomach
piagebba, *piaibbadi* – (no.ina)
a sleepy person, sleepy head
piag·i, *piatki* – (v.ui. inf. *piaksu*)
to fall asleep
pjaha, *pjara* – (no.ani)
healer, doctor
pialjekk·a, *pialjekkia* – (v.ut/.at. inf.
pialjekmu/pialjekmi)
to make flush, to make red
pialjen·i, *pialjedi* – (v.ui. inf. *pialjentu*)
to seem red, to flush, to be reddish
pjanni, *pjanja* – (no.ina)
harvester, worker | slave (often *abbjanni*)
pjap·pa, *pjarpa* – (act.nom)
(our) shaman
piddani, *pittśa* – (no.ani)
maternal grandmother
piegjist·a, *piegjistia* – (v.at. inf.
piegjistami)
to allow (life/animals) to recover, to give a
chance
piegjino, *piegjindi* – (adj.)
healthy, in good health
pjeskko, *pjeskkue* – (no.ina)
snowflake
pigji~pigjil~piddji~piddjil, *pijila* – (no.ina)
health, vigor
pigj·i·ma, *pidjima* – (v.adj)
to be/look/feel healthy
pigjuoma – (interj.)
take care, goodbye
pihh·u, *pivvu* – (v.aux.utrans. inf. *pihlu*)
may, to be possible (+INF)
pìdna, *pînadi* – (no.ina)
direction, orientation | way, course
sauspîdna 'grammar'
pihha, *pîhra~pîhdi* – (no.ani/.ina)
yew

pigjon, *pī̮jos* – (no.ina)
maternal (uncle's family)/family
pini, *pī̮ndi* – (no.ina)
corn, bean
pikś·i·ma, *pikśuima* – (v.adj)
to be hurt
pila, *piladi~pildi* – (adj.)
red
pil·m·i, *pidlmi* – (v.adj)
to be red(dish)/orange (of light)
pjoki, *pjokko* – (no.ina)
flint
pirin, *piśis* – (no.ina)
nugget, chunk, piece
piśisusi~piśśuśi~puśiś~puspus~puśpuś~pů śpůś 'not at all, not in the slightest'
piśkel·i, *piśkedli* – (v.ui. inf. *piśkelsu*)
to be in a coma
piśvi, *piśśumi* – (no.ani)
lynx
pitsġ·a, *pitska* – (v.at inf. *pitsġami*)
to scold, to yell at, to discipline
pitt·a, *pittia* – (v.at. inf. *pitmi*)
to pay attention to
pittabmot, *-bmotta* – (adj.)
attentive, observant, alert (adv. *pittamoi~pittamil*)
pittami~pittamil, *pittamila* – (no.ina)
attention, attentiveness
pittśa-, *pittśaś-* – (act.nom)
maternal grandmother
piust·i, *piustui* – (v.ai/.ui. inf. *piustisa/piustisu*)
to thrive | to flourish, to burgeon, to blossom
poakn·u, *poantu* – (v.utrans. inf. *poaknoru*)
to be very busy | to make the mistake of (+ELAT)
poaśśi, *poaśka* – (no.ina)
sleep
poaśv·a, *poaśvia* – (v.ut/.at. inf. *poaśvamu/poaśvami*)
to make sleepy | to put to sleep (.at)
poavvi, *poagga* – (no.ina)
seal
pohhj·i, *posti* – (v.ui. inf. *pośśu*)
to sleep
pohi, *pohiko* – (adj.)
chubby, fat, round

polbi, *polumi* – (no.ani)
northern cardinal
polra, *polramo* – (no.ina)
cranberry
pȯbi, *pomumi* – (no.ani)
(young) seal
puḥḥu – (onom.)
woosh, go away
puilo, *puilma* – (no.ina)
nerve
pulġemis, *pulġemhi* – (no.ina)
Monday
puna, *pummo* – (no.ina)
deer skin, deer leather
puodus, *puolhi* – (no.ina)
navel, belly button | focus, nucleus
půa, *půama* – (no.ina)
(head)louse
půadlva, *půadlvamo~půalvamo* – (no.ina)
otter
půbma, *půmamo* – (no.ina)
point, position | level, degree
půdů, *pêuma* – (no.ina)
log
půkka – (onom.)
woosh, go away
půlġůn, *půlġůs* – (no.ina)
bud (on a tree)
půmr·a, *půmria* – (v.at. inf. *půmrami*)
to situate
ujopůmra 'to pinpoint'
pyddji, *pyttśa* – (no.ani)
male cousin (mother's brother's)
pydna, *pytva* – (no.ani)
female cousin (mother's brother's)
pykn·ů, *pyntů* – (v.ut inf. *pyknůrů*)
to swell up | to throb | *hę~* to get an erection
pymi, *pyndi~pymmo* – (no.ina)
(bad) bark, (hard) bark
pyry, *pyhma* – (no.ina)
wind | fart
pẏbme, *pẏmedi* – (no.ina)
seal skin, seal lather
pẏ·ka, *pyby* – (no.ina.pl)
canvas, material, cloth

R r

r·a, *ria* – (v.at/.ut inf. *rami/ramu*)
to bite
rȧmi, *rȧmka* – (no.ina)
rock protruding out of water | protrusion, projection, outgrowth, bulge
rabma, *ramaka* – (no.ina)
canoe (for one man)
rad·a, *radda* – (v.at. inf. *rabmi*)
to stop, to cease
rad·eddō – (adv.)
unceasingly, non-stop, constantly
radlv·a, *radlvia* – (v.at/.ut. inf. *radlvami/radlvamu*)
to disturb, to interrupt
hę·radlv·a 'to agitate' (.at/.ut)
i·rahk·a, *irahkia* – (v.adit. inf. *rahkanin*)
to advise, to give advice (to someone +ALLAT)
rahot, *rahotta* – (adj.)
crisp, crispy, dry
rahtsġ·i, *rahtski~rahtsġui* – (v.ai inf. *rahtsġisa*)
to run (on all fours, of animals)
raḥḥ·i, *raḥḥui* – (v.ui inf. *raḥḥisu*)
to rupture, to tear
raibma, *raimaka* – (no.ina)
tail
raiksi, *raigsika* – (no.ina)
fresh water source
rakana, *rakakka* – (adj.)
fragile
rakm·a, *rakmia* – (v.at/.ut inf. *rakmami/rakmamu*)
to take something from somewhere, to rely on
rapa, *rapra*, -*śi*- or *raḍga* – (no.ina)
small hill, hillock, mound, knoll
rapuppa, *rapupra~rapuppaka* – (adj.)
hilly
rarp·i·ma, *rarpuima* – (v.adj)
to feel furious, enraged
rarpo, *rarpoka* – (adj.)
furious, enraged: *rarpo ůrjůjů~ůrjůjemi* 'madly furious' (lit. furious like a female wolf)
ratta, *rattaka* – (adj.)
dry, hardened, rough

raunko, *raunkoka~raunkka* – (no.ina)
(fox/wolf) litter
redlmen, *redlmes~relmes* – (no.ina)
cricket
rehh·a, *rehra* – (v.at/.ut. inf. *rehmi/rehmu*)
to drag, to haul | to have an attitude
rehhji, *reṡie* – (no.ina)
secret
reibo, *reibbe* – (no.ina)
beam (of light), ray | expression, look
rekkot, *rekkotsta~rekkoddja* – (adj.)
open | clear, safe
remmy, *remme* – (no.ina)
issue, (state of) affaire, thing, material | (arch.) pimple
soġemmy 'economy'
rendl·i, *rendlui* – (v.ai/.ui. inf. *rendlisa/rendlisu*)
to graze, to eat slowly | to talk (a lot)
rentim·a, *rentibma* – (v.at/.adit. inf. *rentimmi/rentimnin*)
to feed (seeds, to birds/animals)
rento, *rentue~rentobi* – (no.ina)
seed, grain
reri, *reṡie* – (no.ina)
bladder on foot
rerreki, *reregge* – (no.ina)
sudden change of mind; *ituvvibma reregge* 'X had a sudden change of mind/mood (lit. ~ turned onto X)
reṡet, *reṡetsta* – (no.ina)
mussel
retema, *revva* – (no.ani)
fox (pl. **sitema**)
retro, *retue~retobi~retsta* – (no.ina/.ani)
northern pike
reymkena, *reymkedi* – (no.ina)
dangerous spot in a river/lake due to hidden rocks
i·r·i, *irui* – (v.adit. inf. *irinen*)
to bite into
riakkabi, *riakkabid* – (no.ina)
key
rjanna, *rjanka* – (no.ina)
hip
rjaḍba, *rjaubba* – (no.du)
hips
riehpi, *riekumi* – (no.ani)
wife

riehu, *rieudi* – (no.ina)
woman (pej.)
rjeinkena, *rjeinkedi* – (adj.)
thorny, shaped like a thorn | difficult, tricky
rietki, *rietkid* – (no.ina)
where the forest ends
ri, *ritśa* – (no.ani)
tooth
ridbi, *rîpid* – (no.ina)
socket, hole, fitting
ridni, *rînid* – (no.ina)
thorn, spike, barb: *idi rînîta(ra)*
rihko, *rîhta* – (no.ani)
skin, membrane, film
rikki·a, *rikkua* – (v.at. inf. *rikkimi*)
to open
rikvu, *rigvudi* – (no.ina)
parcel | bag carried on animal (gen. caribou)
riskkotan, *riskotas* – (no.ina)
joke, funny story
riso, *risodi* – (no.ina)
sandy ground
roahi, *roahika* – (adj.)
simple, normal, usual
roaht·a, *roahtia* – (v.at. inf. *roahtami*)
to hollow out, to gouge, to scoop
roakken, *roakkes* – (no.ina)
circle
soku·roakken 'society'
roatme, *roatmeka* – (no.ina)
crust, hard layer, tough layer
robůakken – (adv.)
everyday (also **rokendai**)
rodlot, *rolotta* – (no.ina)
folds, detail (in clothes) | fine clothes
rodlůl·i, *rodlůdli* – (v.ai. inf. *rodlůlsa*)
to be wearing beautiful clothes
rogo, *rotsa* – (no.ani)
(young/heroic) man | character, hero
rogo – (postp.)
in the way (*rośta* 'into ~' *rośka* 'from ~')
rogo·ni – (det.)
the one in the way, obstacle
roihho, *roihma* – (no.ina)
droplet, drop (of water)
rokloma, *roklomamo~roklommo* – (adj.)
round, rounded
roko, *rokoma* – (adj.)
hollow, void, worthless
rom·estot, *~estodna* – (num.quard/.adj)
the very first | primal, fundamental, primeval, primitive (adj. GEN. *romestotsta~romestoddja*)
rom·ni – (pron.)
every
rokni 'pl.'
rebomni 'both'
retsomni 'every (one of)'
rovus, *rẙhhi* – (no.ina)
shore (of a lake)
rudlu, *ruluma* – (no.ina)
wrinkle
rukso, *rugsoma* – (no.ina)
circle, ring
rumu, *rumma* – (no.ina)
fog
ruogjia – (adv.)
everywhere
ruogjita 'everywhere (movement to)'
ruogjika 'everywhere (movement from)'
ruogju – (adv.)
every time
ruoikne·i, *ruoiknui* – (v.ui inf. *ruoknesu*)
to wake up a little (also *růiknei, ryvvoiknei*)
ruovva – (adv.)
in every way, completely, quite
rutr·a, *rutria* – (v.at. inf. *rutrami*)
to hate, to despise
rů, *rumu* – (no.ina)
limit (of territory), border
růtůmmi, *růtůmmid* – (adj./no.ina)
idiot
rybmy, *rymyma* – (no.ina)
dress
rymėul·i, *rymẻudli* – (v.ai. inf. *rymẻulsa*)
to be wearing a dress, to be in a dress
rymyry, *rymyhma* – (no.ina)
mosquito, problem: *syngydni rymyry-yli* 'no problem'
rytgy, *rytgyma* – (no.ina)
hammer
rẏ, *rymy* – (no.ina)
tremmor, shaking | earthquake

S s

såhk·a, *såhkia* – (v.at. inf. *såhkami*)
to dare to, to have the courage to (+INF)

såhpa, *såmġa* – (no.du)
lungs, torso

såhta, *såhhu̧a* – (no.ani)
lung, breath

såma-, *såmġa-* – (act.nom)
maternal grandfather

sabbas, *sabahi* – (no.ina)
sole (of shoe), underside of foot

saddama, *sadakka* – (no.ina)
callus, wart

saḍbi, *sapika* – (no.ina)
forest fire

sagna~svagna, *sagva~svagva* – (no.ani)
bride

sahh·a, *sahra* – (v.at/.ut. inf. *sahmi/sahmu*)
to burn

sahh·i, *savvi* – (v.ui. inf. *sahsu*)
to burn

saibb·a, *saipra* – (v.aux.atr. inf. *saipmi*)
must/may/shall not (+ELAT)

saiddon, *saidonta* – (no.ina)
big catch, big fish | jack pot

saidli, *sailika* – (no.ina)
burnt food

saiḍḍe, *saihheka* – (no.ina)
burning sensation | *hẹ~* heartburn

saiḍgena, *saikekka* – (no.ina)
burnt forest

saigi, *saitsa* – (no.ani)
moose

saihkena, *saihkekka* – (no.ina)
point, cap, spit

s·ail·a, *taila* – (v.at.irr inf. *sailmi*)
to trust

saimn·i, *saimui* – (v.ui./.ai. inf. *saimnisa*)
to run, to flow | to sprint, to dash | to flee | to disappear
   tat·saimn·a 'to belong to'

saipi, *saiḍga* – (no.ina)
race, contest | rivalry, opposition

sais·a, *saiha* – (v.at inf. *saismi*)
to warn, to caution | *kat~* to notify, to advise | *tama~* to hint at, to predict

saitk·i, *saitkui* – (v.ui/.asubj. inf. *saitkisu/saitkina*)
to disappear, to go out of sight | to hide (in shame, in fear, cowardly) (.asubj, *osaitki*)

saiu̧u, *sajuka* – (no.ina)
pot (usually for boiling)

saksla, *sakslaka* – (no.ina)
(loose) ice in a river | (med.) discharge, menstruation

sakva, *sagvaka* – (no.ina)
soap

salama, *salakka* – (no.ina)
antlers | caribou(s)

sale·koahibmis, *~mhi* – (adj.)
which has many caribou

salla – (adv.)
well (COMP. *sahne*, SUPER. *sagjoba~saiba*)

salśin·hi, *salśijagi* – (no.ani.pl)
caribou head sacrifice

saluli~saluri, *salulka* – (no.ina)
tar

Samho, *Samtsa* – (no.ani)
(male personal name)

samna – (postp.)
while, during

-samnanha, *-samnanhaka* – (adj.)
belonging to X time/period: *oapi kelgosamnanha* 'war-time help'

samna·ni – (det.)
the one during, the one from X period

sappiska, *sappiskka* – (no.ina)
paw, big hands

sapr·u, *sapraju* – (v.aux.utrans. inf. *saproru*)
to be likely to, may very well (+INF)

sara, *sarġa, sakka* – (adj.)
good (COMP. *sohta*, SUPER. *saisla* [GEN. *saisilda*])
sarv·a 'is good'

sarah·m·i, *sararrima* (*sarar-*) – (v.adj)
to (become/be) more narrow

sarana, *sarakka* – (adj.)
narrow, tight, cramped | limited

saroko, *sarokka* – (no.ina)
piece, part, section, portion (also **soroko**)

sasame, *sasakka* – (no.ina)
tent, tipi

sasat, *sasatta* – (no.ina)
protective spirit | benevolence, kindness

sask·i, *saskui* – (v.ui/.ai. inf. *saskisu/saskisa*)
to wake up, to awake
sasli, *saslika* – (no.ina)
responsibility (towards one's land)
saś·i~sahhį·i, *satsi~sasti* – (v.ai. inf. *saśśa*)
to speak, to talk
saśi·ba~saś·pa, *saśkaba* – (act.nom)
Siwa | (our) language
saśkoge, *saśkokka* – (no.ina)
victim (of murder)
sata, *savva* – (no.ani)
ear
saubus, *samuhi~sauvvuhi* – (no.ina)
small flame, small fire, candle
saudd·a, *sauddia* – (v.at)
to catch (with ones hands)
saudn·u, *saundu* – (v.utrans. inf. *saudnoru*)
to catch on fire
saugen·i, *saugedi* – (v.ui. inf. *saugenta*)
to smell something burning, for something to smell burnt
sauhna, *sauhnaka* – (no.ina)
narrowing point in lake/river
saumi, *saumka* – (no.ina)
caribou (owned/domesticated)
saupihtsġa – (adv.)
generally, customarily, in many cases, time and time again
savi – (conj.)
than
saḍba, *saubba* – (no.du)
ears
saḍḍa, *sahhaka* – (no.ina)
fire (in house/forest)
sat·a, *sadda* – (v.at inf. *sabmi*)
to whistle at someone
savvu, *savvutta* – (v.pat.part)
burn (on skin)
savvù, *sauri* – (no.ina)
goal, destination, aim, target
saykl·a, *sayklia* – (v.at. inf. *sayklami*)
to protect, to defend, to shield
sayna, *saynka* – (no.ina)
hiding place
seba, *sebġi~sepri~sepsi* – (adj.)
bad | evil | harmful, dangerous (COMP. *seutta~sůtta*, SUP. *baidla*, SUP.GEN *bailda*)
segaka, *sevaġi -śi-* – (no.ina)
burnt (out) embers, cinder, coal
seġa, *seġari* – (adj)
barren, infertile, arid | *kat~* sterile
seġu, *seume* – (no.ina)
barren soil, rocky soil
sehhųe, *sehhųeri* – (adj.)
fervent, passionate, intense | eager, keen | impatient
sehi, *sehie* – (adj.)
thin (not thick) | fine
sehka, *sehkari* – (no.ina/.adv)
south-east
  sehkaśa 'in the south-east'
  sehkahta 'to the south-east'
  sehkahteri 'towards the south-east'
  sehkahtsi 'along the south-east (face/side)'
  sehkahka 'from the south-east'
seh·m·i, *sevvima* – (v.adj)
to (be/feel) eager/keen, impatient | to be sexually aroused, to be horny
seį·a, *sedįa* – (v.at/.ut. inf. *seimi/seimu*)
to hear
seidlġa, *seidlġari* – (no.ina)
pregnant fish
seidlo, *seilue~seilobi* – (no.ina)
push, help, support
seitkv·a, *seitkvia* – (v.ut/.at. inf. *seitkvamu/seitkvami*)
to put to shame, to shame
seitu·a, *seitia* – (v.at. inf. *seitomi*)
to threaten
seįuli, *seįulle~seįultśa* – (no.ina/.ani)
someone who hears well, someone with fine hearing
seky, *segme* – (no.ina)
cliff, rock face
sel-, *seus-* – (act.nom)
(my) herd
selga, *seltsa* – (no.ani)
(young/pretty) woman
(t)selgoni, *(t)selgoįa* – (no.ani)
girlfriend
selion, *selios* – (no.ina)
caribou herd (small)
selo, *selue~selobi* – (no.ina)

(big) river
seng·i, *send·i* – (v.ai. inf. *sengisa*)
to sound, to sing, to chant, so make a sound | to shine (of the sun only)
sengẏ, *sengyla* – (no.ina)
song, chant
senni, *sennie* – (no.ina)
time, period
seppi, *seppie~seppi̯e/seppen* – (quant.)
very, quite, exceedingly, quite (the)
seri̯ekk·a, *seri̯ekkia* – (v.at/.ut. inf. *seri̯ekmi/seri̯ekmu*)
to fix, to make good/amends, to make up for | to make feel/seem good
seri̯en·i, *seri̯edi* – (v.ui. inf. *sei̯entu*)
to feel good, to seem good, to appear good
serula, *serusta~serulli* – (no.ani/.ina)
larch
sesġ·u, *seskku* – (v.utrans. inf. *sesġoru*)
to happen (of accidents)
sesġō 'by accident'
seskken – (adv.)
sometimes
seskora, *seskosta* – (no.ani)
tree used to find one's way: *tåsa seskostimi~seskotemi~seskotebi* 'to be obvious/evident' or 'to be obvious' (lit. to stand like a *seskora*)
seskv·i, *seskvui* – (v.ui. inf. *seskvisu/seskosu*)
to be clear, to be obvious | (**kat·-**) to be safe, to be away from danger
sesoi̯aka, *sesoi̯aġi -ṡ-* – (no.ina)
group of tents, camp, temporary settlement
set~sem~sę̯ – (neg.adv)
not
s·et·a, *teta* – (v.at inf. *sebmi*)
to place, to put (also *setġa*)
seto, *setue* – (no.ina)
threat
setul·a, *sedla* – (v.at inf. *sedlmi*)
to push | to help
sėu, *sůbů* – (no.ina)
river, creek
seu̯is, *sůhhi* – (no.ina)
(small) river (also *seu̯iṡ*)
seumi, *seumme* – (no.ina)
soil, land | clay (arch.)

seuvvi, *seuvve* – (adj.)
sweet
sġaht·a, *sġahtia* – (v.at. inf. *sġahtami*)
to be able to (uncertain)
sġaum·i, *sġaubmi* – (v.ai inf. *sġaumsa*)
to breathe
sġidlġa, *sġidlġadi~sġiladi* – (no.ina)
reins (pl. if *sġiladi*)
sġo·a, *sġia* – (v.at. inf. *sġomi*)
to feed (animals)
sġoakke, *sġoakkeka* – (no.ina)
ghost
sġodna, *sġonamo* – (no.ina)
shade, shadow
sġotrage, *sġotahmo* – (no.ina)
enemy
sġůdl(k)·i, *sġůlli~sġůdlkui* – (v.ai. inf. *sġůdl(k)isa*)
to shit (-k- often found, originally translo.)
sġůgi̯i·ia – (adv.)
nowhere
sġůita 'nowhere (movement to)'
sġůika 'nowhere (movement from)'
sġůgi̯ů – (adv.)
never
sġům·ni, *sġů-* – (pron.)
no one
sġebůmni 'neither'
sġetsůmni 'none (of)'
sġůvva 'in no way'
misġů 'for no reason'
sġvelmi, *sġveltta* – (no.ani)
gland
sġvi~sġvil, *sġvila* – (no.ina)
brains
sianta, *siantadi* – (no.ina)
horizon, skyline
siari̯i, *siari̯id* – (no.ina/.adv)
south-west | front (direction WEST)
siari̯a 'in the south-west'
siari̯ata 'to the south-west'
siari̯ateri 'towards the south-west'
siari̯atsi 'along the south-west (face/side)'
siari̯aka 'from the south-west'
sibema, *sibekka* – (no.ina)
North | back (direction, EAST)
sibemla 'northern most'
sibm·a, *sinda* – (v.at/.ut)
to catch

sibma, *simadi* – (no.ina)
claw
sibmuli, *simuldi~sibmultśa* – (no.ina/.ani)
good/lucky/skilled hunter/fisherman
sid·i~si~svid·i, *siddi~sui~sviddi* – (v.ai/.at. inf. *sitsa~sisa~svitsa*)
to understand: *tsengita~tsengista sîsa* 'to realize' (lit. to understand [into] clear')
sidn·i, *sindi* – (v.imp/.ui)
to last (for a long time)
siḍbi, *sipid* – (no.ina)
shoe, boot
sieddo, *sietodi* – (no.ina)
understanding, intelligence (also **svieddo**)
sieḍbi, *siehhumi* – (no.ani)
eagle
sieḍḍo, *siehhodi* – (no.ina)
foot (also *siḍḍo*)
siehdia – (adv.)
south
siehta 'southwards, to the south'
siehteri 'towards the south'
siehtsi 'along the south(face/side)'
siehka 'from the south'
siehhi·hidoha, *~hidohdi* – (adj.)
long-haired
siehhin, *siehhis* – (adj.)
long (in length) | tall (.ina)
siehhumi, *siehhõdi* – (no.ina)
dried meat
siehhủ~siehhul, *siehhula* – (no.ina)
length, height
sieh·m·i, *sievvima* (*siehh-*) – (v.adj)
to (be/become) elongated, stretched out: *ůvvika siehmi suśta syjahmo* 'from here the tributaries stretch out/ spread out far'
siggini, *sigindi~siggija* – (no.ina/.ani)
sparrow
sigv·i·ma, *sigvuima* – (v.imp)
it is dusk
sihh·i, *sihri* – (v.imp.)
to rain
sihhju·ita – (adv.)
along the length: *sihhjuita hohtsi* 'down along the length'
sihi – (adv.)
only
sihts·a, *sihtsta* – (v.at inf. *sihtsami*)
to look for (something lost) | *hẹ~* to find something (lost)
sihuha, *sihuhadi* – (adj.)
(the) only (one)
sihḥe – (interj.)
isn't it, right?
sihpi, *sîhhumi~sîrumi* – (no.ani)
whale
siub·m·i, *sîuddima* – (v.adj)
to be hungry (*siut-*)
siutả, *sîutẹgịi* – (no.ina)
glutton, giant
sijula, *sịjuldi* – (no.ina)
spruce (usually as a material)
sikk·a, *sikkia* – (v.at. inf. *sikmi*)
to refuse, to send back | to leave, to abandon | to kick
o·sikk·i, *osikkui* – (v.ut. inf. *sikna*)
to sneak
sikvi, *sikvid* – (adj.)
white, bright, shiny | beautiful, pretty, attractive
sikvut, *sigvutsta~sigvuddịa* – (no.ina)
bonfire, large fire, bright light
sili, *sildi* – (no.ina)
breast(s)
simśi~semśi, *simohta~semohta* – (no.ani)
human, person, Siwa
singel·i, *singedli* – (v.imp)
to last for a long time, to be permanent
singelibmis 'permanent'
sinin, *sinis* – (no.ina)
large fish
sinka – (adv.)
(from) a long time (ago)
sinnena, *sinnendi* – (adj.)
long (duration)
sipob·m·i, *sipostima* (*sipoḥ-*) – (v.adj)
to (be/feel) confused | to be entangled, for there to be a knot: *gangakia sipobmi* 'the net is entangled'
sipoḥi, *sipoḥid* – (adj.)
entangled, twisted, intertwined, in a knot
sipoḥủ, *sipoḥula* – (no.ina)
confusion, knot, twist
sira, *sîhdi~sîsta* – (no.ina/.ani)
fish
sirit, *sịsịtsta~sịsịddịa* – (no.ina)
fish stock of a lake or river

siriu, *siriudi* – (adj.)
fishy, fishlike
sise, *sised(i)~sisti* – (adj.)
tall (ani.)
siseri, *sisehdi* – (no.ina)
South | front (direction, EAST) | left (WEST)
sisella 'southernmost'
sisġ·i, *siskki* – (v.imp. inf. *sisġisu*)
to thunder
sisi, *sisti* – (no.ina)
thunder
siskko, *siskuni* – (no.ani)
thunder (diety)
siś·i, *sidji* – (v.ai/.ui. inf. *siśśa/siśśu*)
to lie (low)
i·siśib·i, *isiśiḍbi* – (v.uditr. inf. *siśimnon*)
not to be able to stand (+ELAT)
sismu, *sismudi* – (no.ina)
bottom (also *śiśmu~śiśmo*)
sitema, *sivva* – (no.ani.pl)
foxes
sitġobi, *sitġobid* – (no.ina)
fishing rod
sitkȧ, *sitkęgji* – (no.ina)
experiencer fisherman
sitkȧts, *sitkeibme* – (no.ani.poe)
experienced fisherman, skilled fisherman
sitkeh·i, *sitkehri* – (v.imp)
to be the right time to fish
sitk·i, *sitkui* – (v.ai. inf. *sitkisa*)
to fish
  tama·sitk·i 'to fish on a lake (in a boat)'
sitro, *sitodi* – (no.ina)
fish soup
siura, *siusta* – (no.ani)
Siwa (person)
sivi, *sîd* – (no.ina)
honey
sivu·tabbubmi, *~tabbubmika* – (adj.)
nice, goodhearted, pure, innocent, naive | generous
smairu·i, *smairi* – (v.ai/.ui. inf. *smairosa/smairosu*)
to laugh
smoro, *smosta* – (no.ani)
snail, slug | idiot, fool
soappa, *soapra* – (no.ina)
fellow, lad, pal, guy, chap
soaġa, *soaġaka* – (adj.)
which burns well, combustible
soaġġo, *soaġġoka* – (no.ina)
culture, identity, ethnicity, clan
soaki, *soakka* – (no.ina)
house, home
soakubmi, *soakubmika* – (adj.)
cozy, homely, snug, comfortable | welcoming
soakubmú, *soakubmuri* – (no.ina)
coziness, comfort | welcomingness
soalu, *soalka* – (no.ina)
scent, smell | hint, trace, dash | clue, indication | fragrance, perfume
soalusk·u, *soaluskaja* – (v.utrans. inf *soaluskoru*)
to lose ones antlers | to lose face, to lose
soamba, *soambaka~soamu* – (no.ina/ani)
buttercup
soapri, *soapika* – (no.ina)
split, separation, divorce | division
soarut, *soarutta* – (no.ina)
lower back
soasuld·i, *soasuldui* – (v.ai. inf. *soasuldisa*)
to share a tent, to share living space
sodlmot, *sodlmotta* – (no.ina)
snowdrift
soḍḍos, *sohhohi~sohhi~sôi* – (no.ina)
evening
  sôi – in the evening
  sohma – in the evenings
soḍmen, *soḍmes* – (no.ina)
cricket
sogjiekk·a, *sogjiekkia* – (v.ut. inf. *sogjiekmu*)
to dry out, to make feel dry
sogjientsġ·i, *sogjentsġui* – (v.imp)
to be (far) too dry, to be dry season, to be drought
sogji~sogjil, *sojiri* – (no.ina)
dryness, draught
sogjon, *sogjonta* – (adj.)
dry
soġabi, *sovabiko* – (no.ina)
insult, swear word
soġġon, *soġġonta* – (adj.)
which does not burn well, incombustible | wet | good-for-nothing, useless, vain, pointless | hung-over

soġġot, *soġotta* – (no.ina)
wood that burns poorly
soġl·i, *soġlui* – (v.ui inf. *soġlisu*)
to thaw, to melt
soġōrita~sōġōrita – (adv.)
in vain
sohpa, *sohhu* – (no.ani)
skis
sokmi, *sokmiko~sohta–* (no.ina/.ani)
seagull
sokubmue – (adv.)
welcome!
sokum·a, *sokubma* – (v.at. inf. *sokummi*)
to welcome
solha, *solra* – (no.ani)
female caribou (mother)
solka, *solkamo~solluni* – (no.ina/.ani)
aspen
solra, *solramo* – (no.ina)
cervidae, antlered animal
solt·a, *soltia* – (v.at. inf. *soltami*)
to punish | to compensate
soluna, *solummo~solunamo* – (adj.)
fragrant, balmy
soluset, *solusetta* – (no.ina)
losing of antlers | humiliation, degradation, losing face
somi, *sŏkko* – (no.ina/.ani)
man, adult male
somkkoro, *somkohmo* – (no.ina)
larva, pupa | maggot
somodġe, *somodġemo* – (no.ina)
pray, victim
somolken, *somolkes* – (no.ina)
(summer/little) butterfly
somora, *somohmo* – (no.ina)
gold
sompo, *sompoma* – (adj.)
swift, sudden
somuka, *somuhmo* – (adj.)
manly | courageous
somukė~somukeu~somukel, *sokumeri* – (no.ina)
manliness | courageousness
sonnjot, *sonnjotta* – (adj.)
lukewarm, tepid | apathetic, indifferent | cool, trendy, genuine
sŏ-, *sŏma-* – (act.nom)
mother

sopon, *soponta* – (adj.)
evil, wicked, foul, vile | cruel
sopr·a, *sopria* – (v.at/.ut. inf. *soprami*)
to split (in two: *eśita*)
sori, *sohko* – (no.ina)
blister
soroko, *sorohma* – (no.ina)
piece, part, section (also **saroko**)
sorppo, *sorpoma* – (no.ina)
a big drink, big slurp
soś·idl·u, *-utta* – (v.pass.part)
famous, reknown
sot·a, *sodda~(i)sta* – (v.at/.adit. inf. *sobmi/sodnin*)
to make | to give (.adit)
u·sot·i, *usoddi* – (v.pass)
to be allowed, may: *usotiki* I am allowed
Sotsġo, *Sotsa* – (no.ani)
(male personal name)
subo, *suoui~suovvi* – (no.ani)
fruit
sudl·u, *sullu* – (v.utrans inf. *sudloru*)
to bear berries, to blossom
sudna, *sutva~sunamo* – (num.ani/.ina)
six
sunnet 'sixteen'
suntsġa 'sixty'
sutven 'six times'
sudnet 'sixth'
sug·a, *sutka* – (v.at inf. *suhmi*)
to visit
sugagi, *suagimo* – (no.ina)
pea
suikild·i, *suikildui* – (v.ai/.at. inf. *suikildisa/suikildamu*)
to live together (in a house) | to cohabit (.at), to inhabit
suikna, *suingamo* – (no.ina)
ground (to build a house on), place suitable for a house, even ground | base, foundation
suinge- 'basic'
sukin~suggin, *sukis~suggis* – (adj.)
straight
sukli, *suglimo* – (no.ina)
protection, defence, shielding
suklu, *sugluma* – (no.ina)
whale meat
sukno, *sungoma~sukva* – (no.ina/.ina)

large isolated conifer
sumana, *sumammo* – (adj.)
irritated, sore, aching
suod·u, *suoddu* – (v.utrans. inf. *suodlu*)
to bloom | to burst; *tsuoddu marvahta*'X burst out into laughter'
suorpp·i, *suorppui* – (v.ai ind. *suorppisa*)
to drink (of animals)
suosa, *suotta~svotta* – (no.ani)
mother
suoḑga, *suogga~svogga* – (no.du)
mother and son(s)
suoḑba, *suobba~svobba* – (no.du)
mother and daughter(s)
suṡ·u, *suddju* – (v.utrans. inf. *suṡoru*)
to move away, to become more distant, to distance
sutot, *sutotta* – (no.ina)
permission
sùbma, *sůpma/sůmma* – (adj.)
black
sùmůl·i, *sůmůdli* – (v.ai. inf. *sůmůlsa*)
to be wearing black, to be black
sùro, *sůhma* – (no.ina)
berry bush, berry land
sùḑbi, *sůpima* – (no.ina)
winter house/camp
suvi, *sůimo* – (no.ina)
stream, creek | flow, run, course
suvo, *sýma* – (no.ina)
berry
sůddů, *sůtůma* – (no.ina)
infection (inside the body), pus
sůiggi, *sůigid* – (no.ina)
dry weather
sůi·m·i, *sými* – (v.adj)
to be dry (of weather/landscape) | to be low on (+ELAT)
sůite – (conj.)
as (much X) as (Y): *tavvi ohhjo sůite holpo* 'as strong as (he/she is) dumb' | in the same way, by the same (quantitiy)
sůitů, *sůitůma* – (no.ina)
thank
sůivvi, *sůimmo* or *sůiụid* – (no.ina)
proof, sign
sůppi – (adv.)
badly, poorly (COMP. *sůdne*, SUP. *sůiba*)
sůra, *sůhmo* – (no.ina)

part, piece, fraction
sůtro·m·i, *sůtrima* – (v.adj)
to feel frustrated, to be frustrated
sůtrů, *sůtrůma* – (adj.)
frustrated, annoyed
sůrůna, *sůrůmmo* – (adj.)
rough, uneven | coarse, prickly
svabmen, *svamenta* – (no.ina)
boy, young man
(t)svabmesi, *(t)svabmetta* – (no.ani)
boyfriend
svaḑma, *svaḑmaka~svahmaka*
foam (especially on a lake)
svahi, *svaika* – (no.ina)
neck
svahku, *svahkuka* – (no.ina)
skin disease
svaimer·a, *svaimehra* – (v.at. inf. *svaimehmi*)
to buy, purchase
svaltton, *svaltonta, -õri-* (no.ina)
punishment, sentence, correction (also *soaltton*)
svamenha, *svamenhaka* – (adj.)
handsome
svamiskon~soamiskon, *-miskonta* – (adj.)
free (of charge)
sveṡṡi, *sveṡie* – (no.ina)
distance
sesveṡieika 'over long distances, from far away'
sviest·a, *sviestia* – (v.at. inf. *sviestami*)
to translate, to interprete
svilla, *sviladi* – (no.ina)
braid
svohk·a, *svohkia* – (v.at inf. *svohkami*)
to slam, to bang, to clap
svysġ·i, *svysġui* – (v.ui. inf. *svysġisů*)
to be (easy/hard, lit. *salla/sůppi*)
sygja·, *sygjia* – (v.at. inf. *sygjami*)
to invite, to host
syhhi, *syhdi* – (no.ina)
bent tree | something bent
sykly, *syglyma* – (no.ina)
team, party, squad
sykni, *syngid~syngimo* – (no.ina)
generation
syll – (onom.)

sound used to quiet someone down
Syly, *Syltśa* – (no.ani)
(female personal name)
syngey – (adv.)
never
syngogja – (adv.)
nowhere
syngoita 'nowhere (movement to)'
syngoika 'nowhere (movement from)'
syngym·ni, *syngy-* – (pron.)
no one
syngebymni 'neither'
syngetsymni 'none (of)'
syngua 'in no way'
misůn 'for no reason'
synty~syntů, *syntyma~syntůma* – (no.ina)
zero
sytka – (interj.)
please
sytů·a, *sytoja* – (v.at. inf. *sytymi*)
to thank (honorific)
sytvi – (interj.)
please
Sẏ, *Sytśa* – (no.ani)
(female personal name)
sẏgjaka, *sẏjahmo* – (no.ina)
branch(es) of a river | tributary

Ś ś

śahhj·u, *śastu* – (v.utrans.neg. inf. *śahhjoru*)
(not to be able) to stand, to bear, to endure (+ BARE INF)
śahhjuli, *śaśulka~sahhjultśa* – (no.ina/.ani)
wimp, coward, weakling, sissy, wuss
śailkko, *śailkoka* – (no.ina)
swelling, bulge
śainni~śainniu~śainnil~śainnir, *śainiri* – (no.ina)
courageousness, fearlessness
śainno, *śainnoka* – (adj.)
courageous, brave, fearless (adv. *śaigji~śaigjil*)
śaiten·i, *śaitedi* – (v.ui. inf. *śaitentu*)
to feel hungry

śaitśel·i, *śaitśedli* – (v.ui. inf. *śaitśelsu*)
to starve (to death)
śatśilo, *śatśilka* – (no.ina)
starvation
śautr·i, *śautrui* – (v.ui. inf. *śautrisu*)
to (be hungry enough to) want to eat; *ōsi maśautri* 'I am full, I can no longer eat'
śavvi, *śagga* – (no.ina)
courage, bravery
śeim·a, *śeibma* – (v.at. inf. *śeimmi*)
to prevent from (+INF)
o·śeint·i, *ośeintui* – (v.usubj. inf. *śeintinu*)
to get hurt
śeira, *śeirri~śeirari* – (no.ina)
bearberry
śengyts, *śengoibme* – (no.ani.poet)
maid, maiden, young girl | beautiful daughter
śeśkvo, *śeśkvue* – (no.ina)
slush, wet snow on the ground
śevviskon, *śevviskos* – (adj.)
coward, cowardly
śiabuna, *śiabundi* – (adj.)
energetic, active, lively, able-bodied, good to work
śiaggel·i, *śiaggedli* – (v.ai. inf. *śiaggelsa*)
to stay for a while, to visit, to be a guest
śiaggelibmis, *-mhi* – (adj.)
permanent
śib·a, *śidba* – (v.at. inf. *śibmi*)
to be able (to +ILLAT/ELAT), to have enough energy for
(see **i·siśib·i**)
śidda! – (interj.)
stop!, stay!
śiemme, *śiemedi* – (no.ina)
bear skin
śihhjiksus, *śiśiksuhi* – (no.ina)
whizz, buzz | mosquito, fly
śi, *śîd* – (no.ina)
wound or infected or damaged part of tree or plant or piece of meat | *gem~* insanity | pus
śink·a, *śîhta* – (v.at. inf. *śînkami*)
to know how to, to be able to (because of enough knowledge/experience (+ INF.)
śinket, *śinketsta* – (no.ina)
knowledge
śimi, *śitta* – (no.ani)

bear head
śimśi~śintśi, *śimśid* – (no.ina)
bear ritual
śini, *śiśa* – (no.ani)
daughter
śinnen, *śines* – (no.ina)
lake
śiv·i, *śivvi~ahvi~aġvi* – (v.ai/.ui. inf. *śissa/śissu*)
to stay, to remain
śośi – (pron.)
all
  AG. *śośi*
  PAT. *śośva~śośko*
  GEN. *śośō~śośśi~śośko*
  DAT. *śośi*
  śebśi 'both'
  śetsośi 'all (of the)'
  śośśu 'all the time'
śośia – (adv.)
everywhere
  śośta 'everywhere (movement to)'
  śośka 'everywhere (movement from)'
śośva – (adv.)
completely, entirely
śůdġů, *śůtůma* – (no.ina)
fizz, froth
śůśků, *śůśkůma* – (no.ina)
nipple
śvam·a, *śvabma* – (v.at inf. *śvammi*)
to be responsible for something
śvaimmet, *śvaimetta* – (no.ina)
responsability
śvi, *śumi~śvid* – (num.ani/.ina)
seven
  śůnet 'seventeen'
  śůra 'seventy'
  śvivven 'seven times'
  śvoit 'seventh'
śygjana, *śyjammo* – (no.ina)
summer gathering/camp
śyśś – (onom.)
pfew, sound to show that one is tired (also **hįyhhį**)

T t

o·t·i, *otui* – (v.asubj. inf. *otina*)
to unite, to organize, to come together, to pair up
ta – (pron.)
it (ina.sg)
  atta PAT.
  en~taga GEN.
  atsi DAT.
  noni- LOC.
  –ha POSS.
  teta PREC
tȧġ·i, *tȧsti* – (v.ai/.ui. inf. *tȧhsa/tȧhsu*)
to stand up
tȧhma, *tȧhka* – (no.ani)
heart
tȧ·i, *tęgji~teyvi* – (v.ai/.ui. inf. *tȧsa/tȧsu*)
to stand
tȧ·i·ga, *tęmeiga~teyviga* – (v.ai/.ui.semel. inf. *tȧksa/tȧksu* or *tȧhsa/tȧhsu*)
to stand up
tabbi, *tahumi* – (no.ani)
kidney(s)
tab·m·i, *tatmi~tattima* – (v.ai.inconcl. inf. *tabmi*)
to think
taḍma – (postp.)
furthest back, last
  taḍḍebma 'to'
  taḍḍeska 'from'
tagassi, *tagasta* – (no.ani)
traveler, visitor
tagjen~tagjil – (adv.)
much, a lot (COMP. *tainne*, SUP. *taiba~taibba*)
tahama, *tȧkka~tahamatta* – (no.ina~v.ag.part)
world, universe
tahhangųeri, *tahhangųetśa~tahangųehka* – (no.ani/.ina)
team | five people
tahha, *tahhi* – (no.ina)
tree (inanimate)
taikla, *taiglaka* – *(no.ina)*
snail
tairr·a, *tairta* – (v.ut inf. *tairmu*)
to overcome with excitement, to make someone go crazy, to make ecstatic
tairron, *taironta* – (no.ina)
ecstasy, pure joy: *talśa tairron* pure genius

tairven, *tairventa* – (adj.)
ecstatic, crazy with joy/excitement
taja, *taba* – (quant.)
much (COMP. *tata*, COMP.GEN. *tatanna/tadna*, SUP. *talla*, SUP.GEN. *tahla*)
taja-ahmabmot, *~bmotta* – (adj.)
greedy
taja·myroiha, *~myroihmo* – (adj.)
where mosquitoes
taintsġi, *taintsġika* – (adj.)
numerous, many (adv. *taintsġui* 'very often')
taintsġu̇, *taintsġuri* – (no.ina)
number, quantity, amount
taite – (adv.)
still (then)
taju – (interj.)
then, well, in that case
tairsi, *tairtta* – (no.ani)
worker, slave
taiskani, *taiskaja* – (no.ani)
seamstress, sewer
takeri, *takehka* – (no.ina)
person
takeulmo~takůlmo, *takeulka~takůlka* – (no.ani)
righteous man/person, real person/man
takeumuri, *takeumutsa~takeumuhka* – (no.ani/.ina)
foursome, group of four, quattro
takęni, *takekka* – (no.ina)
East
takęnla 'easternmost'
takụ·u, *takụaju* – (v.aux.utrans. inf. *takụoru*)
to be worth (doing) (+ILLAT)
Talgo, *Taltsa* – (no.ani)
(male personal name)
talśa, *talśaka* – (adj.)
nothing but, pure, unadulturated | clear, transparent, potable
tama, *tammi* – (quant.)
many (COMP. *tonda*, SUP. *tabba*, SUP.GEN. *tahba*)
tamepsusi, *tamepsutta* – (no.ani)
net repairer | someone who finds solutions, problem solver
tamoni, *tamoja* – (no.ani)
female friend | female hunter

tamori, *tamohka~tamotśa(gi)* – (no.ina/.ani)
hunters, hunting partners, partners | close (to each other)
tamosi, *tamotta~tamoska* – (no.ani/.ina)
hunter, friend, man
tamoskari, *tamoskahka~tamoskatśa(gi)* – (no.ina/.ani)
people, nation, Siwa | inhabitants
tamụi – (adv.)
many times, repeatedly
tamyna~temyna, *tamykka~temydi* – (adj.)
joyful, cheerful, happy: *tamykkia* 'happy'
tanudni, *tanudja* – (no.ani)
(female) singer
tanutsi, *tanutta* – (no.ani/)
(male) singer
tapa, *tadga* – (no.ina)
bulb
tara, *tarka~tahka* – (no.ina)
root
taru- – (pref.)
special, private, one's own
tarutaru-go 'my very own, just for me, me myself and I'
o·tarv·i, *otarvui* – (v.asbj. inf. *tarvina*)
to specialize (in +ILAT)
otarvodlima~-imo 'specialized, special'
tasko, *taskka* – (no.ina)
woods, woodland
tamalagjo, *~lajoka* – (no.ina)
hindrance, obstacle
tamja – (adv./postp.)
on (the surface of)
tanta 'onto'
tantairi 'towards (the surface)'
tantsi 'along the surface/face, side-by-side'
tanka 'off'
tamiemi – (adv.)
alone, by one's self, on one's own
tamima, *tamikka* – (no.ina)
(place) on/over, surface
tamoskari, *tamoskatśa* – (no.ani)
people, nation, inhabitants, Siwas
taneġġuri, *taneġġutśa~taneġġuhka* – (no.ani/.ina)
threesome, group of three, trio

taneġġuri taneġġuren 'three by three'
tatama, *tatakka* – (no.ina)
 (place) inside, interior
tatami, *tatatta* – (no.ani)
 wolf
 tatamġo 'male'
 tatamha 'female'
tatammuri, *tatammuhka* – (no.ina)
 many people, crowd
tatkatka – (adv.)
 inside-out
tatśa~tatsa – (adv./postp.)
 inside
  tadda 'into'
  taddairi 'towards the inside, at (missing)'
  tatsi 'along the inside'
  tatka 'from inside': *notsa sȋhdi tatka* 'to gut a fish'
Tatimra(gi), *Tatimsta(gi)* – (no.ani)
 eastern Siwa
tatriki, *tatikka* – (no.ina)
 wife's family
tatskairi, *tatskaihka* – (no.ina)
 scarab beetle(s)
tatsůi – (postp.)
 in addition to, along with, and
tatsůi·ni – (det.)
 the additional one | additional, extra
taubmuri, *taubmutśa~taumuhka* – (no.ani/.ina)
 group of four people
taukuna, *taukukka* – (adj.)
 valuable, worthy
taul·hi, *tautśagi* – (no.ani.pl)
 army, force, military
tausġiu, *tausġiri* – (no.ina)
 rigidity, stiffness, difficulty, inflexibility | firmness, discipline
tausġon, *tausġonta* – (adj.)
 rigid, stiff, hard, inflexible | firm, disciplined
tauri, *tautśa* – (no.ani)
 soldier
taḍḍet, *taḍḍedna* – (num.)
 last
tavvi – (equ.)
 as (much) as (~...*te*)
taysġ·i·ma, *tayśguima* – (v.adj)
 to have sore muscles/muscle aches | to ache | to be frozen hard: *longamoja*

taysġima hiedi nivvos 'wet hair freezes hard in the cold'
tȇlv·u, *tȇlvaju* – (v.utrans inf. *tȇlvoru*)
 to clear up, for the sun to shine again
tėmi, *tȇtta* – (no.ani)
 moose head
tėrhi, *tȇhtśa* – (no.ani)
 sun
tėrhudna, *tȇrhudnari* – (adj.)
 sunny
tegjuset, *tejusetsta* – (no.ina)
 going blind, losing one's sight
o·teigjld·i, *oteigjildui* – (v.asbj/.at. *teigjildena/teigjildami*)
 to face (each other), to feud
teigji·a, *teidjia* (*teigje-*) – (v.at/.ut. inf. *teigjemi/teigjemu*)
 to support, to maintain, to sustain
teivi, *teivve* – (no.ina)
 nit: *neivuteivi* trifle
tegj·a, *tetsa~teddja* – (v.at/.ut. inf. *tegjami/tegjamu*)
 to be able to see | to seem to see, to perceive (.ut)
tehteren – (adv.)
 in pair
tehteri, *tehtetśa~tehterre* – (no.ani/.ina)
 pair (of people), duo
 tehteri tehteren 'two by two'
tekskon, *tekskos* – (no.ina)
 not poisonous
tembem·a, *tembebma* – (v.at. inf. *tembemmi*)
 to clean, to swipe
tembi, *tembie* – (no.ina)
 broom, tool to clean
Temhi, *Temtśa~Tentśa* – (no.ani)
 (female personal name)
temmu~temmy, *temme* – (no.ina)
 shore, beach, waterside
temyt, *temytsta* – (no.ina)
 moose antlers | prize, display
tenga, *tentsa~tengari* – (num.ani/.ina)
 eight
 tennet 'eightteen'
 tenra 'eighty'
 tengen 'eight times'
 tenget 'eightth'
terhekken, *terhekkes* – (no.ina)

mayfly
teroma, *terommi* – (no.ina)
twilight, nightfall | gloom, murkiness
terv·i·ma, *tervuima* – (v.imp)
to be twilight (also *termi~terymi*)
tetśõ·ka, *tetśunne* – (no.ina.pl)
guts, bowels, innards
tetra, *tetari* – (no.ina)
mountain
tetsli, *tetśa* – (no.ani)
american coot
tetsni, *tetsnie* – (no.ina)
dried fish
teugjusk·u, *teugjuskaju* – (v.utrans. inf. *teugjuskoru*)
to become blind, to lose ones sight | to disappear, to go out of sight
teuke, *teuġi, -śi-* – (no.ina)
silhouette, outline, contour | profile, figure, shape
teuriri, *teuśirre~teuritśa* (no.ina/.ani)
a few, a couple
tèul·ů, *tẻullů* – (v.utrans. inf. *tẻulůrů*)
to subside, to dwindle, to diminish, to wane
tevu~deu~dů – (postp.)
before
tevuka~teuġġa – (adv.)
beforehand
tevu·ni~deu·ni~dů·ni – (det.)
the one before, the former | ancestor(s)
tevvulo, *teulue* – (no.ina)
relent, diminishment, subsiding, calm
tey, *tůme* – (no.ina)
egg (archaic gen. *tůe*)
teyksl·a, *teykslia* – (v.at. inf. *teykslami*)
to punish
kat·o·~ to avenge oneself
teylba, *teylbari~teylu* – (no.ina/ani)
cotton grass
tęġů – (postp.)
for (someone's benefit)
tęlaskon, *tęlaskos* – (adj.)
not improving, worsening
tęli, *tętśa* – (no.ani)
spring
tęmu, *tęmme* – (no.ina)
egg (also *tey*)
tiebb·a, *tiepra* – (v.at. inf. *tiepmi*)
to have to (morally) (+COP +ILLAT)

tiebba, *tiehba* – (no.du)
hands
tiegibi, *tieibid~tśeibid* – (no.ina)
twig, branch
tiemo, *tieka* – (no.ani)
hand
tigjo, *tijodi* – (no.ina)
irritation, annoyance
tihhjen·i, *tihhjedi* – (v.ui. inf. *tihhjentu*)
to seem fresh/young, to look young
tiba, *tĩu~tĩadi* – (no.ani/.ina)
salsify
tiddji, *tĩddjid* – (no.ina)
stimulus, irritant, annoyance, thing that bugs you
tingi, *tingid* – (no.ina)
mating period
tinin, *tinis* – (no.ina)
fire wood
tinni, *tinja* – (no.ani)
partner, spouse
tiod·a, *tiodda* – (v.at/.ut inf. tiobmi/tiobmu)
to hold, to contain | to block (flow), to stop
tiselmo, *tiselka* – (no.ina)
experienced person, expert
tiuhhen~tyhhyn~tyġġyn,
tiuhhes~tyhhys~tyġys – (quant.)
a little
tkihhen – (adv.)
non-stop, steadily, ongoing, ceaselessly
tkollo, *tkoloma* – (no.ina)
breastmilk
tkųaggi, *tkųakka* – (no.ina)
wooden duck | hoax, scam, trojan horse
tmetvi, *tmettumi* – (no.ani)
cow vetch
tmisas, *tmisahi~tmisġi* – (no.ina)
stone, rock
tmůġla, *tmůġlamo~tmůġġůsta* – (no.ina/.ani)
type of psychedelic mushroom
to – (pron.)
he/she/it (ani.sg)
otta PAT.
ůn~ůhõ GEN.
otsi DAT.
neni- LOC.
–ho POSS.
tyta PREC

toabi, *daumi* – (no.ani)
  older sister
toahhoko, *toahhokka* – (no.ina)
  sapling, little tree
toahhun, *toahhunta -ōri-* – (no.ina)
  large tree, big tree
toaibi, *toagjid* – (no.ina)
  cap, lid | fur hat
toam·ni, *to-* – (pron.)
  someone (known)
  teboamni 'either, one or the other'
  tetsoamni 'some (of)'
  toagju '(at) sometime'
  toavva 'in a way'
  mito 'for a certain reason'
toarra, *toarka* – (no.ina)
  root vegetable | root
o·toat·i, *otoaddi* – (v.asubj. inf. *toadna*)
  to join, to team up with
toatti, *toatka* – (no.ina)
  trade
    toatkita~toaddjita (in exchange) for (postp.)
toaḍba, *daubba* – (no.du)
  twin (sisters)
tobi-, *toumi-* – (act.nom)
  older sister
tobi·m·i, *tobimitta* – (v.act.part.pl)
  sisters
toge, *tohmo* – (no.ina)
  eyelash(es)
tohabmot, *-bmotta* – (adj.)
  skillful, dexterous
tohami, *toamiri* – (no.ina)
  skillfulness, dexterity
tohate, *tohaika~toaika* – (no.ani)
  urine
tohhobben, *tohhobbes* – (no.ina)
  treehopper, little bug, bug on a tree/plant
tohhot, *tohhotta* – (adj.)
  green
tohhus, *tohhuhi~toġġi* – (adj.)
  young
toḥḥ·a, *toḥḥia* – (v.at. inf. *toḥḥami*)
  to know how (+COP +ILLAT)
i·toḥḥ·i, *itoḥḥui* – (v.aditr. inf. *toḥḥanin*)
  to know how (+ILLAT)
tokkil·ka, *tokkiri* – (no.ina.pl)
  fish trap

tokorů, *tokohma* – (no.ina)
  fox (when white)
tokura, *tokuhmo* – (no.ina)
  amphibian
tomri~tomśi, *tomriko~tomśiko* – (no.ina)
  velvet | skin on antlers
o·tomrōt·i, *otomrōtti* – (v.as inf. *tomrōdna*)
  to rub skin off antlers | *o·tomrōt·a* to get rid of something
tona, *tommo* – (no.ina)
  West | right (direction WEST)
  tonla 'westernmost'
tonk·a, *tonkia* – (v.at/.adit. inf. *tonkami/ tonkanin*)
  to sew clothes (on someone +ALLAT)
tonku·a~tonko·ma~tonkō, *tonkamo* – (no.ina.pl)
  sinew
tontsori~tsontsori,
  tontsohko~tsontsohko – (no.ina)
  puffin *(also tōtsōri~tsōtsōri)*
tȯ, *tobo* – (no.ina)
  rock
tȯhni, *tȯhhja* – (no.ani)
  late spring
tȯm·ba, *tȯmmaba* – (act.nom)
  Siwa people, (our) people
tȯmo, *tȯmma* – (no.ina)
  people, tribe, band
toron, *toronta -ōri-* – (no.ina)
  big bear, male adult bear
torttiu, *torttiutta* – (v.pp)
  paralyzed
tosġora, *tosġosta* – (no.ani)
  reject, outlaw
tosmi, *tosmiko* – (no.ina)
  hay
toś·m·i, *totsmi~toddjami* – (v.adj)
  young
totami, *todatta* – (no.ani)
  head
totomma, *totośśi* – (no.ani)
  family member, close relative
toton, *totonta -ōri-* – (no.ina)
  family (direct)
totta – (equ.)
  as (much) as (~... *te*)
tottamo, *tottaśi* – (no.ani)

trader, merchant
toḍgo, *tokoma* – (no.ina)
tree trunk | torso
toskvi, *toskkumi* – (no.ani)
caribou without antlers
tovv·ia – (adv.)
somewhere (known)
tovvita 'somewhere (movement to)'
tovvika 'somewhere (movement from)'
tõkkia·u·ki, *tõkkiauttaki* – (v.pat.part.pl)
litter
tõtani, *tõtaja* – (no.ani)
(female) dancer
tõtari, *tõtahko~tõtatśa(gi)* – (no.ina/.ani)
dancers, group of dancers
tõtasi, *tõtatta* – (no.ani)
(male) dancer
tsåp·mi, *tsåppuima* – (v.imp)
to bleed
tsalbi – (adv.)
rarely
tsammi, *tsamġa, -śi-* – (no.ina)
forest
tsarppa, *tsarpaka* – (no.ina)
button
tsasġ·a, *tsaskka* – (v.ut. inf. *tsasġamu*)
to forget (+ ELAT)
tsaupr·i, *tsauprui* – (v.ui. inf. *tsauprisu*)
to happen rarely
tsatsaupri 'to be unheard of'
tsengi~tsengin, *tsengie~tsengis* – (adj.)
clear, comprehensible, lucid | obvious | pure, clean, fresh (also *tsengy*)
tsengů~tsengul, *tsengula* – (no.ina)
clarity, comprehensiveness, lucidity | obviousness | purity, cleanness, freshness
(i)·tsep·i, *(i)·tseḍbi* – (v.ai./.ditr inf. *tsepsa/tsemnin*)
to wait (.ai) | to wait for, to have the patience to (+ELAT)
tsepsu, *tsebsue* – (quant)
a little
tsebséu – (adv.quant.)
a little (also *tsůbsů, tsůbsêu*)
tsepu, *tsepume* – (adj.)
unfrozen, defrosted, thaw
tsero·gi, *tsestagi* – (no.ani.pl)
sweat lodge (ceremony)
tsġe, *tsġeje* – (no.ina)
cedar
tsġebb – (onom.)
sound to encourage someone
tsġėut, *tsġêutsta* – (no.ina)
skeleton
tsġiami, *tsġiandi* – (no.ina)
cedar stripe(s) | arms
tsġiauga, *tsġiauḍḍi* – (no.ina)
cedar wood
tsġin, *tsġîs* – (no.ina)
cedar
tsġokli, *tsġoglimo~tsġogliko* – (no.ina)
type of fire made by splitting a log, *rakovalkea*.
tsġumi, *tsġummo* – (no.ina)
worm
tsġůli, *tsġůldi* – (no.ina)
skull, cranium
tsidå, *tsilala* – (no.ina)
rabbit
tsieltami, *tsieltandi* – (no.ina)
idiot
tsik·i, *tsiḍgi* – (v.ui. inf. *tsiksu*)
to shine (dimmly) | to be hardly visible:
tsikimaika saitkisa 'to disappear from sight'
tsoair·i, *tsoairri~tsvarri* – (v.ai inf. *tsoarha*)
to ski
tsoggis, *tsogihi~tsohki* – (no.ina)
hope
tsoihhi, *tsoihko* – (no.ina)
sleigh
tsuggi, *tsugimo* – (no.ina)
hope
tsulra, *tsulramo* – (no.ina)
vapor-pressed or vapor-moulded wood | mould, cast | frame
tsuogg·a, *tsuotka* – (v.at inf. *tsuokmi*)
to hope | *hę~* to assume, to count on, to expect
tsusina, *tsusimmo* – (adj.)
fresh | untrained, inexperienced
tsutġasi, *tsutġatta* – (no.ani)
lunar eclipse
tsůiro, *tsẙhmo* – (no.ina)
spot, place, slot, space
tsyġy, *tsẙma* – (no.ina)
reach (of a throw) | aim, goal
tulmu, *tulmuma* – (no.ina)
clothing, clothes

tulvi~tulbi, *tulvimo~tulbimo* – (adj.)
  nutrient | nourishment | provisions (*tulvie~tulbie* pl.)
tulvusta~tulbusta, *tulvustamo~tulbustamo* – (adj.)
  lacking in nutrient, nourishment | without provisions | infertile, barren, arid
tunna, *tunnamo* – (adj.)
  important, heavy, major, great
tuobi, *tuovvumi, tubimo* – (no.ani/.ina)
  juniper tree
tuono~tvono, *tuomma~tvomma* – (adj.)
  the same
tusta, *tustamo* – (no.ina)
  barricade, steep hill
tuśkvasi, *tuśkvatta* – (no.ani)
  murderer
tuvala~toala, *tuvalmo~toalka* – (adj.)
  heavy, hefty, big, fat (adv. *tuvavvi~toavvi*)
tuvavven – (adv.)
  heavily, very (especially negative) (also *tůavven*)
tuvė~tuveu~tuvel, *tuveri* – (no.ina)
  heaviness, weight
tuv·a, *tuvva* – (v.at inf. *tummi*)
  to turn | to change
tuv·i, *tuvvi* – (v.ai/.ui. inf. *tussa/tussu*)
  to turn | to change
tůġni, *tůġnima* – (no.ina)
  youth
tůh·m·i, *tůvvima* – (v.adj)
  to feel anxious, worried
tůhna, *tůhnamo* – (adj.)
  anxious, worried, stressed
tůhnė~tůhneu~tůhnel, *tůhnela* – (no.ina)
  anxiety, worry, stress
tůlri, *tůlrimo* – (no.ina)
  younger sibling
tůmkki, *tůmkid~tůmkkid* – (no.ina)
  boulder
tůnůkśi, *tůnůkohta~tůnůhta* – (no.ani)
  attack leader, general
tůppi~tůppiu~tůppiů~tůppil~tůppir, *tůppila* – (no.ina)
  clumsiness, awkwardness, unhandiness
tůppů, *tůppůma* – (adj.)
  clumsy, awkward, unhandy
tůpra, *tůpamo* – (no.ina)
  juniper berry

tůreisk·ů, *tůreiskeju* – (v.utrans. inf. *tůreiskůrů*)
  to shed ones fur | to mature, to come to maturity
tůrů, *tůrůma* – (no.ina)
  fur
tůrůppů, *tůrůppůma* – (adj.)
  fluffy | furry
tvelėl·i, *tvelėdli* – (v.ai. inf. *tvelėlsa*)
  to be covered in blood, to be bloody
tveli, *tvelle* – (no.ina)
  blood (outside the body), bloodshed | tragedy, horror
tvel·iu, *tvel·ibi* – (no.ina)
  uncles and aunts (mother's brother or father's sister)
tveluri, *tvelurre* – (no.ina)
  cousins (mother's sister's or father's brother's)
tvimyn, *tvı̊mys* – (no.ina)
  vagina
tvonna, *tvonnamo~tvommo* – (adj.)
  equal
tvonnė~tvonneu~tvonnel, *tvoneri* – (no.ina)
  equality
tvuni – (adv./postp.desti)
  down
    tvunda 'down (to)'
    tvunga '(from) down'
tvů – (adv./postp.direct)
  down
    tvůda 'down (to)'
    tvůdari 'downward | out to sea/away from land'
    tvůtsti 'down along | along the bottom'
    tvůga 'down below'
(o·)tvůd·i, *(o)tvůtti* – (v.ai/.asubj. inf. *tvůtsa~tvůdna*)
  to embark, to leave, to go fish/hunt
tvůmma, *tvůmamo* – (no.ina)
  (place) down | bottom
    tvůmamoja 'safe, in a secure position/state/place'
tygi, *tůid* – (no.ina)
  poison, toxin
tygyha, *tygyhma* – (adj.)
  poisonous
tylla, *tylmo* – (no.ina)

little brother, little bro, bro
tym·m·i, *tyvvima* (*tyv-*) – (v.adj)
to be heavy/full/heavier | to become (temporarily) heavy: *tymmi bengommeibma* '(rain) is heavy on the roof'
tym·oagjon, *oajonta* – (no.ina)
recording, record, account
tyry~tvoro, *tolba~tvolba* – (no.ani)
son
tẏi – (interj.)
please, I beg you
tẏs·ka, *tẏhhi* – (no.ina)
joint

Tṡ tṡ

tṡadn·a, *tṡanda* – (v.at. inf. *tṡadnami*)
to find | (~adn·a) to recover
tṡairri, *tṡairka~tṡaihtṡa(gi)* – (no.ina/.ani)
row men
tṡalta, *tṡaltaka* – (no.ina)
clay
tṡaltira, *tṡaltihka* – (adj.)
made of clay
tṡanni, *tṡagja* – (no.ani)
female guest
tṡassi, *tṡatta* – (no.ani)
male guest
tṡeddjet, *tṡeddjetsta~tṡeddjeddja* – (no.ina)
old man
tṡeḍḍa, *tṡevva* – (no.ani)
arm (from elbow to wrist)
tṡegma, *tṡegmari~tṡekṡi* – (no.ina/.ani)
child, youngster
tṡegni, *tṡengja* – (no.ani)
childhood
tṡeidobi~tṡeilobi, *tṡeilobid* – (no.ina)
torch, branch (on fire)
tṡellu, *tṡelue~tṡelobi* – (no.ina)
catkin(s)
tṡem·i, *tṡebmi* – (v.ai inf. *tṡemsa*)
to crawl
tṡemi, *tṡebi* – (adj.) IRR
small, tiny
tṡemkk·a, *tṡemkkia* – (v.at/.ut inf. *tṡemkkami~tṡemkkamu*)
to diminish, to lessen | *tû~* to shrink
tṡemmi, *tṡemme* – (no.ina)
animal tracks (usually in snow)
tṡengibmi, *tṡengibmid* – (adj.)
childish | immature
tṡeyntġ·i, *tṡeyntġui* – (v.ut.imp. inf. *tṡeyntġisû*)
to be allergic to: *tatṡeyntġika* 'I'm allergic to it'
tsġaġe, *tsġaika* – (no.ina)
hammer
tsġatsġva, *tsġatsġvaka* – (no.ina)
bug, insect (flying)
tsġin, *tsġîs* – (no.ina)
cedar
tṡibes, *tṡiehhi* – (no.ina)
sign, omen | letter, character
tṡibi, *tṡîd* – (no.ina)
baby, toddler
tṡibmis, *tṡimhi* – (no.ina)
chain, string
tṡiebġo, *tṡiebġodi* – (no.ina)
letter
tṡieka, *tṡieġi~tṡieuni* – (no.ina/.ani)
snake
tṡiella, *tṡieladi* – (no.ina)
island
tṡiempa, *tṡiempadi* – (adj.)
sinuous, stiff, rough, tough (of meat/muscles)
tṡihi, *tṡihid* – (adj.)
tiny, minute
o·tṡil·i, *otṡilli* – (v.asub inf. *tṡilna*)
to dry (oneself)
tṡild·i, *tṡildjui* – (v.ai inf. *tṡildisa*)
to scream
tṡil·u, *tṡillu* – (v.utrans. inf. *tṡillu*)
to dry, to (be hung to) dry
tṡipr·a, *tṡipria* – (v.at inf. *tṡiprami*)
to write
tṡirri – (onom.)
sound to make animal go away
tṡoadjun, *tṡoadjunta -ōri-* – (no.ina)
intestines, innards, guts
tṡoair·u, *tṡoairru* – (v.utrans inf. *tṡoairlu*)
to rot (of wood)
tṡoammus, *tṡoamuhi~tṡoahmi* – (no.ina)
unit (of circumference, roughly 5 inches)
tṡoati, *tṡoatṡika* – (no.ina)

cooperation | harmony, accord, agreement
tśoatolot, *tśoatolotta* – (no.ina)
cooperation, teamwork, collaboration
tśodli, *tśoddja* – (no.ani)
last summer: *tśoddjai* 'last summer'
tśot·i, *tśotti* – (v.ai. inf. tśotsa)
to work together, to cooperate
tśuoppi, *tśuoppimo~tśuopmo* – (adj.)
shallow
tśůnůni, *tśůnůja* – (no.ani)
animal that ahs not left its parents/nest | rookie, beginner
tśvaila, *tśvailġa* – (no.ina)
waterfall, rapids
tśven·a, *tśvetta* – (v.at/.ut. inf. tśvemmi/ tśvemmu)
to destroy
tśyśp·i, *tśyśpůi* – (v.ai inf. tśyśpisa)
to speak with an accent

U u

ųahnoke, *ųahnokka* – (no.ina)
dandruff, dust | thick snowfall
ųala, *ųalka* – (no.ina)
calf, newborn
ųanuahmo, *ųanuahmoka* – (no.ina, adj.)
lichen covered spot | sweet spot
ųar·a, *ųahra* – (v.cop)
to be (somewhere)
ųauvvu, *ųauvvuka* – (adj.)
soft, juicy | sexy, (sexually) exciting | horny (then a patientive participle, -utta)
uba, *oama* – (no.ina)
knee, joint
uboko~ubboko, *uohma~ubohma* – (no.ina)
pipe
ųeit, *ųeitsta* – (no.ina)
quality of water | clear water:
  tåi ųeitstia sebġi 'to be in a bad situation'
ųeśis~ųeśiś, *ųeśihi* – (no.ina)
young (of animal), offspring
uḍḍemi, *uḍḍemta* – (no.ani)
black bird, raven
uḍḍ·u, *utġu~ukku* – (v.utrans inf. *uḍlu*)
to clear up (of night/afternoon sky)
uhkime, *uhkimmo* – (no.ina)
alder bark
uhkjų, *uhkjuma* – (no.ina)
alder
uja, *ůki* – (no.ina)
water
ujeisk·u, *ujeiskaja* – (v.utrans. inf. *ujeiskoru*)
to become dehydrated | to lose water (of lakes/rivers)
uini, *uinila* – (no.ina)
truth
uino, *uinoma* – (adj.)
true
ujoaimi, *ujoaimka* – (no.ina)
ceremonial or traditional story telling prosody/language register
uitse, *uitsemo* – (adj.)
aquatic, which lives in water
uljè~uljeu~uljel~uśè~uśeu~uśel, *uljeri~uśeri* – (no.ina)
seriousness, earnestness, soberness
ulju~uśu, *uljuma~uśuma* – (adj.)
serious, earnest, sober, stern
umeḍgas, *umeḍgahi* – (no.ina)
wound, being wounded
umi·ma – (adv.)
on the ground: *umibma* 'to ~' *umiska* 'from ~'
umna, *umnamo* – (no.ina)
(place) under, below | bowels (deepest part)
umpa, *ůppa* – (no.du)
knees
umui·gi, *umutśagi* – (no.ina)
autumnal equinox (ceremony)
ungo·keśen, *ungokeśes* – (no.ina)
effort
unka – (adv.)
from under, from below
unnaśka, *unaśkamo* – (no.ina)
vocabulary
unnja – (adv./postp.)
under
unta '(to) under' : *kůimpa mîhu unta* 'a pair of boots for your feet'

untairi 'under, not enough, not far enough, too low'
   untsi 'along the underside/back'
   unka '(from) under | without permission, unexpectedly'
uolda~volda – (sup.)
   least
ussů~ussul, *ussuri* – (no.ina)
   smoked fish
us·u, *usutta* – (v.pat.part)
   smoked (of food)
uśkv·a, *uśkvia* – (v.at. inf. *uśkvami*)
   to murder
utegjas, *utegjahi* – (no.ina)
   support
ututa, *utubmo* – (adj.)
   still, calm, motionless
ůdno, *ůnoma~ůtva* – (no.ina/.ani)
   angelica
ůġi, *ůśimo* – (no.ina)
   unedible berry
ůhtakemi, *ůhtaketa~ůhtakemmo* – (no.ani/.ina)
   balsam fir
ůlnuma, *ůlnumatta* – (v.ap)
   milky way (also *gigemoni*)
ůma, *ůmatta* – (v.act.part)
   a lot, a great deal of
ůrhu, *ůrhuma* – (no.ina)
   bank of (little) fish
ůs, *ůhhi* – (no.ina)
   young fish
uvvů~uvvul, *ůri* – (no.ina)
   abundance, profusion, plentifulness

Ů ů

ůaddja – (proadv.)
   right here
   ůadda 'to ~'
   ůatka 'from ~'
ůad·ni – (det.)
   like this, like such, such
ůarro, *ůaroma~ůasta* – (no.ina/.ani)
   wild turkey
ůaśků, *ůaśkůma* – (no.ina)
   (salmon) migration
ůat, *ůatta* – (det.)
   this (proximal) (also *êut*, *ŷt*)
   ůadba, *ůappa* 'this (out of two)'
   ůats, *ůatsta~ůaddja* 'this (out of many)'
   ůatteųi 'this manieth'
   ůattê̊ 'this time'
ůbġi, *ůpimo~ůpima(?)* – (no.ina)
   ungulate
ůbůra, *ůbůhma* – (quant.)
   several, 2-4
ůdlġůt, *ůdlġůtsta~ůdlġůddja* – (no.ina)
   throat
ůdůt, *ěutta* – (no.ina)
   power (left), energy (left)
ůḍvů, *ůḍvůma* – (no.ina)
   whetstone | practice
ůhhja – (proadv.)
   here
   ůhba 'to ~'
   ůhka 'from ~'
ůigjůs, *ůijůhi* – (no.ina)
   (little) hedgehog
tat·ůiġ·a, *tatůista* – (v.at/.ut. inf. **tatůiġmi**/**tatůiġmů**)
   to swallow
ůiġ·i, *ůisti* – (v.ai/.ui. inf. *ůihsa/ůihsů*)
   to swallow
ůiki, *ůikid* – (no.ina)
   marsh, bog
ůikků, *ůikkůma* – (no.ina)
   fight, brawl
ůil·m·i, *ůidlmi* – (v.adj)
   to be caustic, corrosive, abrasive | to smell bad
ůilů~ůilul, *ůilula* – (no.ina)
   pungency, power | causticity, corrosiveness, abrasiveness
ůilve, *ůilvemo* – (adj.)
   pungent, powerful (ina) | caustic, corrosive, abrasive
ob·ůkků·i, *obůkkei* – (v.asubj)
   to fight, to quarrel
ůkkůibba, *ůkkůibma* – (no.ina)
   quarreler, someone who likes to fight
ůngegj·a – (adv.)
   anywhere

ůngeita 'anywhere (movement to)'
ůngeika 'anywhere (movement from)'
ůngům,ni, ůngů- – (pron.)
  anyone
  ůngebůkni 'either'
  ůngetsůkni 'any (of)'
  ůngegju 'anytime'
  ůngua 'in any way'
  miůn 'for any reason'
ůre, ůrmo – (no.ina)
  rash, breakout, hives
Ůrjůa, Ůrjůra – (no.ani)
  (female personal name)
ůrjůni, ůrjůja – (no.ani)
  female wolf
ůrkůdden~ůrkůddil – (adv.)
  similarly, relatedly
ůrkůt, ůrkůtsta~ůrkůddja – (adj.)
  close, related, similar
ůrkyno, ůrkynoma – (adj.)
  close to, closely related to, akin to
ob·ůrůk·i~ob·ůrk·i, obůrůdgi~obůrkeji –
  (v.usubj. ůrůkna~ůrkina)
  to drown
ůrůma, ůrůmmo – (no.ina)
  place near, vicinity, area
ůrůt, ůrůtsta~ůrůddja – (no.ina)
  nature, environment
ůrůuen~ůrůin~ůrůn – (adj.)
  the following, the next
ůrvi, ůrvimo – (no.ina)
  surroundings
ůskky, ůskyma – (no.ina)
  fold, roll | curve
ůt·a, ůtta – (v.ut. inf. ůbmů)
  (not) to be able to (because of cold) (+INF)
ůt·ů, ůttů – (v.aux.utrans. inf. ůdlů)
  to be too cold (for +ELAT)
ůtsů – (postp.)
  without
ůtůna, ůtůmma – (adj.)
  porous, rough | spongy
ůvvia – (proadv.)
  around here
    ůvvita 'to ~'
    ůvvika 'from ~'

V v

vå, veja – (no.ina)
  lake
vadn·u, vandu – (no.utrans)
  to clear up (of sky/weather)
vagjon~vagjōka, vajonta – (no.ina)
  memory, remembrance
i·vagl·a, ivaglia – (v.dit.itr, inf. vaglanon)
  to lack
vahs·u, vahsaju – (v.utrans. inf. vahsoru)
  to grow (in strength/power)
vaik·a, vaidga – (v.ut. inf. vaikmu)
  to be ashamed to (+INF)
valo, vålka – (no.ina)
  tea, brew (also ualo)
varppi, varpika – (no.ina)
  rude person
varru·a~varro·ma~varr·ō, varoka –
  (no.ina.pl)
  ladle
vaśi, vaśka – (no.ina)
  strength
vatro, vatoka – (no.ina)
  lichen cover
vaukke, vaukkeka – (no.ina)
  hook¡
vauri, vauhka – (no.ina)
  position, whereabouts, location | existence
  (also tama·vauri) | status | thing, item, issue
vebo, vivve~viobi – (no.ina)
  knot
vedgo, vekue~veddubi – (no.ina/.ani)
  crow
o·veim·i, oveibmi – (v.asubj. inf. veimna)
  to get married | to marry (v.asubj.tr)
Vengy, Ventśa – (no.ani)
  (female personal name)
velba, velu~velbari – (no.ani/.ina)
  dandelion
velken, velkes – (no.ina)
  moth
vellu, velume – (adj.)
  nightly, night-
vess·u, vessaju – (v.utrans. inf. vessoru)
  to abound, to be(come) abundant
vetśo, vetśue~vetśobi – (no.ina)
  rash
věurhů, věurhůma – (no.ina)

scar, would healing, cicatrization
vėut, *vėutsta*   – (no.ina)
   ices (in river, lake)
viamu·a, *viamaja*   – (v.ut/.at. inf. *viamumu/ viamumi*)
   to enrage, to make very angry
viekso, *viegsodi*   – (no.ina)
   high-pitched noise
vihla, *vihladi*   – (no.ina)
   flesh (especially of fish/raw)
vim·i, *vı̂bmi*   – (v.ai/.ui. inf. *vı̂msa/vı̂msu*)
   to scream
vinjaka, *vı̂njakadi*   – (no.ina)
   theorem, doctrine, thesis
virke, *vı̂rkedi*   – (adj.)
   stumpy | thick, fat
vike, *vikedi*   – (adj.)
   bruised, damaged, hurt
vilo, *viltsa*   – (no.ani)
   maternal aunt
vilśi, *vilśid*   – (adj.)
   verdant, lush, leafy, green
vilvi, *vil(l)umi*   – (no.ani)
   bird (poetic) | woman (poetic)
viviksu·i, *viviksi*   – (v.ui inf. *vivikksosa*)
   to winnow
voakna, *voaknaka*   – (adj.)
   fearful, afraid, terrified
voall·a, *voadla*   – (v.at. inf. *voalmi*)
   to have still to (do/finish), to have left (+ILLAT)
i·voall·i, *ivoadli*   – (v.aditr. inf. *voalnin*)
   to have still to (do/finish), to have left (+COP +ILLAT)
voamme, *voameka*   – (no.ina)
   ghost
voa·mm·i, *voavvima*   (*voavv-*)   – (v.adj)
   to be afraid, to be frightened
voanna, *voakka~voanka*   – (adj.)
   strange, scary, foreign, curious, odd (adv. *voagji~voagjil*)
Voġġo, *Vohtsa*   – (no.ani)
   (male personal name)
voġon, *vovvonta*   – (no.ina)
   sample, small amount of something to test | bait (for fishing)
voho, *vǒma*   – (no.ina)
   fear, fearfulness, terror
voli, *volko*   – (no.ina)

arthritis, bone pain
vuihl·i, *vuihlui*   – (v.at.itr, inf. *vuihlisa*)
   to whistle (also **vyhli**)
vulma, *vulśi~vulmamo*   – (no.ani/.ina)
   leaf
vůvvů   – (onom.)
   sound to calm animals/children

Y y

ybi, *ybid*   – (adj.)
   clear, cloudless
ydni, *ynja*   – (no.ani)
   character, person in a story, fellow
   åḥ-ydni   'good guy'
   yḥ-ydni   'bad guy'
ygji, *yjima*   – (no.ina)
   spike
yhhy, *yhyma*   – (no.ina)
   salmon (fairly large)
ykj·a, *ykjia*   – (v.at. inf. *ykjami*)
   to go around collecting
yly, *ylyma~ŷl*   – (no.ina)
   night
ymen   – (adv.)
   terribly, horribly
ymina~ymna, *ymimma~ymma*   – (adj.)
   lost, missing, not present
ymmẏ~ymmyl, *ymyla*   – (no.ina)
   bad fishing waters
ymni, *ymja*   – (no.ani)
   early fall
ymy, *ymma*   – (adj.)
   terrible, horrible
yṡi, *yhta*   – (no.ani)
   (adult) salmon
ẏ, *yby*   – (no.ina)
   ice
ẏksy, *ẏgsyma*   – (no.ina)
   bow
ẏlys, *ŷlhi*   – (no.ina)
   little leaf, leaflet | child (endearing)
ẏm·m·i, *ŷvvima* (*ŷv-*)   – (v.adj)
   to (become/be) wide, to widen
ẏrh·ů, *ẏrhejů*   – (v.utrans. inf. *ẏrhůrů*)
   to scar, to grow, to cicatrize
ẏstǔ·a, *ẏsteja*   – (v.at inf. *ẏstůmi*)

to kiss
little leaf, leaflet | child (endearing)

ẙm·m·i, *ẙvvima* (*ẙv-*)   –   (v.adj)
to (become/be) wide, to widen

ẙrh·ů, *ẙrhejů*   –   (v.utrans. inf. *ẙrhůrů*)
to scar, to grow, to cicatrize

Table of vowel-final inanimate declension, abridged.
Vertical represents stressed vowel. Horizontal is the word-final vowel (see §4.1.3.1.1)

	-a	-e	-i	-o	-u/-y/-ů
A-declension a á au ai oa	-ka or -ġa/-ra tsammi : tsamġa 'forest' pagi : pakka 'back' takeri : takehka 'person'				
E-declension e ė ę ei ay	-ri/-ġi/-di/-li helva : helvari 'female moose' eleba : elepri 'flower' teuke : teuġi 'shape' męrana : męradi 'difficult' biele : bielli 'fat'		-e/-obi kepsi : kebsie 'mushroom' benho : benhue~benhobi 'dog' seumi : seumme 'soil'		-me tsepu : tsepume 'not frozen' ennju : enjume 'pole'
I-declension i ì ie ia			-id or -di dida : diadi 'girl' hide : hiedi 'hair' kì : kid 'new'		
-o- / -ou- / -oi- o ò ou oi	-mo njobba : njobmo 'beard' kokve : kokvemo 'lightweight' onona : onommo 'little'		-ko or -ġo kori : kohko 'boy' tosmi : tosmiko 'hay' somi : sōkko 'man'		-ma
U-declension u ù uo ui	-mo butta : buttamo 'bad weather' njukli : njuglimo 'finger' nubba : nubmo 'eyelid'				obeno : oimma 'smoke' nobemo : noimma 'fire' kydly : kylyma 'bell'
Y-declension y ỳ ů ėu eu ůi ůa	-mo tylla : tylmo 'little brother'		-id or -di kyni : kyndi 'nest' tsġůli : tsġůldi 'skull' pymi : pyndi 'hard bark'		

Table of consonant final inanimate declension, abridged.

	-s	-t	-n	-l / -ʔ	-V¹ts
Front e i y ů	-hi or -h-Ø-i	-tsta or -ddja	-s	-la	-V²bme
Back a o u		-tta	-nta (-ōr-)	-ri	

Table of animate noun declension.

unmarked		marked	
singular	plural	singular	plural
-mo	-mogi	-ka or -śi (if stressed o u)	-kagi or -śigi
-ma	-magi		
-mi	-migi -mśi / -mhi	-ta -tta	-tagi -ttagi
-ba -pa -va	-bagi -pagi -vagi	-u	-ugi
-bi -pi -vi	-bigi / -bśi -pigi / -bśi -vigi	-umi	-umśi
-bo -po -vo	-bogi -pogi -vogi	-oųi	-ośi
-na -no	-nagi -nogi	-va / -ųa -vva	-vagi / -ųa -vvagi
-ni	-nigi / -nśi / -nhi	-ja	-jagi
-ta -to	-tagi -togi	-va / -ųa -vva	-vagi / -ųa -vvagi
-te -ti	-tegi -tsi	-ika	-ikagi
-sa -so	-sagi -sogi	-hi (-ḥi) -tta	-higi (-ḥigi) -ttagi

unmarked		marked	
singular	plural	singular	plural
-si	-sigi -sġi	-tta	-ttagi
-ṡi	-ṡigi	-hta -ohta	-htagi -ohtagi
-ro -ra -la	-rogi -ragi -lagi	-sta	-stagi
-ri -li	-rigi / -rhi -ligi / -lhi	-tṡa	-tṡagi
-lu	-lugi -lhi	-da	-dagi
-ka -ko	-kagi -kogi	-uni	-unhi
-ki	-kigi / -kṡi	-tṡa	-tṡagi
-ga -go -gi	-gagi -gogi -gigi	-ubi -tsa	-ubigi / -ubṡi -tsagi
-ha -ho	-hagi -hogi	-ra	-ragi
-hi -i	-higi -igi	-tṡa	-tṡagi

§19 Glossing

ABL	ablative	PROADV	proadverb
ACT	active case (agentive subject)	PRON	pronoun/pronominal
ACT.NOM	action nominal	QUANT	quantifier
ACT.PART	active participle	SEMELF	semelfactive
ADV	adverbial	SG	singular
AG	agentive	STAT	stative case (unagentive/ subject/object)
ALLAT	allative		
ASS	assertive	SUBJ	subjective
COMP	comparative	SUP	superlative
COMPL	complementizer	TR	transitive
	relativizer	TRANSLO	translocative
CONCL	conclusive	TRANSL	translative
COND.IRR	conditional irrealis	UNAG	unagentive
COP	copula	V.ACT.PART	active verbal participle
DAT	dative	V.ADIT	agentive ditransitive verb
DET	determiner	V.ADJ	verbal adjective
DIT	ditransitive	V.AI	agentive intransitive verb
DIMI	diminutive	V.ASUBJ	agentive subjective verb
ELAT	elative	V.AT	agentive transitive verb
EXPL.PART	explicative particle	V.IMP	impersonal verb
FREQU	frequentative	V.PAT.PART	patientive verbal participle
GEN	genitive	V.UDIT	unagentive ditransitive verb
HAB	habitual		
HABIL	habilitive	V.UI	unagentive intransitive verb
ILLAT	illative		
INA	inanimate	V.USUBJ	unagentive subjective verb
INCONCL	inconclusive		
INESS	inessive	V.UT	unagentive transitive verb
INF	infinitive		
INFER	inferential	V.UTRANS	(unagentive) translative verb
INSTRU	instrumental		
ITR	intransitive		
LINK	linking clitic		
MEDI	medial		
NO.ANI	animate noun		
NO.INA	inanimate noun		
OBLI	obligative		
OBV	obviative		
PART	particle		
PASS	passive		
PASS.PART	passive participle		
PAT	patientive		
PERF	perfective, perfect		
PERSI	persistive		
PL	plural		
POSTP	postposition		
POSTP.DESTI	destinal postposition		
POSTP.DIRECT	directional postposition		

§20 Siwa Swadesh List

megi	'I'	sira	'fish'
negi	'you'	hemi	'bird'
to	'he'	benho	'dog'
måra	'we (inclusive)'	půa	'louse'
nåri~ît	'you (plural)'	tsġumi	'worm'
ki	'they'	tahha	'tree'
ůat	'this'	tsamma	'forest'
hait	'that'	nokos	'stick'
ůhhja	'here'	subo	'fruit'
hahhja	'there'	rento	'seed'
mîmni	'who?'	ôlma	'leaf'
nîdni	'what?'	tara	'root'
nîvva	'where'	pymi	'bark'
nîġju	'when'	eleba	'flower'
nînni	'how'	elki	'grass'
set	'not'	gůme	'rope'
śośi	'all'	kehma	'skin'
tama	'many'	mine~vihla	'flesh'
kůtůdni	'some'	amoi~tveli	'blood'
euma	'few'	demo	'bone'
todni-ne	'other'	kŷ~kvŷ	'grease'
mî	'one'	tey	'egg'
eśi	'two'	gybi	'horn'
neġvi	'three'	atkana~raibma	'tail'
aits	'four'	kvon	'feather'
akno	'five'	hide	'hair'
atana	'big'	totami	'head'
siehhin	'long'	sata	'ear'
ouala	'wide'	kita	'eye'
otġa	'thick'	njarri	'nose'
tuvala	'heavy'	kuki	'mouth'
onona	'small'	rî	'tooth'
ġůla~itvi	'short'	oadi	'tongue'
sarana	'narrow'	nykki	'fingernail'
sehi	'thin'	motona	'claw'
îski	'woman'	sieḍdo	'foot'
somi	'man'	uba	'knee'
simśi	'person'	tiemo	'hand'
tśegmi	'child'	moukki	'belly'
riehpi	'wife'	svahi	'neck'
nalbi	'husband'	sili	'breasts'
suosa	'mother'	tåhma	'heart'
atri	'father'	bîlin	'liver'
imisi	'animal'	moġi	'to drink'
		ha	'to eat'
		ra	'to bite'
		sůvůli	'to suck'
		hiḍga	'to spit'

hopsai	'to vomit'	ivu	'to freeze'
sı̃la	'to blow'	sı̃lku̇	'to swell'
seyġu̦i	'to breathe'	te̊rhi	'sun'
mairui	'to laugh'	gasi	'moon'
nuja	'to see'	aihhji~aiśśi	'star'
seja	'to hear'	uja	'water'
neta	'to know'	siġva	'rain'
tabma	'to think'	selo	'river'
(k)nira	'to smell'	śinnen	'lake'
voammi	'to fear'	vetra	'sea'
pohhji	'to sleep'	hego	'salt'
ı̃ngi ~iljili	'to live'	misas	'stone'
niki	'to die'	neu̦o	'sand'
ira	'to kill'	vihi	'dust'
obu̇kku̇i	'to fight'	seumi	'earth'
mahha	'to hunt'	kolo	'cloud'
hu̇tva	'to hit'	ġedlvi	'fog'
aka~eta~ljasa	'to cut'	rekken	'sky'
sopra	'to split'	ġu̦eni	'wind'
nu̇imġa	'to stab'	omi	'snow'
rı̃nta	'to scratch'	ibme~hadlna	'ice'
geḍda	'to dig'	obena	'smoke'
noni	'to swim'	nobemo	'fire'
hȧbmi	'to fly'	asġa	'ashes'
koni	'to walk'	sahhi	'to burn'
maki	'to come'	moni	'path'
siśi	'to lie'	tetra	'mountain'
neni	'to sit'	pila	'red'
tȧi	'to stand'	tohhot	'green'
tuvi	'to turn'	ġilka	'yellow'
idi	'to fall'	magja~maiki	'white'
sota	'to give'	su̇bma	'black'
tenda	'to hold'	yly	'night'
resi	'to squeeze'	kengi	'day'
ukia~ukesta	'to rub'	gjekes	'year'
gjia	'to wash'	hı̃mi	'hot'
debba	'to wipe'	heje	'cold'
		pahla	'full'
tekigoa	'to pull'	kı̃	'new'
katagoa	'to push'	iśi	'old'
bia	'to throw'	sara	'good'
aunta	'to tie'	seba	'bad'
aiska	'to sew'	ljoġna	'rotten'
atadia	'to count'	lu̇rha	'dirty'
oai	'to say'	sukin	'straight'
nori	'to sing'	rokloma	'round'
biohtsi	'to play'	gigjes	'sharp'
lehhi	'to float'	holpo	'dull'
suvvi	'to flow'	kengy	'smooth'

711

nivvon	'wet'
sogjon	'dry'
keunenima	'correct'
ŭrja	'near'
suhhja	'far'
sŭaron	'right'
kamġon	'left'
nokkiu	'name'

§21 Map

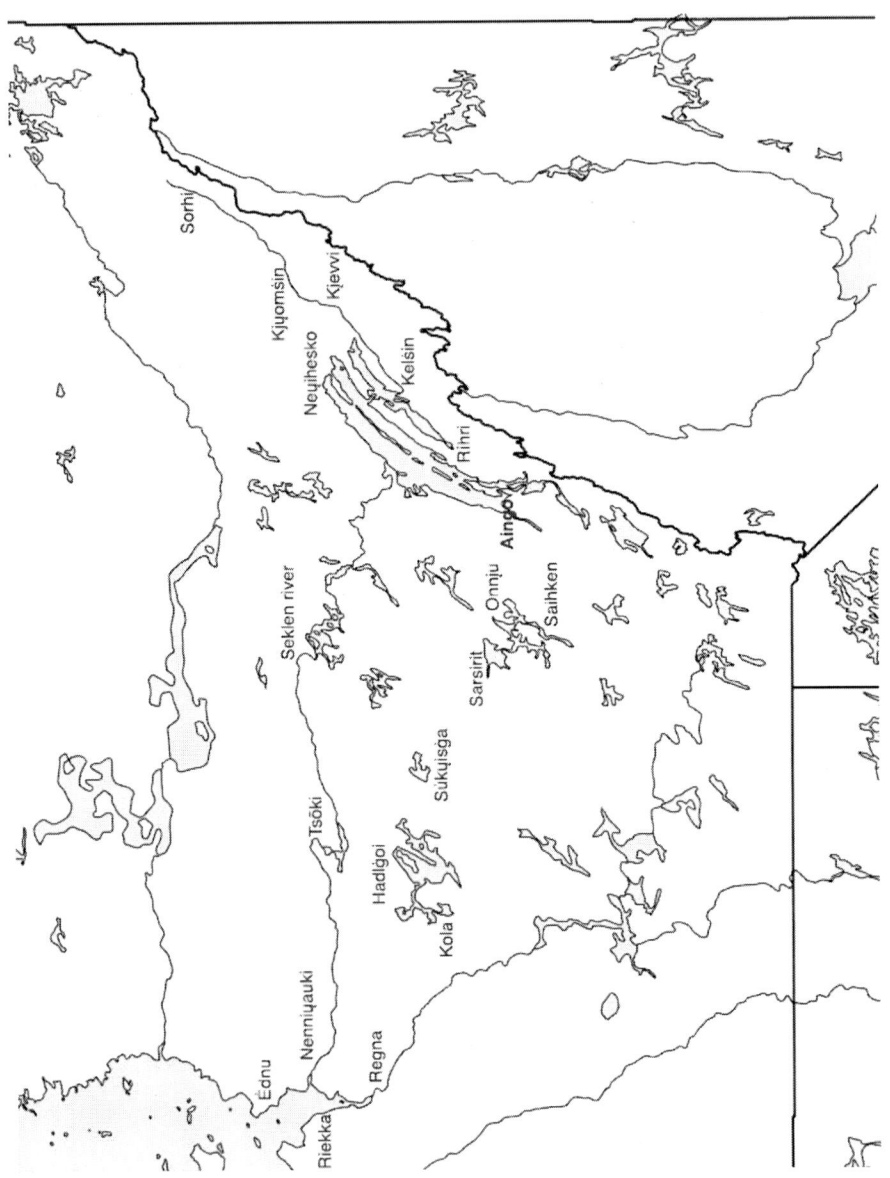

Appendix A: Modernization

Because of its pre-Columbian historical context, the Siwa language lacks vocabulary for some of the even most basic ideas of modern thought. For example, there exists no word for *wheel* and there is no vocabulary relating to science, technology or medicine in the language herein described. However, in an effort to make it possible to use Siwa in a modern day context, a number of neologisms have been created.

Because Siwa lends itself so easily to descriptions of life and natural phenomena, the vocabulary was developed from such a perspective. Thus, one find neologisms derived in great number from words describing nature. For example, the word for 'car' is *gjelvis* which comes from **ta·gjàli** 'X will spin' and *ouis* 'turtle', and the word for 'computer' is **dionyaddi** which consists of *(*ata·*)dion* 'counting' and **nyaddi** 'beehive'.

Technology	*Katageidlot*	
airplane	mjaridmi	(from *mjari* 'shield' and *idmi* 'raven')
alcohol	tugjai	(from *tygy* 'poison' and *aji* 'clear')
arch	kjomkamo	(cf. *kjuomon* 'bent' and *kaibmu* 'support')
bicycle	gjolba	(lit. two-wheel)
book	valtsa	(cf. from *òl-* 'leaf' and *-(a)tsta-* absolutive descriptive)
bottle	mohhy̌	(from *moġ-* 'drink' and *vevva* 'glass')
bus	gjelkobo	(from *gjel-* 'wheel' and *kobbomora* 'salamander')
camera	huḍḍjolus	(from *huḍḍe* 'light' and *jolus* 'reader')
car	gjelvis	(from *ta·gjǻli* 'X will spin' and *ouis* 'turtle')
chair	keulme	(cf. *kekli* 'X will sit in a circle')
clock	itsiku̇s	(cf. *itski* 'X will spend time')
compass	sibejolus	(from *sibema* 'north' and *jolus* 'reader')
computer	dionyaddi	(from *hę·dion* 'counting' and *nyaddi* 'beehive')
dome	puntsġůli	(cf. *puna* 'deerskin' and *tsġůli* 'skull')
electricity	hallu	(cf. *hauma* 'bright')
farm	ailki	(cf. *ilja* 'X will grow Y')
glass	vevva	(cf. *věut* 'ice')
gun, riffle	tiemihpi	(lit. hand-arrowhead)

internet	tśikkekot	(from *tśîkka* 'X will connect Y' and *kekot* 'web')
kettle	lossa	(cf. *luhha* 'X will boil Y')
laser	huḍḍirri	(lit. light-arrow)
light bulb	tėhtumus	(from *tẻrhi* 'sun' and *tẹmu* 'egg')
machine	tśoatus	(cf. *tśoati* 'X will work together')
microscope	pirikiḍbi	(from *pirin* 'nugget' and *kita* 'eye')
microwave	mukkalsa	(cf. *ta·muhu* 'X will be invisible' and *kalsa* 'oven')
military	taulva	(cf. *taulhi* 'army')
mobile-phone	tśagjemun	(lit. hand-box)
money	soami	(cf. *somora* 'gold')
movie	teukśi	(lit. silouhette-time)
oven	kalsa	(lit. bowels)
paper	keihko	(diminutive of *kehhe* 'birch bark')
photograph	kehhy̨ůn	(from *kehhe* 'birch bark' and *vẻume* 'reflection')
plastic	kjommit	(from **kjom-** 'bend' and **-mit** 'metal')
press	tamġotus	(from *tama·goa* 'X will press Y')
telephone	kjauhlun	(lit. thread-box)
toaster	hу̨inin	(cf. *honomi* 'embers')
toilet	eiskun/eskona	(cf. *eskot* 'empty')
toilet	euna/gjeuna	(cf. *gjia* 'X will bathe Y')
train	mjahkobo	(from *mjari* 'shield' and *kobbomora* 'salamander')
radio	jamnon	(lit. smoke-box)
refrigerator	geimin	(lit. frost-box)
saw	ikurit	(cf. *iki* 'axe' *rî* 'tooth' and **-(a)tsta-** absolutive descriptive)
scissors	djehbi	(cf. *djiki* 'X will carve')
ship	tśahhun	(cf. *kehkjo* 'canoe')
shower	kvilki	(cf. *kuilva* 'drizzle')
steel	vahmit	(cf. *t·vahsu* 'X will grow stronger and **-mit** 'metal')
technology	katageidlot	(from *kata·gedla* 'X will work Y out')
telescope	suśkiḍbi	(from **suś-** 'far' and *kita* 'eye')
television	teuknomi	(from *teuke* 'silouhette' and *nuobmo* window')
toothbrush	vekis	(lit. little comb)
umbrella	sihmjari	(cf. *sihhi* 'it is raining' and *mjari* 'shield')
vaccination 'bee')	sinukkon	(cf. *sinukka* 'to vaccinate', from *sinni*
wheel	gjeulke	(cf. *ta·gjåli* 'X will spin')
wool	pahmieri	(from *pagi* 'back' and *mieri* 'moss')

zero	dęsi	(lit. 'not-counted')

Food

coffee	moġasġa	(from **moġ-** 'drink' and *asġa* 'black ashes')
garlic	sahtapa	(lit. good-bulb)
onion	rihtapa	(lit. skin-bulb)
tomato	subbi	(from *subo* 'fruit' and *pila* 'red')

Science — *Haljonka te Kistonka*

agriculture	iljokadlas	(from *iljon* 'vegetation' and *kadlas* 'tradition')
algebra	tamulgeulva	(from *tamů* 'number' and *geulva* 'function')
anatomy	horedġenipjagjė	(from *horet* 'body' and *gena* 'section')
anthropology	somukiston	(cf. *somi* 'man')
architecture	soketsġovon	(from *osoken* 'building a house' and *kata·tsġovon* 'description')
astrology	aihhjuhaljon	(from *aihhji* 'star')
astrophysics	aihhiosvarhaljon	
biology	ilhajon	(cf. *t·iljili* 'X is alive')
botany	elikiston	(from *ě* 'plant')
chemistry	pẏhaljon	(from *pẏka* 'material')
CO_2	kuihletka	(from *kuihla* 'X will breathe Y out' and *etka* 'gas')
dentist	ripjaha	
dentistry	ripjagjė	(from *rî* 'tooth' and *pjagjė* 'doctoring')
doctor	pjaha	
ecology	golkakiston	(from *ta·guolki* 'X will live gregariously')
economy	gemkot	(cf. *gemk·a* 'to make advantageous')
education	nitśiyon	(cf. *nitśiya* 'X will make Y (want to) learn')
engineering	jeiton	(lit. building)
engine	einsa	(cf. *om·eini* 'X will propel itself')
evolution	austas	(cf. *t·yst·i* 'X will develop')
gas	etka	(cf. *edġe* 'air')
gene	aġo	(cf. *kat·iġa* 'X will inherit Y')
genetics	aġihaljon	
geology	ůmeihaljon	(from *ůmů* 'earth')
geometry	ġerttitsġovon	(from *ġertto* 'line' and *kata·tsġovon* 'description')

histology	rihehaljon	(cf. rȋhet 'tissue, skin')
history	unenjas	(cf. u·nynnjyli 'X is said')
hydrogen	ùtka	(cf. ujo 'water' and etka 'gas')
law	ketsġasko	(cf. ketsġo 'according to customs' asko 'control')
and		
linguistics	sauhhjakiston	(from sauhhjas 'language')
logic	saskaun	(from t·saiskia 'it will follow that')
magnet	tekkat	(from **tek·** 'toward' and **kat·** 'away')
mathematics	diokiston	(from ata·dion 'counting')
medicine	pegmopjagjė̂	(cf. pegme 'cure' and pjagjê 'doctoring')
microbe	elů	(from el- 'to grow' and ȇu 'sand')
mycology	kepsukiston	(cf. kepsi 'mushroom')
nuclear fission	angilpurrùn	(from angȋ 'pit' and purrůn 'squeezing')
oxygen	sġametka	(from sġam- 'breathe' and etka 'gas')
philosophy	galdekiston	(from ogalden 'meditation, discussion')
physics	mangamehaljon	(from mangama 'nature of the world')
planet	hoknun	(lit. big boulder)
psychology	komukiston	(cf. komi 'mind')
radioactivity	hamiljuhhya	(from hamit 'ore' and ljuhhya 'rot')
science	haljon	(cf. haljukka 'to stalk')
science	kiston	(lit. 'studying')
seismology	guġokiston	(cf. ta·guġurui 'X will growl')
silver	omit	(from oi 'moon light' and -mit 'metal')
space	iḍḍatsio	(cf. iḍḍi 'night-sky' and atsio 'glade')
statistics	tameikiston	(cf. tamů 'number')
zoology	mautsġehaljon	(cf. mautsġa 'animal')

Society

farmer	tailko·mi	(cf. ailki 'farm')
government	auskun	(cf. asko 'control')
judge	ketsġotauski·si	(cf. ketsġasko 'law')
politician	taiskjak·si	(cf. aiskjaka 'politics')
politics	aiskjaka	(cf. asko 'control')
president	tauski·mi	(cf. auskun 'government')
professor	keis·ki	(cf. kesġa 'X will teach Y')
school	keinta	(cf. kesa 'X will learn Y')
soldier	ataulmi	(cf. taulhi 'army')

teacher	anotsvi	(cf. *nitśiųa* 'X will make Y (want to) learn')
university	mikeinta	(from **mi-** 'specialized' and *keinta* 'school')
week	śukengi	(from *śvi* 'seven' and *kengi* 'day')

Geography

America	Aimrika/Okokna	(cf. *oaki* 'home' and *-kna* 'country')
Asia	Åsia	
Canada	Kanata	
US	Tśoamkena(ka)	(cf. *tśoami* 'unition')
Europe	Ůropa/Maikna	(cf. *magįa* 'white' and *-kna* 'country')
Finland	Sȯma	
Iceland	Vėutkįala	(cf. *vẘut* 'ices')

Biology

Order (similar animals)	kenet	(cf. *kekna* 'organize, put together')
species	kemomi	
vertebrates	nįydůheret	
invertebrates	nįydeskiret	

Chemistry

hydrogen	ůtka
helium	kekki
lithium	haukmit
carbon	hỏ
nitrogen	toḥḥet
oxygen	sġametka, sayt
sodium	haggi
phosphor	gebmit
sulphur	ylmit
chlorine	vasvi
potassium	halget
calcium	debmit
copper	melmit
zink	dįemit
gold	somora
silver	omit
mercury	oilut
iron	bengy
lead	tummit

acid — bel, osil
base — igjon

Months - Gaisġua

January	-	mitvigas
February	-	itvogas
March	-	soġġelkas
April	-	aylkkas
May	-	tvohkas
June	-	iknas
July	-	koggas
August	-	ymġas
September	-	guknas
October	-	enśugas
November	-	ilkkas
December	-	hejogas